Pedro Menéndez de Avilés and the Conquest of Florida

UNIVERSITY PRESS OF FLORIDA

Florida A&M University, Tallahassee
Florida Atlantic University, Boca Raton
Florida Gulf Coast University, Ft. Myers
Florida International University, Miami
Florida State University, Tallahassee
New College of Florida, Sarasota
University of Central Florida, Orlando
University of Florida, Gainesville
University of North Florida, Jacksonville
University of South Florida, Tampa
University of West Florida, Pensacola

Pedro Menéndez de Avilés and the Conquest of Florida

A NEW MANUSCRIPT

Gonzalo Solís de Merás

Edited, translated, and annotated by David Arbesú

UNIVERSITY PRESS OF FLORIDA

Gainesville / Tallahassee / Tampa / Boca Raton

Pensacola / Orlando / Miami / Jacksonville / Ft. Myers / Sarasota

Frontispiece. Portrait of Pedro Menéndez de Avilés.
Reprinted from Gannon, *New History of Florida*, 45.

This book may be available in an electronic edition.

22 21 20 19 18 17   6 5 4 3 2 1

Names: Solís de Merás, Gonzalo, active 16th century, author. |
Arbesú-Fernández, David, 1978– editor, translator.
Title: Pedro Menéndez de Avilés and the conquest of Florida : a new manuscript / Gonzalo
Solís de Merás; edited, translated, and annotated by David Arbesú.
Other titles: Memorial que hizo el Doctor Gonzalo Solís de Merás, de todas las jornadas
y sucesos del adelantado Pedro Menéndez de Avilés. English
Description: Gainesville : University Press of Florida, [2017] | Includes bibliographical
references and index.
Identifiers: LCCN 2016030100 | ISBN 9780813061245 (cloth : acid-free paper)
Subjects: LCSH: Menéndez de Avilés, Pedro, 1519–1574. |
Florida—History—Spanish colony, 1565–1763.
Classification: LCC F314.M54 S62813 2017 | DDC 975.901092—dc23
LC record available at https://lccn.loc.gov/2016030100

The University Press of Florida is the scholarly publishing agency for the State University
System of Florida, comprising Florida A&M University, Florida Atlantic University,
Florida Gulf Coast University, Florida International University, Florida State University,
New College of Florida, University of Central Florida, University of Florida, University
of North Florida, University of South Florida, and University of West Florida.

University Press of Florida
15 Northwest 15th Street
Gainesville, FL 32611-2079
http://upress.ufl.edu

Para Alonso, con cariño, por los últimos treinta años.

Y para Genaro e Isabel,

por haberme acogido siempre como a uno más de la familia.

Contents

PART 2

LA CONQUISTA DE LA FLORIDA POR EL ADELANTADO
PEDRO MELÉNDEZ DE VALDÉS

Illustrations

Acknowledgments

First and foremost, I would like to express my deepest gratitude to Genaro Llano-Ponte and Isabel Coello de Portugal, marqueses de Ferrera, for their kindness and support. It was in their private archive in Asturias, Spain, that I stumbled upon this important copy of the chronicle written by Gonzalo Solís de Merás, and it is only due to their generosity that we now have an edition and translation of the most complete account of the conquest and settlement of Florida by Pedro Menéndez de Avilés.

I am also greatly indebted to the William A. Freistat Center at Augustana College in Rock Island, Illinois, for a generous grant to support my research at the Archivo General de Indias in Seville and at the St. Augustine Foundation in St. Augustine, Florida, where I consulted several letters and documents related to Pedro Menéndez de Avilés, as well as a microfilmed copy of the Revillagigedo manuscript—until now the only known copy of the Solís de Merás narrative. My gratitude goes to Joy McMillan, director of the St. Augustine Foundation, for all her help and support during my visits in November 2012 and 2013, and to Eugene Lyon, whose knowledge of Pedro Menéndez is unsurpassed, for helping me locate the box with the Revillagigedo microfilm and for all his suggestions to improve the book. Likewise, during my research I have benefited from the generosity of Pilar Lázaro de la Escosura at the Archivo General de Indias, James G. Cusick at the George A. Smathers Library, University of Florida, and Michael Gallen and Katherine Owens at the Proctor Library, Flagler College.

I also acknowledge the assistance of many friends and colleagues who helped along the way. Chief among these are Philip C. Allen, who proofread the entire manuscript, Michael Francis, Charles Moore, Óscar Perea Rodríguez, Gemma Avenoza, Francisco Gago Jover, Nina M. Scott, Francisco J. Borge, María José Álvarez Faedo, Lucía Fernández, Charles Faulhaber, David Mackenzie, James D'Emilio, and Daniel Gullo. I thank Ann Marlowe, the best copy editor an author could hope for, for the expertise in maritime history she brought to the honing of my translation. I also thank the editorial team at the University Press of Florida, who have been unfailingly supportive and helpful throughout the process. Special thanks go to Meredith Babb, director of the press and acquiring editor, who believed in this project from the beginning.

Finally, I would like to thank all those who came before me, for the present volume owes much to Woodbury Lowery's and Eugene Lyon's research on the Florida enterprise, to Eugenio Ruidíaz y Caravia's edition of the Revillagigedo manuscript, and to the talented translation of Gonzalo Solís de Merás by Jeannette Thurber Connor. Without their pioneering work on the conquest of Florida and Pedro Menéndez de Avilés, writing this book would have been a much more trying task.

Pedro Menéndez de Avilés
and the Conquest of Florida

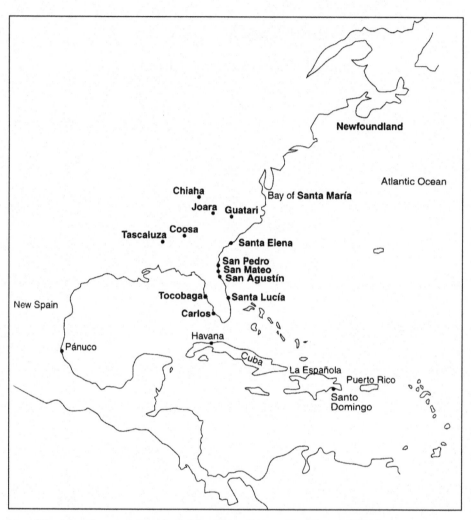

Map of Spanish settlements in Florida. Reprinted from Gannon, *New History of Florida*, 47.

Introduction

In 2013 Florida celebrated the 500th anniversary of the pioneering expedition commanded by Juan Ponce de León, which culminated with his arrival in a land he chose to name Florida on account of its copious vegetation, and because he had discovered it during the time of Pascua Florida, or Easter.[1] The year 2015 also had a special significance in the history of the state, since it marked the 450th anniversary of the nation's oldest city, St. Augustine. Some fifty-two years after Ponce's expedition, Pedro Menéndez de Avilés and his crew reached the coast of Cape Canaveral on 28 August 1565, the feast day of St. Augustine of Hippo. Not long after, on 8 September, they anchored in a pleasant harbor that they named San Agustín in honor of the saint, thus setting the foundations of what would become, with time, the oldest continuously occupied European settlement on the mainland of what is today the United States of America.

Menéndez's expedition was by no means the first attempt to settle in a land that had been claimed for the Spanish Crown half a century earlier,[2] but it turned out to be the only successful one. Ponce's initial voyage marked the beginning of what historian Eugene Lyon has aptly described as "the enterprise of Florida," but the Spaniards' efforts to build a permanent settlement north of the Bahama Channel proved ineffective time after time. To Ponce's expeditions in 1513 and 1521 we must add those of Alonso Álvarez de Pineda (1519), Lucas Vázquez de Ayllón (1526), Pánfilo de Narváez (1528), Hernando de Soto (1539–43), Luis Cáncer de Barbastro (1549), and Tristán de Luna y Arellano (1559–61), but all of them failed miserably. Ponce himself died in Cuba from wounds inflicted by the native Indians of south Florida; Barbastro was beaten to death near Tampa Bay; Ayllón and de Soto were taken ill and died in their respective camps;

and Narváez disappeared after he was shipwrecked off the Gulf of Mexico. After all these failed expeditions, Florida was discredited as a land with impossible weather, dangerous coasts, and indomitable natives, so it is not surprising that, on 23 September 1561, King Philip II of Spain decided that there would be no more attempts to settle the region.

Needless to say, the enterprise of Florida did not come to an end in 1561. Reports of the French activities in North America forced Philip II to reconsider his decision and license Lucas Vázquez de Ayllón the younger to settle Florida, but he never sailed. In 1565, amid unsubstantiated rumors that the Portuguese and English had also settled in that land, the king entered into an *asiento* or agreement with one of his most experienced seamen, Pedro Menéndez de Avilés. Menéndez's exploits in Florida from 1565 to 1567, most notably the expulsion of the French Huguenots, made the Asturian soldier famous at home (and infamous abroad), and paved the way for Spain's control over the present states of Alabama, Florida, Georgia, Louisiana, Mississippi, South Carolina, and part of Texas, a long "Spanish period" that (apart from a twenty-one-year interregnum) came to an end only with the transfer of Florida to the United States in 1821.

From a literary and historical point of view, the failures and successes of Spanish attempts to settle Florida have left some of the most compelling accounts written in or about the southern United States. Álvar Núñez Cabeza de Vaca, one of the few men who survived the shipwreck that killed Pánfilo de Narváez, wrote in 1537 a *Relación* of his perilous journey through the lands bordering the Gulf of Mexico. The *Relación*, in which Cabeza de Vaca gave a detailed account of how he managed to survive his eight-year ordeal, was published in 1542 with the title *Naufragios*, and to this day it is one of the most fascinating accounts of the Spaniards' exploration of the southeast. Likewise, the *Memoir* (1575) of Hernando de Escalante Fontaneda (who was shipwrecked off the coast of Florida and lived with the Caloosa Indians for seventeen years), Antonio de Herrera's *Descripción de las Indias Occidentales* (1601), and Garcilaso de la Vega's *La Florida del Inca* (1605) are literary and historical monuments that predate the founding of Jamestown in 1607 by several years. Sadly, most of these interesting narratives have been somewhat neglected and their protagonists denied their rightful place in Spanish and American history. The attention paid to these narratives has improved considerably in the last century, and at least the *Relación* by Cabeza de Vaca is now considered an essential account to study the history of the United States. The case of Pedro Menéndez de Avilés has also improved since Aureliano Fernández Guerra declared in 1865 that "Spain owed him a monument; History, a book; and the Muses, a poem,"[3] but, as recently as 1983, Florida historian Michael V. Gannon still wondered how "such a man, such a giant in the American epic, has otherwise fallen into academic as well as popular oblivion."[4]

The main reason for this lack of interest is that the national identity of the United States is rooted not in Florida but in the northern colonies. Thus Pedro Menéndez, Adelantado (captain-general or colonial governor) of Florida, is seldom studied in the United States as a founding father of the nation, for he was not from the British Isles and his field of action was not their Thirteen Colonies. A second reason is that the Spanish conquest of America has always been associated with the Black Legend disseminated by the enemies of Spain. Still, some of the blame must be transferred to historians and scholars of literature, for otherwise it would be impossible to explain why, 450 years after the founding of St. Augustine, we still do not have an authoritative edition of its longest, most complete and important account, the *memorial* written by Gonzalo Solís de Merás.

Menéndez's expedition was documented by two firsthand witnesses, Father Francisco López de Mendoza Grajales, who wrote a brief diary of the events, and the Adelantado's brother-in-law, Gonzalo Solís de Merás, who left a detailed and passionate account of the events that led to the capture of the French Fort Caroline, the massacre of the French Huguenots at Matanzas Inlet, Menéndez's exploration of the Florida river system, and his dealings with several Indian tribes of the Florida Peninsula. A third narrative, written by Salamanca professor Bartolomé de Barrientos, relied heavily on the previous two, and its author was never in Florida. Therefore the chronicle written by Gonzalo Solís de Merás is the single most important narrative of the conquest and settlement of Florida by Pedro Menéndez, and one of the oldest accounts written in and about the region. Until recently, the only known copy of this important work was the Revillagigedo manuscript, a very defective copy which is missing many folios and contains hundreds of corrections. This manuscript was transcribed in 1892–93 by Eugenio Ruidíaz y Caravia, the first and last editor to ever see the original. The present edition corresponds to a second, complete copy, the Ferrera manuscript, which I located in the private archive of the marqués de Ferrera in 2012. With the discovery of this manuscript, we finally have a complete version of the *memorial* written by Solís de Merás, which I will now call *The Conquest of Florida* to accord with what is indeed stated in both manuscripts.

Pedro Menéndez de Avilés

Pedro Menéndez was born in the town of Avilés on Spain's northern coast on 15 February 1519.[5] The son of Juan Alfonso de Avilés and María Alonso de Arango, Menéndez was raised in a family of skilled seamen, a circumstance that, no doubt, contributed to his permanent life at sea. According to his most important biographer, Gonzalo Solís de Merás, when Menéndez returned to Avilés in 1567 from his voyage to Florida, it was eighteen years since he had gone away to serve the king, "and in all that time he had been home only four times, and for twenty-two days in all."[6] His brother-in-law also tells us that the Adelantado's family was one of the most prominent in the northern region of Asturias, or at least in the area of Avilés, where it had blood ties to other notables such as the Cascos, Valdés, Arango, Bustio, and Vigil families. In the Ferrera version of *The Conquest of Florida*, Solís de Merás makes it very clear that "the Adelantado and his relatives are among the first families of that region,"[7] but if we follow the Revillagigedo manuscript we will see that the Adelantado's brother-in-law went too far when he tried to establish a connection between Pedro Menéndez and the semi-legendary first king of Asturias, Pelayo. In a long narrative detailing the Adelantado's ancestry and younger years, the Revillagigedo manuscript states that Menéndez would have owned

> one of the oldest houses in that region, which is the house of Doña Paya, where the kings of old used to dwell, after the death of King Rodrigo and the coronation of Pelayo, and this is why the place where it is located is called the King's Hill. The village of Pravia, where many of these kings used to be interred, is located one league from there, and the town of Avilés is located two leagues from there.[8]

Another of Menéndez's biographers, Bartolomé de Barrientos, followed Solís de Merás and took his narrative one step further, creating a foundational fiction in which the Menéndez family was made to descend from three gentlemen from Ávila who had gone to Asturias in the eighth century as personal guards of King Pelayo. Because these men were from Ávila, said

Barrientos, they were called *avileses*. Not content with giving us a fictitious story and an erroneous etymology for the town of Avilés, the Salamanca professor went on to say that King Pelayo himself "granted that town to the ancestors of the most illustrious Pedro Menéndez de Avilés, which attests to the antiquity of his lineage and ancestry."[9] This, of course, is also pure fantasy, and there are absolutely no records indicating that King Pelayo ever set foot in that part of Asturias, but at the time these little genealogical tales were so common that the oddity is not that a prominent family is made to descend from an important character associated with Pelayo; it would be odd if it were not. The motif is not exclusive to the seventeenth century, and one needs only to consult the works of Eugenio Ruidíaz y Caravia or, more recently, José Antonio Crespo-Francés to find an excessive zeal in parading the noble ancestry of the Adelantado. For Ruidíaz, Menéndez de Avilés belonged "to an illustrious family of the Principality of Asturias," but in truth, as Eugene Lyon has put it, Menéndez "was a descendant of minor Asturian *hidalgos* and had blood and marriage connections with the important Valdés family as well as with other noble *norteño* families."[10] Being a minor hidalgo and having connections with important families of the region is quite a step down from having one's ancestry linked to the Visigoth nobility of Pelayo's time.

What we do know for certain is that Menéndez's family was not wealthy. It is Solís de Merás again who tells us that the family's assets had to be divided among no fewer than twenty brothers and sisters, a circumstance that forced Menéndez and some of his brothers to opt for a life at sea. This idea is reinforced in many episodes of the chronicle, where we are constantly reminded of how Menéndez started out in life with very little, how he incurred great expense to carry out his most famous enterprise, how he asked most of his relatives and friends to provide financial support, and how he lost most of the wealth he had accumulated serving the interests of the Spanish Crown. Although this chronicle is clearly trying to exaggerate Menéndez's poverty to accentuate his achievements, the fact is that, in 1893, Ruidíaz still described the Adelantado's material legacy as just a "very modest tomb in the Church of San Nicolás, in Avilés, [and] some portraits of dubious authenticity."[11] In any case, the best evidence regarding the sorry state of the family's finances comes from the Adelantado's own relatives. In 1577, after Menéndez's death, his wife María de Solís (1517–1594) wrote a *consulta de gracia* or supplication to the king explaining that she had no money with which to travel to Asturias to bury her husband, and that she had had no other option but to live in Cádiz with Pedro del Castillo.[12] Likewise, his daughter Catalina had to appear before the Council of the Indies to speak about her financial worries, claiming that she had been forced to take up residence in the Asturian village of Grado, not being able, as Ruidíaz has put it, to live at court according to the dignity of her person.[13] Finally, in a report on the various services rendered by Pedro Menéndez de Avilés drafted in Mexico in 1595, several witnesses mentioned that the Adelantado was "poor" or "very poor," and a witness named Miguel de la Vega, who was acquainted with Pedro Menéndez since childhood, claimed—alluding to the rural practice of reckoning payment in grain—that the Adelantado "owned only six or seven bushels of bread in Gozón," an Asturian county, "from which he collected rent."[14]

It has also become customary for Menéndez's biographers to speak of his restlessness as a young boy, his adventurous spirit, and his desire to break free of the confines of his home, although the harsh economic conditions in which he found himself must have played a role in his leaving home at the age of thirteen. After the death of his father, Menéndez signed on as a cabin boy aboard one of the ships that had been sent by the king to strike at French corsairs in the Bay of Biscay. Since the young boy was bound to leave home again, his family looked for an excuse to keep him close. According to Solís de Merás,

> he was an orphan, for his father had died and his mother had married in second nuptials. He fled the country [and] the house of the tutors who had been raising him. They sent for him, and six months later he returned from Valladolid. To prevent him from leaving the country, they married him to Ana María de Solís, who was ten years old, although the two were relatives within the fourth degree of consanguinity. This, however, was not enough to keep him from leaving the country.[15]

This short narrative appears at the very beginning of the Revillagigedo manuscript of *The Conquest of Florida* (but not the Ferrera manuscript, which contains no genealogical data on Menéndez). At least, it appears this way in Ruidíaz's 1893 edition of the work, and therefore in its subsequent renditions by Gómez Tabanera and Mercado,[16] but a quick look at the microfilm of the Revillagigedo manuscript reveals that it contains hundreds of lines that the author has crossed out, which Ruidíaz has neither transcribed nor mentioned. What is particularly interesting is that Solís de Merás, Ana María's brother, had actually given us a more interesting reason for the Adelantado's departure, claiming not only that the marriage did not suffice to keep him from leaving, but also that he was unhappy to be married. Perhaps this can also explain why, in eighteen years, the Adelantado spent only twenty-two days at home.[17]

In any case, once Menéndez began his life at sea, he was very successful. The fleet in which the young man enlisted to pursue the corsairs in the Bay of Biscay, Eugene Lyon suggests, must have been the fleet of the famous Álvaro de Bazán, dispatched by the king in 1543. Lyon's intuition is supported by the fact that Bazán himself—one of the most famous admirals in Spanish history—is credited in the Ferrera manuscript with having provided Menéndez with two galleys and two galliots for his expedition to Florida in 1565.[18] Upon his return to Spain around 1545, Menéndez bought a small *patache* and became a privateer, capturing three French vessels off the coast of Vigo. His exploits at sea secured him two royal commissions to pursue corsairs, first in 1548 from the future emperor Maximilian II, who was acting as a representative of Charles I in Spain, and again two years later from Charles I himself. The king instructed Menéndez to capture the famous pirate Juan Alfonso Portugués, whom Menéndez killed off La Rochelle, and then the pirate's own son Antonio Alfonso, who suffered the same fate, for he was later killed by Menéndez in Santa Cruz de Tenerife. In 1550 Menéndez was allowed to travel to the Indies in order to strike at the French and English corsairs in those waters, and for this purpose he bought two galleons, the *Santa María de la Antigua* and the *Concepción*.[19]

When Menéndez returned from the Indies in 1551, war broke out again between France and Spain. This was the ninth of the so-called Italian Wars, which began in 1494 with the French invasion of the Italian Peninsula, where King Ferdinand the Catholic ruled over the Kingdom of Naples. For Menéndez, war with France meant that the "seas were filled with French pirate ships."[20] During his second voyage to the Indies in 1552, his vessel was overtaken by a French galleon, and he was held prisoner for fifteen days. He managed to pay his ransom and continue his voyage to New Spain and Cuba. There he observed firsthand the threat that French privateers posed to the Spanish Empire, and he came up with a strategy to counterattack. In the words of Lyon, to meet the danger, Menéndez had a plan. He appeared before the Council of the Indies as an expert seaman experienced in dealing summarily with the corsair menace. Drawing upon this reputation and his expertise, Menéndez proposed to counter the French and build four ships and four smaller *zabras* at his own cost. He urged the Crown to bear the expense of outfitting the ships and paying him a salary as captain-general. . . . Pedro Menéndez made his point. He received a commission as captain-general for the Indies voyages and prepared to sail.[21]

As a result of these voyages, he was appointed to the prestigious office of General of the Fleet of the Indies in 1554, but his assumption of that command had to be postponed because he was also chosen as one of the captains who were to accompany Prince Philip—the future Philip II—to England for his wedding to Mary Tudor. Navigation in the Canal de la Mancha, or English Channel, was very dangerous, as evidenced by the calamitous fate of the Invincible Armada which Philip II sent against England thirty-four years later, so the fact that Menéndez was chosen for this mission is proof that he was already considered one of the best sailors of his time. In October 1555, Menéndez's ships sailed for the Indies again, but a storm forced some of them to return to Seville. There the ships were inspected by an official of the House of Trade, who found several violations of shipping laws. Menéndez was thrown in jail.[22] José Manuel Gómez Tabanera has argued that Menéndez had "abused the duties of his office and transferred his obligations and attributes to his brother and lieutenant, while he traveled to New Spain to take care of private affairs."[23] While little is known of these private affairs, we do know that Menéndez's ships returned to Seville much sooner than anticipated, for they were back as early as September 1556, although they were not expected until April of the following year. According to Lyon, Menéndez and his brother "were arrested and charged with having brought a half million ducats' worth of cochineal and sugar outside of legal registry [as well as] with having brought passengers disguised as soldiers."[24]

The Revillagigedo version of *The Conquest of Florida* makes ample reference to this incident,[25] and even though the Ferrera manuscript has omitted all events prior to Menéndez's departure for Florida, it still refers to this traumatic episode when it summarizes the whole enterprise at the end:

And because the Adelantado had had such good and prosperous outcomes in His Majesty's service, there were many slanderers against him, and he had been imprisoned for twenty months in the shipyards and in the Torre del Oro in Seville, and at this court, and in all this time he had not been able to kiss His Majesty's hands, until, after being sentenced, he gave him license to do so. [The Adelantado] feared that His Majesty might have thought ill of him because of what his ministers had said of him, having given credit to those who had spoken ill of the Adelantado, and that he was in disfavor with [His Majesty], who would think much less of him than was just.[26]

While most of Menéndez's biographers insist on the Adelantado's innocence, it is clear that his imprisonment had several causes, one of them being that he had indeed committed many irregularities during his 1555 voyage to the Indies.

At this point we must turn our attention to Pedro del Castillo, who was a distant relative of Menéndez. Later in life Castillo became a *regidor* (city councillor) of Cádiz, but in 1555 he was only a young merchant involved in illegal trading with the Indies. According to Lyon, Menéndez had allowed him "to send goods under his command in violation of the laws of the Casa de Contratación, [and] enmity against Cádiz, Pedro del Castillo, and Pedro Menéndez began to build in Seville."[27] The Ferrera manuscript makes the connection between Castillo and Menéndez so clear that he is the last person to be mentioned in the narrative.

The incident with the House of Trade must also be explained by the rivalry between the cities of Cádiz and Seville regarding control over commerce with the Indies. Following the recommendation of Christopher Columbus, in 1493 Cádiz was designated as the sole port of entry and departure for ships trading with the West Indies, but later on, in 1503, the city lost its monopoly to Seville, the wealthiest and most populous city of the realm.[28] The rivalry between the two cities, together with the jealousy of some of Philip II's advisers, contributed to the imprisonment of Menéndez and his brother Álvaro, but we must not forget that the charges brought against them were not fabricated.[29]

In any case, partly because of the support of King Philip II, Menéndez and his brother were acquitted of all charges. In 1557 Menéndez was named captain-general of the Fleet of Flanders, assigned to transport more than a million ducats to the Spanish troops in northern Europe. His successful escort of these monies was credited with having helped the Spanish offensive that led to the victory over the French at St. Quentin in August 1557. As a reward for his services, the king conferred upon Menéndez the Encomienda de Santa Cruz and knighthood in the Order of St. James.[30] In October 1561 he was confirmed as captain-general of the Fleet of the Indies, but his voyage was again delayed for various reasons, among them a renewed conflict with the House of Trade, which refused to pay him an increased salary.[31] However, the Peace of Cateau-Cambrésis in 1559, which put an end to the lengthy Italian Wars, also freed France to follow up on Giovanni da Verrazano's exploration of the North American mainland, and even though the treaty did recognize Spain's claim to all the Indies, the events that ensued would forever change the fate of Florida.

In January 1562, under the direction of French admiral Gaspar de Coligny, General Jean Ribault sailed from Le Havre de Grâce and landed near the St. Johns River in Florida, then sailed northwards and arrived at present-day Port Royal Sound, South Carolina. The Spaniards had already explored the area, which they called Punta de Santa Elena, in 1561, when Ángel de Villafañe was dispatched to assist Tristán de Luna after his failed expedition. However, the Spaniards discarded Santa Elena as a possible site to settle because Villafañe's report indicated that the place was not suitable. The Ferrera manuscript explains the mistake in detail, for the Spaniards had entered the port of Santa Elena "not through its main entrance (because it has two entrances), and that is why the sailors and the pilot considered it a poor harbor."[32] Ribault, on the other hand, erected a fort at Santa Elena called Charlesfort, named in honor of King Charles IX of France. On 11 June of the same year, he returned to France, leaving thirty soldiers in the fort and promising to return within six months with more ships and supplies.[33] Life must not have been easy for the men who remained behind, and in 1564, when Spanish authorities in Cuba sent a frigate to destroy the French settlement in Florida, its commander, Hernando Manrique de Rojas, found that the French fort was deserted, with no sign of recent habitation. Rojas ordered it burned and returned to Cuba confident that there was no French presence in Florida.

Indeed, the French soldiers whom Ribault had left in Charlesfort had grown dissatisfied with the land and the hardships they had to endure on a daily basis, and they had eventually abandoned the fort and returned to

France. Only one soldier, Guillaume Rouffi, stayed behind.[34] However, had Manrique remained on the east coast of Florida for an additional week, he would have seen the three French ships commanded by René de Laudonnière arrive at the Matanzas River on 22 June 1564. Laudonnière, who had traveled to Florida in 1562 with Ribault's expedition, sailed northwards in search of the River May (present-day St. Johns River), where he established a French settlement called Fort Caroline to replace the failed Charlesfort. When Ribault returned to Florida a year later, he joined Laudonnière and the other French settlers at Fort Caroline. Little did he know that, on the very day of his arrival, 28 August 1565, Pedro Menéndez's fleet had also reached the sandy beaches of Florida.

In the *asiento* or contract signed by King Philip II on 20 March 1565,[35] the king appointed Pedro Menéndez adelantado of Florida. The events that followed, from his arrival in Florida in 1565 to his return to Spain in 1567, are precisely what Gonzalo Solís de Merás recorded in *The Conquest of Florida*, so I shall let the narrative speak for itself. Let it suffice to say here that, within two months of his arrival, Menéndez had captured Fort Caroline and killed Ribault and most of his men at the site now called Matanzas Inlet—the inlet of the massacre. The few soldiers who survived were either captured by the Indians or chased by Menéndez along the coast of Florida. France's attempts to build a permanent settlement in Florida had been brought to an abrupt end in less than two months, and for the first time since Ponce's voyage in 1513, a Spanish expedition to Florida was not to end in disaster.[36]

Upon his return to Spain, Menéndez was called to replace one of his most bitter enemies as governor of Cuba. Francisco García Osorio, who had been the governor of that island during the crucial years 1565–67 when Menéndez was trying to settle Florida, had denied any assistance to the Adelantado, and his insistence on ignoring Menéndez's pleas for help posed a serious threat to the wellbeing of the soldiers stationed in Florida, to the point that, if the reinforcements sent by Philip II had not arrived in July 1566, the entire enterprise might have failed. Thus it must have been a small victory for Menéndez when Osorio was deposed and sent to Spain in chains, although the Adelantado's own governorship, which he held from 1568 to 1572, also ended in disaster. According to Juan Carlos Mercado, after several accusations of smuggling goods, mistreating the citizens of Cuba, and failing to effectively administer the finances of Florida, the Council of the Indies was forced to carry out an investigation, which resulted in Menéndez's removal from office.[37] In 1574, King Philip II entrusted Menéndez with organizing a great fleet in order to travel to Flanders to build several forts to assist in controlling the rebellious territories. On 8 September 1574 he was appointed captain-general of the fleet, but on the very same day an epidemic broke out and killed several of its sailors and soldiers. Menéndez fell ill and died in Santander a few days later. He was buried in his hometown of Avilés, in the church of San Nicolás, where his tomb can still be visited, and where an inscription reads:

> Here lies buried the most illustrious knight Pedro Menéndez de Avilés, a native of this village, Adelantado of the Provinces of Florida, Commander of Santa Cruz de la Zarza, of the Order of St. James, Captain-General of the Ocean Sea and of the Fleet that Lord Philip II gathered in Santander in the year 1574, when he died, on 17 September of the said year, when he was fifty-five years old.[38]

The Enterprise of Florida and Its Sources

Apart from archival sources such as contracts, royal edicts, proceedings, and letters regarding the conquest and settlement of Florida, there are only three main narratives in Spanish detailing the enterprise of Pedro Menéndez de Avilés.[39] The oldest is the journal of Father Francisco López de Mendoza Grajales, from Jerez de la Frontera, who was the chaplain of the expedition and who, according to the manuscript edited here, was appointed vicar of the forts of St. Augustine and San Mateo.[40] His narrative, titled *Memoria del buen suçeso . . .* , was written in the year 1565 or shortly thereafter, and the only surviving manuscript can be found in the Archivo General de Indias in Seville. It is one of the best-known sources on Menéndez's expedition to Florida, and perhaps because of its brevity—it is just eleven folios—it has been edited and translated into English several times.[41]

The second narrative is that of Solís de Merás, but before we deal with the chronicle edited here, let us consider the third account.

In 1568, Salamanca professor Bartolomé de Barrientos wrote a chronicle titled *Vida y hechos de Pedro Menéndez de Avilés*,[42] and although Barrientos did not take part in the enterprise of Florida, his admiration for the Adelantado led him to consult as many documents as he could find and write his own version of the events. It has now been established that Barrientos used Solís de Merás's narrative as one of his sources, although certain details—such as the fact that Solís himself killed Jean Ribault—are exclusive to his chronicle.[43]

The relationship between the Barrientos and Solís narratives has long been the cause of debate. At first it was believed that they were both based on a lost *relación* written by Menéndez himself. The lost document is mentioned in Barrientos, who tells us that Menéndez wrote a "Relación de lo que había hecho y se había de hacer para la conservación de la Florida" [Account of what he had done and what should be done to preserve Florida],[44] but this fact was already recorded by Solís de Merás, who informs us that, upon his return in 1567, the Royal Council of the Indies asked the Adelantado "to write a report on many issues in order to remedy them. He did so."[45] In any case, it is now widely accepted that this document—if it ever existed—would have been of a very different nature, and that the narrative of Solís de Merás is not just one of the documents consulted by Barrientos but rather his main source.[46]

The problem with the Barrientos narrative is twofold. First, the author had declared his intention to write the chronicle "in our common language for the Spaniards, and in Latin for the foreigners," but the Latin translation was probably never written, and the Spanish original is hard to track down. The earliest reference to the Barrientos manuscript was made by Gonzalo de Illescas in the second part of his *Historia pontifical y católica*, published in 1573. Writing about the papacy of Pius IV, he says of the conquest of Florida:

> I have seen this praiseworthy enterprise, with all the particulars thereof, and with the description and qualities of Florida, which is a firm land, bordering on its northern part with the right [i.e., eastern] part of New Spain, written by Master Bartolomé de Barrientos, Chair and Professor of Latin in the distinguished, most notable, and no less Catholic University of Salamanca, to which I shall refer.[47]

This allusion to the manuscript is the last for more than three centuries. It is mentioned in the *Ensayo cronológico* written by Andrés González de Barcia in 1723, but simply to point out the author's inability to locate the copy mentioned by Illescas.[48] Thus nothing was known about the manuscript until 1885, when it was suddenly announced that the Mexican bibliophile José

María de Ágreda y Sánchez had purchased it from the book dealer Gabriel Sánchez.[49] Fortunately, Ágreda was kind enough to allow Genaro García to transcribe the manuscript, resulting in the first publication of the Barrientos chronicle since it was set down in writing in 1568. The problem is that the manuscript disappeared again, and in the interim there was much confusion as to the whereabouts of the original *Vida y hechos de Pedro Menéndez de Avilés*. In the introduction to his translation of the text in 1965, Anthony Kerrigan stated that "very recently, a fair copy of the original manuscript dating almost certainly to the sixteenth century turned up in the Netherlands, where it has been offered for sale by a book dealer."[50] Likewise, in the prologue to the 1993 edition by Elviro Martínez, Justo Ureña y Hevia stated that he did not know "where the original manuscript of this interesting work was," but then asserted that the edition could be considered the "editorial unveiling of a seventeenth-century manuscript, owned by the historian Javier López de Lerena, which has never been published before."[51] Since Genaro García had assumed that he was editing the text "as it appears in the original manuscript,"[52] we are left with no fewer than three different manuscripts of the Barrientos chronicle: the supposed original edited by García, the sixteenth-century copy mentioned by Kerrigan, and the seventeenth-century text published by Martínez.

Obviously, it is very likely that the manuscripts mentioned by these three authors are one and the same. The lack of attention to textual, codicological, and paleographical matters is at the root of the problem, for if García and Martínez had provided specifics of their manuscripts—measurement, binding, cover, folios—we would know exactly which copy they used, if indeed there is more than one. In any case, a comparison of the editions shows that their texts are identical, which implies either that these authors were consulting two exact copies of this work or, more reasonably, that Ureña's claim to an "editorial unveiling" of a never-before-published manuscript is inaccurate. In a recent newspaper article on the dispersion of important Mexican libraries in the last two centuries, Yanet Aguilar has shed some light on the whereabouts of the Barrientos manuscript. According to Aguilar, one of the most significant private libraries in Mexico, belonging to José María de Ágreda y Sánchez, was sold by his heirs in 1916.[53] Thus, at the beginning of the twentieth century, the Barrientos manuscript was back on the market, and since there is no evidence to the contrary, this copy once owned by Ágreda is most likely the same one consulted by Illescas in the sixteenth century, the one that appeared later in the Netherlands, and the one owned today by Javier López de Lerena.[54]

The Grajales and Barrientos manuscripts are, together with the chronicle written by Solís de Merás, the essential witnesses to the conquest and settlement of Florida by Pedro Menéndez de Avilés. However, the lack of codicological information in all existing editions of these works has made it very difficult to know the precise source of their narratives, and while the diary written by Grajales can be easily consulted at the Archivo General de Indias,[55] there are no reproductions of any folios from the Barrientos manuscript, all editions of this work lack information on their source other than what I have referred to, and therefore all data given for this important chronicle are hypothetical at best. Furthermore, this problematic aspect is shared with the third and most important textual account of the enterprise of Florida, the so-called *memorial* written between 1565 and 1568 by Pedro Menéndez's brother-in-law, Gonzalo Solís de Merás.

Gonzalo Solís de Merás and the Revillagigedo Manuscript

There is little biographical information regarding Gonzalo Solís de Merás, and most of what is known about him was recorded in a single entry of the *Biblioteca asturiana*, an eighteenth-century catalog of Asturian authors sometimes attributed to the conde de Campomanes. In this entry Solís de Merás is presented as Menéndez's brother-in-law, and we are told that he was a captain in the enterprise of Florida, that his son Pedro de Merás was there with him, and that he was the nephew of Garci Fernández de Tineo, a man who participated in the siege of Tlemcen in 1518 and became famous for killing Aruj Barbarossa during the battle that ensued.[56] This information is not confirmed by any other source, and it is highly suspicious that neither the Ferrera nor the Revillagigedo copy of the Solís de Merás chronicle makes any mention whatsoever of his son, or the fact that he was a captain, two details to which he certainly would have referred. Therefore we must be cautious with the information provided in the entry, most of it unsubstantiated.[57] What is known is that he was related to Menéndez not only through his sister Ana María, the Adelantado's wife, but by his own marriage to Menéndez's niece Francisca de Quirós. This fact was recorded in a petition written by Solís de Merás to request a copy of the Adelantado's last will and testament, so we can be quite certain of its accuracy.[58] However, the existence of a second document, in which the archdeacon of the Church of Benavente, a certain "Don Gonzalo de Solís," is credited with having paid the expenses to bring the Adelantado's body to his hometown of Avilés, has created much confusion, and scholars disagree as to whether *Doctor* Gonzalo Solís de Merás is the same person as *Don* Gonzalo de Solís.[59]

The sole contribution we can make to the discussion is a letter in the Archivo General de Indias that seems to have gone largely unnoticed by critics, except for Eugene Lyon. The letter, written in Havana by Pedro Menéndez on 1 July 1566, explains how his brother-in-law joined the expedition:

> Gonzalo de Solís, a servant of Your Majesty, will inform you of the same particulars. And since he longed to serve me, he has always been with me in all the enterprises I have undertaken, except the one in Santa Elena. And since he is a relative of mine, he learned of this enterprise that I was undertaking in the service of Your Majesty, and he left [the University of] Salamanca, where he had just concluded his studies, and went to Cádiz searching for me. And since he was a married man I did not want to bring him along, so he embarked against my will.[60]

These few lines are the only information we have on how Solís de Merás came to join Menéndez's expedition. They also confirm that he was a student at the University of Salamanca, where he must have completed his studies, for all the chronicles refer to him as *Doctor* Solís de Merás. Furthermore, the letter confirms something already known, namely that Solís de Merás was a firsthand witness of the events that took place in Florida between 1565 and 1567. This gives him precedence over Barrientos, who was never there, and such other secondary authors as Andrés González de Barcia, who also used the Solís de Merás narrative in his *Ensayo cronológico*.

The oldest narrative, that of Father López de Mendoza Grajales, is extremely valuable because it was written by yet another firsthand witness of the conquest of Florida, but the priest's eleven folios cannot compete with Solís de Merás's detailed account, which is more than ten times larger.[61] It may seem surprising, then, that the latter work, the longest and most important account of the conquest and settlement of Florida by Pedro Menéndez, has suffered so much critical and textual neglect.

As we have mentioned, the Solís de Merás chronicle is extant in two manuscripts, the Revillagigedo and Ferrera copies. This was not always so. For a long time the only known copy was the Revillagigedo manuscript, which all editions of Solís de Merás have followed until the present one. To explore the problematic editorial history of this chronicle we must begin, then, with its manuscript sources, which have never been described in detail. The Revillagigedo copy is housed in the archive of the conde de Revillagigedo, a direct descendant of Pedro Menéndez de Avilés who still holds the title of Adelantado of Florida. Fortunately for us, the manuscript was microfilmed in the 1960s, and the film can be seen at the St. Augustine Foundation.[62] Unfortunately, the manuscript is not in good condition, and the order in which the folios were photographed is perhaps not the way they were meant to appear. According to Pérez Bustamante, the manuscript "belonging to the conde de Revillagigedo is deteriorated,"[63] and for Lyle N. McAlister, "the manuscript used by Ruidíaz was torn and illegible in several places."[64] From my own inspection of the microfilm, I can say that the manuscript is missing many folios, and others have been lost and restored by a later hand. Some pages appear in an incorrect order, and numeration—when it appears—is erratic at best.[65] My description of the manuscript is as follows:

Revillagigedo Manuscript. Archive of the Count of Revillagigedo (Madrid, Spain). I have consulted a microfilmed copy at the St. Augustine Foundation. Box labeled 1964 (Michael V. Gannon). Spain. Archivo del conde de Revillagigedo. Selected papers of Pedro Menéndez de Avilés relating to Florida. A handwritten note in the box reads "Contains Solís de Merás." The manuscript has 113 folios. The chronicle by Solís de Merás is in ff. 1r–109v. Folios 110r–112r contain, in a later hand, a letter signed by Pedro Menéndez. Folios 112v–113v are blank or have marginal annotations. The manuscript is extremely difficult to read, it has been copied in procesal script, and it contains hundreds of lines which have been crossed out and corrected either by the same scribe or by a later hand. Of particular interest are ff. 20r, 20v, 22r, and 22v, which have been left blank or contain marginal annotations, and ff. 21v–28v, which have been restored in a later hand. A comparison with the text of Ferrera shows that the manuscript is missing at least twelve folios (twenty-four pages), and this is confirmed by a note in f. 82v that mentions that the "memorial" has one hundred and nineteen folios.[66]

The fact that none of the existing editions has given us a description of the manuscript would be less problematic were it not that the first and last person ever known to consult the original was Eugenio Ruidíaz y Caravia, who edited the Solís de Merás narrative in his monumental 1893 work *La Florida*. From that moment on, all editions and translations of Solís de Merás—Connor (1923), Gómez Tabanera (1990), Mercado (2006), Callahan (2010)—are renditions of the text as it appears in Ruidíaz, not in the original manuscript, and thus everything that Ruidíaz did—and did not do—has been perpetuated. Ruidíaz's work is commendable if only for his having been the one to unearth this important manuscript and provide the first and only transcription of its contents. A quick look at the microfilm of Revillagigedo is enough to understand how difficult it must have been for him to read more than one hundred folios of an incredibly challenging *procesal* script filled with corrections and marginal annotations, and to make sense of a chronicle with many folios out of order or missing.

On one hand, then, it is not surprising that Ruidíaz's work was praised as a model of historical erudition and awarded the prestigious prize of the Spanish Real Academia de la Historia. On the other hand, we must discuss its shortcomings, because Ruidíaz's rendition of *The Conquest of Florida* has been perpetuated to our day. In the introduction to the first volume of *La Florida*, Ruidíaz claims only to have divided the manuscript into chapters and paragraphs and to have supplied the missing text with extracts from Barcia's *Ensayo cronológico*. In truth, his editorial intrusion went much further. He reorganized the contents of the chronicle at will and failed to transcribe all instances where words or sentences had been crossed out, without even indicating that they were there. Most notably, the order in which the narrative is displayed is incorrect, but since I was not able to consult the original manuscript, I do not know if the fault is in the Ruidíaz transcription or in the manuscript itself. In other words, since the manuscript was microfilmed in 1964 and Ruidíaz consulted it in 1890–92, it could have been Ruidíaz himself who rearranged the folios, which now appear in this specific order in the microfilm.[67]

In the Ferrera manuscript, events prior to the Adelantado's departure for Florida are narrated, not only at the beginning, but at the end of the manuscript (chapter 33 in this edition), and thus we are reminded several times that these events have already been mentioned. For example, on folio 105v, we are told that the Adelantado was afraid the French might receive reinforcements and insisted on sailing for Florida as early as possible. Since this fact was already stated on folio 1r, here we are reminded that this has been "mentioned before." The same occurs twice on folio 108v, where we are told that the Adelantado departed on 28 June 1565 and, in the very last paragraph of the Ferrera manuscript, when we are reminded once more that the Adelantado wanted to depart as soon as possible. In all such instances the formula "como está dicho" [as is mentioned before] is repeated. In Ruidíaz's edition of the Revillagigedo manuscript, however, these events are narrated just once in chapters 7 and 8 (folios 18r onward in Revillagigedo). This makes sense if we order the events in a strictly chronological fashion, but the phrase "como está dicho" is then out of place, as these facts have not been previously stated.[68] Chapters 1 to 6 in Ruidíaz's edition—which presumably follows the order in Revillagigedo—describe Pedro Menéndez's ancestry and his exploits as a young man, mainly his first encounters with French and English corsairs and the important missions later entrusted to him by Maximilian II, Charles I, and Philip II. However, none of this information is found in Ferrera, and the two narratives only become the same one in Ruidíaz's chapter 7 (folios 107v–108v in Ferrera) and chapter 8 (folios 105r–106r). Chapter 9 has been supplied from Barcia, and then, in chapter 10, the narrative coincides with Ferrera's folio 3r and continues—with some discrepancies and passages supplied from Barcia—until folio 109v.

Just as troublesome is the transcription of the text, for even though Ruidíaz claimed to have "copied its contents literally,"[69] a quick comparison with the microfilm shows that his transcription has several significant mistakes. In order not to dwell on this, I shall quote Charles Hudson, who encountered the same problem when he consulted Ruidíaz's transcription of the so-called Juan Pardo Relation, included in volume 2 of *La Florida*. According to Hudson, "the reader should be aware that in checking my text against Ruidíaz's and the microfilm I found that he made a number of paleographic errors, consistently modernized spellings, and even made grammatical errors."[70] Likewise, Gómez Tabanera, who admits to having copied Ruidíaz's transcription verbatim, has to concede that "some expressions were not faithfully transcribed from the manuscript."[71] Among them are several abbreviations that he did not understand (such as *españoles* for *cristianos* and *quinientos* for *cincuenta*), a few instances where he read the numbers wrong (including *cuatro* for *cinco* and *doscientos* for *seiscientos*), and hundreds of other words that were incorrectly transcribed. To give one of the most notable examples, the dialogue between Captain Martín Ochoa and the French sentinel moments before the Spanish attack on Fort Caroline is reproduced in Ruidíaz (and all subsequent editions) as "—¿Quién va? —Francés" [—Who goes there? —A Frenchman], when in truth Revillagigedo agrees with Ferrera in giving us the dialogue in French: "—Qui là? —Fra[n]soi."[72] Keeping in mind that Martín Ochoa is trying to pass for a French soldier, it makes sense for him to answer in the sentinel's native language.

Finally, the textual and critical mistreatment of this important chronicle extends even to its being given an incorrect title. According to Ruidíaz, Solís de Merás "accompanied his brother-in-law as a chronicler in his conquests and journeys, writing the *Diary* of those events, which he titled *Memorial que hizo el Dr. Gonzalo Solís de Merás, de todas las jornadas y sucesos del Adelantado Pedro Menéndez de Avilés, su cuñado, y de la conquista de la Florida, y justicia que hizo en Juan Ribao y otros franceses*."[73] As usual, Ruidíaz's assertion that Solís de Méras titled his work *Memorial* was perpetuated in all subsequent editions, with some authors going so far as to claim that "as is well known, the original title of the book that we present here today, *Memorial*, was given to it by its own author, Dr. Gonzalo Solís de Merás."[74] However, it is unlikely that Solís de Merás would have written a title in which he referred to himself in the third person ("that Dr. Solís de Merás wrote of . . . his brother-in-law"), and a quick look at the microfilm of the Revillagigedo manuscript reveals that this title is nowhere to be found. There is no title on folio 1r, where the narrative begins, and on the cover, in a later hand, we see only a description of its contents: "The following proceedings concern the enterprises and events of the Adelantado Don Pedro Menéndez de Avilés, of the conquest of Florida, how the forts were captured, the Indians and chieftains of those provinces conquered and subdued, the Catholic faith implanted there. Written by Dr. Solís de Merás, brother-in-law of the said Adelantado."[75]

The title *Memorial* is not found on the Ferrera copy either, which raises the question of where it originated. Not surprisingly, the answer is found in Barcia's *Ensayo cronológico*, where the author—writing under the pseudonym Gabriel de Cárdenas y Cano[76]—made a list of all the chronicles and documents to which the reader could refer to learn more about the conquest of Florida. Among them he mentioned the *memorial* written by Dr. Solís de Merás, which was found among his documents, of all the enterprises and dealings of his brother-in-law, the Adelantado Pedro Menéndez de Avilés, and of the conquest of Florida, how the forts and the French fleet were captured, and Juan Ribao [Jean Ribault], General of the King of France, killed with all his people, and the Indian chieftains of those provinces conquered and subdued, implanting the Holy Catholic Faith in them, which the said Dr. Solís was writing as he accompanied him in his journey to Florida, when he conquered it, etc. The original is in the aforementioned archive, and its copy, and the other aforementioned [documents], in the library of Don Andrés González de Barcia.[77]

The same title is mentioned again, 140 years later, in the entry for Gonzalo Solís de Merás in the *Biblioteca asturiana*. Apart from a handful of biographical facts about the author, we are told that he wrote the "*memorial* of all the Adelantado's enterprises and the conquest of Florida," and that "its original is in the archive of the Adelantado, marqués de Canalejas, and a copy was owned by Andrés González de Barcia."[78] Aside from these two sources, no other indication as to the title of the work is given except in Ruidíaz's edition, and it is obvious that the entry in the *Biblioteca asturiana* is copied from Barcia's *Ensayo cronológico*. It is here that we find the word *memorial* for the first time, but when Barcia referred to a *memorial* written by Solís de Merás, he was using the word in its broadest sense, meaning a book or a journal, and he did not imply that this was the title of the work. It was Ruidíaz, then, who jumped to the conclusion that the author had titled his chronicle *Memorial*, an error repeated by Connor, Gómez Tabanera, Mercado, and Callahan.[79]

In the present edition, and to clarify the matter, I have chosen not to refer to this chronicle as *Memorial* but rather as *The Conquest of Florida*, because that title is given in the Ferrera manuscript several times. On folio 1*r the title reads "the conquest of Florida, and all the events that took place in it, by the Adelantado Pedro Menéndez de Avilés"; folio 3*r repeats the title as "the conquest that Pedro Menéndez de Avilés . . . made in Florida," and even the spine of the manuscript is labeled "Conquista de la Florida de Meléndez." Although Revillagigedo is not titled, its cover—written in a later hand—does refer to "the conquest of Florida," a much more accurate title than *Memorial*.

The Conquest of Florida and the Ferrera Manuscript

In the summer of 2012, visiting the private archive of the marqués de Ferrera in my hometown of Oviedo, I stumbled upon a manuscript titled *La Conquista de la Florida por el Adelantado Pedro Meléndez de Valdés* (signature 428). While I immediately recognized the importance of this volume, at the time I was unsure of its contents, and I did not know if it was a new account of the conquest and settlement of Florida (judging from some passages exclusive to this manuscript) or a copy of one of the three main narratives already known. As it turns out, the Ferrera manuscript is the second and most complete textual witness of the narrative written by Solís de Merás, and it supersedes the Revillagigedo manuscript because it is not lacking any folios. Moreover, it is written in a clear script, and its contents are displayed in the correct order. The manuscript is in very good condition, although the acidity of the ink has contributed to its deterioration and a few words are illegible on a handful of folios. It has 120 folios, and its contents are as follows:[80]

- [1*r] *Title*: The conquest of Florida, and all the events that took place in it, by the Adelantado Pedro Menéndez de Avilés. It tells of the disposition of the land and the Indians that inhabit it, and of a fort the French had built.
- [1*v, 2*r, 2*v] *Blank*.
- [3*r] *Title*: The conquest that Pedro Menéndez de Avilés, Knight of the Order of St. James, made in Florida, with the title of Adelantado of that land and other honors bestowed on him by His Majesty King Philip II in that land, if it happened to be subdued. He died in the greatest of events, and all that had been conquered was lost with his death, as well as the friendship he had forged with the chieftains. He went there in 1565.
- [3*v] *Index of captains and noblemen who participated in the conquest of Florida. Index of Indian chieftains in Florida. Index of forts built by Pedro Menéndez.*
- [1r–108v] *The Conquest of Florida, written by Gonzalo Solís de Merás.*
- [109r–112v] Description of the land of Florida, its good qualities, and its climate.

- [113r–114r] Title of Adelantado of the coast and land of Florida that His Majesty bestowed on Pedro Menéndez.
- [114r–115r] Title of Captain-General of the Fleet of Florida for Lord Pedro Menéndez de Avilés.
- [115r–116r] Title that His Majesty bestowed on Pedro Menéndez de Avilés, giving him the staff belonging to the Chief Bailiff of the Royal High Court of Florida.
- [116r–116v] Royal edict in which His Majesty grants the Adelantado Pedro Menéndez de Avilés power to distribute lands and *repartimientos* to those who settle in Florida.
- [117r–117v] Royal edict in which His Majesty grants favors to those going to settle Florida, so that, for a period of six years—I mean ten years—those going to settle Florida will pay only the tenth part of the gold, silver, and pearls found there.

Although the chronicle was originally written or dictated by Solís de Merás, the Ferrera manuscript was copied by the scribe Diego de Ribera, a citizen of Madrid, who has left us a detailed account of his activities on the last folio of the manuscript (117v). We do not know where Ribera came across this account of Pedro Menéndez's expedition, but it appears that he enjoyed it so much that he decided to investigate "what all these things amounted to and how it all ended," transcribing the chronicle together with a description of the land of Florida and several letters and royal edicts pertaining to the titles conferred upon the Adelantado by King Philip II. According to his own testimony, this was all he could find regarding these matters, and his sole purpose was to provide us with a narrative that would please anybody who read it. He finished his work on 16 March 1618.

There is not much we can say about Diego de Ribera, for there are several scribes with the same name in the sixteenth and seventeenth centuries. The most famous of these is the author of *Escrituras y orden de partición y cuenta* (1563) and *Instrucciones y aranceles de los escribanos del reino* (1577), who Blasco Martínez cites among the great authors of legal writings in Castile.[81] However, since this scribe was already one of the greatest notaries in the kingdom by the mid-sixteenth century, it seems unlikely he could be the same man who copied the Solís de Merás chronicle in 1618. A scribe of essentially the same name, Diego de la Rivera, transcribed certain municipal laws in the northern town of Logroño in 1630,[82] but again we have no way of knowing if he is the same person who copied the manuscript. In light of this, we must look for the connection between Ribera and the Solís de Merás chronicle elsewhere. From a look at the extant records, it appears that the Ribera family to which this scribe must have belonged had northern origins and was very much invested in the conquest of America. An Asturian named Diego de Ribera Valdés, son of Diego González de Rivera and Doña María de Hevia, was the general of the fleets of New Spain under Philip III (r. 1598–1621), and he was married to Catalina de Arango.[83] As we have seen, the Valdés, Hevia, and Arango families were connected to Pedro Menéndez de Avilés. Furthermore, a certain ensign called Gonzalo de la Ribera is mentioned as a witness in the "Long" Bandera Relation regarding the expeditions of Juan Pardo in Florida.[84] Menéndez himself had appointed a man called Diego de Ribera y Cepero as governor of Cuba,[85] and yet another Diego de Ribera appears in 1575 as the author of a statement declaring that a nephew of the Adelantado, also called Pedro Menéndez de Avilés, and his wife Doña Mayor de Arango were not related by blood.[86] Most important, Pedro del Castillo, the *regidor* of Cádiz who was so closely connected to the Adelantado and who is mentioned in such a favorable light in the last paragraph of the chronicle by Solís de Méras (Ferrera manuscript), was married to a woman named Isabel de Ribera.

As we have discussed, Castillo himself was a distant relative of the Adelantado, and his close ties to Menéndez are evidenced by the fact that after the Adelantado's death, his widowed wife lived in Cádiz with Castillo for some time. Furthermore, Menéndez appointed Castillo executor of his 1577 last will and testament, a copy of which is found in the Archivo de Protocolos de Cádiz, "office [escribanía] of Diego de Ribera." Finally, a man called Diego González de la Rivera who served as lieutenant of the *corregidor* in the Principality of Asturias is listed as belonging to the house of Báscones, which is, together with Avilés, one of the historic strongholds of the marqueses de Ferrera.[87] Although there is no way of knowing who Diego de Ribera was, what this means is that it is likely that his family was originally from Asturias—as the surname itself suggests—and connected in some way to Pedro Menéndez de Avilés and Pedro del Castillo. This would explain Ribera's enthusiasm at having found the narrative of the Adelantado's exploits in Florida and his eagerness to copy "all that he could find" about it, and it would also explain why Castillo was the last person to be mentioned in the manuscript. In the very last paragraph of the chronicle we are informed that Castillo was the person who rendered the greatest assistance to Menéndez in mounting his expedition: "Pedro del Castillo, a resident and city councillor of Cádiz and a great friend of the Adelantado, distinguished himself in this more than anybody else, helping him with his properties and those of his friends. He alone lent him twenty thousand ducats."[88]

One problem regarding the Ferrera copy is that only the folios at the beginning and end of the manuscript are the originals written by Diego de Ribera in 1618, for the rest were later replaced by a different hand.[89] The replacement of so many folios casts some doubt on the integrity of the Ferrera copy as it has come down to us, but the cohesion of all its contents is evident throughout the manuscript. There is no break or alteration between folios 1v and 2r, where the handwriting changes; the chronicle written by Solís de Merás continues uninterrupted. At the very beginning, on folio 1*r, Ribera states that the manuscript contains "the disposition of the land and the Indians that inhabit it," a promise that is fulfilled at the end with the "Description of the Land of Florida"—where the folios are, again, from 1618. When he copied the "Description" at the end of the manuscript, Ribera made several references to the chronicle that precedes it. This proves that the two narratives followed one another. For example, he mentioned that the Adelantado informed the Indians that the French were false Christians, that the first time the Indians had killed any Christians was because the mutineers had killed three of the Indians, that the Adelantado had made the trip back to Spain in seventeen days, that Juan Pardo explored the land of Florida, that the Adelantado ordered war waged on Saturiwa, and that God helped the Spaniards by performing a miracle. In all these instances, the "Description" contains the formula "as is mentioned before," which can only refer to the text of the chronicle written by Solís de Merás.[90]

Furthermore, in the "Description" Ribera again connects what he has just copied with the letters and royal edicts he is about to include, for in order to satisfy the requirements of the Royal Council, Ribera recorded "the benefits that His Majesty has conferred on the Adelantado and the other persons who went on this expedition and conquest of Florida."[91] Additionally, at the end of one of these letters Ribera states that he has transcribed it to include it "at the end of the conquest that the Adelantado made in Florida."[92] As we can see, the different elements of the manuscript—*The Conquest of Florida* by Solís de Merás, the "Description of the Land of Florida," and the royal edicts—were conceived as a unit, although, for some reason, most of the folios containing the narrative of Solís de Merás had to be replaced later on.

This gives us a very strong connection between the Ferrera and Revillagigedo manuscripts, for whoever replaced these folios in Ferrera was, without a doubt, the same person who replaced folios 21–29 in Revillagigedo and made hundreds of corrections throughout that manuscript. As we have mentioned, not only is the complicated *procesal* script of Revillagigedo difficult to read, but the manuscript contains hundreds of insertions and lines that have been crossed out. Some of the corrections were made by the same person who wrote the original manuscript, but others, including the replacement of folios 21–29, were made by the same eighteenth-century hand that replaced most folios in Ferrera. This is confirmed by the fact that both manuscripts have left a blank in very specific passages, such as omitting the name of a soldier or the date of an event. For example, recounting the second massacre of French Huguenots at Matanzas Inlet, both Revillagigedo and Ferrera say, "The Adelantado ordered them to march. He told one of his captains, named . . . , to march with them in the vanguard."[93] What is interesting is that the same person who replaced the missing folios in both manuscripts has included this information in Ferrera, so the sentence reads "He told one of his captains, named Juan de San Vicente, to march with them in the vanguard." Other instances in which both manuscripts have omitted a fact and a later hand has inserted it in Ferrera can be seen throughout the manuscript.[94]

That there existed more than one copy of this chronicle has been known since it was noted by the anonymous author of the *Biblioteca asturiana*, where it was mentioned that the original was in the archive of the marqués de Canalejas, who held the title of Adelantado of Florida, and that a copy was owned by Andrés González de Barcia. We know that the original is now in the archive of the conde de Revillagigedo, but according to Francisco Mellén Blanco, "in Asturias one of the archives related to this work is that of the marqueses de Santa Cruz de Marcenado, due to their connection to the house of Navia and the marqueses de Ferrera."[95] Although the title of Adelantado of Florida has been inherited by the conde de Revillagigedo, the two families were at one point connected, so it should not be surprising that both of them own a copy of the chronicle written by Solís de Merás.

Is the manuscript edited here the one owned by Barcia in the eighteenth century? The premise is tempting. The reference in the *Biblioteca asturiana* makes him the owner of the only known manuscript, and somebody in the eighteenth century used the Revillagigedo manuscript to replace the damaged or missing folios of the Ferrera copy. Judging from the contents (and the missing words) of both manuscripts, it is clear that the person who replaced folios 21–29 and made hundreds of corrections to the text of Revillagigedo was the same person who transcribed folios 2–108 in Ferrera. This monumental work of replacing hundreds of folios was surely the work of a scholar interested in the history of Florida, and since Barcia relied heavily on the chronicle by Solís de Merás to write his *Ensayo cronológico*, published in 1723, it is not far-fetched to assume that it was he who studied and amended these two manuscripts at the beginning of the eighteenth century.

The only problem with this theory is that Ferrera shows indications of having been copied by someone from the south of Spain, for there are many instances of *seseo* (pronouncing /s/ instead of /Θ/) throughout the manuscript, as well as several cases in which the final consonant of a word has been omitted.[96] These are too common to be ignored, and since Barcia was originally from Galicia and spent most of his life in Madrid, we cannot attribute them to him. While we could postulate that Barcia followed Diego de Ribera's spelling when transcribing the manuscript, it is reasonable to think that he would have added the missing consonants as he copied. In any case, the matter is difficult to settle, for different persons could have been involved in the transcription of the manuscript (one dictating, one writing), or perhaps Ferrera is not, after all, the copy that Barcia owned.[97]

To conclude, both Revillagigedo and Ferrera contain the same narrative of *The Conquest of Florida* by Gonzalo Solís de Merás—except for the genealogical data given at the beginning of Revillagigedo and the hundreds of strike-outs in that text, which appear neither in the Ferrera copy nor in Ruidíaz's 1893 edition. A transcription of all these deleted passages would indeed give us a very different text of the chronicle, and while some of them are irrelevant, others give us very interesting details that were later omitted. The fact that the two manuscripts are closely linked is ascertained by all the instances where both narratives have left a blank for a specific date or name, and it is only logical to suppose that the replaced folios in Ferrera are a copy of Revillagigedo. Judging from the *procesal* script in which it was written, Revillagigedo is surely from the sixteenth century, while the original folios of Ferrera were penned in 1618. Finally, as we have also discussed, even if most of Ferrera was replaced by a later hand, whoever replaced these folios followed the original structure of the manuscript, for several references in the original folios from 1618 attest to the fact that *The Conquest of Florida* was copied first, the "Description of the Land of Florida" second, and the letters and royal edicts third.

Editorial Criteria

This volume presents the first Spanish edition and English translation of the Ferrera manuscript, which contains *The Conquest of Florida* by Gonzalo Solís de Merás, a "Description of the Land of Florida," and six letters or royal edicts pertaining to Pedro Menéndez de Avilés. I have included the "Description" because it contains important references that allow us to connect all the contents of the manuscript, and because it has never been fully edited.[98] I have omitted the letters at the end of the manuscript because they can be consulted elsewhere.[99]

For the Spanish edition, I have checked the text of Ferrera against the Revillagigedo manuscript in order to make some minor corrections, although the Ferrera copy presents a far more complete version of the chronicle than that of Revillagigedo, since the latter is missing many folios and parts of the text are illegible. As I have mentioned, the variants in Revillagigedo have been quoted from Ruidíaz's edition, which I have checked against the microfilmed copy at the St. Augustine Foundation to ensure that Ruidíaz's transcription was accurate. I have consulted the original Ferrera manuscript at the archive of the marqués de Ferrera in Oviedo, Asturias.

I have attempted to present a clear and readable transcription of the text, without modifying words or sentences, except when the text was erroneous. In those instances, I have checked the text of Ferrera against that of Revillagigedo, and when the latter was more accurate, I have followed its transcription in Ruidíaz. Needless to say, all corrections to the text of Ferrera are indicated in the notes to the edition, but I indicate textual variants between the two texts only when Ferrera is mistaken or when the differences are substantial or important. I do not indicate minor variations in the way the text was copied, for it is not my intention to offer an edition of Revillagigedo, although this is much needed. Therefore, alternative versions of the text, such as "y que estaba cargando" (Ferrera) / "y que estaba ya cargando" (Revillagigedo), or "la gente que pudiese caber y que el despacho que Su Majestad" (Ferrera) / "la gente que pudiese tomar y que cualquier despacho que Su Majestad" (Revillagigedo), to give but two examples, are not indicated.[100] Apart from being all too frequent, these minor discrepancies are irrelevant to the main content of the chronicle.

Spanish in the seventeenth century was not much different from modern Spanish, and only a handful of words present difficulties to the modern reader (for example, *lengua* meaning *intérprete*). What is radically different is the spelling of words, which in the seventeenth and eighteenth centuries was chaotic at best, and which modern editors often maintain in order to "be faithful to the original." As Pedro Sánchez-Prieto Borja has shown in his essential *Cómo editar los textos medievales*, this widespread practice of transcribing the text with its original spelling has more to do with the inability of editors to interpret the text correctly than with preserving the alleged essence of the original, since variant spellings do not indicate, in many cases, any variation in pronunciation. In this specific case, a (semi) paleographic transcription retaining, for example, *mandaua* for *mandaba*, *hizquierda* for *izquierda*, *triumfar* for *triunfar*, or *scriuio* for *escribió* would not indicate a difference in pronunciation and would only make the text inaccessible to the modern reader. The absurdity of observing the spelling of a different time period is best seen in Gómez Tabanera's 1990 edition, in which he not only copied the 1893 text of Ruidíaz y Caravia word for word but also preserved the accentuation and punctuation systems of the nineteenth century, thus making his edition very difficult to read for a contemporary audience.

My editorial policy is taken largely from Sánchez-Prieto's manual, but in making sense of this text, and in order to facilitate comprehension, I have adhered to these specific criteria:

- In those cases in which a specific spelling could suggest a specific pronunciation, I have retained the original. The same is true for alternative spellings such as *agora*, *mejtad*, *pudían*, *prencipales*, or *frechado*, and the double consonant *ll* when it represents the merger of a verb and a pronoun (*echalles*, *dalles*). I have also retained the use of *ç* in many words, which indicates that the scribe had a tendency toward *seseo*.

- The manuscript has several marginal notes that I have not transcribed, since they were added by a later hand in order to call attention to specific passages. For example, on folio 8r the word *Milagro* [*Miracle*] has been added next to the line that reads "God performed a miracle."
- I have indicated all insertions into the text with square brackets.
- Capitalization, accentuation, and punctuation follow modern standards.
- All abbreviations have been expanded. The common abbreviation *xpiano* is resolved as *cristiano*.
- Vowels merged in the process known as "merger by phonetic syntax" have been expanded (*della* > *de ella*).
- Words and pronouns have been separated or joined following modern standards. Notice the special case of *por que*, which in addition to *porque* and *por qué* was used with the meaning of *para que*.
- I have altered the spelling of *R*, *rr*, and *r* to conform to modern standards (*Villa roel* > *Villarroel*).
- I have altered the spelling of the phoneme /x/ from *x* to *j* to conform to modern standards (*dixo* > *dijo*; *truxo* > *trujo*; *caxas* > *cajas*).
- I have altered the use of *u/v* and *i/y/j* according to their vocalic or consonantal values (*yndios* > *indios*; *mandaua* > *mandava*; *iucatan* > *Yucatán*). Similarly, I have altered *b/v* according to modern standards (*vergantin* > *bergantín*; *brebedad* > *brevedad*; *contentaua* > *contentava* > *contentaba*; *mandava* > *mandaba*).
- I have altered the use of *g/j* to conform to modern standards (*magestad* > *Majestad*).
- I have altered the use of *qu* to conform to modern standards (*quatro* > *cuatro*; *cinquenta* > *cincuenta*; *qual* > *cual*; *qualquier* > *cualquier*).
- I have altered the consonant combinations *nb* and *np* to *mb* and *mp* (*canpaña* > *campaña*; *onbres* > *hombres*; *tienpo* > *tiempo*). Similarly, I have altered such words as *triumfar* to *triunfar*.
- I have added or eliminated the "silent h" to conform to modern standards (*heran* > *eran*; *allar* > *hallar*; *horden* > *orden*; *hahorcar* > *ahorcar*; *desonestas* > *deshonestas*; *uaia* > *bahía*).
- I have modified all archaic and fossilized spellings that do not indicate a difference in pronunciation (*fructa* > *fruta*; *thesorero* >

tesorero; *matheo > Mateo; bartholome > Bartolomé; sancta elena > Santa Elena; sanct(o) agustin > San Agustín; instruction > instrucción; districto > distrito*).

- All superfluous double consonants or vowels, which are very common in the manuscript, have been rendered as a single consonant or vowel (*officiales > oficiales; possible > posible; apposento > aposento; fee > fe; successos > sucesos; succedio > sucedió; sucçedió > suçedió; apellacion > apelación; mill > mil; commoda > cómoda*). In the sixteenth century, the pairing "s/ss" did not indicate a difference in pronunciation.

About the Translation

The chronicle by Solís de Merás was first translated into English by Jeannette Thurber Connor in 1923, and the book was given a facsimile reproduction with an excellent introduction by Lyle N. McAlister in 1964. In 2010 Laura Callahan translated the 2006 edition of the *memorial* by Juan Carlos Mercado. Both translations are based on the Revillagigedo manuscript—or, rather, on the transcription of its contents made by Ruidíaz in 1893, since neither translator consulted the original manuscript. The present translation is the first one based on the Ferrera manuscript, taking into account significant variants in Revillagigedo. I have not consulted Callahan's translation, because I agree with Gagliardi that "Mercado's edition presents some errors of transcription,"[101] but I have relied heavily on Connor's expertise whenever a passage proved to be challenging.

On occasion, I have found instances where Connor misinterpreted the text, either because the transcription in Ruidíaz was mistaken or because she did not understand the Spanish of the time. To give but one example, in chapter XIV of Connor's edition we read that "the Adelantado commanded, with great secrecy and diligence, that there should be a soldier near each Indian, and 66 [others] near them." The editions of Gómez Tabanera and Mercado follow Ruidíaz blindly, but Connor is at least suspicious of the number, mentioning that it "must be a mistake in the text, for we are told that there were only thirty soldiers in the brigantine."[102] Indeed, the problem lies with Ruidíaz, who mistranscribed "e se sentasen cabe ellos" as "e sesenta e seis cabe ellos," and thus the correct translation should be that "the Adelantado ordered each soldier to place himself next to an Indian and be seated next to him." There are other instances where Ruidíaz's transcription was faulty, the translation inaccurate, or a whole paragraph missing, but I will not dwell upon these.[103] No edition is free of mistakes, and Connor's excellent rendition into English of the *memorial* has proved invaluable in guiding my hand through the complicated process of translating this chronicle.

When translating the words of Solís de Merás, I encountered several challenges. One of them had to do with those words that have no easy translation into English, such as *asiento, oidores, fusta,* or *zabra.* Following Connor, Lyon, and other scholars, I have opted to leave these words in Spanish and offer an explanation in the notes to the edition. Likewise, I do not translate *adelantado*—nobody does—but, while Connor leaves *cacique* in Spanish, I have used "chief" or "chieftain." I have translated the names of monarchs (such as Charles I or Philip II), but all other names are given in Spanish (Pedro and not Peter). If a place has an accepted name in English, I have used it (Seville, Havana, London, Spain, New Spain), but the names of most locations have not been translated (Cádiz, Coruña, Avilés, Los Mártires, Las Tortugas). This is especially true of the names of the Spanish forts in Florida, which I have rendered as San Mateo, Santa Lucía, Santa Elena, San Felipe. The only exception is St. Augustine, since it would be awkward for an English audience to read "San Agustín" instead of St. Augustine. Finally, although they do not completely convey the meaning of the original, I have strived to give an English translation of the names of governing bodies. Thus Casa de Contratación has become House of Trade, Consejo de Indias has become Council of the Indies, and Real Audiencia is rendered as High Court.

A greater challenge was posed by the syntax of the seventeenth century, which differs greatly from modern Spanish. At that time, sentences were much longer than they are now. Keeping in mind that even modern Spanish sentences are too lengthy for English syntax, I chose to alter punctuation to break large sentences—sometimes the size of a whole paragraph—into smaller ones. The challenge extends to the way in which the text was written. Digression is so common that, sometimes, four or five different ideas will be inserted into the same paragraph, often with no punctuation or divisions to help the reader make the transition from one to the other. The reader will also notice that the text is filled with the copulative conjunction *y* [and], which is often used out of place by modern standards, or is used to join sentences that add to the aforementioned digression. Thus, even though I was always aware while translating the text that there was a simpler, more elegant way to convey the meaning of the Spanish original in English, I decided—following Connor—to be as faithful to the original as possible, and therefore some of the syntactic and stylistic idiosyncrasies of seventeenth-century Spanish have carried over to the translation. I have, however, departed from the original in several respects in order to make the text more readable. I have eliminated certain repetitive structures, such as "the said Adelantado," "the said fort," "the said ship," and rendered them as "the Adelantado," "the fort," "the ship." Finally, in order to make the translation as clear as possible, I have added in brackets several names and dates not mentioned in the original that could be inferred from other passages.

Pedro Melendez de Auiles Cauallero del Abito de
sanctiago de nacion Asturiano, Hombre, nomenos noble que bali
ente general, por su mag. en la carrera delas yndias, y adelantado de
la florida, por particular md. de su mag despues que tomo asiento con
su mag para yr ala conquista dela florida. ya plantar enella el Sagrado
eVangelio// Bisto, que Juan Ribao, frances lutero, dela nueua
Religion Abia venido de francia con nueua Armada y auia tomado puerto en la florida y junto a un rrio Caudaloso que atrauiesa gran parte
dela florida, Auian fabricado Un fuerte y puesto le por nombre, el fuerte

de francia, Afin de tener en aquel puerto, nauios y baseles para salir
a rrobar los pasageros y a los nauios que bienen Con la plata, de todo lo
qual dio cuenta a su mag y señores de su real conseso y el peligro que deno Re
mediallo se seguiria que con benia la breuedad, antes que se fortificasen y gana
sen la boluntad alos caciques, porque tiniendo alos yndios naturales por
enemigos y alos franceses que los yndios triaua para pelear en compaña de
ellos nueua bastante Recaud el que se le daua para poner pie en la fondo
niechar alos luteranos della, y aun que esta particularidad, el Adelantado
dixo al sum en santa Maria, de nieua por abril de 65. y lo dixo alos señores
del Real conseso del estado de guerra que con el estauan, y des pues le binoa dezir
a mandil donde estaua la corte y señores del veaconseso delas yndias, que le
diesen para la sornada, dos galeras y a lestos del cargo de don Aluaro Bacan
para que con ellas y sus Cobras, y pataxes se adelantase ala florida antes que
los franceses fuesen socorridos, y quando lo fuesen, el desenbarcario en otro puerto
el mas corcano que al los al delos franceses, que por ver los nauios que peñase
poca Agua, lo podria muy bien sacar, y alli se fortificaria, procurando sacarles
todo el mal que pudiese y ganar la boluntad alos Caciques, y ala primd Vera
con la Caua lleria que le biniese delos yndios seria señor dela Canpaña, y su
puerto, por tener el fuerte dos leguas por ce vio a Riba, por que no fuesen socorridos
mil os yndios trata sen con ellos, y que por esta sorden se les auia de aer la guerra con
yndustria y breuedad. con lo qual serian echados dela florida, por que no sustan
tasen

First folio of *The Conquest of Florida*. Facsimile of the Ferrera manuscript, f. 1r. Reproduced with permission of the marqués de Ferrera.

Part 1

The Conquest of Florida by
the Adelantado Pedro Meléndez de Valdés

BY GONZALO SOLÍS DE MERÁS

The conquest of Florida, and all the events that took place in it, by the Adelantado Pedro Menéndez de Avilés.[1] It tells of the disposition of the land and the Indians that inhabit it, and of a fort the French had built.

The conquest that Pedro Menéndez de Avilés, Knight of the Order of St. James,[2] made in Florida, with the title of Adelantado of that land and other honors bestowed on him by His Majesty King Philip II in that land, if it happened to be subdued. He died in the greatest of events, and all that had been conquered was lost with his death, as well as the friendships he had forged with the chieftains. He went there in 1565.

The captains and noble persons who went on this expedition:

- Alonso Menéndez Marqués, the Adelantado's nephew.
- Bartolomé Menéndez, the Adelantado's brother.
- Don Pedro de Valdés, married to [Ana Menéndez,] the Adelantado's oldest daughter.
- Gonzalo de Villarroel, Captain and Sergeant Major.
- Captain Juan de Zurita.
- Diego Flores de Valdés, Admiral of the Fleet.
- Captain Juan de San Vicente.
- Captain Francisco de Recalde.
- Captain Diego de Amaya.
- Captain Martín Ochoa [de Argañaras], from Vizcaya.

- Captain San Vicente.[3]
- Captain Francisco de Castañeda.
- Captain Andrés López Patiño.
- Ensign Rodrigo Troche, who was the first to hoist his flag in the fort taken from the French.
- Ensign Cristóbal de Herrera, who was the second to hoist his flag in the fort.
- Captain Juan Vélez de Medrano, from Medina del Campo.
- Captain Diego de Alvarado.
- Captain Esteban de las Alas.[4]

The Indian chieftains with whom the Adelantado forged a friendship:[5]

- Chief Carlos, lord of many Indians and villages.
- Chief Guale.
- Chief Orista.
- Chief Utina.
- Chief Mayaca.
- Chief Saturiwa.
- Chief Ais.
- Chief Tequesta.
- Chief Calibay.
- Chief Tocobaga.
- Chief Emola.

The forts made by the Adelantado:

- San Mateo, which was the one taken from the French on St. Matthew's Day. It is located next to a river that flows from the lagoon named Maymi, which is forty leagues in circumference, and several large rivers flow from the uplands into it.[6] It flows toward Fort San Mateo and empties into the Bahama Channel,[7] and another river runs from the same lagoon through the lands of Chief Carlos into the channel.
- Fort St. Augustine, located on the site where the Adelantado arrived on St. Augustine's Day, 28 August 1565.
- Fort San Felipe, next to Santa Elena's harbor.

Chapter 1

Voyage to Florida

Pedro Menéndez de Avilés, Knight of the Order of St. James, Asturian by birth, a man no less noble than brave, His Majesty's general of the Fleet of the Indies[8] and Adelantado of Florida by a particular honor bestowed on him by His Majesty after he had granted him an *asiento* to conquer Florida and to spread the word of the Holy Gospel in this land—seeing that Jean Ribault,[9] a Frenchman of the new Lutheran religion, had come from France with a big fleet and had arrived in Florida, and that the [French] had built a fort they called Fort of France next to an affluent river that crosses most of the land of Florida[10] in order to detain there all ships and vessels, and capture the passengers and the silver in the ships—informed His Majesty and the lords of his Royal Council of all of this, as well as of the perils that would ensue if they did not put an end to it, saying that it had to be done quickly, before the French could fortify themselves and earn the trust of the chieftains, for if the Adelantado were to have the native Indians as enemies as well as the French, who were inciting the [Indians] to become our enemies, whatever supplies he had been given to go to Florida and expel the Lutherans from that land would not suffice.

The Adelantado informed His Majesty of this in Santa María de Nieva[11] in April [15]65, and he informed the lords of the Royal Council of State and War who were there with him, and then came to Madrid,[12] where the court and the lords of the Royal Council of the Indies[13] were, to ask them to give him two galleys and [two] galliots in charge of Don Álvaro [de] Bazán [y Guzmán],[14] so that with those ships and with his *zabras* and *pataches*,[15] he might go to Florida before the French were reinforced, and that if they were, he would disembark in another harbor, the closest he could find to theirs, which he could do because the vessels he had requested were of a shallow draft. There he would fortify himself and attempt to harm the enemy as much as possible, and to earn the trust of the chieftains. In the spring [of 1566], with the cavalry he was to receive from the Indies, he would be master of the field and of their harbor, because they had their fort two leagues inland up the river, so that they could not receive reinforcements or deal with the Indians. Accordingly, he would wage war on them quickly and with all discipline, and they would be driven out of Florida, to prevent them from implanting their evil sect in it.

His Majesty looked favorably upon this, but because he had news that the Turks were descending in force on Malta[16] and he had very few galleys to oppose them, he did not consent that any be given to the Adelantado, although he agreed with what he had said.

The next day in La Mejorada,[17] His Majesty provided that the Adelantado be given five hundred men, provisioned and paid for, with four warships, all at His Majesty's expense, so that with the five hundred men and ten shallops and *zabras* the Adelantado was taking at his expense, he should go to the islands of Puerto Rico, Hispaniola, and Cuba[18] to collect the cavalry, infantry, warships, and supplies that were already provided for.

The deal was referred to Francisco de Eraso,[19] who informed [the Adelantado] that His Majesty had ordered him to go to Valladolid to collect the authorization to recruit men and seize ships, and sureties for the officials of the House of Trade,[20] who were to take care promptly of the provisioning and payment of the men, borrowing some money for this purpose. The Adelantado replied that he was not pleased with the long delay this would entail in assembling the men, especially for Florida, which had been discredited among all countries as having a perilous coast. And since seven fleets with many men, which had gone to Florida by order of the emperor [Charles I] and of His Majesty [Philip II], had been lost at sea, it was hard to find soldiers and sailors. The five hundred men he was bringing along were from Asturias and Vizcaya, gathered and sought out by his relatives and friends, who were important people, accompanying him more to serve God and their king than for their own profit. But since so much time had already passed, the Adelantado would go post-haste to Seville by way of Madrid, so the lords of the Royal Council of the Indies might write to the officials of the House of Trade to give the Adelantado the fifteen thousand ducats they had offered him in the *asiento* to defray the great costs he would have to make. He wrote to his relatives and friends, asking them to recruit as many men as possible in his name, and he said to Francisco de Eraso that delay would not be in His Majesty's best interest. He went to Seville, where he collected the fifteen thousand ducats, and arrived in Cádiz[21] on a large vessel that he owned. He gathered his men in his *zabras*, and in the ships that came from Asturias and Vizcaya he gathered two thousand one hundred fifty soldiers and sailors.

He made such good time that he sailed from Cádiz on St. Peter's Day [29 June 1565], with a fair wind.[22] Within thirty days of his departure he was hit by a great storm called a "hurricane,"[23] and was in great danger of being sunk with all his fleet, having lost all masts, sails, and rigging of the galleon in which he traveled. When all was calm again he found himself with only three ships, and since he had much spare sailcloth and rigging, he remedied the situation as best he could and landed in Puerto Rico, where with great diligence he got fitted out again within a week and left, having collected another of his ships that had gone astray during the storm. From there, from Puerto Rico, he took another one—making five ships in all—with one thousand soldiers and sailors, and announced to his men that he was going straight to Havana.[24]

After putting out to sea where it was suitable, navigating carefully as he went, being in a place where the sandbanks prevented going to Havana except by taking a much longer route, he called his captains together and entered into council with them, telling them privily that it was much less dangerous to go straight to Florida while the weather was good, before winter came, than to travel to Havana to gather the ships that had gone astray, as well as the rest of the fleet, cavalry, and infantry that His Majesty had ordered him to gather in Santo Domingo[25] and in that island [of Cuba], for if he did this he would be delayed and would not be able to go to Florida until spring, when the Lutherans would be stronger. Therefore, because he was not in a position to do anything else, he determined, with their consent, to go straight to the French fort and harbor in Florida, for he believed he had more than enough [forces] to take their harbor, as long as the French fleet had not arrived yet. He begged them to agree with him, and asked them, individually and collectively, to reassure their soldiers and sailors and to tell them that this was a very good decision, that the enterprise they were undertaking was of Our Lord God and of our king, and that they should have great confidence that His Divine Majesty would grant them victory in everything, and have great courage and patience to endure all the ordeals and perils that were to follow.

Some of the captains then answered, approving the Adelantado's decision, and showed themselves content with it, offering to set themselves with full will to all the ordeals and perils that were to follow, and [saying] that they would encourage their soldiers and lead them in all good discipline to be most obedient in their service. And without awaiting the opinion of the captains who had not replied (who the Adelantado thought were distressed by his decision), he said to all of them:

—Brothers, do stay in this cabin for two hours in the company of God, so that our secret not be known, and address this matter and talk it over so that you can tell me if you find any problems with my resolution. He who speaks out more will be the more my friend. Then, once your reasoning and mine are heard, let us determine what is best. Each of you, individually and collectively, and all the sailors and soldiers will be content to see that whatever is provided for in this matter has been thoroughly discussed and agreed upon.

The Adelantado left them closeted in that cabin and went out on to the ship's deck, where he ordered prayers and litanies to be recited. He asked all the men in the fleet—everyone in his ships—to kneel and beseech Our Lord to enlighten the Adelantado so that, in a decision he wanted to make, he would decide what was best for the service of Our Lord God and the spreading of His Holy Catholic Faith. All of which they did with great devotion. After this was done, the Adelantado withdrew to the sterncastle of the galleon with a Book of Hours in his hand, and he prayed for an hour in front of a crucifix and an image of Our Lady. Then he left there, since the two hours' time he had given his captains would have passed, and went to them in the cabin where he had left them closeted, and asked each and every one of them to tell him openly and clearly what they felt in their hearts and souls, what they thought about his plan, and if he should change it.

Addressing and talking over this matter for an hour, they resolved to follow the Adelantado's determination and go straight to Florida to the French harbor. When they left the cabin and the decision was announced in the galleon with her six hundred and four men and in the other ships, which sailed together all around her with a fair wind, the Adelantado ordered the decision to be celebrated as if he already had the victories that Our Lord God was to grant him on the appointed day. He ordered the men to play all the fleet's trumpets, fifes, and drums, and to deploy on all the ships the banners, pennants, and campaign flags that he had brought for this enterprise, and to hoist the royal standard, giving it a royal salute by firing all the arquebuses and artillery on the ships. He ordered that all the men should get double rations that day, which gave the greatest of pleasure. This was seen very clearly in the happiness and rejoicing of all the men, who talked of nothing except to praise the Adelantado's decision.

On the evening of that day the Adelantado gave orders that all the weapons in the ships be given to the captains so they could distribute them among their soldiers, who were to keep them clean and ready. Since most of the soldiers were raw recruits, each of them was to shoot three rounds every day until they arrived in Florida in order to lose their fear of the arquebuses and be properly trained. Each round was to be shot with bullets into a target erected in the said galleon, with prizes awarded to the soldiers in the companies that did best, and to their captains, so they would take great care to make them skilled. With this daily drill, they also recited the catechism and the litanies, praying to Our Lord and beseeching Him to give them victory in everything. They sailed until 28 August 1565, St. Augustine's Day,[26] when they sighted the land of Florida. Falling to their knees and reciting the Te Deum Laudamus,[27] they all praised Our Lord, continuing their prayers and beseeching Our Lord to make them victorious in all their endeavors.

Chapter 2

Capture of Fort Caroline

Since they did not know where the Lutherans had fortified themselves, they sailed for four days along the coast, very afflicted and perplexed, not knowing whether the French were to the north or the south, where the Adelantado with his fleet was navigating by day and anchoring by night. One morning he saw some Indians on the coast.[28] He ordered his *maestro de campo*, or brigadier[, Pedro de Valdés,][29] to land with twenty arquebusiers. Fearing that the Indians would be afraid and flee, he did not let more people disembark, and when the brigadier went ashore with these twenty soldiers, the Indians came out with their bows and arrows. When our men went toward them, they retreated into the woods. The Christians were afraid to follow them, thinking they would be ambushed by many people, but they realized that if they did not take one of them [to use him] as an interpreter in order to know where the Lutherans were, things would not look good for them, because neither the Adelantado nor his pilots knew the coast or the sandbanks, and in case of a storm they were at risk of being shipwrecked with their fleet. To remedy this, the brigadier ordered a soldier who had committed a crime to put down his weapons and go to the Indians with some gifts, which he did. The Indians waited for him, received him well, and were reassured. Then the brigadier arrived and spoke to them with hand signs, asking them about the French. Also with signs, they replied that they were about twenty leagues from there, to the north.

The Indians asked if the general of the fleet was there with them or on board the ships. They told them that he was on the ships. [The Indians] replied that they were really eager to see and meet him. The men wanted to take them to the ships, but the Indians refused, saying that they were afraid, and that they would wait for him on land. So the brigadier returned with his twenty soldiers to the flagship where the Adelantado was, informing him of all that had taken place with the Indians, and that they were waiting for him on land. With his desire to see them and confirm what the Indians had told them by signs—that the French were twenty leagues north of there—he went ashore with two boats and fifty arquebusiers.

When the Indians saw the Adelantado on land, they put down their bows and arrows and came toward him. They began to sing and gesture toward Heaven in the manner of adoration, which was truly an incredible sight. The Adelantado gave them many presents and fed them sweets that he brought on the boat, and they reiterated what they had said, that the French were twenty leagues from there. The Adelantado left them very happy and embarked on his ships, sailing along the coast with his fleet. Eight leagues from there he discovered a good harbor with a good bank, which he named St. Augustine because it was the first land he had discovered in Florida, on the very day of St. Augustine [28 August 1565].

The next day [4 September 1565] at three in the afternoon, sailing along the coast, he saw four large galleons anchored.[30] Gathering that this was the harbor where the French were located, that they had already received reinforcements, and that those galleons belonged to the French fleet, he entered into council with his captains and asked what they thought should be done, it being certain that the French fleet had already come, and that the fort, the harbor, and the fleet could not be taken. There were different opinions. Most captains said the Adelantado should return to Santo Domingo with his five ships in order to collect the remaining vessels of his fleet that had gone astray in the storm and the other six ships of the fleet from Vizcaya and Asturias that were waiting there (since they had been ordered in the Canary Islands[31] to go to Puerto Rico), and he would also collect two warships, as well as the cavalry, infantry, and supplies that His Majesty had commanded be given to him in Santo Domingo and Cuba. This way, having gathered everything, he could go to Havana, and in the coming month of March [1566] he would go back to Florida strong enough to carry out any plan successfully.

The Adelantado feared that if he followed this line of thinking he would risk being defeated, for the French fleet had already spotted him and his five ships. There was no wind, the sun promised fair weather, and from the storm they had been through, four of the ships were left without topmasts and missing other spars that had broken. The French fleet could overtake them, especially since they had been informed that [the French] had ships with oars. He replied that it stood to reason that the French could not have expected him so soon on that coast, and therefore they would have their infantry on land, and they would be unloading their supplies, as those four vessels were large and could not enter the harbor laden. He was of a mind to go and fight, for if they succeeded in taking them, the French would not have enough of a fleet to chase them at sea. They could return to the port of St. Augustine, which was twelve leagues from there,[32] and disembark in that port and fortify themselves, sending the ships to Hispaniola to alert the fleet he had left there. The infantry, cavalry, and supplies that His Majesty ordered him to collect in Santo Domingo could come together in March [1566] to the port of St. Augustine, and once they arrived, they could go against their enemies by land and sea, taking control of their harbor. Their fort was two leagues upriver, and they would not be able to receive any reinforcements from France. With the cavalry, [the Spaniards] would be masters of the field, so that [the French] could not deal or speak with the Indians, and this way [the Spaniards] would wage war on [the French] briefly, without risk to the fleet, the Adelantado, or his men. This was to be done after reconnoitering their fort. [The Adelantado felt his forces] were so strong that they might just attack and capture it by force of arms.

For the reasons the Adelantado mentioned, all the captains approved this opinion and advice and, before reaching a decision, they prayed to Our Lord, beseeching Him to favor them in all their endeavors and grant them victory over their enemies. When their prayers were finished, the Adelantado told them what he had decided—that he was determined to attack the French fleet—which they all approved. He then ordered the captains to go to their ships and told them what they needed to do. He ordered [Diego Flórez de Valdés],[33] the admiral of the fleet, to take two ships that he pointed out to him as well as the one he would be on, making three, telling him where to go and in what order. The Adelantado commanded that the remaining ship, a *patache*, should not leave the side of his flagship. Thus, sailing along with fair weather, they came to a point about three leagues from the [French] fleet, which consisted of four large galleons anchored off the harbor.

Then the wind died down and there was much thunder, lightning, and heavy rain, which lasted until nine in the evening, when the sky became serene and clear with an onshore breeze. The Adelantado realized that by the time he came up on the enemy it would be almost midnight, and it would be wrong to grapple with the ships, because they would be at the mercy of the incendiary devices that the enemy usually carried (and which can be used more effectively at night than during the day). And in case the vessels of both fleets should burn, the enemy could easily escape in the boats and skiffs they had at the stern, since they held the land, and they would be victorious and the Adelantado would be defeated. So he decided to anchor in front of their bows in such a manner that when the anchors were dropped and the cables paid out, the sterns of the Adelantado's ships would be poised over the prows of the enemy ships. At dawn, loosing the cables, they would board the enemy ships, which could receive no help from the ships inside the harbor because it was night and the gravel bar was long and treacherous, and at dawn it would be low tide and they would have to wait until it was high, which would be noon. The Adelantado ordered the captains to come aboard his flagship and told them his decision, which they all endorsed as very good.

When they came close to the French fleet, about eleven-thirty at night, the enemy began firing artillery, but the balls passed through the masts and rigging of the Adelantado's ships without doing any harm. He did not permit or consent to any artillery being fired from his ships, but rather commanded that on all his vessels—including the one he was aboard—all the soldiers should go below in order not to be injured, for since they were to anchor and not board the enemy ships, it was not appropriate for them to be on deck with the artillery. With great courage and dignity, ignoring the artillery pieces that were firing, he passed by the French flagship (since the four ships were together), paying no attention to them. They had pennants and banners; on the mainmast of the flagship were a command flag and a royal standard, and at the top of the foremast on the other galleon was an admiral's flag. When the Adelantado had anchored with the prows of his five ships turned toward shore, he had the cables paid out, and the stern of his flagship ended up between the prows of the enemy flagship and the admiral's ship. Their prows reached his vessels like long pikes. Then he commanded the trumpets to hail the enemy, and they responded, hailing him with their own. After these salutes were over, the Adelantado spoke to them courteously, saying to those on the flagship:

—Gentlemen, where is this fleet from?

One of them said it was from France. He went on to say:

—What is it doing here?

They replied:

—We bring infantry, artillery, and supplies for a fort which the King of France has in this land, and for others that he is yet to build.

The Adelantado said to them:

—Are you Catholics or Lutherans? And who is your general?

They replied that they were all Lutherans of the new religion and their general was Jean Ribault. Then they asked [the Spaniards] who they were, who was the man asking them questions, whose fleet that was, why it had come to that land, and who was its general. The Adelantado replied:

—He who asks this of you is called Pedro Menéndez, this fleet belongs to the King of Spain, and I am its general. I have come here to hang and behead all the Lutherans I may find on this land and sea. These are the instructions I have from my king, which I will fulfill when day comes, for I will board your ships, and if I find any Catholic, I will treat him kindly.

Many replied at once with various insults and abusive words against our lord the king, calling him by name, and against the Adelantado, saying:

—Let this and that be for King Philip and for Pedro Menéndez, and if you are a brave man, as they say you are, come now and do not wait until tomorrow.

The Adelantado, on hearing so many insulting words against his king, ordered the cables to be paid out in order to board the enemy. Since the sailors were reluctant to do it, he leaped down from the bridge to hasten them, but the cable was wound round the capstan and it could not be done so quickly. Seeing this and hearing the call to arms that the Adelantado sounded, the [French] became afraid of him. They cut the cables, hoisted the sails, and fled. The Adelantado did the same with his ships and followed them. As he was amid the French ships, he followed two of them northwards in his flagship with a *patache*, and his admiral followed the other two southwards with his three ships. The Adelantado sent a message with the *patache* to the admiral, telling him to return to the harbor at the break of dawn and [saying] that he would do the same, to see if it could be captured. Otherwise they would disembark at the port of St. Augustine, as agreed, because if none of the French ships could be captured (they sailed faster than the Adelantado's ships, which were missing some spars from the storm they had endured), it would take the enemy three or four days to regroup, and in that time the Adelantado would be able to either capture their harbor or disembark at the port of St. Augustine. The other French vessels anchored inside the harbor would not dare to come out unless the four returned, and even if they did, there was no reason to fear them.

And it so happened that the Adelantado chased the two French galleons northwards until dawn for about five or six leagues, and his admiral traveled the same distance southwards chasing the others. At ten in the morning the Adelantado was off the French harbor with his five ships. When they went into the harbor he saw two infantry flags at the end of the bar, five vessels anchored within, and artillery being fired. It seeming to the Adelantado that if he tried to take the harbor he could be defeated, and in the meantime the four ships that had fled could rejoin the five ships within and he would not be able to escape by land or sea, he decided to get his flagship under full sail without losing any time and to command the other ships to do the same. He headed for the port of St. Augustine, where he arrived on that same day [7 September 1565], on the eve of Our Lady of September. Upon his arrival he ordered some three hundred soldiers to disembark, and the next day at dawn he sent them off with two captains to explore the land and the likeliest places to erect a stockade quickly, while meanwhile considering where to build a fort, so that another day, when the Adelantado landed, they could show him what they had observed and decide what was best to do.

On the following day, the day of Our Lady of September,[34] the Adelantado came ashore around noon and found many Indians waiting for him, since they had been told about him by the others who had seen and spoken to him four days before. He had a solemn mass said in honor of Our Lady and, when it was finished, took possession of the land in His Majesty's name. He received solemn oaths from the officials of His Majesty's Royal Exchequer, the brigadier, and the captains that they would all serve His Majesty with fidelity and loyalty. This done, he ordered that the Indians be fed and himself ate. Then he went to see the places the captains had thought suitable for a stockade, and leaving the site marked out he returned to the vessels, having first held a council where it was decided that, in the next three days, they should unload as much as possible from the vessels, and that the two large ones that could not enter the harbor should be sent to Hispaniola, for if the French fleet were to come, it would capture them. The Adelantado, thinking that the French fleet would attack in four days' time, was so diligent in unloading these vessels in order to send them away so the enemy would not capture them that all those who were there were astonished, because even if the ships were anchored more than a league and a half from the landing stage, the men unloaded the artillery and ammunition and a good part of the supplies in two and a half days.

One night at midnight he had a premonition that the French fleet would be upon him at dawn, and not waiting until the third day, he ordered the ships to sail to Hispaniola without unloading more supplies. He embarked the hundred and fifty soldiers he had with him in a shallop of about a hundred tons,[35] and he himself embarked in a large boat he had had with him at the stern of his flagship when he chased the French fleet. In order to better be able to flee, he launched the boat and anchored it and the shallop off the bar in two fathoms of water. At dawn the French fleet was just a quarter of a league away, where the Adelantado had been at midnight when he ordered the ships to go to Hispaniola. There came one enemy ship and three of their shallops, and because the tide was extremely low and the sea was not calm, it was dangerous to cross the bar. When the Adelantado saw the enemy so close to him, and that he could not escape, everyone prayed to Our Lord God and to His Precious Mother to deliver them from that peril. When the Lutherans were close to him, he let go the rope with which his boat and the shallop were anchored and at great risk he got in over the shallows, as Our Lord was pleased to place them inside the bar and in safety. The enemy were afraid of the entrance and waited for high tide.

At that time the ships the Adelantado had sent to Hispaniola were approximately five or six leagues away from there, and thus they were saved from that peril without being discovered. Two hours after the enemy began waiting for high tide, God performed a miracle:[36] even though the weather was calm and clear, all of a sudden the sea became very rough, and from the north came a strong wind that was contrary to what [the French] needed to go [back] to their harbor and fort. The Adelantado became aware of this. He was already ashore with his men, having a mass said in honor of the Holy Spirit which everyone was to attend, beseeching Him to enlighten him and guide him in a decision he wanted to make. When the mass was over, he entered into council with his captains, the first council he had held in the land of Florida. None of them knew why they were gathered. When they were together he said:

—Gentlemen and brothers, we have a great, difficult, and dangerous task on our shoulders, and if it were only for our lord the king, I would not be

surprised if some of us grew weary and committed the weak acts of cowards, not being able to endure as many hardships as we have ahead of us.
But since this burden we carry is the enterprise of Our Lord God and of
our king, let that person among us who shows weakness and does not encourage the officers and soldiers under his command be accursed, for this
is of great importance to us. Thus, gentlemen, I beg you of your goodness,
as earnestly as I can, [to consider] that, since in this we serve God and our
king, the prize of Heaven will not be denied us, and we should not worry
about the few supplies we have, or about being isolated in this land. I ask
of you, of your goodness, that we all take courage and try to endure [these
hardships] with patience.

They all replied very appropriately, agreeing individually and collectively
that for their part they would do their best. Having thanked them for their
good responses, the Adelantado said:

—Gentlemen, it occurs to me to tell you about a very good opportunity
that I can clearly perceive in my senses and my soul. We should not waste it,
we should take advantage of it and not let it pass by. I think (and it is common sense to think so) that since the French fleet fled from me four days ago
and has now come back to chase me, they must have reinforced themselves
with part of the garrison that they had in their fort—the best part and the
best captains. The wind is most unfavorable for them to return to their fort
and harbor, and it seems that this wind will last for many days. These men
are Lutherans, something we knew before departing from Spain because of
the proclamations General Jean Ribault issued in France when he embarked:
that, on pain of death, only men professing the new religion should embark,
and that, under the same penalty, they should bring only books belonging
to this sect. They themselves assured us of this when our fleet was anchored
with theirs outside the harbor, since they said there was not a Catholic
among them, and when we wanted to punish them, they set sail and fled.
For this reason our war with them—and theirs with us—has to be one of
blood and fire, since they as Lutherans seek us Catholics to prevent us from
spreading the Holy Gospel in these provinces, and we seek them for being
Lutherans, to prevent them from spreading their harmful and hateful sect in
this land and teaching it to the Indians. It seems to me that we should take
five hundred soldiers—two parts arquebusiers and one part pikemen—and
rations for a week in our packs, without porters, carrying our weapons on
our backs, and that each of you ten captains should take his banner, officers,

and fifty men, and we should all go and explore the route, the land, and the fort where the Lutherans are, for even though we do not know the way, I will be able to guide you with a compass (give or take two leagues to the right or to the left). Where we find wooded areas, we will clear the path with axes in order to pass and know how to return. I am taking with me a Frenchman [Jean François][37] who was in that fort for more than a year, and he says that he knows the land for two leagues around the fort and that he knows how to take us there. If we are not spotted, it could be that, a quarter of an hour before dawn, by setting up twenty ladders that we shall make when we are close, we might capture the fort at a cost of fifty soldiers. And if we find that we have been spotted, well, we know the woods are less than a quarter of a league away. We will plant our ten banners, each for its own camp, along the edge, and it will appear to them that we have more than two thousand men. Then we can send them a trumpeter to say that they should surrender the fort and harbor and leave the land, and that they will be given ships and supplies with which to go back to France, and if not, we will put all of them to the sword. Even if they do not comply, we will have gained much from exploring the route, the land, and the fort, and they will fear us, which will make them leave us undisturbed this winter, until next March, when we will have enough men to seek them out by land and sea.

There was much debate regarding what the Adelantado had said, as some thought that they should not embark on this expedition and others thought they should. It was finally decided that they would. The Adelantado ordered that they all hear mass on the third day at dawn and then depart. He ordered the brigadier Pedro de Valdés (a relative of his and espoused to his oldest daughter) and Captain and Sergeant Major Gonzalo de Villarroel[38] to arrange for the selection of men who were to go and to give them a sufficient supply of powder, fuses, and lead to make bullets and shot. He decided that his brother Captain Bartolomé Menéndez should be in charge of the soldiers who were to remain there [at St. Augustine], with artillery, weapons, ammunition, and supplies, and that Diego Flórez de Valdés, who was the admiral of the fleet, should remain as captain of the artillery and general of the three vessels that remained of the fleet, keeping them and their sailors ready. After having agreed to this, the council ended, and then it was made public throughout the camp and the things the Adelantado had ordered began to be prepared and provided, with which the whole camp showed the greatest satisfaction.

On the morning of the next day, the Adelantado was informed that some of the captains were criticizing his decision to go in search of the French at the fort. They spoke so openly and justified it in such a way that it became clear that the soldiers who had been pleased with this decision the first day were now disheartened. Some of the captains, in particular Juan de San Vicente, Francisco de Recalde, and Diego de Amaya, had decided that on behalf of most of the captains and people there, and as friends of the Adelantado, they would tell him, once he had finished eating, that he needed to change his mind and not go to the French port under any circumstances. When the Adelantado was notified of this, he ordered a fine meal to be prepared and had the captains and most of the ensigns summoned to dine with him and some gentleman soldiers of the expedition. When they had finished eating he said:

—Gentlemen and brothers, after we landed, we gathered the captains in council, which was done with great secrecy, and only those of us who were there and no others knew of the words that passed between us. I now understand that all the soldiers and women here know of it, and are having bitter arguments and fights among themselves regarding whose opinion is better or worse, so that people are criticizing our decision and saying that it would be unwise to carry out what has been agreed. I think this was a very bad idea, worthy of a strong reprimand and punishment, and even though I know who should most be blamed (and they are here), I do not want to condemn anyone, but rather ask you, gentlemen, of your goodness, that from here onwards each of you shall remedy this by observing great secrecy in the matters we discuss in our councils. Success is seldom attained in times of war when there is no secrecy—and diligence—and in this respect I will punish those of you who commit a lesser sin as if it were a mortal sin. It is very easy to tell from the soldiers which captain is most disheartened and afraid of the expedition: If the fifty soldiers who have to go with him are disheartened, it is because of the captain and his ensign, not them; and those soldiers who look sharp, cleaning their weapons and readying their packs for their rations, it is clear that their captains and officers encourage them by being themselves in good spirits, and they wish to undertake the expedition.

And [he said] that if they still thought he should change his mind, they should tell him, [but] that once they were out of there, he would order that the captain who spoke against what was arranged be punished by taking his company away from him and not admitting him to councils. They all replied that what His Lordship had said was very well said, and that some of them thought he should change his mind and others thought the opposite, that they should follow the agreement and decision that had already been made. Then the Adelantado told the captains that each of them should take the packs to the storekeeper, with one person to collect the rations, in order to depart at dawn of the following day after hearing mass, as was agreed. He ordered each of them to go and attend to what they had to do, and they departed.

The next day at dawn they sounded reveille with the trumpets, fifes, and drums, and the bells chimed. Everyone came to hear mass, and afterwards they departed to good-luck wishes, all setting out marching in order. The Adelantado took twenty soldiers from Asturias and Vizcaya with their axes, and with them a captain from Vizcaya called Martín de Ochoa, and two Indian brothers who had shown up there, who appeared to be angels sent by God, and who told them by signs that they had been at the French harbor six days before. He marched on, going as far ahead as he could and marking the path by blazing the trees with the axes so that the men would not get lost and would know their way back, leaving the brigadier and the sergeant major to march in good order, because they were afraid that the Indians, being friends of the French, might ambush them, shooting them from the woods with their bows. When the Adelantado thought best to halt in a suitable place with water in order for the men to regroup and rest, he did so, and he would wait until all of them had been assembled to tell them how long they could rest, and then he would depart, clearing and marking the path as mentioned, and he would halt again in the place that he deemed best to spend the night.

Proceeding in this way, on the fourth day at sunset he went to explore the land half a league from the fort, where he halted. The night was stormy, it was pouring rain, and it seemed best to him to draw closer in order not to be discovered. Thus he came into a pine grove less than a quarter of a mile from the fort, where he decided to spend the night in a very bad and swampy place. He turned back to look for his rear guard and help them find the way through the dreadful night, but they did not arrive until after ten o'clock. As it had rained a lot in the past four days and they had had to cross many marshes carrying their weapons and packs with food on their backs, the men arrived exhausted and weak. Since the rainfall that night was so heavy, there was no way to prevent the powder and fuses from getting wet, or the little biscuit they had in their packs, and none of the men had anything on them that was not soaked.

At this point the Adelantado was afraid to enter into council with his captains on whether to go back or go to the French harbor, because some of them—as well as their officers—were showing signs of insolence, saying offensive words against him so openly that he heard many of them, especially [Fernán Pérez,] an ensign of Captain [Juan de] San Vicente, who came close to the Adelantado and said loud enough for him to hear:

—Look how we are being misguided by this fainthearted Asturian, who is as ignorant of land warfare as an ass! If it had been up to me, the same day he left St. Augustine on this journey, he would have gotten what is now coming to him!

Then the Adelantado was more afraid and pretended that he had not heard him.

The Captain San Vicente of whom this man was the ensign had, at the time of their departure from St. Augustine, claimed to have pain in his leg and a stomachache, and remained behind. There was much grumbling at his staying behind and at the insolent words of his ensign, because it was later discovered that, when some other men who had stayed behind criticized Captain San Vicente for not having gone with the Adelantado, he had replied by saying:

—I swear to God that I am waiting for the news that all our soldiers are dead, so that those of us who have remained here can embark in these three ships and go to the Indies, for it is not reasonable that we should all die like beasts.

Two hours before daylight, the Adelantado sent four soldiers who were near him, servants of his, to run to the men and tell the brigadier, the sergeant major, and the [other] captains to join him there, and they did so. When they were all together, he said to them:

—Gentlemen, although I am a great sinner, I have beseeched Our Lord and His Precious Mother, all through the night, to favor us and put us on the right path regarding what we must do. And I am sure, gentlemen, that you must have done the same. Let us discuss what is best for us to do, considering where we find ourselves, without ammunition or food, and with all the men tired, lost, and disheartened.

Some of them replied that they did not see why they would agree to anything other than retreating and returning to St. Augustine at dawn, eating palm hearts [on the way], and that it seemed imprudent to discuss any other option. The Adelantado approved it and said to them:

—Gentlemen, for the love of God, listen to my reasoning and do not be displeased with me for sharing it with you, as this is not to make you do as I say, but so that you will do whatever you wish and that which seems best to you, for until now you have followed my opinion and counsel, and now that I see myself in this great danger I want to follow yours.

They said that His Lordship should speak, for they were happy to listen to him and share their opinion with him. Then he said:

—Gentlemen, are you confident that the woods are very close to the fort?

They replied that they were. He said to them:

—It seems to me that we must go and test our luck as was agreed. When we send them the trumpeter, if the fort cannot be captured we must not fear the thought of the French coming out of it to chase us to the edge of the woods where we will have camped, hoisting our flags. For this we shall have little need of fuses or powder. If we are spotted in the morning and we retreat, the enemy will take heart and hold us to be cowards and men of little worth, and this will be for them a great beginning to victory.

Some of the captains, and especially the brigadier and the sergeant major, replied that this reasoning seemed sound, and that the plan and decision agreed upon should be carried out to the end. After a give-and-take with those who thought differently, they all agreed that it should be done.

Then the Adelantado ordered them all to kneel and say their prayers to Our Lord, beseeching Him to make them victorious against their enemies in the enterprise and risk they were undertaking. They prayed then with as much devotion as if their enemies were in front of them, inviting them to give battle. When they were done, after designating the captains who were to go in the vanguard and the rear guard and the places and the way in which each of them should attack the fort, and asking them for the love of God to encourage their soldiers, he ordered them to march. He guided them, marching at the front, taking with him as a guide the Frenchman [Jean François], who had his hands bound behind him with a rope of which the Adelantado held the other end.

This must have been an hour before daybreak. Because of the great darkness and the severity of the wind and rain, and the path being so narrow, they lost their way before a quarter of an hour had passed, so that some of them thought they were marching forward when they were really going in the opposite direction. When the Adelantado realized this, considering that the rear guard could be marching in a different direction than the vanguard, by word of mouth he ordered them to halt and remain where they were until daybreak, for fear they should be separated from one another. Many of them, including the Adelantado, halted in a swamp where the water reached above the knees. When day came, the Frenchman recognized the place where he had to take them, and the Adelantado marched out of formation in a great hurry, ordering everyone by word of mouth to follow him on pain of death, for the captains were far apart from one another and he did not think it was time to enter into council about what they should do. When they came to a rise, the Frenchman told him that the fort was behind it, down below, at a distance of approximately three arquebus shots, and that the water from the river washed against it. The Adelantado gave the Frenchman over to Francisco de Castañeda, who was the captain of his guard and who never left his side, and coming down very quickly from the high terrain, he saw the river and some houses, but he could not make out the fort, even if it was next to them. Returning to where he had left the captain of the guard with the Frenchman close by, he found the brigadier, who had just arrived, and Captain Martín Ochoa. He said to them:

—Brothers, I would like to go down with five or six soldiers into this valley, where there are some houses, to see if I can find the sentinel in order to learn about their strength and the men they have, because the sun has already risen and the day is clear, so we cannot attack the fort without powder unless we reconnoiter.

Then the brigadier said that His Lordship should stay [there], since that was his duty, and took with him only Captain Martín Ochoa, not wishing to take anyone else in order not to be discovered. When they arrived near the houses, they saw the fort. Returning with this news, they encountered two paths and did not take the one by which they had come. After following it for a short distance they came upon a fallen tree, and the brigadier said that they had lost their way. Since Captain Martín de Ochoa had been walking behind him, when they turned around he was in front. It seems they were discovered by the sentinel, who thought they were French and came to see who they were. As he did not recognize them when he was in sight of them, he stopped and said:

—Qui [va] là?

Martín de Ochoa replied:

—Fra[n]soi.

The sentinel came closer, thinking they were French. Martín Ochoa did the same. When the Frenchman did not recognize him, he stopped. Captain Martín Ochoa closed with him and, scabbard and all, gave him a slash across the face, although it did not hurt him much because he warded it off with his sword. They both drew their swords, and the brigadier arrived with his own sword unsheathed, buckler in hand. As he lunged at him, the Frenchman retreated, fell backwards, and began to shout. The brigadier put the tip of his sword on his chest and told him to shut up or be killed, and the Frenchman did so. They pulled him up and took him, bound, to the Adelantado, asking him about the fort and the people in it. From the Frenchman's screams, the Adelantado thought they were killing the brigadier and Captain Martín Ochoa, and as some of his captains and flag bearers were gathered near him—especially the sergeant major [Gonzalo de Villarroel], Francisco de Recalde, Diego de Amaya, and Andrés López Patiño, with their flags and men—the Adelantado said in a loud voice:

—St. James![39] At them! God is helping! Victory! The French are beheaded! The brigadier is inside the fort and has captured it!

Then they all broke ranks and went running along the path, while the Adelantado stayed where he was, never ceasing to repeat these words. The men took it as certain that many soldiers had gone with the brigadier and the fort had been captured. They felt great joy and happiness, so much so that the one who could outrun the rest was considered the bravest, and none of them were crippled, maimed, or cowardly. When they reached the place where the brigadier and Martín Ochoa were marching with the Frenchman, Martín Ochoa came running pell-mell to the Adelantado to seek his reward for good news and to tell him that they had captured the sentinel. Fearing he would be discovered, the brigadier ran the Frenchman through with his sword and, leaving him for dead, took the lead and said to the men:

—Brothers, do as I do, for God is with us.

Then he encountered two Frenchmen in their nightshirts. He killed one of them, and the other was killed by Captain Andrés López Patiño, who was behind him. He ran on, and when he arrived near the fort, the people outside were screaming, for they had seen the two Frenchmen get killed. The postern of the main gate opened. The brigadier closed in and killed the man who had opened the gate. He slipped inside, and after him came all those who had run the fastest. Since they could not close [the door], they opened it. When they were inside, they found many Frenchmen coming out of their houses in their nightshirts, and others fully clothed, [trying] to find out what had happened. These were killed at once. Others retreated and jumped from the walls. Two flags were brought in, one the sergeant major's, raised by his ensign called Rodrigo Troche, from Tordesillas, on a cavalier,[40] the other belonging to Diego de Amaya, raised by his ensign Cristóbal de Herrera, from Cantabria,[41] on another cavalier. These two ensigns could not agree who had been the first, and it was never determined. Two trumpeters entered at the same time as these two flag bearers and placed themselves next to the flags, sounding victory, whereupon the French were disheartened, and all our men came at once through the gate, which had been opened wide for them, going into the French barracks and leaving no one alive.

The Adelantado waited until half of the men had gone inside and told the captain of his guard, Francisco de Castañeda (to whom he had given over the Frenchman [Jean François] with his hands bound behind him), to remain where he was, crying out victory, until the rearguard arrived, because he himself had to catch up with the vanguard and get into the fray. [The captain] did so, and [the Adelantado] ran with the utmost speed and arrived at the fort, where our soldiers were killing the French. Then, running from one place to another, he said in a loud voice that, on pain of death, no one should harm or kill any woman, or any child under fifteen years of age. This being so, seventy people were saved, but all the rest were killed, except fifty or sixty who jumped from the walls and took refuge in the woods from which the Adelantado had come.

The Adelantado left the fort and went toward some houses that were close to the wall, where Captain Castañeda was approaching with the Frenchman [Jean François]. This man pointed to a large house which he said they called La Granja, which was full of articles for barter, cloth and linen, and other munitions. The Adelantado left six men guarding the house to prevent anyone from going inside, so that everything there would belong to the camp in general and be used and distributed among those who were most in need. Then he went to the shore, where three very well armed ships were moored. He called a trumpeter and made him sound a peace call, using a white cloth as a flag, telling them to come ashore in their boat. The French replied that they did not want to, and the Adelantado assured them on his word that they could come [safely]. They refused.

He went to the fort, had four bronze artillery pieces set up to sink the ships, and went looking for powder. He found two barrels with approximately a hundredweight of powder, and some twenty balls, in the house of a gunner that a Frenchwoman pointed out to them. They served the pieces, loading balls inside, and before opening fire they asked them again to come ashore on their boat. [The men on] the ship the Adelantado was addressing replied that they would send a boat for someone to speak to them and tell them what the Adelantado wanted. He replied that they should come to him. In order for them to believe what he said, he took the Frenchman [Jean François] whom he held bound and set him free, telling him to go to those ships and inform the man in charge that they could take any ship they wanted of the three and, with God's help, go to France with the women and children who had been spared and the necessary supplies, but without any artillery or ammunition, for he would give them permission to leave, as well as letters of safe-conduct that would allow them to go to France safely and be treated well wherever they went. If they chose not to do this, he would sink them and have them beheaded and hanged, without leaving anyone [alive]. The boat came ashore and the Frenchman went back in it with this message. By then the Adelantado had already ordered the sergeant major to distribute among his soldiers one barrel of very good arquebus powder which was found with the powder for cannons in the house of that gunner.

The Frenchman came back to the Adelantado with the answer, telling him that the man in charge of those vessels was Jacques Ribault, the oldest son of Jean Ribault,[42] who claimed that the king of France had made [his father] viceroy and captain general of that land, and that he had come together with his father, by order of his king, to bring in those ships men, artillery, and supplies for that fort, in which he had committed no crime but had rather done what he was bound to do as a good subject, and that if the Adelantado meant to wage war against him, he would wage war against the Adelantado. Then the Adelantado ordered the men to aim the best piece of bronze artillery at what appeared to him to be the best ship, a new one on her maiden voyage, and which was appropriate, for the other two were not in such a suitable place to be shot at. Thinking he could aim better than anyone else, Captain Diego de Amaya did this and fired the cannon. He hit the ship at the water line, in such a way that the French realized that they were sinking, and that they could not use the pump, because to do this they would have to be exposed on deck and could be killed by the artillery.

When they saw they were doomed, the Frenchmen in the ship took to their boat on one side, and the two boats from the other vessels came to bring to those two the people of that ship, which was sinking. The other two cut the cables and let themselves go downstream with the strong current, anchoring at a place where the artillery could not really harm them, especially since the Adelantado did not dare to waste powder because he had not yet been able to find any more in the fort. During all this time the wind and the water from the sky were a marvel to behold. The soldiers were rejoicing over the victory and booty, and they did not care to retire and rest from all their hardships and the dreadful night they had had. For the good of all, the Adelantado had them lodged in groups of twenty in the many houses outside the fort, giving them all sorts of shirts and clothes, because there were many inside the house of La Granja, and good rations of bread, wine, lard, and bacon, since there was much of this. Around noon he undressed and went to bed, where he was fed. Since he wanted to enter into council with his captains, he ordered them to come to him at four in the afternoon. They did so, and the Adelantado, having gotten up and dressed, said to them all, his eyes brimming with tears:

—Gentlemen and brothers, God works these miracles once and again for His cause. Let us be able to serve and praise Him for the great mercy He has shown to us. It is now time to commend ourselves to Him more than ever and get our things ready to defend this fort against the French fleet when it returns, and to secure the men, artillery, weapons, ammunition, and supplies we have left at St. Augustine. For this purpose, let us make a list of all the men here—because it seems to me that we are missing many of the five hundred soldiers who set out from St. Augustine—in order to see who is to remain here and who is to go back to St. Augustine. I should return the day after tomorrow with those who will go with me, since it is necessary to keep [St. Augustine] well protected. We shall defend this [fort] against the French, preventing them from setting foot ashore when they come back with their fleet, and they shall not disembark at St. Augustine, which is a better port.

He appointed as warden of the fort and governor of that district Captain Gonzalo de Villarroel, the sergeant major, who had worked very well, with much order and care, and who was a trustworthy soldier and very fit for command. [The fort] was delivered to him, he took the usual oath, and they named it Fort San Mateo, because it was conquered on [21 September

1565,] St. Matthew's Day. [The Adelantado] commanded that, from that day onwards, he should hold it and defend it in His Majesty's name with three hundred soldiers he would leave with him to serve as guards. He ordered the brigadier to go and make a list of all the men there, [selecting] those who were to remain [in San Mateo] and those who were to return with the Adelantado [to St. Augustine]. He did so, taking the sergeant major with him. In this council the Adelantado had first appointed Rodrigo Montes as the storekeeper in that fort. [He said] that all the supplies there should be handed over to him and that, the following day, they should bring him a list of what had been given out, so he could leave instructions on how to distribute the rations. In that council the Adelantado commanded that the two coat of arms belonging to the admiral and the king of France, which were over the main gate of the fort, be removed, [but] when they went to do so, a soldier had already removed them, cut them into pieces, and burnt them. Then he ordered them to make an escutcheon with the Spanish royal arms of King Philip [II], our lord, with the Cross of the Angels[43] on top of the crown, which was very well painted by some Flemish soldiers who were there, and it was placed where the others had been.

The morning of the following day [22 September 1565], having heard mass, the Adelantado had two crosses erected in those parts that seemed best to him. He marked the spot for a church where a wooden chapel was to be built in order to say mass every day, for the French had lots of timber there for a galley they had been building. Having received the list of supplies that had been found, he gave instructions to Gonzalo de Villarroel, warden of the fort and governor of the district, regarding how he should distribute the supplies and the rations. They brought him a list of the men there, and out of five hundred [who departed from St. Augustine] they found fewer than four hundred, since the rest had either been too tired to make it there or were cowards who, because of the danger they imagined, had returned to St. Augustine, claiming—as it was later found out—that they had lost their way.

The Adelantado commanded three hundred soldiers to remain there and the other hundred to march with him and with captains Andrés López Patiño, Juan Vélez de Medrano, and [Diego de] Alvarado, but the soldiers and captains said they were in no condition to march, especially since it had rained so hard that it was impossible to cross the swamps, rivers, and brooks on the way.[44] Even though the Adelantado made great efforts to get them to go, he realized it would not be possible, as they were largely right and had no desire to go, for they were very tired and fatigued from the hardships of the journey. Then he went about the houses where the soldiers were lodged and, of those he knew better and who were less tired, he found thirty-five who wanted to follow him. Together with the captain of the guard, he asked them to be ready to leave the following day at dawn.

At nine o'clock that day, the Adelantado ordered the brigadier to go at once with fifty soldiers to where the French ships were anchored, one league from there. That morning they had weighed anchor and had gone to that place, since it seemed to them that the fifty or sixty Frenchmen who had jumped from the walls when the fort was taken from them had gone through the woods straight toward the ships in order to call out to the boats and be taken aboard. The brigadier scattered his men throughout the woods, and they found about twenty Frenchmen who had escaped. Not being able to catch up with them, they shot at them with the arquebuses and killed them. The remaining thirty or so had embarked, among them Captain [René Goulaine de] Laudonnière,[45] warden of the fort, who had escaped by jumping from the wall like the rest. The other ten had gone to the Indian chieftains and were later rescued and sent to France by the Adelantado. [It was they who] told how Laudonnière and his thirty men had embarked on those ships.

When the brigadier returned that night with Captain Martín Ochoa and Diego de Amaya and the men they had taken with them, the Adelantado asked all the captains to enter into council with him and told them that the next morning [24 September 1565] he would depart for St. Augustine. He would then send two of the three ships he had left there, well armed with good artillery, to capture those two French ships and force them to leave the harbor, because according to the Frenchmen there, they had very few men on board. When [the French ships] had left, they could set the artillery that the two ships brought in the most necessary parts of the fort, in order to be better fortified when the French came, for the Adelantado always feared that when the French fleet came back with their Indian allies, they would be eager to conquer that fort again and take revenge. [He said] that one of these ships would take the women and children to the island of Santo Domingo, that he would write to the High Court[46] to have them sent to Seville and from there to France, and that he would give instructions to the masters of these two ships to take supplies from the galleon *San Pelayo*, which the Adelantado had sent to that island of Santo Domingo.

On the morning of the following day, having heard mass, the Adelantado departed with the captain of his guard, Francisco de Castañeda, and the thirty-five soldiers he had singled out, ordering the brigadier and the other captains to remain in that fort until he gave them different orders. Whenever the three captains [Diego de] Alvarado, [Juan Vélez de] Medrano, and [Andrés López] Patiño and the balance of the hundred-man contingent were fit to walk, they should leave for St. Augustine without wasting time. They did so within the week.[47]

Chapter 3

First Massacre of Huguenots

The perils and hardships the Adelantado and the [thirty-five] men who returned with him endured on the day he left San Mateo—and the second and the third, until they arrived at St. Augustine—were so great that only those who saw them could believe them. On the day he departed from San Mateo, at around two in the afternoon, having marched for two leagues, he entered some woods he had been through before and, after about half a league, encountered a lot of water. Thinking he would be out of it quickly, he walked more than a league farther, finding more and more water, until he could not go ahead. On the way back the water in the woods and the creeks was rising, and he lost his way, so that he did not even know whether he was advancing or retreating. He wished to go back to a place where he could halt and build a fire for the night's rest, but he could not find it. He wanted to climb the trees, but they were so tall and straight that it was not possible. At that point he realized he was completely lost and his men were discouraged. Not knowing how to remedy the situation, he had the most agile soldier he could find climb the tallest tree he could find in order to check if he could spot any flat country or anywhere dry, but once he was up he said that all he saw was water, and that he did not see any level or dry terrain. The Adelantado ordered him to see if he could make out which way the sun was moving. He said that he could not. He ordered him to stay there until later, when by God's will the weather cleared a little. The soldier saw where the sun was about to set, and he pointed in that direction. The Adelantado saw a way to get out of the woods, for there was no undergrowth and the trees were far apart. Cutting down some pine trees in the places with deep water, he came to a narrow and deep river which he and his men had crossed at a different point when they went from St. Augustine to San

Mateo.[48] He had the trees on the bank cut down at the base with five axes the soldiers were carrying, so they fell across to the other bank, and they crossed the river at much peril. When they were crossing, two soldiers escaped miraculously from drowning. He ordered the soldier who had previously climbed the tree to climb another one, and he saw some dry land in a place they had previously passed through, and they came out on the path and camped in a dry place where they built great fires. They dried their clothes, which were all soaking wet.

Toward daybreak it began to rain very hard, and as it was already light, they left. It took them three days to get to St. Augustine, but owing to the victory that Our Lord had given them, they did not mind the journey or its dangers, because they were very eager to share the good news with their comrades. One league before they reached St. Augustine, that soldier asked the Adelantado, as a favor, to allow him to run ahead and tell the good news, and the Adelantado granted it. Given the bad weather they had endured and the news from those who had turned back, the people who had stayed behind were of the opinion that they had been lost, because they knew they did not have any food, powder, or fuses. When they heard the good news, all the clerics who were there came out in a procession with a cross, and with all the sailors, soldiers, women, and children, chanting the Te Deum Laudamus. They greeted the Adelantado with great happiness and pleasure, everyone laughing and crying with joy, praising Our Lord God for such a great victory. They went triumphantly with him into the stockade and settlement of St. Augustine, where he told them all the specifics of the great mercy that Our Lord had granted them with this victory. He then prepared the two warships. Within two days, as he was about to depart with them for San Mateo, news came that the two French vessels had already crossed the bar. He dispatched one of the ships with artillery, powder, and ammunition to place in the fort so that it could be ready with the best defenses, and he busied himself fortifying [St. Augustine] as best he could to await the French fleet, if it should come there.

The following day [28 September 1565],[49] some Indians arrived and told him by signs that four leagues away there were many Christians unable to cross an arm of the sea, albeit narrow, an estuary inside a bar, which one must perforce cross to get to St. Augustine. That evening the Adelantado took with him forty soldiers, and after midnight he arrived near that inlet, where he called a halt. In the morning, leaving his soldiers in ambush, he saw from the top of a tree what was happening. On the other side of the river he saw two flags and many people, and in order to prevent them from crossing, he came close enough for them to be able to count his men, so they would think there were many [more].[50] Once they were spotted, a man swam across the river. He was French, and he said that the people there were all French, that they had been shipwrecked in a storm, and that they had all escaped.[51]

The Adelantado asked him who the French were. He said there were six hundred,[52] captains and people of Jean Ribault, the king of France's viceroy and captain general of that land. He asked if they were Catholics or Lutherans. [The man] said they were all Lutherans of the new religion—although the Adelantado already knew this, for they had said so when he encountered their fleet, and so had the women and children whose lives he spared when he conquered the fort [San Mateo], and he had found six coffers filled with bound and gold-tooled books, all pertaining to the new religion, which he had burned, sparing none; and [he knew] that they did not say mass, and that their Lutheran sect was preached to them every evening.

The Adelantado asked him why they had come there. He said that their captain had sent him to see who they were. The Adelantado asked him if he wanted to return. He replied that he did, but he [also] wanted to know who they were. This man spoke [Spanish] very clearly, because he was a Gascon from Saint-Jean-de-Luz.[53] Then the Adelantado asked him to tell his captain that he was King Philip [II]'s viceroy and captain general of that land, that his name was Pedro Menéndez, that he was there with some soldiers to find out who they were, because the day before they had had news that they were there, and that he was just now arriving.

The Frenchman left with the message and later came back asking that they give a safe-conduct for his captain and four other gentlemen who wanted to meet with him, and loan them a boat that the Adelantado had there, which had come down the river with supplies. [The Adelantado] asked the Frenchman to tell his captain that he could come safely on his word. Then he sent for them with the boat, and they came. The Adelantado received them very well with about ten of his men and ordered the rest to stay back among some bushes where they could all be seen, so the French would think there were more men. One of the Frenchmen said that he was the captain of those people, that four galleons and several shallops belonging to the king of France had been shipwrecked in a storm twenty leagues from one another, that they were the people from one of those ships, and that they wanted the Adelantado to help them by letting them use that boat to cross that inlet, as well as another one located four leagues away, which was that of St. Augustine, as they wished to go to a fort they had twenty leagues [northwards] from there.[54] (This was the fort the Adelantado had taken from them.) The Adelantado asked him whether they were Catholics or Lutherans. He said they were all of the new religion. Then the Adelantado said to them:

—Gentlemen, your fort has been captured and its people killed, with the exception of the women and the children under fifteen years of age. In order for you to be certain of this, among some of the soldiers here there are many things [from that fort], and two Frenchmen whom I brought with me because they claimed to be Catholics. Be seated here and eat, for I shall send you the two Frenchmen and the things the soldiers have taken from the fort in order for you to be convinced.

The Adelantado did this, ordering his men to feed them and sending them the two Frenchmen and many things the soldiers had taken from the fort so that they could see them, and then withdrew to eat with his men. An hour later, when he saw that the Frenchmen had eaten, he went to where they were, asking them if they were convinced of what he had said to them. They said that they were, and they asked that he kindly give them ships and provisions with which they could go to France. The Adelantado replied that he would gladly comply if they were Catholics and he had ships to spare, but he did not have them, because he was sending two to San Mateo with the artillery, and then to take the French women and children to Santo Domingo, [and] to fetch supplies. The other was to be sent to His Majesty with news of what had happened in that land so far.

The French captain asked the Adelantado to spare their lives and [allow them] to stay with him until there might be ships [bound] for France, for the kings of France and Spain were friends and brothers and there was no war between them.[55] The Adelantado replied that this was true, and that he would help Catholics and friends, for he believed he would be serving both kings in this. However, since they belonged to the new religion, he considered them enemies. He had a war of blood and fire with them, and he would wage it with all cruelty against those he found on that sea or land where he was viceroy and captain general for his king. He had come to implant the Holy Gospel in that land so that the Indians might be enlightened and live in the knowledge of the Holy Catholic Faith of Jesus Christ, Our Lord, as preached and practiced by the Church of Rome, and if they chose to surrender their weapons and flags, placing themselves at his mercy so he might do with them as God wished, they could do so. Otherwise, they should do as they pleased, for he would not come to any other truce or agreement with them.

Even though the French captain protested, he could not make the Adelantado agree to anything else. He went back to his men in the boat in which he had come, saying that he was going to tell them what had happened and decide what they must do, and he would return within two hours with an answer. The Adelantado told them that they should do as they thought best, and that he would wait.

Two hours later the same French captain returned with the same men as before, and he told the Adelantado that there were many noblemen there who would give him fifty thousand ducats if he spared all their lives. The Adelantado replied that, even though he was a poor soldier, he did not want to do such a weak thing, so as not to be branded as greedy; that whenever he chose to be liberal and merciful he would be so without self-interest. The French captain persisted, but the Adelantado disabused him: even if the earth were to join with the heavens, he would not do anything other than what he had told him. So the French captain returned to where his men were, telling the Adelantado that he would return with whatever decision they made. Half an hour later he came back, and he had put in the boat all the flags, some sixty arquebuses, twenty pistols, a quantity of swords and bucklers, and some helmets and breastplates. He came to where the Adelantado was and said that all those Frenchmen gave themselves up to his mercy, and he surrendered the flags and weapons.

Then the Adelantado ordered twenty of his soldiers to get into the boat and bring back the French in groups of ten. The river was narrow and easy to cross. He ordered the admiral of the fleet, Diego Flórez Valdés, to receive the flags and weapons, and to be diligent in bringing the French in the boat, [saying] that the soldiers should not mistreat them. The Adelantado withdrew from the shore to some bushes behind a sand dune, at a distance of two arquebus shots, where he could not see the people bringing the Frenchmen across in the boat. Then he said to the French captain and to another eight Frenchmen who were with him:

—Gentlemen, I have but a few inexperienced soldiers, and there are many of you. Walking unbound, it would be easy for you to take revenge on us for the people we killed when we captured the fort. Therefore, it is necessary that you march with your hands tied behind your back to my camp, eight leagues [north] from here.[56]

The French agreed to this, and their hands were tied securely behind their backs with the soldiers' fuse cords. The ten men coming in the boat could not see the others whose hands were tied until they were close to them. It was best to proceed in this manner so that the Frenchmen who had not yet crossed the river would not see this and become alarmed, so they tied up two hundred and eight French soldiers. The Adelantado asked if any among them were Catholics who wanted to make confession. Eight of them said they were. He took them out of there and placed them in the boat to be taken by the river to St. Augustine. The others replied that they belonged to the new religion, that they considered themselves to be very good Christians, and that they had no other creed but this one.

When [each] ten men arrived, the Adelantado gave them food and drink before tying them up, which was done before the next ten arrived. Then he ordered them to march. He told one of his captains, named Juan de San Vicente, to march with them in the vanguard until he came to a sandy stretch, at a distance of a crossbow shot, that they needed to cross in order to go to the port of St. Augustine. There he would find a line that [the Adelantado] would draw with a short lance he carried in his hand, where he should kill them all. He ordered the one in the rear guard to do the same, and it was done like this, leaving all [the French] dead. He got back to St. Augustine that night toward dawn, for the sun had already set when those men died.

Chapter 4

Second Massacre of Huguenots

On the day after the Adelantado's arrival in St. Augustine, the same Indians as before came and told him that there were many more Christians on that part of the river where the others had been. The Adelantado realized that this must [be the men of] Jean Ribault, general of the Lutherans on land and sea, whom they called viceroy of that land for the king of France. Then he departed with one hundred and fifty soldiers in formation, and at midnight he set up camp in the same place as before. At dawn he and his men were lying on the ground next to the river and, as the day got clearer, they saw a lot of people on the other side of the river, at a distance of two arquebus shots, and a raft they had made to take them across to where the Adelantado was. When they spotted the Adelantado and his men, the French sounded the call to arms and unfurled a royal standard and two campaign flags, playing fifes and drums in very good formation, ready to fight the Adelantado, who had ordered his men to sit and eat without showing any signs of turmoil. His admiral [Diego Flórez de Valdés] and two other captains walked along the shore paying no attention to the turmoil and the battle cries of the French, in such a way that [the French] must have been disconcerted, for they halted their forming up, ceasing to play the fifes and drums. Sounding a bugle, they raised a white cloth of peace.

The Adelantado called a very good bugler he had brought with him and took a handkerchief out of his pocket and began to wave it as a sign of peace. A Frenchman climbed on the raft and in a loud voice said we should cross over there. By order of the Adelantado, they were answered that if they wanted something, they should cross to where he was, since they had a raft and he was calling to them. The one on the raft replied that it was unsuitable for crossing, since the current was strong, and that they should send him a canoe they had there, which belonged to some Indians. The Adelantado gave his word that he could swim over to get it. Then a French sailor came over, but the Adelantado did not allow him to speak. He told him to take the canoe and go and tell his captain that if he wanted something, he should send word, since he had called to him. This sailor came back presently with a gentleman who said that he was the sergeant major of Jean Ribault, viceroy and captain general of that land for the king of France, and that he had sent him to say that he had been shipwrecked with his fleet during a storm at sea, that he had approximately three hundred and fifty Frenchmen there, that he needed to go to a fort he had about twenty leagues from there,[57] that he should be given boats to cross that river and another that was four leagues away, and that he wished to know if they were Spaniards, and who their captain was.

The Adelantado replied that they were Spaniards, that their captain was the same person with whom he was speaking, that his name was Pedro Menéndez, and that [the man] should tell his general that [the Adelantado] had captured the fort he claimed to have twenty leagues[58] from there and had killed its Frenchmen, as well as many others who had come from the shipwrecked fleet, because they had not behaved well. He walked over to where the dead men were and showed them to him, [telling him] that there was no reason for him to cross the river to his fort.

Without showing any sign of grief at what the Adelantado had told him, this sergeant asked the Adelantado with great composure if he would do him the kindness of sending one of his gentlemen to communicate this to his general so they might negotiate a safe-conduct for the Adelantado to go and see him on a boat he had there, because his general was very tired. The Adelantado replied:

—Go with God, brother, and give him my reply, and if your general would like to come to speak to me, I give him my word that he can come and return safely with five or six men of his council, so that he might think about what suits him best.

This French gentleman left with this message. Within half an hour he returned to accept the assurance the Adelantado had given and to request the boat, but the Adelantado did not want to give it to him, sending him back to say they might steal it, and since the river was narrow, it was safe to cross over in the canoe. This gentleman returned with this message, and then came Jean Ribault, whom the Adelantado received very well, with another eight gentlemen who came with him, all treated very well as persons of rank and authority. He served them light refreshment from a certain barrel of preserved victuals, and drink, [saying] that they would give them food if they desired it. Jean Ribault replied with much humility, thanking him for the kind reception given him. He said that in order to cheer their spirits, which were sad because of the news they had been given about their comrades, they would like to have the preserved food and the wine for breakfast, and that, for the time being, they did not want any other food. They did so.

Jean Ribault said that his comrades who died there (whom he saw, because they were nearby) could have been deceived, and he did not wish to be. Then [the Adelantado] ordered the soldiers who were there to approach, each bringing the things he had taken from the fort, and [Jean Ribault] saw so many things that he knew for certain it was true. He already knew the news but couldn't believe it. There was among them a French barber whom the Adelantado had ordered to be killed with the rest, who had let himself fall after the first knife-thrust, playing dead, and they had left him for dead among the other men. When he [Jean Ribault] arrived, the barber swam over to him and said he was sure the Adelantado had deceived them, claiming that the fort had been captured when it was not, and this is what he [Jean Ribault] had believed until then. The Adelantado said that, in order for him to believe it more and satisfy himself, he should speak separately with two Frenchmen who were there and who had been present.

Then Jean Ribault came to the Adelantado and told him that he was certain that everything he had told him was true, that whatever was happening to him could happen to the Adelantado, and that—since their kings were brothers and such great friends—the Adelantado should treat him likewise as a friend, giving him ships and supplies with which to go to France. The Adelantado gave him the same reasons he had given to the first Frenchmen he had executed, and [even] after discussing with him, Jean Ribault could not make the Adelantado agree to anything else. Then Jean Ribault told them that he wanted to inform his men, because there were many noblemen among them, and he would send him word of whatever they agreed. Ribault returned within three hours in the canoe, saying that there were different opinions among his men, as some wished to place themselves at the Adelantado's mercy and others did not. The Adelantado replied that he did not care whether they all came, or only some of them, or none at all, that they were free to do whatever suited them best. Jean Ribault told the Adelantado that half of them wanted to place themselves at his mercy and would pay him more than one hundred thousand ducats in ransom, and that the other half could pay even more, because among them there were wealthy persons of large income who intended to settle in that land. The Adelantado replied:

—It really grieves me to lose such good ransom and booty, for I have dire need of those monies to help with the conquest and settlement of this land in the name of my king, where it is my duty to spread the Holy Gospel.

Jean Ribault used much cunning here to see if he could profit from it. It seemed to him that, coveting the money they would give him, the Adelantado would spare him and those who placed themselves at his mercy, believing that by not killing either group, according to an agreement Jean Ribault would make with him, they would be worth more than two hundred thousand ducats to him. He said to the Adelantado that he was to return to his men with his reply, and asked him as a favor to stay there until the following day, when he would come back with their decision, because it was now late. The Adelantado told him that he would wait, and that he should rejoin his men, as the sun was already setting.

The next morning [12 October 1565], he came back in the canoe and gave the Adelantado two royal standards, one belonging to the king of France and the other to the admiral, and two campaign flags, a sword, a dagger, a very good gilded helmet, a buckler, a pistol, and a seal he carried that the admiral of France had given him in order to seal the documents and titles he was to confer. He said to the Adelantado that, out of the three hundred and fifty persons that were there, about one hundred and fifty wished to place themselves at his mercy, that the rest had fled during the night, and that the boat should go over to bring back those who wished to come and their weapons. The Adelantado instructed Captain Diego Flórez de Valdés, admiral of the fleet, to have them brought over as he had the others, in groups of ten. The Adelantado took Jean Ribault into the bushes behind the sand dune, where he had taken the others. He had Ribault's hands and those of all the rest tied behind their backs, as had been done to the others, telling them that, since they were to march four leagues on land, and at night, he could not allow them to go unbound. When they were all tied up, he asked them if they were Catholics or Lutherans, and if anyone desired to confess.

Jean Ribault replied that he and all those who were there were of the new religion, and he began to recite the psalm "Domine Memento Mei." When it was over, he said that dust they were and unto dust they must return,[59] that another twenty or so years were of little account, and that the Adelantado should do with them as he pleased. The Adelantado ordered them to march, as he had done to the others, in the same formation and toward the same line, and commanded the same be done to these as he had done to the others. He excepted only the fifers, drummers, trumpeters, and four other men who claimed to be Catholics, sixteen men in total. All the rest were put to the knife.

That night he returned to St. Augustine, where some people believed he had been cruel and others thought he had acted as a very good captain. It was decided that if the French had been Catholics and he had not finished them off, they would have killed [us] Catholics, for they were more numerous, or we would all have died of hunger due to the scarcity of supplies the Adelantado had, since Fort San Mateo, which the Adelantado had taken from them, burned down with a lot of property and supplies within a week of being captured.[60] In a house where Captain Francisco Recalde was lodged, one of his servants had set it on fire by sticking a lit candle on a post that fell down. This was suspicious because there had been much discord between Captain Villarroel—the sergeant major—and Francisco Recalde, and some soldiers had started to suggest that, since the fort had been captured and there were no supplies, they should raze it and move on to the Indies in the two ships the Adelantado had sent to them from St. Augustine with the artillery.[61] Some captains did not dare to voice their opinions because the brigadier and Villarroel and the most important men among the soldiers were the Adelantado's friends, and he had some relatives and servants there. At that time it was not known in San Mateo that the Adelantado had been victorious against Jean Ribault and his men, and that he had killed them. It was later found out from the French women and children who had been spared when the French fort was captured that, at the time Jean Ribault and his men had embarked in their fleet, they had drunk two casks of wine, toasting each other and saying:

—I drink to the heads of Pedro Menéndez and his men, who are Spanish pigs![62] We shall punish them by hanging them from the yards of their ships and our own, and they shall not come back to look for us in this, our land!

[This was said] in such a way that many noblemen who were there with Jean Ribault were offended by those words and insults uttered against the Spaniards.

Chapter 5

Expedition against the French

After these men were put to the knife, some Indians came to the Adelantado twenty days later[63] and told him by signs that, a week's march from there to the south, within the Bahama Channel at Cape Canaveral, many men—brothers of those whom the Adelantado had had killed—were building a fort and a vessel. Then the Adelantado suspected what this could be; that the [two hundred] Frenchmen who had escaped were fortifying themselves with the timber, artillery, supplies, and ammunition from the French fleet that had been shipwrecked, and building a ship to send to France and request relief. He dispatched ten soldiers from St. Augustine to San Mateo to tell them all this and how he wanted to proceed, requesting that enough soldiers should come to him to make up a unit of one hundred and fifty, counting the thirty-five he had brought with him when he captured the fort and returned to St. Augustine. The brigadier sent them at once with Captains Juan Vélez de Medrano and Andrés López Patiño, and they arrived in St. Augustine on 23 October [1565].

On the morning of the twenty-sixth, having heard mass, the Adelantado departed with three hundred men and with three vessels carrying the weapons and supplies by sea. The vessels went at the same pace as the men marching on land, and wherever they camped at night the vessels anchored, as the whole coast was sandy and clear. Before departing from St. Augustine, the Adelantado appointed judicial and administrative officers, and held a council with the captains. Consulting with them, it was noted in the council books that they should give out the appropriate rations with the supplies they had, and do the same with future supplies. He left the fort traced out, divided the work of building it equally among squads of men, and [designated] the soldiers who were to work daily on the fortification, three hours in the morning and three in the afternoon. He left Captain Bartolomé Menéndez, his brother, as warden of the fort and governor, as he had always been and still remains. He decreed that all criminal sentences be imposed by the council, since the captains themselves were the councilors, and that all appeals be heard before the brigadier,[64] on whom he conferred enough authority to be his lieutenant general, as His Majesty had given him power to appoint whomever he wished whenever he was absent.

He sent the same orders and instructions to San Mateo to Gonzalo de Villarroel so he would observe the aforementioned, and before his departure he dispatched the admiral of the fleet, Diego Flórez de Valdés, with the ship that was there,[65] to go to His Majesty and inform him of everything that had happened until that day.

All the men and women of the St. Augustine complement asked the Adelantado kindly not to return to that port with his men without bringing food, as the supplies would last longer if there were fewer of them there, and they would [. . .] better. In the three vessels, the Adelantado took with him supplies to last the three hundred men forty days, with a daily ration lasting two days. He promised that, in every matter, he would strive to do what was best for the general good, despite the dangers and hardships, because he had faith in the kindness and mercy of God, who would help them in all ways to succeed in such a good and holy endeavor. Thus he bid farewell to them, while most of them wept, for he was loved and feared, esteemed and respected by all.

Making good time each day, he arrived at the fort the Frenchmen were building at dawn of All Saints' Day [1 November 1565], for some Indians were guiding him. He marched on foot with the soldiers, and the three vessels—commanded by Captain Diego de Amaya—followed him by sea. When the French inside the fort spotted them, they fled to the woods, leaving no one behind. The Adelantado sent them a trumpeter, assuring them that he would spare their lives, and that if they came back he would treat them as he would treat a Spaniard. About one hundred and fifty of them came to the Adelantado, but twenty other men stayed behind with their captain, who sent word that he would much rather be eaten by Indians than surrender to Spaniards. The Adelantado received these men very well and treated them kindly. He set fire to the wooden fort and destroyed it, burned the ship they were building, and buried the artillery, because the [Adelantado's] vessels were so small that they could not carry it with them.

Chapter 6

In the Country of Chief Ais

Later in the afternoon that day the Adelantado went south along the coast. The three vessels sailed down, looking for a port or river located fifteen leagues from there,[66] where there were some Indian villages. The Adelantado wanted to see if he could leave his men quartered there with some chieftain and he himself could go within the Bahama Channel to the island of Cuba in order to get supplies. On the third day, 4 November of the said year of [15]65, they arrived at that port and named it Ais, because that was the name of the chieftain who lived there, a very good Indian who received the Adelantado very well.[67] Neither he nor his people left their homes, but rather waited for the Adelantado with all the people in the village. This was a demonstration of trust that gave the Adelantado much pleasure, because up until then all the people of the Indian villages where he arrived had fled into the woods, leaving their homes deserted.

The Adelantado did not allow any damage to be done to their houses or to the things they left inside, but instead he left, in return for hospitality in the chieftains' houses, some gifts such as mirrors, knives, scissors, and some bells, things of which they were very fond. He was there four days, during which he went along a river to see some sites the chieftain had told him were good to settle, and without going out to sea he arrived at a small harbor located about fifteen leagues from there, inside the Bahama Channel. He was not pleased with the land, and he returned. Not having much food—and neither did the Indians of that land, other than fish, coco plums, and palm hearts—it was agreed and requested by all the people there, in view of the danger that they would all die of starvation, that even though it was the middle of November,[68] a dangerous time to sail through the Bahama Channel, which is very stormy, and the vessels were very small, the

Adelantado should go with two of the [three] vessels to Cuba to send supplies to the men at St. Augustine and San Mateo.

The Adelantado did so, taking with him fifty men, counting both sailors and soldiers, and twenty of the French soldiers from Canaveral—for he had taken them all with him, which was why the rations for forty days he had brought from St. Augustine were consumed sooner, because they gave as much food to the French as to the Spaniards, and the Adelantado did not receive special treatment in his ration, which was half a pound of biscuit daily for each soldier (although it should have been one and a half pounds), without any wine or any other kind of food, other than the palm hearts and coco plums they gathered in the countryside.

There was a soldier there in Ais who sold four pounds of biscuit at twenty-five reales each,[69] but he ate so many palmetto berries and other kinds of fruit that were tasty that one day at nightfall he was well and then at midnight he was dead.

Everybody was astonished at how much the Adelantado marched on foot, because for this expedition he had not taken any horses with him, and on the third day there were still fifty soldiers left in the rear guard that could not catch up to him, with many so tired that they could not even walk. Two of the strongest soldiers who were marching with the Adelantado in the vanguard, each between twenty-five and thirty years of age, who had been among the first to go into Fort San Mateo when it was taken from the French, were ashamed to see how much the Adelantado could walk, and in order not to fall behind they forced themselves more than was reasonable, and as they walked along one of them said to the other:

—Comrade, I would like to sit down for a while, for I am very tired.

Without the Adelantado being aware of it, these two remained behind, seated. Within fifteen minutes, without ever getting up from there, this soldier had surrendered his soul to God. The other forced himself to keep up with the Adelantado and one night he disappeared, never to be seen again, because all the men marched on a sandy stretch along the coast from two hours after midnight until sunrise. Then they halted, and the soldiers went into the savannahs to eat palm hearts and coco plums, gathering some to take with them. They stayed for two hours and then marched until eleven or noon, then they rested until two in the afternoon and marched on until the sun set once more. There was not a day in which they did not walk upwards of eight leagues, and everyone marveled at how much they walked, without any food, and on such a route with such treacherous sands.

Chief Ais was much grieved at the Adelantado's departure from that land, and he and his children wept, for the Adelantado had treated him very well during those days when he was there and had given many gifts to him and likewise to his children and to the most important Indian men and women. Since the Adelantado feared that war would break out between his soldiers and the Indians—in which they were at risk of being killed—because of the lack of food, and since they did not know the land and were very feeble, the Adelantado before he departed for Havana arranged to leave [his soldiers] three leagues from there in a place on the river that the Indians said was very good and had palmitos, coco plums, and fish.[70]

The men arrived there with the vessels in two days. [The Adelantado] dreaded his departure, first because he thought the soldiers were feeble and disheartened, and for another thing because no ship had ever been known to reach the island of Cuba from within the Bahama Channel, although many had attempted it, because the current always runs very strong toward the north, and the Adelantado had to sail south toward the island of Cuba, so that the current was against him and struck the ships' prows. If it were not for the relief of these men and those who remained in St. Augustine and San Mateo, he would much rather have sent another person in the two vessels, he himself staying behind with the other vessel and his men, instead of exposing himself to such great peril. But the soldiers wanted him to go because they hoped that, if he went there personally, they would be relieved with supplies.

Chapter 7

First Voyage to Havana

And so he decided to depart from that port of Ais [which he named Santa Lucía] on 6 November [1565], with fifty sailors and soldiers and twenty Frenchmen, leaving Captain Juan Vélez de Medrano in charge of those [other] men,[71] sitting down with him and all those who remained with him, encouraging and comforting them, asking them to pray for him daily, because he was placing himself, on their behalf, in a very great danger in which no man had ever placed himself before, and to beseech Our Lord God and His Precious Mother to grant him safe passage. Kneeling, they all chanted the litanies and prayed. The Adelantado embarked and had such a favorable wind that, even though there were one hundred leagues from there to Havana, as well as contrary currents, he made the journey in two days, a deed worthy of admiration, because all the pilots that had sailed in the Indies were of the opinion that it was impossible to go against that current with galleys equipped with oars. He sailed all along the coast and land of Florida. Crossing over to the island of Cuba, he encountered a great storm with a wind from the north, so they ran before the wind to protect themselves from the contrary seas.

One night while this storm lasted, the Adelantado himself steered, not trusting the helm to any of his sailors. Among the twenty Frenchmen he had with him were Jean Ribault's chief pilot and another who seemed to him a very efficient sailor. The Adelantado asked him if he was a good helmsman. He replied that he was. The Adelantado gave him the helm toward dawn, and this Frenchman steered very well. So the Adelantado and the Frenchman steered until they arrived in Havana. The vessel in which the Adelantado traveled carried no compass, because on leaving Ais, when he had it taken out of its housing, he discovered it was broken. Captain

Diego de Amaya said that the vessel he was in could sail faster than the Adelantado's, and it carried a compass. As the Adelantado's was broken, he should trim the sails and not travel far from land, and be careful not to be separated from him. On the second night, when the storm ceased almost at daybreak, the Adelantado lost sight of the other vessel, and he sailed past the port of Havana, thinking that they had not yet arrived.

Around ten in the morning he recognized the port of Bahía Honda,[72] which is fifteen leagues beyond Havana. He saw a small boat going in, followed it, and caught up. They were some Indians from Havana who were going hunting. They gave the Adelantado a lot of meat, cassava (which is the bread of that land), and palmitos, and the Indians told him that his nephew Pedro Menéndez Marqués was there in Havana with part of the fleet from Vizcaya and Asturias that had been separated from General Esteban de las Alas during a storm, and that all the men were very sad because they did not know what had happened to the Adelantado, and they were afraid that he had perished at sea in a storm, or that his enemies had defeated him, for they could not conceive or believe he would dare to go to Florida with so few ships, nor did it ever cross their minds that he was there.

The Adelantado and all his men landed at the port of Bahía Honda, and kneeling on the ground they thanked Our Lord for the mercy He had granted them in carrying them through to safety. He called the Frenchmen and urged them to consider the power and kindness of God and, if they were Lutherans, to repent and become Catholics. He would treat them kindly, regardless of their creed, and give them leave to go to Spain on the first available ships, and from there to France, for he was only thinking of their salvation when he said these words. Some of them began to cry, beating their chests, praising Our Lord and begging Him for mercy, saying that they had been Lutherans and bad Christians, that they repented, and that from that moment on they wanted to renounce their evil sect and be Catholics, making confession and taking communion, and that they wanted to observe what was dictated by Holy Mother Church. The Adelantado comforted and encouraged them, telling them that they should be happy and not resent their hardships, that he would take care of them as though they were his brothers. And so he did for these men as he did for each of the others whose lives he had spared, each according to his rank: he supplied the noblemen with clothes and sat them at his own table, and the sailors [he sat] with his pilots and sailors, and the soldiers with his captains and soldiers.

That night the Adelantado departed from the port of Bahía Honda to return to Havana. As the wind was very contrary and strong, and it was pushing him out to sea toward Florida farther than he wished, he did not arrive at Havana until midnight the following day. Since Diego de Amaya had arrived two days before, he feared that the Adelantado had been lost, and they all believed his ship had been ripped open and sunk by the great winds, for the storm had been so great and he was carrying no compass. It was said that all the people of Havana and the men of his fleet felt very sorry about him.

On the day he arrived, he rowed into the harbor, as the wind was off-shore. The sentinel on watch to guard the harbor asked whose ship was entering. They replied that it was the Adelantado Pedro Menéndez. The sentinel replied, saying:

—Blessed be Our Lord that Lord Pedro Menéndez is alive!

[He told them] to wait a bit while he went to notify [Francisco] García Osorio, the governor of that island,[73] so that they would not be shot at from the fortress. The Adelantado himself said to the sentinel, who was very close:

—Brother, go with God, for I shall wait.

He waited there long enough for the sentinel to go and return but, as he saw that he was taking too long, he ordered the yard to be adjusted and went inside. As he passed the fortress, they shot at him—knowing it was the Adelantado—with the balls of four artillery pieces, but none hit their mark. They arrived at the dock where part of his fleet from Vizcaya, commanded by his nephew Pedro Menéndez Marqués, was anchored, and they began to fire many artillery pieces on the ships and sound the trumpets out of happiness. The Adelantado saw the governor standing on the dock with many people with lit torches, a campaign flag, and a drum and a fife being played. Thinking that they were waiting for him, he went straight to disembark at the dock where the governor was, without going aboard any of his ships or stopping among them, but when [the governor] saw him coming, he left with most of the people he had there. Only Juan de [Rojas] Hinestrosa, His Majesty's treasurer on that island, remained there with some of the regidores, or city councillors.[74] He took the Adelantado to his house and entertained him and all those with him very well.

The governor summoned the Adelantado, but everyone was shocked at the little pleasure and joy the governor had shown at the Adelantado's safe arrival, and his ordering the artillery fired, because in Florida the Adelantado, to console his soldiers whenever he thought they were unhappy, always took as his refrain:

—Be strong, brothers, for García Osorio, governor of the island of Cuba, will send us a sufficient supply of food for all of us who are in Florida, for so he promised me in Seville, and His Majesty has commanded and charged him to do so.

The morning of the following day the Adelantado went to mass. As he was leaving, the governor came in and they spoke to each other. Everybody noticed how brusquely the governor spoke to the Adelantado, as if he had never seen him or met him before, and thus they took their leave. On the same day, after he had eaten, the Adelantado went to the governor's house and informed him of the great necessity in which the people of Florida found themselves. He notified him of certain provisions whereby His Majesty had ordered him to give [the Adelantado] a warship with fifty soldiers and twenty horses, paid for and with supplies for four months, and to give him all the service and help he asked for and needed for the conquest and settlement of Florida. He explained to him how there were five hundred men at His Majesty's expense in Florida who were without supplies and would die of hunger if they did not receive assistance. [He said] that he did not care about the warship, the horses, or the soldiers, all of which would cost more than twenty thousand ducats, while with [only] three or four thousand he would be able to give relief to the soldiers who were in Florida at His Majesty's expense until the spring [of 1566].

The governor replied that he would not give them to him. [The Adelantado] said he might loan them to him, and that he would procure a bondsman for them and guarantee payment himself. [The governor] said that he did not have them. [The Adelantado] said that [the governor could advance them] from the ten or twelve thousand ducats he had seized from a Portuguese caravel that Captain Juan de la Parra had captured when on the flagship of the Fleet of New Spain,[75] because that ship and its sailors and soldiers owed obedience to the Adelantado and were under his command, and those monies belonged to the Adelantado and to the men of that ship as the persons who had captured the caravel and whatever was inside, because it was trading in the Indies unregistered and counter to His Majesty's provisions and decrees. [The governor] replied that he would not give those to him either, because he said [the caravel] did not belong to him. The Adelantado asked to be loaned four thousand of those ducats on endorsed bonds, and whenever His Majesty commanded him to return them, he would. [The governor] refused.

He had imprisoned Juan de la Parra, captain of the flagship.[76] The Adelantado asked him to deliver [la Parra] to him with the proceedings of his crime. [The governor] said that, even though [the captain] was [the Adelantado's] soldier, he as governor of the land had to punish him, as well as any of the Adelantado's soldiers who did unlawful things in his district. The Adelantado replied:

—Sir, the reception Your Honor has given me in your district, let it be, for the love of God. I am determined to arm myself with patience and endure these things Your Honor does to me, because I know that, in doing this, God grants me a greater victory than the one against Jean Ribault and the other Lutherans in Florida, because I know that, in doing this, I am doing a great service to His Majesty.

[The Adelantado] doffed his hat and went out the door without waiting for the governor's reply. Then the Adelantado ordered a proclamation to be issued that all the sailors and soldiers from Asturias, Vizcaya, and the flagship of the Fleet of New Spain who were there [in Havana] should board the ships before the day was over, for he wanted to inspect and take the muster roll of all the men he had there in order to employ them in His Majesty's service.

On the morning of the following day, having heard mass at daybreak, he went to the vessels, inspected them, and took the muster roll, [finding] that he had five hundred and fifty men. He called the captains and pilots to the flagship, entered into council with them, and when they were all together he said to them:

—Gentlemen and brothers, we have been told here that many French and English corsairs are going about and robbing His Majesty's subjects. As we are at peace, they deserve to be punished, and it is held for certain—and some of you gentlemen who came from those parts have mentioned it—that among these corsairs are two vessels from England and three from France that are carrying on board more than half a million in monies they have stolen, as well as from blacks and merchandise they have sold, and that they are spending the winter in the northern part of the island of Santo Domingo in order to go to France in the spring. I have here with me four very yare ships and this flagship, all well armed, and much good ammunition, and there are five hundred and fifty sailors and soldiers on board, all very good men. It seems to me that in these ten days we should be able to stock up on water, timber, and meat—since we have most of the supplies on board, as the ships brought them from Asturias and Vizcaya—and grease and rig the ships, and put out to sea with the first [favorable] weather and go in search of these corsairs. We will do great service to Our Lord God and to His Majesty in punishing them, and this will be for the general good of all the Indies, and we will be able to profit very much. As soon as we get there, we will send two or three ships with supplies to our comrades in Florida, and in the spring we will take our ships, laden with food and livestock, to Florida in order to make our inland explorations and discoveries. And we have to remove ourselves from the risk that I perceive that some of us are running with this governor, that is, of losing our patience and being ruined. For my part I tell you, gentlemen, that even though we are in December and navigation through the Bahama Channel is perilous, I would much rather sail through it and be at sea than be in this town, because even though I know how to conduct myself with this governor, I fear that some of you might not, and if anything should happen, I would be blamed for it, having perceived the danger and not having prevented it. I ask you kindly, gentlemen, to advise me whether or not I should follow this plan.

They all approved it as good and showed great contentment. Then the Adelantado ordered the captains and pilots to get ready to sail within twelve days, and he had the masters, boatswains, storekeepers, and officers of all ships summoned and informed them of his resolution, giving them orders and charging them to get their ships ready. They agreed to do so, showing great contentment and good cheer about the voyage, and so did the sailors, ship's boys, and cabin boys of the fleet. And in the presence of all he made his nephew, Pedro Menéndez Marqués, admiral of the fleet.[77] The ships were ready to set sail within the agreed time, which was twelve days. The Adelantado embarked, sending a petition to the governor to have Captain Juan de la Parra delivered to him, but he refused to do so. In these fifteen days there had been some bitter disputes between the Adelantado and the governor, and many men had noticed the Adelantado's patience. He set sail on his voyage in the beginning of December [1565].[78]

Chapter 8

Expedition against the Corsairs

On the third day after departing from the port of Havana he spotted a sail. Thinking it was a corsair, he gave chase and followed it until they put in at Matanzas, a port on the island of Cuba,[79] where on arrival he found no one on board, as all the men had fled into the woods. He commanded the admiral of the fleet, his nephew Pedro Menéndez Marqués, to board the ship with some sailors in order to keep her cargo safe, and to anchor her near the Adelantado's flagship, because he wanted to anchor in that port.

As soon as he anchored, they heard voices in the woods, for the fleet was anchored close by. The Adelantado sent a boat to land to see what it was. Some Portuguese approached, and realizing that the fleet was from Spain and that the Adelantado was its general, they rejoiced greatly and called out to their comrades. They got into the boat and were brought before the Adelantado aboard the flagship, telling him with great pleasure that they had come from Spain aboard that caravel under orders from His Majesty with dispatches for [the Adelantado], which they gave him. His Majesty informed him that France was organizing a great fleet to be sent to Florida against him, and that he was sending him seventeen ships and one thousand five hundred soldiers, with many supplies, so that he could defend himself and aid the fortresses and islands of Puerto Rico, Hispaniola, and Cuba, [telling him] that he should distribute them as he pleased, on land as well as on the sea, in order to attack that fleet if it should come upon him or his lands. Then the Adelantado summoned his captains to a council and, having shown them the letter, said to them:

—Gentlemen and brothers, I am of the opinion that, in all things, and especially in war, "for each new occasion, a new consideration." It seems to me that I should stay close to Havana, because they write to me that the reinforcements will arrive there in March. Let us return there, and I shall send one or two of these vessels to Campeche to be laden with corn for Florida, and I will send another one to Puerto de Plata to be laden with cassava and meat, and the other one I will have laden in Havana as quickly as I can.[80] And even though I have no money, I will sell or pawn some of the artillery or the munitions I have with me, even if it be for a lower price, and the gold jewelry and chains that some of us have, and we shall pass the time as best we can, trying to avoid confrontations with the governor no matter what, because now that I have received this dispatch, if I were to go with this fleet against the corsairs and the reinforcements were to come to Havana from another direction, and the French fleet were to go to Florida, I would deserve to be punished by His Majesty for any misfortune that might come our way.

They all thought the Adelantado's resolution was wise, and good advice, and they approved it. The following day the whole fleet left for Havana, and once it had arrived, the Adelantado dispatched the vessels as he had agreed and sent his nephew Pedro Menéndez [Marqués] to Spain in a *patache* to inform His Majesty of what had happened up to then.

At the beginning of January of the following year of [15]66, Esteban de las Alas, who was the general of the fleet from Vizcaya and Asturias that had been separated from Admiral Pedro Menéndez Marqués during the storm, arrived there, and [it turned out] he had been in Yaguana.[81] The joy and happiness that the Adelantado felt at his arrival was great, for he brought with him two ships and two hundred men. The Adelantado then ordered those two ships and the two he had brought from Florida to be fitted out within the month, and also a new brigantine that Diego de Amaya brought from Florida where he had gone with supplies, and another French *patache* that [the Adelantado] bought in Havana, and a new shallop. He had all seven ships caulked, greased, and made ready.

Chapter 9

In the Country of Chief Carlos

On 10 February [1566] he sailed for Florida with five hundred sailors and soldiers on board, in order to discover if there was adequate passage and good navigation between Las Tortugas and Los Mártires,[82] because it was most necessary to know this for the fleets of New Spain and Tierra Firme,[83] as well as for whatever other vessels might sail in those parts. Finding it very good, he proceeded to the coast of Florida in search of some men and women who, it was rumored, had been captured twenty years ago and were being held captive by a chieftain named Carlos.[84] Each year he killed some of these people, sacrificing them to the devil, and they all went about naked, having become savages like the Indians themselves. The Adelantado, taking pity on these Christians, wished to undertake this expedition and go from there to the provinces of Santa Elena, which are fifty leagues north of the port of San Mateo (the one taken from the Lutherans), because the Indians had told the soldiers in that fort that some Frenchmen had recently arrived at the port of Guale.

Having had many masses said to St. Anthony to intercede with Our Lord so [the Adelantado] might find the harbor where those Christians were (as well as the Christians themselves), he found it within a week of leaving Havana, and it happened like this: The Adelantado left the flagship in which he was traveling, turning her over to Esteban de las Alas, making him his lieutenant and general of those vessels. He embarked with thirty men in a brigantine[85] that did not draw more than half a fathom of water. He ordered Captain Diego de Amaya, who served as admiral of the ships,[86] to accompany him with another thirty men aboard another brigantine that drew very little water. The two brigantines went sailing together along the coast, and the other ships out at sea, because the coast was shallow. On the third day, in bad weather, the two brigantines were separated from the other five ships, and on the fourth day, as they sailed along the coast, a canoe approached Diego de Amaya's brigantine, which was half a league ahead. When the man paddling it came close to the brigantine, he spoke and said:

—Spaniards! Brothers! Christians! Welcome! We have been expecting you for a week, for God and St. Mary told us you were coming! The Christian men and women who are here alive have sent me here with this canoe to wait for you in order to give you a letter I carry with me.

Captain Diego de Amaya and those who were with him in the brigantine were much delighted and pleased at having found those whom the Adelantado was seeking and was so eager [to find]. He welcomed aboard the brigantine this man who, transformed into an Indian, was painted and naked, only his private parts covered. The captain embraced him and asked him for the letter. The man took a cross out of the deerskin with which he covered his private parts and told the captain that this was the letter the captive Christian men and women there were sending to him, beseeching him—by the death that Our Lord suffered on that cross to save us—not to pass by without going into that harbor and attempting to deliver them from that chieftain and take them to Christian lands.

Meanwhile the Adelantado arrived with his brigantine and the man came aboard. The Adelantado heard from this Christian many more details about the condition of the Indians, the characteristics of that land, and all that had happened there. They all worshiped the cross on their knees, giving thanks to Our Lord. The Adelantado went into the harbor and anchored [so] near the shore that they were able to jump ashore from the brigantine without wetting their shoes. There were said to be five Christian women and four Christian men in the village half a league from there, and farther inland two other men and one woman. Of more than two hundred Christians from the Fleet of the Indies shipwrecked in the country of this chieftain twenty years earlier—and they had all been taken to him—he and his father had killed them in their feasts and dances, sacrificing them to the devil. The Adelantado did not dare to reveal to this Christian how he was planning to free the Christian men and women who were there, because it appeared to him that he knew little and whatever he said could be repeated to the chieftain. He only asked him to tell the chieftain that he was bringing many things for him and his wives, and that he should come to see him.

The next morning, the chieftain—knowing how few men the Adelantado brought—came with about three hundred Indian archers. The Adelantado had a platform set up so that the chieftain could sit down—as he did, with his principal Indians around him—next to the brigantines, along the shore, with the prow of one touching the stern of the other, and with the artillery being set up on the land side [of those ships], loaded with much grapeshot ready for whatever might happen. The Adelantado disembarked from the brigantines, with thirty arquebusiers with their fuses lit, and sat next to him. The chieftain and his principal men paid much homage to him. He gave him a shirt and breeches of taffeta, a doublet, and a hat in which he looked very nice, for he was a fine-looking man of about twenty-five years of age. He also gave him presents for his wives, and the principal Indians, and he gave them biscuit and honey, which they ate very willingly.

The chieftain gave the Adelantado a bar of silver worth two hundred ducats in weight and asked him for more presents or more things to eat. The Adelantado told him that he did not have food for so many people, that if he and his principal Indians were to board the ships he would give them and their wives many things to eat. The chieftain did so, driven by greed, and took about twenty Indians with him. With great secrecy and diligence, the Adelantado ordered each soldier to place himself next to an Indian and be seated next to him, not letting them throw themselves overboard if they were to attempt it. He ordered the cables with which the brigantines were moored to be paid out, and stood offshore. This made the Indians somewhat nervous, but the interpreter told them not to be afraid, since they were only going there to prevent more Indians from coming aboard the brigantines, which were small and would capsize. The chieftain and the Indians believed them, and they were given many things to eat.

The chieftain wanted to leave, but the Adelantado told him that his lord, the king of Spain, had sent him for the Christian men and women he had there, and that if he refused to release them he would have him killed, that he begged him to give them up, for he would give him many things in exchange and would be his great friend and brother. The chieftain said that he was satisfied and he would fetch them. The Adelantado said that if [Carlos] went, his men [the Spaniards] would kill [the Adelantado] for having released him, and that he should send some Indians for them. The chieftain did so, out of fear, and within an hour they brought five women and three Christian men, to whom the Adelantado had shirts given. He told four or five tailors who were there to make clothes for them out of some London kersey that he had brought. And all this time the Christians were weeping for joy, which was a sight to behold. The Adelantado comforted and consoled them very much, and they said that they were very sad about the children they were leaving behind. The Adelantado gave the chieftain and his people many things and sent him away very pleased. The chieftain said that in three months' time he would bring him another two Christian men and one Christian woman who were inland, and begged him to go to his village the next morning, before he departed, so that his wives could see him. The Adelantado said he would do so.

In the morning the cacique sent many canoes for him. The Christian who had gone out to sea with the cross—and who had now left with the chieftain to visit his wives and give them presents on behalf of the Adelantado, who was suspicious of his departure—came back in a canoe. This Christian advised the Adelantado not to go to the village, because the chieftain planned to kill him. The Indians in the canoes, who were aware of this treachery, suspected that the Christian was revealing it, and they fled. The Adelantado, so that the chieftain and the Indians would think he did not know about the treachery, hoisted the brigantines' anchors and rowed to the village, where he dropped anchor. There, sounding two bugles and waving the flags, he signaled that the canoes should come for him, because the brigantines could not sail any farther. Since no canoe wanted to come, the Adelantado left the harbor to look for his five ships and get them together. When they did not appear, the Christians told him that there was a very good harbor fifty leagues farther along from there, where the Indians held another three Christians captive. The Adelantado thought his ships could have gone there, and he wished to rescue those three Christians. He went there and did not find the Christians or the ships. When he returned, he found his five ships anchored off Carlos's harbor. Esteban de las Alas had gone to the village with one hundred soldiers. The Indians, upon seeing so many ships and people who had gone there with their canoes to reconnoiter, were afraid and received Esteban de las Alas very well. In exchange for trifles, the soldiers obtained there more than two thousand ducats' worth of gold and silver.

The Adelantado resolved to send the Christian to Carlos to make him think the Adelantado knew nothing of his treacherous plan to kill him. Carlos believed it and, prompted by his greedy desire to be given more things and to take the Adelantado as a friend, came to see him with only five or six Indians. He told him that he wanted to take him for his elder brother and do anything he commanded, and that he wanted to give him as wife an older sister whom he loved very much, so that he would take her to Christian lands and then send her back. When she returned, he would go too and become a Christian with all his men, because it seemed to him that this was better than being Indians, and he begged him to go fetch her and see his wives and village.

The Adelantado, saying that he would go some other day, gave him many presents and sent him away. The captains and soldiers would have preferred that the Adelantado not let the chieftain go, because it was said that he had a lot of money and would have given it all to be set free. The Adelantado did not want to do this, for he thought it would be dishonest, given the re-assurances he had made to the chieftain, and that the Indians would never become Christians.

All the captains, soldiers, and sailors there were astonished at the Adelantado's reply, for they knew how much he had spent in this enterprise and how little assistance His Majesty had given him, and that he was indebted in Havana, that he and his relatives and friends were indebted in Spain, and that he had sent to borrow money in New Spain. They took him for an ill-advised man, for he could have obtained from that chieftain at least one hundred thousand ducats, for even if he did not have them, his Indians [would], and his friends among the chieftains who had some gold and silver from shipwrecked vessels and did not know what it was or what it was [worth]. With this he could free himself from debt, and also those who were indebted for his sake, and be in a stronger position to carry out such a holy enterprise as this, to try—according to his inclination and that of all the soldiers—as they were already trying, to implant the Holy Gospel, because the Indians did not know what gold or silver was [worth]. One soldier was given a piece of gold worth seventy ducats in exchange for a playing card, which was an *as de oros*,[87] and in exchange for a pair of scissors half a bar of silver worth one hundred ducats. At that time, all the soldiers who arrived there first with Esteban de las Alas and those who arrived with the Adelantado in the two brigantines obtained by barter about three thousand five hundred ducats' worth altogether, which made them cheerful and happy, and they began to gamble, holding the money of little account. The Adelantado did not take anything from what each of them had traded for, nor did he trade anything himself, so the Indians would not think that they had come looking for that.

And then, the day after Chief Carlos departed from the brigantines, the Adelantado went to eat with him, taking with him two hundred arquebusiers, a flag, two fifes and drums, three trumpets, a harp, a bowed *vihuela*, a psaltery,[88] and a tiny dwarf he had with him, who was a great singer and dancer. There was a distance of about two arquebus shots from the place where he had landed to the chieftain's house, which could easily fit two thousand men inside without being very crowded. The Adelantado's men marched in order to the house, but he did not allow them to go in and [told them] to be ready, with their fuses lit, outside. He took only twenty men and the musicians into the chieftain's house, where there were large windows from which he could see his men. The chieftain was in a good position, seated by himself in great estate, and with an Indian woman seated next to him at some distance, on an elevation half an *estado* off the ground.[89] There were approximately fifty principal Indian men and another fifty Indian women, the men seated next to him and the women next to her, below them.

When the Adelantado ascended to that place, the chieftain gave him his seat and drew quite a distance apart, [but] the Adelantado had him seated next to him. Then the chieftain got up and went toward the Adelantado to take his hands, according to their custom, performing a ceremony equivalent to when people kiss the king's hand here, and which the Indian vassals perform with their chieftains. This is the utmost sign of deference among them. The Indian woman came afterwards and did the same, and so did all the principal Indians who were there. Outside the window were seated more than five hundred Indian women of ten to fifteen years of age, who began to sing, and other Indian [boys] began to jump and spin. The principal Indian men and women who were seated next to the chieftain began to sing, and they said—it was later learned—that this was the highest sign of joy, respect, and obedience that this chieftain or any other chieftain of that land could have shown the Adelantado, because among those who danced were the brothers, uncles, and aunts of the chieftain, and there were Indian women who were ninety and one hundred years old, and they all danced and showed much happiness and joy.

After the principal Indians were done dancing and singing (although the Indian women who were outside never stopped doing so until the Adelantado left, and they sang in good form and were seated in groups of one hundred, and fifty of them would sing for a while and then stop, and the other fifty would resume singing), the chieftain asked the Adelantado (after his principal Indians had danced) if he wanted food to be brought to him and his Christians. The Adelantado said not so quickly. He had in writing many kind and loving words in the Indian language to speak to the principal wife of Carlos and to his sister. Thinking that the woman there was the chieftain's principal wife, he said to her the words he intended to say to her in her language. The chieftain and the Indians were astonished, thinking that the words were spoken by the paper itself and whatever was written on it, and the chieftain realized that the Adelantado thought that woman was his principal wife. He told him, through the interpreter they had there to communicate with each other (who was one of the captive Christians), that she was not his wife but his sister, whom he had already given to the Adelantado as a wife.

Then the Adelantado got up, took her by the hand, and sat her next to him, between himself and the chieftain, and from what was written he said to her in her language—reading from the paper—many things at which they, as well as all the Indian men and women who were there, rejoiced. This Indian woman was about thirty-five years old, not at all beautiful, although very dignified—so much that, as time went on, all of us were astonished because it seemed that she had been brought up from birth to behave with dignity. The Adelantado asked the chieftain to bring his principal wife there, and he did so. She was twenty years old, very comely and beautiful, with very fine features. She had very good hands and eyes, and looked very decorously and with great modesty from one side to the other. She had a very good figure and, even among all the beautiful Indian women who were there, none was as beautiful as she was. She had her eyebrows very well done, and around her throat she wore a beautiful collar made of pearls and gemstones, and a necklace of gold beads. She was naked like the other—the chieftain's sister—with only her private parts covered. The Adelantado took her by the hand, seated her between the Indian woman and the chieftain, and spoke many words to her in her language (for he had them written down on the paper) at which she greatly rejoiced, especially because the Adelantado had been told that she was very beautiful, and he had copied down some words to tell her so, with which she showed herself not displeased. She blushed and looked with modesty at her husband. The chieftain seemed to regret having brought his wife there and ordered her to leave, because he thought [the Spaniards] wanted to take her away. The Adelantado asked him through the interpreter not to send her away, [saying] that she should eat there with him, because he had many things to give to her.

He then had the offering brought to him and had the chieftain's sister clothed in a shirt and the chieftain's wife in another and both in green robes in which the chieftain's wife looked very beautiful. He gave them beads, scissors, knives, and bells, with which they were delighted, especially with the mirrors when they looked at themselves, and the Indian men and women who were there laughed greatly at this. He gave the chieftain another garment, on top of another one he had given him before, and some other trifles of trading goods, and two hatchets and two machetes. He also gave some goods to the principal Indian men and women who were there, without their giving the Adelantado anything in exchange or his asking for it. He ordered the food to be brought, which consisted of many kinds of very good poached and baked fish, as well as raw, poached, and baked oysters, in addition to many other things the Adelantado had had brought ashore: a hundredweight of very good biscuit, a cask of wine, and another one of cane syrup, which he distributed among the principal people. Through the interpreter he asked them to bring bowls to put some of that syrup in. He gave them some preserves and quince paste. The Adelantado ate from his own plate and the chieftain's sister from another, and the chieftain and his wife from another, the table set with tablecloths and napkins that the Adelantado had had brought. They understood very well that our food was better than theirs.

When the food was brought they sounded the trumpets, which were outside, and as soon as the Adelantado had eaten, they began to play the instruments very well and the dwarf danced. Five or six gentlemen with very good voices who were there began to sing in very good form, because the Adelantado is really fond of music and always brings with him the best he can afford. The Indians were strangely pleased to hear it, and the chieftain told the [young Indian] women not to sing, because they knew little and the Christians knew a lot. The music stopped, and the chieftain begged them to play the instruments and sing until they departed. The Adelantado ordered it so. They finished eating, the table was removed, and then [the Adelantado] told him that he wished to depart.

The chieftain told him that, since he had given him his sister as a wife, he should go to a room nearby and rest with her, and if he did not, his Indians would be outraged, claiming that they and she were being mocked, and that he did not value her much. In that village there were more than four thousand Indian men and women. The Adelantado was somewhat distressed and told him, through the interpreter, that Christian men could not sleep with women who were not Christians. The chieftain replied that, since he had taken him for his elder brother, he and his sister and his people were already Christians. The Adelantado replied that, before they could be considered Christians, they had to know and believe many things. He told them about God, His knowledge, power, and kindness, and that all the creatures born on this earth have to obey only Him and do what He commands. When the Christians who do so die here on this earth, they go to Him in heaven, and there they dwell forever without dying, and they see their wives and children and brothers and friends, and they are always happy, singing and laughing. But since the [Indians] do not know about this and they do not adore or serve God, but rather a very wicked and mendacious chieftain called the devil, when they die they go to him and they cry perpetually, because sometimes they are very cold and sometimes very hot, and nothing gives them satisfaction.

This Indian and his sister appeared to be intelligent. They spoke with each other and the Indian woman replied with great modesty and dignity— because the brother so desired—that she already knew about that, for the Christians who were there had spoken of it, although [the other Indians] refused to believe it, thinking that they were lying, as they did in other matters, but [she and her brother] clearly saw, and she believed what the Adelantado said, and she was a Christian. And if she needed to know and believe something else, the Adelantado should tell her, and she would do as the Adelantado himself did, because she was his wife, and she should be a Christian like him and not an Indian, and that if he did not want to sleep with her he should take her to the ships and to Christian lands. The chieftain's wife said that she too wanted to go with him, for the Christians seemed better to her than the Indians, and that her husband would also go, and that they would come back in a month or two.

The Adelantado replied courteously that he also wanted this, and that he was very happy about it. The chieftain removed [his wife] from where she was and moved her to a different place, thinking that the Adelantado wanted to take her with him. The Adelantado replied to the chieftain's sister that, since she wanted to be a Christian, he loved her a lot more than she loved him, and that he wished to know if her brother and most of the Indian men and women knew what it was to be Christians. She replied that they all knew what the Adelantado had said because the Christians who were there had told them (although they did not believe them) and that, if [the Adelantado] should take her with him, some of the principal Indian men and women would accompany him and see the things of the Christians, how they lived and how they did better than them in being Christians, and upon their return they would inform all the Indians of this and all of them would be Christians. The Adelantado said that he was satisfied, that he wanted to depart, and that another day she should come with the people that were to accompany her to Christian lands and he would take her with him. She said that both she and the chieftain were satisfied and very pleased with this.

It was believed among those who were there that, if the chieftain's wife had been a Christian, the Adelantado would have been very pleased to sleep with her and take [Carlos's] sister to Christian lands, so that she could go and come back with news about the way the Christians lived.

The Adelantado bid them farewell and the chieftain's wife and his sister took him by the hands. The chieftain's sister placed herself on his right side and told her sister-in-law to go to his left, with the chieftain and his principal Indian men and women before them, singing and dancing. Thus they escorted the Adelantado from the house until he was outside, where these Indians remained with the other women. The chieftain accompanied him with the Indians to the boats, and he embarked and went to his ships, where the next day he ordered wood and water to be taken on.

It was already late when Chief Carlos came with his sister and some three hundred Indian men and women who accompanied him, as well as two other chieftains who had recently arrived, eager to see the Adelantado and the Christians. The Adelantado received them very well, had food served for them, and gave them some items of barter. At sunset Carlos said that he wanted to depart and that he was leaving his sister with six Indian men and six Indian women of the most elite and wise of that land, that he requested her return within four or five months, and that if she and they said that being Christian was a good thing, he and all his people would be that. The Adelantado was troubled at her presence, for he meant to go straight from there to Guale and to Santa Elena, which was more than two hundred leagues north of there, to look for the Frenchmen who the Indians claimed were there, before they could receive reinforcements in the summer. He feared that this could be Jacques Ribault (the oldest son of Jean Ribault, the general of the Lutherans in Florida, whom the Adelantado had had beheaded with all his men), who had escaped with two ships from the fort when it was taken from them, and he did not know that his father was dead. It seemed to the Adelantado that, since Guale and Santa Elena were good ports, [Ribault] could better fortify himself there, and that he had much artillery, munitions, supplies, and more than a hundred men, that he could build a fort there and send the ships to France to ask for reinforcements, and that, therefore, it was necessary to defeat him and expel him from the land before help could come.

Because of this, he replied to Chief Carlos that he was going to wage war against his enemies and had to be at sea for a very long time, through many ordeals and perils, and if the sea were to harm or kill his sister and those who wanted to go with her, or if the Adelantado were defeated and his enemies were to kill her and the rest, then [Carlos] would think that the Adelantado had killed them. [He said that Carlos] should bring from his land the four Christian men and women who were captives, and that he would return within four months, bringing him many things and taking [his sister] with him.

The chieftain and the Indian woman were very sad and spoke to each other for a while. Then the Indian woman replied that, since the Adelantado was her husband, she wanted to be with him at sea and at war, live and die with him. She said that he should take her with him, because otherwise those chieftains [there] and their Indian men and women, as well as their enemy chieftains, would laugh at her and her brother, saying that the Adelantado held them in little esteem and had tricked them. The Adelantado replied that he loved her and her brother very much and he promised to come back for her within four months. Then, when it was almost nightfall, her brother got up, very annoyed and angry, took his sister by the hand, and went to embark in the canoes, saying that the Adelantado and all the Christians told many lies, and that all they had said about God and St. Mary was also probably a lie. The Indian woman was crying.

The Adelantado, taking pity at what they were saying and at seeing the Indian woman cry, went after them, telling them to wait. They refused to wait and embarked in the canoes. The Adelantado, to prevent them from leaving (and because the Indians were somewhat agitated with him), waded into the water in his hose and shoes until it came up to his belt. He reached the canoe, took the Indian woman by the hand, and asked the interpreter to tell her and her brother that it was only because he loved her so much that he did not want to put her in that peril with his enemies, but that he would gladly take her with him if she still wished to go. She said that she did, bid farewell to her brother, raised her skirts, and jumped into the water, which, as she was not very tall, reached above her waist. Three of the six Indian men who were to go with her did the same, and four Indian women. Carlos departed with his people and she remained behind with the Adelantado, who appeared to be in distress. He said to Esteban de las Alas and the other captains who were there that he did not know how to conduct himself with her, since they had a contrary wind and could not depart, and if he did not make her happy and satisfy her, he feared she might leave the next day, especially because the Indian men and women would come to see her and she would be bound to tell them what had happened. And since the Indians of that chieftain were very numerous and bellicose, it seemed to him that this could be the cause of a rupture between them, which did not suit the Adelantado's purpose, for all that he had done since his departure from Spain showed that his particular interest was to convert these Indians to Christianity.

The captains replied that it would be best to have a big party for her and the Indian men and women with her, that there should be much rejoicing and music that night, that she should be baptized and given a [Christian] name, and that the Adelantado should sleep with her. This would be a fine start for him and the other Christians to earn [the Indians'] trust, and all those Indians and the neighboring chieftains would convert to Christianity. In no way would it be advisable to do anything else. The Adelantado tried his best to find another solution but, since none could be found or agreed upon, he gave his consent. Then the Christian women who were there bathed her, combed her hair, and clothed her, and she looked much better than before, when she was naked. The captains adroitly praised her beauty and modesty. Because of the Adelantado's devotions to St. Anthony to find those Christian men and women he sought, they gave her the name Doña Antonia, and they named that harbor San Antón. They gave the dinner on land, in some tents the Adelantado had set up near his ships, with music and rejoicing until two in the morning. The Adelantado had her seated next to him, and with the help of the interpreter he said to her many courteous words, which pleased her. Everyone was astonished at how she replied so modestly and in so few words. Her Indian women and the Christian women and some of the soldiers danced, and once this was over, they took her to a bed that the Adelantado had prepared, and he went to her. The next morning she woke up happy, and the Christian women who spoke to her said that she was very satisfied.

Then she sent two Indian men and two Indian women to her brother in a canoe that was there. He came to see her, and the Adelantado received him very well. The Adelantado said that he wished a large cross to be set up near Carlos's house, that every day in the morning the men, women, and children should go to kiss and worship it, that they should regard it as their most important idol, and that he should give up the other idols he had, explaining the reasons. The chieftain said that he would do so, but that he could not give up his other idols so soon, [not] until his sister and the Indians who accompanied her came back to tell them what they had to do. This chieftain was named Carlos because it was his father's name, and his father had taken this name because the Christians he held captive had told him that the emperor Charles was the greatest king of the Christians.[90]

The cross was made and the Adelantado had it set up there, and with much music and great devotion he went toward it on his knees and kissed it, and so did all of us Spaniards who were there. Then the Indian Doña Antonia and most of the [Christian] women and Indian women with her did the same. Then Carlos and his Indians kissed and worshipped it. This Carlos had a captain, a very good Indian, who was married to one of Carlos's and Doña Antonia's sisters, and the chieftain was married to this captain's sister. According to what the Christians said, it seemed that the Indians were more afraid of this captain than of the chieftain. He said to the chieftain that he needed to be the "captain" of that cross so that all of them should do as the Adelantado commanded, kissing and worshipping it every morning. So the Adelantado gave it to him, and he carried it on his shoulders, with much reverence, to the canoes. Then the Adelantado proceeded to embark, taking with him Doña Antonia, three Indian men, four Indian women, and seven Christian men and women who were captives (for two of the [Christian] women had gone back to the Indians because they longed for the children they were leaving behind).

He ordered Esteban de las Alas to go to Havana with this Indian woman and her people and deliver her to [the royal] treasurer, Juan de [Rojas] Hinestrosa, who was the Adelantado's lieutenant on that island for Florida matters. He wrote to him that he should arrange for the Indian woman and those who were with her to be instructed in the Catholic faith, that they should be treated well and, when the time came, be converted to Christianity, and that he would return to Havana within three or four months to take her back to her land. [The treasurer] should give Esteban de las Alas as many supplies of livestock and poultry as he could, and then dispatch him so that he could return with the five ships to the port of St. Augustine, where the Adelantado would be waiting for him in order to go against the French who were rumored to be in Guale and Santa Elena. Meanwhile he was going to explore the entire Los Mártires coast with two brigantines to see if he could find a good harbor in the Bahama Channel and try to form alliances with the villages and chieftains he might encounter. Thus they departed with a fair wind, Esteban de las Alas with five ships for Havana, and the Adelantado with two brigantines along Los Mártires.

Chapter 10

Mutinies in Santa Lucía, St. Augustine, and San Mateo

A week after [the Adelantado] departed from the port of Santo Antonio, where Chief Carlos lives, he entered a harbor that he found in the Bahama Channel. The next day, when he was leaving it, he sighted a ship, and when he went to examine her he realized she was a caravel he had dispatched from Havana to Campeche to be laden with corn. He went aboard and found more than one hundred and thirty people on her, and she was all laden with corn. And it had happened like this: In accordance with letters from the Adelantado and at his request, Fray Francisco de Toral, bishop of Yucatán, and Don Luis de Céspedes, governor of that island,[91] had loaded the caravel with corn, chickens, honey, sandals, and other things. On the way to Florida the caravel had put in at Havana, where Juan de [Rojas] Hinestrosa, the Adelantado's lieutenant for Florida matters, had dispatched her at once, ordering that she should go to the land of [Chief] Ais and the harbor of Santa Lucía—where Captain Juan Vélez de Medrano had remained when the Adelantado left him there with the three hundred Spaniards and Frenchmen and went to Havana with the two vessels to get supplies (and the Adelantado had already sent him relief with a loaded *patache*)—and that she leave them some *fanegas*[92] of corn, chickens, and meat, and go to St. Augustine with the rest. The master of the caravel, setting out to do so, arrived at Santa Lucía and tried to unload the corn, but the soldiers seized the master and took possession of the caravel. Because Captain Juan Vélez de Medrano tried to prevent it, they tried to kill him, and they wounded his ensign, Pedro de Ayala, who was also opposing their takeover of the caravel. And now they had all embarked and were on their way to Havana, and they had already sailed more than fifteen leagues.

The Adelantado embarked with some of his gentlemen and went to St. Augustine, where he entered with [the caravel] on 20 March [15]66. He found the field commander [Pedro de Valdés] there very ill and with no supplies. There had been great mutinies there, and in Fort San Mateo, as some of the captains and most of the soldiers were in accord.[93] Since neither the field commander, who was in St. Augustine, nor [the sergeant major] Gonzalo de Villarroel, who was in charge of Fort San Mateo, had been able to remedy matters, they had put up with some ill-advised and reckless things in order not to be killed. When Captain Diego de Amaya had arrived at the end of December [1565] with an eighty-ton ship laden with cassava, meat, and livestock—although altogether it was not very much—he left some at the port of St. Augustine and went on to San Mateo with the rest. At the entrance of the bar the ship and the supplies were lost, though the people were saved.

The Adelantado was then notified, and at the beginning of February [1566] he sent them a seventy-ton frigate[94] laden with corn, wine, oil, cloth and linens, some rigging, and quality oakum, all of it worth more than six thousand ducats. From one merchant alone he bought four thousand ducats' worth of the clothes and supplies, to be paid after one year. When the frigate arrived at St. Augustine, before she could be unloaded, the soldiers mutinied one night and captured the field commander, the judicial and administrative officers who were there, and the storekeeper. They spiked the artillery and elected one person as well as a sergeant major to govern them, for these were obeyed and respected. They stayed like this for six days, at the end of which about one hundred and thirty men went aboard the frigate. Because she could not hold all the mutineers, the sergeant major whom the mutineers had elected went about choosing those who were to embark, which had to be those who had been most rebellious and treasonous to His Majesty in the mutiny. This sergeant had twelve arquebusiers and six halberdiers with him as his bodyguard, and when he was trying to embark with these men of his guard, the field commander took the opportunity to free himself and eight of His Majesty's officials. Taking their arquebuses, they approached them without being heard.

These men abandoned the skiff and the field commander seized it. As they realized they were lost, they surrendered and gave him their weapons, and he had them taken into custody. He charged them, since some friends of these captives who had not been able to embark in the frigate were becoming restless. Having taken their confession after nightfall, the field commander had the sergeant hanged before daybreak. He took pity on the elected leader, whom he also captured, because he was a halfwit, and he had accepted that office very much against his will. In the morning the field commander released him and the other captives, giving them a reprimand. In order to prevent the frigate from leaving, the field commander armed a *patache* he had there to go against her. Once he had done this, and taking with him on the *patache* the men he trusted most, he began to fire in order to sink her, but they cut the cable with which the frigate was anchored, hoisted the sails, and fled.

The field commander returned to the fort, disarmed the *patache*, and brought his men under orders and discipline as before. When the Adelantado arrived there on 20 March [1566], it pained him greatly to see the field commander so thin, and the suffering caused by his being disrespected. The Adelantado's brother Bartolomé Menéndez, governor and warden of that fort and district, was also very ill in bed. When the mutiny began, he had gone with some soldiers to see if the enemy Indians had any corn. Otherwise, if he had been there when the mutiny broke out, they would have killed him because he was so disliked. Everyone was sad and afflicted, which was a great pity, but with the Adelantado's arrival they became cheerful and the sick became well, because the caravel brought much corn, honey, chickens, and sandals.

That same day Esteban de las Alas returned from Havana, where he had left Doña Antonia and the rest of the Indians, and he too brought supplies, meat, and livestock. Everybody rejoiced and was happy and merry.

At the time this mutiny broke out in St. Augustine, another one broke out in San Mateo, for it turned out that this was a preconceived piece of double dealing among some captains, officers, and soldiers of both forts, who arranged to urgently request of the field commander [Pedro de Valdés] that a galley-type vessel that the French had left on the stocks at San Mateo be finished, that a patache that was in St. Augustine be prepared, and that they seize the first supply ship that might arrive. Provided with all this, [the mutineers] would leave the land with the three ships, the soldiers taking captive the captains who wished to leave, so it would be understood that they were taken by force. And if one of those captains who had taken part in the mutiny were to remain behind, it seemed to them that he must perforce leave on whatever other ship there might be, for with so few men he would not be able to defend himself from the Indians, if they should be enemies. This way, His Majesty would acknowledge their service [both] in remaining at the time of the mutiny and in leaving the land afterwards so they would not all be killed. [They had] to do this in total secrecy, because they were afraid of the field commander and could not bend to their will the governors and wardens of the forts, who were the Adelantado's brother Bartolomé Menéndez in St. Augustine and Gonzalo de Villarroel in San Mateo.

The field commander, even though he was aware that getting the ships ready was wrong, did not dare to do anything else because the [men] were already stirred up. He said they should write the letter to be sent to San Mateo and he would sign it, and this was done. He wrote another one to Gonzalo de Villarroel and had it sewn into the back of the messenger's coat so that it would not be found. In this letter he said that Villarroel should prevent the ship from being finished, because he had had no choice but to give the men the letter they demanded, as they were all stirred up, and that if the men in San Mateo also wished to mutiny, he should deal with them as best he could, according to the circumstances, so as not to get killed.

The planning of these mutinies began five days after the Adelantado departed from St. Augustine for Cape Canaveral to look for the Frenchmen who were building a fort, as is mentioned before. He departed from St. Augustine on 26 October [15]65, and some letters written from one fort to another on November first were found in which the men were beginning to look for the best way to leave the land, there being no motive or reason for it except that it seemed to them that they had had no news of gold or silver in that land, and that most of them thought the Adelantado's victory against the Lutherans (which Our Lord God granted him) was impossible, and that from Santo Domingo and the island of Cuba they would be able to pass on to Peru[95] and New Spain, which were rich and fertile lands—and these had been their main motivations when they set out from Spain. And because they had not reached those islands, and [because] God granted victory against the Lutherans, casting them out of the land, and [because] they did not want to be conquerors and colonizers there, it seemed to them a good opportunity to claim that they were doing it for lack of food. As for the food, if we follow the guidelines, since the Adelantado had removed three hundred men for the second fort [of Santa Lucía, in the country of

Ais] which he later left under the command of Captain Juan Vélez de Medrano, and the sailors aboard the vessels he sent for supplies and the one he sent to Spain with dispatches, there was [enough food] until the end of March [1566], with large quantities of very good fish, oysters, crabs, palmitos, and a large quantity of oil that the Adelantado had landed. And even before he had taken the fort [San Mateo] from the enemy, the Adelantado had arranged to give a ration of one pound of biscuit, which is very generous on campaign, and sometimes meat, other times cooked chickpeas with oil and vinegar, other times fish.[96]

Juan de San Vicente replied for all of them. He was a soldier from Medina del Campo who had arrived in Seville when the Adelantado was about to depart for Florida. He was just back from Italy about an issue he had there, and he brought the Adelantado a letter of introduction from Luis [de] Quintanilla saying that he was a very good soldier who seemed worthy of the spirit and courage of his brother Captain San Vicente, and he entreated [the Adelantado] to honor and favor him in any way he could. The Adelantado was a good friend of Luis de Quintanilla, and this was the first thing he had asked of him. He had heard that Captain San Vicente, this soldier's brother who was in Italy, was a good captain, and it seemed to him that this one would be the same, so he appointed him captain. And as his ensign he appointed a companion he brought with him who had been his comrade in Italy, whose name was Fernán Pérez and who was also from Medina del Campo. This captain and his ensign said to the Adelantado that a ration of one pound of biscuit per soldier was not much, and even though the Adelantado gave plenty of arguments that it was reasonable and that, considering their needs and circumstances, he should not increase it, [San Vicente] persisted and came back with some of his soldiers to say that a ration of one pound of biscuit was not enough. For this reason, the Adelantado agreed that it be one pound and a quarter. [From then on] he remained very suspicious of this captain and his ensign.

After they captured the fort from the French, which then burned down with its supplies, there still remained more than a hundred casks of flour. Many soldiers began to eat more, without discipline and refusing to have their rations cut. By the middle of February [1566] there were no more—and, it was later learned, they wished that they had run out much sooner because, when a seventy-ton frigate arrived laden with supplies, they seized her and fled. Then other ships the Adelantado had brought from St. Augustine came with supplies, and the men in San Mateo had risen in mutiny and had not yet departed.

He informed them at once of the sufficient amount of supplies he was bringing and that he had news that the French were coming against them. [He said] that he forgave them for their uprising, and that if he had been there with them he would have left the country so as not to perish from hunger, that he did not blame them for having rebelled in order to leave the country when they did not have any food, but now that there was plenty, abandoning the two forts that His Majesty had in that land would be a great treason against him, especially because the Indians would immediately become enemies of the few Christians who were to remain behind, and there were some Frenchmen among them who would train them to wage war on those who remained in the forts, for [surely] some would want not to abandon them, in order to be of service to His Majesty and be loyal vassals to him. They received this message the Adelantado sent them by a notary, who notified them of it in the name of His Majesty, and [told them] that, under penalty of being considered traitors, they should return to the fort and guard it and obey. They replied that they did not know how to plough, till, or farm; that the land was not good for anything else; and that they wished to go to the Indies to live as Christians and not dwell in that land like beasts.

In that vessel there were more than one hundred and twenty soldiers who had risen in mutiny, thirty-five of them noblemen. These replied that they wished to return to the fort to serve their king and obey their general, and that they should be put ashore, because they were only about two leagues from the fort. The rest of them said that they did not want to, and these thirty-five replied that, if they took them along, they would be lost, for in whatever place they might land, they would have to inform the authorities of their plans to mutiny, and how they had deserted the land, leaving the fort abandoned save only for the warden, Gonzalo de Villarroel; his ensign, Rodrigo de Troche; Don Hernando de Gamboa; the field commander's first cousin Rodrigo Montes[97]; four additional relatives and servants of his; Captain Martín Ochoa with his ensign, his sergeant, and other friends; and Captain Francisco de Recalde with one of his servants; in total, twenty-five men.

When this became evident to the rebels and the main leaders—the ensign and sergeant of Captain Francisco de Recalde, as well as some of the

Guzmán family, who enlisted the disaffected: all the soldiers in their company, without exception, were mutineers—they jumped from the ship into a boat and went ashore, where they killed three Indians, two of them principal ones. Then they returned to the ship and put ashore these thirty-five soldiers, unarmed and deprived of their clothes. All in all, [the thirty-five] went forth happily, not knowing that [the others] had killed the Indians, for up until then they had not been at war with any of them, [but] rather many Indian men and women came to the forts to bring them fish, and were good friends with the Christians, and wanted to unite their communities and come to live next to the forts with the Christians. Within one hour of this, they disembarked and set off for the fort. The Indians came after them and, with their arrows, shot and killed them.

Gonzalo de Villarroel, who had remained with the twenty-five men in Fort San Mateo and who was not aware of the war the mutineers had started with the Indians, dispatched his ensign Rodrigo Troche and another soldier with a message for the field commander—for he did not know that the Adelantado had already arrived [in St. Augustine]—telling him how he had remained there with only a few men, and that the route from San Mateo was secure. Thus [these two soldiers] went through the Indian villages, where they were treated courteously, and Rodrigo Troche did not suspect anything when some Indians with whom he was acquainted approached them and said:

—Christians! Brothers! Friends!

They seized him and his companion and took them to their chieftain, Saturiwa,[98] who knew them very well. He commanded that [Troche] be ripped open and his heart taken out and pierced with arrows. The same was done to his comrade.

When the notary had completed his errand with the mutineers, he returned at once to St. Augustine without going to San Mateo. When the Adelantado learned about this, he resolved to go after this vessel and seize it in order to hang the ringleaders. As he was about to leave, Juan de San Vicente and his ensign [Fernán Pérez] came to ask him for permission to embark in a caravel the Adelantado was dispatching to Hispaniola to take on supplies. The Adelantado replied that if he granted it, many others would ask for it too, and he needed to go with his four vessels and three hundred men to Guale and Santa Elena, as agreed, to expel the French who were said to be there and to fortify himself in Santa Elena, which was said to be a good harbor. And since many Indians had joined forces and were on the warpath, he needed to send one hundred soldiers as reinforcements to Gonzalo de Villarroel [in San Mateo] and leave as many others with the field commander in St. Augustine. Thus he begged that [San Vicente] not speak openly about his desire to leave the land, and that neither he nor his ensign ask to be discharged, because it was not appropriate to request this at a time when the French were expected to come against them, as His Majesty had informed him.

[San Vicente] replied that he and his ensign were in poor health and that the Adelantado would do them a kindness in discharging them. [The Adelantado] replied that they should present petitions and he would decide whatever was appropriate. They presented them, and after them more than one hundred other soldiers did so, since each petition contained twelve or fifteen requests. The Adelantado answered that there wasn't room, but he feared that once he departed for Santa Elena, the mutinies in that fort [St. Augustine] and San Mateo would be worse than the previous ones, and that, to carry out their intentions, they would kill the field commander, the wardens of the forts, and some others of His Majesty's officials.

He stipulated this: Since, in order to better serve His Majesty, it was not appropriate for them to leave the land or ask him to be discharged, once he departed for Santa Elena they should not rise up in rebellion or mutiny. He would discharge them when more soldiers arrived from Spain. If they wished to appoint any persons to be sent to Spain, they should do so, for they could embark in the caravel the Adelantado was dispatching to Hispaniola to take on supplies, and from there go to Spain in the ships departing from Santo Domingo. However, if after he left for Santa Elena they still intended to leave and mutiny, abandoning the forts, they should leave them [now], for in order to prevent greater harm he would discharge them. But he ordered them—on pain of death, confiscation of property, and branding as traitors—to remain in the fort without abandoning it, warning them that he would carry out this punishment on any man who did otherwise. If they still refused to keep and comply with this, he would discharge them so they could go to Spain as prisoners to the House of Trade in Seville, with the evidence, so that His Majesty might pronounce on it as he wished.[99]

In spite of this, and [knowing] the requirement and penalties, they still asked to be discharged, and he granted it. The caravel could fit some sixty people, but they squeezed in and made room so well that it took more than one hundred. The caravel was told to sail to Puerto Rico to take on supplies and return to Florida, and the men were ordered, under penalty of death and branding as traitors, to depart from Puerto Rico for Spain on the first ships they could find, to which they agreed. [However], once they were at sea they forced the pilot to head for Havana, because it seemed to them that from that place they could go more easily and faster to Peru, New Spain, Honduras,[100] and Campeche. But they had a contrary wind. They did not want to sail to Puerto Rico, so they went instead to Puerto de Plata, on the island of Santo Domingo. Before they arrived there they prepared a statement, each one backing up the others, claiming that they had completed their service and had been discharged. The authorities were notified of the opposite through a secret dispatch the pilot brought, which he gave to Francisco de Ceballos, a citizen of that town [of Puerto de Plata], who received the dispatch and held on to it. These men were treated kindly and favorably by the authorities and citizens, mainly Francisco de Ceballos, who gave them food and horses. And because there was a royal edict from His Majesty ordering the authorities in that town and all the Indies to arrest any person from Florida who might arrive in their district and send him back to Florida, well guarded, to wherever the Adelantado might be, for this reason some men were arrested, but later released, and most of them went on to Peru and New Spain. Some died there [in Puerto de Plata] because they had arrived very weak, since so many came in the caravel, far more than she could carry, and they were very crowded, the heat was intense, and a voyage of ten or twelve days took more than thirty, and the supplies and water ran out, so it was a miracle that anyone survived.

The Adelantado was informed of all this, and of the fact that the other hundred and twenty soldiers who had seized the frigate with supplies in St. Augustine had arrived there and had been shown much courtesy and honor. He notified the High Court of that island [of Hispaniola] that, according to His Majesty's royal edict, if they were not going to send these soldiers back to Florida, they should send them to Spain, for His Majesty would be very ill served if they were to go to the Indies. This was ignored, for most of them went on to those parts of the Indies where they wished to go, and others went to the High Court claiming that they had served very well and were guiltless. And they were freed, especially Captain San Vicente and his ensign, a thing that caused much wonder and set a very bad example for all the other soldiers who remained in Florida in the service of His Majesty, for His Majesty in the royal edicts presented before that High Court had not ordered that the cases pertaining to Florida be tried but rather, specifically, that every man who abandoned Florida without the Adelantado's permission be returned to him, well guarded, as a prisoner. And even though these decrees were made public and presented before the authorities throughout the Indies, out of five hundred soldiers who had left Florida as mutineers and five hundred more who, bound for Florida, went instead to the Indies—all one thousand of whom the Adelantado had brought from Spain at his own expense, giving them passage and provisions—to this day they have sent not ten of them back to him in Florida.

The Adelantado informed His Majesty of everything so he might dispatch throughout the Indies his edicts saying that they should send them as prisoners to this kingdom [of Spain] so that there not be so many rebellious men in those parts [of the Indies]. In order to justify their wrongdoing, most of these men, wherever they went, and those who came back to this kingdom, spoke poorly of the land [of Florida], of the Adelantado's enterprise, and of the officials, relatives, and friends who remained there to endure the hunger, hardships, and perils that might come to them. And this was the reason why at the beginning, when the Adelantado sailed, many persons wanted to go and settle [in Florida], but because of what these men were saying and the detrimental letters that Captain San Vicente and his ensign Fernán Pérez and others who had behaved badly had written against the Adelantado and his officers and agents, speaking ill of the land, without any trace of justice or truth, they say this is why it was [now] impossible to find any man wishing to come to live, conquer, or settle in [this land]. People gave so much credence to these reports and letters throughout Spain and the Indies that it is said that many condemn the Adelantado for his insistence in wanting to settle in this land, to such an extent that it is said that several of His Majesty's ministers blame him for this, without realizing that the men who said these things had only traveled along the coastline, on the shore and the sands and the swamps, defending the forts and waging war against the Lutherans, and that none of them had gone one league inland in Florida.

Because Captain Juan de San Vicente and his ensign had left Fort St. Augustine for Puerto de Plata with more than one hundred men in the caravel—as is mentioned before—the Adelantado changed his mind, and of the three hundred men he had intended to take to Guale and Santa Elena, he left one hundred and fifty in the two forts of St. Augustine and San Mateo with the people he had first left there, and he departed with the other one hundred and fifty straight to Guale in two brigantines and a one-hundred-ton ship. On the way he called at San Mateo, leaving the men and provisions there and visiting that fort. Gonzalo de Villarroel and all those who were there with him were greatly cheered by his arrival.

Those in St. Augustine and San Mateo blamed Captain Francisco de Recalde and held him largely responsible for the mutinies. From the general investigation made of those who had been convicted, he was held to be more guilty than any other. The Adelantado refused to punish any of them, sending the proceedings of the trial to His Majesty and sending Francisco de Recalde as a prisoner to the House of Trade in Seville. When the proceedings arrived, it was discovered that Francisco de Recalde's conviction had been excised, and when he arrived in Seville he did not appear before this court. As he saw that there was no verdict against him in the proceedings, he asked His Majesty kindly to suspend them until the Adelantado arrived in Spain. It was held as certain that the Adelantado would order Captain Francisco de Recalde to be executed for the crime of which he was convicted in the trial—and because there were found in his coffer certain letters from a priest from Seville, called Licentiate Rueda, who had been in Fort St. Augustine and was one of the main leaders of the mutiny and who, thanks to a statement that he made before the authorities of Santo Domingo, calling on other rebellious soldiers as witnesses, now serves as a priest in that town, and is shown much courtesy there.

Chapter 11

In the Country of Chief Guale

Having repaired the two forts of St. Augustine and San Mateo as best he could given the time and supplies he had, the Adelantado left San Mateo for Guale at the beginning of April of the said year of [15]66. After sailing for three days he discovered a harbor and entered it with the two brigantines and about fifty persons. Leaving Esteban de las Alas with the other hundred [men] in the one-hundred-ton ship, the Adelantado went along the coast to examine a harbor that he discovered there and landed about a quarter of a league from the village. Many Indian archers showed up there with their bows and arrows, and one Christian man among them, also naked. He spoke in Spanish and said to them:

—What people [are you?] Where are you from, brothers?

The Adelantado replied:

—Friends, we are Spaniards.

And [the Adelantado] asked them:

—Brothers, who are you and what are you doing here?

The man replied:

—I am a Frenchman, although I was born and raised in Córdoba. Fifteen years ago I escaped from the Castle of Triana,[101] where I was a prisoner. I fled to France, and there I got married in Havre de Grace.[102] From that time onwards I have always been at sea. I spent six years in Brazil learning the language of the Indians in a harbor and land of Brazil with Captain [Nicolas Durand de] Villegaignon, the captain general of that country, who [in 1559] left for France to request reinforcements. A large Portuguese fleet came [in 1560] and captured the fort he had there.[103] Some of us died and some survived. I escaped among the Indians, for I know their language very well. Afterwards a French vessel went there and I returned to France in it, and then the admiral of France assembled a fleet and sent me to this land as an interpreter. And Jean Ribault, who was the general of the fleet, came as viceroy of all Florida. I came with him and I have been here ever since as an interpreter.

The Adelantado asked him the name of that land and of its chieftain. He said that it was called La Florida, that the lord of that land and the village nearby was called Guale, and that he had sent him to find out who they were, for if they happened to be Spaniards, the Indians would not let them disembark, because that chieftain and his people were friends of the French. The Adelantado said to him:

—We do no harm to the Indians, but rather much good, and we do not want to go to their land against their will. Come closer, brother, because it grieves me to see you go about like this.

He gave him a new shirt and some breeches and a hat, and some food, telling him that if the Indians wished to eat, they should come there.

He called the Indians and they came at once. They sat down on the sand and they gave them biscuit—which they ate very willingly—and some dried figs. There were approximately forty Indians, and the Adelantado gave them all some trifles, in which they took much pleasure. They spoke to the Adelantado by signs, bidding him to go to their land. The Adelantado asked the interpreter what they were saying. He replied that they were very happy with the Adelantado and were inviting him to go to their village to meet their chieftain. The Adelantado told the interpreter to tell them that he wished to do so. He landed, taking with him thirty arquebusiers and four crossbowmen, and leaving sixteen men guarding the brigantines. The Indians were not afraid [of them].

As he walked toward the village the Adelantado was talking with the interpreter, and he asked him who had left him there. He said that it was six months since Jean Ribault had been shipwrecked with part of his fleet while he was looking for General Pedro Menéndez, who had come to that land to convert the Indians to Christianity. Jean Ribault and the captains and men who came with him were [Lutherans] of the new religion, and the admiral of France and all the Frenchmen who had come in that fleet desired that all the Indians be Lutherans of the new religion, like themselves, and to subdue them and bring them to obedience to the king of France. [They intended] to keep galleys there to capture the fleets and vessels of the [Fleet of the] Indies that might pass through there. His general was shipwrecked in a storm, but the people were saved, and in a boat he sent a son-in-law of his and some other captains and twelve sailors, [the interpreter] himself among them, to go to a fort they had and ask them to send two or three ships to collect the people, because these ships were in the harbor where the fort was. And on their entering the harbor where the fort was, their Indian allies told them that other Christians like them had captured their houses and property and fort, and had slain the men inside.

Then a Frenchman who had escaped among the Indians ran down to the shore and told them everything that had happened [at Fort Caroline], and the men on the boat decided to go to Santa Elena, because the Indians there were their allies and they knew the language and the country, for six years previously they had had a castle[, Charlesfort,] there for three or four years. And since the captain refused to go back to France, his soldiers killed him and built a ship and sailed in it to England [in 1562]. One servant of this dead French captain fled to the woods where the Indians were, and he remained there with them in order not to be killed (for in France he would have revealed what had happened). They married him to one of the chieftain's daughters. His name was Guillermo and he was very well schooled in Latin.[104]

The Royal Council of the Indies learned about this through the ambassador in France and England, and they wrote to Diego de Mazariegos, who was the governor of the island of Cuba,[105] asking him to send a light vessel to that coast to discover if there were any Frenchmen there. He sent a very light frigate, and in good order they entered the port of Santa Elena, but not through its main entrance (because it has two entrances), and that is why the sailors and the pilot considered it a poor harbor. When the frigate arrived near the village, the Frenchman Guillermo approached them. He told them how he had come to that land, how many years it had been, and that he was a Catholic and the Frenchmen who had been there were all Lutherans and were not fond of him. They asked him if there were any Frenchmen in that land. He said that he was the only one, and [asked] if they were Spaniards. They said they were. He asked them to take him with them. They said they were happy to do so, and they did. They returned to Havana with this news and handed Guillermo over to the governor of Cuba, Diego de Mazariegos, who in turn—following a royal edict from His Majesty—handed him over to the Adelantado Pedro Menéndez.[106]

When the Adelantado arrived in Guale and was walking toward the village speaking with the French interpreter, he had Guillermo there with him, who also understood the language of Guale because it was no more than twenty leagues from Guale to Santa Elena. The interpreter he had found in Guale was telling the Adelantado, as they were walking toward the village [. . .], that fifteen Frenchmen had arrived in Guale, and that the chieftain had received them very well, giving them food and making them a house in which they could live. They had been there for five months, in which they had enlarged their boat, and fifteen days earlier they had departed for Terranova[107] in order to embark on the vessels that went fishing there. The chieftains of Guale and Santa Elena were enemies, and the chieftain of Guale had taken these Frenchmen with him to wage war against the chieftain of Santa Elena, whom they call Orista, even though the Frenchmen went unwillingly because Orista and his Indians knew them and they did not want to become their enemies. Guale went to Santa Elena in the Frenchmen's own boat, and with that boat they captured four Indians traveling in a canoe—two of them principal ones, relatives of Orista—who recognized most of the Frenchmen in the boat. They returned with this prize to Guale, [but] before they reached the village, two of the four Indians (those who were not principal ones) jumped overboard and swam back to Santa Elena, informing the chieftain of what had happened: that the Christians who had been there six years before had captured them with their boat. Chief Orista sent a message from Santa Elena to threaten the Frenchmen at Guale. All of this the interpreter told the Adelantado, and that Chief Guale meant to kill those two principal Indians from Santa Elena within two days.[108]

The Adelantado showed great satisfaction at hearing this. He told the interpreter that he was sorry to hear about the war between these two chieftains and would like to make them friends. The interpreter was happy to hear this and told him that he would try, because he wanted those in Santa Elena to be allies of the French.

The Adelantado arrived at the village and was very well received by Guale and all his people. They gave him the same house they had given the Frenchmen. All the Indian men and women, adults and children, came to see the Adelantado. He had there with him three boys who every morning and evening, wherever they were, on land or at sea, raised a cross and recited the catechism, and they did so that evening there in the village of

Guale. All the soldiers attended the catechism, and when it was over, they went and kissed the cross. This was [12 April,] the day of Good Friday of the year of [15]66,[109] and the Frenchman Guillermo always attended the catechism.

The other interpreter there, the one born in Córdoba, laughed at Guillermo and all of us because, as it was later found out, he was a great Lutheran, and he reproached Guillermo. Guillermo reproached him in turn and told the Adelantado what had passed between them. The Adelantado called him and asked him if he was a Catholic or a Lutheran. The interpreter [from Córdoba] replied that he was a Lutheran of the new religion, and that this was the reason why he had remained in that land [of France]. The Adelantado told him then who he was, for until then he did not know, and [said] that he was there to convert the Indians to Christianity, and that if his soldiers found out he was a Lutheran, they would kill him at once. [He said] he would not tell them anything, that [the interpreter] should tell everyone that he was a faithful Catholic, and tell the chieftain and the rest of the Indians that those Frenchmen who had been there [before] were not true Christians and were not from his land, that he was a true Christian, and that we were also true Christians, servants of God, and were going to kill those Frenchmen because they were reprobates and bad Christians. If the chieftain and his people wished to be Christians, the Adelantado would be very pleased and would defend him from his enemies.

Fearing that the Adelantado's soldiers would kill him, the interpreter conveyed that message to the chieftain and his principal men very well, because the Frenchman Guillermo was present to see if he said something else. Guillermo understood the language very well and was very fond of the Adelantado, who treated him very kindly, and he went about in full freedom to leave when he pleased. And in the two years he was in Havana he could have left if he wished.

The chieftain replied to the Adelantado that he wanted to be a true Christian and not a false one like the other Christians who had been there. The Adelantado told him about God's mercy and power, and all the things he had said to the other chieftains, [saying] that he should order his people to listen to the chants the boys recited, which were the Christian doctrine, and to come and kiss the cross, for afterwards they would tell him what those chants meant. He said he would do so, and the Adelantado had a large cross set up there. When all of them had gathered and recited the litanies, they went on their knees to worship and kiss the cross. The chieftain and all the Indian men and women did the same.

The Adelantado implored the interpreter, since he was [born] a Spaniard, to convert to Catholicism, to the faith of Jesus Christ, for he would hold him in great esteem and give him many things, and if he wished to go to France he would send him to Spain so that he could go from there, and if he wanted to stay there [in Florida], he could also do so. He replied that he wanted to be there and stay, that he wished to be a Christian and a Catholic, and that he would endeavor to convert the Indians. The Adelantado thanked him very much and told him that, the next morning, they would discuss a peace treaty between that chieftain and the one in Santa Elena, and that he should try to be a good mediator for that, so that they would not kill the two principal Indians from Orista. The interpreter promised he would do what he could in this matter.

The next morning, when the chieftain and all the Indian men and women and boys and girls saw that they were reciting the catechism, they went there and kneeled. When it was over and the soldiers went to kiss and worship the cross on their knees, the chieftain and all the Indians did the same. Then the Adelantado took the chieftain by the hand and led him to his house, asking him to summon his principal Indians, because he wanted to speak to them. Ten or twelve of them indeed came. The Adelantado said through the interpreter that he had learned they were warring with the Santa Elena Indians and he begged them to be friends. He would negotiate a peace [treaty], and [the chieftain] should give him the two Indians he held and he would take them there, and if the Santa Elena chieftain refused to be his friend, he would bring them back. Guale spoke with his Indians and replied that he did not want to, because Orista would take these two Indians and refuse to be his friend.

It was eight months since it had rained in that land. The cornfields and farmlands were dry, and everybody was sad about the scarcity of food. The Adelantado told him that God was angry with him because he was at war with Orista and another two chieftains, and because he had killed the men he had captured, and for this reason God did not want to give him water. [He said] that in exchange for the two Indians he would leave with him two Christians, whom he could kill if [the Adelantado] did not make peace with Orista and did not bring back the two Indians. Guale spoke with his

Indians for a while and replied that he was satisfied. The Adelantado told him that he would depart the following day.

All the Indians, old and young, showed great pleasure at the Adelantado's intentions to negotiate a peace treaty, for the Santa Elena Indians were more powerful and killed many of the Guale chieftain's Indians. Then the Adelantado went to eat with his soldiers and took with him the chieftain and two of his sons, who were very good men. He walked for two leagues from there in order to inspect the island and the lay of the land, but the chieftain, being old, turned back after walking half a league. The land was found to be very good and suitable for bread and wine. When the Adelantado returned to the village, the chieftain asked him to show him the two Christians who were to remain behind with him. He showed them to him at once, because in his own mind he had them picked out. The two soldiers were silent and did not say a word, looking very sad. The chieftain said that he did not want those two Christians, that he would take two of his choice. The Adelantado said that he was satisfied and that he should choose them now. The chieftain chose a nephew of the Adelantado named Alonso Menéndez Marqués and Vasco Zabal, the ensign of the royal standard, because he had noticed that they ate at the Adelantado's table (and it was also believed that the interpreter had told him that they were two of his principal men).

The Adelantado told him that he was satisfied that those two would remain behind, that both of them were among the captains he loved most, and that he would leave a Christian with each of them to wait on them, as well as the boys who were to teach the catechism.

The chieftain was very happy about this and went to embrace them in their manner, thanking them, as a sign of respect, but they were very sad and said that it was not good to remain behind with those savages.

The Adelantado replied that he himself would gladly stay behind, and that they had nothing to fear. He begged them to try their best, with the help of the interpreter, to make [the Indians] understand what bestial lives they led and how good it was to be a Christian. He then told the chieftain to treat his Christians well, and [said] that if he harmed them, he would command that [the chieftain] and all his people have their heads cut off. He would negotiate peace [with Orista], he would bring back principal Indians from Santa Elena to settle it, and he would return as soon as possible. The chieftain was frightened, and if the Adelantado had pressed him, he would have given him the Christians and the Indians willingly just to see him out of his land, because the Indians were really afraid of the Adelantado. They had already learned of his victories against the French Lutherans, for in that land news of the things that happened traveled fast from chieftain to chieftain. This chieftain replied to the Adelantado that he would treat his people kindly and that neither he nor his Indians would kill them, [that is,] unless the Chieftain of Heaven did so.

Chapter 12

In the Country of Chief Orista

The Adelantado departed for Santa Elena the following morning, leaving these six Christians behind as hostages and to teach the Indians the Christian doctrine.[110] He embarked in his brigantines, put out to sea at noon, saw a ship, went toward her, recognized her as his own, riding at anchor, and boarded. Great was the joy that Esteban de las Alas and his men felt when they saw the Adelantado, because they were much afraid that he had been lost, for it was four days since he had left them to explore the harbor, which should have taken only two or three hours, and that night there had been a huge storm. They sounded the trumpets with joy and fired the artillery. The two Indians from Santa Elena whom the Adelantado had brought along, as well as another principal Indian from Guale who came to attend the peace negotiations, were very afraid of the artillery, claiming that it hurt their heads and hearts greatly, and that they should sound the trumpets—which was a good thing—and not fire anymore. The Adelantado commanded that it be so, and he told the interpreter Guillermo that, since he understood the Indians, he should keep an eye on them and comfort and cheer them as much as he could, and he asked all the soldiers to treat them very well. The Adelantado ordered the ship to weigh anchor and sailed for Santa Elena with her and with his two brigantines. He related to Esteban de las Alas and the other people what had happened to him, and they were pleased, although they were very sad that Alonso Menéndez Marqués remained behind, because everyone was fond of him.

The following evening they arrived in Santa Elena, for the three Indians who accompanied them knew the port very well. He entered it, following the directions given by the Indians, who were skillful pilots and were used to fishing there in their canoes. Once they entered and traveled one league inland, the Indians told them to anchor the large vessel, as she could go no farther, and to embark in the brigantines and go to the village. The Adelantado did so and embarked in the brigantines, taking with him Esteban de las Alas and about a hundred men. He arrived in the Indian village, which was two leagues from there, and found that it had been burned and that they were rebuilding some of the houses. Some very agitated Indians appeared with their bows and arrows, ready for war. The Indians whom the Adelantado had brought along told him that those Indians thought that he and his people were some of the false Christians who were on Guale's side and had captured them during the war. [They said] that they would land and tell them that we were very good, and enemies of those people, and why we had come there.

The Adelantado let them go, and within half an hour he landed with all his people, leaving ten men in each brigantine as guards. Then the Indians came to the Adelantado without their bows and arrows, with great humility, showing great signs of respect. Many ran off, some on one road and some on another, because they were already sending word to the villages, chieftains, and captains to come see the Adelantado. Then they made a large fire and brought a large quantity of shellfish, and the Adelantado and his men dined. Many Indians came to speak and pay their respects to him, and the love and joy these Indians showed to the Adelantado was something to see. Three chieftains, subjects of Orista, came that night and told him to go to a village one league from there, because Orista and some of his captains and chieftains were coming there to eat. The Adelantado did so.

Orista came at daybreak with two other chieftains and captains, and great was the joy they all had with the interpreter Guillermo, whom Orista had married to one of his daughters when Guillermo was there. The Adelantado ordered him to tell Orista to convene with his principal men, because he wanted to speak to them. They did so. The Adelantado ordered Guillermo, who was the interpreter, to inform them of all that had happened in Guale concerning the peace negotiations, all of this in front of the three Indians the Adelantado had brought with him. Orista said that he would reply presently and spoke with his Indians for more than half an hour, deliberating back and forth, and not allowing Guillermo to be there, so that he would not understand what was happening and what they were discussing. Then they called the interpreter and talked with him for a long time. Then the interpreter told the Adelantado on behalf of Orista that it pleased him greatly to make peace, as the Adelantado commanded, and that he and his people would be even more pleased to be true Christians, as those in Guale wanted to be, so those [in Guale] would not be better than them. His two Indians that the Adelantado brought back had told him who God was and how good it was to be a Christian, and they wished very much to have the Adelantado live in that land and would take him for their elder brother in order to do as he commanded, [adding] that they would consider the false Christians their enemies, since they were enemies of the Adelantado.

The Adelantado replied with great joy in his heart that he loved them very much but that he did not intend to live in that land, because it was bad and his was better. [He said] that his Indians would kill his Christians, because the Christians he had brought with him did no harm to the Indians, and if they did any harm, the Adelantado would kill whoever did it, and that he would want to live there only to teach them how to be Christians so they would go to Heaven when they died. He told them about God's power and mercy, and the same things he had told the other chieftains in order for them to convert.

They showed great satisfaction at hearing this and repeated that they wanted to become Christians, and that, if the Adelantado did not wish to live there, he should leave them some Christians to instruct them. The Adelantado said that he would leave some, but if their people were to kill any of them, he would come back to wage war against them and would cut all their heads off. They said they were very satisfied, and then many Indian women came carrying food: corn, acorns, oysters, and poached and baked fish. The Adelantado ordered biscuit, wine, and some cane syrup to be brought, and he divided it among the Indians, who drank the wine very willingly and enjoyed the biscuit dipped in water mixed with that honey, because they are very fond of sweet things.

When the meal was over, they performed certain ceremonies with the Adelantado, taking him for their elder brother and seating him in the chieftain's place of honor. The chieftain and all the others there went to show obedience, performing certain ceremonies, taking his hands (which is a ritual equivalent to when we kiss the king's hand here). Then all the Indian men and women came to do the same, and it was a wonderful sight to see the mothers and relatives of the two principal Indians whom the Adelantado had brought from Guale—who were mere lads—weep with joy together with the Adelantado. Then the Indians danced and sang all day until midnight.

The Adelantado stayed the night there, and the next morning he told the chieftain that he wanted to go and look for a place to build a village, because it was not appropriate for his Christians to live with his Indians, so as not to quarrel with each other. The chieftain said that he should do as he pleased most, begging him to go to the village where he lived, because there was a very good site nearby, next to the harbor where his vessel was anchored. The Adelantado was pleased with this and asked if they were to go by land or by sea. The chieftain said however he wanted. The Adelantado decided to go in his brigantines, and Chief Orista, his wife, and another dozen Indians went with him. Great was the joy and happiness the Adelantado showed at seeing the Indians' trust in him. He kept them very merry and diverted all the way, and when they disembarked he gave them refreshments. After they disembarked, they proceeded on land for approximately half a league to the village and the chieftain's house, where they were entertained very well that night.

In the morning the chieftain had [the Adelantado] seated in the place of honor in a big house he had, and he went there with the other Indian men and women to obey him and take him for their elder brother, as was done the day before in the village where he had been. They made several proclamations, ordering that no harm be done to the Christians, and the Adelantado gave them the usual trifles, as he did everywhere he arrived. They gave him some tanned deerskins and burnt pearls (for there are many in that land, but because they do not prize them, in order to eat the meat they roast the shell where the pearl is, and the pearl is burned and thus rendered worthless).

The next morning the Adelantado went with Chief Orista to examine a site to build a fort. He found it very pleasant and appropriate, for it is an island of about four leagues with a very suitable harbor which could very well be fortified. It was about a league from the bar, so that vessels entering the harbor would see the fort. He decided to build the fort there and, having consulted with Esteban de las Alas and the other captains he had with him, he marked it out. He entrusted its completion, quickly and without delay, to Captain Antonio Gómez, whom he had taken out of the flagship of the Fleet of New Spain that was wintering in Havana and who with another fifty soldiers and sailors—all very good people—came from Havana with the Adelantado in order to be anchored with him in Florida until the month of May [1566] had passed, and they were there and served well in this expedition. Then all the men, one hundred and fifty soldiers, were divided into squads, some to cut and carry timber, others brushwood, and others to sink stakes and dig the trench. The Adelantado was there for two weeks, during which, with the help of his people and some Indians, he left the defenses [of the fort they called Fort San Felipe] half ready and placed in it six bronze artillery pieces. He appointed Esteban de las Alas warden of the fort and governor of that land, leaving one hundred and ten men there with him. He dispatched the one-hundred-ton vessel with another twenty men to Hispaniola to be laden with supplies for the people there, because they had little left. He himself dispatched a brigantine to San Mateo and St. Augustine to tell them what had happened and to say he was on his way back.

Then Chief Orista sent dispatches throughout the country giving notice of how there were very good Christians there who did no harm, who shared what they had, and who wanted to live in that land. [He said] that he and all his people had taken [the Adelantado] for their elder brother so that he would defend them against their enemies, that they were very happy about this, that he and all his Indians wished to become Christians, that the Christian chieftain of these men was a very good man, and that he wished to depart, so they should come at once if they wanted to see him.

At the end of the fortnight when the Adelantado wished to depart, many chieftains came to see him. They all took him for their elder brother, to do as he commanded, and they wanted to be Christians and be given a cross and some Christians to live in their lands to teach them how to become Christians. The Adelantado did so, giving each chieftain a Christian or two, together with supplies so they could erect a cross in the villages where they were to live and recite the catechism every day, morning and evening, and to try to get the Indians to worship and kiss the cross. The Adelantado gave these chieftains some gifts, and a hatchet to each, with which they were very happy.

Chapter 13

Return to the Country of Chief Guale

The Adelantado departed in the beginning of May [1566] and took with him two principal Indians [of Orista] as guides in order to negotiate peace with Guale. Esteban de las Alas and the men who stayed with him were happy, because it seemed to them that they were making a good start in converting the Indians to Christianity, which—next to driving the Lutherans out of the land—was what they desired most. But they were very frightened by the lack of food, for they had very little remaining and there was still much work left to finish their fort. They were daily expecting the French Lutherans, who—since they had tidings of the Adelantado's victories against them on land and sea and of how he had defeated and expelled them from that land to prevent them from teaching their evil sect to the Indians—were building a great fleet to avenge the defeat they had suffered at the hands of the Adelantado and his men, and to return and settle that land. (Knowing that the Adelantado was waiting for them, they did not dare to go in search of him. Instead they went to the island of Madeira, which belongs to the King of Portugal, and seized, sacked, and pillaged it, then returned to France.[111]) And even if the Indians wanted to give food to Esteban de las Alas and his men, they did not have any, for it was many months since it had rained.

The Adelantado arrived in Guale with twenty men on 8 May [1566]. Guillermo was the first to disembark. He told the chieftain about the peace that had been concluded, and [told] Alonso Menéndez [Marqués], Vasco Zabal, and the other four Christians who had remained there with them all that had happened, and they were very pleased. The Adelantado disembarked and was very well received by Guale and all his Indians. Then the two Indians from Orista communicated their message to Guale, who had all his principal Indians around him, and he and all his people, old and young, appeared to be very pleased [with it], but he was troubled by the Adelantado's friendship with those of Santa Elena and by the fact that those chieftains had taken him for their elder brother. Then he said to the Adelantado through the interpreter that he was glad about the peace, that he wanted to take him for his elder brother to do as he commanded, that they wanted to be true Christians and not false ones like the Frenchmen who had been there, and that he should leave him people to live in his land, since he had done that for Orista.

The Adelantado said that he had none, but that he would soon send some. The chieftain replied that he should leave those who had remained there, who were good, to teach them how to be Christians, and afterwards send him more. The Adelantado said he would give him a reply in the morning. Then the chieftain told the Adelantado that, since he was already a Christian and had made peace with Orista in order not to anger God, he should ask Him to give him water for his cornfields and other cultivated lands, for it had not rained in nine months. The Adelantado said that God was very angry with him because He had commanded him to do many things with which he had not complied, and this was the reason why He did not want to give him water, even if he begged Him.

The chieftain became very sad again and went home. When the boy catechists heard this, they went with the interpreter to the chieftain and told him not to be sad, for they would pray to God for rain. The chieftain gave them many chamois cloths, which are tanned deerskin, and corn and fish, which they accepted and went off with. When the Adelantado heard about this, he ordered that everything be taken from them and they be stripped in order to be whipped. When the chieftain heard this, he came to the Adelantado looking very sad and saying that [the Adelantado] had deceived him because he did not want to ask the Chieftain of Heaven for water and wished to whip the boys because they had asked Him. [He begged him] not to whip them, for he no longer wanted them to ask God for water, and it should rain whenever it pleased God. The Adelantado said to the chieftain that those boys were rascals who had deceived him and were telling him lies so he would give them the food and deerskins, and that God was angry with them for being such rascals. He ordered the boys not to be whipped, declaring that if the chieftain was truly a Christian, God would sooner give water to him than to the Adelantado or to the boys who had told him many falsehoods. The chieftain replied with sorrow that he had been a true Christian from the very first day. He went straight to the nearby cross and knelt and kissed it. He turned to where the Adelantado was and said through the interpreter:

—Behold how I am a true Christian!

This happened around two in the afternoon. Less than half an hour later there came thunder and lightning, and it began to rain very hard. A thunderbolt struck a tree near the village and splintered it into many pieces. All the Indian men and women came to get the pieces of the tree and take them home and keep them. The chieftain and all the Indian men and women went to the Adelantado's house, some of them in tears, some throwing themselves at his feet, others asking for his hands, begging him to leave some Christians with them.

The Adelantado's nephew Alonso Menéndez [Marqués] and Vasco Zabal had told the Adelantado that the French interpreter [from Córdoba] who was there was a Lutheran and a great sodomite, that when the Adelantado had left for Santa Elena he had tried to convince the Indians to kill them, and he could inform himself about what happened by talking to Guillermo or to two Indians with whom [the interpreter] slept (one of them rumored to be the chieftain's oldest son). The Adelantado did so in great secrecy and, learning that it was true and that [the interpreter] had been seen many times mocking the Christians and spitting on the cross in front of the Indians, he spoke with his nephew Alonso Menéndez [Marqués] and with Vasco Zabal, ensign of the royal standard, for both of them had witnessed it and knew about it. He told them that it was not appropriate to leave that chieftain and his people disconsolate, for they wished to be Christians, and that it would please him much if they would remain there as they had before.

Vasco Zabal replied that he would sooner have the Adelantado behead him than be left there. Alonso Menéndez [Marqués] replied that it would pain him much to stay there, but since His Lordship commanded it, he would comply, on condition that the Adelantado took the Frenchman [from Córdoba] with him or had him killed, for otherwise nothing would be accomplished and he and those who remained with him would be killed, for the chieftain's son was more powerful than his father, and he was really fond of this interpreter, so that if they were to kill [the interpreter], the Indians would be angered and break out in war. This reasoning seemed very good to the Adelantado, and since he trusted Guillermo and held him to be a Catholic, he called him and told him to talk with that interpreter [from Córdoba] about going with him to Santa Elena, which they could reach in two or three days by canoe—through a river without going out to sea—[and tell him] that Esteban de las Alas, who was a good and generous captain, would give him many things, and that he would bring back a present for his chieftain that the Santa Elena chieftain had said should be delivered [only] by the interpreter. The interpreter was pleased with this and, without realizing that the Adelantado knew about it, he came to beg him for a letter of introduction to Esteban de las Alas, and a hatchet, for he wished to go and fetch the gift that the Santa Elena chieftain was sending to his own Chief Guale. The Adelantado asked to be given paper and ink, for he wished to write the letter at once, and he wrote it very favorably and gave it to him.

Chief Guale dispatched this interpreter in a canoe with another two of his Indians, that they might go and return at once. The chieftain's son seemed very sad at the interpreter's departure and wept, begging him to return at once. The Adelantado sent a soldier with a letter to Esteban de las Alas, [ordering him] to have the interpreter killed in great secrecy (because he was a sodomite and a Lutheran, and if he were to return alive the people of Guale, who wished to be Christians, would not be converted so soon); to treat the two Guale Indians who accompanied him very well; to do the same to Orista, giving him a handsome present; to send another one to Guale, offering him his friendship; and to pretend to be very concerned when the interpreter went missing [and say] that, since he was a false Christian, he must have hidden in the woods in order not to return to Guale, so that if a ship came from his country [France] he could depart on it. Thus it was that Esteban de las Alas had [the interpreter] strangled in great secrecy, and the two Indians returned to Guale.

Chapter 14

Return to San Mateo and St. Augustine

The Adelantado had already departed for San Mateo and St. Augustine, leaving there in Guale his nephew Alonso Menéndez [Marqués] and the four Christians who had been there with him before. He took Vasco Zabal with him. The rain in Guale lasted twenty-four hours and extended over the whole island, which is about four or five leagues in length. While the Adelantado was sailing toward San Mateo in the brigantine on the inland [water]way, without going out to sea, many canoes came to meet him and said:

—Spain! Friends! Christians! Brothers! Give us the cross!

For these Indians had learned of what had happened in Santa Elena and Guale, and how it had rained, and they wanted to be Christians. The Adelantado was very pleased with this. He disembarked, gave them some trifles, and had many little crosses made to be given out—the Adelantado and his soldiers kissing them first—one for each village.

He bid them goodbye and arrived in San Mateo on 15 May [1566], where he found the people of that fort well but in great need of supplies, and all the Indians in a state of war. He learned that they had shot arrows at the sentinels in St. Augustine twice and had killed two soldiers and set fire to the powder magazine, for its roof was made of palmetto leaves, and thus the fort was burned. At night they put artificial fire on their arrows and with their bows they shot the house, and the fire caught, because it was windy. It spread in such a manner that it could not be remedied, and all the powder and munitions, cloths and linens, flags and standards, both the Adelantado's and those captured from the Lutherans, were burned, and nothing escaped. The field commander [Pedro de Valdés] and the rest [of the men] were in great difficulties due to the lack of food and the Indian threat, for they set up ambushes in small bands so that, if a Christian went out in search of palmitos or shellfish, they would shoot their arrows at him. And since these Florida Indians are so agile and so certain that they cannot be caught, they are very bold in approaching the Christians, and other times they wait for them, and when the Christians retreat they are in great danger from them, for [the Indians] draw their bows with such force that an arrow will penetrate the clothes and coat of mail the soldier wears. They shoot very quickly. And once a soldier has fired his arquebus, before he reloads, the Indian with his agility closes with him and shoots four or five arrows at him before the soldier finishes tamping the wad in the arquebus, and when he is pouring in the powder to prime it, the Indian retreats among the high grass and woods in which that land abounds and he waits for the powder to take fire, and he ducks. Since he is naked, he moves [easily] through the grass, and once the arquebus fires, he pops up in a different spot from where he ducked when they wanted to aim at him. [The Indians] are so subtle in this that it is a thing worthy of admiration. They all fight in skirmishes, they leap over the bushes like deer, the Spaniards less agile by far than they are, and if the Christians follow them and they become afraid, they go where there are rivers or swamps (for there are many on the seacoast), and since they go about naked, they swim across, for they swim like fish, holding their bows and arrows out of the water with one hand so they do not get wet. Once they are on the other side they start yelling and mocking the Christians, and when the Christians retreat they cross the river again and follow them until they are back inside the fort, coming out from the bushes and shooting arrows at the Christians, for they do not miss the opportunity when they see it. This is why waging war against them is quite ineffective unless we go to their villages in search of them and cut down their crops, burn their houses, take their canoes, and destroy their fisheries and all their plantations, so they are forced to leave their lands or keep their word to the Christians, so that the chieftains and the Indians may become friends with them and treat them well. When they go to the forts of St. Augustine and San Mateo, if they are not given food, clothing, iron hatchets, and trifles, they leave very angry and break out in war, killing the Christians they find. They are very treacherous Indians, and in this manner, by treason, under [the pretense of] friendship, they have killed more than one hundred soldiers. The Indians at these two forts, San Mateo and St. Augustine, where the French used to be, are the most treacherous.

The Adelantado was much troubled by the burning of the powder magazine, fort, supplies, and munitions [in St. Augustine], and by the great need and danger in which the field commander and his brother Bartolomé Menéndez and the rest of the people found themselves. He departed with dispatch for St. Augustine, taking some men, munitions, and supplies from the little there was in San Mateo. He took with him [the sergeant major, Captain] Gonzalo de Villarroel, who was very sick from past hardships, in order to send him to Havana to be cured, and in his place he left the ensign of the royal standard, Vasco Zabal.

He arrived in St. Augustine on 18 May [1566], and great was the joy of those who were there. They wept with happiness at the mercy that Our Lord was granting them in succoring them with the Adelantado's arrival at such a time. He informed them of the good things that had happened in Guale and Santa Elena and of their fine start in converting the Indians to Christianity, at which everyone rejoiced most greatly. He had the supplies and munitions they had brought unloaded, and he had rations given out. He entered into council with the field commander and captains. They agreed that they should relocate from there and erect a fort at the entrance of the bar, where Fort St. Augustine is now, because there the Indians would not be able to do them as much harm, and that they should place the artillery in it, because from there they would be able to better defend themselves against whatever enemy ships might want to enter the harbor. This done, if the supplies did not arrive within two weeks, the Adelantado should go in search of them in three brigantines he had there, because the ships he had sent under the command of other men had never returned.

This decision was made public and gave great happiness to everyone, even though they were very sorry that the Adelantado would leave them, because they understood that the field commander had to go to San Mateo because of the absence of Villarroel, for that was what the soldiers who had remained there had requested and the Adelantado had promised. Then, that day and the next, they crossed the bar and began to trace the fort and build it with the greatest diligence. They worked from three in the morning, before daybreak, until nine, and from two in the afternoon until six. They divided the people into four parts, and the tasks the same, and cast dice to decide who should do which. So great was the order observed in building this fort speedily, for fear that the Indians might attack them, that it was a joyful sight. Approximately one hundred and seventy persons were working on it, and within ten days it was in a reasonable state of defense, with the artillery in position.

Since no ship with supplies came, they were all at risk of dying from hunger. It was agreed unanimously that the Adelantado should depart at once for Havana with the three brigantines and take one hundred men [with him], for most of them were from the flagship of the Fleet of New Spain and the Adelantado had agreed to take them back to Havana during the month of May, and with only seventy rations left, they could not feed themselves for more than a few days unless some vessel arrived.

Chapter 15

Second Voyage to Havana

Thus the Adelantado embarked with the hundred men in the three brigantines at the beginning of June [1566]. On the day he left he encountered one of his sixty-ton ships laden with supplies that Francisco Cepero was bringing. Diego de Amaya was aboard, very ill, and if the Adelantado had not encountered them at that moment, they would have sailed near the banks. They were already in a place where, had they not dropped anchor, they would have been lost, for while they thought they were entering over the bar at high tide in two fathoms of water, at low tide there was none. The sea was running high, and when the ship loosed her cable she hit bottom. The Adelantado boarded her and brought such skill that he pulled them out to safety, for otherwise all those aboard would have drowned and died.

He wrote to the field commander that he should distribute all those supplies between those forts [of San Mateo and St. Augustine] and go at once to San Mateo and not leave that fort until [the Adelantado] returned, which would be in a very short time, and that they should load a brigantine left in that harbor with corn and send her to Esteban de las Alas [in San Felipe], and so it was done. Once the ship was unloaded, they were to sink her, so that the twenty men she was bringing, all good men, would stay in the fort, and so that the soldiers would not mutiny, having no ship with which to leave the country. The field commander did so.

It was very fortunate and lucky that the Adelantado encountered this ship, for otherwise all those who remained in the fort would have starved to death.

The Adelantado made sail at once and arrived in Havana within a week with two of the brigantines, for the other had not been able to turn her bow (the wind and the sea were high) and instead put in at the island of Santo

Domingo. The Fleet of New Spain had arrived in Havana two days earlier. On board was Licentiate [Jerónimo de] Valderrama of the Royal Council of the Indies, whom His Majesty had appointed *visitador*[112] of New Spain and who, having served his term, was returning to Spain.

On disembarking in Havana the Adelantado went with his soldiers to the church to pray, and before going to his lodgings he went to visit Valderrama, thinking that since he was there, he could quickly relieve the fort with men and supplies, because there were more than three hundred soldiers from Florida who had fled there. Valderrama was staying at the governor's house, and the Adelantado and Valderrama spoke to each other standing up, without sitting down, greeting and embracing each other very courteously. The Adelantado said he was very fortunate to find him there, because he was to return [to Florida] in four or five days, and he asked him kindly to choose a time when he could speak to him and give him particulars of the state of affairs in Florida and of the great necessity in which those forts were left, for His Majesty had five hundred men there at his own expense, and even though he had brought many messages and decrees for the governor of that island, he had not helped him with anything. Valderrama replied that anytime the Adelantado wished to get together with him, he would be happy to do so.

On the following day the Adelantado noted when Valderrama went to church and went there himself. When mass was over, he told him that he was indebted in that country [of Cuba] for the supplies he had bought for Florida, and that for eight months he had been providing for the soldiers that His Majesty had there, who had been left in extreme want and danger, both as to food and the Indians. [He said] that those [Indians] in the land where the forts of St. Augustine and San Mateo were located were all in a state of war, and there were few soldiers in the forts, most of them sick, ill-treated, and very discontented due to the great hardships and perils they had had to endure and still endured daily. Also there had been mutinies and double dealings among some of the captains wherein more than four hundred soldiers had abandoned those forts, and on that island of Cuba there were more than five hundred men, [not only] those mutineers who had abandoned the forts but also men who had sailed from Spain for Florida but had been separated from the Adelantado in a storm and had landed in Cuba and remained there, not wanting to go to Florida. [He said that] even though he had asked the governor [Francisco García Osorio] many times to relieve him with supplies at His Majesty's expense, and by having these men picked up and turned over to him, he never would do it. And since [Valderrama] was there in order to inform His Majesty of everything, he begged him to write a report and, so he could return [to Florida] soon, help him with two or three thousand ducats that His Majesty carried in that fleet, which he undertook to give back if His Majesty was not pleased. Also he should ask the governor to give him two hundred of those soldiers from Florida who were in that town and island, in order to fortify the two forts at San Mateo and St. Augustine.

[The Adelantado] told him what had happened in Guale and Santa Elena, how all the Indians of that land were his allies and wanted to be Christians, and that he had built a fort and left in it one hundred and ten soldiers with Esteban de las Alas as governor of that district [of San Felipe], and that he wanted to depart in the morning for the country of Chief Carlos in order to take back to him his sister [Doña Antonia], who was there in Havana, because the principal Indian men and women whom she had brought with her had died, so that only two remained, and if she and the others were to die, the chieftain and his Indians would think the Adelantado had had them killed. This chieftain ruled over much land, plus Los Mártires and the Bahama Channel, where navigation was most dangerous for the Fleet of the Indies, and it would be very desirable to have him for a friend and try to convert him and his Indians to Christianity. He himself would return there in ten or twelve days, in which time the two hundred soldiers and the supplies he was to take with him could be assembled.

Valderrama responded dryly that he could not give him the money; on the matter of the soldiers, he would speak to the governor and charge him with gathering them; as for the report [the Adelantado] was asking him to write on how badly the governor had treated him, so that His Majesty would know the truth—he had no brief to do that.

It seemed to those of us who were present that the Adelantado went pale with grief, and he said to Valderrama:

—Sir, until I return from [the land of] Carlos, Your Lordship may consider how you can serve His Majesty in this, and you will do me the kindness you think most appropriate, for it is in Your Lordship's hands to do what I am begging of you in order not to lose Florida, to save the souls and the natives thereof, and to further His Majesty's purpose, which is to prevent the Lutherans from setting foot in that land, and to endeavor to implant the Gospel in it.

Valderrama did not reply. The Adelantado took his leave and went to his lodgings feeling much distressed. He informed Juan de [Rojas] Hinestrosa, the treasurer of that island and his lieutenant for all matters concerning Florida, of the little help he had received from Valderrama and of everything that had passed between them. Juan de Hinestrosa consoled him greatly, saying:

—Sir, with my property and my person I have done all I could for Your Lordship, and now I will try to do the same with that of my friends. Let Your Lordship not be distressed. Go to [the land of] Carlos tomorrow, as you have decided, and I will send to find some corn, cassava, and meat that you might take with you for the men to eat. Meanwhile I will talk to Licentiate Valderrama, who, because he is of His Majesty's Council and understands how important it is to give this aid, for which His Majesty will hold himself to have been well served by him, I am certain he will do it.

The Adelantado thanked him and charged him to do so. [Hinestrosa] also told him that the Indian woman Doña Antonia, Carlos's sister, was very discreet and so dignified that everyone in town was astonished. In only a few days she and a maidservant of hers whom she loved very much had learned with great ease everything, all the prayers and Christian doctrine needed to be baptized, which they were. She was very sad about His Lordship's absence and the deaths of her Indian men and women, [but] after she had been informed of His Lordship's arrival, her delight and happiness were great, and she wept with joy. It behooved him to pay attention to her and treat her well because, as he wished to take her with him, it would be best if she were to report good things [about them], for [Hinestrosa] and all those in Havana had devoted great attention to treating her well and making her happy.

The Adelantado told him that the day before, upon disembarking, he had sent [someone] to call upon [Doña Antonia], telling her that he would visit her the following day, and he was planning on doing it as soon as he finished eating. This he did, first sending her some of what he was eating, and a few shirts and clothes that he had asked the treasurer to buy, so that the Indian woman would see that he had brought something for her and be pleased. When [the Adelantado] went to see [Doña Antonia] he took with him many persons of agreeable manners who kept her company, as well as his musicians, for the Adelantado never went about without them. He found the Indian woman very sad, and even though the Adelantado gave her many presents, she would not cheer up. With the help of the interpreter, he asked her many times to tell him why she was sad. She replied that she wanted God to kill her because when he disembarked the Adelantado had not sent for her in order to take her to his house to eat and sleep with him. When the Adelantado realized that she was a woman of the first rank, with such fine understanding, and that she was right, he told her that the Christians who wore that cross (for the Adelantado is a knight of the Order of St. James) could not sleep with their wives when they returned from an expedition against their enemies until one week had passed, and that he wished them to be over, because he loved her very much.[113] The Indian woman half laughed and half cried, saying that she would be happy if she only knew that he spoke the truth. The Adelantado begged her to be happy, because he spoke it. She said, beginning to count on her fingers, that two days had already gone by, and she indicated the six after which she would go to his house. The Adelantado said she should do so, and he rose and embraced her with great rejoicing. He ordered the instruments to be played, because she had never seen them in that land, and they seemed to her very good. The Adelantado was there for more than an hour cheering her up.

This Indian woman was under the care of a *regidor* of that town called Alonso de Rojas.[114] He had a high-ranking wife who had stood godmother to this Indian when she was baptized, and who loved her very much and instructed her in doctrine. [This woman] told the Adelantado many things about her good understanding and her good and clear judgment, with which the Adelantado was very pleased. He asked the Indian woman if she had any desire to go to her land. She replied that she did, a very great one. The Adelantado asked her if she wanted to leave the following day. She said that she did, and she pleaded that they go. The Adelantado said that they would do so. He took leave of her and went to his lodgings, which were near there.

That night after midnight, when the Adelantado was sleeping in his room with a lit candle, it so happened that the Indian woman asked a woman friend whom she loved very much—one of those [Christians] that her brother Carlos had enslaved and the Adelantado had brought from Florida—to go with her to the Adelantado's house, because he had commanded her to go there. The woman believed it, and she went with [Doña Antonia] and her Indian maidservant, and she knocked on the door of the Adelantado's residence. They opened it to see who it was and they recognized her. This [Christian] woman said that the Adelantado had commanded her to go there with the Indian woman [Doña Antonia], and the young man who opened the door, thinking she spoke the truth, let them in and took them to the Adelantado's room, where there was a lit candle. The Indian woman took it in her hand and looked to see if any woman was in bed with the Adelantado, and then she looked around the bed and underneath. The Adelantado, although he was very tired and exhausted, awoke, and when he saw her with the candle in her hand, he was disturbed and demanded of the woman who had come with her:

—Sister, what does this mean?

Doña Antonia sat on top of the bed with the candle to see what the Adelantado was saying. The [Christian] woman replied that Doña Antonia had told her that His Lordship had commanded her to be brought to him at that time, and that she, believing it, had done so. The Adelantado, with a happy and amused countenance, laughed much at this and asked her to tell [Doña Antonia] that he would be very pleased if the week had [already] passed so she could sleep there with him. Doña Antonia begged him through the interpreter to let her lie in a corner of the bed, promising not to come close to him; this way her brother Carlos would know that they had slept together, for otherwise he would think that he was mocking her, and he would refuse to be a true friend of the Christians or be a Christian like she was, which would distress her very much. The Adelantado thought that she was right, but [he said] God would kill him, and if she wanted him to die she should undress and get into bed with him. Then she began to embrace the Adelantado and told him that she did not want to lie with him, so that he would not die.

The Adelantado called one of his servants to take some things from a chest, which were three shirts, a couple of mirrors, and necklaces of glass beads—trifles that the Adelantado had had gathered that day to take to her brother Carlos. The Christian woman who was with her said that if the Adelantado had not woken up, [Doña Antonia] would have put out the candle and gotten into bed with him. And at this they went away satisfied.

Chapter 16

Second Voyage to the Country of Chief Carlos

The Adelantado went to embark the next morning, taking with him the Indian woman [Doña Antonia], her maidservant, and two of the Christian women who had been captives [in Florida]. He went in a *patache* and a little shallop with about thirty soldiers and sailors. Sailing with a fair wind, he arrived at the village of Carlos on the third day. He anchored at the entrance of the harbor because, since he had brought few men, he did not dare to go to the village. Then the Indian woman told the Adelantado to disembark with her and go to the village. The Adelantado said that there was no way he could do this, for he needed to depart at once in order to look for Christians to leave there and teach her brother and the Indians of that land how to be Christians, if they wished to convert. Then he promised her to remain there for a few days and build her a house in which to live in the Christian village. [The Adelantado said] that the relatives of those Indian men and women who had died in Havana would think he had killed them and would want to harm him and his soldiers. War could break out with her brother, and this would grieve him very much, for he loved [Carlos] much (due to his love for her) and held him to be his brother, and he wished to return soon. The Indian woman replied that she was very distressed because the Adelantado would not disembark, and that he should remain a few days on land until the week had passed, in order that she might sleep with him. But she also feared that the Indians might be hostile and might do him some harm, so she begged him to return as soon as he could and bring Christians to leave there and convert her brother and the rest of the Indians to Christianity.

There came many canoes, and Doña Antonia sent word to her brother that she was there and that he should come for her. The joy that the Indians had with her was something to see, although others were grieved and weeping for the Indian men and women who had gone with her and died. Carlos came within two hours with as many as twelve canoes, two of them fastened to each other and covered by an awning fashioned of arches and woven mats. The captain, the chieftain's brother-in-law, first boarded the Adelantado's *patache* with six other principal men, and the ceremonies with which Doña Antonia and her brother greeted each other were a sight to see. The Adelantado ordered that food be brought and instruments played, and that the Indians in the canoes be given some corn and cassava and some knives, scissors, mirrors, and bells. When lunch was over he gave a present to Carlos for himself and his wife, and another to the captain for himself and his wife, who was Doña Antonia's sister, and he gave [presents] to the principal Indians who were there, and to Doña Antonia some things that he had brought for her.

The Adelantado asked Carlos if he wanted to become a Christian and cut his hair, and go to Christian lands as promised, [adding] that he should bring him the Christians he said he would give him upon his return. Carlos asked that they let him speak privately with his captain before replying. They withdrew for more than a quarter of an hour, and they told the Adelantado that for the next nine months there was no way that [Carlos] could go to Christian lands or become a Christian, lest his Indians rise against him and kill him. The Adelantado should return after that time had passed[, Carlos said,] and justified his words with plenty of reasons. When those nine months had passed and [the Adelantado] returned, he would become a Christian and go to Spain with him to visit his king. Also he had those Christians [the Adelantado] had requested in a village four leagues from there, and the next day at noon he would send them to him.

Then he took his sister [Doña Antonia] with him and they bid the Adelantado farewell. The following day at noon the Christians had not yet arrived, and Carlos sent six of his principal Indians in a canoe to tell the Adelantado that he should eat with him, that the Christians would come at once, and that he would bring them. The Adelantado had those Indians seated in his *patache* and very well fed. He gave them each a present and told them to go and tell Carlos that he was an evil and mendacious man, that if he was thinking of betraying him and his soldiers, he commanded him to come to his *patache* at once in order to be there with him until he sent him the Christians he had to deliver to him. If not, he would order his head cut off and those of his Indians, and his villages burnt, and he would be a friend and brother to his enemies. The Indians went away very distressed.

The Adelantado was eager for high tide in order to leave, because neither he nor the men who were there with him ever thought for a moment that Carlos would come. [But] within an hour Carlos came with his twelve Indians, bringing his captain with him, and the Christians had already come by a different path. Carlos boarded the *patache* with his people, duly performed the handover, and told the Adelantado that if he wanted to kill him or take him to his country against his will, he could [now] easily do it. The Adelantado treated him very well, from which Carlos and those who were with him took satisfaction. Carlos gave the Adelantado two Indians to take with him, one a young man of twenty years, his first cousin who was to inherit the rank [of chieftain], and the other one to wait on him. The Adelantado bid him farewell and sailed away.

Chapter 17

Third Voyage to Havana

On the way the wind was contrary, and the Adelantado entered a harbor where one of Carlos's villages was located, and remained for four or five days. The Indians took much pleasure in him and received him with much respect. They asked him for a cross to worship, for this had been done throughout Carlos's country ever since the first time the Adelantado had left one there. He gave it to them and sailed for Havana with fair weather, arriving there within ten days of his departure. The Tierra Firme fleet had already arrived. The treasurer [Juan de Rojas Hinestrosa] told the Adelantado not to expect any help from [the *visitador* Jerónimo de] Valderrama or the governor [Francisco García Osorio], whether money or supplies or soldiers, and that he had not been able to obtain any help even from his friends. The Adelantado was much distressed.

He spoke to Valderrama and the generals of the fleets of Nombre de Dios[115] and New Spain who were there, Cristóbal de Eraso and Bernaldino de Córdoba, who were relatives, and represented to them his dire necessity and that he wished to return to Florida with some supplies, for he did not have any, nor the money to buy them, thinking that once his great need was understood, they would speak to the governor or to Valderrama, or that from the fleets or armadas—for there were more than thirty vessels—they would each give him a hundredweight of biscuit and a cask of wine. And with some corn and cassava that he would beg from his friends in Havana (from each his own fair share as charity) he would be able to return to Florida with fifty or sixty sailors and soldiers he had there. They did not help him with anything. In view of this, and of the few men he had left in the forts, the Adelantado took a frigate, a brigantine, and a shallop, and he embarked about sixty-five men, of whom the governor gave him five. And [in exchange for] a gold-embroidered suit, some garments, and other household items, he obtained five hundred ducats with which he bought corn, meat, and cassava.

Chapter 18

Reinforcements from Spain
Arrive in San Mateo

He sailed from Havana on 1 July [1566] together with the fleets of New Spain and Tierra Firme, which were bound for Spain, and later that day he drew away from them. Within a week he arrived in Florida, at Fort San Mateo, where he found a vessel anchored off the bar. He went to identify her and learned that she had come from Spain with supplies. The men aboard her said that there were another fourteen vessels in the harbor at St. Augustine, two more at Santa Elena, and that all of them came laden with supplies. They brought one thousand five hundred infantrymen to reinforce those forts and the Indies, because they had news that the French Lutherans were assembling great fleets for those parts. The joy that the Adelantado and his people received from this was great, for he had come there much distressed about the little help and support he had found in Havana, for even though so many of the king's servants—all of them such good gentlemen—held prominent positions there, they had given him no help, alms or charity, especially as they were aware of His Majesty's ample edicts and stipulations ordering the governor of that island, García Osorio, to give him from his Royal Exchequer whatever he requested and needed.

The Adelantado crossed the bar of San Mateo, went to the fort, and found Captain Aguirre there. He had come from Spain as a soldier due to the absence of Juan de Orduña, who had been colonel of these men but remained in Sanlúcar [de Barrameda][116] on orders of His Majesty, to whom it seemed he was not needed in Florida on account of the good captains the Adelantado had there with him. The day they arrived in St. Augustine, Sancho de Archiniega,[117] who came as general of the fleet and the relief expedition, gave the colonel's company of two hundred and fifty men to this Aguirre so that he could go and reinforce San Mateo, for once the field commander [Pedro de Valdés] knew that the reinforcements had come, he went at once from San Mateo to St. Augustine, leaving Vasco Zabal in charge of [San Mateo].[118] [The Adelantado] found Vasco Zabal with the veteran soldiers inside the fort and Aguirre quartered outside, in disagreement with one another because Vasco Zabal wanted Captain Aguirre to go inside the fort with his soldiers, and [Aguirre] said that he would do it, but he must [be the one to] place the sentinels and give the password,[119] while Vasco Zabal argued that he was in charge of the defense and safekeeping of the fort and must not consent to this.

The Adelantado ordered that Captain Aguirre put fifty soldiers in the fort every night and that Vasco Zabal place the sentinels and give the password. Leaving them much in accord, he departed for St. Augustine. Sailing there, he met en route the field commander in a brigantine, coming to San Mateo to settle the dispute between Captain Aguirre and Vasco Zabal. The Adelantado was extremely pleased to see him. [Valdés] told him all the miseries, hardships, and perils they had suffered before the arrival of the reinforcements, and how the Indians near Fort San Mateo had treacherously killed Captain Martín Ochoa and other soldiers, and that in Fort St. Augustine they had killed Captain Diego de Hevia, a relative of the Adelantado, in the same manner, and that as they had no food, they were forced to go out in search of oysters, crabs, and palmitos, but it had been necessary for most of the men to go out [in a group]. Otherwise, the man who went [alone] never came back.

The Adelantado was much distressed at the death of these two captains, for he loved them very much, and Martín Ochoa had greatly distinguished himself when they took the fort [Caroline] and had served faithfully in all other things related to his office, so that the mutineers had thought many times of killing him for returning with high spirit to His Majesty's service, reprimanding them for their failings. The Indians had also treacherously shot with their arrows an interpreter and five other soldiers whom the Adelantado loved very much and who had been among the first to share in the hardships and perils when the fort [Caroline] was captured, obeying the governor in everything, and never wishing to abandon the fort and join the mutineers. One of them was Don Prudencio de Avendaño's illegitimate son Don Hernando de Gamboa, another the field commander's first cousin Juan de Valdés, another the Adelantado's cousin's son Juan Menéndez. The Adelantado was very sorry about this, but since he realized how distressed the field commander must have been, he concealed his sorrow and said:

—In enterprises such as this one there is no way to avoid these deaths, hardships, and perils. May Our Lord forgive them, for I am truly sorry.

Then the field commander told him in detail about the reinforcements that had come, the names of the captains, and how badly they had behaved with him, because as soon as they had disembarked and landed they quartered themselves around the fort. The first two nights after his arrival, the field commander had the sentinels stationed at the points where they needed to be and he gave them the password, for they were all in agreement that the field commander, with the ample powers the Adelantado had given him, was their lieutenant. But when the captains realized that the powder magazine and Fort St. Augustine where they previously stood had burned down with everything inside, including all the papers and directives, and among them the powers that the field commander had received from the Adelantado, they agreed to station their own sentinels and give their passwords and appoint a field commander and sergeant major. Some of them thought this was right and others wrong, and there was some disagreement among them, [but] in effect they went on in this fashion. The field commander was surprised at this development because they had never, before or after, said a word to him or asked for those authorizations. He sent word that they should all get together, that he wished to speak to them, and he said to them:

—Gentlemen, the Adelantado has left me in these provinces as his lieutenant, in accordance with the commission he received from His Majesty for this, and he gave me ample powers, which have been burned. The notary before whom they were executed is here, and the wide knowledge that everyone had of it, and how they respect and obey me as their lieutenant. Your Lordships can be informed and satisfied of this by the captains and soldiers who are in this province, for most of them are here. They are Bartolomé Menéndez, regular captain to His Majesty, brother of the Adelantado, warden of this Fort St. Augustine and governor of the district, and another is Gonzalo de Villarroel, warden and governor of Fort San Mateo and its district, and another is Esteban de las Alas, warden and governor of Fort San Felipe and its district, which is in Santa Elena. All three are persons of worth, noblemen and very good soldiers, from whom Your Lordships can be satisfied of this. It being as I say it is, His Majesty will be [better] served if you obey me [while I am] in this office. Let us give our attention to the provision of all appropriate things, as befits His Majesty's service, sending supplies and men to Esteban de las Alas in Santa Elena, for he is in great need, and to fortifying ourselves, for if the enemy should come upon us—as it is said that they are coming strong—we are not [behaving] as soldiers [should be].

[He said] that Sancho de Archiniega—who was general of the fleet and whom they all considered their leader—had replied to him that he could not give him the men before the Adelantado returned, because that is what he and his captains had decided. And it was rumored that His Lordship had drowned, because when he departed from St. Augustine for Havana to fetch supplies with the three brigantines, one of them could not turn her prow and landed in Hispaniola, and since the sea and the wind had been very strong for two days, they believed he had been shipwrecked. [Therefore] they were determined to be the leaders, name the necessary officers, and dwell in that land until they could inform His Majesty. The field commander had replied to Sancho de Archiniega that he was truly sorry to hear those things, because he realized that His Majesty would not be served thereby and his royal service would cease in those provinces. And since they were determined to do so, he and the wardens of the forts, with the soldiers inside, would hold the forts as they had been holding them in His Majesty's name, and would defend them with their lives against friends and enemies. [Archiniega and his men] would be quartered in the fields, accomplishing nothing, spending His Majesty's money and supplies. If this enterprise were to continue, they should be good friends.

[Archiniega] replied to the field commander that it would be so and they would have this friendship, and that he had put up with those things because there was nothing else he could do, and that in the service of His Majesty it would be best to overlook them, and that for the last twelve days, ever since the fleet with reinforcements had arrived, they had been conducting themselves in that manner, without going into the forts or doing anything else.

The Adelantado thanked the field commander very much for how wisely he had conducted himself and [said] that he had acted as a very good captain, because when it came to settlements and conquests of new lands, those in command had to endure such insubordinations at times, for there was nothing else they could do, and that this was the true way to serve His Majesty and do what was appropriate.

The Adelantado arrived in St. Augustine that day and was very well received by all. General Sancho de Archiniega was on board his ships, and as it was late, he did not land. The next morning, when the Adelantado had heard mass, he sent to ask the captains to come to the fort because he wanted to speak to them and enter into council with them, and this was done. There came Sancho de Archiniega, who was general of the fleet and of the men in that relief expedition, and who was carrying a mandate from His Majesty to deliver everything to the Adelantado and do whatever he ordered and commanded. He brought with him Captain Juan de Ubilla, admiral of the fleet.[120] The Adelantado received them very well, because Sancho de Archiniega had been a great friend of his for many years. General Sancho de Archiniega delivered the men, the fleet, and the dispatches from His Majesty to him, and once the Adelantado had received the dispatches, he acknowledged receipt of all and told the general that he had brought with him some poor counselors, for he had not performed the task, on the day he arrived, with the field commander, as his lieutenant in those provinces by His Majesty's commission. [The Adelantado said] that he could hardly be everywhere in Florida at once, the land being so large, that if [Archiniega] were as familiar with warfare on land as at sea, he would not trust his counselors nor allow himself to be deceived by them, that the Adelantado did not blame him as much as he blamed some captains who, wishing to rule and follow their private interests, did not advise him well in what best served His Majesty. But that was over and remedied with his arrival, he did not intend to speak any more of it, and asked them kindly to consider him their brother and friend and to advise him in all the things that seemed to them best to serve His Majesty. In its own time, he would beg His Majesty to reward those who had served him well, and he would be very distressed by those who did the opposite, and would have them punished.

Sancho de Archiniega reassured the Adelantado, and what the Adelantado had said to the captains seemed very fine to everyone. They were not familiar with the Adelantado, and they learned that his manner held both bile and honey, to be loved and feared. Then he asked each captain to bring his officers there, because he wanted to speak to them, and they did so. The Adelantado received them very cheerily and spoke warm words to them, encouraging them to strive to endure the hardships and perils that were to come, because all of this would be to better serve Our Lord God, and the King. He begged them to comfort and reassure all the soldiers, and to help those who were disheartened, cheering them and advising them to be strong and firm in His Majesty's service, which was the reason they had gone to that land.

They all replied that they would do so and showed great satisfaction at the discussion the Adelantado had with them. Then he ordered them to go and gather the soldiers at once because he wished to speak to them, and they did so. The Adelantado entered into council with his captains and, having read His Majesty's dispatch to them, decreed that Sancho de Archiniega be general of the fleet—which he turned back over to him—and be in charge of the sailors, supervising and disciplining them, adjudicating all future disputes. Captain Juan de Ubilla was to be his admiral as before, to which they agreed.

Since His Majesty had ordered that the forts in Florida be reinforced with as many of the one thousand five hundred infantrymen as seemed appropriate to the Adelantado, and that the fortresses of Puerto Rico, Hispaniola, and Cuba be secured with the rest, [the Adelantado asked] that they all come and eat with him, and that once they had finished, they endeavor to fortify themselves as best they could, so that if the enemy were to come, they would find them [prepared] as soldiers, and that they build a powder magazine in order to unload the supplies, and that the ships be unloaded as quickly as possible. He ordered that General Sancho de Archiniega and Admiral Juan de Ubilla be in charge of this, and have the sailors bring in their boats many pine trees to be sawn to make wooden planks for the powder magazine.

Thus they went to eat with great pleasure and satisfaction. When that was over, with the troops assembled, the Adelantado spoke to the soldiers, thanking them for having gone to that land, and [saying] they could be certain that he would love and be very fond of them, especially of those who did their duty and served better than the others. He begged them to be cheerful and to arm themselves with patience to endure the hardships and perils that were to come. He gave them his word that he would support and defend them as much as possible, treating them as well as he could. [He said] that in that land [of Florida] he would honor, in His Majesty's name, any man who served well and deserved it, and that he would implore His Majesty to do so too, that they should all be cheerful and most willing to obey their captains and officers, doing all the things they commanded and ordered, for this was the chief service that they could render to His Majesty.

They all replied that they would do so, and received great satisfaction from the fine words the Adelantado said to them. Then the Adelantado went to visit the women who had come in that fleet, who numbered fourteen, and he sent them word that they should all be assembled in one house, congratulating them on their arrival. They were delighted with the Adelantado's visit and the kindness he showed them. He spoke to the priests who were there with these people, five of them, urging them to be good Christians in all the things pertaining to their charge, and gave them the vicar whom they were to obey, who was Chaplain [Francisco López de] Mendoza [Grajales], from Jerez de la Frontera, a very good cleric and soldier who had come from Spain with the Adelantado.[121] He appointed him vicar of that fort [St. Augustine] and of San Mateo. They replied that they would do so and pledged obedience to the vicar.

The Adelantado took his leave with all the captains who accompanied him here and, taking into account everybody's opinion and the general consensus, and debating about it in order to better decide, they marked out the site, the place and space where they were to fortify themselves, which was the same place where the Adelantado had fortified himself [before], but since the sea was eating into the fort, they retired farther inland, taking a cavalier from the fort already built for the one that was to be erected. The men were divided into companies and squads, and the same was done with the work. They cast dice to leave to chance which section each one would work on, and it was settled in this manner to the satisfaction of all, so that in the morning each captain and squad would know what part in the making of the fort had fallen to their lot.

The next morning at dawn they rang the bells, which was the signal for all to rise, and they beat the drums, assembling the men. It was a pleasure to see them come to work. On the third day, when the Adelantado saw that it was progressing as it should, he summoned the captains to a council and told them that it would be well to discuss the reinforcements that His Majesty ordered and how they should be done. Upon discussion, it was agreed that half of the one thousand five hundred soldiers were to stay in those parts, in the three forts of St. Augustine, San Mateo, and San Felipe, and that the Adelantado should depart with the rest in six ships and a frigate and a *patache* together with their crews (making one thousand men altogether) to cruise about the islands of Puerto Rico, Santo Domingo, and Cuba in order to harass the corsairs there and to fortify those places. The other ships should be dispatched quickly to Spain under the command of Sancho de Archiniega and Juan de Ubilla, who—as is mentioned before—had come as general and admiral of that relief expedition. In the meantime while the frigate, the *patache*, and the six ships the Adelantado was to take with him were being unloaded and prepared, he wanted to go and visit the port of San Mateo and leave there Gonzalo de Villarroel (who was [in St. Augustine], having returned from Havana) in charge of all the men, and go on to Guale and Santa Elena in order to visit Fort San Felipe and put it in good defensive order, because two vessels had gone there, the flagship and a larger ship, with three hundred soldiers under the command of Captain Juan Pardo, and it was not known if they had arrived, nor the state of things in those parts.

Chapter 13

In the Country of Chiefs Utina,
Mayaca, and Calibay

With the accord and general consensus of all the captains, [the Adelantado] appointed Captain Juan de Zurita to succor Puerto Rico and Captain Rodrigo Troche[122] to succor Santo Domingo (these two being among the first who had gone to Florida with the Adelantado) and Ensign Baltasar de Barreda[123] to succor Havana.

He himself went to San Mateo, where he left Gonzalo de Villarroel in that fort with Captain Aguirre's company and the other veteran soldiers who were there. In three brigantines he went upriver from San Mateo (for he had not done so until then) with one hundred soldiers and some sailors, in order to befriend the chieftains and solve the mystery as to whether that river[124] reached the lands of New Spain.

The day following his departure from San Mateo he disembarked after having gone twenty leagues up the river. Together with a guide he had brought along, he walked five leagues through very nice grasslands in the land of a chieftain called Utina.[125] When he was one mile from his village, he sent six soldiers with this guide, who was an interpreter, and on arriving there they gave [Utina] a present the Adelantado had sent him and told him that the Adelantado was coming to see him because he considered him his friend. [Utina] received the six soldiers very well and replied that he was afraid of the Adelantado, [asking] that if he wished to come to his village, he not bring more than twenty men, and that he ask God for rain for his cornfields that were dry, as he had done for Chief Guale. The Adelantado marched behind the six soldiers, and when the answer came back to him, he was about one-quarter of a league from the village. He halted and ordered eighty of the men to remain there, proceeding with twenty, and laughing at the chieftain's request for water. But when he arrived at the village, where it had not rained in more than six months, it began to rain heavily.

He went to the chieftain's house and did not find him there. He asked five or six Indians who were there to go in search of him and tell him that he had come with the twenty men and the water. One of the Indians went and came back with an answer, saying that the chieftain was hiding in the forest and that he had sent him word that he was very afraid of a man who had such an influence on God, that he should depart with God, since He was a friend of his. The Adelantado was very sorry to hear this, for he greatly wished to meet this chieftain, as people said he was very knowledgeable and very powerful on that riverbank of San Mateo. He sent word back, begging him to come and meet him and not be afraid, since the Adelantado had only twenty men and he had more than one thousand Indians, all with bows and arrows. [Utina] replied that if the Adelantado was getting help from his Chieftain (who was God), then those twenty men were a great force. He begged him to leave and [told him] that, from that moment onwards, he would take him for his elder brother and be his friend, as long as the cacique remained in his own land and the Adelantado in his, and that he did not want to fight with the Adelantado or his men, but his Indians did, and that he was very distressed because he refused to leave. The Adelantado said that he would leave in order to please [Utina], and that he was not afraid of him or his people, but that he would go upriver from San Mateo, [and Utina should] send word to the villages through which the Adelantado was to pass that the men and women should keep calm and not be afraid of him, for if they fled he would wage war on them, burning their villages, canoes, and fisheries.

And so the Adelantado returned to where the eighty soldiers had halted and, taking them with him, he went back to the brigantines at dusk. Everybody was astonished at how [fast] he could march, because it was an hour after daybreak when he left the brigantines to go to Utina, and he was there for two hours and still returned in daylight, a distance of a good ten leagues, although many estimated twelve. He had a very bad night, for it was raining very hard and he could not embark, and as they had camped in a wet field they fared poorly.

In the morning, the Adelantado sent the largest brigantine with fifty men to San Mateo and went upriver with the other fifty and some sailors in the two brigantines, since he had supplies for [only] ten or twelve days, and if all the men had gone, they would not have lasted that long and he would not have learned the secret of that river. He was very well received in the villages along the river banks because they said that their chief Utina had sent the order. The Adelantado tried to take a guide to discover the secret of the river, but despite the presents he gave them and his kind treatment, none wanted to go with him. He went up the river as far inland as the French had gone [before], taking some Indians as guides. The tide rose and fell for a good forty leagues, which greatly impressed the Adelantado. He went upriver approximately fifty leagues, two leagues farther than the French had gone, to [the land of] a chieftain called Mayaca, a friend of Saturiwa, who was a powerful chieftain of the country and coast where the forts of San Mateo and St. Augustine are located. This Mayaca retired with his Indians, leaving the village deserted.

The Adelantado landed and went into the houses. He did not consent to any damage being done, withdrew, and sent the interpreter to see if any Indians appeared. They came to meet him, for they knew him, and they took much pleasure at seeing this interpreter. He told them how the Christians and their captain general were there, and that they should send word to Chief Mayaca to come to the village with his people and not be afraid. Some Indians went to look for him to tell him this, while some others came to their houses and brought the Adelantado a great deal of fish. He gave them some presents and received them very well, begging them to call their chieftain, because he wanted to give him many things he had brought for him and his wives. The ones who had gone first went [to where Mayaca was], and they told the Adelantado that their chieftain was very afraid of him and did not want to come, that he and his Indians were his friends because they knew that he did no harm to any chieftain, and that he should turn back and not go farther upriver, for his Indians were angry because he had gone to their land without their permission.

The Adelantado sent him word that he wished to go upriver to see some Christians, begging him to give him two or three Indians as pilots. The chieftain sent him word that he refused. The Adelantado ordered his men to row and started upriver, going approximately one league. It was already late. He saw many bellicose Indians with bows and arrows, and when he came to a narrows he found the river blocked with stakes. He broke down the entrance and went in, but the river became barely two pikes wide and very deep. The current was very strong against him there, and up until then there had been none except the ebb and flow of the tide, and the Adelantado feared that the [Indians] might kill the oarsmen with their arrows. Two or three Indians went down to the riverbank and told him on behalf of Chief Mayaca that he should turn back and not continue any farther, for otherwise they would wage war on him. The Adelantado replied that he was not there to do them any harm, and that they could come and wage war on him whenever they pleased, but he needed to go up that river and, as it was night, he wanted to stay there until morning, which he did.

The guide and interpreter the Adelantado brought with him had been a slave of a chieftain of [the country of] Ais whom they called Peracho,[126] who lived twenty leagues up the river and was acquainted with Mayaca. [The interpreter] told the Adelantado to turn back because there were many hostile Indians in that land and he had been told that, from that point on, the river would become very narrow for more than thirty leagues until it reached a large lagoon called Maymi, which is said to be more than thirty leagues in circumference and to receive the waters of many rivers from the sierra. And this lagoon emptied in the country of Chief Carlos, which is on the coast of New Spain, and another branch emptied around Tequesta, which is in Los Mártires.[127] The Adelantado had a great desire to find out this secret because of the alliance he had forged with Carlos and to know if that river was navigable, which was a very advantageous thing for the settlement and conquest of Florida. On the other hand, he feared that if hostile Indians came at him in their canoes in that narrow stretch, within the blockade of stakes, he could be harmed, especially because the soldiers' fuses and powder were wet on account of how much it had rained.

He retreated for approximately one league with his two brigantines and in the morning he decided to turn back. On the way, after about seven or eight leagues, he landed in a village where some Indians were waiting for him. He gave them presents and asked them to summon their chief, whom they called Calibay.[128] He came, and the Adelantado told him through the interpreter that Mayaca had sent to ask him not to go up the river and that his soldiers had become infuriated with [Mayaca] and wished to land and burn his village and canoes and destroy his fisheries, and that to prevent them from doing this, he was on his way back. Calibay replied that he wanted to be his friend and take him for his elder brother, to do as he commanded, and he begged [the Adelantado] to give him a cross as he had done for Guale and another six Christians, for he and his Indians wanted to become Christians. He would show the river as far as the Maymi lagoon to the six Christians who were to remain there with him, because the Indians were not afraid of a few Christians but they did fear many, and he would do them no harm.

The Adelantado was afraid of this chieftain because he was a subject of Utina and would rise against him, and because he was a good friend of Chief Saturiwa, [but] as it was less than twelve leagues by land from there to St. Augustine, he agreed to give him the cross and leave the men there, warning him that if he killed any of them he would return to wage war against him, burning his houses and canoes, destroying the fisheries, and cutting off his head and those of his men, women, and children, for he was a friend of his true friends and an enemy of his enemies. The chieftain said that he was satisfied, and then many soldiers requested to be left there. The Adelantado selected those who seemed most willing and able to instruct the Indians. He gave this chieftain a present for himself and another for Mayaca, asking him to send it to him together with three of those Christians, so they could live with him and instruct him and his Indians.

Calibay said that he would do so, and thus he sent [Mayaca] the gift and the Christians, but Mayaca took the gift and refused to receive the men. He sent word to the Adelantado that he was his friend and had taken him for his elder brother, which is all the obedience the chieftains of Florida can give, but [warned him that] if he came to his land, he would consider him his enemy. When Saturiwa heard that Calibay had the Christians, he sent two of his sons and other Indians to kill them. Calibay did not allow it. Saturiwa sent to tell him that he should either kill them or deliver them to him, and if he did not comply, he would consider him his enemy. Calibay, for fear of Saturiwa, sent them to San Mateo, and when the Adelantado was returning to San Mateo, passing through three or four of Utina's villages that he had previously visited, all the people—old and young—were awaiting him with much delight. He gave them some presents and had the instruments played. They all rejoiced at this, and they were sorry he departed so soon. He arrived where he had disembarked when he went inland to see Utina. He sent word to Utina that he should come to visit him there, as the Adelantado had gone to visit him in his village, and that if he didn't, he would consider him his enemy. Utina was afraid to upset the Adelantado and, considering how friendly he had been in those villages where he stopped, and that everyone was fond of him, he came to see the Adelantado with three hundred warriors. When he was a quarter of a league from the brigantines he halted and sent word to the Adelantado that he should go there with twenty Christians, which he did, taking with him twenty skillful arquebusiers, marching in good order.

When he was approaching, Utina became afraid of him and sent word to him that he should come there with only two men. At a distance of about half an arquebus shot, he halted with the twenty soldiers and continued with only two of them and the interpreter toward Utina, who was surrounded by his three hundred archers, seated. Utina was very humble toward the Adelantado and showed him the greatest obeisance that is customary among them. Then came his principal men, one by one, to do the same, and then the rest of the Indians who were there. The Adelantado clothed Utina in a shirt—for he was naked, with only his private parts covered, and so were all his Indians—and a pair of breeches, a doublet of green silk taffeta, and put a hat on him. This Indian was very gentlemanly in features and disposition, about twenty-five years old, and very modest. He told the Adelantado that he took him for his elder brother to do as he commanded, and that he should leave him a cross as he had done in Guale, and some Christians to instruct him and his people, and a trumpeter, for he was his true brother. The Adelantado did so, leaving him a cross and six Christians, among them the trumpeter. He gave him some presents for his wife and for the principal Indians who were there. They parted very good friends.

The Adelantado embarked and went [back] to San Mateo within twelve days after he had departed. He found everything there in good condition and Gonzalo de Villarroel pleased with the men, although some of them had gone without orders from him to rob certain of Saturiwa's houses two leagues from there. The Indians came out to meet them, and eight of the twelve arquebusiers who had gone there were killed. The other four hid in the woods and returned to the fort within three days, very badly injured. The Adelantado was there [in San Mateo] for two days.

Chapter 20

Voyage to Santa Elena
and the Country of Chief Tequesta

He departed for Santa Elena and sent a message to His Majesty about the state of affairs and how the reinforcements had arrived. He sent a captain with thirty soldiers and two Dominican friars to St. Marys Bay [Chesapeake Bay], which is at 37° latitude, with an Indian, a brother of the chieftain of that country, who had been with the Adelantado for six years. He was very articulate and intelligent, and a very good Christian, by name Don Luis de Velasco, with whose help they might settle in that land and attempt to convert the Indians to Christianity. The friars were from Peru and New Spain, a very fertile country. They had suffered hunger, hardship, and peril in Florida, and thinking that they could not endure such a hard life, they secretly stirred up some of the soldiers (which was not difficult) and the pilot as well. With everyone's agreement, swearing in writing that they had not been able to go there [to St. Marys Bay] because of a storm, they went to Seville, speaking ill of the land and of the king and the Adelantado for wanting to conquer and settle it.[129]

The Adelantado arrived in Santa Elena. He found Esteban de las Alas installed in the fort with the veteran soldiers and Juan Pardo quartered outside, building houses to lodge the men, because he had been told by General Sancho de Archiniega that he was to give out the password one night and Esteban de las Alas was to do so the next night, and he showed him his orders. Esteban de las Alas told Juan Pardo that he was very pleased with his arrival and that he had been ordered by the Adelantado Pedro Menéndez, his captain general, to guard and defend that fort in His Majesty's name, and that he was to place the sentinels and give the password, he and no one else. On this condition Juan Pardo could either go inside the fort with all his men or some of them or remain quartered in the field, as he wished. Juan Pardo is a good soldier, zealous in His Majesty's service, and it seemed to him that Esteban de las Alas was right, that Sancho de Archiniega had been wrong, and that once in Florida he was bound to obey and follow the orders of the Adelantado and not others. He pledged obedience to Esteban de las Alas for the defense of the fort, giving him a squad of soldiers for the sentinels' guard, and [told him] that when necessary he would come in with the rest. He quartered himself with them in the field and they all began to work to ready the fort for its defense.

Great was the joy and happiness they all received with the Adelantado's arrival. He learned that the Indians were very friendly and that Esteban de las Alas had great need of men and food [before] Juan Pardo had arrived with two ships laden with supplies and three hundred soldiers, for it was a month since the Adelantado had sent him a laden vessel [of supplies], but on the day she arrived, before anything could be unloaded, the soldiers mutinied and sailed away with her, leaving Esteban de las Alas a prisoner along with the officers who had come with him from Havana with some sixty men. In the Bahama Channel [the mutineers] ran into a storm which forced them to enter a harbor back in Florida, at the tip of Los Mártires. They found a village of a chieftain called Tequesta, a close relative of Chief Carlos and the Indian woman Doña Antonia.[130] Christians who were captives there, who had arrived long ago in a canoe, told them this, and also that those Indians used to kill all the Christians from shipwrecked vessels, now they loved them very much because they knew that the highest-ranking man among them had taken a relative of theirs, Carlos's sister, as a wife. [The Spaniards] should not be afraid, because the chieftain had sent them to find out if they came from that group of Christians (they said they did), and that near there, in a coastal village, there were many of those Christians. This was true, because approximately twenty of the soldiers who had mutinied in San Mateo had landed there on their way to Havana. A strong wind hit the ship, which set sail and left them in that land. The Indians treated them very kindly, giving them of what they had out of love for the Indian woman Doña Antonia.

Another twenty soldiers had also deserted Esteban de las Alas to go inland, so when Juan Pardo arrived, he had only about twenty-five men in the fort and no food beyond what the Indians sent them. After Captain

Juan Pardo arrived, he had hanged two soldiers for mutiny and imprisoned another three. Six had deserted. The men were somewhat unnerved, as it seemed to them that there was discord between [Juan Pardo] and Esteban de las Alas (when there was not, but rather much harmony, and no less than what has been stated).

The Adelantado entered into council [with them] and they decided upon the way in which they would fortify themselves. He was there for a week, during which the friendly chieftains came to see him and begged him to stay there for a month, because many chieftains who lived inland wanted to come and see him and take him for their elder brother. The Adelantado could not do it, for he needed to return quickly to St. Augustine to reinforce the Indies as His Majesty had commanded. He freed the three soldiers Juan Pardo had imprisoned, giving them a reprimand, and spoke to all of them, encouraging them and entreating them to remain steadfast in His Majesty's service. He appointed Esteban de las Alas as his lieutenant general in those provinces because along with the reinforcements he wanted to take the brigadier [Pedro de Valdés] with him as his lieutenant and admiral of the fleet, which he did.

He ordered Juan Pardo to go inland with one hundred and forty soldiers and visit the chieftains who wished to come see the Adelantado. With all friendliness possible, in the place he thought best for the protection [of the Indians] and their conversion to Christianity, they should fortify themselves wherever he thought best for their own safety, in the direction of New Spain.[131]

The Adelantado departed from Santa Elena at the end of August [1566], having confirmed the peace with the chieftains, and ordering Esteban de las Alas to preserve it.

Chapter 21

Second Voyage to the Country of Chief Guale

He arrived in Guale within two days and found the Indians very sad about the death of the Adelantado's nephew, Alonso Menéndez Marqués, who was the leader of the Christians there and whom they loved very much. They worshipped the cross with much devotion and all the boys and girls attended the Christian doctrine and knew it by heart. Many chieftains of that district came there with a great desire to see the Adelantado. He remained there eight days, in which fourteen or fifteen of them came. They asked him for crosses and Christians who could teach them how to be Christians. The Adelantado agreed to leave one captain with thirty soldiers there, most of them important men who asked to be left there, for it seemed to them that, [this way], they could serve God and their king better. The Adelantado departed.

Chapter 22

Return to San Mateo and St. Augustine

He arrived two days later in San Mateo, where he found all the people well. He took Gonzalo de Villarroel with him to St. Augustine, where he found that many soldiers wanted to mutiny and leave the land. The brigadier had hanged three of them and had imprisoned others, including Captain Pedro de Rodabán, one of the captains His Majesty had sent with the reinforcements, who had disrespected the brigadier and was accused of being the most to blame for giving the [soldiers] orders and occasion to mutiny. And even though the Adelantado found enough grounds to have him brought to justice, he spoke to the brigadier and told him that, since they were not familiar with those captains and soldiers, and that most of them had been disobedient from the start, it was necessary to tolerate things and do what they could, not what they wished. To keep the peace, it would be best for the Adelantado to rebuke this captain and set him free, leaving the proceeding against him as it was. The brigadier thought this was just, and it was done like this. The Adelantado was received very joyfully by all the captains, sailors, and soldiers there, [and] he dispatched the ships to Spain.

Chapter 23

Voyage to Puerto Rico, Hispaniola, and Cuba

[The Adelantado] sailed with the fleet to look for corsairs and provide reinforcements to the islands of Puerto Rico, Hispaniola, and Cuba as had been decided. Although he was ready to set out at the end of September [1566], with the winds contrary he could not do so, and he sailed on 20 October. He arrived on 5 November at La Mona with half of the fleet and the brigadier [Pedro de Valdés] arrived at San Germán[132] with the other half, in order to take the corsairs by surprise, because those were places where the thieving corsairs habitually went, but they did not find any.

The captains of the six warships were:

- the Adelantado, general of his warship;
- the brigadier, captain and admiral of his own;
- Juan Vélez de Medrano, of another;
- Ensign Cristóbal de Herrera (who was the first to plant the flag inside Fort San Mateo when it was captured from the French, he being the ensign of Captain Diego de Amaya), of another;[133]
- Captain Pedro de Rodabán, of another;
- Baltasar de Barreda, of another;
- García Martínez de Cos, of the frigate;
- Rodrigo Montes (a first cousin of the brigadier and also one of the first to enter the fort), of the brigantine.

As soon as the brigadier anchored his vessels at San Germán, he was notified by the locals that a message boat, a *patache* bound for Santo Domingo, was in Guadianilla,[134] fifteen leagues from there, and that the crew said that on 25 September 1566, twenty-seven warships had departed from France.

The fleet, carrying six thousand soldiers and sailors, had been divided into three parts; one had captured the island of Madeira on 6 October, but where the other parts had gone they did not know. At once the brigadier sent Hernando de Miranda, His Majesty's factor in Florida, to inform himself and find out more details about this. He went to Guadianilla and spoke to the master and the pilot of the *patache*, who were his friends, and they told him the same thing. They gave a written statement of what had happened, signed by a city councillor from La Palma who was on the island of Madeira when the French captured it (and were there seventeen days). And on the ships there came some Portuguese men whom that councillor knew, who informed him of all that had happened.

On the third day, Hernando de Miranda returned to San Germán and recounted all of this to the brigadier, who, thinking that the Adelantado should know this in order to regroup his fleet and decide what to do, sent word to the island of La Mona, which was twenty leagues from there, where the Adelantado was with three ships. Once the Adelantado received the dispatch, he sent the fleet to San Germán with orders to the brigadier to careen and grease the ships and put them in total readiness. He went to the city of Santo Domingo, fifty leagues from there. He was very well received by the High Court and citizens of that city because they had already heard the news about the French fleet two days earlier and were very afraid that it would come there.

The Adelantado went to the High Court, where the president and *oidores*, or judges, were assembled, and showed them the order he had from our lord the King to make those reinforcements. He told them that he had brought one thousand sailors and soldiers, all very good people, and good pilots and seamen, because for this purpose he had withdrawn all the sailors he had in Florida, who were very good and who came there with the intention of harassing and pursuing all the corsairs in those parts in order to punish them, so that they would not go about extorting, robbing, and injuring His Majesty's subjects in times of peace. Because of the news he had received that that French fleet was coming to those parts, he would ask their opinion and advice on what he should do, asking them kindly to share with him their views on this matter. The High Court, after discussing the matter, summed it up by telling him that their advice was to fortify that city and fortress [of Santo Domingo] and those in Puerto Rico and in Havana and neighboring ports, as His Majesty ordered, and then to return promptly to Florida.

The Adelantado was greatly grieved by this advice, for he was looking forward to encountering one of the three parts of the French fleet, as well as other corsairs who went about independently in those parts, much enriched from the plundering they had done, but it seemed to him that His Majesty had commanded him in his order to do what the High Court had advised him, and therefore he resolved to do it. He asked them to make themselves available that afternoon and the next day to look into the best way to fortify the city and fortress and to look into and figure out the places where the enemy could disembark, so as to station sentinels and to make carriages and wheels for the artillery (because the ones they had were rotten) in order to mount it and place it in readiness at the most necessary sites. It was all done with great diligence and care.

The Adelantado left Captain Rodrigo Troche in that city with one hundred and fifty soldiers, two-thirds arquebusiers and one-third pikemen. He left Captain Antonio Gómez as captain of artillery, for he was very skilled and a fine gunpowder man.

Within six days the Adelantado headed back to San Germán and arrived there in three days. He sent Captain Cristóbal de Herrera in his carrack with supplies, munitions, and twenty hundredweight of gunpowder for cannons and arquebuses for the defense of the fortress and city [of Santo Domingo]. In that city there were ten vessels being laden with hides and sugar for Spain. The High Court made that carrack their flagship and appointed Cristóbal de Herrera as its general, for he was a good fighting man at sea. The fleet departed from that city within six days and arrived safely in Seville with all of them.

As soon as the Adelantado arrived in San Germán, he found the vessels fully prepared for war. He entered into council with the brigadier and the captains. He told them the decision he had made with the advice of the president and *oidores* of the High Court of Santo Domingo, and that he intended to abide by it and fulfill it. Then he dispatched Juan de Zurita in his warship to [San Juan de] Puerto Rico[135] with one hundred arquebusiers, four artillery pieces, and a supply of powder and munitions. The Adelantado went by land from San Germán to [San Juan de] Puerto Rico, where he was very well received by the governor and the citizens, who were in great fear that the French fleet might come. He told them what His Majesty commanded. He showed the order to the governor and regiment, and [told them] that one hundred soldiers, four artillery pieces, and munitions would soon be there on a warship, because he had just dispatched them from San Germán. He visited the fortress and the entrance to the harbor, where he commanded that a tower there be fortified with a different and better design he had brought, and he visited the other danger spots for enemy disembarkation. Following the opinion and agreement of the governor and warden of the fortress, Juan Ponce de León,[136] and other city councillors, they decided the way they were to fortify and defend themselves in case the French fleet, or part of it, should come there. Most of the citizens had fled to the woods with their wives, children, and belongings, fearing the French fleet might come there. The governor could not draw them back to the town, but with the Adelantado's arrival they all returned. They rejoiced and organized processions, praying to Our Lord to make them victorious against the enemy, for if the enemy came, all the citizens were determined to die rather than surrender.

On the fourth day the Adelantado departed for San Germán. The third day after his arrival there he sailed for Puerto de Plata, where, with the advice and consent of the judicial authorities, local regiment, and residents of Puerto de Plata, he laid out plans for a tower at the harbor entrance, where it had been laid out before. He left fifty soldiers, all of them arquebusiers, to work on it, as well as four very good artillery pieces of bronze, to defend the entrance against the corsairs who tried to enter, for they would come there often with the consent of the townsfolk to trade large quantities of merchandise and black [slaves] for gold, silver, pearls, sugar, and hides. At other times they came not come to trade but to plunder the town, which they had twice set on fire. On one hand, the people were happy about the reinforcements, and on the other hand, they regretted it because it cost them their profits from dealing with the corsairs.

It so happened that within four months there came, trying to get into the village, four very well armed vessels which had as their general a corsair named Jean Bontemps,[137] who had been trading between the Indies and France for some years and had become very rich. When he tried to enter the harbor, Captain Aguirre, whom the Adelantado had left with the fifty soldiers to defend that tower and harbor, prevented their entrance, so that the French turned back without being able to enter. Of the townsfolk only five came to its defense—something that astonished Captain Aguirre and his soldiers. The people were very sorry about the retreat of the French because their earnings were taken from them, and above all from Francisco de Ceballos, who was the richest and one of the most important men in the village, for he had a sugar mill and refinery, many hides, and a lot of cattle.[138] Every year when Jean Bontemps arrived, he treated him very cordially and concluded a great deal of business and deals with him, selling his hides and sugar. From that day on, he started following Captain Aguirre and his soldiers, giving false reports to the High Court that they were being unruly in the village.

The High Court wrote to His Majesty [to request] that Francisco de Ceballos be the warden of that tower, and since His Majesty had not been informed of how ill Francisco de Ceballos served him in that village, permitting and carrying on trade and transactions with the French, Portuguese, and English, who went there to pillage and [to trade] without license, against the provisions and decrees His Majesty had issued for these matters. Francisco de Ceballos had been married to a sister of Lucas Vázquez de Ayllón, a legitimate daughter of Lucas Vázquez de Ayllón, [Ceballos's] father-in-law. Both father and son had contracted with His Majesty and had been appointed adelantados of Florida and settlers and conquistadors of that land. But because of how badly they behaved, and because it did not please God, they could not succeed in their enterprise. When the father died, His Majesty took it away from the son, and in those days he entered into an agreement with the Adelantado Pedro Menéndez.

Francisco de Ceballos was resentful of this, but he concealed his hatred, and when Esteban de las Alas and the Adelantado's nephew Pedro Menéndez Marqués passed through [Puerto de Plata] on their way to Florida with a fleet from Asturias and Vizcaya, Francisco de Ceballos wrote to the Adelantado that he should send him some ships. He [said he] would load them with supplies and cattle, and offered them many things, for that port was suitable and had supplies. [He requested] to be appointed his lieutenant in these matters. The Adelantado was certain that Francisco de Ceballos would do as he had said, for he had mentioned it in writing in three [different] letters, and to better validate his point he had sent him a servant of his. The Adelantado, thinking that it was true, gave him enough powers, and at different times he sent six of his ships there. [Ceballos] detained some of them, claiming that he would dispatch them [soon], but instead he let them be until they were riddled with teredo worms and unseaworthy. Others sailed away because he would not load them, and one that he did load sank to the bottom on the second day after leaving the harbor.

It came to pass that some of the mutineers from Florida arrived there in two ships with two hundred and fifty men, among them the ringleaders, the captains and soldiers who had rebelled most against His Majesty's service in Florida.[139] And even though the Adelantado and the brigadier had informed [Ceballos] that these men had committed treason against His Majesty, he received them very well and gave them lodging and horses, and they played cane games with them and ran bulls, saying many offensive words about the Adelantado, the brigadier, and those who had remained in that land in the service of His Majesty. [Ceballos] enjoyed this greatly and laughed, saying that they remained there [in Florida] as beasts, and would soon be beasts, slaves to the Indians, or they would all get killed. He helped all these men, so that most of them got to Peru and New Spain and those parts of the Indies where they wished [to go]. And since Francisco de Ceballos had married, the second time, a daughter of the licentiate who then presided over the High Court in Santo Domingo, and he had married off one of his sons (a grandson of this president) to a daughter of Don Cristóbal Colón, and Don Cristóbal had married off a daughter to Licentiate Ortegón, *oidor* of the High Court in Santo Domingo, there was no *oidor* in that High Court [free of Ceballos's influence] other than Cáceres, who was a friend of his friends.[140] In order to undermine all things pertaining to Florida—knowing that His Majesty wanted them to be successful—Francisco de Ceballos did and said as he pleased. And he got away with protecting the corsairs because he was protected by the High Court. Instead of being punished for so many foul and grave crimes, since neither His Majesty nor the lords of his Royal Council of the Indies were informed of this, instead of having him punished, they make him warden of the tower that Captain Aguirre and his soldiers built, with the result that, once the decree arrives in which His Majesty grants this favor, Captain Aguirre and his soldiers depart for the Indies very displeased—which is what these others intended, and His Majesty will not be served by this, while Francisco de Ceballos will remain very happy and content with the wardenship, because he will be able to trade and deal with the corsairs as he used to, seeing that he has not been punished for what went on, which is rather esteemed to have been in [His Majesty's] service.

After Captain Aguirre prevented Jean Bontemps from entering the harbor with his four armed vessels, Jean Bontemps set sail for other ports on that island, which were Monte Cristo, Puerto Real,[141] and La Yaguana, where he captured twelve vessels and many goods in them and set fire to Puerto Real, then returned to France. The Adelantado had gone to all three of these towns, but they refused to accept any soldiers.

In those days two other vessels came upon Santiago de Cuba,[142] where the Adelantado had left fifty arquebusiers with Captain Diego de Godoy, a good soldier, as their captain, as well as four pieces of bronze artillery with their powder and munitions, which prevented entrance. These vessels went to Cabo de Cruz and Manzanillo, a port of Bayamo.[143] They captured five vessels carrying a great quantity of money and hides. The Adelantado reinforced Havana with six artillery pieces and two hundred soldiers, and as their captain—as had been agreed and provided—Baltasar de Barreda, who took these reinforcements to Havana at the beginning of January [1567]. It seems magical that the Adelantado could place so many reinforcements in so few days, and with such difficult navigation, for he had departed from Florida on 20 October [1566] and traveled to San Germán, La Mona, Santo Domingo, and [San Juan de] Puerto Rico. He had hurried with the fleet to Puerto de Plata, reinforced it, and sent the brigadier with the three ships through the old channel to reinforce Havana—who on his way encountered a very great storm from the north and was many times on the brink of foundering.

The Adelantado went with the other vessel to Monte Cristi, Puerto Real, and La Yaguana and offered them soldiers to defend them against the corsairs, but they did not want them. [He went] to Santiago de Cuba, Cabo de Cruz, and Macaca, a town near Bayamo. He left the ship laden with supplies to go to Havana, and from there to Florida. He embarked in a *zabra* and, sailing through the islands, arrived at a harbor south of Havana called [. . .] and by land reached Havana, arriving there on [. . .].[144] He made this journey from Bayamo to Havana by sea and land in eight days, which astonished everyone, for it is a journey of at least a month. Great was the joy that the brigadier and the captains, sailors, and soldiers felt at [seeing] the Adelantado.

He ordered that the city and harbor be fortified, as His Majesty commanded, and he gathered all the munitions onto one of the three warships that were there. The other two he dismissed and sent to Spain, leaving Captain Baltasar de Barreda there with the two hundred soldiers to defend the fortress and harbor, as His Majesty had told him to reinforce that city with the men he thought best. He sent the brigadier to Florida with the surplus munitions and the supplies brought by the vessel the Adelantado had left in Macaca being laden with supplies from Bayamo. He dismissed this vessel from His Majesty's expenses, like the others, and later he would dismiss the one from Puerto Rico and the carrack that had arrived in Santo Domingo, in order to spare His Majesty the expense. And if His Majesty had been required to cover the cost of that fleet—not counting the men and supplies, just the fortifications and the other things necessary for the warships—more than twenty thousand ducats would have been outlaid at His Majesty's expense, and in the Indies more than forty thousand. The Adelantado did not spend a single ducat [of His Majesty's], because he did it all with the officers he had in Florida, whom he had taken with him at his own expense, some other materials, and a part of the ships, supplies, and men who had gone there to reinforce Florida and the islands, as well as another one hundred and fifty sailors, pilots, and men he had there. The frigate and the brigantine, with their crews, were the Adelantado's, at no expense whatsoever to His Majesty.

Chapter 24

Third Voyage to the Country of Chief Carlos

When the brigadier departed for Florida, the Adelantado ordered him to take his men and, once he arrived in St. Augustine and inspected that place and San Mateo, to go up the San Mateo River with one hundred and fifty men and three brigantines that the Adelantado had in Florida for explorations, until he reached [the country of] Chief Mayaca where the Adelantado been when he turned back.

The same day the brigadier departed, the Adelantado set off from Havana for the country of Chief Carlos with six *pataches* and brigantines. He told the brigadier that he would attempt to find out if there was a river in [the land of] Carlos that led to [the land of] Mayaca, and that he would explore that coast up to the Maymi Lagoon.

Before the Adelantado departed from Florida to deploy the reinforcements, he had decided to send thirty men with Francisco de Reinoso, one of His Majesty's men-at-arms and a fine soldier, to Chief Carlos and to send him his cousin, who was his heir, whom they had given the name Don Pedro when they baptized him, and another Indian man who waited on him. It seemed to [the Adelantado] that this Indian, Carlos's heir, was very intelligent and a great friend of his. The Adelantado didn't want [Don Pedro] to die and, since he showed strong signs of being a good Christian, the Adelantado sought to marry him to the Indian woman Doña Antonia, for they would succeed Carlos and strive to convert the Indians to Christianity.

He appointed Francisco de Reinoso as captain of those thirty soldiers, instructing that he build a blockhouse in Carlos's village and that they all try to worship the cross with great devotion morning and evening, reciting the catechism, so the Indians would do the same, and to endeavor to instruct them as best they could. Winning the Indians' friendship, they should try to find out if a river located two leagues from there[145] led to the Maymi Lagoon, and how many leagues it was, for the Adelantado already knew how many from this lagoon to [the land of] Mayaca, and that it was navigable, because he was to go to Carlos within three or four months with enough vessels to find out if he could use that river to go to San Mateo and St. Augustine, which was what the Adelantado greatly desired, for he realized this would be of great service to His Majesty, to the merchants in the Indies, and to the overall well-being of those involved in the conquest and settlement of Florida. He gave [Reinoso] a present for Carlos, another for his wife, and another for the Indian woman Doña Antonia.

When Francisco de Reinoso in his brigantine arrived in [the country of] Carlos with his thirty soldiers and the Indian Don Pedro, Carlos's heir, and the other Indian, they landed the two Indians so they could speak to Carlos and Doña Antonia, and all the Indians rejoiced at seeing them. Then Carlos came to the *patache* and offered his friendship to Captain Francisco de Reinoso and the soldiers, for the Adelantado was his elder brother and had sent word that he should receive them and treat them kindly, which he would do, and neither he nor any of his Indians would do them harm. Thus they disembarked with great joy and happiness and he took them to his village, where Francisco de Reinoso gave him the gift he had brought, as well as a letter. [The captain] with the interpreter explained what it said, which was that he and his Indians should treat the Christians very kindly. Carlos promised Captain Reinoso that he would do so and had a house built for them, where they gathered. They erected a cross near it and went to worship it morning and evening, reciting the catechism, and all the Indian men and women attended it with great devotion.

As the Adelantado had commanded, the brigantine sailed for Havana with five or six sailors, carrying the Indian woman Doña Antonia and five or six principal Indians, as the Adelantado had ordered for the safety of Captain Francisco de Reinoso and the thirty soldiers who remained there with him. The Adelantado did not have much trust in Carlos because, in his dealings with him, he had seen him show many signs of being a traitor. Six days after leaving Carlos, the brigantine arrived in Havana. Then Alonso de Rojas, a city councillor, came to the shore and took Doña Antonia and her Indians to his house, as he had done before. His wife, who was Doña Antonia's godmother, received her very well, entertaining her and treating her very kindly. Then the brigantine and a *patache* were laden with livestock and some supplies, and sailed with these to [the country of] Carlos.

Captain Francisco de Reinoso wrote of the travail and peril they were enduring, [stating] that Carlos had tried to kill them treacherously two or three times, and that [for this purpose] he had sent to his sister Doña Antonia and the other Indians, [claiming] that he had a very great desire to see them and asking that they return promptly. Having them with him, he could kill Francisco de Reinoso and the soldiers who were there with him, for this chieftain and his father were very fierce in killing Christians, and the captive men and women the Adelantado found there had told him that, in the twenty years they had been there, father and son had killed more than two hundred Christians, using them in their feasts and dances, and sacrificing them to the devil.[146] This was done to all the people from the shipwrecked vessels of the Fleet of the Indies, for even if they were shipwrecked one hundred leagues from there they were taken to [Carlos], as he was the chieftain of much of the land on the coast, Los Mártires, and the Bahama Channel, which is where the ships sailing from the Indies to Spain run the greatest risk. This is why the Adelantado was so diligent in trying to settle in that coast and draw the Indian chieftains into friendly relations.

And so [the Adelantado sailed for the land of Carlos] with one hundred and fifty men in the six brigantines he took from Havana on the same day that the brigadier departed for St. Augustine with a vessel laden with the surplus supplies and munitions from the armed fleet that had gone to New Spain. The brigadier had been ordered to go up the River of San Mateo until [the country] of Mayaca, for the Adelantado was going to find out if he could go to Mayaca from the country of Carlos in order to go to St. Augustine and San Mateo from there. The Adelantado was taking with him Doña Antonia and the Indian men and women she had with her, and he arrived [in the land of Carlos] in two days. He brought with him Father [Juan] Rogel, of the Society of Jesus, a very learned and religious man, and Father Francisco [de Villarreal], of the same [Jesuit] society.[147]

He was taking [with him] principal Indians of Tequesta, which is where the ship coming from San Mateo with the mutineers had left twenty soldiers. When a brigantine the Adelantado had dispatched from Florida to

Havana to fetch supplies was sailing by, she encountered contrary winds and went into that harbor, finding those Christians who had risen up in mutiny very well. They told them how nicely the chieftain and his Indians had treated them on account of the Adelantado's marriage to Doña Antonia, and that five or six of them had gone inland. The men in the brigantine took approximately fifteen of these soldiers, and the chieftain [Tequesta] sent one of his brothers with three Indian men and three Indian women in this brigantine to tell the Adelantado that he and his Indians wished to become Christians, [asking him] to go and see him, because he wanted to take him for his elder brother and do as he commanded.

This chieftain was at war with Carlos, and the reasons were known: Chief Tequesta used to be one of Carlos's subjects, and when Carlos learned that he had those Christians, he sent for them, but Tequesta would not give them up, so he later sent to have them killed treacherously. Tequesta learned about this, protected the Christians, and killed two of his Indians who were trying to kill them. On this third visit [to Carlos] the Adelantado was taking with him the messengers from Tequesta with Doña Antonia, all of them together, to negotiate a friendship and peace treaty between Carlos and Tequesta.

When the Adelantado entered Carlos's harbor two days after he departed from Havana—as is mentioned before—he was spotted by Captain Francisco de Reinoso and his soldiers, and by Chief Carlos and his people. The canoes came at once to the brigantines and the Adelantado landed. He was very well received by both Christians and Indians. He had a house built for Doña Antonia next to the Christians' house, and a chapel where Father Rogel said mass. The next day, Father Rogel preached to the soldiers—who were in great need of instruction—and he gave them such good examples that they asked the Adelantado to leave him there with them, for otherwise they would soon be savages like the Indians themselves. This was because the Indian women were very fond of them, in such a manner that, if the Adelantado had not arrived there at that time, Carlos and his Indians had determined to kill Francisco de Reinoso and all the Christians who were there with him, even if that meant losing his sister Doña Antonia and the six Indian men and women she had with her. In any case, because the Indian women had warned the Christians that Carlos and his Indians wished to kill them, they went about their lives with great caution.[148]

Francisco de Reinoso informed the Adelantado of the particulars of the habits and customs of Carlos and his Indians and the many times they had tried to kill them, [saying] that the Indians were becoming very devout toward the cross, but that Carlos himself was very stubborn and laughed at our ceremonies. The Adelantado was very kind to Carlos and his people, taking him, his wife, and the principal Indians to eat with him twice. The Adelantado learned that the passage he was seeking [from Carlos to Mayaca] was not to be found there, and that fifty leagues from there, in a village called Tocobaga, he would find a waterway. The chieftain of that land was a great enemy of Carlos and was at war with him.[149]

Carlos had asked the Adelantado and Francisco de Reinoso to go with him and his people to Tocobaga and wage war on them. Francisco de Reinoso replied that he could not do so without the Adelantado's permission, for if he did the Adelantado would have his head. The Adelantado replied to Carlos that his lord, the king of Spain, had not sent him there to wage war on the chieftains and Indians, and that, if they were at odds, he would strive to make them friends and ask them if they wanted to become Christians. He would teach the catechism to those who wished, so they would learn how to become Christians and go to Heaven with God, Lord of all the world, when they died here on this Earth. Therefore, if Carlos wished to be friends with Tocobaga, the Adelantado would go and negotiate a peace [treaty] with him.

Carlos regretted very much the Adelantado's refusal to wage war on Tocobaga. He told him that he wanted to sail in his brigantines with about twenty of his principal men to [the country of] Tocobaga, where the Adelantado could negotiate the peace. The Adelantado was pleased with this. He discussed at once the peace and friendship between Carlos and Chief Tequesta, together with Tequesta's brother who was there with him and another two or three Indians, and this was settled. The Adelantado confirmed that there was peace between the Indians and the soldiers, and he left the Tequesta Indians with the Christians there, as well as the two Jesuit priests, until he returned from Tocobaga. Father Rogel hastened to learn words in the language of Carlos and Tocobaga in order to start preaching to the Indians, and Father Francisco was learning the language of Tequesta, because the Adelantado intended, when he returned from Tocobaga, to leave Father Rogel there and take Father Francisco to Tequesta.

Chapter 25

In the Country of Chief Tocobaga

After [the Adelantado] had been with Carlos for three days he left with all six brigantines for [the country of Chief] Tocobaga, taking Carlos and another twenty principal Indians with him. He arrived at the harbor on the second day, at night. The chieftain lived twenty leagues inland, but one could reach the side of his house by a saltwater channel. Even though it was night and there was no moon, one of the Indians who accompanied Carlos steered by the North Star in such a way that, with a fair wind, the Adelantado arrived near Tocobaga's house one hour before daybreak, without being discovered. He ordered the brigantines to anchor with great secrecy.

Carlos begged the Adelantado to disembark, burn the village, and kill the Indians. The Adelantado refused to do so, telling him that his lord, the king of Spain, would have his head for it, since neither Tocobaga nor his Indians had ever done him any harm, [but] if they had, then he would do what Carlos asked. Carlos was grieved by this and asked the Adelantado to land him and his Indians, [saying] that he would burn the chieftain's house and then swim back to the brigantines. The Adelantado told him not to do it, that he would not allow it, for Carlos had come with him to negotiate friendly relations and a peace [treaty]. Carlos was very angry and cried out of sorrow. The Adelantado comforted him the best he could and told him that he would try to negotiate an honorable peace with Tocobaga, who would give him ten or twelve Indian men and women he held captive. Carlos was very happy to hear this, because a sister of his and Doña Antonia's was among them, and he told the Adelantado that he was satisfied with this.

The Adelantado ordered a small shallop to approach the chieftain's house with eight oarsmen and one of the Christians who had been captives of Carlos, who knew the language of Tocobaga. He ordered him, once at the chieftain's house, to call out in his language not to be afraid, because the people in the vessels that had come there were true Christians and friends of his. When he had done this, the Indians woke up, saw the vessels next to their houses, and started to flee with their wives and children. The chieftain remained behind with five or six Indian men and one woman, and at daybreak he sent one of the Christians he had there to tell the Adelantado that he was very grateful that he had not killed him or his people or burned his village, and that the Christian he had sent to him was the only one he had, and no others, and that his people had fled and he had remained in his house of prayer with his gods, for he would sooner die than forsake them, and that if the Adelantado wanted him to go to his vessels he would do it, and if he wanted to land, whether to kill him or spare him, he could do so, for he was waiting for him.

The Adelantado was very pleased with the message and with the Christian who brought it, who was a Portuguese man from Tavira, which is in the Algarve. He said that he had been a prisoner there for six years, and that he was traveling from Campeche in New Spain in a boat laden with corn, chickens, blankets, and honey when a storm drove them ashore there. Within one hour the Indians had killed all the men, but he had hidden in the woods so they could not find him, and he stayed there for a month, eating palmitos, acorns, and some shellfish. It happened that some Indian fishermen saw him, seized him, and brought him to this chieftain [Tocobaga], whom he served by fetching water and wood and cooking for him. From the day he was shipwrecked until now, he prayed every day to Our Lord to free him from captivity, and he had been expecting Christians for eight days, for every night of these eight days he dreamed that Christians were coming to live there, which made him very glad. He told the Adelantado things about that land, although he knew very little, for he had never traveled farther than twenty leagues from the village.

Out of consideration for Carlos, the Adelantado did not want to tell this Christian that Carlos had come there or that Tocobaga should come to his vessel. He sent him to tell [Tocobaga] that he would land to speak to him and that he should not be afraid, asking the Christian to assure him that he would do him no harm, and that [Tocobaga] should send word to his Indians to return to the village. The Christian left with that message, and the Adelantado landed at eight o'clock in the morning and spoke to the chieftain, who received him very well and had him seated close to him in the highest and most prominent place. He had six Indian men and one Indian woman with him. Through the interpreter he told the Adelantado that he never thought

Christians could be so good, that he was fully aware they could have killed him and his people and burned their idols and their village, and that he had known for many days that there were Christians in that country, because they had sent word to his chieftain allies that they should give them corn, and if not they would kill them. And because it was not given to them, they had killed many, and he was very afraid of them, but other Christians had later come and killed these ones, and it was said that the chieftains and Indians loved these latter Christians very much. [He asked them] which ones they were.

The Adelantado replied that he and his men belonged to the latter group of Christians and were there to kill the first ones, who had come to enslave the chieftains and the Indians. They were false Christians, which was why he killed them. He and his people were true Christians and had not come there to kill them or enslave them or take their corn. He came only to ask them if they wanted to become Christians and teach them how to do it, and to have them as friends and brothers. He did not come to wage war on them or kill any chieftain or Indian, except those who wanted to harm him or kill a Christian, and it would make him very happy if [Tocobaga] and his people wanted to convert.

The chieftain was much pleased at what the Adelantado told him. He rose with his six Indians and they all did reverence and made obeisance to the Adelantado, kissing his hands. Then they sat down again. The Adelantado said to the chieftain that he was a friend of Carlos and that he had left some Christians in his land, but that this was no reason why he should be Tocobaga's enemy. He had Carlos with him in the brigantines and had brought him to negotiate friendly relations and a peace [treaty] with him, and [Tocobaga] should return to him the twelve persons he held captive. If he and his Indians wished to convert, [the Adelantado] would be very happy and would leave Christians there as in [the country of] Carlos to defend them from their enemies and teach them to be Christians. [Tocobaga] replied that all his people, the principal ones, and his chieftains, his subjects and allies, were far from there, and that until they came and he spoke to them, he could not answer him. If the Adelantado would [only] wait three or four days, he would send for them. The Adelantado said that he was satisfied. The chieftain sent to summon his principal Indians and chieftains, begging the Adelantado to tell his soldiers not to go near the house of his gods, whom that chieftain held in great veneration. That night the Adelantado and his men went back to the brigantines to sleep.

The next morning Chief Tocobaga went to see him. He and Carlos had a lengthy discussion. Carlos wished to disembark with Tocobaga and his Indians, but because the Adelantado considered Carlos very treacherous, he did not dare [allow it], thinking that Carlos would speak ill of him and his Christians, and that the two chieftains would conspire to have Carlos kill the Christians that he had and Tocobaga those that [the Adelantado] was to leave there. On the other hand, the Adelantado did not dare to anger Carlos, and for this reason he allowed him to land with two interpreters, who were to be always at his side so he would not speak ill of the Christians to the chieftain or the Indians. In those three days, more than one thousand five hundred Indians came there with their bows and arrows, all of them people of very good disposition. When the Adelantado saw so many people, he told the chieftain that his soldiers were happy because they thought that his Indians wanted to act unruly and fight with them, and that he should ask the principal ones to stay with him to negotiate the peace [treaty] and send the others away. The chieftain did this.

On the fourth day, when twenty-nine of these chieftains and about one hundred other principal Indians who remained there had gathered, the chieftain sent word to the Adelantado that he should come to negotiate the peace. He went there, taking Carlos with him. Once they were assembled, with the Adelantado seated in the most prominent place, Chief Tocobaga said to him that he had told the Indian chieftains who were there everything the Adelantado had said, and that, if he truly meant those things, all of them would be happy to take him for their elder brother and become Christians, and to make peace with Carlos, and give him back his people, with [the proviso] that should Carlos wage war on him again, the Adelantado would help him, and that if [Tocobaga] waged war on Carlos, then the Adelantado would help Carlos. [Tocobaga said] that he wanted to make peace with the true Christians, not the false ones, and that he should leave him another captain with thirty Christians to teach him and his chieftains how to be Christians.

It was all done in this manner, the peace made with Carlos and his people returned to him. The Adelantado left thirty soldiers there under the command of Captain García Martínez de Cos, who stayed quite against his will. The Adelantado left him because he was displeased with him over a disobedience he had committed, but also because he was level-headed and a good Christian.

Chapter 26

Fourth Voyage to the Country of Chief Carlos

Since Tocobaga told the Adelantado that he could not go with so few men to [the land of] Mayaca, because they were very numerous and hostile, the Adelantado departed with his brigantines four days after he arrived, and within a week he returned with Carlos to his village. On the way, he noticed that Carlos was very angry and irritated at the good friendship the Adelantado had forged with Tocobaga. The Adelantado tried very hard to cheer him up, but he could not. When a sailor passing in front of Carlos let the end of a thin rope fall on his head by mistake, Carlos, thinking the sailor had done it on purpose, gave him a hard slap in the face and grappled with him to try to throw him overboard. The Adelantado came to the rescue and freed him. The sailor was one of the highest-ranking there and took great offense at this. The Adelantado was even more offended, but since he had brought Carlos away from his country in his brigantine, it seemed to him that he was bound to take him back there. Otherwise, it was understood he would have ordered him hanged for that blow, and also because he had learned from the interpreters that [Carlos] was threatening the Adelantado and his Christians, [saying] that he would give orders that none should escape.

The Adelantado left him in his village and had the Christians [there] fortify themselves better than before. He left a complement of fifty soldiers beyond those already there, and some culverins, and Father [Juan] Rogel of the Society of Jesus to teach the catechism to the Indians. He departed with [Rogel's] companion, Father Francisco [de Villarreal], and with the Tequesta Indians in order to take them back to their chieftain and tell him about the peace [treaty] concluded between him and Carlos. The Adelantado left Doña Antonia there with the Christians. He did not have a good opinion of her because she was much on the side of her brother Carlos and was very sad about what [the Adelantado] had said in [the land of] Toco-baga. She spoke very resentful words to the Adelantado because they had not burned and killed Tocobaga and his Indians and burned the village and the house of his idols, and [she said] he had two hearts, one for himself and another for Tocobaga, and for herself and her brother he had none. The Adelantado reassured her as best he could, took leave of her, and went to embark to go to Tequesta.

When he was on the ships and ready to sail and go to Tequesta in order to take back the Indians he had there and confirm the peace treaty, and to go from there to the forts of St. Augustine and San Mateo, he saw a ship entering the harbor. He was startled, not knowing what it could be. When it anchored, he learned it was a vessel[150] of his which he had left in St. Augustine when he departed with the fleet against the corsairs, and which the captains of the forts of St. Augustine, San Mateo, and San Felipe had dispatched to Havana notifying the Adelantado to relieve them with supplies. When the brigantine reached Havana, Treasurer Juan de [Ro-jas] Hinestrosa, the Adelantado's lieutenant in that island and town for all things pertaining to Florida, sent her [back] to the Adelantado with mes-sages and with letters from all the city councillors in Havana. The situation was this: When the Adelantado departed from Havana on his last voyage, at the moment when the Adelantado was ready to sail, a captain named Pedro de Rodabán, one of the men His Majesty had sent to the Adelantado with the reinforcements, had fled to the woods with the flag with the intention of passing over to New Spain, which at that time was in a disturbed state.

The Adelantado was alarmed by his departure, and he lingered for sev-eral days thinking that he could capture him. He instituted proceedings against him, making public pronouncements to summon him, declaring him a rebel, and notifying Governor [Francisco] García Osorio of the sen-tence, so that if this captain were captured, he would be sent to His Maj-esty in Spain with the proceedings of the case. They wrote to him [by] this brigantine that the day after the Adelantado left that town of Havana, Cap-tain Rodabán was walking openly about the town, keeping the governor company and dining with him, together with many of the mutineers who had fled and come there from Florida, and that six days after the Adelan-tado departed, the governor had sent word to Captain Baltasar de Barreda, whom the Adelantado had left in that town with two hundred soldiers for the defense of its harbor and fortress as His Majesty had commanded, [to come and see him]. He went there and found the governor in the company of His Majesty's officials on that island as well as the city councillors. [The governor] made the captain sit in a chair next to him and ordered his ensign and other gentlemen who had gone there with him to leave. He said to the captain that he wished to see the order he had from His Majesty to defend that fortress and harbor. The captain replied that the Adelantado had sent it to him originally with a notary, as His Majesty commanded, and that he had a certified copy there, together with the orders the Adelantado had given him. He put his hand in his pocket and took it out and gave it to the governor, who said that if it was not the original he did not wish to see it. The captain replied that the notary by whom it was signed was one who were present there. The governor refused to accept it and ordered a notary who was there to tell the town drummer to make a public announcement that, on pain of death, all the soldiers in Captain Baltasar de Barreda's company were to keep to their barracks and none were to come out without his permission and order. Captain Barreda was astonished [but] remained calm, without giving any reply. After some time he took off his cap, saying to the governor and those who were there that he kissed their hands, and he rose to go. The governor rose and embraced him, saying:

—Prisoner in the name of the king!

Two constables came out at once with seven or eight bailiffs.[151] They seized the captain, but since they could not take the sword from his hand, they fought back and forth. His ensign, a good soldier and gentleman from Trujillo called So-and-so,[152] who was outside, heard the noise and went in. Seeing how roughly they were treating his captain, he grabbed his sword and charged like a lion at those who were holding him. They let him go and retreated with the governor into a room, locking the door from the inside. Captain [Barreda] and his ensign went out. They saw many restless soldiers coming toward them, and the captain ordered them to keep to their guardhouse, on pain of death. Captain Rodabán had many of Captain Barreda's soldiers mutinous and had assembled many of those mutineers. And it was said he was inside the governor's house in order to be given Captain Barreda's flag and company once he had been captured.

The brigantine had brought the Adelantado a certified statement of all this, as well as a letter that all the city councillors had written to him, begging him to come at once to Havana to remedy these things, for otherwise great harm could happen.

Chapter 21

Return to Havana

When the Adelantado read those dispatches, he sent the Indians to Tequesta and himself returned to Havana. He arrived in three days, and Captain Rodabán immediately fled into the woods. [The Adelantado] investigated what had happened and was compelled to remain there for a month to see if he could capture this Captain Rodabán, who went about in the woods with fifteen or twenty arquebusiers. [The Adelantado] acted in such a clever way and had such good spies that he captured him, brought him to justice, and sentenced him to be beheaded. When he was about to execute him, many men came to ask him to grant him an appeal, advising him that in order to better justify the case to His Majesty, he should do it, to which he agreed.

Chapter 28

Second Voyage to the Country of Chief Tequesta

Leaving affairs there as settled as he could, he sailed to Florida, to [the country of] Tequesta, with some supplies that he gathered from other vessels he had sent to Campeche to be laden with corn. He was very well received by this chieftain and Indians, he made peace with them, they took him for their brother, and he left thirty soldiers there with Pedro [Gutiérrez] Pacheco,[153] a good soldier, as captain. He also left them a saw and some carpenters to build a blockhouse. He erected a cross, which the Indians worshipped with much devotion. He left there Father Francisco [de Villarreal], of the Society of Jesus, and remained in that village for four days. Great was the joy at seeing that all the Indians, old and young, went to worship and kiss the cross with great devotion morning and evening. The chieftain gave the Adelantado one of his brothers and two principal Indians (one of whom was the captain of one of Carlos's villages) to be taken to Spain.

Chapter 23

Return to San Mateo
and the Country of Chief Saturiwa

The Adelantado sailed with [these Indians] in good weather, and on the third day he arrived in San Mateo, where he found Gonzalo de Villarroel and all his men very well. [He learned] that Saturiwa had many men, and that some chieftains and their Indian subjects had killed all the livestock. [Villarroel] had captured Chief Emola[154] and one of his sons, as well as two other chieftains' heirs and two other principal Indians of Saturiwa, in all sixteen Indians, all of whom he held in chains.

The Adelantado learned how the brigadier had gone with three brigantines up the San Mateo River for fifty leagues to [the land of] Mayaca and how, encountering a large number of Indians and finding the river narrow and densely wooded along both banks, he had turned back since he had no news of the Adelantado, who had told him that he would [attempt to] come from the land of Carlos. And even though they had informed the Adelantado in Tocobaga (when he was there with the brigantines and left the Christians) that there was a river there that crossed over to Mayaca, he had [too] few men to go there, because there were many Indians, all very hostile and enemies of Tocobaga, [but this chieftain said] that the next time the Adelantado came there, he and his warriors would go with him.

On the second day after he arrived in San Mateo the Adelantado decided, in agreement with Gonzalo de Villarroel, to free one of the Indians that were prisoners and send him to Saturiwa to tell him that the next morning he should be at the point of the bar, two leagues from there, because the Adelantado needed to go to His Majesty and he wished to see Saturiwa and speak to him, because the Adelantado had never met this chieftain and very much wished to speak to him. It was said that the chieftain greatly admired the Adelantado but was very afraid of him. Saturiwa, who was two leagues from there, from Fort San Mateo, received the message and replied to the Adelantado that he would go to the bar, as he commanded, begging him to bring the Indians with him, because he wanted to see and speak to them.

The next morning, the Adelantado left the fort, having heartened the soldiers as best he could, entreating them to be steadfast in His Majesty's service, because he had to sail at once to Spain—as they were all begging him to do—so that His Majesty would relieve them with supplies and payments for their clothing, for they were now going about almost as naked as the Indians. The Adelantado took Gonzalo de Villarroel with him. They found Saturiwa at the bar, at quite a distance from the shore, with many Indians. The Adelantado had Emola and another six principal Indians with him. He set one of them free and sent him to ask Saturiwa to come down to the shore under his word [of safe-conduct]. Saturiwa replied that the Adelantado should allow Emola and the Indians he had brought along to land, because he wanted first to speak to them. The Adelantado did so, but with their shackles that they had on their feet, and placed them opposite a brigantine that held twenty arquebusiers and two culverins with grapeshot ready, so that if any Indians attempted to carry them off on their backs, they could kill them.

Saturiwa did not want to come and speak with Emola and sent two of his principal men, who spoke with him. These men came and went between Saturiwa and Emola for more than two hours. It was later found out that all their dealings were to [try to] free the Indians and make the Adelantado land in order to shoot arrows at him and the soldiers he had with him, for the Indians that Saturiwa had placed in ambush were many. The Adelantado learned of the plot from a soldier, a great friend of Emola, who was in charge of feeding him and his Indians and who understood their language, although they did not know it. The Adelantado pulled Emola and the other Indian prisoners back to his brigantines. He sent word to Saturiwa that he had always wanted to be his friend, and still did, and that he was very sorry that [Saturiwa] did not want to be; that from now on he should consider him his enemy, and that on account of the Christians he had treacherously killed, he would order him beheaded or driven from his land.

The chieftain replied with many threats and said that, although he had told the Adelantado's captains many times that he was a friend of his, he had not said it from the heart, because he considered all Christians enemies, and that the Adelantado and his soldiers were cowardly chickens, [adding] that they should disembark and fight him and his Indians. The Adelantado left him and refused to reply.

Chapter 30

Return to St. Augustine
and War against Saturiwa

He crossed the bar and went to St. Augustine, where he found the brigadier and other captains very well, although the men of that fort were very unhappy about their poor treatment by Captain Miguel Enríquez (one of the captains that His Majesty had sent with the reinforcements), and about the great disobedience and lack of respect he had shown, in the Adelantado's absence, to their governor and warden of the fort, [Bartolomé Menéndez,] whom they respected and went to for the password. Among other things, he showed his insubordination in changing—against the governor's will—the sentinels the Adelantado had ordered to be kept, and in ordering—against the governor's will—that weapons be given to soldiers who had been deprived of them for crimes they had committed, and appointing them as sentinels. [Once,] when the governor wanted to inflict injury on a soldier who had disobeyed him, the captain came out, sword in hand, and took him away. And within a week of this, as the captain could not punish any of his soldiers because the governor was there, he injured two of them without bringing formal charges against them. He clubbed a constable and committed other ugly and serious offenses, all of them in disobedience of his governor, whom he had acknowledged as such.

The Adelantado instituted formal proceedings against him. He denounced him and charged him, receiving his answer. He abstained from executing the sentence because the governor was his brother, Captain Bartolomé Menéndez. The Adelantado gave this captain's company to his ensign, Francisco Núñez, and to his sergeant and officers. He consigned the captain's person to His Majesty and to the gentlemen of the Royal

Council of the Indies, together with the proceedings [of the case]. The Adelantado appointed Esteban de las Alas, who was there, as his lieutenant in those provinces, as he had done before. He discussed in council the way in which they should wage war on Saturiwa, and it was agreed upon. He left instructions concerning this, and before his departure he undertook it on four different fronts. The Adelantado went in person, with seventy soldiers, to the area where Saturiwa was believed to be, and in order not to be discovered, that night he marched ten leagues until daybreak. Neither he nor the others could find Saturiwa. About thirty Indians were killed. The Indians killed a sailor and two soldiers, and they injured another two, although they did not kill or injure any of those whom the Adelantado took along. They went back to Fort St. Augustine. He spoke to the captains and soldiers who remained there, encouraging them and begging them to be steadfast in His Majesty's service.

Chapter 31

Return to San Felipe

He embarked for Santa Elena, where Fort San Felipe is located, in a brig-antine, and the brigadier [Pedro de Valdés] did the same in a frigate. The Adelantado was bringing with him as prisoners the two captains Miguel Enríquez and Pedro de Rodabán, in order to take them to Spain,[155] and three principal Indians, one of them being Emola's son. He had freed Emola and all the other Indians [that Villarroel had captured], telling them that he would treat well the three Indians he was taking to Spain, and the other three from Tequesta, and would bring them back. But if Saturiwa were to wage war on the Christians, and if Emola and his Indians and the other principal men the Adelantado was freeing were to help him, the Adelan-tado would cut the heads off those three Indians he was taking with him.

With a fair wind he arrived on the third day at Santa Elena and Fort San Felipe, where he found Captain Juan Pardo and all the soldiers very well, and much pleased with the good land they had seen when they went inland about one hundred and fifty leagues. [There] they had erected the fort [San Juan] at the foot of the sierra in the country of Chief Joara. Since the Adelantado had received a warning from His Majesty that a large fleet of Lutheran corsairs had sailed from France and was rumored to have gone to those parts, and that he should be prepared for war, the Adelantado had sent orders to Cap-tain Juan Pardo that, once he had left some soldiers inland to take care of the Indians and friendly chieftains and to teach them the catechism, he should return immediately to the coast and install himself in Fort San Felipe in order to defend it if the French fleet should come there. Captain Juan Pardo told the Adelantado how friendly the chieftains and Indians of the inland country had been to him, how much they desired to be Christians like him and take him for their elder brother to do as he commanded. And the chieftains of the coast and the Indians of that district, neither more nor less, were very friendly and all greatly wished to meet him and become Christians.

Chapter 32

Voyage to Spain

The Adelantado would have liked very much to stay there for a month for the confirmation and the friendship of these chieftains and Indians [of Santa Elena], but the supplies that remained in the forts were very low and the soldiers were on very short rations. And it was ten months since he had written to His Majesty that he would soon be in Spain, and he had had news that Flanders was in rebellion against His Majesty's service and that His Majesty was to go there.[156] Therefore—in order to assist the soldiers who were in Florida under his charge as well as those in the islands of Puerto Rico, Hispaniola, and Cuba (that they might receive their supplies and salaries, for they were in great need of food and clothes), and in order to inform His Majesty of the particulars of the state of things in Florida and all the islands and the Indies, and of the depredations that the corsairs were committing (for if this was not remedied they would all be lost), and of how he could remedy this and maintain the forts in Florida at much less cost to his Royal Exchequer, and in order to be able to serve him in the expedition to Flanders—he embarked in the frigate, which was made to order, very swift under both oar and sail, of about twenty tons, because the brigantine he had brought from St. Augustine with this frigate was not very sturdy. He sent [the brigantine] to St. Augustine and San Mateo laden with fifty hundredweight of biscuit that had been saved because some soldiers from that fort [San Felipe] had gone inland.

The Adelantado took with him in the frigate the brigadier [Pedro de Valdés]; Francisco de Castañeda, captain of the Adelantado's guard; Captain Juan Vélez de Medrano, whom the Adelantado had granted leave to come to Spain because of his poor health; Francisco de Cepero; Diego de Miranda; Álvaro de Valdés; Juan de Valdés; Pedro de Ayala, ensign to Captain Medrano; Diego de Salcedo; Juan de Aguiniga; Alonso de Cabra; Licentiate [. . .] who was a priest; Captain Blas de Merlo; and other gentlemen, numbering twenty-five—all with their arquebuses and good weapons—persons who usually accompanied the Adelantado, most of them eating at his table, plus another five sailors (for the rest of those soldiers were sailors and knew well how to sail), and the six Indians, and the two captains that the Adelantado held prisoner, Pedro de Rodabán and Miguel Enríquez, altogether thirty-eight men.

The frigate was so swift and he had such fair wind that he sighted the islands of the Azores in seventeen days, having sailed an average of seventy-two leagues per day, as can be seen in the navigation chart. The Adelantado was very pleased to have sighted the islands in so few days because he realized how fast his frigate was. He entered the island of Terceira, where he was informed that His Majesty was going to embark in La Coruña for Flanders.[157] It seemed to him that if he followed that course he might overtake him before his departure from La Coruña, and that with oars and sails he could flee the corsairs in large vessels that he might encounter there, whereas going toward Cape San Vicente and Seville, if he came across Moorish *fustas*, they could overtake him with their oars.[158]

He had some contrary winds going from Terceira to La Coruña and entered that port on St. Peter's Day, [29 June 1567].[159] About three leagues from the port he encountered two French ships and one from England, which gave chase, and he fled. On the second day he entered [the harbor of] Viveiro, twenty leagues from La Coruña, where he learned that His Majesty was at court and had not yet left for La Coruña.[160] From that place he sent the two captive captains, [Pedro de] Rodabán and Miguel Enríquez, and placed them in the charge of Ensign [Pedro de] Ayala to take them, as prisoners in secure custody, to the court prison and hand over the proceedings of the case to the Royal Council of the Indies. He wrote to His Majesty that he had arrived at that port and would soon go to kiss his hands.

The day after the Adelantado arrived there he departed at noon for Avilés, where he had his wife and household, and which was twenty-eight leagues from Viveiro. He had such a fair wind that he sailed twenty-five leagues that day, and he entered a bay called [La Concha de] Artedo,[161] where there were ten ships anchored. Their crews, when they saw this new kind of frigate with so many oars that she resembled a Turkish vessel from the Eastern Mediterranean,[162] were afraid of her, deserted their vessels, and fled to land in their boats. There were many vessels loading there, and one of them that was taking on iron ran aground in the sand so that if the Adelantado was a corsair, he could not make off with her. The Adelantado anchored his frigate in the midst of those ships. There was not a single man or boat on board. He was distressed when he saw that one of them was stranded and made great efforts [to free her]. He ordered a sailor in the frigate to call out for some boat to come there. He had three small bronze artillery pieces, and two of the five sailors were very good buglers. The Adelantado did not want them to sound them or fire the artillery, so as to not disturb anyone. Since it was already ten o'clock at night, the men of the frigate were asleep, and no boat had come to identify the frigate.

At midnight there came a small boat equipped with many oars, and from a distance they called to the men in the frigate, asking what vessel she was and where she was coming from. From the frigate they replied that it was the Adelantado Pedro Menéndez, who was coming from Florida, and that they should come aboard. Those in the boat were afraid it was a trick, and since many of the sailors there knew the Adelantado well, they said they were afraid they were being tricked, and that if the Adelantado spoke to them, they would recognize him. The Adelantado, who was listening, said to them:

—Brothers, do me the favor of going to that vessel which is aground, sinking, to tell them that I am the Adelantado Pedro Menéndez, and that I come from Florida, so that they might try to save their ship. And tell the same to the men of those other [vessels], for it seems to me that they have fled to the woods, leaving their boats adrift. And once you have told them that, come back here, because I wish to speak to you.

[He asked them] to tell the same to the masters of the other ships, that they should come in their boats and board the frigate. From the boat they replied that His Lordship was welcome and that they were going to do as he commanded, and they did so at once. The men in the boat stayed until dawn, sending messages to the people who had come in the boats to lend a hand in order to save the ship [laden with] iron. At dawn they came in their boats alongside the frigate, where the Adelantado had a flag of crimson damask deployed as a standard, and a campaign flag, and had the bugles play and the three artillery pieces fire. The men in the boats were alarmed, thinking that he was a corsair, so they turned and fled; only the boat whose men had spoken to the Adelantado and recognized him drew up alongside. ([The ships in the harbor] were five Portuguese caravels laden with salt, another three fishing vessels, and the other two were one laden with iron and one with wood.) This boat turned back at once to reassure the rest, and they came on board the frigate to speak to the Adelantado. They were all very happy to see him, and they marveled at how much sea he had sailed in such a small vessel—and it is true that this is one of the [most wonderful] things seen at sea to this day.

He set sail and within two hours entered his town [of Avilés], where they already knew he was coming because a man who had landed in order to make known who [the Adelantado] was had gone that night by land to ask the Adelantado's wife and relatives for his reward [for bringing good news]. The joy that the whole town—his wife, relatives, and neighbors—felt at his arrival was so great that it cannot be described, for besides the fact that the Adelantado and his relatives are among the first families of that region, he is so loved and treasured by all that many dropped to their knees and raised their hands to Heaven, praising Our Lord for having brought him back to safety. And they looked at the frigate, which had them marveling to see on such a small ship so many banners and pennants, arquebuses, bronze artillery pieces (which the men fired), bugles (which they played), and dashing and well-disciplined soldiers. And they all stared at one another as if enchanted.

The Adelantado went straight to church to give thanks to Our Lord and His Blessed Mother for the mercy He had shown him in bringing him back to safety. He was accompanied by the townspeople to his house, where he was welcomed by his wife and daughters, and his sisters and nieces, who were keeping them company (as one might have guessed). It had been eighteen years that the Adelantado was away in the service of His Majesty as captain general of the fleets on the coasts of Asturias and Vizcaya, Flanders, and the Fleet of the Indies, and in all that time he had been home only four times, and for twenty-two days in all. This time he stayed for eighteen days, for he was notified that His Majesty was not yet on his way [to La Coruña]. In those days the brigadier [Pedro de Valdés] went to the town of Gijón,[163] which is four leagues from there, to see his parents, because he had embarked on this expedition against their will and without their consent, for he was their only son and they loved him very much. From the age of ten he had been raised in Italy. Years ago his parents and relatives had arranged with the Adelantado that he should marry a daughter of his, [Ana Menéndez]. They sent to Italy for him, and he returned [just as] the Adelantado was about to bid his wife farewell in the year [15]65 in order to embark on this expedition to Florida. Since [Pedro and Ana] were doubly related within the fourth degree of consanguinity, they could not get married without a dispensation, according to ecclesiastical law, and once the marriage papers had been drawn up, they petitioned to Rome for one.[164] [Pedro] importuned the Adelantado to take him with him to Seville and to Cádiz, where he was to embark, [saying] that by then the dispensation would have arrived and he would return to get married. The Adelantado was happy to do this, but when the time came to depart from Cádiz, [the young man] asked the Adelantado's permission to go on the expedition, and when the Adelantado would not grant it, he insisted to the point of saying that if the Adelantado did not take him along, he would embark on the first vessel bound for Florida. The Adelantado regretted his determination, and—as is mentioned before—[Pedro de Valdés] embarked on this expedition secretly and against his will.

Chapter 33

Information Regarding
the Conquest of Florida

The Adelantado came to Madrid on 20 July [1567] to kiss His Majesty's hands, bringing with him the six Indians, as naked as they went about in Florida, with their bows and arrows. He was very well received by His Majesty, who considered that the expedition had been of great service, and [who said] that he would reward him. The Adelantado informed him of the state of affairs in Florida and the great need of supplies in which the soldiers had been left, and of some of the damage done by the corsairs in all the Indies and the danger they posed to the fleets carrying the treasure if they were to encounter them, [saying] that it was necessary and essential that His Majesty should remedy both things.

His Majesty then ordered that the soldiers be assisted and that a report be written on the best way to strike at the corsairs who in times of peace went about stealing from his subjects in those places and in the Western Mediterranean,[165] to spare them the damages they might inflict. [He said] he considered himself fortunate that [the Adelantado] had arrived at such a crucial moment to remedy this and to accompany him to Flanders, [ordering] that he be available for this, and that one of the captains he had brought with him would take the reinforcements to Florida.

The Adelantado replied that in both of these matters he would pray to Our Lord to favor and support him in assisting His Majesty as best he could. Then the brigadier [Pedro de Valdés] kissed His Majesty's hands, and since he had served with distinction and conducted himself well in this enterprise, although he was only twenty-four years old (but had experience as a soldier before), His Majesty thanked him and credited to his service the expedition and how well he had served in it. He also received the other captains and gentlemen who came with the Adelantado and who kissed his hands. His Majesty ordered the Royal Council of the Indies to give a hearing to the Adelantado in council, specifically on the matters of Florida, which they did, asking him to write a report on many issues in order to remedy them. He did so.

Among the things he mentioned, one was this: Many of the captains and soldiers who had mutinied in Florida had made statements before the governor of Havana and other officers of the law wherever they arrived, each swearing for the others that they had served well and with greater distinction than those who remained [in Florida] in His Majesty's service, who [in truth] had distinguished themselves in his royal service, both in the capture of the forts from the Lutherans and in enduring the hardships, food shortages, and perils of that land, and war with the Indians. And with these statements made by the mutineers being so favorable to themselves, they got so cocky that, as they spread all over the Indies and Spain, captains as well as soldiers, in order to justify their transgressions at the time when they mutinied (they had seized the brigadier and the officers of the law and the regiment, spiked the artillery, taken the supplies, leaving them none, and, with the Indians being at peace, had killed three of the principal ones so the chieftains of that land might unite—as they did—and kill the brigadier and the other captains and soldiers who remained in the forts without supplies so that all those who had remained in Florida would perish, and His Majesty would reward the mutineers liberally in return for what they reported), wherever these mutineers found themselves, they spoke ill of the Adelantado and those who remained with him. They based this on many lies and falsehoods to [produce] the best reasons they could in order to be believed. Some of them asked His Majesty to grant them rewards for their good service, which His Majesty postponed until the arrival of the Adelantado, and since [the Adelantado] gave information on some of these things, they left.

The Adelantado found that some of the lords of the Royal Council of the Indies believed in their hearts that what these mutineers said to them was true. Some other ministers of His Majesty, who were close to his royal person, believed that in certain matters the Adelantado had gone beyond what was reasonable, and they thought that he had embarked on that expedition and enterprise more for his own interest than for the service of Our Lord God, and His Majesty. This, as we have seen and explained, is quite the opposite, and the same was true of all the times he served His Majesty, for it is well known from experience that in his eighteen years as captain general on missions and naval commands of such prominence, trust, honor, and usefulness, he could have become rich if he so desired, without being inattentive or spending excessively. Before becoming general of His Majesty's fleets, he had thirty thousand ducats and two very good galleons, and from that time onward he made prosperous dealings and voyages with many of his galleons and ships, *pataches* and *zabras*, earning great benefits from the brief and prosperous voyages he made. He carried out his transactions without prejudice to his position or His Majesty's service, making more than two hundred thousand ducats, all of which he has spent—as a good captain—in His Majesty's service, on things necessary to bring to fruition the affairs in his charge, since neither His Majesty nor his ministers wanted to provide for them. And in order to bring with him very good captains and soldiers, important and trustworthy people, both sailors and soldiers, in all the fleets under his command, to whom he provided many amenities, as neither His Majesty nor his ministers wished to do so—and since he never drew stipends from His Majesty, or even salary except when he served (and this was less than what was given to other generals on expeditions), and once the mission was over, His Majesty would dismiss them until another assignment came along—he remained responsible for the captains, officers, and noblemen who followed him in His Majesty's service, and he had to provide for them.[166]

For the Florida expedition, His Majesty gave him enough assurance and written documents [stating] that in the Indies he should be given two hundred cavalrymen and four hundred infantrymen paid for four months, three warships, artillery, munitions, supplies, and all the things that he might need and ask for in order to expel the French Lutherans from Florida.[167] It seemed to him that if he were to depart from Cádiz in June [15]65, as he was forced to do, going about the islands and the Indies to collect the cavalry, infantry, and warships would delay him much, and he would not be able to go to Florida until the spring of [15]66, and by that time—as is mentioned before now—many reinforcements of men, artillery, weapons, munitions, and supplies would have reached the French, and they would have fortified themselves, so that when the Adelantado arrived there in March [15]66, he would not be as successful as if he went straight from Cádiz to Florida where the French were, before they received reinforcements or, if they had already received them, before they fortified themselves and earned the trust of the chieftains. This was the Adelantado's greatest fear, for if he were to have the native Indians of Florida as enemies, and the French were to get them to fight, the forces that he was bringing with him would not be enough to set foot in that land or expel the Lutherans from it.

The Adelantado informed His Majesty of this in Santa María de Nieva in April [15]65, and in La Mejorada, and he informed the lords of the Royal Council of State and War who were there with him, and then came to Madrid, where the court and the president of the Royal Council of Castile and the lords of the Royal Council of the Indies were, to ask them to give him two galleys and two galliots in charge of Don Álvaro de Bazán [y Guzmán], so that with his *zabras* and *pataches* he might go to Florida before the French were reinforced, and that if they were, he would disembark in another harbor, the closest he could find to theirs, which he could do because the vessels he was taking were of shallow draft. There he would fortify himself and attempt to harm the enemy as much as possible, and to earn the trust of the chieftains. In the spring [of 1566], with the cavalry he was to receive from the Indies, he would be master of the field and of their harbor, because they had their fort two leagues inland up the river, so they could not receive reinforcements or deal with the Indians. Accordingly, he would wage war on them with all discipline and diligence, and they could be driven out of the land of Florida at once, to prevent them from implanting their evil Lutheran sect in it. But because His Majesty had news that the Turks were descending in force on Malta and he had very few galleys to oppose them, [he said] that he could not give them to the Adelantado, although he believed his reasoning to be sound, and the other aforementioned lords with whom he spoke told him the same thing.

The next day in La Mejorada, His Majesty provided, through his Council of State and War, that they give the Adelantado five hundred men, provisioned and paid for, with four warships, all at His Majesty's expense, so that with the five hundred men and ten shallops and *zabras* the Adelantado was taking at his expense, in accordance with the *asiento* he had made with His Majesty concerning the conquest and settlement of Florida, he should go to the islands of Puerto Rico, Hispaniola, and Cuba to collect the cavalry, infantry, warships, and supplies that were already provided for. When the lords of the Royal Council of State and War had agreed to this and emerged from the council, they did not inform the Adelantado because, seeing that they could not give him the galleys and galliots he had requested, they referred the matter to Francisco de Eraso, who had been present at that council, so he might inform him of their decision.

That same day His Majesty went to El Abrojo, which is two leagues from Valladolid, to spend the night. The Adelantado accompanied him because Francisco de Eraso had told him that he would inform him that night of what the council had decided. At nine o'clock that night, the Adelantado and Francisco de Eraso took leave of His Majesty and went from El Abrojo to Laguna to spend the night. And even though the Adelantado dined and stayed that night with Francisco de Eraso, he refused to tell him the decision, saying that he would tell him the following day. The Adelantado was eager to know what had been decided because, if they were to give him the two galleys and galliots he had requested, he had faith in God that this good and holy enterprise would be successful, and otherwise he was feared for it, for the reasons he had expressed.

At noon the next day, Francisco de Eraso asked the Adelantado to come and have lunch with him, and the Adelantado replied that he would not enjoy the food if he did not tell him what the council had decided. Francisco de Eraso told him, saying that His Majesty had ordered him to go to Valladolid, where he would give him the authorization to recruit men and seize ships, as well as sureties for the officials of the House of Trade in Seville, who were to take care promptly of the provisioning and the payment of the men, borrowing some money for this purpose. The Adelantado replied to Francisco de Eraso that he was not pleased with that provision, because there would be much delay in looking for the money and the ships, in careening them and fitting them out, and in getting the supplies and gathering the men, especially for Florida, which was discredited among all countries as having a perilous coast. And since seven fleets with many men, which had gone to those parts by order of the emperor [Charles I] of glorious memory and of His Majesty, had all been lost at sea, it was hard to find soldiers and sailors. The five hundred men he was bringing along were from Asturias and Vizcaya, gathered and sought out and entreated by his relatives and friends, and he was accompanied by important people who, aside from service to God and His Majesty, were going more to please him and keep him company than for the benefits and riches there might be, for they knew well that they were embarking on a difficult and dangerous adventure, in no way profitable. [Also] His Majesty would not at all be served by his going to Valladolid for the orders; since so much time had passed already, he wished to go post-haste to Seville by way of the court so the members of the Royal Council of the Indies might write to the officials of the House of Trade to give the Adelantado the fifteen thousand ducats they had offered him in the *asiento* to defray the great costs and expenditures he would have to make for the conquest and settlement of Florida, and other things specified in the *asiento*, which were favors of little substance.

But the Adelantado had just come out of a long imprisonment due to being falsely accused by Licentiate [Diego] Venegas, the prosecutor for the House of Trade in Seville,[168] of having exceeded the orders given to him when he was general of that fleet—for the breaking of them enabled His Majesty's best interest to be served, and if he had followed them it would have been the opposite. And because the Adelantado had had such good and prosperous outcomes in His Majesty's service, there were many slanderers against him, and he had been imprisoned for twenty months in the shipyards and in the Torre del Oro in Seville, and at this court, and in all this time he had not been able to kiss His Majesty's hands, until, after being sentenced, he gave him license to do so. [The Adelantado] feared that His Majesty might have thought ill of him because of what his ministers had said of him, having given credit to those who had spoken ill of the Adelantado, and that he was in disfavor with [His Majesty], who would think much less of him than was just. He wished to restore his reputation, which he had earned through such hardships and perils, and at the expense of his property, and the loss and death of his son [Juan Menéndez][169] and of his brothers, relatives, and friends, and having to see the captains and noblemen who had followed him, and who had served His Majesty in his company, poor and needy, and not be able to help them because he was in the same situation. [Yet] no mission he undertook seemed difficult to him, and especially that of Florida—which was of such great service to Our Lord God, to His Majesty, and to the general well-being of this kingdom—in which, if he were to serve well, he understood that even if a reward from His Majesty was lacking, he would not lack reward and aid from Our Lord God, which was what he needed, and what he particularly sought in this.

Three months later, he dispatched three messengers to different parts, writing to his friends and to Francisco de Reinoso, a man-at-arms of His Majesty, [asking them] to recruit as many men as they could. He told Francisco de Eraso that delaying his departure for Florida would be a disservice to His Majesty, and that he thought it was ill-advised to stay there [waiting] for these ships, supplies, and men, because he did not know where he would find ships. [He said] that he had a one-thousand-ton galleon, the best ship at sea, which was very fast and well armed, readied for war, and that [although] the merchants of Seville were giving him twenty-five thousand ducats' worth of freight to take her laden to Nombre de Dios, and she was now loading, he would lose that interest and would go about in her and collect as many men as he could. [He said that] notice should be sent to the officials in Seville to take her and provision her to carry as many people as she could hold, and His Majesty could order that any dispatches he wished to give him in Valladolid be sent to Seville.

Francisco de Eraso thought this was very appropriate and urged him to do so, and to make the voyage quickly. The Adelantado went so smartly on the way from Cádiz and Vizcaya that he set out from Cádiz on St. Peter's Day [29 June 1565] with the galleon *San Pelayo* and ten other ships, and another five from Asturias and Vizcaya, and two thousand one hundred and fifty soldiers and sailors, as is mentioned before. And of all these His Majesty paid for only three hundred soldiers and one ship. All the rest was at the expense of the Adelantado, who sought all the aid he could from his relatives and friends, who helped him very much, knowing that this enterprise was of such great service to God and His Majesty.

Pedro del Castillo, a resident and city councillor of Cádiz and a great friend of the Adelantado, distinguished himself in this more than anybody else, helping him with his properties and those of his friends. He alone lent him twenty thousand ducats, as the Adelantado understood the great service he was doing for His Majesty in going straight to Florida, as he did, in order to destroy the enemy before they could fortify themselves and earn the trust of the chieftains and Indians of that land, as is mentioned before.

Chapter 34

Description of the Land of Florida, Its Good Qualities, and Its Climate

The land of Florida stretches from Pánuco,[170] a port of New Spain, to Terranova, which is one thousand three hundred leagues of coastline. It is all dry land along the coast. There are many islands and keys, and very good harbors, for within three hundred leagues the Adelantado has discovered four harbors that each have four fathoms of water at high tide, some of them more, and he has discovered another ten of two and one-half to three fathoms of water. All of these he himself has gone to and entered three times, with four or five or six brigantines, in order to explore, sound, and mark them, and other pilots also with his brigantines. In these three hundred leagues of coastline the chieftains and Indians are his friends, and he has built settlements in seven places near these harbors—three forts and four villages, which make seven settlements—where all of the chieftains and Indians are his friends.[171] Only in the forty leagues of coastline and ten leagues inland where the French Lutherans used to be are the chieftains and Indians enemies of the Adelantado and the Spaniards. This is because the French Lutherans had settled in that country and built a fort three years before the Adelantado arrived, [in 1562,] and when he did, they were already on very good terms with the Indian women—the sisters, daughters, and wives of the chieftains—and [had] some children by them. When the Adelantado captured their fort, some of these Frenchmen fled to the woods and went to the chieftains in the villages, and were well received and treated by them. The Indians were astonished that one group of Christians would fight with another, and that those who had arrived could kill those who had been there with such ease. The Frenchmen told them that we were Spaniards who had gone there to kill them, and the Indians we did not kill would have to be our slaves, as well as to take their wives, children, and houses. Because of this, the chieftains of that district united and agreed that neither they nor their Indians should be friends of the Spaniards.

The Adelantado was notified of this, and he endeavored to treat them very well and earn their trust, so they would see that the Frenchmen had lied, and that we were better men than they and more truthful. As has been mentioned before, he told them as best he could that the Frenchmen were false Christians. He gave them many presents, as well as some of what he had, and did not permit any harm to be done to them. In this way he earned the trust of many chieftains, who would come to the fort with their wives, sons, and daughters. But later, when the Adelantado left to fetch supplies and [the Indians] realized how little those who remained there had, they became very treacherous, and with cunning and deceit they killed more than one hundred and twenty soldiers at different times, although the first outbreak was because the mutinous soldiers had killed three of the Indians—as is mentioned before—so that the rest of the Indians and their chieftains would kill the few Christians who remained there.

Most of the seacoast is poor land; since there are many rivers and inlets, and the tide rises and falls so much and the land is flat, the tide flows inland fifteen or twenty miles up the rivers. The rivers branch out sideways to one another in such a way that one can navigate them in canoes and boats without going out to sea, and the coastline is turned into islands. When the tide rises or the rivers are swollen, after it falls all that remains is swamp, in which men and horses are swallowed and cannot pass. The islands on the coastline are well forested with abundant groves of holm oak, white oak, pine, walnut, mulberry, sweet gum, very good cedar, and juniper. There is good fresh water on all of them, and forage for cattle. They all have many deer, rabbits, and hares, and around them there are many shellfish, oysters, and large quantities of fish. Some of them are inhabited, as well as the eight villages and forts that the Adelantado has settled.[172] These islands are suitable for [production of] much wine, wheat, and all kinds of crops, and much sweet sugarcane, and for raising much cattle. The islands are mostly six or eight leagues in length—some more and some less—and in order to be able to navigate these three hundred leagues in boats or canoes by an inland route, there are only five places—none wider than half a league—to be dredged, places that the Adelantado is thinking of settling.

[Florida] has been settled from a latitude of 26° to 36° on the Bahama Channel side, and has friendly Indian chieftains as far [north] as 37°, which is St. Marys Bay. On the New Spain side it is settled as far [north] as 30°, from where one can sail to Veracruz[173] and Pánuco—ports of New Spain—in six days, and to Honduras and Campeche in a few more, and to Havana in [just] three or four. [The Adelantado] has settled the side that empties into the Bahama Channel with forts and villages as far [north] as 33°, and from these forts one can reach Hispaniola and Puerto Rico in twelve and fifteen days [respectively]. With good weather one can sail to the islands of the Azores in twenty days, although the Adelantado came in seventeen days because his vessel was very swift.

The entire coastline [is known to us], as well as what is known of the country inland that Juan Pardo explored on orders from the Adelantado, which—as is mentioned before—was one hundred and fifty leagues. He built a fort called San Juan at the foot of the sierra in the country of Chief Joara, and since then the men of that fort have explored another hundred leagues to the west, toward New Spain, at a latitude of 36° or 38°, which is about two hundred leagues from the rich mines of Zacatecas in New Spain.[174]

All of it is a land of very good climate and [clear] skies, very healthy, and very good for all kinds of large and small livestock, bread [grains] and wine [grapes] and all kinds of crops, where there are many mulberry bushes for silk[worms], which will produce a great quantity. Because of its many river banks, it will yield much hemp and flax, and tar and resin, because there are a large number of pine groves for this purpose. There will be many good woods of all kinds to build houses and ships, and masts for the vessels, for these are things that are usually brought from Germany to Spain, even though the ones in Florida are better [and] could be brought to Spain very easily and at less cost to You[r Majesty]. [There are large] numbers of fish of all kinds, and many whales. Much metal with a low gold content has been found, which is a sign that there must be a great quantity of it, although the Indians do not know how much there is, nor do they hold gold or silver to be valuable, even if some falls into their hands from shipwrecked vessels coming from the Indies. Some ambergris, which the Indians value because they are fond of sweet scents, has been found on the coast, as well as emeralds and unicorns.

Between the fear that the chieftains have of the Adelantado, from learning of his victories against the French and how easily he expelled them from the land, and his good treatment of [the Indians], they are both fond and afraid of him in great measure. This is also due to the great acts of treason that the Indians and chieftains who were enemies of the Adelantado committed against his men, for when they saw that the Adelantado and his captains were doing their best to treat them well, they thought that we were afraid of them, and many became arrogant, insulting the Spaniards, saying that they were chickens and refusing to be their friends; unless they gave them so many shirts and hatchets and machetes, mirrors and scissors, and other things by way of tribute each moon—which is a month—they would not be [our] friends and would sooner be [our] worst enemies, and that they were waiting for the French, who could assist them in killing us, and they would assist the French in taking revenge on us, and that they wished there were more of us Spaniards in that land so they could kill them all. They had seven or eight Frenchmen with them, very good soldiers, who encouraged them, and their leader was called Captain Bayona.[175] The Frenchmen had sent a message to France, and they—and the Indians—were waiting for a French fleet to expel the Spaniards from the land.

The Adelantado considered that the time for pleasantries was over. He ordered war waged on them, as is mentioned before, and he began to fight them from the houses and fort [that with] horses and dogs [were positioned] every five leagues. He left orders with the captains regarding how they should wage war on them from that time onward. With the help of a Frenchman, the Adelantado wrote two letters to Captain Bayona, [saying] that if he wanted to come to him or to the captains that were with him in that land he could do so safely with the men he had there, because they would do them no harm but rather would give them a ship and supplies to go to Spain and, from there, to France. Captain Bayona received the letters and did not reply, but when he saw that his chieftain friends were losing the war ordered against them, he came with two Frenchmen to Fort San Mateo and surrendered to Captain Gonzalo de Villarroel, as Captain Villarroel has recorded.

Letters from the captains of those provinces, dating from the end of July [15]67, have been received [telling] how they waged the war on the Indians as they had been ordered, and how the Indians had lost and were abandoning the land and leaving their villages deserted. The friendly chieftains offered the Adelantado many of their Indians to wage war on his enemies both Indian and French. Even though the Adelantado was in great need of them, he never wanted to take them, in order not to lose his reputation with the Indians. He told them that his lord, the king of Spain, had commanded him not to kill or harm any Indians, but to take them for friends and brothers, and that if any chieftains were at war with each other, he should strive to make peace between them. But if the chieftains and Indians were to tell him that they wanted to be his friends and take him for their elder brother and the king of Spain for their lord, and later break their word and kill the Christians, then he should consider them his enemies, wage war on them, and enslave them. [He said] that he had several times forgiven Saturiwa, his chieftain allies, all of their Indians, and all the Indians who were enemies of the Adelantado and the Spaniards, and that he had forgiven them many times for the lies they had told and the Christians they had killed, thinking that they would be good friends. But if he had to consider them enemies, he would know how to wage war on them, expelling them from their lands, killing them all, and taking their houses, canoes, fisheries, and cornfields, which is all they have. And he would do the same to the chieftains with whom he had become friends, if they should lie to him. And since the chieftains would soon realize the Adelantado [was a man who] did what he said, [even if] there were very few Christians and many Indians, they would be very afraid of him—and, on the other hand, they would love him very much because he was very friendly to them, and his reputation would grow. In a land so large, even without his going to conquer them they would pay obedience to him in His Majesty's name. And this would open the doors for the missionaries who would come with the catechism to spread the Holy Gospel, for these were the two things that were his particular interest, not expecting other benefits or riches, nor looking for pearls or mines. And since his departure from Spain he said and made openly known to all the captains and soldiers that they should publicize and strive to settle and conquer that land, and that they should not break off with a chieftain and his Indians unless they forced them to do so, with the cause justified before Our Lord that it would be appropriate to wage war on them—and then do it with total cruelty, in such a manner that [the Indians] would fear them and they would gain great renown, and the friendship of the friendly chieftains would be preserved.

Since leaving that province, the Adelantado has received letters, among them some sent by his nephew Captain Pedro Menéndez Marqués, who is his lieutenant on that coastline for maritime matters and governor of the lands of Chief Carlos, which can be produced and which record the truth about this, as do those written by Esteban de las Alas, his lieutenant in that land, and the other captains, so that no event be recorded in the chronicles that is not checked and verified. [And] to satisfy [the requirements of] the Royal Council, we shall record the benefits that His Majesty has conferred on the Adelantado and the other persons who went on this expedition and conquest of Florida.

And if the French were to rule over Florida, they would gain mastery with great ease over all the Indies, Islands, and Mainland of the Ocean Sea without waging war or [needing] large fleets and armies, for their evil sect is very close to that of the Indians, who do not endure any hardships in their daily lives but pursue earthly pleasures like beasts, not knowing or fearing God, and unaware of where they will end up when they die. For this reason the French Lutherans very easily brought all those provinces under the sway of their evil sect, because of the inhabitants being unenlightened savages who took everything [the French] taught them to heart.

Apart from this, there are very many black men and women, mestizos, and mulattoes in all the ports that have been settled in the Indies, Islands, and Mainland of the Ocean Sea. Most of them are unruly people with bad tendencies, too restless, and with an arrogant disposition. In that land the black women give birth often, and this race and kind grows greatly in number because of their birth rate. Since the land is hot as in Guinea, few of those who are born [to them] die, while of those borne by Spanish women, those who survive are few. Thus the Spaniards do not reproduce much in that land, but rather many die, others live in sickness, because that climate and geographic location are different from those of Spain and very similar to those of Guinea, and that is why black men and women get on well there, and live long and healthy lives, and few die and they reproduce in large numbers.

In all those parts there are thirty or forty black men and women for every Spaniard. Those people could not be slaves in France, because everyone lives in freedom there, and when the French considered this—and that [the blacks] had little faith in God (rather they loathed His divine law because it seemed harsh to them) and little love for the king of Spain (because they had been enslaved by his subjects), and that their new Lutheran religion meant living more in accord with their tastes and their vices—within a month of when the Adelantado arrived there, the French decided to go from Florida with the fleet to all the parts of the Indies to free the black people, who would rise up in rebellion and take the land, killing their masters. The French would then establish their fortresses and their governing bodies, letting the black people, mulattoes, and mestizos live in their Lutheran freedom and not be slaves, and conducting trade, contracts, agreements, and business deals with them. This [plan] was seen and read by many people, because when the Adelantado took the fort called Fort of France [Fort Caroline] and renamed it San Mateo (because he captured it on that day), they found a little coffer of documents that Jean Ribault, the general of the French troops, had in his room. And among other papers, they found in this coffer an instruction from the Admiral of France, signed with his name, ordering this general, once he had arrived in Florida and fortified himself, not to neglect taking care of this mission. Since the fort burned down within a month of when it was captured, with everything inside, the fire destroyed the coffer and all the papers where this instruction was being kept with the intention of presenting it with the other papers.

At this same time, New Spain had begun to rise in rebellion against His Majesty, and it is held certain that if the Lutherans had succeeded in their attempt to settle in Florida, all of New Spain would have been lost at once and all the people of the Indies would have risen in rebellion against His Majesty. But the Divine Majesty of Heaven, in His kindness, aware of the many souls that would have been lost by this, miraculously remedied the situation, as is mentioned before.

End of the description.[176]

And I, Diego de Ribera, scribe of our lord the king, citizen of Madrid, out of curiosity, coming across this narrative and seeing in it the expedition that the Adelantado Pedro Menéndez de Avilés made to Florida and the things that happened to him there, and how it lay abandoned and quite lost after his death, while I investigate what all these things amounted to and how it all ended, and if the French, after the death of the Adelantado,

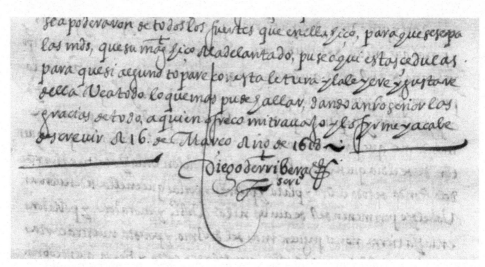

Signature of Diego de Ribera. Facsimile of the Ferrera manuscript, f. 117v. Reproduced with permission of the marqués de Ferrera.

captured all the forts he had built in that land, I set down here these edicts in order to make known the rewards granted by His Majesty to the Adelantado, so that if anyone should come across this narrative, and read it and take pleasure in it, he can see all that I was able to find. I give thanks for all of this to Our Lord, to whom I offer my work.

And I signed it and finished copying it on 16 March 1618.

Diego de Ribera, scribe.

Part 2

La Conquista de la Florida
por el Adelantado Pedro Meléndez de Valdés

[1*r]¹ Conquista de la Florida y de los acaecimientos que hubo en ella por el adelant[ad]o Pedro Meléndez de Valdés. Cuenta la dispusición de la tierra y de los indios que la habitan, y de un fuerte que tienen hecho los françeses.

[3*r] La conquista que Pedro Meléndez de Avilés, caballero del Hábito de Santiago, hiço a la Florida con título de adelantado de aquella tierra, y otras mercedes que Su Majestad el² rey don Felipe II, le hiço en [a]quella tierra, si se acabara de sujetar. Murió en la mayor ocasión, y con su muerte se perdió lo que estaba ganado y el amistad que había cobrado con los caçiques. Fue a ella el año de 1565.

[3*v]³ Los capitanes y personas nobles que fueron a esta jornada:

- Alonso Menéndez Marqués,⁴ sobrino del Adelantado.
- Bartolomé Menéndez, hermano del Adelantado.
- Don Pedro de Valdés,⁵ casado con la hija⁶ mayor del Adelantado.
- Gonçalo de Villarroel, capitán y sargento mayor.
- El capitán Juan de Çurita.⁷
- Diego Flores de Valdés, almirante de la armada.
- El capitán Juan de San Viçente.
- El capitán Francisco de Recalde.
- El capitán Diego de Maya.
- El capitán Martín Ochoa, vizcaíno.
- El capitán San Viçente.⁸
- El capitán Francisco de Castañeda.
- El capitán Andrés López Patiño.

- El alférez Rodrigo Troche. Fue el primero que enarboló bandera en el fuerte que ganaron de los françeses.
- El alférez Cristóbal de Herrera. Fue el segundo que enarboló bandera en el fuerte.
- El capitán Juan Vélez de Medrano, de Medina del Campo.
- El capitán Diego de Alvarado.[9]
- El capitán Estébano de las Alas.

Los indios caciques que el Adelantado trujo a su amistad:

- El cacique Carlos, señor de muchos indios y pueblos.
- El caçique Guale.
- El cacique Orista.
- El cacique Otina.[10]
- El cacique Mocoya.
- El cacique Saturiba.
- El cacique Ais.
- El cacique Tequesta.
- El cacique Calabay.
- El cacique Tocobaga.[11]
- El cacique Emoloa.

Los fuertes que hiço el Adelantado:

- San Mateo, que fue el que se ganó de los franceses día de San Mateo, y está cabe un río que viene de la laguna Maimi, que tiene cuarenta leguas de cercuíto, y en ella entran grandes ríos que de[s]cienden de las sierras. Desagua hacia el Fuerte de San Mateo y entra en la Canal de Bahama, y otro río corre de la propia laguna por las tierras del cacique Carlos y entra en la canal dicha.
- El Fuerte de San Agustín, que fue a dónde tomó puerto el Adelantado el mismo día de San Agustín, 28 de agosto, año de [15]65.
- El Fuerte de San Felipe, junto al puerto de Santa Elena.

Capítulo 1

El viaje a Florida

[1r]¹² Pedro Meléndez de Avilés, caballero del Hábito de Santiago, de nación asturiano, hombre no menos noble que valiente, general por Su Majestad en la Carrera de las Indias, y adelantado de la Florida por particular merced¹³ de Su Majestad, después que tomó asiento con Su Majestad para ir a la conquista de la Florida y a plantar en ella el Sagrado Evangelio, visto que Juan Ribao, françés luterano de la nueva religión, había venido de Francia con gruesa armada y había tomado puerto en la Florida, y junto a un río caudaloso que atraviesa gran parte de la Florida habían fabricado un fuerte y puéstole por nombre el Fuerte de Francia, a fin de detener en aquel puerto navíos y bajeles para salir a robar los pasajeros¹⁴ y a los navíos que vienen con la plata, de todo lo cual dio cuenta a Su Majestad y señores de su Real Consejo (y el peligro que de no remediallo se seguía, que convenía la brevedad, antes que se fortificasen y ganasen la voluntad a los caciques), porque tiniendo a los indios naturales por enemigos y a los françeses que los industriaban¹⁵ para pelear en compañía de ellos, no era bastante recaudo el que se le daba para poner pie en la Florida ni echar a los luteranos de ella.

Y aunque esta particularidad el Adelantado dijo a Su Majestad en Santa María de Nieva por abril de [15]65, y lo dijo a los señores del Real Consejo del Estado y Guerra que con él estaban, y después lo vino a decir a Madrid, donde estaba la Corte y señores del Real Consejo de las Indias, que le diesen para la jornada dos galeras y galeotas del cargo de don Álvaro Baçán para que con ellas y sus çabras y patajes se adelantase a la Florida antes que los françeses fuesen socorridos, y cuando lo fuesen él desembarcaría en otro puerto, el más cercano que hallase al de los françeses—que por ser los navíos que pedía de poca agua lo podría muy bien hacer—y allí se fortificaría, procurando haçerles todo el mal que pudiese y ganar la voluntad a los caçiques. Y a la primavera, con la caballería que le viniese de las Indias, sería señor de la campaña y de su puerto, por tener el fuerte dos leguas por el río arriba, por que no fuesen socor[r]idos ni los indios tratasen con ellos. Y que por esta orden se les había de haçer la guerra con industria y brevedad, con lo cual serían echados de la Florida, por que no plantasen[16] [1v] en ella su mala se[c]ta.

Pareció bien a Su Majestad, y respe[c]to de la nueva que había que el Turco venía sobre Malta, y las pocas galeras que había para resistillo, no consintió que se le diesen, aunque aprobó por bueno su pareçer.

Y otro día, estando Su Majestad en La Mejorada, mandó que se le diesen a el Adelantado quinientos hombres —bastecidos y pagados— y cuatro naos de armada, todo a costa de Su Majestad, para que, con los quinientos hombres y las diez chalupas y zabras que el Adelantado llevaba a su costa, se fuese[17] por las islas de Puerto Rico, Española y Cuba y recogiese la caballería e infantería y navíos de armada y bastimento que estaba proveído.

Quedó el negocio remitido a Francisco de Eraso, el cual le dijo que Su Majestad mandaba fuese a Valladolid para que allí recibiese las provisiones para levantar la gente y embargar los navíos y reca[u]dos para los oficiales de la [Casa de la] Contratación, que con brevedad hiciesen los mantenimientos y pagasen la gente tomando el dinero a cambio. A lo cual respondió el Adelantado que no le contentaba por la dilación que habría en ello y en juntar la gente, y en especial siendo para la Florida, que estaba desacreditada de todas las naciones ser de costa brava. Y porque siete armadas con mucha gente que por mandado del emperador y Su Majestad habían ido a la Florida, y se habían perdido, y por esta causa los soldados y marineros serían malos de hallar, y que los quinientos hombres que llevaba eran de Asturias y Vizcaya, buscados y rogados por deudos y amigos suyos que le acompañaban, gente prinçipal, más por servir a Dios y a su rey que por el interés que esperaban, que por estar el tiempo tan adelante se iría por la posta a Sevilla y pasaría por Madrid para que los señores del Real Consejo de las Indias escribiesen a los de la [Casa de la] Contratación le diesen los quinçe mil ducados que conforme a el asiento le ofrecieron para ayuda [de] los grandes gastos que había de haçer. [Él] escribió a sus deudos y amigos para que en su nombre levantasen la más gente que pudiesen, y dijo al señor Francisco de Eraso que de la dilación no sería servido Su Majestad, que él se partía a Sivilla, donde recogió los quinçe mil ducados, y llegó a Cádiz, y en un [n]avío grueso que tenía y en sus zabras recogió su gente, y en los navíos que le vinieron de Asturias y Vizcaya recogió dos mil ciento cincuenta hombres de mar y guerra.[18]

Y tal prisa se dio que día de San Pedro partió de Cádiz con próspero viento.[19] [2r] Y dentro de treinta días que partió de Cádiz tuvo una tormenta muy grande que llaman furaca. Estuvo en gran peligro de perderse con toda la armada, quedando sin árbol ninguno, perdiendo todas las velas y jarçias del galeón en que él iba. Luego que vino la bonança se halló con solos tres navíos, y por el bastante recaudo que llevaba de lonas[20] y jarcias se remedió lo mejor que pudo y entró en Puerto Rico, donde con gran diligençia dentro de ocho días volvió a aparejarse y salió, habiendo recogido otro navío de los que se le apartaron con la tormenta. Y de allí, de Puerto Rico, sacó otro, que fueron çinco navíos[21] que llevaba[n] dentro de ellos mil personas de mar y guerra, y publicó a su gente que iba derecho a La Habana.

Y salido a la mar en la parte que convino, yendo navegando, estando en parte que no era posible ir a La Habana sino era haçiendo gran rodeo por los muchos bajíos que había, hizo llamar y juntar a sus capitanes, y entrado en consejo con ellos les dijo con gran secreto el menos peligro que se corría en irse derechos a la Florida en buen tiempo, antes que el invierno entrase, que no ir a La Habana a recoger los navíos que se le habían apartado y los más de armada, caballería e infantería que Su Majestad le mandaba tomar en Santo Domingo y en aquella isla, que en esto se había de detener, de manera que no podría ir a la Florida hasta la primavera, y que entonces los luteranos estarían fuertes, y que se corría mayor peligro, y que con su parecer de ellos él determinaba, pues estaba en parte que no podía hacer otra cosa, de se ir a la Florida derecho al puerto y fuerte que los franceses tenían, porque si la armada francesa no era llegada le parecía llevaba recaudo bastante para les ganar el puerto que tenían, que les rogaba lo tuviesen por bien y que cada uno de por sí y todos juntos animasen mucho a sus soldados y a los marineros, diciéndoles que era muy buena determinación y que la empresa que llevaban era de Dios Nuestro Señor y de nuestro rey, que tuviesen grande esperança[22] en [que] la Divina Majestad les daría [2v] victoria en todo, y que tuviesen grande ánimo y paçiençia para pasar los trabajos y peligros que sucediesen.

Y luego[23] algunos capitanes respondieron, aprobando la determinaçión del dicho Adelantado, y mostraron tener contento, ofreciéndose a ponerse con toda voluntad y ánimo a los trabajos y peligros que sucediesen, y que animarían a sus soldados y los traerían en toda buena di[s]ciplina para que sirviesen con toda obediençia. Y sin aguardar respuesta de otros capitanes que no respondían a esto (y le pareció al dicho Adelantado les pesaba de su determinaçión) les dijo a todos juntos:

—Hermanos míos, quedaos con Dios ençerrados en este aposento por dos horas por que no se entienda nuestro secreto. Trata[d] y platica[d] sobre esto, para que si algunas dificultades viéredes en ésta mi determinación me lo digáis, y el que más pusiere será mayor mi amigo, para que oídas vuestras razones y las mías determinemos lo más açertado. Y cada uno de por sí y todos juntos, y la gente de mar y guerra tendrá contento con ver que lo que en esto se proveyere será con consejo pensado y acordado.

Y así los dejó encerrados el dicho Adelantado en un aposento y se salió a la cubierta de la nao, donde hizo hacer plegarias y rezar las letanías y hacer que toda la gente de la armada, cada uno en sus navíos, hincados todos de rodillas, suplicasen a Nuestro Señor alumbrase al dicho Adelantado para que en una determinación que quería tomar proveyese lo que conviniese para el serviçio de Dios Nuestro Señor y para acrecentamiento de su Santa Fe Católica, lo cual todo se hizo con gran devoçión. Y después de hecho esto el dicho Adelantado se retiró a la cámara de popa del galeón, donde iba con unas horas en la mano, y delante de un crucifijo y de una imagen de Nuestra Señora estuvo rezando y haciendo oraçión por espaçio de un hora. Y salió de allí, ya que serían pasadas [3r] las dos horas del término que había dado a sus capitanes, y fuese para ellos al aposento donde los dejó çerrados y pidioles le dijesen abierta y claramente cada uno lo que sentía en su pecho y alma de lo que les pareçía cerca de su determinación, y si debía mudar consejo.

Y tratando y platicando un hora en esto resolviéronse en la determinaçión del dicho Adelantado para que se fu[e]sen derechos a la Florida al puerto que los franceses tenían. Y salidos de este aposento y dicha esta determinación públicamente en el galeón donde iban sei[s]cientas y cuatro[24] personas, y dicho en los otros navíos que iban juntos al derredor de él navegando con viento de bonança,[25] mandó el Adelantado triunfar esta determinación como si hubiera tenido ya las victorias que después Nuestro Señor Dios les dio en la dicha jornada. Y mandó tañer las trompetas, pífanos y atambores de toda la armada, y desplegar por todos los navíos estandartes y gallardetes y banderas de campaña que llevaba para la dicha jornada, y arbolar el estandarte real, al cual se le hizo una real salva disparando toda la arcubecería y artillería de los navíos. Y mandó dar la raçión doblada aquel día a toda la gente. Dio esto grandísimo contentamiento, y esto se vio muy claro por la alegría y regocijo que todos tenían, que no hablaban de otra cosa sino alabando la determinación del dicho Adelantado.

Aquel[26] día a la tarde el Adelantado mandó en todos los navíos entregar las armas a los capitanes para que las repartiesen por sus soldados, que las tuviesen limpias y listas, que hasta llegar a la Florida cada día tirase tres tiros cada soldado para que perdiesen el miedo a los arcabuces y se ejerçitasen, porque era la más de la gente bisoña. Y el un tiro que lo tirasen con pelota en un terrero que se hizo dentro del dicho galeón, ofreciendo [3v] precios a los soldados de las compañías que mejor lo tirasen y a sus capitanes, por que tuviesen gran cuidado de hacerlos diestros. Y con este ejercicio[27] que cada día se hizo, diciendo cada día la doctrina cristiana y las letanías, haciendo plegarias y oraçiones a Nuestro Señor, suplicándole les diese en todo victoria, fueron navegando hasta veintiocho de agosto [de 1565], día de San Agustín, que descubrieron la tierra de la Florida. Hincándose todos de rodillas, diciendo el Te Deum Laudamus, alabaron a Nuestro Señor, prosiguiendo toda la gente sus oraçiones, suplicando a Nuestro Señor les diese en todo victoria.

Captura de Fort Caroline

Y por no saber la parte [en] que los luteranos estaban fortificados anduvieron cuatro días navegando al luengo de la tierra muy afligidos y suspensos, no sabiendo si los franceses estaban al norte si al su[r], donde el dicho Adelantado andaba con su armada navegando de día y surgiendo de noche. Y una mañana vio indios en la costa. Envió a tierra a su maestro de campo con veinte arcabuceros. No quiso que desembarcase más gente por que los indios no hubiesen miedo y huyesen, y en desembarcando el maestro de campo con los veinte soldados en tierra los indios salieron con sus arcos y flechas. Y como los nuestros se iban para ellos, ellos se iban retirando al monte, temiendo los cristianos que habría emboscada de mucha gente y correrían peligro seguirlos, y que si no tomaban lengua de ellos para saber en la parte que los luteranos estaban sería mal caso, porque como la costa y bajíos que tenían no eran sabidos por el dicho Adelantado ni sus pilotos, corriendo alguna tormenta tenían peligro de perderse con la armada. Y para el remedio de esto mandó el maestro de campo a un soldado que había cometido delito dejase las armas y con cierto rescate se fuese a los indios, y así lo hizo el soldado. Los indios le aguardaron y recibiero[n] bien, y se aseguraron. Entonces llegó el maestro de campo y habló [4r] con ellos por señas, preguntándoles por los françes[es], los cuales también por señas[28] respondieron que estaban como veinte leguas de allí a la parte del norte.

Preguntaron los indios si el general de la armada estaba en las naos o si estaba entre ellos. Dijéronles que estaba en las naos. Respondieron que deseaban mucho verle y conoçerle. Quisieron llevarlos a las naos y ellos no quisieron. Dijeron que habían miedo y que allí en tierra le agu[a]rdarían. Y así se volvió el maestro de campo con sus veinte soldados a la capitana donde estaba el dicho Adelantado y le contó todo lo que había pasado con los indios, y que le estaban agu[a]rdando en tierra. Y con el deseo que tuvo de verlos y satisfacerse de lo que los indios decían por señas—que los franceses estaban veinte leguas de allí a la parte del norte—fue en tierra con dos bateles y con çincuenta arcabuceros.

Y luego que los indios lo vieron en tierra, dejando sus arcos y flechas se vinieron al dicho Adelantado. Empeçaron a cantar y hacer ademanes con las manos al çielo a manera de adoraçión, que fue cosa harto de ver. El Adelantado les dio muchas cosas de rescates y les hizo dar de comer cosas dulçes que llevaba en el batel. Afirmáronse en lo que habían dicho, que veinte leguas de allí estaban lo[s] franceses. Dejolos el Adelantado muy contentos y embarcose en los navíos, y fue navegando al luengo de la tierra con su armada, y descubrió ocho leguas de allí un puerto bueno con una buena ribera a que puso por nombre Santo Agustín, por ser allí la primera tierra que descubrió de la Florida y ser el mismo día de San Agustín cuando la descubrió.

Otro día siguiente, yendo navegando al luengo de la tierra, siendo las tres horas después de mediodía descubrió cuatro galeones grandes que estaban surtos, y pareciéndole[29] ser allí el puerto donde los franceses estaban, y que el socorro les era venido, y que aquellos galeones eran de su armada, entró en consejo con sus capitanes [4v] y les dijo que, teniendo por çierto que la armada francesa era venida y que no se les podía ganar el fuerte ni el puerto ni la armada, que le dijesen lo que les pareçía debía de hacer. Y habiendo diferentes pareçeres, en que los más capitanes decían se volviese el dicho Adelantado con los çinco navíos que llevaba a Santo Domingo, y que allí recogería los demás navíos de su armada que con la tormenta se le apartaron y otros seis navíos de la armada de Vizcaya y Asturias que aguardaban (que le había dejado orden en Canaria[s] se fuesen a Puerto Rico), y que también recogería dos naos de armada y la caballería, infantería y bastimentos que Su Majestad le mandó dar en aquella isla de Santo Domingo y en la de Cuba. Y así, recogido todo, se iría a La Habana, y el mes de março venidero [de 1566] iría poderoso a la Florida para hacer cualesquier buenos efectos.

Y este parecer temió el dicho Adelantado, porque si lo tomaba corría peligro de perderse a causa que ya él era descubierto con sus çinco navíos de la armada françesa, y el viento era calma, y el sol demostraba grandes bonanças, y de la tormenta que habían tenido habían quedado los cuatro navíos sin mástiles de gavia y tenían otros árboles menos que se habían rompido, y la armada francesa los alcançaría, en espeçial que tenían aviso traían navíos del remo. Y respondioles que, conforme a razón, los franceses no le podían aguardar tan presto en aquella costa, y que ternían la infantería en tierra, y que estarían descargando los bastimentos, y que por se[r] aquellos cuatro navíos grandes no podían entrar en el puerto cargados, que le pareçía fuesen a combatir con ellos, porque si los tomaban no ternían los franceses armada sufiçiente para les salir a buscar a la mar y se podría volver al puerto de San Agustín, que estaba doce leguas de allí, y desembarcar en aquel [5r] puerto y fortificarse, y enviar los navíos a la Española a dar aviso a la armada que le faltaba. Y que la infantería, caballería y bastimentos que Su Majestad le mandaba tomar en Santo Domi[n]go viniese todo junto el mes de março [de 1566] a aquel puerto de Santo Agustín, y que llegado que fuese podrían ir por mar y por tierra contra los enemigos, ganándoles el puerto, porque tenían el fuerte dos[30] leguas por una ribera adentro y que no les podría venir socorro de Francia. Y que con la caballería serían señores de la campaña, para que no tuviesen trato ni conversaçión con los indios, y para que, de esta manera, les harían la guerra en breve tiempo, sin peligro de su armada ni del dicho[31] Adelantado ni de su gente. Y que esto se haría habiendo reconocido su fuerte, y que estaban tan fuertes que corrían peligro de dalles batería y ganarlo con las armas.

Y con estas razones que el dicho Adelantado dijo todos los capitanes aprobaron este parecer y consejo, y antes de la determinación hicieron oración a Nuestro Señor suplicándole les favoreciese en todo y diese victoria contra sus enemigos. Y acabada la oración, el dicho Adelantado dijo la determinación que determinaba acometer a la armada francesa, la cual todos aprobaron. Luego mandó irse los capitanes a sus navíos y dioles instrucción de lo que habían de hacer. Y mandó al Almirante de la Armada que con dos navíos que le señaló y en el que iba,[32] que eran tres, a la parte que había de acudir y la orden que había de tener, y al otro navío, que era un patax, mandó el Adelantado no se le quitase de a bordo de su nao capitana. Y así, yendo navegando con bonança, estarían como tres leguas del armada que estaba surta sobre su puerto, que eran cuatro galeones grandes.

Vino el viento a calmar y mucho trueno y relámpago y aguaceros, que duró hasta las nueve de la noche, y entonces el cielo quedó muy sereno y claro, el viento a la tierra. Pareçiéndole al Adelantado que cuando llegase a los enemigos sería cerca de medianoche y no convenía aferrar con los navíos por el peligro de los artifiçios de fuego que los enemigos suelen

[5v] traer (y de noche pu[é]dense aprovechar más de ellos que de día) y a trueque que se quemasen los unos navíos y los otros que escaparían los enemigos en los bateles y esquifes que tenían por popa, lo cual pudieran hacer con facilidad, pues la tierra estaba por ellos, y quedar ellos victoriosos y el dicho Adelantado perdido, acordó de surgir por las proas de ellos de manera que, dando fondo con las áncoras y largando los cables, quedasen las popas de lo[s] navíos del dicho Adelantado sobre las proas de los enemigos, para que al alba del día, largando el cable, abordase con los enemigos, los cuales no pod[r]ían ser favorecidos de su[s] navíos que estaban dentro del puerto a causa que, por ser la barra larga y mala, [y] de noche, no pod[r]ían salir, y al amanecer estaba bajamar y hab[r]ían de aguardar que fuese llena, y esto era mediodía. Y así mandó venir los capitanes a bordo de su nao capitana y les dijo su determinación, la cual aprobaron todos por muy buena.

Y llegando como a las once y media de la noche çerca de la armada françesa empeçaron a tirar de ella[33] pieças de artillería, y las balas pasaban por entre los mástiles y jarcias de los navíos del dicho Adelantado sin que en cosa ninguna hiciesen daño, el cual no permitió ni consintió que de sus navíos tirasen pieça de artillería. Antes mandó en todos los navíos, y en el que él iba,[34] que todos los soldados echasen abajo por que no los descalabrasen, que pues habían de surgir y no habían de abordar no era bien que estuviesen con la artillería arriba de la cubierta. Y con grande ánimo y gravedad, sin hacer cuenta de las pieças de artillería que tiraban, pasó a luengo de la capitana francesa (que estaban todos cuatro navíos juntos) sin hacer cuenta de ellos, los cuales tenían banderas y gallardetes, y en el mástil mayor una bandera de nao capitana y un estandarte real arbolado. Y en el otro galeón estaba en lo alto del mástil del trinquete una bandera de nao almiranta. Y como hubo surgido [6r] el dicho Adelantado con sus çinco navíos por la proa a tierra de ellos, hizo largar los cables, y la popa de su capitana quedó en el medio de las proas de la nao capitana y almiranta de los enemigos, que como una pica larga se llegaban las proas a sus navíos, y entonces hizo tocar las trompetas, salvando los enemigos. Y los enemigos le respondieron salvándole con las suyas. Y luego, acabadas estas salvas, el dicho Adelantado les habló con mucha cortesía, diciendo a los de la nao capitana:

—Señores, ¿[de] dónde es esta armada?

Respondió uno que de Françia. Volvioles a decir:

—¿Qué hace aquí?

Dijéronle:

—Traemos infantería, artillería y bastimentos para un fuerte que el Rey de Françia tiene en esta tierra, y otros que ha de hacer.

Díjoles el Adelantado:

—¿Sois católicos o luteranos? ¿Y quién es vuestro general?

Respondieron que todos eran luteranos de la nueva religión, y que su general era Juan Ribao, y que quiénes eran ellos y el que se lo preguntaba, y de quién era aquella armada y a qué venía a aquella tierra, y quién era el general de ella. El Adelantado les respondió:

—El que os lo pregunta se llama Pero Menéndez, y esta armada es del Rey de España, y yo soy general de ella, y vengo para ahorcar y degollar a todos los luteranos que hallare en esta mar y tierra, y así lo traigo por instrucción de mi rey, la cual cumpliré en siendo de día, que iré a vuestros[35] navíos y si hallare algún católico le haré buen tratamiento.

Respondieron muchos juntos palabras muy desvergonçadas y deshonestas diciendo contra el rey nuestro señor, nombrándole por su nombre, y contra el dicho Adelantado:

—Tal y tal sea para el rey don Felipe y para Pero Menéndez, y si eres hombre valiente como se dice, ven y no aguardes a la mañana.

Y el Adelantado, oídas tantas deshonestidades que decían en [6v] perjuicio de su rey, mandó largar el cable para abordar con los enemigos. Y como esto hicieron de mala gana los marineros, saltó abajo de la puente para que lo hiciesen con brevedad, y [como] el cable estaba guarnecido en el cablestante no se pudo hacer tan presto. Como esto vieron los enemigos, y la arma que el dicho Adelantado mandó tocar, temiéronle y cortaron los cables y guindaron las velas y echaron a huir. El dicho Adelantado hizo lo mesmo con sus navíos y siguiolos, de manera que como estaban en el medio de ellos él siguió los dos [en su nao capitana] con un patax que llevaba la vuelta del norte, y su almirante siguió los otros dos con los tres navíos la vuelta de su[r], y con el patax dio aviso el dicho Adelantado a su almirante que al alba del día revolviese sobre el puerto, que él haría lo mismo, para ver si le podrían ganar, y si no se irían a desembarcar al puerto de Santo Agustín, como estaba acordado, porque en caso que no se tomase ningún navío de lo[s] dichos franceses (porque navegaban más que los navíos del dicho Adelantado, que llevaban mástiles [de] menos de la tormenta que habían tenido), que se pasarían tres o cuatro días primero que los enemigos se volviesen a juntar, en los cuales ganaría el dicho Adelantado el puerto o desembarcaría en el puerto de Santo Agustín, porque los otros navíos franceses que estaban dentro de[l] puerto no se atreverían a salir no pareciendo los cuatro, y cuando saliesen no había por qué temerlos.

Y así suçedió que el dicho Adelantado siguió a los dos galeones franceses la vuelta del norte hasta el alba como çinco o seis leguas [7r] y su almirante otras tantas a los otros en la vuelta del su[r], y el dicho Adelantado a las diez del día estaba con sus çinco navíos sobre el puerto de los françeses. Y cuando entraron en el puerto vio dos banderas de infantería a la punta de la barra, y tirar pieças de artillería, y estaban çinco navíos dentro surtos. Pareciendo al dicho Adelantado que corría peligro de perderse si procuraba ganarles el puerto, y que en el entretanto se podrían juntar los cuatro navíos que habían ido huyendo con los çinco que estaban dentro, y que no se podía escapar por mar ni por tierra, acordó sin perder tiempo cargar de velas con su nao capitana y mandar a los otros hacer lo mesmo, y se fue al puerto de Santo Agustín, donde llegó aquel mismo día [7 de septiembre de 1565], víspera de Nuestra Señora de Septiembre. Y desembarcó luego que llegó hasta tre[s]cientos soldados, y envió con ellos dos capitanes que reconociesen luego a otro día en amaneçiendo la tierra y lugares que les pareciesen más fuertes para que hiciesen con brevedad una trinche[r]a, en el entretanto que se miraba dónde pudiesen hacer un fuerte para que, otro día, cuando el dicho Adelantado desembarcase, le mostrasen[36] lo que hubiesen visto y acordasen en esto lo que más conviniese.

Y otro día siguiente, día de Nuestra Señora de Septiembre, el dicho Adelantado desembarcó ya çerca de mediodía, donde halló muchos indios que le estaban aguardando porque habían tenido notiçia de él de los otros que cuatro días antes le habían visto y hablado. Hizo decir misa solemne de Nuestra Señora y, acabada, tomando la posesión de la tierra en nombre de Su Majestad, tomó juramento solemne a los ofiçiales de la Real Hacienda de Su Majestad y al maestro de campo [7v] y capitanes, que todos servirían a Su Majestad con toda fidelidad y lealtad. Y, hecho esto, hizo dar de comer a los indios y comió el dicho Adelantado, y en acabando luego fue a ver los sitios que para la trinche[r]a les pareçió a los capitanes que había enviado, y dejándola señalada se volvió a las naos, habiendo primeramente entrado en consejo y acordado que dentro de tres días se sacase de las naos todo lo que se pudiese sacar, y que luego enviasen las dos de ellas a la Española, que por ser grandes no podrían entrar en el puerto, porque si la armada francesa venía las tomaría. La diligençia que el Adelantado hizo en descargar estas naos para las enviar por que los enemigos no se las tomasen, pareciéndole que al cuarto día la armada françesa había de venir sobre ellos, fue tanta que se admiraron todos los que allí se hallaron, porque en dos días y medio, con estar surtas las naos más de legua y media del desembarcadero, sacó la gente artillería y muniçiones y mucha parte del bastimento.

Y sin aguardar los tres días, una noche a la medianoche, revelándosele que la armada françesa había de amaneçer con él, sin atender a que descargasen más bastimentos les hizo hacer a la vela la vuelta de la Española, y metió hasta çiento y çincuenta soldados que consigo tenía en una chalupa de hasta cien toneladas, y él se metió en un batel grande que cuando corrió tras la armada françesa lo llevaba por la popa su nao capitana, y para poder mejor huir se lo largó, y fue a surgir con este batel y con la chalupa sobre la barra en dos braças de agua. Y al amaneçer estaba la armada françesa junto de allí cuarto de legua, donde el dicho Adelantado había [8r] estado a la medianoche, donde hizo irse los navíos a la Española. Y vino una nao de los enemigos y tres chalupas, y por ser bajamar de todo y la mar no andar muy buena era peligro entrar la barra. Y cuando el dicho Adelantado vio junto de sí a los enemigos, que no podía escapar, hicieron todos oración a Dios Nuestro Señor y a su Preciosa Madre los salvase de aquel peligro. Y estando los luteranos ya junto de él, largó la amarra con que estaban surtos el batel en que él estaba y la chalupa, y entró para dentro por encima de los bajos con gran peligro. Y Nuestro Señor fue servido de meterlos dentro de la barra a salvamento. Los enemigos temieron la entrada[37] y aguardaban que fuese la mar llena.

En este tiempo estarían las naos que el dicho Adelantado enviaba a la Española como çinco o seis leguas de ellos, y así se salvaron de aquel peligro sin ser descubiertos. Y cuando de allí a dos horas que los enemigos aguardaban que la mar fuese llena hizo Dios un milagro: Que estando el tiempo sereno y claro, súpitamente se alteró mucho la mar y entró viento norte muy recio y contrario para se ir a su puerto y fuerte. Conoçido esto por el Adelantado, que estaba ya en tierra con su gente haciendo decir una misa al Espíritu Santo, y que todos la oyesen, suplicándole lo[38] alumbrase y encaminase en una determinación que quería tomar, y acabada la misa entró en consejo con sus capitanes, y fue el primero que en la tierra de la Florida había tenido, y ninguno de ello[s] sabían para qué se juntaban. Y estando juntos les dijo:

—Señores y hermanos míos, nosotros traemos una carga muy grande a cuestas, y muy trabajosa y peligrosa. Y si fuese solamente por el rey nuestro señor no me espantaría que alguno de nosotros nos cansásemos e hiciésemos algunas flaquezas de cobardes en no poder pasar [8v] tantos trabajos como se nos representan. Mas por ser empresa esta carga que traemos de Dios Nuestro Señor y de nuestro rey, por malaventurado se podrá tener el ministro de nosotros que mostrare flaqueza y que no animare a los ofiçiales y soldados de su cargo, que esto nos importa mucho. Y así, señores, os lo pido por merçed, cuan encarecidamente puedo, que pues en esto servimos a Dios y a nuestro rey, el gualardón del cielo no nos ha de faltar, y no nos desmaye el poco bastimento que tenemos ni el quedar aislados en esta tierra. Pídoos por merced que nos animemos y esforcemos todos a pasallos con paciençia.

Todos le r[e]spondieron muy bien, ofreciéndose cada uno y todos juntos que harían de su parte lo posible. Entonces el Adelantado, habiéndoles agradecido sus buenas respuestas, les dijo:

—Señores, a mí se me ofrece deciros una muy buena coyuntura que se me representa en los sentidos y en el alma, que no la debemos de perder, y nos conviene aprovecharnos de esta ocasión y no la dejar pasar. Y es que yo considero y es razón natural que, pues la armada francesa huyó de mí ha cuatro días y agora me viene a buscar, que se ha fortificado con parte de la gente de guarnición que tenía en su fuerte. Y ésta será de la mejor y los mejores capitanes. El viento lo tienen muy contrario para se volver a su puerto y fuerte, y el semblante es de manera que durará este viento muchos días. Y pues éstos son luteranos, y así lo tenemos entendido antes que partiésemos de España por los bandos que Juan Ribau, general de ellos, echaba en Françia al embarcar, que so pena de la vida no se embarcase ninguno que no fuese de la nueva religión, y so la mesma pena que no llevasen libros que no fuesen de esta secta, y también nos lo han certificado ellos mesmos [9r] cuando sobre el puerto estaba nuestra armada surta con la suya, que dijeron no había católico entre ellos, y queriéndolos ir a castigar dieron las velas y huyeron. Y por esto no se puede hacer la guerra que con éstos tenemos—y ellos con nosotros—sino a sangre y fuego, pues ellos, como luteranos, nos buscan a nosotros, que somos católicos, para que no plantemos en estas provinçias el Santo Evangelio. Y nosotros los buscamos a ellos por ser luteranos, para que no planten su mala [y detestable]³⁹ secta en esta tierra ni la enseñen a los indios. Paréceme que debemos tomar quinientos soldados, las dos partes de arcabuceros y la una de piqueros, y la ración de ocho días en nuestras mochilas, sin moços, con nuestras armas a cuestas, y que diez capitanes que sois, cada uno con su bandera y ofiçiales, con número de çincuenta personas cada capitán, vamos a reconocer el camino, tierra y fuerte donde los luteranos están, que aunque no sepamos el camino, por una aguja de navegar, dos leguas a mano derecha[40] o dos a mano izquierda, yo os sabré guiar. Y donde halláremos bosque abriremos el camino con las hachas para pasar y sabernos volver, que un francés traigo yo conmigo que ha estado en aquel fuerte más de un año que dice que la tierra de a dos leguas al derredor la conoçerá y nos sabrá llevar al fuerte. Y si vemos que no somos descubiertos podría ser que, a un cuarto del alba, plantando veinte escalas que haremos cuando estemos çerca de allá, a trueco de perder cincuenta soldados les ganemos el fuerte. Y cuando entendiéremos que somos descubiertos, pues estamos çiertos que a menos que cuarto de legua está el bosque. Plantando nuestras diez banderas por sus cuarteles a orilla de él, les parecerá [9v] tenemos número de más de dos mil hombres, y les podremos enviar una trompeta diciendo[41] que nos dejen el puerto y fuerte y se salgan de aquella tierra, y que se les dará navíos y bastimentos con que se vayan a Françia. Y, si no, que los pasaremos[42] todos a cuchillo. Y cuando no lo hiciesen habremos ganado mucho en reconoçer el camino, tierra y fuerte, y temernos han, de manera que será causa que nos dejen este invierno estar aquí seguros hasta el marzo venidero [de 1566], que tendremos recaudo para los ir a buscar así por mar como por tierra.

A esta plática que el Adelantado hizo hubo muchos dares y tomares, pareciendo a algunos que no se debía hacer la jornada y a otros que sí. Al fin se acordó que se hiciese. Mandoles allí el Adelantado que para el tercero día al alba oyesen todos misa, y acabándola de oír marchasen luego. Y mandó al maestro de campo—su deudo y desposado con su hija mayor— que se dice don Pero (Menéndez) de Valdés, y a Gonçalo de Villarruel, capitán y sargento mayor, que luego entendiesen en repartir la gente que había de ir y se les diese bastante recaudo de pólvora, mecha y plomo para que hiciesen pelotas y perdigones. Y proveyó que el capitán Bartolomé Menéndez, hermano del dicho Adelantado, quedase a su cargo la gente de tierra que allí había de quedar, artillería, armas y muniçiones y bastimentos, y que Diego Flórez de Valdés, que era almirante de la armada, quedase por capitán de la artillería y general de los tres navíos que allí quedaron de armada, teniéndolos a su cargo diestros y a la gente de mar de ellos. Y salidos de su junta, quedado esto acordado, luego fue público [10r] en el campo y se empeçaron a hacer y proveer estas cosas que el Adelantado había mandado, de que todo el campo mostró tener grandísimo contentamiento.

Otro día siguiente por la mañana, siendo informado el Adelantado que algunos capitanes murmuraban de la determinación que había tomado de ir a buscar al fuerte [a] los franceses (y esto lo dijeron tan público y lo justificaban de [tal] manera, que los soldados que el día primero mostraron tener gran contento de este acuerdo se vio claramente andaban desmayados). Y tenían acordado algunos capitanes, en especial Juan de San Vicente, Françisco de Recalde [y] Diego de Maya, que—como amigos del Adelantado—en acabando el Adelantado de comer le dijesen de parte de los más capitanes y gente que allí había que debía mudar consejo para que en ninguna manera fuese al puerto de los franceses. El Adelantado fue avisado de esto y mandó hacer muy bien de comer y que dijesen a los capitanes que se fuesen a comer con él y otros soldados caballeros que iban en la jornada, y a los más de los alférez. Y acabado de comer díjoles:

—Señores y hermanos míos, después que estamos en tierra hémosno[s] juntado los capitanes a consejo, el cual se hizo con gran secreto, y de las palabras que allí pasamos solos los que allí estábamos lo supimos, y no otros. Entiendo agora que todos los soldados y mujeres que aquí están lo saben, y tienen disputas y porfías entre sí sobre quién habló mejor o peor, de tal manera que se murmura de nuestra provisión y que es temeridad hacer lo acordado. Paréceme muy mal consejo, digno de gran reprehensión y castigo, y aunque sé quiénes son los más culpados de esto y están aquí, no quiero condenar a ninguno, mas de pediros, [10v] señores, por merced, que para adelante cada uno lo remedie con tener gran secreto en las cosas que en nuestros consejos se tratan, pues en las guerras, donde no hubiere esto—y diligencia—pocas veces se pueden tener buenos suçesos, y el que en esto hiciere pecado venial lo haré castigar por mortal, que bien se entiende claramente el capitán que está desmayado y teme esta jornada por sus soldados, porque los cincuenta soldados que han de ir con él, el desmayo que tienen es por él y su alférez, y no por ellos, y los soldados que andan diestros, limpiando sus armas y haciendo sus mochilas para tomar la ración, claro está que sus capitanes y ofiçiales los animan por estar ellos animados, y desean hacer la jornada.

Y [dijo] que si todavía les parecía se debía mudar consejo se lo dijesen, y que, salidos de allí, el capitán que de lo proveído murmurase le mandaría castigar, quitándole la compañía[43] y no le admitiendo en consejo. Todos respondieron que lo que Su Señoría decía era muy bien dicho, y que a unos le[s] pareçía debía de mudar consejo y a [o]tros les pareçía al contrario, que se debía de seguir el acuerdo y determinación que sobre esto estaba tomado. Y así le[s] dijo el Adelantado a los capitanes que cada uno trujese las mochilas al tenedor de bastimentos, y una persona que reçibiese las raçiones, para otro día al alba, en oyendo misa, marchar como estaba concertado. Y les mandó que cada uno fuese a entender en lo que había de hacer, y así se fueron.

Otro día al alba dieron la alborada con las trompetas y pífanos y atambores y repicaron las campanas. Acudieron todos a misa, y habiéndola oído se partieron con la buena ventura, saliendo todos, marchando en ordenança. El Adelantado tomó veinte [11r] soldados, todos vizcaínos y asturianos, con sus hachas, y un capitán vizcaíno con ellos que se decía Martín de Ochoa, y dos indios que allí se allegaron, hermanos, que pareçió ser ángeles que Dios enviaba, los cuales por señas dijeron que había seis días que estuvieron en el puerto de los françeses. Y se adelantó caminando adelante lo que podía, señalando el camino, cortando con las hachas en los árboles, para que la gente no lo errase y lo supiesen para la vuelta, dejando al maestro de campo y [al] Sargento Mayor que caminasen con buen orden, porque tenían temor a los indios [que], siendo amigos de los franceses, no les hiciesen algunas emboscadas, tirándoles de los bosques con los arcos. Y cuando le parecía al Adelantado hacer alto en lugar cómodo y donde hubiese agua para recoger la gente y que descansase, lo hacía, y aguardaba a que toda se recogiese y les dejaba orden de lo que habían de descansar, y se partía luego, abriendo el camino y señalándole, como está dicho, y volvía a hacer alto en la parte que le parecía para alojar aquella noche.

Y por esta orden, el cuarto día al poner del sol fue a reconoçer la tierra del fuerte a media legua de él, donde se paró.[44] Y por parecerle que la noche estaba tempestuosa y de muchas aguas, y que le convenía acercarse más por no ser descubierto, por entre un pinar se allegó a menos de cuarto de legua del fuerte, donde acordó alojar aquella noche, y en lugar harto malo y cenagoso, y volvió a buscar la retaguarda porque acertasen el camino, por la mala noche que hacía, y eran más de las diez de la noche cuando acabaron de llegar. Y como en estos cuatro días hubo muchas aguas y se pasaron muchas çiénagas y traían a [11v] cuestas las armas y las mochilas con la comida, la gente llegó[45] muy cansada y quebrantada. Y como el agua de aquella noche fue tanta no hubo remedio de salvar pólvora ni mecha que no se mojase todo, y el poco de bizcocho que tenían en las mochilas, y no tenían ninguna cosa en su cuerpo que no estuviese bañada en agua. Aquí temió mucho el Adelantado tomar consejo con los capitanes ni para volver atrás ni para llegar al puerto de los franceses, porque se empeçaban algunos a desvergonçar—y sus ofiçiales—diciendo contra él palabras injuriosas, y tan altas que él oía muchas de ellas, en especial un alférez del capitán San Vicente que se puso çerca del Adelantado y dijo alto por que él lo oyese:

—¡Cómo nos trae vendidos este asturiano corito, que no sabe de guerra de tierra más que un asno! Y, si fuera de mi consejo, el primer día que salió de San Agustín para hacer este camino se le había de dar el pago que agora ha de llevar.

Entonces el Adelantado temió más, e hizo que no le entendía.

El capitán San Vicente, de quien éste era alférez, al tiempo del partir de San Agustín dijo que le dolía una pierna y el estómago, y quedose. Y de su quedada se murmuró mucho, y de las palabras disolutas de su alférez, porque se averiguó que, reprehendiendo al capitán San Viçente algunos de los que quedaban porque no había ido con el Adelantado, les respondió[46] diciendo:

—¡Voto a Dios que aguardo cuándo vienen las nuevas que todos los nuestros están degollados, para que los que aquí nos[47] [12r] quedamos nos embarquemos en estos tres navíos e irnos a las Indias, que no es razón muramos todos como bestias!

El Adelantado, como dos horas antes del día, envió a cuatro soldados que estaban çerca de él, criados suyos, que fuesen corriendo a la gente y le llamasen al maestro de campo, [al] Sargento Mayor y [a los demás] capitanes que se juntasen allí con él, y así lo hicieron. Y estando todos juntos les dijo:

—Señores, yo, aunque gran pecador, toda esta noche he suplicado a Nuestro Señor y a su Preciosa Madre nos favorezca y encamine en lo que hubiéremos de hacer, y así creo, señores, lo habréis vosotros hecho. Tratemos qué será bueno que hagamos conforme al punto en que estamos, y sin municiones ni comida, y la gente muy cansada, perdida y desmayada.

Respondiéronle algunos que para qué se había de tratar en otro acuerdo mas de que, en siendo día, se retirasen y volviesen a Santo Agustín, comiendo palmitos. Y que tratar otra cosa parecía temeridad. El Adelantado aprobó esto y les dijo:

—Señores, por amor de Dios que me oigáis una razón y no recibáis desgusto porque la diga, que no es para que hagáis lo que diré, sino lo que quisiéredes y os pareçiere, porque hasta aquí siempre habéis tomado mi pareçer y consejo, y agora que me veo en este gran peligro quiero tomar el vuestro.

Ellos le dijeron que Su Señoría lo dijese, que holgaban de oírle y decir su pareçer. Entonces les dijo:

—Señores, ¿estáis satisfechos que el bosque está muy cerca del fuerte?

Respondieron que sí. Díjoles:

—Pues paréceme [12v] que debemos de ir a probar nuestra ventura como está acordado, que no tenemos que temer, cuando el fuerte no podamos ganar, de pensar, cuando les inviemos la trompeta, que han de salir de su fuerte a buscarnos a la orilla del bosque, donde estaremos hecho alto por nuestros cuarteles, arboladas nuestras banderas. Y para esto poca falta nos ha de hacer la pólvora ni cuerda, porque si cuando fuésemos descubiertos por la mañana nos retiramos, los enemigos cobrarán ánimo y nos ternán por cobardes y nos ternán en poco, y esto les será gran prinçipio de victoria.

Respondieron algunos capitanes, en especial el maestro de campo y [el] Sargento Mayor, que les pareció buena razón, y que se debía llevar hasta el cabo el designio y determinación acordada en este caso. Y dando y tomando con los que les parecía otra cosa, todos fueron de acuerdo que así se hiciese.

Entonces el Adelantado mandó a todos hincarse de rodillas y rezar su oración a Nuestro Señor, suplicándole les diese victoria contra sus enemigos en aquella empresa y peligro que cometían. Y esta oración hicieron luego con tanta devoçión como si sus enemigos estuvieran delante, queriéndoles dar la batalla. Y, acabada, señalando los capitanes que habían de ir en vanguardia y retaguardia y de la manera y por las partes que cada uno había de acometer al fuerte, y encargándoles que por amor de Dios cada uno animase sus soldados, mandó marchar, yendo él en la delantera guiando, llevando el francés que traían por guía las manos atrás amarradas con un cordel, y el cabo de él en la mano.

Sería una hora antes del día, y antes de ser pasado[48] un cuarto de ella, por ser tanta la escuridad[49] y tempestad del viento y agua, errose el camino porque era una senda muy angosta, de tal [13r] manera que algunos pensaban que iban adelante y volvían atrás. Y como esto entendió el Adelantado, y pareciéndole que la retaguarda podía marchar diferente que la vanguardia, de mano en mano mandó hacer alto, y que hasta el día ninguno se meneease de donde estaba, de temor que no se perdiesen unos de otros. Y esto hicieron muchos de ellos en una çiénaga de agua que daba encima de las rodillas, y el Adelantado fue uno de ellos. Y venido el día, el francés reconoció por dónde había de guiar, y el Adelantado marchó sin orden con toda priesa, mandando de mano en mano que todos le siguiesen, so pena de la vida, porque le pareçió no era tiempo de tomar consejo de lo que habían de hacer porque estaban apartados buen trecho unos capitanes de otros. Y llegando a un altecico el francés le dijo que detrás de allí estaba el fuerte en lo bajo, y que el agua del río batía en él, y que habría como tres tiros de arcabuz. El Adelantado dio el francés a Francisco de Castañeda, que era capitán de su guarda, que nunca se le quitaba del lado, y [abajá]ndose muy presto del alto[50] descubrió el río y vio unas casas, y no pudo ver el fuerte, aunque estaba junto a ellas, y volviendo a donde había dejado al capitán de la guarda con el francés que era cerca, halló al maestro de campo, que había llegado, y al capitán Martín Ochoa, y díjoles:

—Hermanos, yo quiero abajar a este llano con çinco o seis soldados, donde están unas casas, a ver si puedo descubrir la centinela, para que nos informemos de la fortaleza de éstos y la gente que tienen, porque como es ya día claro y el sol salido no podemos sin reconocer el fuerte acometer sin pólvora.

Entonces dijo el maestro de campo que Su Señoría [13v] se quedase, que aquel ofiçio era suyo, y tomó consigo a sólo el capitán Martín Ochoa, sin querer llevar otra persona por no ser descubiertos, y llegando cerca de las casas descubrieron el fuerte. Y volviéndose con la nueva hallaron dos sendas, y no tomaron por la que habían ido, y andando un poco por ella encontraron un árbol caído. Entonces dijo el maestro de campo que iban errados. Como el capitán Martín de Ochoa iba detrás, al tiempo que dieron la vuelta anduvo delante. Pareçe que ellos fueron descubiertos de la centinela, el cual pensó que eran françeses e iba a reconocerlos, y encontró con ellos, y como no los conoçió detúvose, diciendo:

—Qui [va] là?

Respondió el Martín de Ochoa:

—Fra[n]soi.[51]

Y pareciéndole a la centinela eran francese[s] se fue allegando más, y el Martín Ochoa hizo lo mesmo, y cuando el francés no lo conoçió, se paró,[52] y el capitán Martín Ochoa cerró con él, y con vaina y todo le dio una cuchillada po[r] la cara, aunque no le hizo gran herida porque se la rebatió con la espada. Y echaron mano a sus espadas, y llegó el maestro de campo, que ya traía la suya desenvainada, con una rodela [en la mano],[53] y calándole una estocada, y el francés, por retirarse de ella, cayó para tras y a esto dio gritos. El maestro de campo le puso la punta del espada sobre el pecho, diciendo que callase, si no que le mataría, y el francés lo hizo así. [Levantáronle][54] y lleváronle asido al Adelantado, preguntándole por el fuerte y la gente que estaba en él. A las voces que este francés dio pareciole al Adelantado mataban al maestro de campo y [al] capitán Martín Ochoa, y estando ya cabe él recogidos algunos capitanes y banderas, en especial el Sargento Mayor y Francisco de Recalde, y Diego de Maya y Andrés López Patiño, con sus banderas y gente, dijo el Adelantado en altas voces:

—¡Santiago y a ellos! ¡Dios! ¡Ayuda! ¡Victoria! ¡Degollados son los franceses! ¡El maestro de campo está dentro [d]el fuerte y le tiene ganado!

Y entonçes [14r] [todos sin orden][55] fueron corriendo por la senda adelante, y el Adelantado se estuvo quedo, diciendo esto siempre sin parar. La gente tuvo por cierto que con el maestro de campo había ido mucha gente y que el fuerte estaba ganado. Recibieron grande alegría y contento, en tanta manera que el que más podía correr se tenía por más valiente, y no había ninguno cojo, manco, ni cobarde. Y como dieron luego por donde el maestro de campo y el Martín Ochoa venían con el francés, el Martín Ochoa vino sin orden corriendo a pedir las albricias al Adelantado y a decirle que la centinela traían presa. El maestro de campo, temiendo no ser descubierto,[56] caló una estocada al francés que le pasó, y dejándole muerto tomó la delantera, diciéndoles:

—Hermanos, hace[d] como yo, que Dios es con nosotros.

Y encuentra luego con dos fra[n]çeses en camisa y mató él uno de ellos, el otro el capitán Andrés López Patiño, que le iba detrás. Y pasó corriendo, y llegando junto del fuerte, a las voces que la gente del arrabal dio cuando vieron matar los dos françeses, abrieron el postigo de la puerta prençipal, y cerró con él el maestro de campo y mató al que lo abrió, y colose[57] dentro, y tras él los que más presto pudieron entrar. Y no pudiendo cerrar, abrieron, y entrados dentro hallaron muchos franceses que salían de las casas en camisa, y otros vestidos, a reconocer lo que era.[58] Éstos fueron luego muertos, y otros se retiraban y echaban de las murallas abajo. Entraron luego dos banderas, la una fue del Sargento Mayor, que arboló en un caballero su alférez que se dice Rodrigo Troche, de Tordesillas, y la otra de Diego de

Maya, que arboló su alférez Cristóbal de Herrera, montañés, en otro caballero. Hubo diferencias entre estos dos alféreces sobre cuál fue el primero, y no se pudo averiguar. Y juntamente con estas dos banderas entraron las trompetas y se pusieron estos dos caballeros junto a las banderas, [14v] tocando victoria, a la cual victoria desmayaron todos los franceses y acudió de golpe toda nuestra gente por la puerta, que se les abrió toda, y dan en los cuarteles de los franceses sin dejar ninguno a vida.

El Adelantado aguardó hasta que hubo pasado la meitad de la gente y dijo a Francisco de Castañeda,[59] capitán de su guarda, a quien había encomendado el francés con las manos atrás, que se quedase cantando la victoria[60] hasta que la retaguarda llegase, porque le convenía alcançar los delanteros y hallarse en aquel peligro, y así lo hizo. Y corriendo con toda furia llegó al fuerte, que andaban matando nuestros soldados a los franceses. Entonçes dijo en altas voces, acudiendo a una parte y a otra, que so pena de la vida ninguno hiriese ni matase mujer ni mochachos de quince años abajo, y así se hizo, que se salvaron setenta personas de éstas. Los demás murieron todos, salvo cincuenta o sesenta que se echaron de la muralla abajo y se acogieron al bosque de que el Adelantado había salido.[61]

El Adelantado se salió luego del fuerte a unas casas que estaban çerca de la muralla donde llegaba el capitán Castañeda con el francés, el cual señaló una casa grande que él dijo que llamaban La Granja,[62] que estaba llena de rescates, paños y lienços y otras municiones. El Adelantado dejó allí seis hombres de guarda para que ninguno entrase dentro, para que todo lo que allí estaba fuese de todo el campo generalmente para lo gastar y destribuir con los que tuviesen más necesidad, y acudió a la marina, donde estaban tres naos con sus proízas amarradas y muy bien artilladas, y llamando una trompeta la hizo tocar con señal de paz, poniendo un paño blanco por bandera y diciendo que viniesen [15r] en tierra con el batel. Los franceses respondieron que no querían, y el Adelantado les hacía segurança que sobre su palabra podían venir. No quisieron.

Acudió al fuerte e hizo poner en orden cuatro pieças de artillería de bronce para los echar a fondo, y anduvo buscando la pólvora, y halló en la casa de un lombardero que una frances[a] les mostró dos barriles que tenían como un quintal y hasta veinte balas, con las cuales atacaron las pieças, y echándoles sus balas. Y antes de poner fuego les volvieron a decir que viniesen con el batel a tierra. Respondieron de la nao [a] donde el Adelantado hablaba que lo enviarían por que fuese alguna[63] persona a hablar con ellos a decirles lo que quería el Adelantado, el cual respondió que viniesen. Para que creyesen lo que les dijese tomó el francés que traía amarrado y soltole, y díjole que fuese a aquellas naos y dijese al principal mandador de ellas que tomasen de todas tres la nao que quisiesen, y las mujeres y mochachos que se habían salvado, y el bastimento que fuese menester, y se fuesen a Françia con Dios, sin que llevasen ninguna artillería ni municiones, porque él les daría pasaporte y salvoconducto para que en cualquier parte que llegasen no les hiciesen maltratamiento y los dejasen ir a Francia seguros, y si esto no hiciesen los echarían al fondo y mandaría degollar y ahorcar sin dejar ninguno. El batel vino a tierra y el francés fue en él con esta embajada, que ya entonces había mandado el Adelantado al Sargento Mayor repartir entre los soldados un barril de pólvora de arcabuz muy buena que estaba en casa de aquel lombardero con la pólvora de cañón.

[15v] El françés volvió con la respuesta al Adelantado y díjole que el mandador principal de aquellos navíos era Ja[c]ques Ribau, hijo Mayor de Juan Ribao, que decía era virrey y capitán-general de aquella tierra por el Rey de Fançia, y que él había venido por mandado de su rey en compañía de su padre a traer gente, artillería y bastimentos con aquellas naos a aquel fuerte, en lo cual no había cometido delito, antes había hecho como buen vasallo lo que era obligado, y que si el Adelantado pensaba hacerle guerra, él se la haría al Adelantado. Entonces el Adelantado mandó hacer puntería con la mejor pieça de artillería de bronce a una nao, de las mejores que le pareçió, que era nueva del primero viaje, y que estaba a propósito, porque las otras dos no lo estaban tanto para las batir. El capitán Diego de Maya, pareciéndole que él haría aquella puntería mejor que otro, la hizo, y dio fuego a la pieça. Acertó a la nao a la lumbre del agua, de tal manera que los franceses entendieron que se anegaban, y no pudían dar a la bomba porque habían de estar descubiertos encima de cubierta y los pudiera[n] matar con la artillería.

Los franceses que dentro de la nao estaban, cuando vieron su perdición, por un lado de ella se metieron en un batel, y acudieron a ella los dos bateles de las otras naos y trujeron toda la gente de aquella nao a las dos, la cual nao se fue al fondo. Y las otras dos cortaron luego los proíces, y con la gran corriente que había dejáronse ir por el río abajo y surg[i]eron en parte que con la artillería no se les pudía hacer mucho daño, en especial [16r] que el Adelantado no se atrevía a gastar la pólvora, porque hasta entonces no se había podido hallar más en el fuerte. Y en todo este tiempo era el viento y

agua del cielo tanta que era cosa de admiración. Y como los soldados andaban alegres de la victoria y saco no atendían a recogerse para repararse de
los trabajos que habían tenido y mala noche. Por lo que tocaba al bien de
todos los hizo alojar en muchas casas que había fuera del fuerte, de veinte
en veinte, y darles todo recaudo de camisas y vestidos, porque había en
cantidad de ello dentro de la casa de La Granja, y darles buenas raciones de
pan y vino, manteca y tocino, que había cantidad de ello. Y él se desnudó y
acostó en una cama, y esto sería a mediodía, donde le dieron de comer. Y
mandó a los capitanes que para las cuatro horas de la tarde acudiesen todos
a él porque quería entrar con ellos en consejo, y así lo hicieron, donde el
Adelantado, habiéndose levantado y vestido les dijo a todos juntos, arra-
sándosele los ojos de agua:

—Señores y hermanos míos, estas cosas Dios milagrosamente las hace
y vuelve por su causa. Sepamos alabarle y servirle por tan gran merced
como nos ha hecho. Y agora es tiempo que nos encomendemos a Él más
que nunca y proveamos nuestras cosas[64] de manera que defendamos esta
plaça a la armada françesa cuando ella vuelva, y aseguremos nuestra gente,
artillería, armas y muniçiones y bastimentos que dejamos en San Agustín.
Y para esto hágase luego reseña de la gente que aquí estamos, porque me
parece falta mucho de los quinientos soldados que salimos de San [16v]
Agustín, para ver la que aquí quedare y para la que se volverá a San Agustín,
porque conviene yo me vuelva pasado mañana con la que hubiere de ir,
porque es necesario que aquello esté a buen recaudo para que, defendiendo
esto a los françeses cuando vengan con su armada, que no pongan pie en la
tierra, y que no se nos vayan a desembarcar a Santo Agustín, que es mejor
puerto.

E hizo alcaide de aquel fuerte y gobernador de aquel distrito[65] al capitán
Gonçalo de Villarroel,[66] que era sargento mayor, el cual había trabajado muy
bien y con mucha orden y cuidado y era muy buen soldado de gobierno y
toda confiança. Se lo entregó y tomó el juramento acostumbrado, y púsole
nombre el Fuerte de San Mateo, por ser aquel día que se ganó día de San
Mateo. Y mandó que desde aquel día en adelante él [lo] tuviese y defendiese
en nombre de Su Majestad con tre[s]cientos soldados que para guarda de
él le dejaría. Y mandó al maestro de campo fuese luego a hacer la lista[67] de
toda la gente que había y de la que había de quedar y volver con el Adelantado, y así lo hizo, llevando consigo al Sargento Mayor, habiendo primero
en este consejo nombrado el Adelantado a Rodrigo Montes, por tenedor de

bastimentos en aquel fuerte, y que se le entregase todo el bastimento que había y le trujesen otro día por la mañana la memoria del entrego para dejar instrucción de la manera que se habían de dar las raçiones. Y acordó el Adelantado en aquel consejo [17r] que luego se quitasen dos escudos de armas que estaban sobre la puerta de este fuerte prinçipal,[68] del Rey de Françia y del Almirante. Y cuando las iban a quitar ya un soldado las había quitado, despedaçado y quemado. Mandó que se hiciese luego un escudo con las armas reales de España del rey don Felipe nuestro señor con una Cruz de los Ángeles encima de la corona, el cual pintaron muy bien unos flamencos que allí iban por soldados, y se puso en la parte que las otras estaban.

Otro día por la mañana, habiendo oído misa, el Adelantado hizo arbolar dos cruces en las partes que mejor le pareçía. Señaló el lugar para una iglesia donde se hiciese luego una capilla para decir cada día misa, de tabla aserrada, que los franceses tenían allí mucha para una galera que estaban haciendo. Y dándole memoria del bastimento que se había hallado, dio instrucçión a Gonçalo de Villarroel, alcaide y gobernador de aquel fuerte y distrito,[69] de cómo se había de gastar el bastimento y dar las raciones. Trajéronle la lista de la gente que había. Halláronse menos de cuatrocientas personas, porque las demás, a cumplimiento de quinientas, unos de cansados no habían llegado, y otros de cobardes—por el peligro que se les representaba—se volvieron a San Agustín, diciendo que habían errado el camino, según después esto se averig[u]ó.

El Adelantado mandó que se quedasen los tre[s]cientos [17v] soldados y se fuesen con él los çiento con los capitanes Andrés López Patiño y Juan Vélez de Medrano y [Diego] de Alvarado,[70] los cuales capitanes y soldados dijeron[71] que no estaban para poder caminar, en espeçial que como había llovido mucho era imposible poder pasar las ciénagas, ríos y arroyos que había en el camino. Y aunque el Adelantado procuró mucho que fuesen, vio no ser posible por la mucha razón que tenían y poca voluntad de ir y estar muy cansados y fatigados del trabajo del camino. Entonçes recorrió los[72] alojamientos donde estaban los soldados, y de los menos cansados y más sus conoçidos halló treinta y çinco que le quisieron seguir. Y con el capitán de su guarda los aperçibió para partir otro día por la mañana.

Mandó el Adelantado que el maestro de campo partiese luego, que serían las nueve del día, con çincuenta soldados, a una legua de allí, derechos a donde las naos francesas estaban surtas, porque aquella mañana se habían alçado las áncoras y se habían ido allí porque les pareçió que los cincuenta o sesenta franceses que se habían echado de la muralla abajo cuando el fuerte se les ganó acudieron por el monte derecho de las naos a llamar los bateles para meterse dentro de ellos.[73] Llevó el maestro de campo esta gente repartida por el bosque. Encontraron con hasta veinte françeses que, yendo huyendo y no los pudiendo alcançar, les tiraron con los arcabuces y los mataron. Y [18r] los demás[74] se habían embarcado como treinta, y entre ellos el capitán Luduniel, alcaide del fuerte, que se escapó echándose de la muralla abajo con los demás. Los otros diez se habían acogido a los caçiques, que después los hizo rescatar el Adelantado e invió a Francia, los cuales dijeron cómo el Luduniel con los[75] treinta se habían embarcado en aquellos navíos.

Y vuelto el maestro de campo aquel día a la noche, y el capitán Martín Ochoa y Diego de Maya con la gente que habían llevado, el Adelantado mandó llamar a todos los capitanes a consejo y les dijo que para la mañana sería su partida para Santo Agustín, donde enviaría lu[e]go dos navíos de los tres que había dejado allí, bien armados con buena artillería, para que tomasen aquellas dos naves francesas y que saliesen del puerto, porque tenían poca gente, según habían entendido de los françeses que allí estaban. Y cuando fuesen idos plantarían la artillería que los dos navíos llevasen en el fuerte, en las partes más necesarias, para estar más fortificados cuando los franceses viniesen, porque siempre el Adelantado temió que cuando la armada francesa volviese con los indios amigos habían de querer volver a ganar aquella plaça y vengarse. Y que uno de estos navíos llevaría estas mujeres y moços a la isla de Santo Domingo y escribiría a la Audiencia para que los enviasen a Sevilla y de allí fuesen a Francia. Y daría instrucción a los maestres de estos dos navíos para que cargasen de bastimentos del galeón *San Pelayo* que el Adelantado había enviado [18v] a aquella isla de Santo Domingo.

Y otro día por la mañana, habiendo oído misa, el Adelantado se partió con Francisco de Castañeda, capitán de su guardia, y con los treinta y cinco soldados que tenía señalados, y mandó al maestro de campo y más capitanes quedasen en aquel fuerte hasta que otra cosa les mandase. Y que los tres capitanes [Diego de] Alvarado y [Juan Vélez de] Medrano y [Andrés López] Patiño, con el cumplimiento de los cien soldados, se partiesen a San Agustín luego que estuviesen buenos para caminar sin perder tiempo, los cuales lo hicieron así dentro de ocho días.[76]

Primera masacre de hugonotes

Los trabajos y peligros que el Adelantado y los que con él se volvieron pasaron este día que partió de San Mateo, y el segundo y tercero hasta llegar a San Agustín, fueron tantos que no se pueden creer sino quien los vio, porque este día que partió de San Mateo, habiendo caminado dos leguas, serían las dos después de mediodía, entró en un monte por donde había ido, y habiendo andado por él media legua halló mucha agua, y pensando salir presto de ella caminó más de otra legua, y hallaba cada vez más agua, de manera que no pudo pasar adelante, y volviendo atrás iban creciendo los arroyos y el agua del monte, y erró el camino, de tal manera que ni sabía si iba para tras o si para delante. Quiso volver a lugar donde pudiese hacer alto y fuego para descansar aquella noche. No lo pudo hallar. Y quererse subir encima de los árboles, eran tan altos y derechos que no fue posible. Allí se vio del todo perdido y sus compañeros desmayados. No sabiendo remedio que se tomar hizo subir [19r] a un soldado, el más suelto que halló, ençima de un árbol, el más alto que halló, para que descubriese si pudía ver algún raso o parte enjuta, el cual dijo—estando arriba—que todo cuanto vía era agua, y que no vía raso ni tierra enjuta. Mandole el Adelantado que mirase si pudía ver algún semblante por donde el sol iba. Dijo que no. Mandole estar quedo hasta más tarde, que quiso Dios que aclaró un poco, y el soldado vido a la parte que el sol se iba a poner y señaló a dónde. El Adelantado reconoçió por dónde había de salir del monte, que eran árboles muy ralos y limpios por debajo. Cortando algunos pinos en las partes hondas vino a salir a un río estrecho y hondo que él había pasado cuando vino de San Agustín a San Mateo con la gente, aunque no por aquel lugar. Y de los árboles que estaban a la orilla del río, con cinco hachas que llevaban los soldados, cortó por el pie, de manera que venían a caer de la otra banda del río, y lo pasaron con harto peligro, y al pasar se escaparon de no ahogarse milagrosamente dos soldados. Y mandó subir sobre un árbol al soldado que primero había subido, y descubrió a una parte tierra enjuta por donde habían venido, y salieron a la senda y fueron a alojar a una parte de tierra enjuta donde hicieron grandes fuegos. Enjugaron lo que llevaban vestido, que todo iba bañado[77] en agua.

Y sobre el día empeçó a llover muy mucho, y siendo ya claro se partieron. Tardaron en llegar a San Agustín tres días, que con la victoria que Nuestro Señor les había dado no [19v] sentían el camino ni los trabajos de él, con el deseo que tenían de dar estas nuevas buenas a sus compañeros. Pidió por merced aquel soldado al Adelantado una legua antes de llegar a San Agustín le dejase adelantar para dar las buenas nuevas. Concedióselo el Adelantado, y cuando la recibieron los que allí habían quedado (que, según el mal tiempo que habían llevado y las nuevas que daban los que se habían vuelto, teníanlos por perdidos, a causa que sabían[78] no tener ningún género de comida ni pólvora ni cuerda), y salen luego todos los clérigos que allí estaban con la cruz y con todas las personas de mar y guerra, mujeres y niños, en procesión y cantando el Te Deum Laudamus. Reçibieron al Adelantado con gran placer y alegría, riéndose y llorando todos de placer, alabando a Dios Nuestro Señor por tan gran victoria. Y así le metieron con este triunfo en la trinche[r]a y lugar de San Agustín, donde les contó particularmente la merced tan grande que Nuestro Señor les había hecho con la victoria. Y proveyó luego los dos navíos armados, y dentro de dos días, estando para partir a San Mateo con ellos, vino aviso que las dos naos francesas habían ya salido de la barra. E invió el uno de ellos con artillería, pólvora y muniçiones para que plantasen en el fuerte y estuviesen con toda buena defensa, y él se ocupó en fortificarse allí lo mejor que pudo para aguardar la armada françesa, si allí viniese.

Y otro día siguiente llegaron unos indios y por señas les dijeron que cuatro leguas de allí estaban muchos cristianos [20r] no pudiendo pasar un braço de mar, aunque estrecho, que es una ría que está dentro de una barra, porque para llegar a San Agustín le habían de pasar forçosamente. El Adelantado tomó luego consigo aquella tarde cuarenta soldados y fue después de la medianoche cerca de aquel braço de mar, donde hizo alto. A la mañana, dejando sus soldados emboscados, de sobre un árbol descubrió lo que había. Vido mucha gente[79] de la otra banda del río y dos banderas, y para impedirles que no pasasen llegose tan çerca el dicho Adelantado que los pudiesen contar,[80] para que pensasen que había mucha gente. Y como fueron descubiertos luego se pasó un hombre a nado. Era francés, y dijo que la gente que allí estaba eran todos franceses que se habían perdido con tormenta, y que toda la gente había escapado.

Preguntole el Adelantado qué franceses eran. Dijo que seiscientas personas, capitanes y gente de Juan Ribau,[81] visrey y capitán de aquella tierra por el Rey de Françia. Preguntoles si eran católicos o luteranos. Dijo que todos eran luteranos de la nueva religión, aunque esto ya lo sabía el Adelantado, que ellos lo habían dicho cuando encontró su armada, y las mujeres y moços a quien dio la vida cuando ganó el fuerte se lo habían dicho, y les halló dentro del fuerte seis cofres llenos de libros encuadernados [20v] y dorados, todos de la nueva religión, y no decían misa, y que se les predicaba cada tarde su secta luterana, los cuales libros mandó quemar sin dejar ninguno.

Preguntole el Adelantado que a qué venían. Dijo que el capitán de ellos le inviaba a ver qué gente eran.[82] Díjole el Adelantado que si se quería volver. Respondió que sí, mas que querría saber qué gente era. Éste hablaba muy claro porque era gascón de San Juan de Luz. Entonçes le dijo el Adelantado que dijese a su capitán que era el visrey y capitán-general de aquella tierra por el rey don Felipe, y que se llamaba Pedro Menéndez, que estaba allí con algunos soldados a reconoçer qué gentes eran ellos, porque habían tenido aviso un día antes que estaban allí y llegaba a aquella hora.

El françés se fue con la embajada y volvió luego, diciendo que le diesen segurança a su capitán y a otros cuatro gentileshombres que querían ir a verse con él, y que les prestasen un batel que allí tenía el Adelantado que había llegado entonces por el río con bastimento. Y respondieron al françés que dijese a su capitán que pudía venir seguramente debajo de su palabra. Y luego envió por ellos con el batel y vinieron luego. El Adelantado los recibió muy bien con hasta diez personas y los demás mandó estar un poco apartados entre unas matas para que se pudiesen [21r] descubrir todos, de manera que los franceses pensasen que había más gente. Dijo uno de estos françeses que él era capitán de aquella gente y que con tormenta se habían perdido cuatro galeones y otras chalupas del Rey de Françia en término de veinte leguas una de otra, y que ellos eran la gente de la una nao, y que querían que los favoreçiese para pasar con aquel batel aquel braço de mar y otro que estaba cuatro leguas de allí, que era el de San Agustín, que se querían ir a un fuerte que tenían veinte leguas de allí. Éste era el que el Adelantado les ganó. Preguntole el Adelantado si eran católicos o luteranos. Dijo que todos eran de la nueva religión. Entonçes les dijo el Adelantado:

—Señores, vuestro fuerte es ganado y la gente de él degollada, si no son las mujeres y mochachos de quince años abajo. Y para que sepáis çierto que es así, entre algunos soldados de los que aquí están hay muchas cosas, y hay dos françeses que yo traje conmigo que dijeron eran católicos. Sentáos aquí y comeréis, que yo os enviaré los dos franceses y las cosas que aquellos soldados han tomado del fuerte para que os satisfagáis.

El Adelantado lo hizo así, mandándoles dar de comer, y les envió los dos françeses y muchas cosas que los soldados habían ganado en el fuerte para que las viesen, y retirose a comer con su gente. Y de allí a una hora, ya que vio que los françeses habían comido, fue donde estaban y díjoles que si estaban satisfechos de lo que les había dicho. Dijeron que sí, que le pedían por merced que les diese navíos y matalotaje con que se pudiesen ir a França. Respondioles el Adelantado que [21v] él lo hiciera de buena gana si ellos fueran católicos y tuvieran navíos para ello, mas no los tenía porque los dos enviábalos a San Mateo con la artillería, y que llevasen las francesas y moços[83] a Santo Domingo, [y] a buscar bastimento. El otro había de ir de aviso a Su Majestad con lo sucedido[84] hasta entonçes en aquellas partes.

El capitán françés le respondió que otorgase a todos la vida y que se estarían con él hasta que hubiese navíos para França, pues no tenían guerra el Rey de España y França, y eran hermanos y amigos. El Adelantado les respondió que era la verdad, y que a los católicos y amigos él los favoreçería, entendiendo que servía a entrambos reyes en ello, mas que por ser ellos de la nueva religión los tenía por enemigos, y tenía con ellos guerra a sangre y fuego, y que ésta la haría con toda crueldad a los que él hallase en aquella mar y tierra donde era visrey y capitán-general por su rey. Y que iba a plantar el Santo Evangelio en aquella tierra por que fuesen alumbrados los indios y viviesen en conocimiento de la Santa Fe Católica de Jesucristo Nuestro[85] Señor, como lo dice y canta la Iglesia Romana, que si ellos quieren entregarles las banderas y las armas y ponerse a misericordia lo pueden hacer, para que él haga de ellos lo que Dios le diere de gracia, o que hagan lo que quisieren, que otras treguas ni amistades no había de hacer con él.

Y aunque el capitán françés replicó no se pudo acabar otra cosa con el Adelantado, y así se partió para su gente en el bajel en el que habían venido, diciendo que les iba a decir lo que pasaba y acordar lo que habían de hacer, y que dentro [22r] de dos horas volvería con la respuesta. El Adelantado les dijo que hiciesen lo que mejor les pareçiese y que él aguardaría.

Pasadas dos horas volvió este mismo capitán francés con los mesmos que primero y dijo al Adelantado que allí estaba mucha gente noble que le darían cincuenta mil ducados de talla porque otorgase a todos la vida. El Adelantado les respondió que, aunque era pobre soldado, que no quería hacer aquella flaqueza porque no le notasen de codiçioso, que cuando hubiese de ser liberal y misericordioso había de serlo sin interés. Volvió a porfiar en esto el capitán francés. Desengañole el Adelantado que si la tierra se juntaba con el çielo no había de hacer otra cosa más de lo que le tenía ya dicho. Y así volvió el capitán françés a donde estaba su gente y dijo al Adelantado que con lo que acordasen volvería luego. Y así volvió dentro de media hora y metió en el batel las banderas y hasta sesenta arcabuces y veinte pistoletes y cantidad de espadas y rodelas, y algunas çeladas y pectos. Y vínose a donde el Adelantado estaba y dijo que todos aquellos françeses se rendían a su misericordia, y entregoles las banderas y las armas.

Entonçes mandó el Adelantado entrar veinte soldados en el batel y que trujesen los franceses de diez en diez. El río era estrecho y fácil de pasar. Mandó a Diego Flórez de Valdés, almirante de la armada, recibiese las banderas y armas y anduviese con diligençia en el batel a hacer pasar los françeses, que no les hiciesen mal tratamiento los soldados. Y apartose[86] el Adelantado [22v] de la marina como dos tiros de arcabuz, detrás de un medano de arena, entre unas matas, donde la gente que en el batel venía que pasaba los franceses no los podía ver. Entonçes dijo al capitán francés y a otros ocho franceses que con él estaban:

—Señores, yo tengo poca gente, y no muy conocida, y vosotros sois muchos. Y andando sueltos fácil cosa sería satisfaceros de nosotros por la gente que os degollamos cuando ganamos el fuerte. Y así es menester que con las manos atrás, amarrados, marchéis de aquí ocho leguas, donde yo tengo mi real.

Respondieron los franceses que se hiciese así, y con los cordones de las mechas de los soldados les amarraban así las manos muy bien atrás. Y los diez que venían en el batel no vían a los otros que les amarraban las manos hasta dar con ellos, porque convino hacerse así a causa que los françeses que no habían pasado el río no lo entendiesen y se ascandalizasen. Y así ataron do[s]cientos y ocho franceses, a los cuales preguntó el Adelantado si había entre ellos algunos católicos que se quisiesen confesar. Y ocho de ellos dijeron que lo eran. Sacolos de allí y metiolos en el batel para que los llevasen por el río a San Agustín. Los otros respondieron que ellos eran de la nueva religión y se tenían por muy buenos cristianos, y que ésta era su ley y no otra.

El Adelantado mandó marchar con ellos, habiéndoles primero dado de comer y beber, cuando llegaban los diez, antes que los amarrase[n], lo cual se hacía antes que los otros diez viniesen. Y dijo a un capitán de los suyos que se decía Juan de San Vicente[87] que marchase con ellos en la vanguardia, y que a un tiro de [23r] ballesta de allí hallaría una raya que haría con una gineta que llevaría en la mano, que era en un arenal por donde habían de caminar al puerto de Santo Agustín, que los degollasen a todos. Y mandó al que iba en la retaguarda hiciese lo mismo, y así se hizo, dejándolos todos muertos. Y se volvió aquella noche al amaneçer al puerto de Santo Agustín, porque era ya puesto el sol cuando éstos murieron.

Capítulo 4

Segunda masacre de hugonotes

Y[88] otro día siguiente que el Adelantado llegó a Santo Agustín vinieron los mesmos indios que de antes y dijeron que muchos más cristianos estaban de aquella parte del río donde los otros. El Adelantado entendió que éste debía de ser Juan Ribao, general de los luteranos en la mar y en la tierra, a quien ellos llamaban visrey de aquella tierra por el Rey de Françia, y luego fue con çiento y çincuenta soldados bien en orden y llegó a alojar donde la primera vez a la medianoche. Y al alba púsose junto del río con su gente tendida, y como aclaró el día vido [a] dos tiros de arcabuz, de la otra banda del río, mucha gente, y una balsa hecha para pasar la gente a la parte donde el Adelantado estaba. Luego los franceses, como vieron al Adelantado y su gente, tocaron arma y desplega[ro]n un estandarte real y dos banderas de campaña, tocando pífanos y atambores con muy buena orden, y representa[ro]n la batalla al Adelantado, el cual había mandado a su gente que se sentasen y almorzasen y que no se hiciese ninguna demostraçión de alteraçión. Y paseándose [por la marina][89] su almirante y otros dos capitanes, no haciendo caso de la alteraçión y demostraçión de batalla de los franceses, de tal manera que ellos se debieron de correr, y en su ordenança como estaban hicieron alto, [23v] dejando de tocar los pífanos y atambores, y con un clarín que tocaron arbolaron un paño blanco de paz.

Y el Adelantado llamó luego a otro clarín que traía muy bueno y sacó de la faltriquera un pañizuelo[90] y empeçó a campear con él a manera de paz. Un françés se metió en la balsa y a voces altas dijo que pasásemos allá. Por mandado del Adelantado se les respondió que, pues tenían balsa, viniesen ellos a donde él estaba, pues que los llamaba, si quería[n] algo. Respondió el de la balsa que era mala de pasar porque la corriente iba grande, que le enviasen una canoa que allí estaba de unos indios. El Adelantado le respondió que viniese a nado por ella debajo de su palabra. Un françés marinero vino luego y no consintió el Adelantado que le hablase. Mandole que tomase la canoa y se fuese y dijese a su capitán que, pues lo llamaba, si lo quería alguna cosa se lo enviase a decir. Vino este marinero luego con un gentilhombre, el cual dijo que él era sargento mayor de Juan Ribau, visrey y capitán-general de aquella tierra por el Rey de Françia, y que le enviaba a decir que él se había perdido con una armada con tormenta en la mar, y que tenía allí como tre[s]cientos y cincuenta françeses, que le convenía irse a un fuerte que tenía como veinte leguas de allí, que le diese bateles para pasar el río y otro que estaba de allí a cuatro leguas,[91] y que deseaba saber si eran españoles y qué capitán traían.

El Adelantado les respondió que españoles eran, y que el capitán que tenían era el mesmo con quien hablaba, y que se llamaba Pero Menéndez, que dijese [24r] a su general que el fuerte que decía tenía veinte leguas de allí él se lo había ganado, y degollado sus françeses y aun hartos que habían venido de la armada perdida porque se habían mal gobernado. Y fuese paseando hacia donde estaban muertos y mostróselos, y que así no tenía para qué pasar el río a su fuerte. Este sargento, con gran semblante, sin hacer demostración [de] tener pena de lo que el Adelantado le dijo, dijo al Adelantado si le haría merced de enviar un gentilhombre de los suyos a decir aquello a su general para que se tratase asegurança, porque su general venía cansado, y el Adelantado le pasase a ver en un batel que allí tenía. Y el Adelantado le respondió:

—Hermano, andad con Dios y dad la respuesta que os doy, y si vuestro general quisiere venir a hablar conmigo yo le doy mi palabra que puede venir y volverse seguro con hasta çinco o seis compañeros que traiga consigo de los de su consejo, para que tome el que más le convenga.

Y así se partió este gentilhombre francés con este recaudo. Dentro de media hora volvió a açeptar la asegurança que el Adelantado le había dado y pedir el batel, el cual el Adelantado no le quiso dar, enviándole a decir que se lo podrían tomar, que pasase en la canoa, que era segura, pues el río era estrecho. Y así se volvió con este recaudo este gentilhombre, y luego vino el Juan Ribau, a quien el Adelantado recibió muy bien, con otros ocho gentileshombres que con él vinieron, todos muy bien tratados de muy buenas personas y autoridades. [24v] Él les hizo dar colación de cierto barril de conserva, y de beber, y que les darían de come[r] si lo quisiesen. El Juan Ribau respondió con mucha humildad, agradeciéndole el buen recebimiento que se le hizo. Él dijo que para alegrar los espíritus, que estaban tristes por la nueva[92] que le habían dado de sus compañeros, querían desayunarse con la conserva y vino, y que por entonces no querían otra comida, y así lo hicieron.

Y Juan Ribau dijo que aquellos compañeros suyos que allí estaban muertos (él los vio, que estaban çerca) pudieron ser engañados, y que él no lo quería ser. Entonçes mandó a los soldados que allí estaban se llegasen cada uno con lo que tenía del fuerte, y fueron tantas las cosas que vido que tuvo por cierto que era verdad. Aunque ya él sabía aquellas nuevas no las pudía creer, porque entre ellos estaba un barbero françés de los que el Adelantado había mandado degollar con los demás, que había quedado por muerto entre los otros, que de la primera cuchillada que le dieron se dejó caer, haciéndose muerto, y cuando él allí llegó se pasó a nado para él. Y que el barbero tenía por cierto los había engañado el Adelantado, diciendo que el fuerte era ganado—no lo siendo—y así lo tenía él hasta entonces por çierto. El Adelantado dijo que, para que lo creyese mejor y se satisfaciese, hablase aparte con dos franceses que allí estaban que se hallaron presentes.

Y luego se vino el Juan Ribau para el Adelantado y le dijo que estaba cierto que todo lo que le había dicho ser verdad, y que lo que de él aconteçía pudiera acontecer del Adelantado, que pues sus reyes eran hermanos y tan grandes amigos lo hiciese el Adelantado con él como tal amigo, dándole navíos [25r] y bastimentos con que se fuese a Françia. El Adelantado le respondió lo que a los primeros franceses de que hizo hacer justicia, y dando y tomando con él no pudo acabar otra cosa el Juan Ribau con el Adelantado. Entonçes el Juan Ribau les dijo que quería dar cuenta a su gente, porque había entre ella[93] mucha noble, y le volvería enviar la respuesta de lo que acordase de hacer. Y dentro de tres horas volvió el Juan Ribau en la canoa y dijo que había diferentes pareceres entre su gente, que unos se querían poner a su misericordia y otros no. El Adelantado les respondió que no se le daba ninguna cosa que viniesen todos, o parte, o ninguno de ellos, que hiciesen lo que mejor les estuviese, pues tenían libertad para ello. El Juan Ribau dijo al Adelantado que la meitad de ellos se querían poner a su misericordia y pagarían de talla más de cien mil ducados, y la otra meitad podían pagar más, porque hay entre ellos personas ricas y de mucha renta que pretendían hacer estados en aquella tierra. Respondiole el Adelantado:

—Mucho me pesa se perdiese tan buena talla y presa, que harta necesidad tengo de ese socorro para ayuda de la conquista y poblaçión de esta tierra en nombre de mi rey, [que] es a mi cargo plantar el Santo Evangelio en ella.

El Juan Ribau usó aquí de un ardid si le valiera, porque le pareçió que el Adelantado, con la codiçia del dinero que todos le darían, no le mataría a él ni a los que a él se viniesen a su misericordia, pareçiéndole que con no los matar, los unos y los otros, por conçierto que Juan Ribau haría con él, valdría[n] al Adelantado más de do[s]cientos mil ducados. Y dijo al Adelantado que él se volvía con [25v] la respuesta a su gente, que porque era tarde le pidía por merced se detuviese allí hasta el día siguiente, que él volvería con la resolución que acordase. El Adelantado dijo que sí aguardaría y fuese a su gente, y ya era a puesta de sol.

Y a la mañana volvió en la canoa y entregó al Adelantado dos estandartes reales, uno del Rey de Françia y otro del Almirante, y dos banderas de campaña, y una espada, daga y çelada dorada muy buena, y una rodela y un pistolete, y un sello que traía que el Almirante de Françia le había dado para sellar las provisiones y títulos que diese. Dijo al Adelantado que hasta çiento y cincuenta personas de las trecientas y cincuenta que había se querían venir a su misericordia, y que las demás se habían retirado aquella noche, y que fuese el batel por los que se querían venir y por sus armas. El Adelantado proveyó luego al capitán Diego Flórez de Valdés, almirante de la armada, que los hiciese traer como a los demás, de diez en diez, y llevando el Adelantado a Juan Ribau detrás del medano de arena entre las matas donde los más, les hizo amarrar las manos atrás a él y a todos, como a los de antes,[94] diciéndoles que habían de caminar cuatro leguas por tierra, y de noche, que no se sufría ir sueltos. Y estando amarrados todos les dijo si eran católicos o luteranos, y si había alguno que se quisiese confesar.

El Juan Ribau respondió que él y todos cuantos allí estaban eran de la nueva religión, y empeçó a decir el salmo de Domine Memento Mei. Y, acabado, dijo que de tierra eran y que en tierra se habían de volver, que veinte años más o menos todo era una cuenta, que hiciese el Adelantado lo que quisiese de ellos. Y man[dan]do el Adelantado marchasen, como a los demás, [26r] con la mesma orden y en la mesma raya, mandó que se hiciese de éstos lo que de los otros. Sólo sacó a los pífanos, atambores y trompetas, y otros cuatro que dijeron eran católicos, que eran en todos diez y seis personas. Todos los demás fueron degollados.[95]

Y fuese aquella noche a Santo Agustín, a donde algunas personas le notaron de cruel y otros que lo había hecho como muy buen capitán. Y hallose que cuando fueran católicos y no hiciera la cuenta que hizo de ellos, por los pocos bastimentos que el Adelantado tenía, perecieran los unos y los otros de hambre, o los franceses degollaran a los católicos, porque eran más, a c[a]usa que el Fuerte de San Mateo que les ganó el Adelantado se quemó con mucha hacienda y bastimentos dentro de ocho días[96] que se ganó, por una casa donde vivía el capitán Francisco Recalde, que un moço con una candela puso fuego y dijo que la había apegado en un palo que se cayó. Túvose mala sospecha de esto, a causa que entre el capitán Villarroel— Sargento Mayor—y el Francisco Recalde estaban muy desconformes. Y empeçaban algunos soldados a decir que, pues no había bastimentos y el fuerte era ganado, que lo arrasasen y se fuesen[97] a las Indias en dos navíos que el Adelantado les invió de San Agustín con la artillería. Y no se atrevían a aclararse algunos capitanes, porque el maestro de campo y el Villarroel y la gente más principal de los soldados eran sus amigos, y estaban allí algunos deudos y criados [del Adelantado]. Y aunque en este tiempo en San Mateo no sabían que el Adelantado hubiese tenido las victorias con Juan Ribau y su gente y los hubiese degollado, y averiguose de las françesas y moços que se salvaron[98] cuando se ganó el fuerte que Juan Ribao y sus capitanes, al tiempo que se embarcaron en la armada, se brindaron dos pipas de vino lo[s] unos a los otros, diciendo:

[26v]—Brindo [a] la cabeça de Pero Menéndez y a [la de] la gente que con él está, que son marranos españoles,[99] y los castigaremos colgándolos de las entenas de sus naos y de las nuestras por que no nos vengan otra vez a buscar a ésta nuestra tierra.

De tal manera que mucha gente noble de la que Juan Ribau tenía consigo, aquellas palabras y ultrajes que decía contra [los] españoles les pareció mal.

Capítulo 5

Expedición contra los franceses

Y dentro de veinte días que éstos fueron degollados[100] vinieron indios al Adelantado y le dijeron por señas que a ocho días de camino de allí, por la parte del sur, dentro de la Canal de Bahama,[101] al Cabo del Cañaveral, muchos hombres, hermanos de los que el Adelantado había mandado matar, hacían un fuerte y un navío. Luego sospechó el Adelantado lo que pudía ser: Que de la madera, artillería, bastimentos y municiones de la armada francesa que se perdió, los franceses que se retiraban se fortificaban y hacían bajel para enviar a Francia a pedir socorro. Y despachó luego de San Agustín a San Mateo diez soldados dando aviso de todo y de cómo quería ir, para que le viniese de la gente que allá estaba a cumplimiento de çiento y cincuenta soldados, con los treinta y çinco que él trajo de allí cuando ganó el fuerte y se volvió a San Agustín. Y luego los envió el maestro de campo con el capitán Juan Vélez de Medrano y Andrés López Patiño, y llegaron a San Agustín a veinte y tres de octubre [de 1565].

Y a los veinte y seis por la mañana, habiendo oído misa, el Adelantado se partió con trecientos hombres y con tres bajeles por la mar con las armas y bastimento. Y no caminaban más [27r] los bajeles que la gente andaba por tierra, que a dondequiera que alojaban de noche allí surgían los bajeles, porque era todo arenal y costa limpia. Antes de su partida de San Agustín nombró el Adelantado justiçia y regimiento en nombre de Su Majestad, e hizo cabildo con los capitanes, y con ellos sentose en los libros de cabildo que del bastimento que quedaba se diese la ración que pareciese, y lo mesmo del bastimento que viniese. Dejó traçado el fuerte y repartido el trabajo de hacerlo por escuadras tanto a unos como a otros, y los soldados que cada día habían de trabajar en la fortificación. Eran tres horas en la mañana y tres a la tarde. Y dejó por alcaide y gobernador al capitán Bartolomé[102] Menéndez, su hermano, como siempre lo había estado de aquel fuerte y gente, y como lo está agora. Dejó proveído que todas las sentençias criminales que hubiese fuesen sentençiadas por el cabildo, porque los mesmos capitanes eran los regidores, y otorgasen todas las apelaçiones para ante el maestro de campo, a quien dejaba poderes bastantes para que fuese su teniente general, que para ello le había dado Su Majestad poder en suma dejase a quien quisiese siempre que hiciese ausençia. Y la mesma orden e instrucción envió a San Mateo a Gonçalo de Villarroel para que guardase lo susodicho. Y despachó, antes que de allí partiese, a Diego Flórez de Valdés, Almirante de la Armada, a Su Majestad con el navío que allí estaba, dándole aviso de lo sucedido hasta entonçes.

Todo el regimiento de Santo Agustín, hombres y mujeres que allí estaban, pidieron por merced al Adelantado no volviese a aquel fuerte [27v] con la gente sin comida, porque cuantos menos allí quedasen les duraría más el bastimento que allí tenían, y lo p[. . .]an mejor.[103] El Adelantado llevó en los tres bajeles bastimento para cuarenta días, [y] a los trecientos hombres, y la ración de un día duraba dos, y les prometió procuraría de hacer en todo el bien general de todos, aunque corriese peligro y trabajos, que esperaba en la bondad y misericordia de Dios, [que] les había de ayudar en todo para salir con tan santa y buena empresa. Y así se despidió de ellos, quedando los más de ellos llorando, porque era de todos amado y temido, querido y respetado.

Y llegó caminando buenas jornadas [el 1 de noviembre de 1565,] Día de Todos Santos, al alba, a dar sobre el fuerte que los franceses hacían, que unos indios le guiaban. Él por tierra marchaba con los soldados, y los tres bajeles por la mar, que los llevaba a su cargo el capitán Diego de Maya. Y como fueron descubiertos del fuerte, los franceses que dentro estaban se huyeron al monte todos sin quedar ninguno, y el Adelantado les envió una trompeta segurándoles la vida, que se volviesen y se les haría el mesmo tratamiento que a los españoles. Viniéronse al Adelantado como çiento y çincuenta, y el capitán de ellos con otros veinte le envió a decir que antes quería ser comido de los indios que rendido de los españoles. El Adelantado reçibió muy bien esta gente y le hizo muy buen tratamiento. Puso fuego al fuerte, que era de madera, y arrasole, y quemó el navío que se estaba haciendo y soterró la artillería, porque no la pudían llevar los bajeles, que eran chicos.

Capítulo 6

En tierras del cacique Ais

Y luego aquel día a la tarde marchó la vuelta del su[r], al [28r] luengo de la mar, y los tres[104] bajeles fueron navegando a buscar un puerto o río que estaba quince leguas de allí, donde había algunos pueblos de indios, para ver el Adelantado si pudía dejar alojada allí su gente con algún cacique y él ver si podría ir por la Canal de Bahama[105] adentro a la isla de Cuba a buscar bastimento. Al tercero día, a cuatro de noviembre del dicho año de [15]65, llegaron a aquel puerto que llamaron de Ais, porque se llamaba así el cacique que allí estaba, muy buen indio y que reçibió muy bien al Adelantado, no dejando él ni su gente sus casas. Antes le aguardó con toda la gente del pueblo, que fue demostraçión de confiança de que el Adelantado recibió gran contento porque, hasta entonçes, [en] todos los pueblos de indios donde llegaba huía toda la gente al monte dejando las casas desmamparadas.

El Adelantado no les consentía hacer mal ninguno en sus casas ni ajuares que dejaban dentro de ellas, antes dejaba por hospedaje en las casas de los caciques algunos rescates de espejos, cuchillos, tiseras, y algunos cascabeles, cosas que ellos estimaban en mucho. Estuvo allí cuatro días en los cuales fue por un río a ver unos sitios que el cacique le decía que eran buenos para poblar, y sin salir a la mar llegó hasta un puerto pequeño que estaba de allí como quince leguas por la Canal de Bahama[106] adentro, y no le contentado la tierra se volvió. Y teniendo poca comida—y los indios de aquella tierra tampoco la tenían, si no era pescado y [i]cacos y palmitos—visto el peligro que tenía que todos pereçerían [de hambre],[107] fue acordado y rogado por toda la gente que allí estaba que el Adelantado, aunque era mediado noviembre, tiempo peligroso para navegar la Canal de Bahama,[108] que es muy [28v] tormentosa, y los bajeles ser muy pequeños, que Su Señoría

se debía de partir con dos de ellos a la isla de Cuba para enviarles bastimento allá a los de San Agustín y San Mateo.[109]

El Adelantado lo hizo así, llevando consigo entre marineros y soldados
cincuenta personas y veinte franceses de los del Cañaveral, que todos los
llevó consigo, que fue causa que el bastimento que sacó de San Agustín de
cuarenta días se le acabase más presto, porque se daba tanta ración a los
franceses como a los españoles y no se hacía ninguna ventaja en la ración
a el mesmo Adelantado, que era media libra de bizcocho para cada soldado cada día[110] (habiendo de ser libra y media), sin vino ni otro género de
comida más de los palmitos y [i]cacos que cogían del campo.

Allí en Ais hubo un soldado que vendió cuatro libras de bizcocho a
veinte y çinco reales cada una, y comió tantas uvas de palma y otro género
de fruta que sabía bien, y un día a la noche estaba bueno y a la medianoche
murió.

Lo que en este camino el Adelantado andaba a pie era cosa que admiraba [a todos][111] porque no llevaba ningún caballo, y al tercero día no
acabaron de llegar cincuenta soldados que dejaba en la retaguarda, con
muchos cansados que no podían caminar. Dos soldados de los más recios
que allí venían, de edad de veinticinco o treinta años cada uno, que habían
sido de los primeros que entraron en el Fuerte de San Mateo cuando se les
ganó a los franceses, que marchaban en la vanguardia con el Adelantado,
de vergüença, [29r] viendo lo que caminaba, por no le dejar esforçábanse
más de lo que era razón, y yendo andando dijo el uno de ellos al otro:

—Compañero, yo me quiero sentar un poco, que estoy muy cansado.

Y sin entenderlo el Adelantado quedaron sentados estos dos, y dentro de
un cuarto de hora—sin levantarse de allí—dio éste el alma a Dios. El otro se
esforçó a caminar tras del Adelantado y desapareçió una noche, que nunca
más le vieron, porque marchaba toda la gente desde las dos después de
medianoche por un arenal, al luengo de la marina, hasta salido el sol. Y entonçes hacían alto y acudían los soldados por las sabanas adentro a comer
palmitos y [i]cacos, y cogían algunos para llevar. Estábanse allí dos horas
y marchaban hasta las once[112] o las doce del día, entonces descansaban, y
hasta las dos después de mediodía, y volvían a caminar hasta que el sol se
volvía a poner. Y no había día que no se caminase de ocho leguas arriba,
cosa que admiraba a todos, por tal camino y tan malo como eran aquellos
arenales, y sin comida, caminar tanto.

Sentía mucho el cacique Ais que el Adelantado se fuese de allí, y lloraban él y sus hijos porque en aquellos días que allí estuvo el Adelantado le regaló mucho y dio muchas cosas de rescates, y lo mismo a sus hijos e indios e indias principales, que temiendo el Adelantado que romperían guerra los soldados y los indios—de lo cual corrían peligro de ser muertos—por la falta de comida, y no saber la tierra y estar tan flacos, acordó el[113] [29v] Adelantado antes[114] de su partida a La Habana dejarles tres leguas de allí en un sitio que los indios decían ser muy bueno, y tener palmitos y [i]cacos y haber pescado, que era sobre la ribera.

Y en dos días llegó allí la gente con los bajeles. Y temió mucho su partida, lo uno porque le parecía que los soldados andaban flacos y desmayados, [y] por otra parte jamás se había visto entrar por la Canal de Bahama[115] a la isla de Cuba ningún navío, aunque muchos lo habían probado, porque va la corriente la vuelta del norte siempre muy recia, y el Adelantado [había de navegar][116] a la isla de Cuba la vuelta del su[r], y tomaba la corriente por la contraria, que le daba en la proa de los bajeles, y si no fuera por el remedio de esta gente y de la que quedaba en San Agustín y San Mateo, él holgara más enviar otra persona en los dos bajeles y quedarse con el uno y con su gente que no ponerse en aquel riesgo, que era grande. Los soldados deseaban ya su partida por la esperança que tenían del remedio de bastimento, yendo su persona.

Capítulo 7

Primer viaje a La Habana

Y así acordó de partirse de aquel puerto de Ais a seis[117] de noviembre [de 1565] con çincuenta hombres de mar y guerra y veinte fra[n]ceses, dejando con cargo de aquella gente al capitán Juan Vélez de Medrano, al cual—y a todos los que con él quedaban—hizo el Adelantado un razonamiento, esforçándoles y consolándoles, y pidiéndoles que cada día hiciesen por él oración, porque[118] él se ponía por ellos en un peligro de los grandes [en] que nunca hombre se había puesto, que suplicasen a Dios Nuestro Señor y a su Preçiosa Madre le diese buen viaje. E hincándose todos de rodilla[s], cantando las ledanías, [hicieron oración].[119] Y el Adelantado se embarcó y tuvo tan próspero viento que, habiendo desde allí a La Habana çien leguas, y de corrientes contrarias, las anduvo en dos días naturales, cosa de admiraçión, [30r] porque con galeras esquifadas al remo tenían opinión todos los pilotos que navegaban a las Indias no era posible romper esta corriente. Navegó todo al luengo de la costa y tierra de la Florida, y al atravesar a la isla de Cuba tuvo gran tormenta de norte y cierço de mar, y corrían en popa, guardándose de una mar y otra.[120]

Una noche que esta tormenta hacía siempre gobernó, no confiando el timón de ningún marinero de los suyos. Iba allí entre los veinte fra[n]-ceses que llevaban el piloto mayor de Juan Ribau, y otro que le pareçió muy escogido marinero, al cual el Adelantado preguntó si era buen timonero. Respondió que sí. Diole el timón cerca de la mañana y gobernó muy bien este francés, y así, hasta llegar a La Habana, gobernaron el Adelantado y el francés. Y el bajel en que el Adelantado iba no llevaba aguja de marear, porque al partir de Ais, que la hizo sacar [de] donde venía, halláronla que-brada. Dijo el[121] capitán Diego de Moya que el bajel en que él iba navegaba más que en el que iba[122] el Adelantado, y llevaba aguja, porque la suya era quebrada, [que] templase las velas y no se partiesen de la tierra, y que tuviese cuenta no se apartar de él. Y la segunda noche, cesando esta tormenta ya casi del día, perdió de vista el[123] Adelantado al otro bajel y pasó por el puerto de La Habana adelante, pensando no habían llegado [aún a La Habana].[124]

Como a las diez del día conoçió el puerto Bahía Honda, que es quince leguas adelante de La Habana. Vio entrar un batel dentro. Fue tras él y alcançole. Eran unos indios de La Habana que andaban a montear. Dieron al Adelantado mucha carne y caçabe,[125] que es pan de aquella tierra, y palmitos. Y dijéronle los indios que estaba allí en La Habana Pero Menéndez Marqués, su sobrino, con parte de la armada de Vizcaya y Asturias que con tormenta se había apartado del general Esteban de las Salas, y que toda la gente estaba muy triste por no saber qué se había hecho el Adelantado, que temían ser perecido en la mar con tormenta, o que los enemigos le habían desbaratado, que no podían sospechar ni creer que con tan pocos navíos que se atreviese a ir a la Florida, ni les pasaba por pensamiento que estaba allá.

Desembarcó el Adelantado con su gente en tierra en aquel puerto de Bahía [30v] Honda, e hincados todos de rodillas dieron muchas gracias a Nuestro Señor por las merçedes que le[s] había hecho en llevarlos en salvamento. Llamó a los françeses y encargoles mirasen el poder y bondad de Dios, y que si eran luteranos se arrepintiesen y tornasen católicos, que él por cualquier ley que tuviesen les haría buen tratamiento y daría libertad que se fu[e]sen en los primeros [navíos][126] a España, y de allí a França, que aquello les decía por desear que se salvasen. Hubo algunos de ellos que, llorando, se empeçaron a dar en los pechos, y alabando a Nuestro Señor, pidiéndole misericordia, diciendo que ellos habían sido malos cristianos y luteranos y que estaban arrepentidos, y que de allí adelante querían dejar su mala secta y ser católicos, confesándose y comulgándose, y que querían guardar aquello que mandaba la Santa Madre Iglesia. El Adelantado los regaló y esforçó, diciendo que se alegrasen y no tuviesen pena de sus trabajos, que tendría cuenta con ellos como si fuesen su[s] hermanos. Y así lo hizo por éstos como por todos los demás que les otorgó la vida, a cada uno en su grado: Al noble sentándole consigo a la mesa, haciéndole vestir, y a la gente de mar con sus pilotos y marineros, y a los de tierra con sus capitanes y soldados.

Partió el Adelantado aquella noche del puerto de Bahía Honda para volverse a La Habana. Y por el viento ser muy contrario y ser muy recio, que lo echaba en la mar la vuelta de la Florida más de lo que quisiera, no llegó a La Habana hasta otra noche a la medianoche; que como Diego de Maya había llegado dos días había temió que el Adelantado era perdido, y todos tuvieron por cierto que como la tormenta había sido tan grande y no tenía aguja, pensaron que el bajel se había abierto y soçobrado con el mucho viento, que era grande la tristeza que la gente de La Habana y la de su armada por él tenían, según se entendió.

Otro día que allí llegó, como entró por el puerto adentro al remo (porque estaba el viento a la tierra), la centinela que estaba en vela para guarda del puerto preguntó quién era el barco que entraba. Respondieron que el Adelantado Pero Menéndez. La centinela respondió diciendo:

—¡Bendito sea Nuestro Señor, que el [31r] señor Pero Menéndez es vivo!

Y que aguardasen un poco, que lo iba a decir a Garçi[a] Osorio, gobernador de aquella isla, para que no tirasen de la fortaleza. El mismo Adelantado dijo a la centinela, que estaba muy cerca:

—Hermano mío, id con Dios, que yo aguardaré.

Y allí aguardó por tiempo que la centinela pudía[127] ir y volver. Y como vio que tardaba, mandó arrancar la ve[r]ga y entrar para dentro. Y al pasar de la fortaleza, sabiendo que era el Adelantado, le tiraron con cuatro pieças de artillería con sus balas y no le acertó ninguno. Llegaron al muelle donde estaba surta parte de su armada de Vizcaya a cargo de Pero Menéndez Marqués, su sobrino, y empeçaron a tocar las trompetas de alegría y tirar mucha artillería de sus navíos. El Adelantado vio estar al gobernador en el muelle con hachas encendidas, con una bandera de campaña, con[128] una caja de atambor y un pífano tocando con mucha gente, y pareciéndole que le estaban aguardando, sin que entrase en ninguno de sus navíos ni hacer parada en ellos, se fue derecho a desembarcar allá, al muelle donde estaba el gobernador, el cual, cuando le vio llegar, se fue de allí con la más parte de la gente que tenía. Sólo quedó allí Juan de Inestrosa, tesorero de Su Majestad [en aquella isla][129] con algunos regidores del pueblo, que llevó al dicho Adelantado a su casa y le hospedó muy bien, y a todos los que con él iban.

El gobernador envió a visitar al Adelantado. Esta demostración, poco contento y ningún regocijo que el gobernador mostró con la llegada del Adelantado en salvamento, y mandar tirar las pieças de artillería, espantó a todos, porque traía el Adelantado por refrán en la Florida, por consolar a sus soldados siempre que los vía descontentos:

—Esforçáos, hermanos míos, que García Osorio, gobernador de la isla de Cuba, nos enviará bastante recaudo de comida para todos cuantos andamos en la Florida, porque así me lo prometió en Sevilla y Su Majestad se lo ha [31v] mandado y encargado.

Y otro día por la mañana el Adelantado se fue a misa, y al salir entró el gobernador y se hablaron, y todos echaron de ver la gran sequedad con que el gobernador habló al Adelantado, que fue como si nunca lo hubiera visto ni conoçido, y así se despidieron. Aquel día, acabando de comer, el Adelantado se fue a casa del gobernador y le dijo la gran necesidad en que quedaba la gente de la Florida, y le notificó ciertas provisiones por donde Su Majestad le mandaba dar una nao de armada con cincuenta soldados y veinte caballos, pagados y basteçidos por cuatro meses, y le diese todo el favor y ayuda que le pidiese y hubiese menester para la conquista y población de la Florida. Y le mostró cómo por cuenta de Su Majestad estaban quinientos hombres en la Florida, los cuales quedaban sin bastimento, y perecerían de hambre todos si no fuesen socorridos, que él no quería la nao de armada ni los caballos ni soldados, que todo costara más de veinte mil ducados, que con tres o cuatro mil que le diese socorrería [a] aquellos soldados que por cuenta de Su Majestad estaban en la Florida hasta la primavera [de 1566].

El gobernador le respondió que no s[e] lo[s] quería dar. Díjole que se los prestase, y que él se obligaría y daría fiador por ellos. Respondiole que no los tenía. Díjole[130] que [se los prestase a cuenta] de diez o doce mil ducados que tenía de una carabela de portugueses que el capitán Juan de la Parra había tomado con la nao capitana de la Flota de la Nueva España (la cual nao y gente de mar y guerra estaba a obedençia y orden del Adelantado, y aquellos dineros eran del Adelantado y de la gente [32r] de la nao, como personas que habían tomado la carabela con lo que dentro tenía, porque contra las ordenanças y provisiones de Su Majestad y sin registro andaba contratando en las Indias). Respondiole que tampoco se los quería dar, porque decía no le perteneçía [la carabela]. Pidiole el Adelantado le prestase de aquéllos lo[s] cuatro mil ducados sobre fianças abonadas, que cuando Su Majestad se los mandase volver los volvería. No lo quiso hacer.

Tenía preso a Juan de la Parra, capitán de esta nao capitana. Díjole el Adelantado que se lo entregase con el proceso de su culpa. Dijo que, aunque fuese su soldado, él le había de castigar como gobernador de la tierra, y los más soldados del Adelantado que en su distrito[131] hiciesen cosas indebidas. El Adelantado le respondió:

—Señor, sea por amor de Dios este acogimiento que V. M. me hace en su distrito.[132] Yo determino armarme de paciençia para pasar por todas estas cosas que V. M. usa conmigo, porque entiendo que en hacer esto me da Dios más victoria que la que tuve contra Juan Ribau y más luteranos que estaban en la Florida, porque en esto entiendo hago a Su Majestad gran serviçio.

Y quitose[133] la gorra y saliose por la puerta [sin aguardar respuesta][134] del gobernador. Y luego mandó echar bando el Adelantado que toda la gente de mar y guerra que allí estaba de Asturias y Vizcaya y de la nao capitana de la Flota de Nueva España se recogiesen en todo aquel día a los navíos, que quería hacer lista y alarde de la que había y tenía para la ocupar en serviçio de Su Majestad.

Y otro día por la mañana, habiendo oído misa al alba del día, se fue a las naos e hizo lista y alarde de quinientos y çincuenta hombres que había, y llamó a los capitanes y pilotos a la nao capitana, recogiose con ellos a consejo, y estando juntos les dijo: [32v]

—Señores y hermanos míos, aquí tenemos aviso que andan muchos co[r]sarios franceses e ingleses a robar a vasallos de Su Majestad, y habiendo paces merecen ser castigados. Y tiénese por çierto—y algunos de vosotros, señores, lo decís, que venís de allá—que entre estos co[r]sarios hay dos navíos ingleses y tres franceses que traen más de medio millón consigo que han robado, [y] de negros y mercadurías que han vendido, que están invernando en aquella isla de Santo Domingo a la parte del norte para se ir a Francia a la primavera. Y pues aquí tengo cuatro muy buenos navíos ligeros de vela y esta nao capitana, todos bien artillados, y muchas y buenas municiones, y hay en ellos quinientos y cincuenta hombres de mar y guerra, toda muy buena gente, paréceme que dentro de diez días podremos hacer nuestra [provisión de][135] agua y leña y carne, porque el más bastimento le tenemos dentro, que lo traen los navíos consigo de Asturias y Vizcaya, y ensebar y aparejar las naos, y salir luego a la mar con el primer tiempo e ir en busca de estos co[r]sarios, en lo cual haremos gran servicio a Dios Nuestro Señor y a Su Majestad en castigarlos, y será gran bien general para todas las Indias y nos podremos muy bien aprovechar. Inviaremos luego, como lleguemos, dos o tres navíos de bastimentos a la Florida a nuestros compañeros, y a la primavera llevaremos cargados nuestros navíos de comida y ganados a la Florida para hacer nuestras entradas y descubrimientos. Y quitarnos hemos del peligro que se me presenta que corremos de perderse alguno de nosotros con este gobernador, y que nos falte [33r] la paciençia, que yo por mi parte os digo, señores, que más quiero—aunque es en deciembre y por la Canal de Bahama ser[136] navegación peligrosa—andar en ella y en la mar, que no estar en este pueblo, porque aunque yo me sepa llevar con el gobernador, temo no lo sepa hacer alguno de vosotros, y de cualquier cosa que suceda se me podría a mí atribuir la culpa, visto el peligro y no lo remediar. Pídoos, señores, por merced, me aconsejéis si debo tomar esta determinaçión.

Todos la aprobaron por buena y mostraron tener gran contentamiento de ello. Y luego mandó allí el Adelantado a los capitanes y pilotos se pusiesen a punto para hacer vela dentro de doce días, e hizo llamar a los maestres y contramaestres, despenseros y oficiales de todos los navíos, a los cuales dijo su determinaçión y les mandó y encargó todos tuviesen cuenta de poner sus navíos a punto. Y así se ofrecieron a hacerlo, mostrando gran contento y regocijo por la jornada, y lo mesmo mostraron los marineros, pajes y grumetes de la armada. Y nombró en presencia de todos por almirante de ella a Pero Menéndez Marqués, su sobrino, y para el tiempo acordado—que fue dentro de doce días—los navíos estuvieron prestos y a la vela. El Adelantado se embarcó e invió a pidir al gobernador con testimonio le entregase al capitán Juan de la Parra. No lo quiso hacer. Hubo en estos quince días algunas cosas peligrosas de dares y tomares entre el Adelantado y el gobernador. Notaron mucho la paciencia del Adelantado, el cual se hizo a la vela [33v] para hacer su viaje a prinçipio de deciembre [de 1565].

Capítulo 8

Expedición contra corsarios

Al tercero día que salió del[137] puerto de La Habana descubrió una vela. Dándole caça, pensando que era co[r]sario, la[138] sig[u]ió hasta meterla en Matanças, puerto de la isla de Cuba, donde llegado a ella no halló hombre ninguno dentro, porque la gente había huido al monte. Mandó entrar dentro a Pero Menéndez Marqués, su sobrino, almirante que era de esta armada, y que con algunos marineros, poniendo a buen recaudo todo lo que traía, fuese a surgir çerca de su nao capitana donde el Adelantado iba, porque quería surgir en aquel puerto.

Como surgió oyeron voces en el monte, que la armada estaba surta junto de él. Envió el Adelantado un batel a tierra a ver lo que era. Acudieron unos portugueses y, entendiendo que la armada era española y que venía por general de ella el Adelantado, se alegraron mucho, llamando a sus compañeros. Se metieron en el batel y los trajeron a la nao capitana delante del Adelantado, los cuales con grande alegría le dijeron que ellos vinían de España con aquella carabela por mandado de Su Majestad con despachos para él, los cuales le dieron, y era que Su Majestad le daba aviso cómo en Francia se hacía gruesa armada para venir contra él a la Florida, y para poderse defender de ella y socorrer las plaças e islas de Puerto Rico, Española y Cuba, le enviaba mil y quinientos infantes con mucho bastimento y diez y siete navíos, que hiciese los socorros que quisiese, así por mar como por tierra, para ofender [34r] aquella armada si sobre él o sus tierras viniese. Entonçes el Adelantado llamó a consejo a sus capitanes y, habiéndoles mostrado la carta, les dijo:

—Señores y hermanos míos, paréceme que en todas las cosas, en espeçial en la guerra, a nuevos sucesos, nuevos consejos. Y paréceme que no debo de apartarme de La Habana, porque este socorro me escriben vendrá allí por todo março [de 1566]. Volvámosnos allá, y enviaré a Campeche uno o dos navíos de éstos a cargar de maíz para la Florida, y otro enviaré a Puerto de Plata que cargue de caçabi y carne, y el otro cargaré en La Habana lo más presto que pudiere. Y aunque no tengo dineros, venderé o empeñaré alguna artillería, o de estas municiones que traigo, aunque sea [a] menos preçio, [y] la cadena y joyas de oro que hubiere entre nosotros, y nos entretendremos lo mejor que pudiéremos, procurando por ninguna cosa que suçeda no responder con el gobernador, porque si yo fuese con esta armada a la guerra contra co[r]sarios y el socorro viniese por otra parte a La Habana, y la armada francesa fuese a la Florida, merecería ser castigado por Su Majestad de cualquier mal suceso que tuviese, ya que se me da este despacho.

Todos aprobaron la determinación del Adelantado y la tuvieron por buena y buen consejo. Y así partieron con toda la armada a otro día para La Habana y, allegados que fueron, el Adelantado despachó los navíos como lo tenía acordado y envió en un patax a Pero Menéndez, su sobrino, a España[139] a dar aviso a Su Majestad de lo sucedido hasta [34v] entonçes.

Y[140] al principio de enero del año venidero de sesenta y seis llegó Estébano de las Salas, que era general de la armada de Vizcaya y Asturias, y con tormenta se había apartado de Pero Menéndez Marqués, almirante de ella, y había estado en Yaguana. Y con su llegada, que trajo dos navíos y do[s]cientos hombres, fue grande el alegría y contento que el Adelantado con su llegada reçibió. Y luego mandó que en todo aquel mes se aparejasen aquellos dos navíos y los dos que el Adelantado trujo de la Florida, y un bergantín nuevo que, yendo Diego de Moya con bastimento a la Florida, trajo de allá, y otro patax françés que allí compró en La Habana, y una chalupa nueva. Y todos estos siete navíos hizo calafetear y ensebar y poner a punto.

En tierras del cacique Carlos

Y a diez de hebrero [de 1566], con quinientos hombres de mar y guerra dentro de ellos, se partió a la Florida, y fue a descubrir a ver si había pasaje bueno y buena navegación entre Las Tortugas y Los Mártires, que para las flotas de Nueva España y Tierra Firme y otros cualesquier navíos que por allí navegaban era muy necesario saberla. Y hallándola muy buena pasó adelante a la costa de la Florida en demanda de unos hombres y mujeres que decían había veinte años que estaban cautivos en poder de un caçique que llamaban Carlos, y cada año mataba de esta gente haciendo [35r] sacrificio de ella al demonio, y que todos andaban desnudos, hechos salvajes como los mesmos indios. Y compadeciéndose el Adelantado de estos cristianos quiso hacer esta jornada,[141] [*34v] y de allí irse a las provinçias de Santa Elena, que es çincuenta leguas al norte del puerto de San Mateo que se ganó a los luteranos, porque los indios decían a los soldados en aquel fuerte que en el puerto de Guale[142] había franceses nuevamente venidos.

[35r] Y habiendo hecho decir muchas misas a Santo Antonio le fuese abogado con Nuestro Señor les encontrase con el puerto donde estaban aquellos cristianos y con los mesmos cristianos, dentro de ocho días que partió de La Habana encontró con él. Y fue de esta manera, que salió de su nao capitana en que iba, dejando a Estébano de las Salas, que le hizo general de aquellos navíos y su lugarteniente, y metiose el Adelantado en un bergantín con treinta hombres, soldados y marineros, que no demandaba más de media braça de agua, y mandó al capitán Diego de Maya, que iba por almirante de estos navíos, que con otro bergantín en que iba con treinta personas, que demandaba muy poca agua, se fuese con él, y entrambos los dos bergantines juntos fuesen navegando al luengo de la tierra, y los más navíos por lo largo, porque era la costa bajía. Y al tercero [día] se apartó

de sus çinco navíos con los dos bergantines con una çer[r]azón que hubo. Y al cuarto día, yendo navegando al luengo de la tierra, salió una canoa al bergantín donde iba el capitán Diego de Maya media legua delante. Y venía en ella una persona[143] bogando, y cuando llegó cerca del bergantín habló, diciendo:

—¡Españoles! ¡Hermanos! ¡Cristianos! ¡Seáis bienvenidos, que ocho días ha que os aguardamos, que Dios y Santa María nos han dicho que venís! Y los hombres y mujeres cristianos que aquí están vivos me han mandado venir a aguardaros aquí con [35v] esta canoa para daros una carta que traigo.

El capitán Diego de Maya y la gente que con él iban en el bergantín recibieron gran gozo y contento de ver que habían descubierto a los que el Adelantado buscaba y tanto deseaba. Y recibió dentro del bergantín a este hombre, que venía desnudo y pintado, hecho indio, con sus vergüenzas cubiertas. El capitán le abraçó y pidió la carta. El hombre sacó[144] de entre el cuero de venado con que traía atapadas sus vergüenzas una cruz, diciéndole al capitán que aquélla era la carta que los cristianos y cristianas[145] que allí estaba[n] cautivos le enviaban, y que le pidían que, por la muerte que Nuestro Señor había recibido en aquella [cruz][146] por salvarnos, no pasase sin entrar en el puerto y procurar de sacarlos de su cacique y llevarlos a tierra de cristianos.

En esto llegó el Adelantado con su bergantín y pasó este hombre en él, donde entendió más particularmente de este cristiano todo lo que pasaba, y de la calidad de la tierra y condición de los indios. Y todos puestos de rodillas adoraron la cruz, dando gracias a Nuestro Señor.[147] Metiose el Adelantado adentro del puerto y surgió al luengo de la tierra, que saltaban del bergantín en tierra sin mojarse los çapatos. Estaría el pueblo media legua de allí, donde estaban cinco mujeres cristianas y cuatro cristianos,[148] y otros dos estaban en la tierra adentro, y otra mujer, porque de más de docientos cristianos[149] de naos de las Indias perdidas en tierra de este cacique veinte años había, y la gente de ellas se los llevaban todos, los había muerto su padre y él haciendo sacrifiçio [en] sus fiestas y bailes al demonio. El Adelantado no se atrevió descubrir a este cristiano el cómo pensaba sacar estos cristianos y cristianas que allí estaban, porque le pareçía sabía poco y cualquier cosa [36r] que le dijese se lo podría decir al cacique. Sólo le dijo que le dijese al cacique que le traía muchas cosas para él y sus mujeres, que le viniese a ver. El cacique, sabido la poca gente que el Adelantado traía, vino otro día por la mañana con hasta tre[s]cientos indios flecheros. Y junto de los bergantines, al luengo de la tierra, estando la proa del uno puesta en la popa del otro, y puestos los versos de la banda de la tierra dentro[150] de los mesmos bergantines, con muchos perdigones dentro para lo que se pudiese ofrecer, hizo poner un estrado en[151] que se sentase el cacique, y así se asentó, y los más de sus indios principales al derredor de él.

El Adelantado salió de los bergantines con treinta arcabuceros con sus mechas encendidas y sentose cabe de él, haciendo el cacique y sus principales mucha obediencia al Adelantado. Vistiole una camisa y unos çaragüelles de tafetán, y una ropeta y un sombrero, y diole otras cosas de rescate para sus mujeres. Pareçió muy bien, porque era muy gentilhombre de hasta veinticinco años, y también dio a sus indios principales, y dioles de comer bizcocho y miel, que lo comieron muy bien. El cacique dio al Adelantado una barra de plata que pesaba como do[s]cientos ducados y le dijo que le diese más cosas o más de comer. El Adelantado le dijo que no tenía comida para tanta gente, que se metiese él en los navíos con sus prencipales y les daría de comer muchas cosas para ellos y sus mujeres. Con la codicia el cacique lo hizo así, y metió consigo como hasta veinte indios. El Adelantado, con gran secreto y delegencia, mandó que cada soldado estuviese cabe su indio y se sentasen cabe ellos, y si se quisiesen echar a la mar no [36v] se lo consintiesen, y mandó largar los cabos con que los bergantines estaban amarrados a tierra y túvose a lo largo. Los indios se alteraron un poco. Fueles dicho con la lengua que no tuviesen miedo, porque se ponían allí a causa que no entrasen más indios en los bergantines, porque como eran pequeños los trastornarían. El cacique y los indios lo creyeron y les dieron de comer muchas cosas. Y el cacique se quiso ir, y el Adelantado le dijo que el Rey de España, su señor, le enviaba por los hombres y mujeres que tenía, y cristianos, y que si no se los daba le mandaría matar, que le rogaba que los diese porque le daría muchas cosas por ellos y sería grande su amigo y hermano. El cacique le dijo que él era contento y que él iría por ellos. El Adelantado le dijo que si él iba, que su gente le matarían porque le dejaba ir, que le rogaba enviase algunos indios por ellos. El cacique—con miedo—así lo hizo, y dentro de un hora trujeron cinco mujeres y tres cristianos, a los cuales mandó el Adelantado dar unas camisas, y de cariseas y Londres que trajo mandó a cuatro o cinco sastres que allí venían les hiciesen de vestir, y lo mesmo los cristianos lloraban de contento, que era cosa de ver. El Adelantado los consolaba mucho y regalaba, y decían que tenían mucha pena por los hijos que dejaban allí. El Adelantado dio muchas cosas al cacique y a su gente y le envió muy contento, diciéndole el cacique que dentro de tres meses le traería allí otros dos cristianos y una cristiana que estaba en la tierra adentro, y que le rogaba fuese por la mañana—antes que se partiese—a su pueblo, para que [37r] sus mujeres le viesen. Dijo el Adelantado que lo haría así.

A la mañana envió el cacique muchas canoas por él. Estando el Adelantado sospechoso de su ida llegó en una canoa el cristiano que había salido a la mar con la cruz, que se había ido con el cacique a visitar a sus mujeres de parte del Adelantado y a llevarles un presente. Y dijo este cristiano al Adelantado que no fuese al pueblo, porque tenía concertado de le matar [a] él. Y los indios con las canoas, que sabían la traición, sospecharon que aquel cristiano los descubría y fuéronse huyendo. El Adelantado, por que el cacique e indios entendiesen que él no sabía la traición, levó[152] las áncoras de los bergantines y con la boga fue a surgir junto al pueblo. Y de allí, tocando dos clarines, campeando las banderas, hizo señal que viniesen las canoas por él, porque los bergantines no podían pasar más adelante. Y como ninguna canoa quiso venir el Adelantado salió del puerto para buscar sus çinco navíos y juntarlos y, como no pareçían, los cristianos le dijeron que çincuenta leguas de allí más adelante había un muy buen puerto y que había otros tres cristianos cautivos en poder de los indios. Al Adelantado le pareçió que sus navíos habrían corrido allá y tuvo deseo de rescatar aquellos tres cristianos. Fue allá y no halló los navíos ni los cristianos, y a la vuelta que volvió halló los çinco navíos surtos sobre este puerto de Carlos y que Esteban de las Salas había ido al pueblo con cien soldados, que como los indios vieron tantos navíos y gente que fueron a reconocer con las canoas, temieron e hicieron buen recebimiento [a] Esteban de las Salas. Rescataron [37v] los soldados allí más de dos mil ducados de oro y plata con los indios a trueco de bujerías.

El Adelantado acordó de enviar el cristiano a Carlos para que le diese a entender que el Adelantado no sabía nada de la traición que le armaba para matarle. El Carlos lo creyó y, con cobdiçia que tuvo de que le diese otras cosas y de tomar por amigo al Adelantado, le vino a ver con solos çinco o seis indios no más, y le dijo que le quería tomar por su hermano mayor para hacer todo lo que le mandase y que le quería dar por mujer una hermana que tenía mayor que él, que la quería mucho, para que él la llevase a tierra de cristianos y se la volviese a enviar. Y cuando volviese él iría también y se haría cristiano con todos sus indios, que le pareçía que era mejor que no ser indios, y que le rogaba fuese por ella y fuese a ver a sus mujeres y pueblo. El Adelantado dijo que otro día iría, y le regaló muy mucho y le envió. Quisieran los capitanes y soldados que el Adelantado no soltara al cacique, porque decían tenía mucho dinero, y que todo se lo daría por soltarlo. El Adelantado, pareciéndole—por la confiança que el cacique de él tenía—que era bellaquería y nunca serían cristianos, no lo quiso hacer.

Todos los capitanes, soldados y marineros que allí estaban, de la respuesta que el Adelantado dio quedaron admirados, porque sabían lo mucho que había gastado en esta empresa y la poca ayuda que Su Majestad le había dado, y que quedaba en España empeñado, y lo mismo dejaba a sus deudos y amigos, y lo estaba en La Habana, y había enviado a tomar dineros prestados a la Nueva España. Y lo [38r] tuvieron por hombre mal aconsejado, que por lo poco sacara de aquel cacique cien mil ducados que, aunque no los tuviera, sus indios y caciques amigos, en cuyo poder estaba algún oro y plata de naos perdidas, que no lo conoçían ni sabían qué cosa era, [se lo darían, y] pudiera con ello desempeñarse, y a los que lo estaban por amor de él, y hallarse más esforçados[153] para una tan santa empresa como ésta, para procurar, como procuraba, según la inclinaçión que él y todos los soldados tenían, de plantar el Santo Evangelio, porque los indios no sabían qué cosa era oro ni plata. Y por un naipe—que era un As de Oros—le venieron a dar a un soldado un pedaço de oro que valía setenta ducados, y por unas tiseras media barra de plata que valía cien ducados. Rescataron aquella vez todos los soldados que habían llegado primero a aquel lugar con Estébano de las Salas, y los que llegaron con el Adelantado en los dos bergantines, hasta tres mil y quinientos ducados en todo, de que andaban ya regocijados y contentos y empeçaban a jugar, teniendo el dinero en poco. No les quitó ninguna cosa el Adelantado de lo que cada uno rescató ni él rescató ninguna cosa, por que no entendiesen los indios que iban a buscar aquello.

Y luego, otro día siguiente que el cacique Carlos se salió de los bergantines, fue a comer con él. El Adelantado llevó do[s]cientos arcabuceros consigo y una bandera, y dos pífanos y atambores, tres trompetas, y una harpa y vigüela de arco, y un salterio y un enano chiquito—gran cantador y dançador—que traía consigo. Había como dos tiros de arcabuz de donde desembarcó a la casa del cacique. Cupieran [38v] dentro de ella dos mil hombres aunque no estuvieran muy apretados. Fue su gente en ordenança hasta esta casa, que no consintió el Adelantado entrasen dentro, sino que fuera de ella estuviesen a punto con sus mechas ençendidas. Sólo se metió dentro al aposento del cacique con hasta veinte gentileshombres y la música, donde había unas ventanas grandes por donde vía su gente. Estaba el cacique en un buen aposento, sentado solo, con grande autoridad, y una india cabe sí, también sentada, apartada algún tanto de él, en un alto [a] medio estado del suelo, y hasta cincuenta indios prencipales y otras cincuenta indias,[154] los indios cerca de él y las indias cerca de la india en lo bajo.

Como el Adelantado subió a aquel aposento el cacique le dejó el lugar que tenía y se apartaba mucho de él. El Adelantado le puso cabe sí y luego se levantó el cacique, y según costumbre de ellos fuese para el Adelantado a tomarle las manos, haciendo cierta çerimonia que es cuando acá besan la mano al rey, que no se puede hacer más cortesía entre ellos, y la que los indios vasallos suelen hacer a sus caciques. Luego vino la india e hizo lo mesmo, y luego todos aquellos indios principales que allí estaban. Y pusiéronse más de quinientas indias, de diez años hasta quince, sentadas de la banda de fuera de la ventana a cantar, y otros indios a saltar y voltear. Cantaron los indios e indias principales que cabe el cacique estaban, que decían—según después se supo—que éste era el mayor regocijo, respeto y obediencia que aquel cacique ni otro ninguno[155] de aquella tierra pudiera hacer al Adelantado, porque dançaron los hermanos del cacique y sus tíos y tías, que había [39r] indias entre estas principales de noventa y cien años,[156] que dançaron todos, y mostraron estar muy contentos y tener mucha alegría.

Después que hubieron acabado sus principales el dançar y cantar (aunque las indias que estaban fuera nunca lo dejaron hasta que el Adelantado se fue, y cantaban por mucha orden, [y] estaban asentadas de çiento en çiento, y las cincuenta cantaban un poco y callaban, y volvían a cantar las otras çincuenta), el cacique dijo al Adelantado (después que sus principales dançaron) que si quería que trajesen la comida para él y sus cristianos. El Adelantado le dijo que no tan presto, y llevaba escritos muchos vocablos en lenguaje de los indios, los cuales eran de mucho comedimiento y amor para hablar a la mujer prencipal de Carlos y a su hermana. Y pensando que aquélla que estaba allí era la mujer prençipal del cacique le dijo las palabras que pensaba decille en su propria lengua. Quedaron admirados el cacique y los indios. Pensaron qu[e] hablaba el papel y lo que en él estaba escrito, y entendió el cacique que pensaba el Adelantado que aquélla era su mujer principal, y díjole con la lengua que tenían para entenderse (que era de los cristianos cautivos)[157] que aquélla no era su mujer, que era su hermana que ya él le había dado por mujer.

Entonces se levantó el Adelantado y la tomó por la mano y sentó cabe sí, en medio de él y del cacique, y por lo que llevaba escrito le dijo en su lengua—leyendo por el papel—muchas cosas de que ellos y todos los indios e indias que allí estaban [39v] se alegraron. Era esta india de hasta treinta y çinco años, no nada hermosa, aunque muy grave, tanto que, andando el tiempo, admiró a todos nosotros, porque parecía que desde su nacimiento la habían criado a saber tener gravedad. Pidió el Adelantado al cacique trajese allí su mujer prençipal, el cual lo hizo. Era de veinte años, muy bien dispuesta y hermosa, de muy buenas faiçiones. Tenía muy buenas manos y ojos y miraba con mucha gravedad a una parte y a otra con toda honestidad. Tenía muy buena mesura, que aunque entre las muchas indias que allí se vio hermosas ninguna lo era tanto como ésta. Traía las çejas muy bien hechas y a la garganta un hermoso collar de perlas y piedras y una gargantilla de cuentas de oro. Estaba desnuda, como la otra—hermana del cacique—con solas sus vergüenças cubiertas. El Adelantado la tomó por la mano y la puso entre la india y el cacique, y habló con ella en su lengua muchas palabras—que las llevaba escritas en papel—de que ella se regocijó mucho, en especial que, como habían dicho al Adelantado que era muy hermosa, llevaba escrito en su lenguaje palabras para decírselo, de que ella mostró no le pesar. Púsosele en el rostro muy buena color, mirando a su marido con honestidad. El cacique mostró pesarle por haber traído a su mujer y mandaba que se fuese, pensando que se la querían tomar. El Adelantado le dijo con la lengua no la enviase, y que comiese allí con él, porque tenía muchas cosas que le dar.

Y luego hizo traer el presente que llevaba, e hizo vestir a la hermana del cacique [40r] una camisa, y otra a la mujer del cacique, y sendas ropas verdes con que la mujer del cacique estaba harto hermosa. Dioles cuentas, tiseras, cuchillos y cascabeles[158] con que se holgaron mucho, en espeçial con los espejos—cuando se miraban—y de esto reían mucho los indios y las indias que allí estaban. Y dio al cacique otro vestido, sin otro que antes le había dado, y otras menudençias de rescates, y dos hachas y dos machetes. También dio a los indios e indias principales que allí estaban algunos rescates, sin que por ello diesen al Adelantado ningún género de interés ni él lo pidiese. Mandó traer la comida, la cual fue muchos géneros de pescados muy buenos, cocidos y asados, y muchos ostriones crudos, cocidos y asados, sin otras cosas que el Adelantado había hecho desembarcar; un quintal de bizcocho muy bueno y una botija de vino, y otra de miel de açúcar. Y repartió por todos aquellos prinçipales y con la lengua les mandó trujesen escudillas para echalles de aquella miel. Dioles alguna confitura y carne de membrillo, y en un plato de por sí comió el Adelantado, y la hermana del cacique en otro, y el cacique y su mujer en otro, puesta su mesa [con] manteles y servilletas que el Adelantado había hecho llevar. Bien entendieron ser nuestra comida muy mejor que la suya.

Cuando la comida se trajo tocáronse las trompetas, que estaban de la parte de fuera, y en cuanto comió el Adelantado discantaron los instrumentos muy bien, y dançaba[159] el enano. Empeçaron a cantar çinco o seis[160] gentileshombres [40v] que allí estaban, que tenían muy buenas voces, con muy buena orden, que por ser el Adelantado muy amigo de música siempre procura de traer consigo la mejor que tiene y puede. Alegrábanse los indios estrañamente de oír aquello. Dijo el cacique a las moças que no cantasen, porque sabían poco y los cristianos sabían mucho. Çesó la música. Rogó el cacique que, hasta que se fuesen, siempre tocasen los instrumentos y cantasen. El Adelantado lo mandó, y así acabaron de comer. Alçóse[161] la mesa. Entonçes le dijo que se quería ir.

El cacique le dijo que se fuese a reposar a un aposento que estaba allí con su hermana, pues se la había dado por mujer, y si no lo hacía que sus indios se escandalizarían, diciendo que se reían de ellos y de ella, y la tenía en poco. Y había en el pueblo más de cuatro mil indios e indias. El Adelantado mostró un poco de turbación y díjole por la lengua que los cristianos no podían dormir con mujeres que no fuesen cristianas. El cacique le respondió que ya su hermana y él y su gente lo eran, pues le habían tomado por hermano. El Adelantado le respondió que antes que fuesen cristianos habían de saber y creer muchas cosas, y díjoles quién era Dios, y su saber, poder y bondad, que a Éste sólo han de obedeçer todas las criaturas que naçen en la tierra y hacer lo que manda. Y que los cristianos que lo hacen, cuando mueren acá en la tierra se van para Él al çielo, y que allí están siempre sin morir, [41r] y ven a su mujer e hijos y hermanos y amigos, y siempre están alegres, cantando y riendo. Y que ellos, porque no conoçen esto ni sirven ni adoran a Dios, antes sirven a un cacique muy bellaco y mentiroso que se llama el diablo, y cuando mueren se van para él y perpetuamente están llorando, porque unas veces tienen mucho frío y otras veces mucho calor, y ninguna cosa les da contento.[162]

Y mostraban este indio y su hermana tener buen entendimiento. Y hablaron el uno con el otro, y respondió la india con mucha mesura y honestidad—que el hermano lo quiso así—que ya ella sabía aquello, que los cristianos que allí estaban se lo habían dicho, y que [los otros indios] no se lo querían creer, pensando que mentían como lo hacían en otras cosas, [pero] que ellos claramente vían y que ella creía lo que el Adelantado decía y era cristiana. Y si otra cosa le faltaba más para saber y creer, que se lo dijese, que ella lo haría como el mesmo Adelantado, pues era su mujer, que había de ser cristiana como él y no india, y que si no quería reposar con ella que la llevase consigo a sus navíos y a tierra de cristianos. Y la mujer del cacique dijo que también se quería ir con él, porque los cristianos parecían mejor que los indios, y que también su marido se iría y volverían dentro de un mes o dos.

El Adelantado le respondió graciosamente que así lo quería él y estaba muy alegre por ello. Y el cacique la quitó [de] donde estaba y la pasó de la otra parte, pensando que el Adelantado se la quería llevar. Y respondió el Adelantado a la hermana del cacique que la quería a ella mucho más que ella a él, porque quería ser cristiana; que deseaba saber si su hermano y los más indios e indias sabían qué cosa era ser cristianos.[163] Dijo que todos sabían aquello que el Adelantado [41v] había dicho porque los cristianos que allí estaban se los decían, mas que no se los querían creer, que como él la llevase consigo irían con él algunos indios e indias principales y verían las cosas de los cristianos, cómo vivían y hacían mejor que ellos en ser cristianos, y cuando se volviesen lo dirían a todos los indios y con esto serían todos cristianos. El Adelantado dijo que era contento y que se quería ir, y otro día que fuese ella con los que con ella habían de ir a tierra de cristianos y que la llevaría consigo. Dijo que era contenta, y el cacique, que holgó de esto bien.

Se juzgó allí entre los que estaban que, siendo cristiana la mujer del cacique, de buena gana se entrara el Adelantado a reposar con ella y llevara a su hermana a tierra de cristianos para que fuera y volviera con las nuevas de la manera que los cristianos vivían.

Y así se despidió el Adelantado, y tomáronlo en el medio por las manos la mujer del cacique y su hermana, y la hermana del cacique púsose a la mano derecha y dijo a su cuñada se pusiese a la parte izquierda, y el cacique de ellos y sus indios e indias principales delante, cantando y bailando. Y así sacaron al Adelantado de casa y hasta fuera de casa, donde se quedaron estos indios con las demás mujeres. Y el cacique con los indios le acompañó hasta los bateles, que estuvo embarcado, y se fue a sus navíos, donde otro día hizo hacer leña y agua.

Y siendo ya tarde vino el cacique Carlos con su hermana y con hasta tre[s]cientos indios e indias que la iban acompañando. E iban con él otros dos caciques que habían llegado nuevamente, deseoso[s] de ver al Adelantado y a los cristianos. El Adelantado los recibió muy bien e hizo dar de comer, y dio [a] aquellos dos caciques algunas cosas de rescates. Y ya que era a puesta de sol dijo el [42r] Carlos que se quería ir, que dejaba a su hermana con seis indios y seis indias de los más prencipales y sabios de aquella tierra, que le rogaba que dentro de cuatro o cinco meses se la volviese, y que si ella y ellos dijesen que era bueno ser cristianos él y toda su gente lo serían. El Adelantado estaba con pena por recebirla, porque desde allí se había de ir derecho a Guale y a Santa Elena, que era de allí más de do[s]cientas leguas a la parte del norte, a buscar los franceses que los indios decían estaban allí, antes que al verano fuesen socorridos. Y temió que era Ja[c]ques Ribau, hijo mayor de Juan Ribau, general de los luteranos que estaban en la Florida (que el Adelantado hizo degollar, y a su gente), que este Ja[c]ques Ribau había escapado con dos naos dende el fuerte cuando se les ganó, y no sabía que su padre fuese perdido. Y pareciole al Adelantado que por ser Guale y Santa Elena buenos puertos se pudo fortificar en él mejor, y que llevaba mucha artillería, muniçiones y bastimento, y más de cien hombres, que podría hacer un fuerte y enviar los navíos a França a pedir socorro, y que convenía—antes que le viniese—desbaratarle y echarle de la tierra.

Y a esta causa respondió al cacique Carlos que él iba a la guerra contra sus enemigos y había de andar por la mar mucho tiempo en muchos trabajos y peligros, y que su hermana y los que con ella querían ir, si la mar les hacía mal o alguno se moriría, o si los enemigos vençiesen al Adelantado, la matarían a ella y a los demás, y que después pensaría él que el Adelantado los había muerto, que hiciese venir de la tierra adentro los cuatro cristianos y cristianas que estaban cautivos y que dentro de cuatro meses él volvería y le traería muchas cosas [42v] y la llevaría.

El cacique se volvió muy triste, y la india, y hablaron el uno con el otro un rato. Y luego respondió la india[164] que, pues el Adelantado era su marido, que en la mar y en la guerra quería andar, morir y vivir con él, y que la llevase, porque aquellos caciques y sus indios e indias, y los caciques sus enemigos de él, reirían de ella y de su hermano, diciendo que los había tenido en poco el Adelantado y los había burlado. El Adelantado respondió que él la quería mucho, y a su hermano, que le prometía de volver por ella dentro de cuatro meses. Entonçes se levantó el hermano y tomó por la mano a su hermana y se fue a meter en las canoas muy enojado y airado, y ya que quería anochecer. E iba diciendo que el Adelantado y todos los cristianos decían muchas mentiras, y que también sería mentira lo que decían de Dios y de Santa María. Y la india iba llorando.

Compadeciose mucho el Adelantado de esto que dijeron y de ver llorar la india, y fuese tras ellos diciendo que aguardasen. No quisieron aguardar y metiéronse en la[s] canoas. El Adelantado, por que no se fuesen y porque los indios se alteraban contra él, metiose al agua con calças y çapatos hasta la cinta y llegose a la canoa y tomó a la india por la mano, y dijo a la lengua que le dijese a ella y a su hermano que, porque la quería mucho, no la quería poner en aquel peligro con sus enemigos, que si todavía se quería ir él la llevaría de muy buena voluntad. Ella dijo que sí. Y despidiose de su hermano y alçó las faldas y saltó al agua. Y como no era muy grande [le] llegaba el agua arriba de la cintura, y lo mismo hicieron [43r] tres indios de los seis que habían de ir con ella, y cuatro indias. El Carlos se fue con su gente y ella se quedó con el Adelantado—el cual se vía turbado—y dijo a Estébano de las Salas y a los más capitanes que allí estaban que no sabía cómo se había de gobernar con ella, porque el viento estaba muy contrario para partirse. Y si no la regocijaba y daba contento temía se le fuese otro día, en especial que los indios [e] indias la vendrían a ver y había de contar lo que con él había pasado. Y porque los indios de aquel cacique eran muchos y muy guerreros, pareçiole podría venir en rompimiento con ellos, y esto no convenía para[165] el designio del Adelantado, que todo lo que él mostraba dende que había partido de España su interés particular era que los indios se volviesen cristianos.

Los capitanes le respondieron que convenía hacerle mucha fiesta a ella y a los indios e indias que con ella estaban, y que hubiese aquella noche muchos regocijos y música, y la bautizasen y pusiesen nombre, y que el Adelantado durmiese con ella, porque sería éste gran principio para que se confiasen de él y de los demás cristianos, y que todos aquellos indios y los caciques sus vecinos serían cristianos, y que por ninguna manera convenía hacer otra cosa. El Adelantado mostró mucho procurar[166] otro remedio, y como no se pudo tomar ni se halló otro, acordó que se hiciese así. Y luego las cristianas que allí estaban la hicieron lavar, tocar y vestir, que pareçió harto mejor que primero, cuando estaba desnuda. Y los capitanes con industria la alababan de muy hermosa y mesurada. Pusiéronle nombre doña Antonia, y a aquel puerto San Antón, por la devoçión [43v] que el Adelantado había tomado al Señor San Antón para que se encontrase aquellos cristianos y cristianas que iba a buscar. Dieron la cena y música y regocijo, y en tierra, en unas tiendas que el Adelantado tenía armadas junto de sus navíos, hasta las dos después de medianoche, que el Adelantado la tenía cabe sí, y con la lengua le decía muchas cosas graçiosas que la alegraban. Y respondía tan discretamente y en tan pocas palabras que a todos les admiraba. Dançaron sus indias y las mujeres cristianas y otros soldados, y acabando esto la llevaron a acostar a una cama que el Adelantado mandó hacer, y él se fue para ella. Y a la mañana ella se levantó alegre y las mujeres cristianas que la hablaron dijeron que ella estaba muy contenta.

Y luego envió con una canoa que allí estaba a dos indios y dos indias a su hermano, el cual vino a verle, y el Adelantado le recibió muy bien. Y dijo que deseaba que estuviese una cruz grande puesta cabe su casa, y que todos los días a las mañanas los hombres y mujeres y los niños la fuesen a besar y adorar, y la tuviesen por su ídolo mayor, y le dijo las causas para ello y que quitase los más ídolos que tenía. El cacique dijo que sí haría, mas que sus ídolos no los podría quitar tan presto hasta que su hermana volviese, y los indios que con ella iban, y les dijesen lo que habían de hacer. Este cacique se llamaba Carlos porque se llamaba así su padre, y su padre se puso aquel nombre porque los cristianos cautivos que tenía le dijeron que el emperador Carlos era el mayor rey de los cristianos.

Hízose la cruz y hízola el Adelantado hincar allí, y con grande música y devoción se iba de rodillas y la besó, y lo mismo todos los españoles que allí estábamos. Luego lo hizo asimismo la india doña Antonia y las más mujeres e indias que [44r] consigo tenía.[167] Luego la besó y adoró Carlos y sus indios. Tenía este Carlos un capitán, muy buen indio, que era casado con hermana de Carlos y de esta doña Antonia, y el cacique con hermana del capitán. Y los indios, al parecer, según los cristianos decían, más temían a este capitán que no al cacique. Y dijo al cacique que él había de ser capitán de aquella cruz, para que todos hiciesen lo que el Adelantado mandaba, irla a besar y adorar en la mañana. Y así se la entregó el Adelantado y con gran reverencia la llevó a cuestas a las canoas. Y fuese el Adelantado luego a embarcar llevando consigo a doña Antonia y a los tres indios y cuatro indias y siete cristianos y cristianas que estaban cautivos, porque otras dos mujeres se habían ya huido a los indios con[168] el deseo que tenían de los hijos que dejaban.

Dio orden a Estébano de las Salas se fuese a La Habana con esta india y su gente y la entregasen al tesorero Juan de Inestrosa, que era lugarteniente del Adelantado en aquella isla para las cosas de la Florida. Y le escribió diese orden cómo fuese doctrinada la india y las que con ella iban y les hiciesen todo buen tratamiento, y cuando fuese tiempo los hiciesen cristianos, que él volvería a La Habana dentro de tres o cuatro meses para la llevar a su tierra. Y que diese el más bastimento que pudiese, [aves][169] y ganados a Estébano de las Salas, y le despachase luego para que, con los çinco navíos que llevaba, se fuese al puerto de Santo Agustín, a donde el Adelantado le aguardaría para ir sobre los franceses que decían estaban en Guale y Santa Elena, porque se[170] iba en dos bergantines, descubriendo a ver toda aquella costa de Los Mártires, si hallaba algún puerto bueno en la Canal de Bahama,[171] y procurando de ir a hacer amistades con los caçiques y pueblos que topasen. Y así se partieron, con próspero viento, el Estébano de las Alas con çinco navíos a La Habana, y el Adelantado con dos[172] bergantines, al [44v] luengo de Los Mártires.[173]

Motines en Santa Lucía,
San Agustín y San Mateo

Y a ocho días que partió del puerto de Santo Antonio, que es donde el cacique Carlos vive, entró e[n] un puerto que halló en la Canal de Bahama. Y saliendo a otro día vio un navío. Fue a reconocerlo y conoció ser una carabela que había enviado desde La Habana a Campeche[174] a cargar de maíz. Y entró adentro y halló en ella más de çiento y treinta personas, y toda ella cargada de maíz. Y fue de esta manera: que esta carabela, por cartas del Adelantado y a ruego suyo, fray [Francisco] de Toral, obispo de Yucatán,[175] y don Luis de Céspedes, gobernador de aquella isla, se la habían cargado de maíz y de gallinas, miel y [alpargatas y][176] otras cosas. Y cuando iba a la Florida entró en La Habana, y Juan[177] de Inestrosa, como lugarteniente del Adelantado para las cosas de la Florida, la despachó luego, y le mandó fuese por la tierra de Ais y puerto de Santa Luçía, donde había quedado el capitán Juan Vélez de Medrano cuando le dejó allí el Adelantado con los tre[s]-cientos[178] españoles y franceses y se fue con los dos[179] bajeles a La Habana a buscar bastimento (y ya le había socorrido el Adelantado con un patax cargado), y les dejase ciertas hanegas de maíz, gallinas y carne, y pasase con lo demás a San Agustín. Y haciéndolo así el maestro de la carabela, que como llegó a Santa Luçía quiso descargar el maíz, los soldados prendieron al maestro y se alçaron con la carabela. Y porque el capitán Juan Vélez de Medrano se los quiso defender lo quisieron matar, e hirieron a Pedro de Ayala[180] su alférez, que defendía también no se alçasen con la carabela, y embarcados todos en ella se iban para La Habana, y habían navegado ya más de quince leguas.

El Adelantado se embarcó en ella con algunos gentileshombres de los suyos y se fue a Santo Agustín, donde entró con ella a veinte de março de sesenta y seis, y halló al maestro de campo muy enfermo y sin bastimento. Y había habido allí muy grandes motines, y en el Fuerte de San Mateo, y fueron acordados entre algunos capitanes y [45r] los más [soldados],[181] que ya que no lo podían remediar el maestro de campo—que estaba en San Agustín—ni Gonçalo de Villarroel—a cuyo cargo estaba el Fuerte de San Mateo—por que no los matasen pasaban por algunas cosas mal proveídas y ordenadas. Y siendo llegado[182] el capitán Diego de Moya por fin de deciembre [de 1565] con un navío de ochenta toneles cargado de cazabi, carne, ganado—aunque todo era poco—dejando parte en el puerto de San Agustín se fue con lo restante a San Mateo, y a la entrada de la barra se perdió el navío y el bastimento, [y] escapó la gente.

Fue luego avisado el Adelantado, y por prencipio de hebrero [de 1566] les envió una fragata de setenta toneladas cargada de maíz, vino y aceite, paños y lienços, alguna jarçia y estopa de valor, todo ello de más de seis mil ducados. A un solo mercader compró los cuatro mil ducados de esta ropa y bastimentos, fiados por un año. Y como la fragata llegó a Santo Agustín, antes de descargarla, una noche amotinose la gente y prendieron al maestro de campo, justiçia y regimiento que allí había, y al tenedor de bastimentos. Clavaron la artillería y nombraron electo y sargento mayor que los gobernase, que eran obedecidos y respetados. Estuviéronse de esta manera seis días, a cabo de los cuales se embarcaron como ciento y treinta hombres en la fragata. Y porque no cabían todos los amotinados dentro, andaba el sargento mayor que los amotinados habían nombrado señalando a los que se habían de embarcar, que habían de ser de los que habían sido más rebeldes y traidores a Su Majestad en este motín. Traía este sargento por la guarda de su persona doce arcabuceros y seis alabarderos, y queriéndose él embarcar con esta gente que le hacía guarda, tuvo lugar el maestro de campo de soltarse y soltó otros ocho de regimiento y ofiçiales de Su Majestad. Y tomando sus arcabuces [45v] fuéronse sin ser sentidos sobre ellos.

Desmampararon la barca. Tomósela el maestro de campo.[183] Como se vieron perdidos, rindiéronsele y diéronle las armas, y los hizo prender a buen recaudo. Hízoles cargo,[184] porque había alteración entre otros amigos que allí tenían estos prisioneros y no habían pudido caber en la fragata. Y habiéndoles tomado su confesión la noche venida,[185] antes del día hizo ahorcar el maestro de campo al sargento. Hubo lástima del electo, que también lo prendió, porque era un simple, y muy contra su voluntad había aceptado aquel oficio. Luego a la mañana lo[186] soltó, y a los demás que tenía presos, dándoles una reprehensión. Y por que la fragata no pudiera[187] salir, armó el maestro de campo un patax que allí tenía para ir sobre ella. Y habiéndolo hecho, llevando consigo dentro del patax la gente de más confiança que tenía, y empeçándola a lombardear para la echar al fondo, cortaron[188] el cabo a la fragata con que estaba surta, y guindó las velas [y] fuese huyendo.

El maestro de campo se volvió al fuerte y desarmó el patax, [y] puso su gente en gobierno y en de[s]ciplina como de antes. Hubo gran lástima el Adelantado al maestre de campo, de verle tan flaco y del sentimiento que había hecho por habérsele desacatado. Fue a veinte de março [de 1566] cuando el Adelantado allí llegó. También estaba Bartolomé Menéndez, gobernador y alcaide de aquel fuerte y distrito, hermano del Adelantado, en la cama muy enfermo. Y cuando fue el motín había ido con unos soldados a los indios enemigos a buscar algún maíz, que si allí estuviera cuando el motín, según era malquisto le mataran. Todos estaban tristes y afligidos, que era gran lástima, y con la venida del Adelantado luego se alegraron y estuvieron buenos los enfermos, porque la carabela [46r] traía mucho maíz y miel y gallinas y alpargates.

Y el mesmo día entró Estébano de las Salas de vuelta de La Habana, donde había dejado a doña Antonia y a los demás indios, que también traía bastimentos, carne y ganado, que fue gran regocijo, contento y alegría para todos.[189]

En el tiempo que hubo este motín en San Agustín lo hubo también en San Mateo, porque se averiguó que fue caso pensado y trato doble[190] entre algunos capitanes, ofiçiales y soldados de un fuerte y de otro, que ordenaron de pedir con toda instancia al maestro de campo que se acabase de hacer un navío que los franceses tenían en el estellero a manera de galera en San Mateo, y se ad[e]reçase un patax que estaba en San Agustín y se alçasen con el primer navío de bastimento que viniese. Y después de proveídos con esto, y con los tres navíos saldrían de la tierra, prendiendo los soldados a los capitanes que se quisiesen ir, para que se entendiese que los llevaban por fuerça. Y si algún capitán se quedase de éstos del motín, parecíales que en cualquier otro navío que hubiese había de ser forçosa la salida, porque con tan poca gente no se pudían defender de los indios, si fuesen enemigos, y que de esta manera les tendría Su Majestad en servicio la quedada, a tiempo que hubiese el motín, y después la salida de la tierra, porque todos no pereciesen. Y para poderlo efectuar con todo secreto, porque temían al maestro de campo y no pudían atraer a sus voluntades a los gobernadores y alcaides de los fuertes, que eran Bartolomé Menéndez, hermano del Adelantado en San Agustín, y a Gonçalo[191] de Villarruel en San Mateo.

Y el maestro de campo, aunque vio que adereçar[192] los navíos era malo, no se atrevió a hacer otra cosa, porque andaban ya alterados. Díjoles que ordenasen ellos la carta para San Mateo, que él la firmaría, y así se hizo. Él escribió otra a Gonçalo de Villarroel y cosiola en las espaldas al mensajero por que no se la hallasen, y decía por ella al Villarroel que impediese [46v] que aquel navío no se acabase, porque no pudiera hacer otra cosa sino dar la carta que pidían, por estar la gente alterada, y que él se gobernase con la gente de San Mateo, si se quería amotinar, lo mejor que pudiese, conforme al tiempo y de manera que no le matasen.

Y estos motines se començaron a tratar cinco días después que el Adelantado partió de San Agustín la vuelta del Cabo del Cañaveral a buscar a los franceses que se estaban fortificando—como está dicho—porque partió de San Agustín a esto a veinte y seis de octubre de sesenta y çinco. Y halláronse cartas escritas de un fuerte a otro de primero de noviembre en que començaban a buscar el remedio de salir de la tierra, no teniendo razón ni fundamento para ello más de parecelles que no tenían nueva de oro ni de plata en aquella tierra, y que los más de ellos tenían por imposible la victoria que Dios Nuestro Señor había dado al Adelantado con los luteranos, y que de Santo Domingo e isla de Cuba pudieran pasarse al Perú y Nueva España, que era tierra rica y fértil, y eran éstos sus principales intentos con que habían salido de España. Y como no aportaron a aquellas islas y dio Dios la victoria contra los luteranos al acabar de echarlos de la tierra, y no querían ser conquistadores y pobladores en ella, parecioles que era buena ocasión decir que lo hacían por falta de comida. Y ésta, si la quisieran reglar a los principios, por haber sacado el Adelantado los tre[s]cientos hombres para el segundo fuerte que después dejó con el capitán Juan Vélez de Medrano, y la gente de mar que llevaron los navíos que envió por bastimento y el que envió a España de aviso, la[193] había hasta todo março [de 1566], con gran cantidad de pescado, y muy buenos, y ostriones y cangrejos y palmitos, y gran cantidad de aceite que el Adelantado desembarcó. Y sin haber ganado el fuerte a los enemigos, trató el Adelantado que se diese a libra de bizcocho por ración, que era muy buena en conquista; algunas veces carnes, y otras garbanços cocidos con aceite y vinagre, otras pescado.

Y en nombre de todos replicó Juan de [47r] San Vicente, que era un soldado de Medina del campo que, al tiempo que el Adelantado quiso partir para la Florida, llegó a Sevilla, que venía de Italia por cierta quistión que allá había tenido, y llevó una carta de favor al Adelantado de Luis [de] Quintanilla en que le decía que era muy buen soldado, pareciéndole que respondería al esfuerço y valor del capitán San Vicente, su hermano, que le pidía le honrase y favoreciese en lo que hubiese lugar. El Adelantado era grande amigo de Luis de Quintanilla y era la primera cosa que le había pidido. Tenía notiçia del capitán San Vicente que estaba en Italia, hermano de este soldado, ser buen capitán. Pareçiole que éste fuera lo mesmo y nombrole por capitán. Y un compañero que consigo llevaba, que había sido camarada e[n] Italia, que se llamaba Fernán Pérez, también de Medina del Campo, le nombró por su alférez. Y dijo este capitán y su alférez al Adelantado que una libra de bizcocho a cada soldado por raçión es poco. Y aunque el Adelantado justificó con razones bastantes que era razonable, y que conforme al tiempo y necesidad no la había de dar mayor, porfió él y acudió con algunos de sus soldados a decir que no se sufría dar a libra de bizcocho por raçión. Y por esto acordó fuese a libra y cua[r]terón. Y quedole mala sospecha de este capitán y alférez.

Y después de ganado el fuerte a los françeses, que se quemó con el bastimento que había, quedaron más de cien pipas de harina. Alargáronse a comer muchos de los soldados, sin orden y sin querer que se les acortase la raçión. Faltoles a mediado hebrero [de 1566] y ellos desearon se les acabara muy antes—según después se vio—pues vino una fragata[194] de setenta toneles cargada de bastimento, y se alçaron y huyeron con ella. Y luego vinieron otros navíos de bastimento que el Adelantado trajo de San Agustín, y los de San Mateo—que estaban amotinados—no se habían partido.

Avisolos luego del bastante recaudo de bastimento que traía, y que había nueva que [los] franceses venían sobre ellos, que él les perdonaba [47v] la alteraçión. Y [dijo que] si estuviera con ellos se hubiera antes salido de la tierra por no perecer de hambre, y que ninguna culpa les daba en haberse amotinado para se salir de la tierra cuando no tenían comida, mas entonces, que había harta, que era gran traición la que harían a Su Majestad en desmampararle sus dos fuertes que en aquella tierra tenía, en especial que, como los cristianos quedasen pocos, serían luego los indios enemigos, y andaban algunos franceses entre ellos que les ad[i]estrarían para hacer la guerra a los que quedasen en los fuertes, que por hacer serviçio a Su Majestad y serle leales vasallos algunos no los querrían desmamparar. Recibieron este recaudo que el Adelantado les envió con escribano, que se lo[195] notificó de parte de Su Majestad, y que, so pena de ser dados por traidores, se volviesen al fuerte y que lo guardasen y cumpliesen. Respondieron que ellos no sabían cavar, arar ni labrar, y que aquella tierra no era buena para otra cosa, que se querían ir a las Indias a vivir[196] como cristianos y no estar en aquella tierra hechos bestias.

Estaban en aquel navío alçados ciento y veinte y tantos soldados, los treinta y cinco de ellos gente noble. Respondieron que ellos se querían ir al fuerte y servir al rey y obedecer a su general, que los echasen en tierra, que estarían como dos leguas del fuerte. Respondiéronles los demás que no querían, y replicáronles estos treinta y cinco soldados, diciéndoles que se echaban a perder en llevarlos, porque a cualquier tierra que llegasen habían de decir a la justiçia el trato [del] motín y cómo se salían de la tierra dejando el fuerte desamparado con sólo el alcaide Gonçalo[197] de Villarroel y su alférez Rodrigo de Troche, y don Hernando de Gamboa,[198] y Rodrigo Montes, primo-hermano[199] del maestro de campo, y a otros cuatro deudos y criados suyos, y al capitán Martín Ochoa con su alférez y sargento, con otros amigos, y el capitán Francisco de Recalde con un criado suyo, que todos eran veinte y cinco personas.

Como esto vieron todos los alterados y cabeças de este motín (que fueron el alférez y sargento del capitán Francisco de Recalde, y algunos Guzmanes—que recogió alterados—y todos los soldados de su compañía,[200] sin faltar uno, fueron amotinados) saltaron del navío en un batel a tierra y mataron tres indios, los dos principales. Y íbanse al navío y echa[ro]n en tierra estos treinta y [48r] çinco soldados sin armas, robándoles los vestidos. Y con todo esto iban [estos treinta y cinco] contentos, no sabiendo que [los otros] habían muerto los indios, porque hasta entonces no tenían guerra con ninguno, antes venían a los fuertes muchos indios e indias y traían pescado, y tenían grande amistad con los cristianos y querían juntar sus pueblos y venirse a vivir cabe los fuertes con los cristianos. Dentro de un hora que esto [fue] fueron desembarcados, yéndose para el fuerte. Los indios salieron a ellos y los flecharon y mataron.

No supo Gonçalo[201] de Villarruel, que quedaba con las veinte y çinco personas en el fuerte en San Mateo, esta guerra que los amotinados habían rompido con los indios, y envió a Rodrigo Troche, su alférez, con otro soldado, con aviso al maestro de campo, no sabiendo que el Adelantado fuese venido, para que entendiese cómo quedaba solo con tan poca gente y cómo este camino de San Mateo era de paz. Y se iban por los pueblos de los indios, donde les hacían cortesía, y por esto no llevaba el Rodrigo Troche ningún reçelo cuando le salieron ciertos indios, sus conoçidos, diciéndoles:

—¡Cristianos! ¡Hermanos y amigos!

Le prendieron a él y al compañero y les llevaron a Saturiba, su caçique, que les conocía muy bien, el cual le hizo abrir y sacar el coraçón y frechárselo, y lo mismo hizo a su compañero.

Como el escribano hizo su diligencia con los amotinados volviose a San Agustín con brevedad sin irse a San Mate[o], y como el Adelantado esto entendió acordó salir al navío y tomarle para ahorcar las cabeças de todos. Y estando para partir saliole de través Juan de San Vicente y su alférez pidiéndole licencia para irse en una carabela que el Adelantado enviaba a la Española a cargar de bastimento. El Adelantado le respondió que si se la daba la pedirían muchos y que a él le convenía ir con sus cuatro navíos y tre[s]cientos hombres, como estaba acordado, a Guale y a Santa Elena, para echar [a] los franceses que decían estaban allí y fortificarse en Santa Elena, que decían que era buen puerto. Y porque los indios se habían juntado muchos y andaban de guerra, que le convenía socorrer a Gonçalo de Villarroel con cien soldados y dejar en aquel Fuerte de San Agustín otros tantos con el maestro [48v] de campo, que le rogaba no hiciese demostración de irse de la tierra ni le pidiese[n] él ni su alférez liçençia, que no era bien pedírsela en tiempo que se espera viniesen franceses sobre ellos, [ya que] esto le había Su Majestad avisado.

Respondió que él tenía poca salud y su alférez lo mismo, que el Adelantado les haría merced de darles licencia. Respondió que diesen petiçiones, que proveería lo que conviniese. Diéronlas, y tras ellos más de otros cien soldados la pidieron, que en una petición venían doce y quince metidos. El Adelantado les respondió que no había lugar, y temió que, ido a Santa Elena, sería el motín de aquel fuerte y el de San Mateo[202] peor que los pasados, y para salir con sus intenciones matarían al maestro de campo y alcaides de los fuertes y otros ofiçiales de Su Majestad.

Hízoles un requerimiento, que al servicio de Su Majestad no convenía saliesen de la tierra ni le pidiesen la dicha liçençia, y que ido de allí para Santa Elena no hiciesen alteración ni motín, que venida gente de España él les daría liçençia, y si querían enviar persona[s a] España la[s] nombrasen y se fuesen en la carabela que el Adelantado enviaba a la Española a cargar de bastimentos, para que pasasen a España en los navíos que fuesen de

Santo Domingo. Y que si partido él de allí a Santa Elena se habían de ir de allí y amotinarse, dejando los fuertes desmamparados, que se lo[s] dejasen, que por escusar mayor mal él les daba liçençia, mas que les mandaba—so pena de muerte y perdimiento de bienes y ser dados por traidores—que estuviesen en el dicho fuerte sin salir de él, so pena que, el que lo contrario hiciese, ejecutaría en él esta pena. Y que si todavía no lo quisiesen guardar ni cumplir que se les dar[í]a la licencia para que vayan presos a España a la Casa de la Contratación de la ciudad de Sevilla con este testimonio, para que Su Majestad proveyese cerca de ello lo que fuese servido.

Sin embargo de esto, y con este requirimiento y penas, le pidieron licencia y él la dio. Podían caber en la carabela como sesenta personas. Apretáronse y acomodáronse tan bien[203] que cupieron çiento y tantas, y diose orden a la carabela que los llevase a Puerto Rico y cargase allí de bastimentos y se volviese a la Florida. Y a ellos se les notificó que—so pena de la vida y ser [49r] dados por traidores—se fuesen de Puerto Rico a España en los primeros navíos que hallasen, el cual auto consintieron. [No obstante,] salidos a la mar hacen fuerça al piloto que se fuesen a La Habana, porque les pareció que de allí pudían ir mejor y más presto al Perú y Nueva España, Honduras y Campeche, los cuales tuvieron el viento contrario para ello. No quis[ier]o[n] que gobernasen a Puerto Rico y fueron a la isla de Santo Domingo, a Puerto de Plata, y antes que allí llegasen hicieron una información, jurando unos en favor de otros, diciendo que habían servido y que iban con licencia. Fue avisada la justicia de lo contrario por aviso secreto que el piloto llevaba, que dio a Francisco de Çaballos, vecino de aquella villa, el cual recibió y guardó el despacho. Y esta gente fue favoreçida y regalada de la justiçia y vecinos, principalmente de Francisco de Çaballos, dándoles de comer y caballos. Y porque había çédula de Su Majestad en todas las Indias y en aquella villa para todas las justiçias, que cualquier persona que de la Florida aportase a su destricto los prendiesen y a buen recaudo los enviasen a Florida[204] a la parte que el Adelantado estuviese, y a esta causa prendían algunos y luego los soltaban, y se pasaban[205] los más de ellos al Perú y Nueva España, y otros se murieron allí, que llegaron muy flacos, que como venían muchos en la carabela, hartos más de los que ella pudía traer, venían muy apretados y la calor era mucha, y era navegaçión de diez o doce días y tardaron treinta y tantos, y faltoles el bastimento y el agua, fue milagro quedar ninguno vivo.

Fue avisado el Adelantado de todo esto, y que los otros çiento y veinte soldados que se habían alçado con la fragata cargada de bastimento en San Agustín habían aportado allí y se les había hecho mucha cortesía y honra. Dio notiçia a la Real Audiençia de aquella isla que, conforme a la cédula de Su Majestad, pues no le enviaban estos soldados a la Florida los enviasen a España, porque sería Su Majestad muy deservido que se pasasen [49v] a las Indias. Hubo en esto descuido, que se pasaron los más de ellos a las partes de las Indias que quisieron, y otros se presentaron en la Audiençia diciendo que habían servido muy bien y no tenían culpa y los dieron por libres, en espeçial al capitán San Vicente y a su alférez, cosa que admiró y fue muy mal ejemplo para los más soldados que quedaban en servicio de Su Majestad en la Florida, porque Su Majestad, por sus reales provisiones que estaban presentadas en aquella Audiençia, no mandaba conoçer de pleitos y cosas de la Florida sino, que expresamente, que cualquier persona que de ella saliese sin licençia del Adelantado se lo volviesen preso a buen recaudo. Y aunque estas provisiones se presentaron y notificaron en todas las Indias a las justiçias, de quinientos soldados que salieron de la Florida amotinados, y otros quinientos que iban para aquella tierra y se quedaron en las Indias, los cuales todos mil llevó el Adelantado de España a su despensa y costa, dándoles pasaje y matalotaje, y hasta hoy no le han enviado diez de ellos a la Florida.

Dio de todo aviso a Su Majestad para que enviase sus provisiones a todas las Indias para que presos los enviasen a estos reinos, para que no haya tanta gente alterada en aquellas partes. Los más de éstos, por dondequiera que iban, y los que vinieron a estos reinos, para justificar sus flaquezas decí[a]n y publicaban mal de la tierra y de la empresa y del Adelantado y de sus ministros, parientes y amigos que en ella quedaban a las hambres, trabajos y peligros que suçediesen. Y esto fue causa que muchas personas al principio—cuando el Adelantado fue—querían ir a poblar, y por lo que éstos decían, y por las cartas que el capitán San Viçente y su alférez Fernán Pérez y otros de éstos que habían hecho flaqueza escribían, tan perjudiciales[206] contra el Adelantado y sus ministros y oficiales, y en decir mal de la tierra, todo contra [50r] razón y verdad, que dicen fue causa que no se halló hombre que a ella[207] quiera venir a vivir, poblar ni conquistar. Dieron tanto crédito [a] estas cartas y nuevas en España y en todas las Indias que se decía que condenaban muchos al Adelantado en porfiar en querer poblar esta tierra, de tal manera que se dijo que algunos ministros de Su Majestad le daban culpa, en no advertir de que todos los que esto decían lo que habían andado era al luengo de la tierra, y por la marina y arenales y ciénagas, guardando los fuertes y haciendo la guerra a los luteranos, y no había ninguno que hubiese andado una legua por la tierra adentro de la Florida.[208]

Por haberse ido el capitán Juan de San Vicente y su alférez con las ciento y tantas personas del Fuerte de San Agustín en la carabela—como está dicho—a Puerto de Plata, mudó consejo el Adelantado, porque de los tre[s] cientos hombres que había de llevar a Guale y Santa Elena dejó los çiento y çincuenta en los dos fuertes de San Agustín y San Mateo con la más gente que primero había dejado y fuese con los otros çiento y cincuenta con dos bergantines y un navío de cien toneladas derecho a Guale. Y de camino entró en San Mateo, dejó la gente y bastimento, y visitó aquel fuerte. Alegró mucho su llegada a Gonçalo de Villarroel y a los que con él estaban.

Condenaban en San Agustín y en San Mateo al capitán Francisco de Recalde sobre que le daban mucha culpa sobre los motines que hubo, y la información general que se hizo de [aqu]éllos que habían sido culpados resultaba contra él más que contra otro ninguno. El Adelantado no quiso castigar a ninguno, envió el proceso a Su Majestad, y envió preso a Françisco de Recalde a la [Casa de la] Contratación de Sevilla. Vino el proceso, hallose sacado de la culpa de él Francisco de Recalde, y como él llegó a Sevilla no se presentó en esta corte. Como vio que no había culpa contra él en el proceso pidió de merced a Su Majestad se le suspendiese hasta la venida del Adelantado [50v] a España. Túvose por cierto que el Adelantado mandara justiciar al capitán Francisco de Recalde por la culpa que contra él resultaba en el proceso, y porque le halló en su cofre ciertas cartas recebidas de un religioso de Sevilla que estaba en el Fuerte de San Agustín, que se llamaba el licenci[a]do Rueda, que fue una de las cabeças de los amotinadores, que por información que hizo en la ciudad de Santo Domingo ante la justiçia, tomando por testigos a otros soldados amotinados, sirve agora de cura en aquella ciudad y le hacen mucha cortesía.

Capítulo 11

En tierras del cacique Guale

Dejando el Adelantado reparados los dos fuertes—el de San Agustín y San Mateo—lo mejor que pudo conforme al tiempo y bastimento que tenía, partió de San Mateo para prencipio de abril del dicho año de sesenta y seis, y habiendo navegado tres días descubrió un puerto y metiose en los dos bergantines con hasta çincuenta personas. Dejó a Estébano de las Salas con las otras çiento en el navío de cien toneles. A lo largo fue el Adelantado a reconocer un puerto que vio y desembarcó en él cerca del pueblo como un cuarto de legua. Acudieron muchos indios frecheros allí, y un cristiano entre ellos, también desnudo, con sus arcos y flechas, y habló español y dijo:

—¿Qué gente? ¿Dónde sois, hermanos?

El Adelantado respondió:

—Amigos, somos españoles.

Y preguntoles:

—Hermanos, ¿quiénes sois y qué hacéis aquí?

El hombre le respondió:

—Soy francés, aunque naçí y me crié en Córdoba. Habrá quince años que me solté del castillo de Triana, que me tenían allí preso, y fuime huyendo a França. Allí me casé en Abra de Graçia.²⁰⁹ Después acá ando siempre por la mar. Estuve seis años en el Brasil a deprender la lengua de los indios en un puerto y tierra de Brasil que estuvo allí el capitán Villaga-ñón,²¹⁰ capitán-general de aquella tierra, y fue a França a pedir socorro, [51r] y acudió allí una armada portuguesa y ganole el fuerte que tenía. Unos murieron y otros quedamos vivos, yo escapeme en[tre los] indios, que sé muy bien la lengua. Fue allí después [un navío fra]nçés y fuime en él para França. Después hizo [una armada]²¹¹ el Almirante de França y enviome en ella a esta tierra para lengua. Y por visrey de toda la Florida venía Juan Ribao, que era general de la armada. Yo vine con él y estoy aquí por lengua [desde] entonces.

El Adelantado le dijo cómo se llamaba aquella tierra y el cacique de ella. Dijo que se llamaba "la Florida," y que el señor de aquella tierra y pueblo que parecía cerca se llamaba Guale, y que él enviaba a saber qué gente era, para que si eran españoles no les dejasen desembarcar los indios, porque aquel cacique y su gente eran amigos de los franceses. El Adelantado le[212] dijo:

—Nosotros no hacemos mal a los indios, antes les hacemos bien, y contra su voluntad no queremos ir a su tierra. Llegaos acá, hermano, que me pesa veros andar de esa manera.

Y diole una camisa nueva y unos çaragüellos [e un sombrero],[213] y de comer, y dijo [que] si los indios querían comer que se llegasen allí. Él llamó a los i[n]dios y luego vinieron, sentáronse en la arena y diéronles bizcocho, que comían muy bien, y unos higos pasados. Podían ser los indios hasta cuarenta. A todos les dio el Adelantado algún rescate con que se holgaron muy mucho, y hablaban[214] al Adelantado por señas, diciendo que fuese a su tierra. El Adelantado preguntó a la lengua qué decían. La lengua dijo que se alegraban mucho con el Adelantado y le decían fuese a su pueblo a ver a su cacique. El Adelantado dijo a la lengua que les dijese que así lo quería hacer, y luego tomó consigo treinta arcabuceros y cuatro ballesteros y saltó en tierra, dejando los diez y seis hombres en guarda de los bergantines, y los indios no tuvieron ningún miedo.

Y yendo caminando hacia el pueblo iba el Adelantado hablando con la lengua, y preguntole quién lo había [51v] dejado allí. Dijo que había seis meses que se perdiera Juan Ribao con parte de su armada andando en busca del general Pero Menéndez que iba a aquella tierra a hacer los indios cristianos. Y el Juan Ribao y capitanes y gente que con él venían eran de la nueva religión, y querían todos los franceses que en aquella armada venían y el Almirante de França que todos los indios fuesen luteranos de la nueva religión, como ellos, y sujetarlos para que viniesen a la obediença del Rey de França, y tener allí galeras para las flotas y naos de las Indias que por allí pasasen tomarlas; el cual con una tormenta se perdió, y su general, y escapó la gente, y envió en un batel a un yerno suyo y otros capitanes y doce marineros, y él entre ellos, para que fuesen a un fuerte que tenían a decir que fuesen dos o tres navíos para la gente, porque estaban estos navíos en el puerto adonde estaba el fuerte. Y entrando en el puerto donde el fuerte estaba, los indios amigos les dijeron que otros cristianos como ellos les habían tomado sus casas y haciendas y el fuerte, y les habían degollado los hombres que dentro estaban.

Acudió[215] luego a la marina un francés que andaba huido entre los indios, que les contó todo lo que había pasado, y entonçes acordó esta gente del batel que se fuesen a Santa Elena porque los indios de allí eran sus amigos y sabían la lengua y tierra, porque había seis años que tuvieron allí un castillo tres o cuatro años. Y porque el capitán no se quería ir a Françia lo mataron sus soldados e hicieron un navío y se fueron con él a Inglaterra. Y un cri[a]do de este capitán françes muerto, por que no le matasen (a causa que diría en Françia lo que había pasado) huyó al monte entre los indios y quedose con ellos. Casáronle con una hija del cacique.[216] Llamábase Guillermo y era muy buen latino.

Supo el Real Consejo de Indias lo que en esto pasaba por la vía del embajador [52r] que estaba en Françia e Inglaterra, y escribió a Diego de Maçariegos, que era gobernador de la isla de Cuba, enviase a aquella costa algún navío ligero para descubrir si había franceses. Y así envió una fragata muy ligera, y en buena orden entraron en este puerto de Santa Elena, aunque no por la entrada prencipal, porque tiene dos entradas, y por esto los marineros y piloto le tuvieron por ruin puerto. Y llegándose cerca del pueblo con la fragata vino allí el Guillermo françés. Díjolos cómo andaba en aquella tierra, cuántos años había, y que él era católico y los françeses que allí habían estado eran todos luteranos y le querían muy mal. Y preguntáronle si había franceses en aquella tierra. Dijo que no había más que él, y que ellos si eran españoles. Dijéronle que sí. Díjoles que le llevasen consigo. Dijeron que eran contentos, y así lo hicieron. Volviéronse a La Habana con estas nuevas, entregaron a Guillermo a Diego de Maçariegos, gobernador de Cuba, el cual él después, por una cédula de Su Majestad, entregó al Adelantado Pero Menéndez.

Y cuando el Adelantado allegó allí a Guale e iba al pueblo hablando con la lengua françesa, llevaba a Guillermo allí consigo, que también entendía la lengua de Guale, porque había de Guale a Santa Elena no más de veinte leguas. Y la lengua que halló en Guale fue diciendo al Adelantado, yendo para el pueblo, [. . .][217] que quince françeses habían llegado[218] allí a Guale, y que el cacique los había recebido muy bien, dándoles de comer, y hízoles una casa en que viviesen. Y que habían estado allí cinco meses, en que habían hecho su batel mayor, y que quince días había se partieron por la

Tierra Nova para irse en las naos que allí van a la pesquería, y que el cacique de Guale y el de Santa Elena [52v] eran enemigos, y que el cacique de Guale llevó a estos franceses consigo a la guerra contra el cacique de Santa Elena, que llaman Orista, aunque los franceses iban de mala gana porque el Orista y sus indios los conocían y no los querían tomar por enemigos. Y fue el Guale a Santa Elena en el mesmo batel de los françeses. Prendieron con el batel cuatro indios que iban en una canoa, los dos de ellos prençipales, parientes del Orista, que conocieron a los más de los franceses que iban en el batel, y volviéronse con esta presa a Guale. Y antes de llegar al pueblo, de los cuatro indios, los dos que no eran prencipales se echaron a nado y se volvieron a Santa Elena, contaron al cacique lo que pasaba, que los cristianos que allí habían estado seis años había los habían preso con su barco. Envió el cacique Orista de Santa Elena a amenazar a los franceses que estaban en Guale. Todo esto contó la lengua al Adelantado y que de allí a dos días el cacique Guale había de matar [a] aquellos dos indios principales de Santa Elena.

De oír esto mostró gran contentamiento el Adelantado y dijo a la lengua que le pesaba porque tuviesen guerra aquellos dos caciques, que holgaría de hacerlos amigos. La lengua holgó mucho de esto y dijo que lo trataría, porque deseaba que los de Santa Elena fuesen amigos de los franceses.

Llegó el Adelantado al pueblo, fue muy bien recebido de Guale y toda su gente. Diéronle la mesma casa que dejaron los françeses. Todos los indios e indias, grandes y pequeños, venían a ver al Adelantado y tres mochachos que traía consigo, que a las mañanas y a las tardes en mar y en tierra, dondequiera que alojaban, arbolando su cruz decían la doctrina cristiana, y así lo hicieron aquella tarde allí en el pueblo de Guale. Todos los soldados iban a la doctrina, [53r] y acabando de decirse iban a besar la cruz. Este día era Viernes Santo del año de sesenta y seis, y el Guillermo francés acudía siempre a la doctrina.

La otra lengua, naçida en Córdoba, que allí estaba, reíase de Guillermo y de todos nosotros porque era muy gran luterano—según adelante se supo—y reprehendió al Guillermo. Y el Guillermo reprendiole a él y dijo al Adelantado lo que con él había pasado. El Adelantado le llamó y le dijo si era católico o si luterano. La lengua le respondió que era luterano de la nueva religión y que para aquello había quedado en aquella tierra. El Adelantado le dijo entonçes quién era, porque hasta entonçes no lo sabía, y que él andaba por allí para que los indios fuesen cristianos, y que si sus soldados supiesen que era luterano le matarían luego, que él no les diría nada, que dijese a todos que era muy católico, y que dijese al cacique y a los demás indios que aquellos[219] franceses que allí estuvieron eran cristianos de mentira y que no eran de su tierra, que él era cristiano de verdad y que nosotros éramos también cristianos de verdad, siervos de Dios, y que íbamos para matar [a] aquellos franceses porque eran bellacos y malos cristianos. Y que si el cacique quería ser cristiano, y su gente, holgaría el Adelantado de ello y le defendería de sus enemigos.

La lengua, de temor que la gente del Adelantado no le matase, dijo muy bien aquella razón al cacique y sus principales, porque estaba presente el Guillermo francés para ver si decía otra cosa, porque entendía muy bien la lengua y quería muy mucho al Adelantado, que le hacía muy buen tratamiento, y andaba en toda su libertad para poder irse cuando quisiese. Y en dos años que estuvo en La Habana se pudiera [53v] haber ido si quisiera.

El cacique respondió al Adelantado que quería ser cristiano de verdad y no de mentira, como los otros cristianos que allí estaban. El Adelantado dijo el poder y bondad de Dios, y lo demás que a los otros caciques, y que mandase a su gente que fuesen a oír los cantares que los niños decían, que era la doctrina cristiana, y besar la cruz, que después le dirían lo que aquellos cantares querían decir. Dijo que así lo haría, e hizo el Adelantado hincar allí una cruz grande. Y habiéndose juntado todos y cantando las ledanías, hincados de rodillas, fueron a adorar y besar la cruz. El cacique y todos los indios e indias hicieron lo mismo.

Rogó el Adelantado a la lengua, pues era español, se volviese católico, a la fe de Jesucristo, que le quer[r]ía mucho y daría muchas cosas, y si se quisiese ir a Francia lo enviaría de España para que de allí se fuese, y si se quisiese estar allí también lo podría hacer. Respondió que allí se quería quedar y estar, y que él quería ser cristiano y católico, y trabajaría que lo fuesen los indios. El Adelantado se lo agradeció muy mucho y le dijo que para otro día por la mañana tratasen con aquel cacique las paces con el cacique de Santa Elena, y que fuese él buen medianero para ello, y para que no matasen a aquellos dos indios principales de Orista. La lengua le prometió que haría en ello lo que pudiese.

Y otro día por la mañana el cacique y todos los indios e indias y mochachos y mochachas, cuando viero[n] que se estaba diciendo la doctrina cristiana, acudieron allí y se hincaron de rodillas. Después de acabado, que los soldados fueron a besar y adorar la cruz hincados de rodillas, el cacique y todos los indios hicieron lo mesmo. Luego tomó el Adelantado al cacique por la mano y le llevó en casa, y le rogó que hiciese llamar [a] sus indios prencipales [54r] porque los quería hablar, y sí vinieron como diez o doce. El Adelantado les dijo con la lengua que había sabido que tenían guerra con los indios de Santa Elena, que les rogaba fuesen amigos, que él haría tratar las paces, y que le diese los dos indios que tenía para se los llevar, y que cuando el cacique de Santa Elena no quisiese ser su amigo, que él se los volvería. Guale habló con sus indios y respondió que no quería, porque le tomaría los indios Orista y no querría ser su amigo.

Y había ocho meses que no llovía en aquella tierra y tenían sus maízes y labranças[220] secas, de que estaban todos tristes por la poca comida que tenían. El Adelantado le dijo que estaba Dios enojado contra él porque tenía guerra con Orista y con otros dos caciques, y porque mataba la gente que les tomaba, y que por esto no le quería dar Dios agua, que le dejaría dos cristianos en prendas de los dos indios, y que cuando no hiciese las paces con Orista y no le trajese los indios, que matase [a] aquellos dos cristianos. El cacique Guale habló con sus indios un rato y respondió que era contento. Y díjole el Adelantado que otro día se había de partir.

Mostraron tener gran placer todos los indios, grandes y pequeños, de estas paces que el Adelantado quería tratar, porque los indios de Santa Elena eran más poderosos y mataban muchos indios a este cacique de Guale. Luego fue a almorzar el Adelantado con sus soldados y llevó al cacique consigo y a dos hijos suyos muy buenos que tenía, y fuese dos leguas de allí a ver la isla y disposición de la tierra. El cacique, por ser viejo, se volvió habiendo andado media legua. Hallose toda la tierra muy buena y apacible para pan y vino. A la vuelta que el Adelantado vino al pueblo, el cacique le pidió le mostrase los dos cristianos que con él habían de quedar. Luego se los mostró, porque los tenía señalados para [54v] consigo. Los dos soldados callaron, sin responder nada, mostrándose muy tristes. El cacique dijo que no quería [a] aquellos dos cristianos, que él había de tomar los dos que quisiese. El Adelantado dijo que era contento, que los señalase luego. El cacique señaló a un sobrino del Adelantado llamado Alonso Menéndez Marqués y a Vasco Çabal, alférez del estandarte real, que vio que comían a su mesa (y también se creyó se lo había dicho la lengua que eran aquellos dos de los más prencipales).

El Adelantado le dijo que era contento que quedasen aquéllos, que eran entrambos sus capitanes, de los que él más quería, y los dejaría a cada uno un cristiano para que le sirviese, y los niños que enseñasen la doctrina cristiana. El cacique se mostró muy alegre por esto y los fue a abraçar a su modo y darles las gracias a manera de respetallos. Ellos se entristecieron mucho, diciendo que no era bien quedarse con aquello[s] salvajes. El Adelantado les respondió que de buena gana se quedara él, que no tenían de qué temer, que él les rogaba mucho procurasen con aquella lengua darles a entender cuán bestialmente vivían y cómo era bueno ser cristianos. Dijo luego al cacique que tratase bien a sus cristianos y que, si les hacía mal, que a él y a toda su gente les mandaría cortar las cabeças, porque haría las paces y traería indios principales de Santa Elena para efectuarlas, y se volvería lo más presto que pudiese. El cacique se atemorizó, y si el Adelantado le apretara, de buena gana le diera los cristianos con los indios para que se fuera de su tierra, porque tenían gran temor los indios al Adelantado, porque ya tenían noticia de las victorias que habían tenido contra los luteranos franceses, porque en aquella tierra corren mucho las nuevas de las cosas que suceden de cacique en cacique. Respondió este cacique al Adelantado que trataría bien su gente y que él ni sus indios no la matarían, si el cacique [55r] del cielo no la mataba.

En tierras del cacique Orista

Así se partió el Adelantado otro día por la mañana para Santa Elena dejando allí estos seis cristianos en prendas y para que doctrinasen los indios. Enbarcose en sus bergantines, salió a la mar a mediodía, descubrió un navío, fue sobre él, reconoció que era el suyo, que estaba surto, entró dentro. Fue grandísima el alegría que Esteban de las Salas y su gente reçibió con el Adelantado, porque temieron mucho que era perdido, que había cuatro días que se apartó de ellos a reconocer el puerto, que era dilaçión de dos o tres horas, y aquella noche hubo mucha tormenta. Tocaron de placer las trompetas e hicieron salva con la artillería. Los dos indios que el Adelantado llevaba de Santa Elena y otro prencipal de Guale que iba para hallarse presente a las paces hubieron mucho miedo a la artillería, diciendo que les hacía mucho mal para la cabeça y para el coraçón, que tañiesen las trompetas—que era buena cosa—[y] no tirasen más. El Adelantado lo mandó así, y dijo a Guillermo lengua que tuviese cuenta de los tres indios, pues los entendía, y los alegrase y regocijase todo lo que pudiese,[221] y encargó a todos los soldados los tratasen muy bien. Hizo el Adelantado levantar la áncora al navío y navegó para Santa Elena con él y sus dos bergantines. Contó luego a Estébano de las Salas y a la más gente lo que le había aconteçido y holgáronse, aunque les pesó mucho de la quedada de Alonso Menéndez Marqués, porque era muy bienquisto de todos.

Llegaron otro día a la tarde a Santa Elena, que los tres indios que llevaban conocieron muy bien el puerto. Entró dentro, por donde los indios le guiaban, que eran diestros pilotos porque solían andar por allí pescando con sus canoas. Habiendo entrado y andado por la vía adentro una legua, los indios mandaron surgir con el navío grande, porque adelante no podría pasar, [55v] y que se embarcasen en los bergantines y fuesen al pueblo. El

Adelantado lo hizo así y se embarcó en los bergantines, y llevó consigo a Estébano de las Salas y hasta cien personas. Llegó al pueblo de los indios, que estaba de allí a dos leguas, y halláronle quemado, y volvían a hacer de nuevo algunas casas. Parecieron algunos indios muy alterados con sus arcos y flechas, y puestos de guerra. Los indios que el Adelantado llevaba le dijeron que pensaban aquellos indios que él y su gente eran de los cristianos de mentira que los habían cautivado en la guerra sirviendo a Guale, que ellos saltarían en tierra y les dirían cómo éramos muy buenos y enemigos de aquéllos, y a lo que veníamos.

El Adelantado les dejó ir, y dentro de media hora desembarcó con toda la gente, dejando en guarda a los bergantines, en cada uno, diez personas. Y luego los indios vinieron al Adelantado sin arcos ni flechas, con grande humildad, haciendo grandes demostraçiones de respetalle, y fueron corriendo muchos, unos por unos caminos y otros por otros. Esto era que ya enviaban a dar aviso a los pueblos, caciques y capitanes que viniesen a ver al Adelantado. E hicieron luego grande fuego, trajeron mucho marisco y cenó el Adelantado y su gente. Acudieron muchos indios, todos le iban a hablar y respetar, que era cosa de ver el amor y alegría que mostraron estos indios con el Adelantado. Vinieron aquella noche tres caciques, sujetos del Orista, y le dijeron que se fuese a un pueblo que estaba de allí una legua, que el Orista y otros capitanes y caciques suyos vernían allí a comer. Hízolo el Adelantado así.

En siendo de día vino el Orista y otros dos caciques y capitanes. Fue tanta el alegría que todos tuvieron con Guillermo la lengua, a quien este Orista[222] había dado [56r] una hija por mujer en el tiempo que Guillermo allí estuvo. Mandole el Adelantado que dijese a Orista que se juntase con sus prencipales, porque le[s] quería hablar. Así lo hicieron. El Adelantado mandó a G[u]illermo, que era lengua, les dijese, estando presentes los tres indios que el Adelantado consigo había llevado, todo lo que había pasado con Guale cerca de las amistades. El Orista dijo que luego respondería, y habló con sus indios más de media hora, dando y tomando, sin que quisiesen que Guillermo allí estuviese por que no entendiesen lo que pasaba y trataban. Y luego llamaron a la lengua, al cual hablaron muy gran rato. Y dijo luego la lengua al Adelantado de parte del Orista que holgaba mucho de hacer las paces, como el Adelantado se lo mandaba, y holgarían mucho más de ser cristianos de verdad él y su gente, como lo querían ser los de Guale, que aquéllos no habían de ser mejores que ellos, que sus dos indios que el Adelantado trajo les habían dicho quién era Dios y cuán bueno era ser cristianos, que querían mucho que el Adelantado viviese en aquella tierra y tomarle por hermano mayor para hacer lo que él les mandase, y que ternían a los cristianos de mentira por enemigos, pues lo eran del Adelantado.

El cual les respondió, con grande alegría que mostraba tener en su coraçón, que los quería mucho y que no pensaba vivir en aquella tierra (porque era mala y la suya era mejor), y que sus indios matarían a sus cristianos, porque los cristianos que traía no hacían mal [a los indios][223] y que, si [les] hacían algún mal, luego el Adelantado mataría a quien lo hacía, que desearía vivir allí sólo para que supiesen ser [56v] cristianos, para cuando se muriesen se fuesen al çielo. Díjoles el poder y bondad de Dios, y lo mesmo que decía a los otros caciques para que fuesen cristianos.

Mostraron gran contento de oírlo y volvieron a decir[224] que ellos querían ser cristianos y, que si el Adelantado no quería vivir allí, que les dejase algunos cristianos para que los enseñasen. El Adelantado dijo que sí dejaría, y que si su gente le mataba alguno él volvería a hacerles la guerra y les cortaría a todos las cabeças. Ellos dijeron que eran muy contentos, y luego vinieron muchas indias cargadas de comida: maíz, bellotas, ostras y pescado cocido y asado.[225] El Adelantado mandó sacar bizcocho y vino, y alguna melaza de açúcar, y repartió con los indios, los cuales todos bebieron bien el vino y les supo bien el bizcocho mojado en agua mezclado con aquella miel, que son muy amigos de esas dulçes.

Acabando de comer hicieron ciertas cerimonias con el Adelantado tomándole por hermano mayor, e hicieron que se sentase en el lugar más prencipal del cacique, adonde el cacique y todos los demás que allí estaban le fueron a obedeçer, haciendo ciertas cerimonias, tomándole las manos (que es cortesía como acá cuando las besan a los reyes). Luego vinieron todos los indios e indias a hacer lo mismo. Fue cosa de ver las madres y parientes de los dos indios principales que el Adelantado trujo de Guale—que eran moços—lo que lloraron de placer con el Adelantado, e hicieron luego los indios muchos bailes y cantaron todo el día hasta la medianoche.

Quedose a dormir allí el Adelantado, y otro día por la mañana dijo al cacique que [57r] quería ir a ver en la parte que podría hacer un pueblo, porque no era bien que viviesen sus cristianos entre sus indios, por que no riñesen. El cacique dijo que como él quisiese más, que le rogaba se fuese por el pueblo donde él vivía, y que allí cerca estaba un sitio muy bueno junto al puerto donde su nao estaba. El Adelantado holgó de esto y dijo si habían de ir por tierra o por agua. El cacique dijo que por donde quisiese. Acordó el Adelantado de se ir en sus bergantines. Metiose el cacique Orista con él y su mujer con hasta otros doce indios. Fue grandísimo el contento y alegría que el Adelantado mostró tener de ver la confiança que los indios hacían de él. Así los llevó muy alegres y regocijados todo el camino, y al desembarcar les dio de merendar. Fueron por tierra como media legua después de desembarcados, al pueblo y casa del cacique, donde fueron bien hospedados aquella noche.

A la mañana el cacique, en una casa grande que tenía, le sentó en su lugar principal, y él y los más indios e indias le fueron allí a obedecer y tomar por hermano mayor, como el día antes en el pueblo donde había estado. Dieron muchos pregones mandando que no hiciesen ningún mal a los cristianos, y allí les daba también el Adelantado, como dondequiera que llegaba, lo [que] acostumbraba de sus rescates, y a él le daban algunos cueros de gamuças[226] adobadas y perlas quemadas (que hay muchas en aquella tierra, mas como no las estiman, para comer el pescado asan la cáscara adonde está la perla y quémase la perla, y así no valen nada).

El Adelantado se fue otro día por la mañana con el cacique Orista a reconocer un sitio para hacer un fuerte. Hallole muy bueno [57v] y apacible, que es una isla de hasta cuatro leguas y que tiene[227] muy escogido puerto donde se podría muy bien fortificar. Y estaba de la barra como una legua, para que entrando los navíos viesen luego el fuerte. Acordó de fortificarse allí. Luego dio la traça del fuerte, habiéndolo acordado con Estébano de las Salas y más capitanes que consigo llevaba. Encomendó el hacerlo con presteza y brevedad al capitán Antonio Gómez,[228] que había sacado de La Habana de la nao capitana de la Flota de la Nueva España que allí estaba invernando, y con çincuenta soldados y otros marineros—toda muy buena gente—había venido de La Habana con el Adelantado para anclar con él en la Florida hasta todo mayo [de 1566], y así lo anduvieron y sirvieron muy bien en esta jornada.[229] Repartiose luego toda la gente por sus escuadras, que eran çiento y cincuenta soldados, unos a cortar y acarrear madera, otros fajina, e hincar estacas y abrir el foso.[230] Estuvo el Adelantado allí quince días, en los cuales con su gente y algunos indios que le ayudaron lo dejó en mediana defensa. Plantó en él seis pieças de artillería de bronçe. Nombró a Estébano de las Salas por alcaide de él y gobernador de aquella tierra. Dejole çiento y diez hombres. Envió el navío de cien toneles con otras veinte personas a la

Española a cargar de bastimento para los de allí, porque les quedaba poco. Envió él un bergantín a San Mateo y a San Agustín, dando aviso de lo que había acontecido, y que ya iba de vuelta.

El cacique Orista despachó luego a toda la tierra dando aviso de cómo estaban allí cristianos muy buenos y que no hacían mal, y daban de lo que tenían, que [58r] querían vivir en aquella tierra, que él y todos le habían tomado por hermano mayor para que los defendiese de sus enemigos, y que estaban de esto muy contentos, que él y todos los indios querían ser cristianos, y que el cacique cristiano de ellos era muy bueno, y que se quería ir, que si le querían ver viniesen luego. Al cabo de quince días que el Adelantado se quiso partir vinieron a él muchos caciques. Todos le tomaron por hermano mayor para hacer lo que él les mandase, y que querían ser cristianos y que les diese una cruz y algunos cristianos que viviesen en sus tierras que les dijesen cómo habían de ser cristianos. El Adelantado lo hizo así, dando a cada cacique un cristiano, y dos, y recaudo para que en los pueblos donde residiesen hiciesen una cruz y dijesen cada día, a la mañana y a la tarde, la doctrina cristiana, y procurasen que los indios la fuesen a oir y adorasen la cruz. Dio el Adelantado a estos caciques algunos rescates, y a cada uno su hacha, con que fueron muy contentos.

Capítulo 13

Regreso a tierras del cacique Guale

Partiose el Adelantado a prencipio de mayo [de 1566] y para guialle llevó consigo dos indios principales, para efectuar las paces con Guale. Quedó Estébano de las Salas y la gente que con él estaba contentos por parecerle llevaban muy buen principio para volver los indios cristianos, que después de echados los luteranos de la tierra era todo lo que deseaban, mas tenían gran temor a la falta de comida—que les quedaba muy poca—y el trabajo mucho de acabar su fuerte, [58v] porque cada día esperaban franceses luteranos, que como habían tenido nueva de los buenos suçesos que el Adelantado había tenido con ellos, así por mar como por tierra, en acabarlos y desarraigarlos de aquella tierra por que no enseñasen su mala secta a los indios, que para vengarse del daño que habían recebido del Adelantado y su gente y volver a poblar aquella tierra hacían gruesa armada. Y sabido cómo el Adelantado los aguardaba no se atrevieron irle a buscar y fuéronse a la isla de la Madera, que es del Rey de Portugal, y la tomaron, saquearon y robaron, y se volvieron a Françia. Y querer dar los indios comida a Estébano de las Salas y a su gente, no la tenían, que había muchos meses que no llovía.

Llegó el Adelantado a Guale con veinte personas a ocho de mayo [de 1566]. Desembarcó primero Guillermo, contó al cacique las[231] paces que quedaban hechas, y [a] Alonso Menéndez y Vasco Çabal y los otros cuatro cristianos que con ellos quedaron todo lo que les había aconteçido, de que se alegraron mucho. Desembarcó el Adelantado, fue muy bien recebido de Guale y de todos sus indios. Luego dijeron los dos indios de Orista a Guale su embajada, estando junto con sus prencipales, de que se holgó mucho él y toda su gente, grandes y pequeños, y le pesó de las amistades que el Adelantado había tomado con los de Santa Elena y que le hubiesen tomado aquellos caciques por hermano mayor. Y luego dijo con la lengua al Adelantado que él estaba contento de las [59r] paces y que le quería tomar por su hermano mayor para hacer lo que les mandase, y que querían ser cristianos de verdad y no de mentira, como los françeses que allí estaban, que le dejase gente que viviese en su tierra, pues la había dejado a Orista.

El Adelantado le dijo que no la tenía, que él se la enviaría presto. El cacique respondió que dejase la que allí había quedado, que era buena,[232] para que los enseñasen a ser cristianos, y que después le enviaría más. El Adelantado le dijo que él le respondería otro día por la mañana. Luego el cacique dijo al Adelantado que, pues ya era cristiano, y que por no enojar a Dios había hecho las paces con Orista, que le pidiese que le diese agua para sus maizales y sementeras, que había nueve meses que no llovía. El Adelantado le dijo que Dios estaba muy enojado con él porque le había mandado muchas cosas y no las había hecho y que, por eso, aunque le suplicase que le diese agua no lo querría hacer.

El cacique se volvió muy triste y se fue a su casa. Los niños de la doctrina, que esto supieron, fuéronse al cacique con la lengua y le dijeron que no estuviese triste, que ellos suplicarían a Dios que lloviese. El cacique les dio muchas gamuças, que son cueros de venado adobados, y maíz y pescado, los cuales lo tomaron y se fueron con ello. El Adelantado, cuando[233] esto supo, mandó que se lo[234] quitasen todo y los desnudasen para los azotar. El cacique, que lo supo, vino al Adelantado muy triste, diciendo que le traía engañado, pues no quería pedir al cacique del çielo agua y quería açotar a los niños porque se la pedían, que no los açotase, y no quería ya que pidiesen a Dios agua, que lloviese cuando Dios quisiese. El Adelantado dijo [59v] al cacique que aquellos niños eran bellacos, que por que les diese aquella comida y cueros de venados le engañaban y decían aquellas[235] mentiras, y que Dios estaba enojado con ellos porque eran bellacos. Y mandó que no açotasen los niños y dijo que si el cacique quería ser cristiano de verdad, que mejor daría Dios agua a él que no al Adelantado ni a los niños que le habían dicho mentiras e[n] muchas cosas. El cacique dijo con tristeza que él era cristiano de verdad desde el primer día, y fuese derecho a la cruz que estaba allí çerca e hincose de rodillas y besola, y volviose al Adelantado y díjole por la lengua:

—¡Mira cómo soy cristiano de verdad!

Esto pudo ser a las dos horas después de mediodía. No pasó media hora cuando vinieron truenos y relámpagos y empeçó a llover mucha agua, y cayó un rayo junto del pueblo en un árbol, que hizo muchas rajas. Todos los indios e indias acudieron a tomar las rajas y llevarlas para casa, guardándolas. Fueron todos los indios e indias con el cacique—y algunos llorando—a casa del Adelantado, echándose a sus pies algunos y otros pidiéndole las manos, rogándole que dejase allí cristianos.[236]

Habían dicho al Adelantado Alonso Menéndez, su sobrino, y Vasco Çabal, que la lengua que allí estaba francesa era luterano y gran somético, y que partido de allí el Adelantado para Santa Elena anduvo con los indios que los matasen, y que con Guillermo se podría informar de lo que en esto pasaba, que hablase con dos indios con quien él se echaba (que el uno decían era el hijo mayor del cacique), que con [6or] gran secreto hizo el Adelantado la diligençia. Y sabiendo ser verdad, y que le vieron escupir la cruz muchas veces delante de los indios, haciendo burla de los cristianos, habló con Alonso Menéndez, su sobrino, y con Vasco Çabal, alférez del estandarte real, que lo sabían y lo habían visto, y díjoles que no era bueno dejar desconsolados a aquel cacique y su gente, pues querían ser cristianos, que holgaría mucho se quedasen allí como antes estaban.

El Vasco Çabal respondió que antes aguardaría que el Adelantado le cortase la cabeça que quedar allí. Alonso Menéndez dijo que mucho le pesaría de quedar, mas como se lo mandase Su Señoría que lo haría, con que se matase [a] aquel francés o lo llevase consigo, porque de otra manera no se hacía nada y le matarían a él y a los que con él quedasen, y que el hijo del cacique mandaba más que su padre y quería mucho [a] aquella lengua, que si la mataban que se escandalizarían los indios y [se] volvería[n] de guerra. Pareçió muy bien esta razón al Adelantado, [y] porque se confiaba de Guillermo y le tenía por católico llamole y díjole que tratase con aquella lengua que se fuese con él a Santa Elena, que en canoa—sin salir a la mar, por un río—van allá en dos o tres días, y que Estébano de las Salas, que era muy buen capitán y liberal, le daría muchas cosas, y que traería a su cacique un presente que el cacique de Santa Elena le enviaba a decir inviase por la lengua. [La lengua] holgó de esto, y sin entender que el Adelantado lo entendía le vino a rogar le diese una carta para Estébano de las Salas que lo conociese, y le diese una hacha, porque él quería ir por el presente que había de enviar el cacique de Santa Elena [6ov] a su cacique Guale. El Adelantado dijo que le diesen papel y tinta, que luego la quería escrebir, y la escribió muy favorable y se la dio.

El cacique Guale despachó luego esta lengua con otros dos indios suyos en una canoa para que fuesen y volviesen luego. El hijo del cacique mostró pesarle mucho porque la lengua se iba, y llorando le rogó se volviese luego. El Adelantado envió a un soldado con una carta a Estébano de las Salas para que con gran secreto lo hiciese matar esta lengua porque era somético y luterano, y si volvía vivo no serían cristianos tan presto los de Guale, que deseaban serlo, y regalase mucho los dos indios de Guale que iban con él, y que a Orista hiciese lo mesmo, dándole[237] buen presente, y que enviase otro a Guale ofreciéndole amistad, y que fingidamente mostrase pesarle mucho porque la lengua no pareçía, que [dijera que] como era cristiano de mentira se habría escondido por los montes por no volver a Guale, para si algún navío de su tierra viniese irse con él. Y así Estébano de las Salas le hizo dar garrote [con gran secreto],[238] y los dos indios se volvieron a Guale.

Regreso a San Mateo y San Agustín

Y ya era partido el Adelantado para San Mateo y San Agustín, dejando en Guale a Alonso Menéndez—su sobrino—y a los cuatro cristianos que con él estaban primero, [y] llevó consigo a Vasco Çabal. Aquella agua que llovió en Guale duró veinticuatro horas y alcançó en toda la isla, que tendrá cuatro o çinco leguas.[239] Por donde el Adelantado iba para San Mateo navegando en el bergantín, por la parte de dentro, sin salir a la mar, salían muchas canoas [61r] y decían:

—¡España! ¡Amigos! ¡Cristianos! ¡Hermanos! ¡Daca la cruz!

Porque estos indios habían sabido lo que había pasado en Santa Elena y en Guale, y el agua que había llovido, y que querían ser cristianos. Alegrose de esto mucho el Adelantado, saltó en tierra y dioles algunos rescates, e hizo hacer muchas cruces pequeñas, y para cada pueblo dio la suya, besándola primero el Adelantado y sus soldados.

Y se despidió de ellos y llegó a San Mateo a quince de mayo [de 1566], donde halló la gente de aquel fuerte buena, con mucha necesidad de bastimento, y los indios todos muy de guerra. Y supo que habían frechado dos veces de noche las çentinelas de San Agustín, que habían muerto dos soldados y puesto fuego a la casa de muniçión, que estaba cubierta con hojas de palmito, por donde se quemó[240] el fuerte. Y de noche pusieron en las frechas fuego artifiçial y con los arcos las tiraron a la casa, y así se pegó el fuego porque hacía aire. Se apegó de tal manera que no fue posible remediarse, y la pólvora y muniçiones, paño y lienço, y las banderas y estandartes, así del Adelantado como de lo ganado a los luteranos, se quemó todo sin escapar nada. Y que estaban el maestro de campo y todos los demás con grandísimo aprieto y necesidad de comida y peligro de los indios, que andaban emboscados en cuadrillas para que, en saliendo algún cristiano a buscar palmitos y marisco, lo frechaban, que como estos indios de la Florida son tan ligeros y están tan çiertos que no los han de alcançar son muy atrevidos en llegar cerca de los cristianos, y otras veces en aguardarlos, y al retirarse los cristianos corren con [61v] ellos mucho peligro, porque tiran tan recio con los arcos que pasa una flecha la ropa y la cota que el soldado trae vestida, y son muy prestos en el tirar. Al disparar el arcabuz el soldado, primero que lo vuelva a cargar, por ligereza que el indio tiene júntase con él y tírale cuatro o cinco frechas primero que el soldado acabe de atacar el arcabuz, y en cuanto echa el polvorín para çebarlo el indio se retira entre yerbas y bosque, que es muy viçiosa tierra aquélla, y mira cuándo el polvorín toma fuego y abájase. Y como está desnudo se muda por entre las yerbas, y en disparando el arcabuz sale el indio a diferente parte donde se abajó cuando le querían hacer la puntería. Y son en esto tan discretos que es cosa de admiraçión, y todos pelean escaramuçando, saltan por encima las matas como venados, no son con mucho los españoles tan ligeros como ellos, y si los cristianos los siguen y ellos tienen miedo caminan a la parte donde hay ríos o ciénagas de agua—que hay muchas en la costa del mar—y como andan desnudos pásanse a nado, porque nadan como peçes, y llevan los arcos y flecha[s] alçados del agua con la una mano por que no se les moje[n]. Puestos de la otra parte empieçan a dar grito a los cristianos y reírse de ellos, y cuando los cristianos se retiran vuelven a pasar el río y seguirlos hasta meterlos en el fuerte, saliendo por entre las matas y frechando los cristianos, que cuando ven la ocasión no la pierden. Y por esto se les puede hacer muy mala guerra si no es yéndolos a buscar a sus pueblos, cortarles las sementeras y quemarles las casas y tomarles las canoas y derrocar las pesqueras y toda su hacienda, para que dejen la tierra o cumplan sus palabras [62r] con los cristianos, por que se hagan[241] amigos con ellos los caciques y los indios, haciéndoles buen tratamiento. Cuando van a los fuertes de San Agustín y San Mateo, si no les dan de comer, vestidos, hachas de hierro y rescates, vanse muy enojados, rompen la guerra, matando los cristianos que hallan. Son indios muy traidores, y que, de esta manera, a traiçión, debajo de amistad, han muerto más de çien soldados. Los indios de estos dos fuertes, San Mateo y San Agustín, donde los françeses residían, son éstos más traidores.

Pesole mucho al Adelantado de la quema de la casa de muniçión y fuerte, bastimento y municiones, y de la gran neçesidad y peligro con que estaba[n] el maestro de campo y Bartolomé Menéndez—su hermano— y toda la más gente. Fuese con diligencia a San Agustín llevando alguna gente, muniçione[s] y bastimento de lo poco que había en San Mateo. Llevó consigo a Gonçalo de Villarroel, que estaba muy enfermo de los trabajos pasados, para le enviar a La Habana para curar. Dejó a Vasco Çabal—alférez del estandarte real—en su lugar.

Llegó a San Agustín a diez y ocho de mayo [de 1566]. Fue mucha la alegría de los que allí estaban. Lloraban de placer por la merced que Nuestro Señor les hacía en socorrelles en tal tiempo con la llegada del Adelantado, el cual le[s] contó los buenos sucesos que había tenido en Guale y en Santa Elena y el buen prinçipio que había para que los indios fuesen cristianos, de que todos se alegraron muy mucho. Hizo descargar el bastimento y muniçiones que traían y que se les diese raciones. Entró en consejo con el maestro de campo y capitanes. Salió acordado que se mudasen [62v] de allí [e hiciesen un fuerte]²⁴² a la entrada de la barra donde agora está el Fuerte de San Agustín, porque allí los indios no les podrían hacer tanto mal, y plantasen en él la artillería, porque de allí podrían defender mejor cualesquier navíos de enemigos que quisiesen entrar en el puerto. Y que, hecho esto, si el bastimento no fuese venido dentro de quince días, que se partiese el Adelantado a buscarlo en tres bergantines que allí tenía, porque los navíos que enviaba con otras personas nunca habían vuelto ninguno.

Publicose esta determinación, dio gran contento a todos, aunque les pesaba mucho de que el Adelantado se fuese de con ellos, porque entendieron que el maestro de campo se había de ir a San Mateo por la ausencia del Villarroel, que así lo pidieron los soldados que allí quedaron, y el Adelantado se lo²⁴³ prometió. Luego aquel día y el siguiente se pasaron sobre la barra, empeçaron a traçar su fuerte y hacerlo con grandísima diligençia, y trabajaban dende las tres de la mañana antes del día hasta las nueve, y dende las dos de la tarde hasta las seis. Repartieron la gente en cuatro partes, y el trabajo en otras tantas, y echaron el dado la parte que cabía a cada una parte de éstas. Fue tanta la orden que se tenía en hacer este fuerte con brevedad, de temor que los indios no cargasen sobre ellos, que era contento verlo. Trabajaban en él como çiento y setenta personas. A los diez días estaba en razonable defensa y plantada la artillería.

No venía ningún navío con bastimento [y] corrían peligro de perecer todos de hambre. Fue acordado de conformidad de todos que el Adelantado se partiese luego a La Habana con los tres bergantines y que llevase las çien [63r] personas, que las más eran de la nao capitana de la Flota de la Nueva España y estaba obligado el Adelantado a llevarlos a La Habana en todo mayo, y que, quedando setenta raciones, no más pudían sustentarse algunos días en el entretanto que venía algún navío.

Segundo viaje a La Habana

Y así se embarcó el Adelantado con los cien hombres en los tres bergantines al principio de junio [de 1566]. El día que partió encontró con un navío suyo de sesenta toneles cargado de bastimento que traía Françisco Çepero. En él venía el capitán Diego de Maya muy malo, y si en aquel momento el Adelantado no le topara, iban navegando por riba del bajo y estaban ya en parte que si no echaban el áncora se perdían, porque pensaban que entraban por la barra y era plenamar y estaban en dos braças de agua, y a la bajamar no quedaba ninguna, y andaba mucha mar, y cuando largó el navío el cable tocó. Y el Adelantado entró dentro de él, y se dio tan buena maña que los sacó a salvamento, y de otra manera todos perecieran y se ahogaran todos los que allí venían.

Escribió al maestro de campo repartiese todo aquel bastimento por aquellos fuertes y él se fuese luego a San Mateo y no saliese de aquel fuerte hasta su vuelta, que sería luego con toda brevedad. Y que un bergantín que les quedaba en aquel puerto lo cargasen de maíz y lo enviasen [a] Estébano de las Salas, lo cual se hizo así. Y que estando aquel navío descargado lo echase al fondo por que se quedasen en el fuerte veinte hombres más que traía—que era muy buena gente—y por que no se [a]motinasen los soldados, no teniendo navío para salir de la tierra. Así lo hizo el maestro de campo.

Fue una gran ventura y suerte la que el Adelantado tuvo en encontrar con este navío, porque de otra manera todos los que en el fuerte quedaban perecieran de hambre.

E hizo vela luego el Adelantado [y] llegó a La Habana dentro de ocho días con los dos bergantines [63v] [y]²⁴⁴ porque el otro no pudo aproejar— porque el viento y la mar era mucha—arribó a la isla de Santo Domingo.

Era llegada a La Habana la Flota de Nueva España había dos días, y el licençiado Valderrama, del Real Consejo de Indias, en ella, que había ido por visitador de la Nueva España por mandado de Su Majestad, y habiéndolo hecho se volvía a España.

En desembarcando el Adelantado en La Habana fuese a la iglesia con sus soldados a hacer oración y antes de entrar en su posada fue a visitar al Valderrama, pareciéndole que en hallarle allí podría presto socorrer el fuerte de gente y bastimento, porque había más de tre[s]cientos soldados de la Florida que se habían huido allí. Posaba el Valderrama en casa del gobernador, y así, en pie, sin sentarse, se hablaron el Adelantado y el Valderrama, saludándose y abraçándose muy cortésmente. El Adelantado le dijo que tenía muy buena ventura de hallarlo allí, porque dentro de cuatro [o cinco]²⁴⁵ días se había de volver, que le pedía por merced le señalase hora para le poder hablar y darle particular cuenta del estado de las cosas de la Florida y de la gran necesidad en que quedaban aquellos fuertes, que Su Majestad tenía en ellos a su despensa quinientos hombres, y, aunque él había traído bastantes provisiones y recabdos para el gobernador de aquella isla, no le había socorrido con ninguna cosa. El Valderrama le respondió que todas las veces que el Adelantado quisiese que se juntasen holgaría él de ello.

Otro día siguiente el Adelantado tuvo cuenta cuándo el Valderrama se iba a la iglesia y se fue él también. Y, acabada de oír la misa, le dijo que él estaba empeñado en aquella tierra por el bastimento que había comprado para la Florida y que había ocho meses que proveía a los soldados que Su Majestad tiene allá, los cuales quedaban con estrema neçesidad [64r] y peligro así de bastimento como con los indios, y que los de la tierra donde estaban los fuertes de San Agustín y San Mateo todos estaban de guerra y había pocos soldados en los fuertes, y los más de ellos enfermos, y maltratados, y muy descontentos por los grandes trabajos y peligros que habían tenido y tenían cada día. Y que había habido motines y tratos dobles entre algunos capitanes por donde se habían salido de aquellos fuertes más de cuatrocientos soldados. Y que en aquella isla de Cuba estaban más de quinientos, así de los que salieron amotinados de los fuertes como de los que venían de España para la Florida, que con tormenta se habían apartado del Adelantado y habían aportado a aquella isla y se habían quedado en ella sin querer ir a la Florida. Y que, aunque había acudido al gobernador muchas veces les socorriese con algún bastimento por cuenta de Su Majestad e hiciese recoger aquella gente y se la mandase entregar, no lo había querido hacer, que pues él estaba allí, para que constase a Su Majestad de todo le suplicaba hiciese información, y para se poder volver luego le socorriese con dos o tres mil ducados de los que Su Majestad llevaba en aquella armada, que él se obligaría a, cuando Su Majestad no fuese de ellos servido, volvérselos. Y que encargase al gobernador que de los soldados de la Florida que andaban en aquella [villa e][246] isla le diese do[s]cientos para fortificar los dos fuertes de San Mateo y San Agustín.

Y contole lo que le había acontecido en Guale y Santa Elena y cómo los indios de aquella tierra eran todos sus amigos y querían ser cristianos, y que había hecho un fuerte y dejado en él a Estébano de las Salas con ciento y diez soldados con título de gobernador de aquel distrito, y que él quería partirse otro día por la mañana a tierra del [64v] cacique Carlos y llevarle a su hermana, que estaba allí en La Habana, a causa de que se le habían muerto los indios e indias principales que consigo había traído, que no le habían quedado más que dos, y si aquéllos y ella murían pensaría el cacique y sus indios que el Adelantado los había hecho matar. Y aquel cacique era señor de mucha tierra y de Los Mártires y del Canal de Bahama, donde las naos de las Indias tienen mayor peligro de aquella navegación, que convenía mucho tenerle por amigo, procurando se volviese[n] él y sus indios cristianos, y que dentro de diez o doce días volvería, en el cual tiempo estarían recogidos allí los do[s]cientos soldados y el bastimento que hubiese de llevar.

El Valderrama le respondió secamente que el dinero no lo podía dar y que, en lo de los soldados, él hablaría al gobernador y se lo encargaría, y aquella información que él decía hiciese sobre lo mal que el gobernador con él lo había hecho—para que constase a Su Majestad de la verdad—él no tenía comisión para hacerla. Al parecer de los que estaban presentes vimos al Adelantado mudársele la color de afligido, y dijo al Valderrama:

—Señor, en tanto que yo vuelva de Carlos Vuestra Merced verá en lo que podrá servir a Su Majestad en esto y a mí me hará la merced que hubiere lugar, que para que no se pierda la Florida y [se] salven las ánimas y naturales de ella, y el designio de Su Majestad vaya adelante—que es impedir no pongan pie los luteranos en aquella tierra y procurar plantar el Evangelio en ella—está en mano de Vuestra Merced en hacer lo que le suplico.

El Valderrama no le respondió, y el Adelantado luego se despidió y fuese[247] a su posada harto afligido. Trató con Juan de Inestrosa, tesorero de aquella isla y su lugarteniente en las cosas de la Florida, el poco remedio que había hallado en Valderrama y todo lo que con él había pasado. El Juan de Inestrosa le consoló muy mucho, diciendo:

—Señor, yo [65r] he hecho por Vuestra Señoría todo lo que he podido con mi hacienda y persona, y agora procuraré de hacerlo con la de mis amigos. No tenga Vuestra Señoría pena. Váyase mañana a Carlos, como lo tiene acordado, y yo haré buscar algún maíz, caçabe y carne que lleve para comer la gente, y en el entretanto soliçitaré al licenciado Valderrama que, pues es del Consejo de Su Majestad y ve lo que importa hacer este socorro de que Su Majestad se tendrá de él por muy servido, tengo por cierto lo hará.

El Adelantado se lo agradeçió y le encargó así lo hiciese. [Inestrosa] díjole también que era muy discreta la india doña Antonia, hermana de Carlos, y de tanta gravedad que espantaba a los del pueblo, y que en pocos días ella y una criada suya a quien quería mucho habían aprendido con gran facilidad todas las cosas, oraçiones y doctrina cristiana para ser bautizadas, y así lo eran, que estaba muy triste por la ausencia de Su Señoría y por la muerte de sus indios e indias, y que después que le habían dicho que Su Señoría era venido era grande su gozo y alegría, y que lloraba de placer, que era menester regalarla y hacer mucha cuenta de ella. Y, pues la quería llevar, convenía fuese diciendo mucho bien, porque él y los de La Habana habían tenido muy gran cuenta con ella de regalarla y que tuviese contento.

El Adelantado le dijo que el día antes, cuando desembarcó, la envió a visitar diciéndole que otro día la iría a ver, y así lo pensaba hacer en acabando de comer. Y así lo hizo, enviando él primero de lo que comía, y ciertas camisas y ropa que encomendó al tesorero le comprase, para que la india estuviese contenta y viese que le traía [alguna]²⁴⁸ cosa. Y llevó consigo cuando la fue a ver [a] muchas personas bien tratadas que la acompañaron, y sus músicos, que nunca el Adelantado andaba sin ellos. Halló la india muy triste, y aunque [65v] el Adelantado le hacía muchos regalos no se quería²⁴⁹ alegrar. Rogole muchas veces con la lengua que le dijese por qué estaba triste. Díjole que ella quería que Dios la matase porque cuando desembarcó no envió por ella y la llevó a su casa para comer con el Adelantado y dormir con él. Entendido el Adelantado ser mujer tan prençipal, de tan buen entendimiento, y que no le faltaba razón, le dijo que los cristianos que traían aquella cruz—que [es] el Adelantado caballero de la Orden de Santiago—cuando desembarcaban de hacer jornada contra sus enemigos no podían dormir con su mujer hasta pasar ocho días, y que él quisiera que éstos fueran pasados porque la quería mucho. La india se rio, medio llorando, y dijo que si ella supiera que decía verdad que estaría alegre. El Adelantado le rogó que lo estuviese porque él la decía. Y dijo [ella]—empeçando a contar por los dedos—que ya eran pasados dos días, y señaló los seis que, pasados aquéllos, ella se iría para su casa. El Adelantado le dijo que así lo hiciese, y se levantó el Adelantado y la abraçó con gran regocijo y mandó tañiesen los instrumentos, porque aquéllos no los había visto en aquella tierra, que le parecían muy bien. Estuvo el Adelantado allí más de una hora regocijándola.

Tenía a su cargo esta india un regidor de aquella villa que se llamaba Alonso de Rojas, que tenía una mujer prencipal, la cual fue madrina de esta india cuando se bautizó y la quería mucho y doctrinaba, que contó al Adelantado muchas cosas del buen entendimiento y del buen y claro juicio[250] de ella, con que el Adelantado se holgó mucho. Y dijo a la india que si tenía deseo de irse a su tierra. Ella dijo que sí, y muy grande. El Adelantado le dijo [66r] si quería que se fuesen a otro día. Ella le dijo que sí, y que le rogaba mucho que se fuesen. El Adelantado le dijo que así lo harían, y se despidió de ella y se fue a su posada, que era cerca de allí.

Aquella noche acontenció que, siendo pasada la medianoche, estando el Adelantado durmiendo en su aposento con una vela ençendida, la india dijo a una mujer su amiga—a quien quería mucho—de las que el Adelantado había traído de la Florida, que tenía por esclava Carlos su hermano, que se fuese con ella a casa del Adelantado porque le había mandado ir allá. La mujer lo creyó y se fue con ella y con la india su criada, y llamó a la puerta de la posada del Adelantado, la cual abrieron para saber quién era. Conociéronla. Dijo la mujer que el Adelantado la había mandado que fuese allá con la india, y el moço que abrió la puerta, creyendo decir verdad, las[251] dejó entrar y metió en el aposento del Adelantado, donde estaba una vela encendida.[252] La india la tomó en la mano y miró si estaba en la cama alguna mujer con el Adelantado, y después miró al derredor de la cama y por bajo. El Adelantado, aunque muy cansado [e quebrantado],[253] despertó, y como la vio con la candela en la mano, turbose y dijo contra la mujer que venía con ella:

—¿Qué es esto, hermana?

Doña Antonia se sentó encima de la cama con la candela para ver lo que el Adelantado decía. La mujer respondió al Adelantado que doña Antonia le había dicho que mandaba Su Señoría que se la trujesen a aquella hora y que ella, creyéndolo, lo había hecho así. El Adelantado, con alegre rostro y regocijado, riéndose mucho de esto, le dijo que le dijese que holgaría mucho que fueran pasados los ocho días para que se acostara allí con él. Doña Antonia dijo por la lengua que le rogaba [66v] la acostase consigo en un canto de la cama, y que no se llegaría a él, para que su hermano Carlos supiese que habían dormido juntos, porque de otra manera pensaría que se reía de ella y no querría ser amigo de verdad de los cristianos ni ser cristiano como ella, de que le pesaría muy mucho. Al[254] Adelantado le pareció que no le faltaba razón, mas [dijo] que Dios le mataría, que si ella quería que él se muriese que se desnudase y acostase con él. Ella empeçó entonçes a echar los braços al Adelantado y díjole [que] por que no se muriese no se quería con él acostar.

Llamó el Adelantado a un criado suyo que sacase de un cofre algunas cosas, que fueron tres camisas y sendos espejos y gargantillas de cuentas de vidr[i]o, que eran rescates que el Adelantado había hecho recoger aquel día para llevar a su hermano Carlos. Y dijo la mujer cristiana que con ella fue que si el Adelantado no despertara,[255] ella quería matar la candela y acostarse con él. Y con esto se fueron contentas luego.

Segundo viaje a tierras del cacique Carlos

A la mañana el Adelantado se fue a embarcar y llevó la india consigo, y a su criada, y a dos mujeres cristianas de las que habían sido allá cautivas. Fue en un patax y una chalupeta con hasta treinta soldados y marineros. Hizo vela con próspero viento. Llegó al pueblo de Carlos al tercero día. Surgió a la entrada del puerto, porque como llevaba poca gente no se atrevió a llegarse al pueblo. Entonces dijo la india al Adelantado que se desembarcase con ella y fuese al pueblo. El Adelantado le dijo que en ninguna manera lo podía hacer, porque le convenía partirse luego a buscar cristianos para que viviesen allí y enseñasen a ser cristianos a su [67r] hermano y a los indios de aquella tierra, si lo quisiesen ser, y que le prometía entonces de estar allí algunos días y hacerle una casa en que viviese en el pueblo de los cristianos. Y que los parientes de los indios e indias que murieron en La Habana pensarían que el Adelantado los había muerto y le querrían hacer algún mal a él y a sus soldados, de que se podría romper la guerra con su hermano, y de esto le pesaría mucho, porque lo quería bien por amor de ella y le tenía por hermano, y que luego se quería volver. La india le respondió que le pesaba mucho porque el Adelantado no desembarcaba, y que estuviera algunos días en tierra hasta ser pasados los ocho días por que durmiese con él, mas que también tenía miedo que los indios fuesen bellacos y le hiciesen algún mal, que le rogaba viniese lo más presto que pudiese y trujese cristianos para que viviesen allí y volviesen a su hermano y a los más indios cristianos.

Luego vinieron muchas canoas y la doña Antonia envió a decir a su hermano cómo estaba allí, que viniese por ella. Era cosa de ver la alegría que los indios tenían con ella, y otros lloraban de pesar de los indios e indias que se murieron, que habían ido con ella. Dentro de dos horas vino el Carlos con hasta doce canoas, y las dos de ellas amarradas una con otra y cubiertas y entoldadas con sus arcos y esteras muy bien. Y primeramente metiose el capitán—su cuñado—y otros seis prencipales en el patax del Adelantado. Fue cosa de ver cómo se recibieron la doña Antonia y su hermano y las cerimonias que se hicieron. Mandó el Adelantado traer de comer y tañer los instrumentos y dar a los indios de las canoas algún maíz y caçabe y algunos cuchillos y tiseras y espejos y cascabeles. Y acabando de comer dio un presente a Carlos para él [67v] y su mujer, y dio otro al capitán para él y su mujer, que era hermana de doña Antonia, y dio a los indios prencipales que allí estaban, y a la doña Antonia le dio algunas cosas que llevaba para ella.

Dijo el Adelantado a Carlos si quería ser cristiano y trasquilarse, y si quería ir a tierra de cristianos como se lo había prometido, y que le trujese los cristianos que dijo que le daría cuando allí volviese. El Carlos le respondió que le dejasen hablar con su capitán aparte y luego le darían la respuesta. Y así se apartaron más de un cuarto de hora y dijeron al Adelantado que por aquellos nueve meses no pudía en ninguna manera ir a tierra de cristianos ni volverse cristiano por entonçes, por que sus indios no se levantasen contra él y le matasen, que pasado aquel tiempo volviese el Adelantado, y justificó con razones bastantes[256] lo que había dicho. Y pasados aquellos nueve meses, cuando él volviese, que él se volvería cristiano e iría con él a España a ver a su rey, y que los cristianos que le pidía él los tenía en un pueblo cuatro leguas de allí, que otro día mediodía los enviaría.

Y así llevó a su hermana consigo y se despidieron del Adelantado. Y otro día a mediodía los cristianos no eran venidos, y envió Carlos una canoa con seis indios prencipales a decir al Adelantado que se fuese a comer con él y que los cristianos vendrían luego y que los traería. El Adelantado hizo sentar a estos indios en su patax y darles muy bien de comer, y a cada uno dio un presente, y díjoles que se fuesen y que dijesen a Carlos que era mal hombre mentiroso, que si pensaba hacerle alguna traición a él y a sus soldados que le enviaba a mandar luego [68r] viniese al patax donde el Adelantado estaba, para que se estuviese con él hasta que le enviase los cristianos que le había de dar y, si no, que le mandaría cortar la cabeça y a sus indios y le quemaría los pueblos y sería amigo y hermano de sus enemigos. Los indios se fueron muy turbados.

El Adelantado deseaba mucho que la marea viniese para irse, que nunca le pasó por pensamiento, ni a los que con él estaban, que Carlos había de venir. Y dentro de un hora vino el Carlos con sus doce indios y trujo a su capitán consigo, y ya entonçes por otro camino eran venidos los cristianos. El Carlos entró en el patax con su gente y dio su descargo cumplidamente, y dijo al Adelantado que si le quería matar, que bien lo p[o]dría hacer, o llevar a su tierra contra su voluntad. El Adelantado le regaló muy mucho, de que el Carlos y los que con él estaban tomaron contento. Dio Carlos al Adelantado para que llevase consigo dos indios, el uno moço de veinte años (su primo-hermano que heredaba el estado) y el otro para que le sirviese. Y así se despidió el Adelantado de él e hizo vela.

Tercer viaje a La Habana

Diole viento contrario en el camino y entró en un puerto donde estaba un pueblo de Carlos donde el Adelantado estuvo cuatro o cinco días. Los indios se holgaron mucho con él y le recibiero[n] con gran respeto. Pidiéronle una cruz para adorar, porque en tierra de Carlos se hacía desde la primera vez que el Adelantado allí la había dejado. Diósela y partiose luego a La Habana con buen tiempo, donde llegó dentro de diez días que había partido. Era ya llegada la Flota de Tierra Firme. Dijo el tesorero al Adelantado que ningún²⁵⁷ remedio tenía e[n] Valderrama ni en el gobernador de dinero [68v] ni bastimento ni soldados, y que [a] él no [le] era posible remedi[a]r nada, ni con sus amigos, de que el Adelantado se sintió muy afligido.

Habló al Valderrama y a los generales de las flotas del Nombre de Dios y de la Nueva España que estaban allí, que eran deudos, Cristóbal de Eraso y Bernaldino de Córdoba, y representoles su estrecha necesidad y que deseaba volverse a la Florida con algún bastimento, que no lo tenía, ni dineros para comprarlo, pensando entendida su estrecha necesidad hablarían al gobernador o al Valderrama, o que de las flotas o armadas—que había más de treinta naos—le diera[n] de cada una un quintal de bizcocho y una botija de vino, y con algún maíz y caçabe que entre sus amigos pidiera en La Habana (a cada uno su carga por limosna) se pudiera volver a la Florida con cincuenta o sesenta marineros [y] soldados que allí tenía. No le socorrieron con ninguna cosa. Visto esto el Adelantado, y la poca gente que había dejado en los fuertes, tomó una fragata y un bergantín y una chalupeta y metió en ella como sesenta y cinco personas. Las cinco le entregó el gobernador, y sobre un hábito de oro y vestidos y otros ajuares halló quinientos ducados que compró de maíz, carne y cazabe.

Los refuerzos de España llegan a San Mateo

Partió a primero de julio[258] [de 1566] de La Habana con las flotas de Nueva España y Tierra Firme que iban para España, y luego aquel día se apartó de ellas. Llegó a la Florida, al Fuerte de San Mateo, dentro de ocho días, donde halló estar un navío surto fuera de la barra. Llegó a reconoçerlo, supo que venía de España con bastimento. Dijo la gente de él que en el puerto de San Agustín estaban otros catorce navíos, y en el de Santa Elena otros dos, y todos venían cargados de bastimento, y que traían mil y quinientos [69r] infantes para socorrer aquellos fuertes y las Indias, porque se tenía notiçia que françeses luteranos hacían grandes armadas para aquellas partes.[259] El contento que el Adelantado y su gente de esto recibieron fue muy grande, porque venía muy sentido del poco socorro y ayuda que había hallado en La Habana, estando allí tantos criados del rey en oficios tan pre[e]minentes, y todos tan buenos caballeros, no le hacer ningún socorro, limosna ni caridad, en espeçial sabiendo las provisiones y cédulas bastantes de Su Majestad para que de su real hacienda le diese García Osorio, gobernador de aquella isla, lo que le pidiese y hubiese menester.

Entró el Adelantado a la barra de San Mateo. Fue al fuerte, halló al capitán Aguirre, que venía de España por soldado y por ausençia de Juan de Or[d]uña, que venía por coronel de esta gente [y que] se había quedado en Sanlúcar, habiéndoselo Su Majestad mandado, pareciéndole que no era necesario en la Florida por los buenos capitanes que el Adelantado traía consigo. Y el día que llegaron a San Agustín, Sancho de Archienaga, que iba por general de esta armada y[260] socorro, dio la compañía del coronel, que eran do[s]cientos y cincuenta soldados, a este Aguirre, para que fuese a socorrer el puerto de San Mateo, porque el maestro de campo luego se vino de San Mateo a San Agustín, como supo que el socorro era venido, dejando encomendado aquel fuerte a Vasco Çabal. Y halló al Vasco Çabal con los soldados viejos dentro del fuerte y el Aguirre alojado fuera, y diferentes el uno con el otro, porque Vasco Çabal pedía que este capitán Aguirre se metiese dentro del fuerte con los soldados—el cual dicía que sí haría, mas que había de poner las centinelas y dar el nombre—y Vasco Çabal decía que la guarda y defensa del [69v] fuerte estaba a su cargo y que no lo había de consentir.

Mandó el Adelantado que el capitán Aguirre metiese en el fuerte cada noche cincuenta soldados y que el Vasco Çabal pusiese las centinelas y diese el nombre. Y dejándoles muy conformes se partió a San Agustín. Halló en el camino, yendo navegando, al maestro de campo en un bergantín, que venía a San Mateo para concordar la diferençia del capitán Aguirre y Vasco Çabal. Holgose estrañamente el Adelantado con él. [El maestro de campo] contole las miserias, trabajos y peligros que habían padeçido antes de la llegada del socorro y cómo los indios junto del Fuerte de San Mateo habían muerto a traición al capitán Martín Ochoa y a otros soldados, y que en el de San Agustín habían muerto de la misma manera al capitán Diego de Hevia, pariente del Adelantado, y que como no tenían ninguna comida les era forçado salir a buscar ostriones, cangrejos y palmitos, y era menester la más gente del fuerte salir a esto. De otra manera, el que iba no volvía.

Pesole mucho al Adelantado de la muerte de estos dos capitanes porque los quería mucho y el Martín Ochoa habíase señalado mucho en la ganada del fuerte, y en todo lo demás de su cargo sirvió con mucha fidelidad, de tal manera que los que se amotinaron le quisieron muchas veces matar por él volver con grande espíritu por el servicio de Su Majestad, afeándoles la flaqueza que hacían. También habían frechado los indios a traición a otros çinco soldados y una lengua, de los muy queridos del Adelantado, y que habían sido de los primeros cuando el fuerte se ganó que habían asistido a los trabajos y peligros, obedeciendo en todo al gobernador, sin querer desmamparar el fuerte e irse con los amotinados. El uno de ellos era don Hernando de Gamboa—hijo natural [70r] de don Prudençio de Avendaño—,[261] el otro Juan de Valdés—primo-hermano del maestro de campo—[y] el otro era Juan Menéndez—hijo de primo del Adelantado—. Sintió esto mucho el Adelantado y, como entendió lo mucho que el maestro de campo lo debió de sentir, disimuló y dijo:

—En semejantes empresas no se pueden escusar estas muertes, trabajos y peligros. Nuestro Señor los perdone, que çierto mucho lo siento.

Luego le contó particularmente el maestro de campo el socorro que había venido y los nombres de los capitanes y lo mal que se gobernaban para con él, porque como llegaron y desembarcaron en tierra se alojaron por sus cuarteles al derredor del fuerte. Las primeras dos noches, cuando el maestro de campo llegó, hizo poner las çentinelas en las partes que convenía y les dieron el nombre, estando satisfechos que el maestro de campo, con poderes bastantes que el Adelantado le había dado, era su lugarteniente. Y entendieron después los capitanes que, habiéndose quemado la casa de munición y Fuerte de San Agustín donde primero estaban, con todo cuanto había dentro, con todas la[s] escrituras y provisiones (y entre ellas los poderes que el maestro de campo tenía del Adelantado), acordaron de poner en él sus centinelas y dar sus nombres y nombrar maestro de campo y sargento mayor. Algunos había que les parecía bien y a otros mal, y entre sí tenían alguna discordia. En efecto, iban adelante con este uso. De esta novedad se admiró el maestro de campo, porque nunca le habían dicho palabra ni pedido los poderes [antes ni después].[262] Envioles a decir que se juntasen todos, que les quería hablar, y estando les dijo:

—Señores, el Adelantado me ha dejado en estas provincias por su lugarteniente por comisión que de Su Majestad tuvo para ello, y de ello me dio bastantes poderes, los cuales se me han quemado, y está aquí el escribano ante [70v] quien pasaron, y la notoridad que todos tienen de ello, y que me respetan y obedecen como a lugarteniente. De los capitanes y soldados que están en esta provinçia se podrán Vuestras Mercedes informar y satisfacer de esto, que los más[263] de ellos están aquí. Son Bartolomé Menéndez, capitán ordinario de Su Majestad—hermano del dicho Adelantado—alcaide de este Fuerte de San Agustín y gobernador de la tierra, y el otro Gonçalo de Villarroel, alcaide y gobernador del Fuerte de San Mateo y su tierra, y el otro Estébano de las Salas, alcaide y[264] gobernador del Fuerte de San Felipe y su tierra, que es en Santa Elena. Todos tres personas de valor, hijosdalgo y muy buenos soldados, de los cuales se podrán Vuestras Mercedes satisfacer de esto. Y siendo así como lo digo, Su Majestad será servido me obedezcan en mi oficio y demos orden en proveer las cosas que convengan como al servicio de Su Majestad conviene, enviando gente y bastimento a Santa Elena a Estébano de las Salas, que está con gran necesidad, y dar orden en fortificarnos, porque si los enemigos vienen sobre nosotros, como se dice vienen pujantes, no estamos[265] como soldados.

Y [dijo] que Sancho de Archinega, que era general de la armada y a quien todos tenían por cabeça, le respondió que no podía entregarle la gente hasta que el Adelantado viniese, porque así lo habían acordado él y los capitanes que con él traía. Y decían que Su Señoría era ahogado, porque cuando salió de San Agustín para La Habana a buscar socorro con los tres bergantines, que el uno de ellos no pudo aproejar, que arribó a La Española, hubo dos días mucho viento y mar, que le tenía por perdido y estaban determinados de ser ellos las cabeças y nombrar los oficiales que conviniesen y estarse en aquella tierra hasta dar aviso a Su Majestad. A [lo] que le había respondido [a] Sancho de Archienaga que le pesaba mucho oír aquellas [71r] cosas, porque entendía no sería Su Majestad servido de ellas y su real serviçio çesaría en aquellas provinçias. Y pues estaban determinados de lo hacer así, que él y los alcaides de los fuertes, con los soldados que dentro estaban, los tendrían como tenían en nombre de Su Majestad, y los defenderían a los amigos y enemigos hasta perder las vidas. Y que ellos estarían alojados en las campañas, no haciendo efecto para ninguna cosa, gastando la real hacienda de Su Majestad y bastimentos, y que si esto había de pasar adelante fuesen buenos amigos.

Respondiole al maestro de campo que así se hiciese, y que esta amistad se la tendrían, y que él había pasado por aquellas cosas (visto que no podía hacer otra cosa) y que convenía al serviçio de Su Majestad disimular, y que de aquella manera estaban gobernándose, sin fortificarse ni hacer otro efecto había doce días, desde que esta armada y socorro había entrado.

El Adelantado agradeció mucho al maestro de campo lo bien que se había gobernado y que lo había hecho como muy buen capitán, porque en poblaciones y conquistas de tierras nuevas es pasar lo[s] que gobiernan por semejantes desobediençias a tiempos, que no pueden hacer otra cosa, y que aquel era el verdadero servir a Su Majestad y hacer lo que convenía.

Llegó el Adelantado aquel día a San Agustín, fue muy bien recebido de todos. El general Sancho de Archienaga estaba en las naos, y por ser tarde no vino a tierra. Otro día de mañana, habiendo el Adelantado oído misa, envió a decir a los capitanes que se viniesen al fuerte, porque les quería hablar y entrar con ellos en consejo, y así se hizo. Y vino el Sancho de Archienaga, que era general de la armada y de la gente que iba en este socorro, que llevaba de Su Majestad cédula para que todo [71v] le entregase al Adelantado e hiciese lo que él mandase y ordenase. Llevaba consigo al capitán Juan de Ubil[l]a, almirante de la armada. El Adelantado le recibió muy bien, porque era grande su amigo el Sancho de Archienaga de muchos años atrás. Entregole el general Sancho de Archienaga los despachos de Su Majestad y la armada y la gente. Habiendo el Adelantado recebido los despachos, diose por reçebido de todo y dijo al general que había traído consigo algunos malos consejeros, pues no había hecho aquella diligencia el día que llegó con el maestro de campo, como su lugarteniente en aquellas provinçias por comisión de Su Majestad, y que mal podía él estar en la Florida en todas partes, siendo tierra tan grande, que si él supiera las cosas de la guerra en tierra como las de la mar, que no creyera a sus consejeros ni se dejara engañar de ellos, que no le daba a él tanta culpa como a algunos capitanes que, por querer gobernar y serles su interés particular, no le aconsejaron el serviçio de Su Majestad ni lo que le convenía, mas que aquello era hecho y remediado con su venida, que no pensaba hablar más en ello, y que les pedía por merced que le tuviesen por hermano y amigo y le aconsejasen en todas las cosas que les pareçiese que Su Majestad podría ser más servido, y que al que bien sirviese, a su tiempo suplicaría a Su Majestad[266] le hiciese merced, y del que hiciese lo contrario le pesaría mucho y le mandaría castigar.

Sancho de Archienaga satisfizo al Adelantado, [72r] y a todos pareció muy bien lo que el Adelantado había dicho a los capitanes. No conocían al Adelantado, y bien conocieron de él en su manera que tenía hiel y miel para ser amado y temido. Luego les dijo que trajese cada capitán allí a sus ofiçiales, que les quería hablar. Así lo hicieron, los cuales recibió el Adelantado muy alegremente y les dijo palabras de mucho amor, animándoles para que se esforçasen a pasar los trabajos y peligros que se ofreciesen, pues todos eran para más servir a Dios Nuestro Señor y a su rey. Y que les rogaba esforçasen y animasen a los soldados y fuesen ayos de los flacos, animándoles y aconsejándoles estuviesen fuertes y firmes en el serviçio de Su Majestad, que era [a] lo que habían ido a aquella tierra.

Todos respondieron que así lo harían y mostraron gran contentamiento del razonamiento que el Adelantado les hizo. Y les mandó que fuesen luego a juntar los soldados, que les quería hablar, y así lo hicieron. El Adelantado quedó entonces en consejo con todos los capitanes y, habiéndoles leído el despacho de Su Majestad, proveyó que Sancho de Archienaga fuese general de la armada y se la volvió a entregar, [y que] estuviese a su cargo la gente de mar, averiguándolos y diciplinándolos, conociendo de cualesquier pleitos que hubiese. Y que el capitán Juan de Ubil[l]a fuese su almirante como lo era de antes, lo cual aceptaron.

Y porque Su Majestad mandaba que de aquellos mil y quinientos infantes se fortificasen los fuertes de la Florida con la gente que al Adelantado le pareciese, y que con los demás proveyese las fortalezas [de] Puerto Rico, Española y Cuba, [les pidió] que[267] se fuesen a comer todos con él y que, acabando, tratasen de fortificarse lo mejor que les pareciese para que, si los enemigos venían, los hallasen como soldados, [72v] e hiciesen casa de muniçiones para descargar los bastimentos y las naos se descargasen con gran brevedad. Y ordenó al general Sancho de Archienaga y al almirante Juan de Ubil[l]a fuese a su cargo esto, y hacer traer a la gente de mar con sus bateles muchos pinos para aserrar y hacer tabla[s] para la casa de muniçión.

Y así se fueron a comer con gran regocijo y contento. Y acabando, estando las compañías juntas, habló a los soldados, agradeciéndoles su ida a aquella tierra, y que estuviesen çiertos que los querría y amaría mucho, [en] espeçial al que hiciese el deber y sirviese más que otro, que les rogaba hubiesen todo contento y se armasen de paciencia para pasar los trabajos y peligros que se ofrecían, que les daba su palabra de ampararlos y defenderlos todo lo a él posible, haciéndolos el mejor tratamiento que pudiese. Y que al que sirviese bien y lo mereciese, en nombre de Su Majestad le haría la merced en aquella tierra que hubiere lugar y suplicaría a Su Majestad se la hiciese, que anduviesen todos contentos y tuviesen gran cuenta de obedecer a sus capitanes y oficiales, que éste era el prencipal servicio que a Su Majestad habían de hacer, haciendo en todo lo que les mandase y ordenase.

Todos respondieron que así lo harían, y reçibieron gran contento de las buenas palabras que el Adelantado les dijo. Luego fue el Adelantado a visitar [a] todas las mujeres que habían ido en aquella armada, que eran catorce, las cuales envió a mandar se ajuntasen en una casa y les dio la [e]n-[h]orabuena de su llegada, de que ellas se alegraron mucho con la visita y favor que el Adelantado les hizo. Habló a los clérigos que con aquella gente estaban, que eran çinco. Encomendoles las cosas de su cargo las hiciesen con toda cristiandad. [73r] Dioles el vicario a quien habían de obedeçer, que era el capellán Mendoça, de Jerez de la Frontera, muy buen religioso y soldado que había ido con el Adelantado de España, y le hizo vicario de aquel fuerte y del de San Mateo. Y así respondieron lo harían, y dieron la obediençia al vicario.

Fuese el Adelantado con todos los capitanes que a esto le acompañaron y, con acuerdo y parecer de todos, dando y tomando en ello para açertar mejor, señalaron el sitio, lugar y compás donde se habían de fortificar, que era en el mismo lugar que el Adelantado estaba fortificado, mas porque la mar le iba comiendo el fuerte retiráronse más a tierra, tomando[268] él un caballero del fuerte que estaba ya hecho para el que se había de hacer. Repartiose la gente por compañías y escuadras, y lo mesmo el trabajo. Echáronse los dados para que por suerte cabiese a cada uno la parte que había de trabajar, y esto quedó asentado de esta manera, a contento de todos, para que otro día por la mañana entendiese cada capitán, gente y escuadras en hacer del fuerte la parte que les había cabido.

Otro día por la mañana, al alboreçer, repicaron las campanas, que era señal para que todos se levantasen. Tocan las cajas, recogiendo su gente, acuden todos a la obra, que era contento verlos.[269] A terçero día, que el Adelantado vio que esto iba encaminado como convenía, llamó a consejo a los capitanes y díjoles que era bien tratar el socorro que Su Majestad mandaba hacer y cómo se había de hacer. Y dando y tomando sobre ello fue acordado que la meitad de los mil y quinientos soldados se quedasen en aquellas partes, en los tres fuertes de San Agustín, San Mateo y San Felipe, y que con los demás se fuese el Adelantado con seis navíos y una fragata y un patax, y con[270] la gente de mar de ellos (que serían en todos mil personas) a recorrer las islas [de] Puerto Rico y Santo Domingo y Cuba para [73v] hostigar los co[r]sarios que hubiese y fortificar aquellas plaças. Y que las más naos se despidiesen con brevedad y se fuesen a España, y las llevasen Sancho de Archinega y Juan de Ubil[l]a que—como está dicho—habían ido por general y almirante de aquel socorro. Y que, en el entretanto que se descargaban y aparejaban estas seis naos que el Adelantado había de llevar de armada, fragata y patax, él quería ir a visitar el puerto de San Mateo y dejar en él a Gonçalo de Villarroel, que allí estaba, que había vuelto de La Habana, con cargo de toda la gente, y pasar a Guale y Santa Elena a visitar el Fuerte de San Felipe y ponerle en toda buena defensa, porque habían ido a ella dos naos, la capitana y otra mayor,[271] con tre[s]cientos soldados, y el capitán Juan Pardo con cargo de ellos, y no se sabía hubiesen llegado ni el estado de las cosas de aquellas partes.

En tierras de los caciques
Otina, Mocoya y Calabay

Con acuerdo y pareçer de todos los capitanes nombró al capitán Juan de Çurita[272] para el socorro de Puerto Rico y al capitán Rodrigo Troche—que eran de los primeros que habían ido a la Florida con el Adelantado—para el socorro de Santo Domingo, y al alférez Baltasar de Barreda para el socorro de La Habana.

Y se partió a San Mateo, donde dejó a Gonçalo de Villarroel en aquel fuerte con la compañía del capitán Aguirre y los más soldados viejos que allí estaban. Subió con cien solados y alguno[s] marineros por la ribera de San Mateo arriba más de çincuenta leguas con tres bergantines, que hasta entonçes no lo habían hecho, para tomar amistad con los caciques y saber el secreto si aquel río pasaba a la parte de Nueva España.

Y otro día que partió de San Mateo por este río arriba, habiendo andado veinte leguas, desembarcó, y con una guía[273] que llevaba caminó çinco leguas por tierra de muy buenas çabanas de un cacique que llaman [74r] Otina.[274] Y estando una legua de su pueblo enviole seis soldados con esta guía, que era lengua, y llegando a él le dieron un presente que el Adelantado le enviaba y le dijeron que el Adelantado le venía a ver porque le tenía por amigo. Él recibió muy bien a los seis soldados y respondioles que él tenía miedo al Adelantado, y que si quería ir a su pueblo no llevase más de veinte hombres, y que pidiese a Dios que lloviese para sus maizales, que los tenía secos, como lo había hecho con el cacique Guale. El Adelantado iba marchando tras los seis soldados, y cuando le volvió la respuesta estaba como un cuarto de legua del pueblo. Hizo alto y mandó quedar allí los ochenta soldados y fuese con los veinte, riéndose de lo que el cacique pidía del agua.

Y llegado al pueblo, habiendo más de seis meses que no llovía, empeçó a llover mucho.

Llegó a la casa del cacique y no le halló. Dijo a çinco o seis indios que allí estaban que le fuesen a buscar [e le dijesen]²⁷⁵ que él iba con los veinte hombres y el agua. Y uno de los indios fue y le envió con la respuesta, diciendo que el cacique estaba en el monte escondido y que le enviaba a decir [que [a] hombre que podía tanto con Dios]²⁷⁶ que él le tenía gran miedo, que se fuese con Dios, que él era su amigo. Y pesole mucho de esto al Adelantado, porque deseaba mucho ver este cacique, que decían era de muy buen entendimiento y muy poderoso en aquella ribera de San Mateo. Y volviole a enviar a decir que le rogaba mucho le viniese a ver, que no tuviese miedo, pues no tenía más de veinte hombres y él tenía más de mil indios, todos con arcos y flechas. Respondiole que si su cacique le ayudaba, que [74v] era Dios, el Adelantado tenía mucha gente en aquellos veinte soldados, que le rogaba que se fuese, que desde entonces le tomaba por su hermano mayor y que era su amigo—estando el cacique en su tierra y el Adelantado en la suya—y que él no quería pelear con el Adelantado ni con su gente, mas que sus indios lo querían hacer, y que le hacía mucho pesar porque no se iba. El Adelantado le dijo que él se iba por hacerle placer, y que a su gente ni a él no les tenía miedo, que subía por el río arriba de San Mateo, que enviase a decir a sus pueblos por donde el Adelantado había de pasar que se estuviesen quedos los hombres y mujeres y no le tuviesen miedo, y que si se huían les haría la guerra, quemándoles sus pueblos, canoas y pesqueras.

Y así se volvió el Adelantado donde estaban los ochenta soldados hechos alto, y llevándolos consigo se volvió a los bergantines al anochecer. Fue cosa que a todos espantó su caminar, porque era una hora de día cuando partió de los bergantines para Otina, y estuvo allá dos horas y volvió de día, que son muy grandes diez leguas, aunque muchos echaban doce. Tuvo aquélla muy mala noche por no se poder embarcar y llover muy mucha agua, que como alojaron en una zabana húmeda todos lo pasaron muy mal.

Otro día por la mañana envió el Adelantado el mayor bergantín con los cincuenta hombres a San Mateo y él se subió con los otros cincuenta en los dos bergantines por la ribera adentro, y con algunos marineros, por tener bastimento para diez o doce días, y yendo toda la gente no pudiera durar tanto y él no pudiera saber el secreto de aquella ribera. De los pueblos que allí había a la ribera del río era muy bien recebido, porque decían que su [75r] cacique Otina se los había enviado a mandar. Procuró el Adelantado de llevar consigo alguna guía para saber el secreto del río, [y] por dádivas que daba y bien que a los indios hacía ninguno quiso ir con él. Caminó por la ribera adentro todo lo que los franceses habían navegado por allí, llevando [in]d[i]os que los guiaban. Llegaba la marea a hinchir y vaciar bien cuarenta leguas, cosa que espantó mucho al Adelantado. Subió como cincuenta leguas por esta ribera adentro, dos leguas más adelante de lo que los franceses habían subido, hasta un cacique que llaman Macoya, amigo de Saturiba, cacique muy poderoso de la tierra y costa donde están los fuertes de San Mateo y San Agustín, el cual Mocoya se retiró con sus indios dejando el pueblo desmamparado.

El Adelantado saltó en tierra y entró en las casas. No consintió hacer daño, volviose a recoger, envió la lengua a ver si pareçía algún indio. Salieron a él, que le conoçían, holgáronse mucho con esta lengua. Díjoles cómo estaban allí los cristianos y el capitán-general de ellos, que enviasen a decir a su cacique Mocoya que viniese al pueblo con su gente y no tuviese miedo. Algunos indios fueron a buscarle para se lo decir, otros vinieron a sus casas y llevaron al Adelantado mucho pescado. Dioles algún rescate y recibioles muy bien, y rogoles fuesen a llamar al cacique, que le quería[277] dar muchas cosas que traía para él y sus mujeres. Fueron los[278] primeros que habían ido, y éstos dijeron al Adelantado que el su cacique le tenía gran miedo y no [75v] quería venir, y que él y sus indios eran sus amigos, porque sabían que no hacía mal a ningún cacique, y que se volviese sin pasar adelante por el río, que sus indios estaban enojados porque había ido a su tierra sin su licençia.

El Adelantado le envió a decir que quería pasar por aquel río adelante a ver unos cristianos, que le rogaba le diese dos o tres indios para ser pilotos. El cacique le envió a responder que no quería. Mandó echar la boga el Adelantado y empeçó a ir por el río adentro, andando como una legua. Era ya tarde. Vio muchos indios alterados con arcos y flechas. Y llegando a una estrechura halló cerrado el río con estacas. Rompió la entrada y entró por ella adentro. Estrechósele el río como dos picas no más y muy hondo. Allí venía la corriente contra él muy recia, porque hasta entonçes no había tenido ninguna sino sus hinchentes y vaciantes. Temió el Adelantado no frechasen los remadores. Abajaron dos o tres indios a la orilla y dijéronle de parte del cacique Mocoya que no pasase adelante y se volviese, si no que le empeçarían[279] a hacer la guerra. Respondioles el Adelantado que él no iba a hacerles mal, y que viniesen a hacerles la guerra cuando quisiesen, que él tenía necesidad de pasar por aquel río adelante y que, por ser noche, quería quedar allí hasta la mañana, y así lo hizo.

La guía[280] y lengua que el Adelantado llevaba había sido esclavo de un cacique [de] [76r] Ais que llamaban Peracho, que estaba veinte leguas por el río arriba y conoçía a este Mocoya. Y dijo al Adelantado que se volviese, porque había muchos indios y muy guerreros por aquella tierra, y que le decían que el río iba muy estrecho por allí adentro, más de treinta leguas, hasta salir a una laguna grande que llaman Maimi, que dicen tiene más de treinta leguas en çircuito y que recoge dentro de sí muchos ríos de la sierra, y que desaguaba esta laguna a la parte del cacique Carlos, que está en la costa de la Nueva España, y que otro braço desaguaba a Tequesta, que es en Los Mártires. Deseaba mucho el Adelantado descubrir este secreto por la amistad que había tomado con Carlos y por saber si aquello era navegable, que era cosa muy provechosa para la poblaçión y conquista de la Florida. Por otra parte temía que si acudían canoas de indios de guerra en aquella estrechura, y estando dentro de la estacada, podría recebir daño, especialmente que por haber llovido mucho tenían los soldados la pólvora y cuerda húmeda.

Se retiró una legua atrás con sus dos bergantines y por la mañana acordó de volverse. Y en el camino—a siete u ocho leguas de vuelta—saltó en un pueblo donde algunos indios le aguardaron. Dioles rescates y dijo que le llamasen a su cacique, el cual vino, que llamaban Calabay.[281] Díjole por la lengua que Macoya le había enviado a decir que no pasase por aquel río, [76v] y que sus soldados se habían enojado mucho contra él y querían saltar en tierra a quemarle su pueblo y canoas y derrocar las pesqueras, y que por que no lo hiciesen se volvía. El Calabay le respondió que él quería ser su amigo y tomarle por su hermano mayor para hacer lo que él le mandase, que él le rogaba le diese una cruz como a Guale y otros seis cristianos, que él y sus indios querían ser cristianos, que él mostraría aquel río hasta la laguna de Maimi a los seis cristianos que con él quedasen, porque a pocos cristianos los indios no tenían miedo (y a muchos sí), y que no les haría mal ninguno.

Temía el Adelantado a este cacique porque, siendo sujeto a Otina,[282] se alçaría contra él, y era muy amigo del caçique Saturiba, y porque no había desde allí por tierra a San Agustín más de doce leguas acordó de se los dejar y darle la cruz, y le dijo que si alguno le mataba él vendría a hacerle la guerra, de manera que le quemaría las casas y las canoas y derrocaría las pesqueras y cortaría la cabeça a él y a su gente, mujeres y niños, porque era amigo de sus amigos de verdad y enemigo de sus enemigos. El cacique dijo que era contento, y luego hubo muchos soldados que pidieron les dejase allí. El Adelantado dijo los que le pareçió tenían más voluntad y parecían mejor podrían doctrinar los indios. Dio un presente a este cacique para sí y otro para Mocoya, que le rogaba se lo llevase con tres cristianos de aquéllos, que viviesen con [77r] él y doctrinasen a él y sus indios.

El Calabay dijo que así lo haría, y fue así que llevó el presente y los cristianos. Mocoya no los quiso reçebir, y tomó el presente y envió a decir al Adelantado que él era su amigo y lo tenía por su hermano mayor, que es toda la obediençia que los caciques de la Florida pueden dar, mas que si iba a su tierra él le tuviese por su enemigo. Saturiba, como supo que Calabay tenía los cristianos, envió a dos hijos suyos y a otros indios para que los matasen. El Calabay no lo consintió. Enviole a decir Saturiba que los matase o se los enviase, y si no que él lo tuviese por su enemigo. El Calabay, de temor de Saturiba, los envió a San Mateo, y cuando el Adelantado se volvió a San Mateo, en[283] tres o cuatro pueblos de Otina por donde había ido le aguardaron toda la gente, grandes y pequeños, con mucho regocijo. Dábales algún rescate y tocaban los instrumentos. Regocijábanse todos, y pesábales porque se partía tan presto. Llegó a donde desembarcó cuando fue a ver a Otina por tierra. Enviole a decir que como él le había ido a ver a su pueblo viniese el Otina a ver al Adelantado allí, y si esto no hacía que lo tuviese por su enemigo. Hubo miedo el Otina de enojar al Adelantado y entendió la mucha amistad que había hecho en sus pueblos donde llegaba, y que todos le querían bien. Vino a ver al Adelantado con tre[s]cientos hombres de guerra, y a un cuarto de legua de los bergantines hizo alto y envió a decir al [77v] Adelantado que fuese allá con veinte cristianos, el cual lo hizo así, llevando veinte arcabuceros diestros y bien en orden.

Llegando cerca, el Otina[284] le tuvo miedo y enviole a decir que llegase allí con dos personas no más. Y como a medio tiro de arcabuz hizo alto con los veinte soldados, y con solos dos y la lengua se llegó el Adelantado a Otina, que estaba rodeado con sus tre[s]cientos frecheros sentados. El Otina se le humilló mucho, haciendo al Adelantado la más obediençia que entre ellos se usa, y luego vinieron sus prencipales de uno en uno, haciendo lo mismo, y todos los más indios que allí estaban hicieron aquello. El Adelantado vistió una camisa al Otina, que estaba en carnes, sólo cubiertas sus vergüenças, y lo mismo todos sus indios, y vistiole unos çaragüelles, ropeta de tafetán verde, y púsole un sombrero. Este indio era muy gentilhombre en disposición y faiciones, de hasta veinte y cinco años, muy discreto. Dijo al Adelantado que le tomaba por su hermano mayor para hacer lo que le mandase, que le dejase una cruz como a Gu[a]le, y cristianos que le doctrinasen a él y su gente, y que le dejase una trompeta, pues que era su hermano de verdad. El Adelantado lo hizo así, que le dejó una cruz y seis cristianos, y el trompeta entre ello[s]. Dio ciertos rescates para su mujer, y dio a los indios prinçipales que allí estaban. Partieron muy amigos.

Embarcose el Adelantado y se fue a San Mateo dentro de doce días [78r] del día que había partido. Halló todo aquello muy bueno y contento a Gonçalo de Villarroel con la gente, aunque algunos sin orden suya se habían ido de allí a dos leguas para robar ciertas casas de Saturiba. Salieron los indios a ellos y, de doce arcabuceros que iban, murieron los ocho, y los cuatro llegaron muy mal heridos dentro de tres días al fuerte, escondidos[285] por los montes. Estuvo el Adelantado allí [en San Mateo] dos días.

Viaje a Santa Elena y tierras del cacique Tequesta

Partiose a Santa Elena. Despachó aviso a Su Majestad cómo el socorro era llegado y del estado de aquellas cosas. Envió un capitán con treinta soldados y dos frailes dominicos a la Bahía de Santa María, que está en treinta y siete grados, con un indio hermano del cacique de aquella tierra, que había seis años que el Adelantado le traía consigo. Era muy ladino y de muy buen entendimiento y muy buen cristiano, llamado don Luis de Velasco, por que con su favor poblasen en aquella tierra y procurasen de hacer los indios cristianos. Los frailes eran del Perú y Nueva España, tierra muy viciosa.[286] Habían pasado alguna hambre en la Florida y trabajo y peligro. Pareciéndoles que no podrían sufrir tan mala vida, de secreto alteraron algunos soldados (que habían menester hacer poca diligençia para ello) y alteraron al piloto. Y de conformidad, tomando testimonio que con tormenta no habían podido ir allí, se vinieron a Sevilla, difamando la tierra y diciendo mal del rey y del Adelantado porque la querían poblar y conquistar.

Llegó el Adelantado [78v] a Santa Elena. Halló a Estébano de las Salas metido en su fuerte con los soldados viejos y a Juan Pardo alojado fuera haciendo casas para alojar la gente, porque llevaba orden del general Sancho de Archinega que una noche diese él el nombre y otra noche lo diese Estébano de las Salas, y así le mostró la orden que llevaba. Estébano de las Salas dijo a Juan Pardo que se alegraba mucho con su llegada y que él tenía orden del Adelantado Pero Menéndez, su capitán-general, para guardar y defender aquel fuerte en nombre de Su Majestad, y que le había de poner los centinelas y dar el nombre, y no otro ninguno. Y que con esta condiçión se podía meter dentro del fuerte con su gente o[287] con la parte de ella que quisiese, [o] alojarse en la campaña, como le pareciese. El Juan Pardo es buen soldado, celoso del serviçio de Su Majestad. Pareçiole tenía razón el Estébano de las Salas y que no la había tenido Sancho de Archienaga, y que él, en llegando a la Florida, estaba obligado a cumplir y obedecer los mandamientos del Adelantado y no otros. Dio la obediençia para la defensa del fuerte a Estébano de las Salas, dándole una escuadra de soldados para guarda de las çentinelas, y que cuando fuese necesario él acudiría con los demás. Y alojose con ellos en la campaña, y empeçaban todos a trabajar para poner el fuerte en buena defensa.

Fue grande el gozo y alegría que todos recibieron con la llegada del [79r] Adelantado. Supo que los indios estaban muy amigos y la necesidad que Estébano de las Salas tenía de gente y comida cuando el capitán Juan Pardo llegó en dos naos cargadas de bastimentos y tre[s]cientos soldados, porque había un mes que, enviando el Adelantado un bajel cargado [de bastimento],[288] otro día que allí llegó, antes de descargar nada, se amotinaron los soldados y se alçaron con él, dejando preso a Estébano de las Salas y a sus oficiales que vinieron con él a La Habana con hasta sesenta hombres. Y en la Canal de Bahama les dio una tormenta que les hizo entrar en la Florida, a un puerto que allí estaba, que es en la cabeça de Los Mártires. Hallaron un pueblo que el cacique de él llaman Tequesta, pariente cercano del cacique Carlos y de la india doña Antonia, porque los cristianos que allí estaban cautivos, [que] había muchos años que en una canoa llegaron, se lo[289] dijeron, y que aquellos indios solían matar todos los cristianos de las naos que se perdían, y que agora los querían mucho porque sabían que el más principal de ellos tenía por mujer una parienta suya, hermana de Carlos, y que no tuviesen mi[e]do, que el cacique les enviaba a saber si eran ellos de aquellos cristianos, los cuales dijeron que sí, y que cerca de allí, en un pueblo de la costa,[290] estaban muchos cristianos de aquéllos. Y era así la verdad, que los soldados que se amotinaron en San Mateo cuando iban a La Habana saltaron allí como veinte de ellos y entró mucho viento al navío. Hízose a la vela, dejolos en aquella tierra y [79v] los indios los trataban muy bien, dándoles de lo que tenían por amor de la india doña Antonia.

También se le habían ido a Estébano de las Salas de allí de Santa Elena como hasta veinte soldados la tierra adentro. Tenía en el fuerte como hasta veintiçinco cuando Juan Pardo llegó, y ninguna comida más de aquélla que los indios [le inviaban].[291] Y había el capitán Juan Pardo, después que allí llegó, ahorcado dos soldados por amotinadores. Tenía presos otros tres. Habíansele ido seis. Estaba la gente medio alterada, pareciéndoles que había división entre él y Estébano de las Salas (la cual no había, sino mucha conformidad, y no menos de lo que está dicho).

Entró en consejo el Adelantado. Acordó de la manera que se había de fortificar. Estuvo allí ocho días, en los cuales le vinieron a ver los caciques sus amigos y le rogaron aguardase allí un mes, porque muchos caciques de la tierra adentro le querían venir a ver y tomar por hermano mayor. No lo pudo hacer el Adelantado por la mucha necesidad que tenía de tornarse con brevedad a San Agustín para hacer los socorros en las Indias que Su Majestad le mandaba. Soltó a los tres soldados que Juan Pardo tenía presos, dándoles una reprehensión, y habloles a todos, animándoles y rogándoles estuviesen fuertes en el servicio de Su Majestad. Nombró a Estébano de las Salas por su lugarteniente[292] general en aquellas provinçias, porque quería llevar consigo los[293] socorros [y] al maestro de campo por su lugarteniente y almirante de la armada, como llevó.

Y dio orden a Juan Pardo que se fuese con çiento y cuarenta soldados[294] [80r] la tierra adentro a visitar los caciques que querían venir a ver al Adelantado, y con toda la amistad posible, en la parte más cómoda que le pareciese para la conservaçión de ellos, y que fuesen cristianos, se fortificasen en la parte que le pareciese, caminando la vuelta de la Nueva España.

Y así se partió el Adelantado de Santa Elena en fin de agosto [de 1566], confirmada la paz con los caciques y encargando a Estébano de las Salas la conservase.[295]

Segundo viaje a tierras del cacique Guale

Llegó a Guale en dos días. Halló a los indios muy tristes por la muerte de Alonso Menéndez Marqués, sobrino del Adelantado, a quien ellos querían mucho, que era cabeça de los cristianos que allí estaban. Adoraban la cruz con gran devoción. Todos los más de los niños y niñas iban a la doctrina cristiana y la sabían de cabeça. Muchos caciques de aquel distrito[296] venían allí con deseo de ver al Adelantado. Detúvose allí ocho días, en los cuales vinieron catorce o quince. Pidiéronle cruces y cristianos para que los enseñase[n] a ser cristianos. Acordó el Adelantado dejar allí un capitán con treinta soldados, los más de ellos gente prençipal que pidieron los dejasen allí, porque les pareció podían mejor servir a Dios y al rey. Fuese el Adelantado.

Regreso a San Mateo y San Agustín

Llegó a San Mateo en otros dos días, donde halló toda la gente buena. Llevó consigo a Gonçalo de Villarroel a San Agustín, donde halló que muchos soldados se querían amotinar e irse de la tierra. Había ahorcado el maestro de campo tres de ellos. Tenía presos a otros y al capitán Pedro de Rodabán,[297] que era uno de los capitanes que Su Majestad había enviado [80v] con aquel socorro, porque se había desacatado contra el maestro de campo, y le daban culpa ser el prençipal que daba orden y ocasión para que se amotinasen. Y aunque el Adelantado halló por dónde poder hacer de él justiçia, habló con el maestre de campo y díjole que, pues no conoçían [a] aquellos capitanes y soldados, y que muchos de ellos venían desobedientes, que era menester pasar por cosas y hacer lo que pudiesen y no lo que quisiesen, que convenía para sosiego dar una reprehensión el Adelantado a este capitán y soltarle, dejando el proceso de su culpa en el estado en que estaba. Al maestro de campo le pareçió bien. Así se hizo.

Fue muy alegremente recibido el Adelantado de todos los capitanes, gente de mar y guerra que allí había. Envió las naos a España.

Viaje a Puerto Rico, Hispaniola y Cuba

Salió con la armada a buscar los co[r]sarios y hacer los socorros a las islas Puerto Rico, Española y Cuba, como estaba acordado. Hizo vela a veinte de octubre [de 1566], aunque estuvo presto para salir al fin de septiembre [de 1566], y con vientos contrarios no pudo. Llegó[298] a cinco de noviembre [de 1566] con la meitad de la armada a La Mona,[299] y el maestro de campo con la otra meitad a San Germán, por ser aquéllos lugares donde los co[r]sarios ladrones suelen andar, para los tomar de repente, y no hallaron ninguno.[300]

Eran capitanes de las seis naos de armada:

- El Adelantado, general de su nao.
- El maestro de campo, capitán y almirante de la suya.
- Juan Vélez de Medrano, de la otra.
- El alférez Cristóbal de Herrera (que fue el primero que metió bandera en el Fuerte de San Mateo cuando se ganó a los franceses, siendo alférez del[301] capitán Diego de Maya), de otra.
- Y el [81r] capitán Pedro de Rodabán,[302] de otra.
- Baltasar de Barreda,[303] de otra.
- De la fragata, García Martínez de Cos.
- Y del bergantín, Rodrigo Montes, primo-hermano del maestro de campo, que también fue de los primeros que entraron en el fuerte.

Luego que surgió en San Germán el maestro de campo con sus navíos tuvo aviso de los de la tierra cómo estaba en Guadi[a]nilla, quince leguas de allí, un patax de aviso que iba para Santo Domingo, y que decía la gente de él que a veinte y çinco de septiembre de aquel año de sesenta y seis habían partido veintisiete naos de armada de Francia, y que se habían hecho tres partes, que la una parte de éstas tomara a seis de octubre a la isla de La

Madera, y que las otras partes de la armada no sabían a dónde fueran, y que toda la armada traía seis mil[304] hombres de mar y guerra. Y envió luego el maestro de campo a Hernando de Miranda, factor por Su Majestad en la Florida, a enterarse y saber más particularmente esto, el cual fue y habló en Guadi[a]nilla con el maestre y piloto del patax, que eran sus amigos, y le dijeron lo mesmo, y dieron un traslado de lo que en esto pasaba firmado de un regidor de La Palma que se hallara en la isla de La Madera cuando los franceses la tomaron, que estuvieron en ella diez y siete días. Y venían [en] los navíos algunos portugueses conocidos de este regidor que le contaron todo lo que pasaba.

Al tercero día volvió Hernando de Miranda a San Germán y dio relación de todo ello al maestro de campo, al cual, pareciéndole lo debía de saber el Adelantado para que su armada se juntase y tomase determinación de lo que debía de hacer, envió aviso de esto a la isla [81v] de La Mona, donde estaba con tres naos, que eran veinte leguas de allí. Reçebido el Adelantado el despacho invió la armada a San Germán y orden al maestro de campo para que luego diese lado y sebo a las naos y las pusiesen muy a punto, y él se fue a la çiudad de Santo Domingo, que era de allí a cincuenta leguas. Fue muy bien recibido de la Audiencia y vecinos de aquella ciudad porque tenían ya las nuevas de la armada françesa había ya dos días y temían mucho no viniese allí.

Fuese el Adelantado a la Audiençia, [y] estando juntos presidente[305] y oidores mostroles la cédula que del rey nuestro señor tenía[306] para hacer aquellos socorros, y les dijo que traía mil hombres de mar y guerra—toda muy buena gente—y buenos pilotos y marineros, porque había sacado para esto la gente de mar que tenía en la Florida—que era muy buena—que venían con determinación de acosar y seguir todos los co[r]sarios que en aquellas partes hubiese para los castigar, por que en tiempo de paces no anduviesen haciendo tantas estorsiones,[307] robos y daños a los vasallos de Su Majestad. Y por las nuevas que tenía de aquella armada francesa [que] iba aquellas partes, les iba a pedir consejo y parecer de lo que debía de hacer, que les pidía por merced le diesen su parecer en ello. Y dando y tomando en el negocio, la Audiençia se resumió con él, diciéndole que el pareçer que le daban era que fortificase aquella çiudad y fortaleza y la de Puerto Rico y la de La Habana y puertos comarcanos, como Su Majestad[308] se lo mandaba, y se volviese con brevedad a la Florida.

Mucho le pesó al Adelantado con este parecer porque deseaba encontrarse con alguna parte de estas tres de la armada françesa y con otros co[r]-sarios que andaban en aquellas partes divididos y muy ricos de los robos que habían hecho, [82r] mas pareciole que Su Majestad le mandaba por su cédula hiciese lo que la Audiençia le dio por pareçer, y así lo determinó de hacer. Pidioles se desocupasen aquella tarde y otro día para ver la mejor orden que se había de tener para la fortificación de aquella çiudad y fortaleza, y ver y entender las partes por donde los enemigos podrían desembarcar, para poner las centinelas y para que se hiciesen las cajas y ruedas de la artillería, porque las que había estaban podridas, para la encabalgar y ponerla lista en las partes más necesarias, lo cual se hizo todo con gran diligençia y cuidado.

Dejó el Adelantado en aquella ciudad al capitán Rodrigo Troche con ciento y çincuenta soldados, las dos partes arcabuceros y la una piqueros. Dejó al capitán Antonio Gómez por capitán de la artillería, porque era de esto muy diestro, y gran polvorista.

Y dentro de seis días se volvió el Adelantado a San Germán. Llegó en tres días. Envió al capitán Cristóbal de Herrera con su hurca con bastimentos, muniçiones y veinte quintales de pólvora de cañón y arcabuz para defensa de la fortaleza y ciudad. Estaban en aquella ciudad diez naos cargando de cueros y açúcar[309] para España. Nombró el Audiençia a esta[310] hurca por capitana, y al Cristóbal de Herrera por general, por ser buen soldado de mar, y partiose la armada[311] de aquella çiudad dentro de seis días y llegó con todas ellas a Sevilla a salvamento.

Luego que el Adelantado llegó a San Germán halló las naos muy a punto de guerra. Entró[312] en consejo con el maestro de [82v] campo y capitanes. Díjoles la determinaçión que había tomado con [el] parecer del presidente y oidores de la Real Audiençia de Santo Domingo, y que aquélla había de guardar y cumplir. Despachó luego al capitán Juan de Çurita con su nao de armada a Puerto Rico con cien soldados arcabuceros y cuatro pieças de artillería, con recaudo de pólvora y municiones. Y el Adelantado se fue por tierra de San Germán a Puerto Rico, donde fue muy bien reçebido del gobernador y vecinos, porque estaban con gran temor si la armada francesa llegase. Díjoles lo que Su Majestad le mandaba. Mostró la çédula al gobernador y regimiento, y que çien soldados y cuatro pieças de artillería y muniçiones serían luego allí con una nao de armada, porque ya los había dejado en San Germán despachados. Visitó[313] la fortaleza y la entrada del puerto, donde se dio orden [de] fortificar un turrión que allí estaba por otra mejor traça que tenía, y vis[i]tó los otros lugares peligrosos para de-sembarcar enemigos. Con acuerdo y parecer del gobernador y del alcaide de la fortaleza—Juan Ponçe de León—y más regidores, se determinó de la manera que se habían de fortificar y guardar en caso que la armada fran-cesa (o parte de ella) allí fuese. Estaban los más de los vecinos huidos en el monte con sus mujeres, hijos y hacienda de temor que la armada francesa allí viniese. No pudía el gobernador traerlos al pueblo, y con la llegada del Adelantado todos vinieron. Hicieron alegrías y procesiones, suplicando [83r] a Nuestro Señor les diese victoria contra los enemigos porque todos los vecinos estaban determinados—si los enemigos allí venían—[a] morir antes que rendirse.

Al cuarto día se partió el Adelantado para San Germán, y al terçero día que allí llegó se hizo a la vela para Puerto de Plata, donde con pareçer, acuerdo y favor de la justiçia y regimiento de Puerto de Plata y vecinos de ella, traçó un torreón[314] a la entrada del puerto, donde antes estaba traçado. Dejó cincuenta soldados para que trabajasen en él, todos arcabuceros, y cuatro pieças de artillería de bronçe muy buenas, para que defendiesen la entrada de los co[r]sarios que allí quisiesen entrar, porque solían allí venir muchas veces, y de conformidad de los vecinos rescataban muchas merca-durías y negros por oro, plata, perlas y açúcares[315] y cueros, y otras veces sin rescatar robaban el pueblo, y dos veces lo quemaron. Por una parte holgábase el pueblo de este socorro, y por la otra les pesaba muy mucho, por las ganançias que les quitaba del trato con los co[r]sarios.

Suçedió que dentro de cuatro meses vinieron para entrar dentro del pueblo cuatro naos armadas muy fuertes, y por general de ellas un co[r]sario que se llamaba Juan del Buen Tiempo, el cual había algunos años que andaba tratando de las Indias a Françia[316] por rescates, que se hizo muy rico. Y queriendo entrar dentro del puerto, el capitán Aguirre, a quien el Adelantado había dejado [83v] con los cincuenta soldados para defensa de aquel turrión y puerto, les impidió la entrada, de manera que los françeses se volvieron sin poder entrar. A esta defensa no acudió vecino del pueblo sino fueron çinco, cosa que admiró al capitán Aguirre y a sus soldados. Sintió mucho el pueblo la vuelta de los françeses porque se les quitaba su ganançia, y en espeçial Françisco de Çaballos, que era el más rico y de los más prençipales del pueblo, que tiene un ingenio de açúcar y un trapi-che, muchos cueros y mucho ganado, que cada año que este Juan de Buen Tiempo allí iba le hacía mucha amistad y tenía con él gran comerçio y contrataçión, vendiendo sus cueros y açúcares. Y empeçó a seguir de aquel día adelante al capitán Aguirre y a sus soldados, dando falsas relaçiones a l[a] Audiençia que vivían revoltosamente en el pueblo.

La Audiençia escribió a Su Majestad diese la alcaidía de aquel turrión al Françisco de Çaballos, y por no ser informado Su Majestad lo mal que el Francisco de Çaballos lo servía en aquella villa, en permitir y tener el comerçio y contrataçión con los françeses, portugueses e ingleses que allí iban sin registro, yendo a robar, y contra las provisiones y ordenanças de Su Majestad que sobre esto tenía proveído, [se la dio]. Había sido este Francisco de Çaballos casado con una hermana de Lucas Vázquez de Ayllón, hija legítima de Lucas Vázquez de Ayllón, su suegro, que padre e hijo tuvieron título de adelantados de la Florida y pobladores y conquistadores de ella con çiertas capitulaciones que Su Majestad con ellos había hecho. [84r] Y por la mala maña que se dieron, y Dios que no fuese cuido de ello, no pudieron salir con la empresa. Muerto el padre quitolo Su Majestad al hijo, y[317] en sus días capituló con el Adelantado Pero Menéndez.

Estaba sentido Francisco de Çaballos de esto y encubriole el odio, y pasando Estébano de las Salas por allí, y Pedro Menéndez Marqués—sobrino[318] del Adelantado—que venían con una armada de Asturias y Vizcaya que iban para la Florida, escribió Françisco de Çaballos al Adelantado que le enviase navíos, que los cargaría de bastimento y ganados, y haciéndoles muchos ofreçimientos, por estar aquel puerto a propósito y haber en él bastimento, y que le hiciese su teniente para esto. El Adelantado tuvo por çierto que el Francisco de Çaballos hiciera lo que decía, que se lo había escrito por tres cartas, y para más justificárselo le envió un criado[319] suyo. El Adelantado, teniéndolo por cierto, le envió poder bastante, y en veces envió allí seis navíos. A unos detenía diciendo que los despacharía, y los dejaba estar hasta que estaban comidos de broma, que no estaban para navegar, y otros por no les dar carga se iban, y uno que cargó se fue al fondo el segundo día que partió del puerto.

Y sucedió que de los amotinados en la Florida llegaron allí dos navíos con do[s]cientos y çincuenta hombres, y entre ellos las cabeças[320] de los capitanes y soldados más rebeldes en el serviçio de Su Majestad en la Florida. Y aunque le fue aviso del Adelantado y maestro de campo que éstos habían sido traidores a Su Majestad él los recibió muy bien y les dio caballos y posada, y jugaban co[n] ellos cañas y corrían toros, diciendo muchas injurias del Adelantado [84v] y maestro de campo, y de los que quedaban en aquella tierra en servicio de Su Majestad, de que él gustaba mucho y se reía, diciendo que quedaban como bestias y que así lo serían presto, esclavos de los indios, o los matarían a todos. Favoreçió a toda esta gente, de manera que los más de ellos fueron al Perú y Nueva España y a las partes de las Indias que quisieron. Y porque este Francisco de Çaballos había casado segunda vez con hija del licençiado que entonces presidía en la Audiençia de Santo Domingo, y había desposado un hijo—nieto de este presidente— con hija de don Cristóbal Colón, y el don Cristóbal había desposado otra hija con el liçençiado Artegón, oidor de la Audiencia de Santo Domingo, no había en aquella Audiençia más de otro oidor que llamaban Cáçeres, amigo de sus compañeros, [y] hacía y decía el Francisco Çaballos lo que quería en desfavoreçer las cosas de la Florida, que entendía tanto deseaba Su Majestad llevarlas adelante, y el favor que daba a los co[r]sarios, que salía con todo por ser favorecido de la Audiencia. Y en lugar de ser casti- gados por tantos delitos feos y graves, por no ser Su Majestad informado de la verdad, ni los señores de su Real Consejo de las Indias, en lugar de mandalle castigar hácenle alcaide del turrión que el capitán Aguirre y sus soldados hicieron para que, en llegando la provisión de Su Majestad en que le hace esta merced, se vayan el capitán Aguirre y sus soldados a las Indias descontentos, que es lo que ellos querían, y de esto no será nada Su Majes- tad servido y el Françisco de Çaballos quedará muy contento y regocijado con la alcaidía, porque podrá tratar y contratar como solía con los co[r]- sarios, y visto que por lo pasado no ha sido castigado, antes se lo tienen en serviçio.

Porque después que el capitán Aguirre estorbó la entrada de Puerto de Plata a Juan [85r] de Buen Tiempo con sus cuatro naos de armada se fue el Juan de Buen Tiempo a otros puertos de aquella isla, que fueron Monte Christe, Puerto Real, y La Yaguana, que tomó doce navíos y mucha ha- cienda en ellos, y quemó a Puerto Real y se volvió a Françia. En todos estos tres pueblos había ido el Adelantado y no quisieron recebir soldados.

Otros dos navíos vinieron en aquellos días sobre Santiago de Cuba. El Adelantado había dejado allí cincuenta soldados arcabuceros, y por capitán de ellos a el capitán Die[go de] Godoy,[321] buen soldado, y cuatro pieças de artillería de bronçe,[322] con su pólvora y municiones, que los impidieron la entrada. Fuéronse estos navíos a Cabo de Cruz y a Mançanillo,[323] puerto del Bayamo.[324] Tomaron çinco navíos con muchos dineros y cueros. Soco- rrió el Adelantado a La Habana con do[s]cientos soldados y seis pieças de artillería, y por capitán de ellos, como antes lo tenía acordado y proveído, a Baltasar de Barreda, que llevó este socorro a La Habana a los primeros[325] de enero [de 1567], cosa que pareçe encantamiento, que en tan pocos días hubiese el Adelantado hecho tantos socorros con navegaciones tan dificultosas, porque a veinte[326] de octubre [de 1566] partió de la Florida, y estuvo en San Germán y en La Mona y Santo Domingo y Puerto Rico. Corrió con la armada a Puerto de Plata. Hecho aquel socorro, envió al maestro de campo con las tres naos por la canal vieja a socorrer a La Habana, el cual tuvo muy gran tormenta de norte en el camino, que estuvo muchas veces a punto de perderse. [85v]

El Adelantado con la otra nao fue a Monte Christi y Puerto Real y a La Yaguana, y les ofreció soldados para defenderse de los co[r]sarios y no los quisieron recebir. Y a Santiago de Cuba y a Cabo de Cruz, Macaca, pueblo de Bayamo.[327] Dejó la nao cargada de bastimentos para La Habana, y de allí a la Florida. Él se metió en una zabra y por entre los cayos llegó a un puerto que está en el sur de La Habana que se llama [. . .], y por tierra llegó a La Habana, que llegó a tantos de [. . .].[328] Hizo este camino del Bayamo a La Habana, por mar y por tierra, en ocho días, y fue cosa que se admiraron las gentes, siendo por lo menos camino de un mes. Fue grande el regocijo que el maestro de campo y capitanes, gente de mar y guerra, recibieron con el Adelantado.

Luego dio orden en fortificar aquella plaça y puerto como Su Majestad se lo mandaba, y en la una de las naos de las tres que allí estaban recogió todas las municiones. Todas las otras dos[329] despidió y envió a España, y dejando allí al capitán Baltasar de Barreda con los do[s]cientos soldados para defensa de la fortaleza y puerto, como Su Majestad se lo mandaba por su real çédula que socorriese aquella plaça con la gente que le pareciese. Invió al maestro de campo a la Florida con las municiones que habían sobrado y el bastimento que había traído la nao[330] que dejó el Adelantado en Macaca cargando de bastimentos del Bayamo.[331] Despidió también [86r] esta nao del sueldo de Su Majestad, como las demás. También hubo luego despedir la de Puerto Rico y la hurca que llegó a Santo Domingo, de que era capitán Cristóbal de Herrera, por no hacer costa a Su Majestad. Y si Su Majestad hubiera de hacer el costo de esta armada, sin bastimentos y gente, sólo de fortificaciones y otras cosas necesarias que las naos de armada han menester, por cuenta de Su Majestad gastara más de veinte mil ducados, y en las Indias gastara más de cuarenta mil. Y el Adelantado no gastó un ducado [de Su Majestad], porque con los oficiales que tenía en la Florida, que había llevado consigo a su costa, y otros materiales, lo hizo todo con parte de los navíos, bastimento y gente que habían ido para socorro de la Florida y de las Islas, y con otros çiento y cincuenta marineros, pilotos y gente que tenía. Y la fragata y bergantín era[n] del Adelantado, y la gente que en él andaba, sin que a Su Majestad se le hiciese costa ninguna.

Tercer viaje a tierras del cacique Carlos

Dio orden al[332] maestro de campo, cuando se fue a la Florida, que fuese luego con su gente y que,[333] llegando a San Agustín, visitando aquello y lo de San Mateo, con tres bergantines que el Adelantado tenía en la Florida suyos para descubrimientos, subiese por el río de San Mateo arriba con ciento y cincuenta hombres hasta llegar al cacique Mocoya, donde el Adelantado había llegado cuando se volvió.

Y el Adelantado partió aquel mismo día de La Habana, cuando el maestro de campo, para tierra de Carlos con seis patajes y bergantines. Y dijo al[334] maestro [86v] de campo que procuraría saber si en Carlos había río para llegar a Mocoya, y descubriría aquella costa hasta la laguna Maimi.[335]

Antes que el Adelantado partiese de la Florida a hacer los socorros acordó de enviar a Francisco de Reinoso, hombre de armas de Su Majestad, muy buen soldado, con treinta soldados al cacique Carlos, y enviarle a su primo, que era heredero suyo, que pusieron nombre don Pedro cuando le bautizaron, y a otro indio su criado, porque le pareçió este indio heredero de Carlos ser de muy buen entendimiento y grande su amigo. Y no quería el Adelantado que se le muriese, y daba muy grandes muestras de buen cristiano, y pretendía el Adelantado casarle con doña Antonia la india, pues habían de ser herederos del estado de Carlos [y] procurarían que los indios fuesen cristianos.

Y nombró por capitán de aquellos treinta soldados a Francisco de Reinoso, y diole instrucción que hiciese una casa fuerte en el pueblo de Carlos y procurasen todos, con gran devoçión, a las mañanas y a las tardes, adorar la cruz, diciendo la doctrina cristiana, para que los indios hiciesen lo mismo, y trabajasen de los doctrinar lo mejor que pudiesen. Y que con la amistad de los indios procurasen de saber si un río que estaba a dos leguas de allí iba a dar a la laguna de Maimi, y cuántas leguas había, porque ya el Adelantado sabía las que había de esta laguna a Mocoya, y que había pasaje, porque él iría dentro de tres o cuatro meses a Carlos con bajeles suficientes para ver si podría pasar por aquel río a San Mat[e]o y [87r] San Agustín, que era lo que el Adelantado mucho deseaba, por el gran serviçio que entendía hacía a Su Majestad y a los tratantes en las Indias, y al bien general de los que andaban en la poblaçión y conquista de la Florida. Y diole un presente para Carlos y otro para su mujer y otro para doña Antonia la india.

Y llegado el Françisco de Reinoso en el bergantín a Carlos con su[s] treinta soldados y con don Pedro el indio, heredero de Carlos, y con el otro indio, echaron en tierra los dos indios para que hablasen a Carlos y a doña Antonia, de que fue grande el contentamiento que todos los indios recibieron con ellos. Y luego vino Carlos al patax, ofreciendo su amistad al capitán Francisco de Reinoso y soldados, que pues el Adelantado era su hermano mayor y le enviaba a mandar que los recibiese e hiciese buen tratamiento, que lo había de hacer, y que él ni ningún indio de los suyos le había[n] de hacer mal. Y así se desembarcaron con gran regocijo y contento y los llevó a su pueblo, adonde le dio el Francisco de Reinoso el presente que llevaba, y dio una carta, la cual él aclaró con la lengua lo que en ella decía, que era encargándole mucho fuesen bien tratados los cristianos de él y de sus indios. Y así lo prometió Carlos al capitán Reinoso y les hizo hacer una casa en que se recogieron, los cuales, arbolando cerca de ella una cruz, la iban a adorar a las mañanas y a las tardes, diciendo la doctrina cristiana, y a ella acudían los indios e indias con gran devoçión.

Partiose el bergantín [de Francisco de Reinoso] para La Habana con çinco o seis marineros, como lo había ordenado el Adelantado. [87v] Llevó consigo a la india doña Antonia con çinco o seis indios prencipales, porque así lo había ordenado el Adelantado para seguridad del capitán Françisco de Reinoso y treinta soldados que con él quedaban, porque era muy poca la confiança que el Adelantado hacía del Carlos, porque cuando le trató le vio tener muchas muestras de traidor. Llegado el bergantín a La Habana[336] dentro de seis días que partió de Carlos, fue luego a la marina Alonso de Rojas, regidor de aquella villa, y llevó a doña Antonia y a sus indias a su casa, como antes las tenía. Y su mujer, que era madrina de doña Antonia, la recibió muy bien, haciéndole mucho regalo y buen tratamiento. Y luego el bergantín y otro patax cargaron de ganados vivos y algún bastimento y fueron con ello a Carlos.

Escribió el capitán Francisco de Reinoso el trabajo y peligro con que vivían, y que por dos o tres veces a traición los había querido matar Carlos, y que enviaba a pedir a su hermana doña Antonia y los demás indios, que tenía muy gran deseo de verlos, que luego se volverían, a fin que, teniéndolos consigo, poder matar a Francisco de Reinoso y los soldados que con él estaban, porque estaba muy encarnecido este cacique y su padre en matar cristianos, que en veinte años que había que aquellos hombres y mujeres que el Adelantado allí halló captivos decían que habían muerto padre e hijo más de do[s]cientos cristianos sacrificándolos al demonio [88r] y haciendo sus fiestas y bailes con ellos. Y que es con toda gente de naos perdidas de la Carrera de las Indias, porque aunque se perdiesen cien leguas de allí se los llevaban a él, como era cacique de mucha costa de mar y Los Mártires y Canal de Bahama, que es donde las naos que van de Indias a España corren el mayor peligro. Y por esto hacía grandes diligencias el Adelantado de poblar aquella costa y querer atraer los caciques [de indios][337] a su amistad.

Y así, [el Adelantado fue a tierra de Carlos] en los seis bergantines que sacó de La Habana con çiento y cincuenta hombres, el día que el maestro de campo partió para San Agustín con la nao cargada de bastimento y municiones que le habían sobrado de la armada que fue a la Nueva España,[338] y llevaba dada orden subiese por la ribera de San Mateo arriba hasta Mocoya, que él iba a saber si por la parte de Carlos podía ir a Mocoya para de allí ir a San Agustín y San Mateo, y llevaba consigo a doña Antonia e indios e indias que consigo tenía, y fue con próspero viento en dos días naturales. Llevaba consigo al padre Rogel de la compañía[339] de Jesús, muy docto y gran religioso, y al padre Françisco de la mesma compañía.

Llevaba indios prencipales de Tequesta, que era dende dejó el navío que venía de San Mateo con la gente amotinada los veinte soldados, que acertando a pasar un bergantín que el Adelantado enviaba de la Florida a La Habana a buscar bastimento, y llegando sobre aquel puerto, diole el viento contrario y entrose en él, y halló los cristianos que allí habían quedado de estos amotinados [88v] todos muy buenos, que les dijeron el buen tratamiento que el cacique y sus indios les habían hecho por tener por mujer el Adelantado a doña Antonia, y que cinco o seis andaban por la tierra adentro. Y la gente del bergantín tomaron hasta quince soldados de éstos, y el cacique envió a un hermano suyo con tres indios y tres indias en este bergantín a decir al Adelantado que él y sus indios querían ser cristianos, que le fuese a ver, porque le quería tomar por su hermano mayor para hacer lo que él les mandase.

Y este cacique y Carlos tenían gran guerra y sabido por qué era, que el cacique Tequesta solía ser sujeto a Carlos, y como Carlos supo que tenía [a] aquellos cristianos envió por ellos y no se los quiso dar, y después envió para que los matasen a traición. Súpolo el Tequesta, defendiolos, y mató dos indios suyos que andaban tratando de matar los cristianos. Y el Adelantado llevaba consigo esta tercera vez estos mensajeros de Tequesta con la doña Antonia, todos juntos, para tratar paces y amistades entre el Carlos y el Tequesta.

Y como entró el Adelantado en el puerto de Carlos dos días después que partió de La Habana—como está dicho—fue descubierto por el capitán Francisco de Reinoso y sus soldados, y por el cacique Carlos y su gente. Luego acudieron con las canoas a los bergantines. Saltó el Adelantado en tierra. Fue muy bien recebido de los cristianos e indios. Hizo hacer junto de la casa de los cristianos una casa a la [89r] doña[340] Antonia, y una capilla donde el padre Rogel decía misa. Predicó otro día siguiente a los soldados, que tenían harta neçesidad de ser doctrinados, y por los buenos ejemplos que les dio pidieron al Adelantado que le dejase con ellos, porque no de otra manera presto serían salvajes como los mismos indios. Y esto era que las indias los querían mucho, de tal manera que si el Adelantado entonçes allí no llegara, el Carlos y sus indios[341] (aunque perdiera a doña Antonia su hermana y a los seis indios e indias que consigo tenía) estaban determinados de matar a Francisco de Reinoso y a todos los cristianos que con él estaban, aunque con el aviso que las indias daban a los cristianos (que Carlos y sus indios los querían matar) vivían con gran recato.

Informó el Francisco de Reinoso particularmente al Adelantado de las costumbres y condiciones de Carlos y de sus indios, y de las muchas veces que los habían querido matar, y que era grande la devoçión que iban tomando a la cruz, aunque Carlos estaba muy empedernido y se reía de nuestras cerimonias. El Adelantado regocijó mucho al Carlos y a toda su gente. Llevole a comer consigo dos veces, y a su mujer e indios[342] prencipales. Supo el Adelantado que el pasaje que él buscaba no le había por allí, y que cincuenta leguas adelante—en un pueblo que llamaban Tocobaga— hallaría pasaje. El cacique de aquella tierra era grande enemigo de Carlos y le hacía guerra.

Había pedido Carlos al Adelantado y al Françisco de Reinoso [89v] fuesen con él y su gente a hacer la guerra a Tocobaga. El Francisco de Reinoso dijo al Carlos que sin orden del Adelantado no lo había de hacer, porque si lo hacía le mandaría cortar la cabeça. Y el Adelantado respondió a Carlos que el Rey de España, su señor, no le enviaba a aquella tierra a hacer la guerra con los caciques e indios, y que si estaban reñidos[343] procuraría de hacellos amigos y decirles si querían ser cristianos, y los que lo quisieren ser enseñarles la doctrina de la manera que lo han de ser, para que cuando se muriesen en la tierra fuesen con Dios—Señor de todo el mundo—al çielo, que así, si él quería ser amigo de Tocobaga que él iría a tratar las paces con él.

Pesole mucho a Carlos de que el Adelantado no fuese a hacer la guerra a Tocobaga, y díjole que él quería ir en sus bergantines a Tocobaga con hasta veinte indios principales de los suyos, y que allá trataría el Adelantado las paces. El Adelantado holgó de ello y trató luego con el Carlos las paces y amistades entre él y el cacique Tequesta, con su hermano que allí tenía, y otros dos indios o tres.[344] Efectuáronse muy bien. Dejó el Adelantado confirmada mucha amistad entre los indios y soldados. Dejó allí hasta que volvi[er]a de Tocobaga los indios de Tequesta con los cristianos, y a los dos padres de la compañía. El padre Rogel dábase prisa a deprender con vocabulario la lengua de Carlos y Tocobaga para empeçar a predicar a los indios. El padre [90r] Francisco deprendía la lengua de Tequesta, porque pretendió el Adelantado—vuelto de Tocobaga—dejar allí al padre Rogel y llevar a Tequesta al[345] padre Francisco.

Capítulo 25

En tierras del cacique Tocobaga

Dentro de tres días que estuvo con Carlos se partió con todos los seis bergantines la vuelta de Tocobaga, llevando consigo a Carlos y otros veinte
principales suyos. Llegó el segundo día a la noche por el puerto, y vivía
el cacique veinte leguas por la tierra adentro, y se iba hasta el borde de su
casa por un brazo[346] de agua salada. Un indio de los que iban con Carlos,
aunque era de noche y no hacía luna, por el Norte guió de tal manera que—
llevando viento próspero—una hora antes del día llegó el Adelantado junto
de la casa de Tocobaga, y sin ser descubierto, y mandó con gran secreto
surgir los bergantines.

El Carlos rogó al Adelantado que saltasen en tierra y quemasen el pueblo
y matasen los indios. El Adelantado no lo quiso hacer, diciéndole que el Rey
de España, su señor, le mandaría cortar la cabeça porque Tocobaga ni sus
indios ninguno le había hecho mal y que, si se lo hubieran hecho, que él
hiciera lo que Carlos decía. Quedó de esto muy triste Carlos y dijo al Adelantado que le echasen en tierra a él y a su gente, que él iría a dar fuego a
la casa del cacique y se volvería a nado a los bergantines. El Adelantado le
dijo que no lo hiciese, ni se lo había de consentir, pues había venido [90v]
con él para tratar las paces y amistades. Enojose mucho de ello el Carlos y
lloraba de pesar. El Adelantado le consoló como mejor pudo y le dijo que él
procuraría hiciese paces muy honrosas con Tocobaga, y que le diese diez o
doce indios e indias que le tenía cautivos. Con esto se alegró mucho Carlos,
porque había entre ellos una hermana suya y de doña Antonia, y dijo al
Adelantado que con aquello estaba contento.

Mandó el Adelantado que junto de la casa del cacique se llegase una
chalupeta con ocho bogadores y un cristiano de aquéllos que habían estado cautivos con Carlos, que sabían la lengua de Tocobaga. Y mandó que

junto de la casa del cacique le dijese con altas voces en su lengua que no hubiese miedo, que los navíos que allí estaban, toda la gente que traían eran cristianos de verdad, sus amigos. Y habiendo hecho así, los indios despertaron, vieron los navíos junto de las casas y echaron a huir con sus mujeres e hijos. El cacique se estuvo quedo con çinco o seis indios y una mujer, y en siendo de día envió un cristiano que tenía al Adelantado a decirle que le agradeçía mucho en que no lo hubiese muerto a él ni a su gente, ni quemado su pueblo, y que aquel cristiano tenía (y no más) que lo enviaron, y su gente había huido, y que él se había quedado en su casa de oraçión y sus dioses, que primero quería morir que desampararlos, y que si quería que fuese a sus navíos iría, y si el Adelantado quería ir a tierra a dalle la vida o la muerte, que lo podía hacer, [91r] que lo estaba aguardando.

El Adelantado se holgó mucho con el recabdo y con el cristiano que lo llevaba, el cual era portugués de Tavira,[347] que es en el Algarve. Dijo que había seis años que estaba allí cautivo, que iban en una barca con maíz y gallinas, mantas y miel dende Campeche a Nueva España y que la tormenta los había echado allí al través. Y que los indios los mataron [a] todos dentro de una hora, y que éste se escondió en el monte, que no lo pudieron hallar, y anduvo por él un mes [escondido,][348] comiendo palmitos, bellotas y algún marisco. Y que acaso unos indios pescadores le vieron y le prendieron y llevaron a este cacique, y que le servía de traer agua y leña y guisarle de comer. Y que desde el día que se perdieron hasta entonçes, cada día suplicaba a Nuestro Señor le sacase de cautivo, y ocho días había que estaba aguardando cristianos, y que soñaba cada noche de estas ocho que cristianos iban allí a vivir, de que estaba muy contento. Contó al Adelantado las cosas de aquella tierra, aunque sabía muy poco, que nunca había salido veinte leguas fuera de aquel pueblo.

Y no quiso el Adelantado decir a este cristiano que Carlos venía allí, ni que viniese Tocobaga al navío, por amor de Carlos. Enviole a decir que él iba en tierra a hablarle y que no tuviese miedo, y encargó [91v] al cristiano que él le esforçase que ningún mal le haría, y que enviase a decir a sus indios que se volviesen al pueblo, y así se fue el cristiano con esta respuesta. Y a las ocho de la mañana fue el Adelantado a tierra, habló al cacique, el cual le reçibió muy bien y le sentó cabe sí en un lugar más alto y pre[e]minente. Tenía consigo seis indios y una india. Dijo al Adelantado con la lengua que no pensaba que los cristianos eran tan buenos, que bien conocía que le pudieran matar a él y a su gente y quemar sus ídolos y pueblo, y que había muchos días que sabía que cristianos andaban en aquella tierra, y habían enviado a decir a [los] caciques sus amigos que les diesen maíz, si no que los matarían. Y porque no se lo daban mataban muchos, y que él les tenía mucho miedo, y que después vinieron otros cristianos y mataron a éstos, y que decían que a estos postreros que los caciques y los indios los querían mucho, y que de cuáles eran ellos.

El Adelantado les respondió que él y su gente eran de los cristianos postreros, y que vinieron a matar [a] aquellos cristianos primeros que venían a hacer a los caciques e indios esclavos, y que eran cristianos de mentira, y que por esto los mató. Y que él y su gente eran cristianos de verdad, y que no los venían a matar ni hacer esclavos ni a tomarles su maíz, que sólo iba a decirles si querían ser cristianos [92r] y enseñarles cómo lo habían de ser, y tenerlos por amigos y hermanos. Y que no iba a hacerles guerra ni matar a ningún cacique ni indio, excepto a los que le quisiesen hacer mal o matar algún cristiano, y que si él y su gente querían ser cristianos, que él holgaría de ello.

El cacique se holgó mucho de lo que el Adelantado le dijo y levantose él y sus seis indios e hicieron al[349] Adelantado grande humildad y obediencia y le besaron las manos, y luego se volvieron a asentar. Entonces dijo el Adelantado al cacique que él era amigo de Carlos y tenía cristianos en su tierra, y que no por eso había de ser enemigo del Tocobaga. Y que tenía consigo a Carlos en los bergantines, y que le llevaba para tratar paz y amistad con él y le volviese las doce personas que tenía cautivas. Y que si él y sus indios quisiesen ser cristianos, que holgaría mucho de ello, y que le dejaría allí cristianos como en Carlos para que los defendiesen de sus enemigos y los enseñase[n] a ser cristianos. Dijo que él tenía su gente y los principales [y] caciques, sus sujetos y amigos, lejos de allí, y que sin que viniesen y les hablase no podrían responderle, que aguardase el Adelantado tres o cuatro días y los enviaría a llamar. El Adelantado dijo que era contento, y así envió el cacique a llamar [a] sus indios principales y caciques, y rogó al Adelantado mandase a sus soldados no llegasen a la casa de sus dioses, a quienes este cacique tenía gran veneración. Y fuese [92v] el Adelantado aquella noche con su gente a dormir a los bergantines.

Otro día por la mañana el cacique Tocobaga le fue a ver. Habláronse él y Carlos y tuvieron algunos dares y tomares. Quisiera el Carlos desembarcar con Tocobaga y con sus indios, y por tener el Adelantado a Carlos por muy traidor no se atrevió, pensando le diría mal de él y de sus cristianos y se conformarían los dos caciques para que el Carlos matase a los cristianos que allí tenía y el Tocobaga los que allí le dejase. Por otra parte no se atrevía el Adelantado enojar al Carlos, y por esto le dejó saltar en tierra con dos lenguas que siempre anduviesen cabe él por que no hablase al cacique o a los indios mal de los cristianos. Acudieron en aquellos tres días más de mil y quinientos indios, toda gente de muy buena disposición, con sus arcos y flechas. El Adelantado, como vido tanta gente, dijo al cacique que sus soldados estaban alegres porque pensaban que sus indios querían ser bellacos y pelear con ellos, que dejase los principales consigo para tratar de las paces y enviase los otros. El cacique lo hizo así.

Al cuarto día, estando juntos veintinueve caciques y como otros cien indios prencipales que consigo dejaron, envió el cacique a llamar al Adelantado que fuese a tratar las paces, y así fue, llevando consigo al Carlos. Y estando juntos (y el Adelantado sentado en el lugar más pre[e]minente) el cacique Tocobaga le dijo que él había dicho [a] aquellos caciques indios [93r] que allí estaban todo lo que el Adelantado había dicho, y que si él decía aquellas cosas de verdad, que todos holgaban de tomarle por hermano mayor y volverse cristianos, y hacer las paces con Carlos y darle su gente, con que si Carlos volviese a hacer la guerra con él que el Adelantado le ayudase, y que si él la rompiese con Carlos ayudase el Adelantado a Carlos, porque él quería hacer las paces con los cristianos de verdad y no de mentira, y que le dejase otro capitán con treinta cristianos para que le enseñasen a él y a sus caciques a ser cristianos.

Todo se hizo de esta manera, quedando las paces hechas con Carlos y vuelta su gente. El Adelantado dejó allí treinta soldados, y con cargo de ellos y por capitán a García Martínez de Cos, el cual quedó harto contra su voluntad. Y el Adelantado le dejó porque estaba contra él desabrido por cierta desobediencia que había tenido, mas porque era de buen entendimiento y buen cristiano le dejó.

Cuarto viaje a tierras del cacique Carlos

Y porque Tocobaga luego dijo al Adelantado que no pudía ir a Mocoya con tan poca gente, porque eran muchos y bellacos, se partió de allí con sus bergantines dentro de cuatro días que llegó, y dentro de ocho volvió a Carlos a su pueblo. Y en el camino fue grandísima la soberbia y enojo que conoçió traía Carlos por la amistad tan buena que el Adelantado dejaba[350] hecha en Tocobaga. Procuraba mucho el Adelantado alegrarle, y no podía. Y pasando un marinero por delante del Carlos, acertó[351] a caerle un cabo de cuerda delgada [93v] sobre la cabeça [de Carlos],[352] y pensando que el marinero lo hiciera adrede diole un gran bofetón en la cara y cerró con él a braços[353] para le querer echar a la mar. Acudió el Adelantado y quitóselo. Era el marinero de los más principales que allí iba, sintiose de esto, y mucho más el Adelantado, y como lo llevaba en su bergantín y lo había sacado de su tierra parecíale que era obligado a volverle a ella, que de otra manera túvose entendido que lo mandara ahorcar por el bofetón, y también porque había entendido de las lenguas que amenazaba al Adelantado y a sus cristianos, que él daría orden que ninguno se le escapase.

Dejole el Adelantado en su pueblo. Hizo fortificarse los cristianos mejor de lo que estaban. Dejoles a cumplimiento de cincuenta soldados sobre los que allí estaban, y ciertos versos, y al padre Rogel de la Compañía de Jesús para que doctrinase los indios. Y partiose con el padre Françisco, su compañero, y con los indios de Tequesta para los llevar a su cacique y decirle las paces que entre él y Carlos quedaban hechas. Dejó el Adelantado allí a doña Antonia con los cristianos. No traía de ella buen concepto porque estaba mucho de la parte de su hermano Carlos, y muy triste por las palabras que él había dicho en Tocobaga. Dijo palabras muy sentidas al Adelantado porque no habían quemado y muerto a Tocobaga y sus indios y quemádoles el pueblo [94r] y casa de sus ídolos, y que tenía dos coraçones, uno para sí y otro para Tocobaga, y que para ella ni para su hermano no tenía ninguno. El Adelantado la satisfizo lo mejor que pudo y la dejó, y se fue a embarcar para[354] ir a Tequesta.

Y estando en los navíos para hacer vela [e] irse a Tequesta a llevar los indios que allí tenía y confirmar las paces, y de allí ir a los fuertes de San Agustín y San Mateo, vio entrar por el puerto un navío, de que se espantó, no sabiendo qué pudía ser. Y llegando a surgir conoçió ser un patax suyo que había dejado en San Agustín cuando salió de armada contra los co[r]sarios, el cual habían despachado los capitanes de los fuertes de San Agustín, San Mateo y San Felipe a La Habana, dando aviso al Adelantado que [los] socorriese con bastimentos. Y llegado el brigantín a La Habana, el tesorero Juan de Inestrosa, teniente del Adelantado [en aquella villa e isla para las cosas de la Florida],[355] le enviaba con aviso al Adelantado, y también llevaba cartas de todos los regidores de La Habana. Y era el caso que, al tiempo que el Adelantado partió de La Habana este postrero viaje, un capitán que se llama Pedro de Rodabán, de los que Su Majestad había enviado al Adelantado con socorro, al tiempo que el Adelantado quiso partir se alçó al monte con la bandera, con designio de pasarse a la Nueva España, la cual estaba en este tiempo alterada.

Temió el Adelantado de su ida, detúvose algunos días pensando poderle recoger [94v] e hizo cabeça de proceso contra él, llamándole por pregones, sentenciándole en rebeldía, notificando la sentençia al gobernador García Osorio, para que [si] este capitán le pudiese prender le enviase [a España][356] a Su Majestad con su proceso. Y le escribieron en aquel bergantín que otro día que el Adelantado partiera de aquella villa de La Habana el capitán Rodabán se paseaba por aquella villa públicamente, y acompañaba al gobernador y comía con él, acompañado de muchos soldados de los amotinados que se habían venido huidos de la Florida. Y que dentro de seis días que el Adelantado partió, el gobernador había enviado a decir al capitán Baltasar de Barreda, a quien el Adelantado había dejado con do[s]cientos soldados en aquella villa para defensa de la fortaleza y puerto de ellas, según Su Majestad se lo mandaba, [que fuera a verle,] el cual fue, y halló al gobernador acompañado de los oficiales de Su Majestad de aquella isla y de los regidores de la villa, e hizo asentar cabe sí en una silla al capitán y a su alférez, y a otros gentileshombres que con él iban les mandó salir. Y dijo al capitán que quería ver la instrucción que tenía de Su Majestad para defender aquella fortaleza y puerto. El capitán le dijo que con un escribano se lo había enviado el Adelantado originalmente, como Su Majestad se lo mandaba, y que el traslado de ello autorizado, con la orden que el Adelantado le había dejado, [95r] tenía allí. Y echó mano a la faltriquera y sacole y le daba al gobernador, el cual le dijo que si no era el original que no la quería ver. El capitán le respondió que el escribano de quien estaba signada era uno que estaba allí presente. El gobernador no la quiso tomar y mandó a un escribano que allí estaba que mandase al atambor de la villa echar bando que, so pena de la vida, todos los soldados de la compañía del capitán Barreda se recogiesen a sus alojamientos y ninguno saliese de ellos sin su licencia y mandado. El capitán Barreda se admiró de esto y estúvose sosegado, sin responder nada. Y pasado un poco se quitó la gorra, diciendo contra el gobernador y los más que allí estaban que les besaba las manos, y se levantó y se iba. El gobernador se levantó y se abrazó con él, diciendo:

—¡Preso! ¡Por el rey!

Luego salieron dos alguaciles con siete u ocho porquerones y asieron al capitán y, no pudiéndole quitar la espada de la mano, andaban a las vueltas. Su alférez, que se llamaba Hulano, caballero de Trujillo,[357] buen soldado, que estaba fuera, [entendió el ruido],[358] entró para dentro y, visto cuán maltratado tenían a su capitán, echó mano a la espada y como un león arremete a los que lo tenían, los cuales le desmampararon y se retiraron a un aposento, y el gobernador con ellos. Çerraron la puerta por de dentro. Saliéronse el capitán y el alférez fuera, vieron que venían muchos soldados [95v] alterados, mandoles el capitán que—so pena de la vida—se recogiesen a cuerpo de guardia. Y el capitán Rodabán tenía amotinados muchos soldados de los del capitán Barreda, y tenía recogidos otros muchos de los amotinados, y decían estaba dentro de casa del gobernador para, en prendiendo al capitán Barreda, entregarle la bandera y compañía al capitán Rodabán.

Y de todo esto fue testimonio autorizado al Adelantado en aquel bergantín y carta que todos los regidores le escribían, suplicándole se viniese luego a La Habana a remediar aquellas cosas, porque de otra manera podría suceder gran mal.

Regreso a La Habana

El Adelantado, como vio estos despachos, envió los indios a Tequesta y él se volvió a La Habana y llegó dentro de tres días, y luego se ausentó al monte el capitán Rodabán. Averiguó lo que pasaba, y fuele forçado detenerse allí un mes para ver si podría prender a este capitán Rodabán que andaba en el monte con quince o veinte soldados arcabuceros. Tuvo tales espías y maña que le prendió, diole en justiçia, sentençiole a cortar la cabeça. Queriéndolo ejecutar acudieron muchos a le rogar, pidiéndole le otorgase la apelación y consejándole que, para más justificar la causa con Su Majestad, lo debía de hacer, el cual se la otorgó.

Capítulo 28

Segundo viaje a tierras del cacique Tequesta

Y dejando en el mejor recaudo que pudo lo de allí, con algún bastimento que recogió en[359] otros navíos que envió a Campeche a cargar de maíz se fue a la Florida [96r] a Tequesta, donde fue muy bien recibido de aquel cacique e indios. Hizo con ellos paces, tomáronle por hermano, y dejó allí treinta soldados, y por capitán de ellos a Pedro Pacheco, buen soldado,[360] y dejoles una sierra y carpinteros que hiciesen una casa fuerte. Arboló una cruz, con gran devoçión los indios la adoraron, y dejó allí al[361] padre Francisco, de la Compañía de Jesús, y estuvo cuatro días en aquel pueblo. Fue grande el contento de ver que a las mañanas y a las tardes todos los indios, grandes y pequeños, acudía[n] a adorar la cruz y besarla con grande devoçión. Dio el cacique al Adelantado un hermano suyo y dos indios principales (que el uno era capitán de un pueblo de Carlos) para que los trujese a España.

Regreso a San Mateo
y tierras del cacique Saturiba

Y partiose con ellos el Adelantado con buen tiempo, y el terçero día llegó a San Mateo, donde halló a Gonçalo de Villarroel y a su gente todos muy buenos, y que Saturiba había gran número de gente, y que le habían muerto algunos caciques e indios sus sujetos todos los ganados. Tenía preso en cadena al cacique Emoloa y un su hijo, y a otros dos herederos de dos caciques, y otros dos indios prencipales de Saturiba, que en todos eran diez y seis indios, [los cuales tenía todos en prisión de cadenas].[362]

Y supo el Adelantado cómo el maestro de campo había subido cincuenta leguas por aquella ribera de San Mateo arriba con tres bergantines hasta Mocoya, y que por hallar gran número de indios y el río estrecho y cerrado de bosque a la orilla, de [96v] una parte y de otra, se había vuelto por no tener nueva del Adelantado, que le había dicho había de entrar por la parte de Carlos. Y aunque en Tocobaga habían dicho al Adelantado (cuando allí estuvo con los bergantines y dejó los cristianos) que había por allí un río que pasaba a Mocoya, llevaba[363] poca gente para ir por allí, porque había muchos indios y muy guerreros todos, enemigos de Tocobaga, y que cuando el Adelantado volviese allí otra vez, con sus indios de guerra iría con él.

Con acuerdo de Gonçalo de Villarroel acordó el Adelantado al segundo día que a San Mateo llegó soltar un indio de aquéllos que estaban presos y enviole a Saturiba, que le dijese que otro día por la mañana estuviese a la punta de la barra, que es dos leguas de allí, porque el Adelantado se quería ir a Su Majestad[364] y deseaba verse con él y hablarle, porque nunca el Adelantado había visto este cacique y deseaba mucho hablar con él, y decían que el cacique quería mucho al Adelantado, mas que le tenía gran temor. Recibió el recabdo Saturiba, que estaba dos leguas de allí, [del Fuerte de San Mateo], y respondió [al Adelantado]³⁶⁵ que él iría a la barra como se lo enviaba a mandar, y que le rogaba llevase consigo los indios, porque los quería ver y hablar.

Otro día por la mañana partiose el Adelantado del fuerte dejando animados los soldados lo más que pudo, rogándoles estuviesen fuertes en el servicio de Su [97r] Majestad porque él se había de partir luego a España, como todos se lo rogaban, para que Su Majestad los socorriese de bastimentos y pagas para su vestir, porque ya andaban poco menos que indios desnudos. Llevó consigo el Adelantado a Gonçalo de Villarroel. Hallaron [a la barra]³⁶⁶ a Saturiba, muy desviado de la marina y con muchos indios. Llevaba el Adelantado allí a Emoloa y a otros seis indios prençipales. Soltó el Adelantado el uno y envió a decir al Saturiba que se llegase allí a la marina debajo de su palabra. El Saturiba respondió que pusiese el Adelantado en tierra [a] Emoloa y a los indios que consigo traía, porque quería primero hablar con ellos. El Adelantado lo hizo así—con sus grillos, que tenían a los pies—y púsolos fronteros de un bergantín, teniendo diestros veinte arcabuceros y dos versos con perdigones, para que si algunos indios se los quisiesen llevar a cuestas poderlos matar.

Saturiba no quiso venir a hablar a Emoloa [y] envió dos prençipales suyos que hablaron con él. Éstos iban y venían del Saturiba a Emoloa por espacio de más de dos horas. Hallose al cabo que todos sus tratos eran para soltar los indios y querer que el Adelantado saltase en tierra para flecharle a él y a los soldados que³⁶⁷ consigo llevaba, porque eran muchos los [97v] indios que Saturiba tenía emboscados. Entendió la trama el Adelantado por un soldado, grande amigo de Emoloa, que tenía cuidado de darle de comer a él y a sus indios y entendía la lengua [de los indios], aunque ellos no lo sabían. Recogió el Adelantado en sus bergantines a Emoloa y a los más [indios] prisioneros y envió a decir a Saturiba que siempre había deseado ser su amigo y entonces lo deseaba también, [y] que [le pesaba mucho]³⁶⁸ porque él no lo quería ser, y que desde entonçes en adelante le tuviese por su enemigo y que, por los cristianos que a traición había muerto, él le mandaría cortar la cabeça o echar de su tierra.

El cacique le envió a hacer muchos fieros, diciendo que aunque muchas veces había dicho a los capitanes del Adelantado que era su amigo, no lo decía de buen coraçón, porque a todos los cristianos tenían por enemigos, y que el Adelantado y sus soldados eran gallinas cobardes, que saliesen en tierra a pelear con él y con sus indios.³⁶⁹ El Adelantado le dejó, sin quererle responder.

Regreso a San Agustín y guerra contra Saturiba

Salió por la barra y se fue a San Agustín, donde halló al maestro de campo
y más capitanes todos buenos, aunque estaba muy descontenta la gente
de aquel fuerte por el mal tratamiento que el capitán Miguel Enríquez les
hacía (uno de los capitanes que Su Majestad había enviado con el socorro)
y de la gran desobediençia y poco respeto que [98r] por ausençia del Adelantado había tenido a su gobernador y alcaide del fuerte, a quien respet-
aban y pidían el nombre, porque entre otras cosas que se le desacató, fue
mudar las çentinelas que el Adelantado había mandado tener—contra la
voluntad del gobernador—[y] mandar traer armas—contra la voluntad
del gobernador—a soldados que estaban privados de ellas por delito que
habían cometido, nombrándoles para las çentinelas. Queriendo estropear
el gobernador un soldado porque se le había desacatado, salió con mano
armada el capitán a quitárselo y, dentro de ocho días, no pudiendo el capitán—estando allí el gobernador como estaba—castigar ningún soldado de
los suyos criminalmente, estropeó dos sin hacer cabeça de proceso. Dio de
palos a un alguacil e hizo otras disoluçiones feas y graves, todas en desacato
de su gobernador, a quien había obedecido por tal.

Hizo el Adelantado cabeça de proceso contra él. Fulminole, haciéndole
cargo, recibiendo su descargo. Dejó de justiciarle porque el gobernador era
el capitán Bartolomé Menéndez, hermano del Adelantado. Dejó el Adelantado la compañía de este capitán a Françisco Núñez, su alférez, y a su
sargento y oficiales. Remitió la persona del capitán a Su Majestad y a los
señores del Real Consejo de Indias con su proçeso, [98v] y nombró el Adelantado por su lugarteniente de aquellas provinçias—como de antes estaba
nombrado—a Estébano de las Alas, que allí estaba. Trató en consejo y acor-
dose de la manera que la guerra se había de hacer a Saturiba. Dejó instruc-

ción de ello, y antes de su partida se la dio por cuatro partes, y fue él en persona a la [parte en] que se tenía entendido estaba Saturiba con setenta soldados. Y por no ser sentido marchó aquella noche hasta el alba diez leguas. Ni él ni los demás pudieron hallar a Saturiba. Muririán como treinta indios. Mataron un marinero los indios, y dos soldados, e hirieron otros dos, aunque de los que el Adelantado llevaba no le mataron ni hirieron ninguno. Recogiéronse al Fuerte[370] de San Agustín. Habló a los capitanes y soldados que allí quedaba[n], animándoles y rogándoles estuviesen muy fuertes en el serviçio de Su Majestad.

Regreso a San Felipe

Embarcose para Santa Elena—donde está el Fuerte de San Felipe—en un bergantín, y el maestro de campo en una fragata. Traía consigo presos el Adelantado a los dos capitanes Miguel Enríquez y Pedro de Rodabán para los llevar a España, y tres indios prencipales—el uno de ellos el hijo del Emoloa—. Y soltó al Emoloa y todos los demás indios, diciéndoles que él trataría bien los tres indios que llevaba a España [con los otros][371] tres de Tequesta y los [99r] volvería a traer. Y que si Saturiba hacía la guerra a los cristianos y Emoloa y sus indios le ayudaban, y los otros prencipales que el Adelantado soltaba, que cortaría la cabeça a aquellos tres indios que llevaba.

Y con viento próspero llegó al tercero día a Santa Elena y Fuerte[372] de San Felipe, adonde halló al capitán Juan Pardo muy bueno y a todos los soldados muy contentos de la buena tierra que habían visto cuando fueron por la tierra adentro hasta ciento y çincuenta leguas y habían dejado hecho el fuerte al pie de la sierra en tierra del cacique Joara.[373] Y por tener aviso el Adelantado de Su Majestad que había salido de Françia una gruesa armada de co[r]sarios luteranos que decían iban a aquellas partes, [y que] estuviese muy a punto de guerra, por lo cual había enviado a mandar el Adelantado al capitán Juan Pardo que, dejando en aquel fuerte de la tierra adentro algunos soldados para la conservaçión de los indios y caciques amigos y para que los doctrinasen, se viniese luego a la marina y se metiese en el Fuerte de San Felipe, para que si armada françesa allí fuese se la pudiesen defender.[374] Contó el capitán Juan Pardo al Adelantado la mucha amistad que los caciques e indios de la tierra adentro le habían hecho y el deseo que tenían[375] [99v] de ser cristianos como él y tomarle por hermano mayor para hacer lo que les mandase. Y que, ni más ni menos, estaban muy amigos los caciques de la marina y sus indios de aquel distrito, y que todos deseaban mucho de verle y volverse cristianos.

Capítulo 32

Viaje a España

Y bien quisiera el Adelantado detenerse allí un mes para la confirmación y amistad de estos caciques e indios, mas era muy poco el bastimento que dejaba en los fuertes y muy corta la raçión que los soldados comían, y había diez meses que había escrito a Su Majestad que sería en España, y tenía aviso que Flandes se rebelaba contra el servicio de Su Majestad, y que Su Majestad pasaba allá. Y así, para el remedio de los soldados que estaban en la Florida a su cargo, como los que estaban en las islas de Puerto Rico, Española y Cuba, que fuesen bastecidos y pagados, porque padeçían grandes necesidades de comida y vestidos, y poder dar cuenta particular a Su Majestad del estado de las cosas de la Florida y de todas las islas e Indias, y los robos que [los] co[r]sarios hacían, porque si no lo remediaba todos se perderían, y cómo lo podía remediar y sustentar los fuertes de la Florida a mucha menos costa de su real hacienda, y para le poder servir en la jornada de Flandes, se embarcó en la fragata, que era hechiza, muy ligera [100r] de remo y vela, de porte de hasta veinte toneles, porque el bergantín que había sacado de San Agustín junto con esta fragata no era de buen sustén. Y cargó en él cincuenta quintales de bizcocho [y] enviolos a San Agustín y San Mateo, porque como algunos soldados de aquel fuerte habían ido la tierra adentro habíanse ahorrado este bizcocho.[376]

Él metió consigo en la fragata al maestro de campo y a Francisco de Castañeda—capitán de la guarda del Adelantado—y al capitán Juan Vélez de Medrano—a quien el Adelantado había dado liçençia por su poca salud se viniese a España—y a Françisco de Cepero,[377] y a Diego de Miranda, y a Álvaro[378] de Valdés, y a Juan de Valdés, y a Pedro de Ayala—alférez del capitán Medrano—y a Diego de Salcedo, y a Juan de Ag[u]iniga, y a Alonso de Cabra. y al liçençiado [. . .][379]—que era clérigo—y al capitán

Blas de Merlo,[380] y a otros hidalgos, en número de veinticinco, todos con sus arcabuces y buenas armas, personas que solían acompañar al Adelantado y comer los más de ellos a su tabla, y otros cinco marineros, porque los demás de estos soldados eran y sabían bien bogar, y los seis indios, y los dos capitanes que el Adelantado traía presos, Pedro de Rod[ab]án y Miguel Enríquez, que en todos eran[381] treinta y ocho personas.

Y tuvo tan próspero viento y la fragata era tan ligera que en diez y siete [100v] días vio las Islas de las Açores, que un día por otro caminó setenta y dos leguas, como se verá en la carta de mar, de que el Adelantado recibió gran contento cuando vio las islas en tan pocos días por reconoçer la gran ligereza de su fragata. Entró en la isla de La Terçera. Tuvo aviso que Su Majestad venía [a] embarcar a La Coruña para ir a Flandes y, pareciéndole que tomando aquella derrota le pudiera alcançar antes de su partida de La Coruña, [y de que los co[r]sarios de alto borde que por allí encontrase les podría huir a remo y vela, [y] que yendo la vuelta del cabo de San Vicente de Sevilla, topando[382] fustas de moros, le podrían alcançar al remo.

Tuvo algunos vientos contrarios dende La Te[r]cera hasta La Coruña y llegó a entrar en aquel puerto [el 29 de junio de 1567,] día de San Pedro. Encontró çerca del puerto, como tres leguas, dos naos francesas y una inglesa que le dieron caça, y echó a huir. Y al segundo día entró en Vive[i]ro, veinte leguas de La Coruña, donde supo que Su Majestad estaba en la Corte, que no era partida aún para Coruña. Envió de allí los dos capitanes presos, Rodabán y Miguel Enríquez, [y] entregolos al alférez Ayala para que—presos y a buen recaudo—los entregase en la cárcel de [la] Corte y diese el proceso en el Real Consejo de Indias. Escribió a Su Majestad su llegada [a] aquel puerto, y que con brevedad [101r] le iría a besar las manos.

Y otro día siguiente que el Adelantado allí llegó se partió a mediodía para Avilés, donde tenía su mujer y casa, que era veinte y ocho leguas de Vive[i]ro. Tuvo el viento tan próspero que en aquel día anduvo las veinticinco[383] leguas y entrose en una bahía que llaman Artedo, donde estaban surtos diez navíos, los cuales, como vieron aquella fragata de nueva invención y tan esquifada de remos (que parecía de turcos en la Mar de Levante), temiéronla y desmampararon sus navíos y echaron a huir a tierra con los bateles. Hubo muchos de ellos que estaban cargando, [y uno de ellos estaba cargando] de hierro, que encalló en la arena del fondo el navío por abajo, para que si el Adelantado fuera co[r]sario no lo pudiese llevar. Surgió el Adelantado con su fragata entre estos navíos. No había hombre ninguno en ellos ni batel.[384] Tenía muy gran pena de ver que el uno daba al través. Hizo grandes deligencias. Mandó a un marinero de la fragata dar voces que algún batel viniese allá. Traía tres pieças de artillería de bronçe pequeñas, y dos marineros de los çinco eran muy buenos clarines. No quiso el Adelantado que se los tocasen ni tirasen pieça de artillería, por no alborotar. Reposó la gente de la fragata, siendo ya las diez de la noche, y no había venido batel a reconocer la fragata.

A la medianoche vino un batel muy esquifado de remos, y de largo llamó a la gente de la fragata, preguntando qué navío era y de dónde venía. [101v] De la fragata le respondieron que era el Adelantado Pero Menéndez que venía de la Florida, y que llegasen a bordo.[385] Temieron los del batel pensando que los engañaba, que muchos de los marineros que allí iban bien conocieron al Adelantado, y dijeron que tenían miedo que los engañaban, que si el Adelantado les hablaba que bien lo conocerían. El Adelantado, que los estaba oyendo, les dijo:

—Hermanos míos, hace[d]me placer que vais a aquel navío que está en tierra perdiéndose a decirle cómo soy yo el Adelantado Pero Menéndez, que vengo de la Florida, para que procure el remedio de su navío. Y deci[d] lo mesmo a la gente de estos otros, que me parece que son huidos al monte y que sus bateles los habrían dejado por ahí perdidos. Y que, dicho esto, os volváis aquí porque os querría hablar.

Y [dijo] que lo mesmo dijese[n] a los maestres de los otros navíos, que fuesen a bordo de la fragata con sus bateles. Respondieron del batel que Su Señoría fuese bienvenido y que ellos iban a hacer lo que les mandaba, y así lo hicieron luego. Detúvose esta gente con el batel hasta el alba a dar aviso a la gente que había venido de los bateles y [a] ayudar a salvar este navío de hierro. Y veníanse con sus bateles a[l] bordo de la fragata a[l] amanecer, donde el Adelantado hizo desplegar un guión de damasco carmesí como estandarte[386] y una bandera [102r] de campo, y tocar los clarines y tirar las tres pieças de artillería. Alteráronse la gente de los bateles pensando que era co[r]sario y dieron la vuelta huyendo. Sólo llegó a[l] bordo el batel que había hablado la gente de él con el Adelantado y le habían conocido. Eran çinco carabelas de portugueses cargadas de sal y otros tres navíos de pescadores, y los otros dos —uno de hierro y otro de madera—. Volvió luego este batel a asegurar a los demás, y vinieron a bordo de la fragata a hablar con el Adelantado. Todos se holgaron mucho de verle y se admiraban navegar tanta mar en tan pequeño bajel. Y çierto es una de las cosas que hasta hoy en la mar se ha visto.[387]

Hizo vela y dentro de dos horas entró en su pueblo (que ya sabían que iba, porque un hombre que fue a tierra a avisar quién él era fue por tierra aquella noche a pedir las albricias a su mujer y deudos). Fue tanta la alegría que aquel pueblo hubo con su llegada—de su mujer, deudos y vecinos—que no se puede encareçer porque, allende de que el Adelantado y sus deudos son de los prençípales de aquella tierra, es tan bienquisto y amado de todos que se hincaban muchos de rodillas, puestas las manos al çielo, alabando a Nuestro Señor que le había traído a salvamento. Y miraban la fragata, que los tenía admirados, en ver en tan pequeño bajel [102v] tanta bandera y gallardete, y pieças[388] de artillería de bronçe—que tiraron—y arcabucería, y tocar los clarines, y los soldados bizarros y bien traídos, que todos estaban como encantados, mirándose los unos a los otros.

Fuese el Adelantado derecho a la iglesia a dar gracias a Nuestro Señor y a su preçiosa madre por la merced que le había hecho en traerle a salvamento. Fue acompañado de los del pueblo hasta su casa, y entonces fue recibido de su mujer e hijas, hermanas [y] sobrinas, que con ellas estaban acompañándolas (como se podrá juzgar). Había diez y ocho años que el Adelantado andaba en servicio de Su Majestad con los cargos de capitán-general de armadas en las costas de Asturias y Vizcaya, Flandes y Carrera de Indias, en el cual tiempo nunca había estado en su casa sino cuatro veces,[389] y en ellas veintidós días. Estuvo de esta venida diez y ocho días, por tener aviso que Su Majestad no estaba tan de camino, en los cuales se fue el maestro de campo a ver a sus padres a la villa de Gijón, que es de allí cuatro leguas, donde había hecho esta jornada contra la voluntad y sin licencia de ellos porque, como no tenían más de a él, le querían mucho, y de edad de diez años se había criado en Italia. Muchos años antes, tratando sus padres y deudos con el Adelantado que se casase con una hija suya, y enviaron por él a Italia, y venido [103r] que fue, yéndose el Adelantado a despedir de su mujer el año de [15]65 para hacer esta jornada[390] a la Florida, porque eran deudos dentro del cuarto grado dos veces no se pudieron casar sin dispensación—conforme al conçilio—y habían enviado a Roma por ella, estando hechas las escrituras del casamiento. Importunó al Adelantado le llevase consigo hasta Sevilla y a Cádiz, donde se había de embarcar, y que para entonces serían venidas las dispensaçiones y se vendría a casar. Holgose de ello el Adelantado y, al tiempo de la partida de Cádiz, habiéndole pedido licençia para hacer la jornada (y no se la habiendo querido dar el Adelantado), apretole tanto que le vino a decir que, si no le llevaba consigo, en el primer navío que fuese a la Florida se iría en él. Pesole al Adelantado de su determinaçión y contra su voluntad y secretamente se embarcó para la jornada, como está dicho.

Información sobre la conquista de Florida

Vino el Adelantado a Madrid a besar a Su Majestad las manos a 20 de julio [de 1567], trayendo consigo los seis indios desnudos, con sus arcos y flechas, según y como andaban en la Florida. Y fue recebido de Su Majestad muy favorablemente, teniéndole en gran serviçio la jornada, y [diciéndole] que le haría mercedes. Y habiéndole dado cuenta del estado de las cosas de la Florida y la neçesidad con [103v] que quedaban de bastimento los soldados, y algún daño que los co[r]sarios hacían[391] en todas las Indias, y el peligro que las flotas que traían el dinero corrían de ellos, si se juntasen, que lo uno y lo otro era forçoso y neçe[sario] remediarlo.

Su Majestad proveyó luego fuesen los soldados socorridos y que hiciese memorial de la mejor orden que se podía tener para castigar los co[r]sarios que en tiempo de paz andaban a robar en aquellas partes y en la Mar de Poniente a sus vasallos, y obviarlos de los daños que podrían hacer. Y [Su Majestad dijo] que tenía a buena dicha el haber venido en tan buena coyuntura para el remedio de esto y para le llevar a Flandes, que estuviese desocupado para ello, que el socorro a la Florida le llevaría uno de los capitanes que con él venían.

El Adelantado le respondió que en lo uno y en lo otro suplicaría a Nuestro Señor que le favoreciese y ayudase para acertar a servir a Su Majestad. Luego besó las manos el maestro de campo a Su Majestad, y porque había servido señaladamente esta jornada y se supo bien gobernar—aunque no tenía más de veinticuatro años (mas por haber sido de antes soldado tenía experiençia)—Su Majestad le agradeçió y tuvo en serviçio la jornada que había hecho y lo bien que en ella le había servido. Y asimismo recibió a los más capitanes y gentileshombres que con el Adelantado iban, que le besaron las manos, y mandó Su Majestad al Real Consejo de Indias oyesen al Adelantado dentro del consejo, particularmente las cosas de [104r] la Florida, el cual lo hizo, pidiéndole memoria de muchas cosas para las proveer. Así lo hizo.

Entre las cosas que dijo fue una: Que muchos capitanes y soldados de los amotinados en la Florida, habiendo hecho informaciones ante el gobernador de La Habana y ante otras justicias donde llegaban, jurando los unos en favor de los otros que habían servido muy bien y más señaladamente que los que allí quedaban en servicio de Su Majestad, los cuales se habían señalado en su real servicio, así en la tomada de los fuertes a los luteranos como en asistir a los trabajos, hambres y peligros que en aquella tierra hubo [e guerra con los indios]. Y con estas informaciones [que los amotinados hicieron tan favorables para sí],[392] hallábanse tan loçanos que, como se estendieron todos ellos—así capitanes como soldados—en todas las Indias y España, para justificar sus flaquezas del tiempo que se amotinaron (y haber preso al maestre de campo y a la justiçia y regimiento, y enclavado[393] la artillería y tomádoles el bastimento, dejándoles sin ninguno, y siendo los indios amigos, mataron tres de ellos prencipales para que los caciques indios de aquella tierra se juntasen—como lo hicieron—y matasen al maestro de campo y a los demás capitanes y soldados que quedaban en los fuertes sin ningún bastimento, porque de esta manera perec[er]ían todos los que quedaban en la Florida, y Su Majestad les haría a ellos mucha merced por virtud de sus informaçiones)[104v], dondequiera que estos amotinados se hallaban decían mal del Adelantado y cuantos con él quedaban. Y esto lo fundaban con muchas mentiras y falsedades por las mejores razones que ellos podían para ser creídos. Algunos pidieron a Su Majestad que les hiciese merced por sus buenos serviçios, los cuales Su Majestad remitió a la venida del Adelantado, y como [el Adelantado] informó de algunas cosas de éstas, se ausentaron.

Halló el Adelantado que algunos señores del Real Consejo de Indias tenían conçebido en su pecho que era verdad lo que estos amotinados les decían. Algunos otros ministros de Su Majestad, que estaban çerca de su real persona, tenían creído que el Adelantado excedía en algunas cosas de lo que era razón, y les pareçía que el Adelantado había tomado aquella jornada y empresa más por su interés particular que por el serviçio de Dios Nuestro Señor y el de Su Majestad, lo cual fue al contrario—según se vio y entendió—y lo mismo había sido todo el tiempo que había servido a Su Majestad, según es notorio por experiençia en diez y ocho años que fue capitán-general en cargos y armadas tan pre[e]minentes, de tanta confiança, honra y aprovechamiento, y que si él lo quisiera tener fuera muy rico, sin ser distraído ni hacer gastos excesivos. Antes de ser general de las armadas de Su Majestad tenía dos muy buenos galeones y treinta mil ducados en dineros, y después acá ha hecho prósperos sucesos y viajes con muchos galeones, naos y navíos suyos, zabras y patajes con que ha ganado gran suma de mercedes en los viajes prósperos y breves que ha hecho. Y [105r] ha tenido sus granjerías, muy en serviçio de Su Majestad y sin perjuicio de su ofiçio, en que ha ganado más de do[s]cientos mil ducados, [que] todos los ha gastado—como buen capitán—en servicio de Su Majestad, en cosas necesarias para que tuviesen buenos sucesos las cosas de su cargo, por no querer Su Majestad ni sus ministros proveerlas. Y [par]a traer muy buenos capitanes y soldados, gente prencipal de confiança, así de mar como de guerra, en todas las armadas de su cargo, a quien hacía muchas ventajas, por[que] Su Majestad ni sus ministros no las quieren hacer, y por nunca tirar gajes de Su Majestad ni sueldo, mas de cuando servía (y éste[394] era menos de lo que se daba a otros generales en las jornadas), y hecho el viaje les despedía Su Majestad hasta que se ofreçía otra jornada, quedaba cargado de capitanes, oficiales y gente noble que le seguían y servían a Su Majestad en su compañía a los cuales entretenía, como[395] era obligado.

Y[396] en esta jornada de la Florida, visto que Su Majestad le daba provisiones y bastante recaudo que en las Indias le di[e]sen do[s]cientos caballos y cuatrocientos infantes pagados por cuatro meses, y tres naos de armada y artillería, municiones y bastimentos, y todas las cosas que pidiese y hubiese menester para echar los franceses luteranos que estaban en la Florida, pareciéndole que partiendo de Cádiz por junio de [15]65, como forçoso[397] había de ser, que irse por las islas [e Indias][398] [105v] a recoger esta caballería e infantería y navíos de armada se detendría mucho y no podría ir a la Florida hasta la primavera del año de [15]66, y que entonçes—como está dicho antes de agora—por irles a los françeses que estaban en la Florida mucho socorro de gente, artillería, armas, municiones y bastimentos, se fortificarían, de manera que cuando el Adelantado fuese por março de [15]66 no podría hacer el efecto que haría si desde Cádiz no se fuese derechamente a la Florida, donde los françeses estaban, antes que fuesen socorridos, o—caso que hubiesen sido—antes que se fortificasen y ganasen la voluntad a los caciques, [que éste][399] era el mayor temor que el Adelantado tenía, porque teniendo a los indios naturales de la Florida por enemigos y a los franceses que los industriarían para pelear, no era bastante recaudo el que el Adelantado llevaba para poner pie en aquella tierra ni echar a los luteranos[400] de ella.

Y aunque esta particularidad el Adelantado dijo a Su Majestad en Santa María de Nieva por abril de sesenta y çinco, y en La Mejorada, y lo dijo a los señores del Real Consejo de Estado y Guerra[401] que con él estaban, y después lo vino a decir a Madrid, donde estaba la Corte y presidente del Consejo Real de Castilla y señores del Real Consejo de Indias, que le diesen dos galeras y dos galeotas del cargo de don Álvaro de Baçán, para que con sus zabras y patajes[402] él se adelantase a la Florida antes que [106r] los franceses fuesen socorridos, y que—cuando lo hu[b]iesen sido—él desembarcaría en otro puerto, el más cercano que hallase al suyo, que por ser los navíos que llevaba de poca agua lo podría hacer. Y allí se fortificaría, procurando de hacerles el mal que pudiese a los enemigos y ganar la voluntad a los caciques. [Y] a la primavera, con la caballería que le fuese de las Indias,[403] ser[ía] señor de la campaña y de su puerto, porque tenía[n] el fuerte dos leguas por el río adentro, porque no fuesen socorridos ni los indios tratasen con ellos. Y que por esta orden se les haría la guerra con toda buena orden e industria y podrían ser presto echados de la tierra de la Florida, para que no plantasen en ella su mala secta luterana. Y porque tenía Su Majestad aviso que el Turco abajaba poderoso sobre Malta y que las galeras que tenía para resistirle eran pocas, que por esto no las podía dar, aunque le parecía que la razón que el Adelantado daba era muy buena, y lo mesmo le respondieron todos los demás señores dichos con quien lo comunicó.

Otro día siguiente proveyó Su Majestad en La Mejorada, por su Consejo de [Estado y][404] Guerra, diesen al Adelantado quinientos hombres bastecidos y pagados, con cuatro navíos de armada, todo a costa de Su Majestad, para que con los quinientos hombres y diez chalupas y zabras que el Adelantado llevaba a su costa, conforme al asiento que con Su Majestad había tomado sobre la población y conquista de la Florida, se[405] fuese por las islas de Puerto Rico, Española y Cuba y recogiese la caballería e infantería [106v] y navíos[406] de armada y bastimento que estaba ya proveído. Y cuando salieron del consejo y esto quedó acordado no se dijo al Adelantado, porque los señores del Real Consejo de [Estado y] Guerra, visto que no se podían proveer las galeras y galeotas que él pedía, remitiéronlo al Señor Francisco de Eraso, que se había hallado en aquel consejo, que él le respondería lo proveído.

Luego Su Majestad se partió aquel día a dormir al Abrojo, dos leguas de Valladolid, y el Adelantado se fue con él porque Francisco de Eraso le dijo que a la noche le diría lo que el consejo proveía. Y siendo las nueve de la noche se fue el Adelantado con Francisco de Eraso del Abrojo de con Su Majestad a dormir a Laguna y, aunque el Adelantado cenó con Francisco de Eraso aquella noche y posó con él, no le quiso decir lo proveído, diciendo que otro día se lo diría. Estaba deseoso el Adelantado de saber lo proveído, porque tenía esperança en Dios—si le mandaban dar las dos galeras y dos galeotas que pedía—él saldría con su buena y santa empresa adelante, y de otra manera temíalo por las razones que tenía dichas.

Otro día a mediodía, llamándolo Françisco de Eraso al Adelantado que se subiese a comer, el Adelantado le dijo que no le haría buen provecho la comida si no le decía lo que estaba proveído. Francisco de Eraso se lo dijo, y que Su Majestad mandaba se fuese a Valladolid, porque allí le daría las provisiones para levantar la gente y embargar los navíos y recaudo para [que] los oficiales de la [Casa de la] Contrataçión de Sevilla hiciesen con brevedad los mantenimientos y pagasen esta gente y buscasen para ello los dineros a cambio. El Adelantado [107r] respondió a Françisco de Eraso que no estaba contento con aquella provisión porque habría mucha dilaçión en buscar los dineros y los navíos, y para aparejarlos y en darles carena, y en hacer el bastimento y recoger la gente, en espeçial para la Florida, que estaba desacreditada de todas naciones ser de costa brava. Y porque de siete armadas con mucha gente que por orden del emperador de gloriosa memoria y de Su Majestad habían ido a aquellas partes, todas se habían perdido, por lo cual los soldados y marineros son malos de hallar, porque los quinientos que él llevaba eran de Asturias y Vizcaya, sacados y buscados y rogados por deudos y amigos suyos, y le acompañaban gentes prencipales que, después del serviçio de Dios y de Su Majestad, más iban por le acompañar y hacer placer que no por las gananças e intereses que habían de haber, que bien entendían iban a jornada trabajosa y peligrosa y no nada provechosa. Y que Su Majestad no sería nada servido en que se fuese a Valladolid por los despachos, por estar el tiempo tan adelante, que se quería ir por la posta a Sevilla y de camino por la corte, para que los del Real Consejo de las Indias escribiesen a los oficiales de la [Casa de la] Contrataçión que diesen al Adelantado quince mil ducados que conforme al asiento le ofrecieron para ayuda a las grandes costas y gastos que había de hacer para la población y conquista de la Florida y otras cosas que estaba obligado conforme al asiento, que eran todas mercedes de poca substançia.

Mas porque el Adelantado había salido [107v] de una larga prisión de que falsamente había sido acusado del licenciado Venegas,[407] fiscal de la Casa de la Contrataçión de la ciudad de Sevilla, sobre que había excedido en las instrucciones que le habían dado cuando era general en aquella navegación de cosas que, por haberla[s] quebrantado pudiera Su Majestad haber sido servido, y si la[s] hubiera guardado lo fuera al contrario. Y por los prósperos y buenos sucesos que el Adelantado había tenido en serviçio de Su Majestad había[408] muchos malsines contra él, y había veinte meses que estaba preso en las ataraçanas y Torre del Oro de Sevilla, y en esta corte, y no había besado a Su Majestad las manos por todo este tiempo, hasta que después de sentençiado le dio licençia para ello. Y temió [Pedro Menéndez][409] que Su Majestad habría conçebido mal de él por lo que sus ministros de él decían, por haber creído a los malsines que habían dicho mal del [adelantado], y que estaba en su desgracia, no teniendo de él tan buen conçepto [como fuera razón, y][410] deseaba volver a ganar su reputaçión, que con tantos trabajos y peligros [y] a costa de su hacienda había ganado, y con la pérdida y muertes de su hijo, hermanos y deudos y amigo[s]; y los capitanes y gente noble que lo habían seguido y servido a Su Majestad en su compañía verlos pobres y necesitados, sin poderlos remediar, porque él lo estaba también, ninguna cosa que emprendiese le pareçía serle dificultosa, en especial ésta de la Florida, que era tanto del servicio de Dios [108r] Nuestro Señor y de Su Majestad y bien general de estos reinos, a donde—por lo bien que sirviese en esto—tenía entendido que cuando el gualardón de Su Majestad le faltase, el de Dios Nuestro Señor no le había de faltar, ni su ayuda, que era lo que él había menester y el interés particular que en esto pretendía.

Y después, dende allí a tres meses, invió tres mensajeros a partes diferentes, escribiendo a sus amigos y a Francisco de Reinoso, hombre de armas de Su Majestad, para que levantasen la más gente que pudiesen. Y dijo a Françisco de Eraso que de la dilación de su ida a la Florida Su Majestad sería muy deservido, que le pareçía no convenía detenerse por estos navíos, bastimentos y gente, porque no sabía dónde hallaría navíos, y que él tenía un galeón de mil toneladas, la mejor pieça que había en la mar, muy ligera y artillada, puesta a punto de guerra, y que los mercaderes de Sevilla le daban veintiçinco mil ducados de flete porque fuese al Nombre de Dios cargado, y que estaba cargando; que él perdería todo aquel interés y la llevaría y recogería la más gente que pudiese, que se enviase recaudo a los ofiçiales de Sevilla para que la tomasen y basteçiesen para llevar en él la gente que pudiese caber, y que el despacho que Su Majestad le había de dar en Valladolid lo podría mandar dar en Sevilla.

Pareçiole muy bien a Francisco de Eraso y encomendole así lo hiciese, y la brevedad del viaje. Y diose el Adelantado tan buena maña por la vía de Cádiz [108v] y Vizcaya, que día de San Pedro salió de Cádiz con este galeón [*San Pelayo*]⁴¹¹ y otras diez velas, y de Asturias y Vizcaya con çinco, y en ellas dos mil y ciento y cincuenta hombres de mar y guerra—como está dicho—que de todos no pagó Su Majestad más de tre[s]cientos soldados y un navío. Todo lo demás fue a costa del Adelantado, que buscó todo el favor que pudo de deudos y amigos que le ayudaron muy mucho, entendido ser esta empresa tan del servicio de Dios y de Su Majestad.

Y Pedro del Castillo, vecino y regidor de Cádiz, grande amigo del Adelantado, se señaló más que todos en esto, y a ayudarle con su hacienda y con la de sus amigos, y que a él sólo le dejó empeñado en más de veinte mil ducados, entendiendo el Adelantado el gran serviçio que a Su Majestad en esto hacía para irse derecho a la Florida—como se fue—para desbaratar a los enemigos antes que se fortificasen y ganasen la voluntad de los caciques e indios de aquella tierra, como está dicho.⁴¹² [109r]

Capítulo 34

Relación que trata qué tierra es la Florida y las cosas buenas que tiene y su temple

La tierra de la Florida se cuenta desde Pánucu, puerto de la Nueva España,[413] hasta la Tierra Nova, que serán mil y tre[s]cientas leguas de costa. Es tierra firme a lo luengo de la marina. Hay muchas islas y cayos, y muy buenos puertos, porque el Adelantado ha descubierto en término de tre[s] cientas leguas cuatro puertos, que cada uno tiene cuatro braças de agua de plena mar, y algunos más, y de dos braças y media y tres ha descubierto diez, y todos éstos los anduvo y estuvo dentro con su persona y con cuatro o cinco o seis bergantines a descubrirlos, sondarlos y marcarlos, entradas tres veçes, y otros pilotos con bergantines suyos. Mas en todas estas tre[s]cientas leguas de costa son los caçiques y los indios sus amigos, y tiene poblado en siete partes en estos puertos tres fuertes y cuatro pueblos, que son siete poblaciones, que todos los caciques e indios son sus amigos. Sólo donde los françeses luteranos estaban, con cuarenta leguas de costa y hasta diez leguas la tierra adentro, son los caçiques e indios enemigos del Adelantado y de los españoles, a causa que, como había tres años cuando el Adelantado llegó que los françeses luteranos habitaban en aquella tierra y tenían su fuerte, que cuando el Adelantado llegó tenían mucha amistad con las indias, hermanas e hijas y mujeres de los caçiques, y algunos hijos en ellas. Y cuando les ganó el fuerte el[414] Adelantado, acogiéronse al monte algunos de estos françeses y fuéronse a los pueblos para los caçiques, y fueron de ellos bien acogidos y reçebidos. Estuvieron admirados los indios que unos cristianos con otros peleásemos y matasen los que habían ido a los que estaban allá con tanta façilidad. Dijéronles los françeses que éramos españoles que los íbamos a matar, y los que no matásemos de los indios que habían de ser nuestros esclavos, y tomarles las mujeres y los hijos y las casas. Con esto juntáronse los caciques de aquel distrito y conçertáronse que ellos ni sus indios no habían de ser amigos de los españoles. [109v]

Fue de esto avisado el Adelantado. Procuró hacerles mucho bien y haçer de ellos gran confiança para que entendiesen que los françeses habían mentido y que éramos mejores hombres que no ellos y de más verdad. Dioles a entender lo mejor que supo que los françeses eran cristianos de mentira—según ya lo tiene dicho—. Dábales muchos presentes y de lo que tenía. No consentía que se les hiciese ningún mal. De esta manera atrajo a muchos caçiques de ellos a su voluntad, y venían al fuerte con sus mujeres, hijos e hijas. Y después, haciendo ausencia de allí el Adelantado a buscar bastimento, entendido ellos lo poco que tenían los que allí quedaban, fueron muy traidores, y por engaño y ardid mataron en veçes más de çiento y veinte soldados, aunque el[415] primer rompimiento de éstos fue por haber muerto los soldados amotinados los tres indios—como está dicho—para que los demás y sus caçiques matasen los pocos cristianos que allí quedaban.

La más de esta costa de la marina es ruin tier[r]a, porque como hay tantos puertos y ríos, y la mar hinche y vacía mucho y la tierra es llana, sube la marea quinçe y veinte leguas por los ríos adentro. Y estos ríos echan ramos a los lados los unos contra los otros, de manera que sin salir a la mar se navegan en canoas y bateles, haçiendo islas la misma costa, y dondequiera que esta marea llega, o los ríos vienen crecidos, al tiempo que vacía todo aquello queda hecho ciénagas, que los hombres y caballos se sumen sin podellos pasar. Y las islas que quedan a la marina son muy buenas florestas de muy copiosa arboleda, de encinas, robles, pinos, y nogales, morales, y árboles de liquidámbar,[416] muy buenos çedros y sabinas. Hay muy buena agua dulce en todas ellas y cebarías[417] para ganados. Tienen todas muchos venados, conejos y liebres, y al der[r]edor de ellas mucho marisco y ostias, [y] cantidad de pescado. Están algunas pobladas, y todos estos ocho pueblos y fuertes que el Adelantado tiene poblados. Son estas islas aparejadas para mucho vino y trigo y todo género de agricultura, y mucha caña dulçe para açúcares. Criarse han muchos ganados. Son por la mayor parte [110r] islas[418] de seis y ocho leguas de largo, y algunas de más y otras de menos, y para poder andar estas tre[s]cientas leguas en bateles o canoas por de dentro no hay más que cinco pasos por romper, que el mayor de ellos no tiene media legua, los cuales piensa el Adelantado poblar.

Está poblado en altura de veintiséis grados hasta treinta y seis de esta parte de la Canal de Bahama, y tienen los indios amigos hasta treinta y siete, que es la Bahía de Santa María. Y por la parte de Nueva España tiene poblado hasta los treinta grados, donde en seis días de navegaçión pueden ir a la Veracruz y a Pánuco,[419] que son puertos de Nueva España. Y en otros tantos a Honduras y Campeche. Y en tres o cuatro a La Habana. De todos los fuertes y pueblos tiene[420] poblados, desemboca[n]do [en] la Canal de Bahama, hasta los treinta y tres grados, y de estos fuertes se va a la Española y Puerto Rico en doçe y en quinçe días. Y a las islas de las[421] Açores es navegación de veinte días, con buen tiempo, aunque el Adelantado vino en diez y siete días porque el navío que traía era muy ligero.

Toda esta marina, y lo que se sabe de la tierra adentro de lo que el capitán Juan Pardo anduvo por orden del Adelantado, que—como está dicho—fueron ciento y cincuenta leguas, y al pie de la sierra, en tierra del cacique Joara,[422] hiço un fuerte nombrado San Juan, y lo que después acá han descubierto los españoles de aquel fuerte han sido otras cien leguas adelante, la vuelta del puniente, camino de la Nueva España. Y van caminando por treinta y siete o treinta y ocho grados, y están como do[s]cientas leguas de las Çacatecas, minas ricas de la Nueva España.

Toda es tierra de muy buen temple y cielo, y de mucha salud, muy buena para todo género de ganados mayores y menores, y pan y vino, y todo género de labrança, donde hay muchas moreras para seda, y que se criará cantidad de ella. Y por las muchas riberas que tiene se criará mucho cáñamo y lino y breas y alquitranes, porque hay mucho número de pinares para ello. Habrá muchas y buenas maderas de todo género para edificios de casas y navíos, y muchos árboles para las naos, que son cosas que suelen venir de Alemania a España, aunque los de la Florida son mucho mejores. Se trairán a España con mucha facilidad, y a menos costa vuestra,[423] número [110v] de todo[424] género de pesquería [y] cantidad de ballenas. Hanse hallado muchos metales de oro bajo, que es señal de haber gran cantidad, aunque los indios no saben lo que se hay ni estiman oro ni plata, aunque a su poder viene alguno de naos perdidas que vienen de las Indias. Hase hallado en la marina ámbar gris, que es cosa que ellos estiman porque son amigos de buenos olores, y se han hallado esmeraldas y unicornios.

Y con el temor que los caçiques han tomado a el Adelantado, y haber sabido con la facilidad que echó a los françeses de aquella tierra y vi[c]torias que con ellos tuvo, y buen tratamiento que les haçen, ámanle y témenle en gran manera. Y también por las grandes traiciones que los indios y caciques enemigos del Adelantado usaron con su gente, visto que de su parte y de sus capitanes había hecho lo posible por llevarlos por bien, y a ellos les pareció que esto era miedo que les teníamos, y se ensoberbeçían muchos, diciendo ultrajes contra los españoles y que eran gallinas, y que no querían ser sus amigos si no les daban cada luna—que es un mes—tantas camisas y hachas y machetes, espejos y tiseras, y otras cosas por vía de tributo, que no habían de ser sus amigos, y que antes habían de ser sus capitales enemigos, y que aguardaban a los françeses para que los ayudasen a matarnos y se vengasen de nosotros, porque ellos les ayudarían. Y que quisieran que fuésemos muchos más españoles de los que estaban en aquella tierra para los matar a todos. Traían consigo hasta siete u ocho françeses, muy buenos soldados, que los industriaban, que la cabeça de ellos se llamaba el capitán Bayona, y por aviso que habían dado a Françia estos françeses, esperaban ellos y los indios armada françesa para echar [a] los españoles de la tierra.

Pareció al Adelantado que ya no era tiempo de haçer más cumplimientos con ellos. Ordenoles la guerra—como está dicho—de las casas y fuerte, caballos y per[r]os cada cinco leguas. Principió a haçérsela. Dejó la orden a los capitanes para adelante cómo se la habían de haçer. Escribió el Adelantado con un françés dos cartas al capitán Bayona, [111r] que si[425] se quisiese venir para él o a sus capitanes que en aquella tierra tenía, que lo podía haçer seguramente con los compañeros que tuviese, porque no se les haría ningún daño, antes se les daría navío y bastimento en que se fuesen a España, y de allí a Francia. Reçibió las cartas el capitán Bayona, no respondió a ellas, y como vio que los caçiques sus amigos iban perdidos por la orden que se les hacía la guerra, se vino con dos françeses al Fuerte de San Mateo y se entregó al capitán Gonçalo de Villa[r]roel, según lo escribió el dicho capitán Villa[r]roel.

Hanse reçebido cartas de fin de julio de sesenta y siete de aquellas provincias y de los capitanes cómo daban la guerra a los indios en la forma que se les había ordenado, y con ello iban los indios perdidos y dejaban la tierra y sus lugares despoblados. Ofrecieron los caçiques amigos del Adelantado muchos indios para haçer la guerra contra sus enemigos—así indios como françeses—y aunque el Adelantado tenía de ellos harta neçesidad nunca los quiso reçebir por no perder la reputación con los indios, diciéndoles que el Rey de España, su señor, le había mandado que no matase ningún indio ni les hiciese mal, antes los tuviese por hermanos y amigos. Y si estuviesen reñidos unos caciques con otros, los procurase haçer amigos, y que cuando los caçiques y los indios dijesen que querían ser sus amigos y lo[426] tomasen por hermano mayor, y al Rey de España por señor, y después mintiesen y matasen los cristianos, que entonçes se les hiciese la guerra y los tomasen por enemigos y los hiciesen esclavos. Y que él había perdonado algunas veces a Saturiba y a sus caciques sus amigos, y a todos sus indios, y a todos los indios enemigos del Adelantado y de los españoles, y les había perdonado muchas veces las mentiras que habían dicho y cristianos que habían muerto, pensando que serían buenos amigos, mas que, en tiniéndolos por enemigos, él les sabría haçer la guerra, echándolos de su tierra y matándolos a todos, tomándoles sus haciendas de casas, canoas, pesquerías y maiçales, que es toda la que ellos tienen. Y que [con] los caciques [111v] que[427] con él han hecho amistad, que le mintiesen, haría otro tanto, y como presto viesen los caciques que el Adelantado cumplía esto que decía, con tan pocos cristianos y tantos caçiques e indios, temerle ían mucho, y amarle ían por otra parte, por la buena amistad que les hacía, y cobraría reputación. Y con una tierra tan grande, que sin ir a conquistarlos le darían la obediençia en nombre de Su Majestad, y era abrir las puertas para los religiosos que entrasen con la do[c]trina a plantar[428] el Santo Evangelio, que éstas eran las dos cosas de su interés particular, sin atender a otros bienes ni riqueças,[429] ni buscar perlas ni minas. Y desde que partió de España decía y publicaba a todos los capitanes y soldados que por esta orden habían de publicar y procurar poblar y conquistar aquella tierra, y que primero que rompiesen con el caçique y sus indios había de ser cuando les forçasen a no poder haçer otra cosa, tiniendo justificada la causa con Nuestro Señor, que les convenía romper la guerra, y entonçes hacérsela con toda crueldad y de manera que los temiesen y ganasen grande reputación, y se conservase con esto la amistad de los caçiques amigos.

Ha tenido el Adelantado cartas después que partió de aquella provincia, de las unas enviadas por el capitán Pero Menéndez Marqués, su sobrino, que es su lugartiniente en las cosas de la mar en aquella costa y gobernador del estado de Carlos el caçique, las cuales se han de mostrar y escrebir sobre ello la verdad. Y lo mesmo las que escribe Estébano de las Alas, su lugartiniente en aquella tierra, y los más capitanes, por que no se escriba en la corónica cosa que no se averigüe y pruebe. Para satisfación del Real Consejo, hanse de escrebir las merçedes que Su Majestad hiço al Adelantado y las demás personas que fueron [a] esta jornada y conquista de la Florida.

Y si los françeses señorearan la Florida serán señores con gran facilidad de todas las Indias, Islas y Tierra Firme del Mar Oçéano, sin que hiciesen guerra ni gruesas armadas, [112r] y sin[430] que tuviesen ejércitos, a causa que su ley viciosa es muy cercana a la de los indios, que no tiene ningún género de aspereça en su vivir sino irse tras los deleites mundanos como bestias, no conociendo a Dios ni temiéndole, sin saber cuando mueren a dónde irán a parar. Y a esta causa los françeses luteranos tiraniçaron a su mala se[c]ta con gran facilidad todas aquellas provincias, por estar los naturales de ellas hechos salvajes desalumbrados, que imprimían en sus coraçones todo aquello que les enseñaren.

Demás de esto, en todos los puertos de las Indias, Islas y Tierra Firme del Mar Oçéano que hay pobladas en todas aquellas partes son muy muchos los negros y negras y mestiços y mulatos, por la mayor parte toda gente de mala inclinación, demasiado de alterados y soberbios en sus condiçiones, gente indómita. Y las negras multiplican mucho en aquella tierra, y esta casta y generaçión creçe con grande acreçentamiento por la multiplicaçión que de ellos hay, por ser tierra caliente como en Guinea, que de los que naçen mueren pocos y de los que paren las mujeres españolas son pocos los que viven. Y así se multiplican poco los españoles en toda aquella tierra, antes se mueren muchas gentes y otros viven enfermos, por ser aquel temple y co[n]stelación diferente de la de España, muy apropiada a la de Guinea, y por eso se hallan allí bien los negros y negras y viven mucho y muy sanos, y mueren pocos y multiplican mucho.

Y hay en todas aquellas partes treinta y cuarenta negros y negras para cada español, y ésos en Francia no pueden ser esclavos porque todos viven en su libertad, y como los françeses vían esto, y que tenían poca fe con Dios (antes aborrecían su ley divina por pareçerles que era áspera), y que tenían poco amor al Rey de España porque eran esclavos de sus vasallos, y que su nueva religión de luteranos era vivir más a sus gustos y a sus vicios, por esto tenían acordado ir con armada desde la Florida dentro de un mes de como el Adelantado llegó a todas estas partes de las Indias a dar libertad a los negros, los cuales se alçaran[431] con la tierra, matando a sus amos. Y los françeses poner entonçes su[s] fortaleças[432] [112v] y gobiernos, y dejar a los negros y mulatos y mestiços vivir en sus libertades de luteranos y de no ser esclavos, y tener con ellos sus granjerías, tratos, conciertos y comercios. Y esto se vió y leyó por muchas personas, que abriendo un cofreçico de papeles que Juan Ribao, general de los françeses, tenía en su aposento cuando se le ganó el fuerte que se llamaba de Francia, y el Adelantado le puso por nombre San Mateo porque le ganó el propio día, y se halló dentro de este cofre—entre otros papeles—una instrución del Almirante de Francia, firmada de su nombre, en que mandaba a este general que—luego que llegase a la Florida y se fortificase—no se descuidase en haçer esta diligençia. Y quemándose el fuerte dentro de un mes de como se ganó, con todo lo que dentro estaba, se quemó el cofre con todos los papeles donde estaba esta instru[c]ción guardada para juntalla con los demás papeles.

Y en este mismo tiempo se principiaba a alterar la Nueva España contra Su Majestad, y si los luteranos salieran con este disignio que habían intentado y poblaran la Florida, tiénese por cierto que de un voleo todo[s] lo[s] de la Nueva España se perdieran y se alçaran todos los de las Indias contra Su Majestad. Y la Majestad Divina del çielo, entendiendo las muchas almas que en esto se perdían, por su bondad lo quiso milagrosamente remediar, como está dicho.

Fin de la relaçión.[433]

E yo, Diego de Ribera, escribano del rey nuestro señor, vecino de Madrid, por curiosidad, topando con esta le[c]tura y viendo por ella la jornada que el Adelantado Pero Menéndez hiço a la Florida y las cosas que en ella pasó, y cómo por su muerte quedó desamparada y todo perdido, en el entretanto que rastreo el fin que tuvieron estas cosas y en lo que paró, y si los françeses por muerte del Adelantado se apoderaron de todos los fuertes que en ella hiço, para que se sepa[n] las mercedes que Su Majestad hiço al Adelantado puse aquí estas çédulas, para que si alguno topare con esta le[c]tura, y la leyere y gustare de ella, vea todo lo que más pude hallar, dando a Nuestro Señor las gracias de todo, a quien ofre[z]co mi trabajo.

Y lo firmé y acabé de escrebir a 16 de março, año de 1618.

Diego de Ribera, escribano.

Notes

INTRODUCTION

1. The specifics of this expedition, as given by historian Antonio de Herrera a century later, have been the cause of much disagreement, and for a long time it was believed that Florida had been sighted on Easter Sunday of the year 1512. Rather, the expedition arrived at the peninsula a year later, a week after Ponce had seen the coast of an island now believed to be either Abaco or Eleuthera, in the Bahamas. Davis, "Ponce de León's First Voyage," 39; Gannon, *New History of Florida*, 18. Ponce did reach this island on Easter Day, 27 March 1513, and observed that it had "many cool woodlands," but he did not reach the mainland of North America until 2 April 1513. Thus Florida was "discovered"—as Herrera says—during the time (but not on the day) of Easter, and the flowers that Ponce supposedly saw on the coast were in fact the woodlands of one of the Bahamas islands. For a detailed explanation of this misconception, see Davis, who emphasizes that "practically all histories and encyclopedias state that Florida was discovered on Easter Sunday" (39). The mistake regarding the year is due to Antonio de Herrera's *Historia general de los hechos de los castellanos en las Islas y Tierra Firme del Mar Océano* (1601-15), the only authoritative account of Ponce's expedition. Herrera (or a later hand) wrote "1512" at the beginning of the narrative, but later on, historians began to question the year, based on the date of Easter Sunday. According to Cappelli, *Cronologia*, 76, in 1512 this day fell on 11 April, so it could not have been the year in which Ponce reached Florida. In 1513 Easter fell on 27 March, which is the correct date. Some historians still give an incorrect date for the discovery of Florida—to cite but a few examples, Ruidíaz, *La Florida*, 1: lix; Miguel Vigil, *Noticias biográfico-genealógicas*, 10; Gómez Tabanera, *Pedro Menéndez de Avilés*, xvii.

2. Evidence suggests that Ponce's was not the first trip to Florida, for Ponce himself found a Spaniard on shore. A land mass that looks like Florida appears on the maps of Alberto Cantino (1502) and Pietro Martire d'Anghiera (1511). For an excellent summary of these expeditions, see Gannon, *New History of Florida*, 16–17, or Pickett and Pickett, *European Struggle*, 17–45.

3. Ruidíaz, *La Florida*, 1: cxvii, my translation. All translations of Ruidíaz, unless otherwise noted, are my own.

4. Gannon, prologue to Manucy, *Menéndez*, n.p.

5. The date of Menéndez's birth is given in Barrientos, although Mellén Blanco in

Pedro Menéndez de Avilés, 2, has argued that it should be questioned. For Pedro Menéndez's biography I have relied on the historical accounts by Gonzalo Solís de Merás (as they appear in the Ferrera and Revillagigedo copies, as the latter contains genealogical data not present in the former), the *Vida y hechos* by Bartolomé de Barrientos, and the *Ensayo cronológico* by Andrés González de Barcia. I have also followed Lowery, *Spanish Settlements*; Ruidíaz, *La Florida*; Lyon, *The Enterprise of Florida*, 10–18.

6. Ferrera, f. 102v, my translation. All translations of Ferrera are my own.

7. Ferrera, f. 102r.

8. Revillagigedo, f. 1r (*apud* Ruidíaz, *La Florida*, 1: 1). All quotations of the Revillagigedo manuscript are taken exclusively from Ruidíaz's edition, checked for accuracy against the microfilm of the manuscript at the St. Augustine Foundation.

9. Mercado, *Ménendez*, 237, my translation.

10. Ruidíaz, *La Florida*, 1: cxviii; Lyon, *The Enterprise of Florida*, 10.

11. Ruidíaz, *La Florida*, 1: cxvii–cxviii.

12. *Consulta de gracia* located in the Archivo Histórico Nacional, legajo 4407, no. 796. See Mellén Blanco, *Pedro Menéndez de Avilés*, 295–96.

13. Ruidíaz, *La Florida*, 1: ccxxvi.

14. For the report (Archivo de Indias, est. I, caja 2, legajos 1–18), see Ruidíaz, *La Florida*, 2: 590–624. See also Mellén Blanco, *Pedro Menéndez de Avilés*, 3, 50, my translation.

15. Revillagigedo, f. 1v (*apud* Ruidíaz, *La Florida*, 1: 2).

16. Ruidíaz, *La Florida*, 1: 2; Gómez Tabanera, *Pedro Menéndez de Avilés*, 3; Mercado, *Menéndez*, 35.

17. The fact that the Adelantado spent only twenty-two days at home has also been revealed by the discovery of the Ferrera manuscript, for the passage is missing in Revillagigedo.

18. Lyon, *The Enterprise of Florida*, 11; Ferrera, ff. 1r, 105v. A galliot was a small galley furnished with oars and sails. Lyon, *The Enterprise of Florida*, 231.

19. Lyon, *The Enterprise of Florida*, 11.

20. Ruidíaz, *La Florida*, 1: cv.

21. Lyon, *The Enterprise of Florida*, 12.

22. Lyon, *The Enterprise of Florida*, 14.

23. Gómez Tabanera, *Pedro Menéndez de Avilés*, xxxi, my translation.

24. Lyon, *The Enterprise of Florida*, 15.

25. See chapter VI in Ruidíaz, *La Florida*, 1: 41–49.

26. Ferrera, f. 107v.

27. Lyon, *The Enterprise of Florida*, 14.

28. Williams, *From Columbus to Castro*, 47–48.

29. The Adelantado wrote several letters to the Crown explaining the situation; see Ruidíaz, *La Florida*, 2: 34–59, letters XI, XII, XIII, XIV, XVI. A good summary of this incident can be found in Pérez Mallaína, *Spain's Men of the Sea*, 110–12.

30. Lyon, *The Enterprise of Florida*, 16; Gómez Tabanera, *Pedro Menéndez de Avilés*, xxxii.

31. Lowery, *Spanish Settlements*, 134–35.

32. Ferrera, f. 52r.

33. Lowery, *Spanish Settlements*, 35.

34. Manrique de Rojas found Rouffi living among the Indians, rescued him, and took him back to Cuba, where he was later given to Pedro Menéndez as an intepreter. Rouffi's ordeal, and his assistance in securing alliances between the Spaniards and the Indians of Florida, is retold in the manuscript edited here. See Pickett and Pickett, *European Struggle*, 69.

35. The *asiento* was drafted five days earlier, on 15 March 1565.

36. Nicolas Le Challeux, one of the very few men who managed to survive the Spanish attack on Fort Caroline and return to France, wrote an account of these events titled *Discours de l'histoire de la Floride, contenant la cruauté des Espagnols* (1566), where, apart from discussing at length the massacres of French Huguenots perpetrated by Menéndez and his men, he gave a vivid portrait of the soldiers' dissatisfaction with the land: "Who wants to go to Florida? / Let him go where I have been, / returning gaunt and empty, / collapsing from weakness, / the only benefit I have brought back / is one good white stick in my hand." Translation in Bennett, *Laudonnière and Fort Caroline*, 164.

37. Mercado, *Menéndez*, 13.

38. The coffin in Avilés is a reproduction, for the original is housed at the Nombre de Dios Mission Museum in St. Augustine, Florida. I am thankful to Francisco J. Borge of the University of Oviedo for sharing a picture of the coffin in Avilés, which I have used to transcribe and translate the inscription.

39. For a good summary of the Spanish and French sources from the sixteenth to the twentieth century, see Connor, *Pedro Menéndez de Avilés*, xxiii–xxxi.

40. Ferrera, f. 73r.

41. Archivo General de Indias (Patronato 19 R17). The complete title is *Memoria del buen suçeso y buen viaje que Dios Nuestro Señor fue servido de dar a la armada que salió de la ciudad de Cáliz para la provinçia y costa de la Florida, de la qual fue por general el Ilustrísimo Señor Pero Menéndez de Avilés, Comendador de la Orden de Santiago. Salió esta dicha armada de la Bahía de Cáliz Jueves por la mañana veinte y ocho días del mes de julio [sic] de 1565 años y entró en la tierra e costa de las provinçias de la Florida a veinte y ocho días del mes de agosto del dicho año.*

42. The complete title is *Vida y hechos de Pedro Menéndez de Avilés, caballero de la Orden de Santiago, Adelantado de la Florida, donde largamente se tratan las conquistas y poblaciones de la provincia de la Florida y cómo fueron liberadas de los luteranos que de ellas se habían apoderado.*

43. According to Barrientos, "Captain San Vicente stabbed [Ribault] in the stomach, and Gonzalo de Solís thrust a pike into his chest, and they cut his head off." Mercado, *Menéndez*, 299, my translation.

44. Mercado, *Menéndez*, 236, my translation; Martínez, *Vida y hechos*, 17.

45. Ferrera, ff. 103v–104r.

46. See Lowery, *Spanish Settlements*, viii–x. For the relationship between the Solís de Merás and Barrientos chronicles, see Connor, *Pedro Menéndez de Avilés*, 13; Pérez Bustamante, "Fr. Bartolomé de Barrientos," 79–80.

47. Illescas, *Segunda parte de la historia pontifical y católica*, 702, my translation.

48. Barcia, *Ensayo cronológico*, 15, writes, "I have not been able to see the enterprise of Pedro Menéndez, with the particulars thereof, and the description and qualities of

Florida, written by Master Barrientos, Chair and Professor of Latin in Salamanca, which the distinguished Gonzalo de Illescas once held" (my translation).

49. For details about the sale of the Barrientos manuscript, see Gagliardi, "La biblioteca de Bartolomé Barrientos," or Pérez Bustamante, "Fr. Bartolomé de Barrientos," 78.

50. Kerrigan, *Pedro Menéndez de Avilés*, xxi.

51. Martínez, *Vida y hechos*, 17, 18, my translation.

52. García, *Dos antiguas relaciones*, xviii, my translation.

53. Aguilar, "La bibliofilia mexicana." Ironically, the library of Genaro García suffered the same fate, for it was sold to the University of Texas after the Secretaría de Educación Pública in México declined to buy it.

54. I am aware of the disparity between the dates given by Ureña in the Martínez edition of Barrientos and by Kerrigan in his translation of Barrientos. Ureña claims that the manuscript is from the seventeenth century and Kerrigan speaks of a sixteenth-century copy, but this could easily be a mistake on the part of one of these authors. Since the text of the first known manuscript, that edited by García in 1902 (and thence reproduced by Mercado in 2006), and the text of the "seventeenth-century copy" edited by Martínez in 1993 are exactly the same, there is no need to postulate the existence of more than one manuscript for the Barrientos chronicle. Elviro Martínez's access to the manuscript owned by the historian Javier López de Lerena might be explained by their close collaboration on volume 32 of the Monumenta Historica Asturiensia—Barrientos is no. 31—where Lerena wrote a prologue to Martínez's edition of the letters by Lorenzo de Cancio on the government of Coahuila.

55. A facsimile can be found online in the database for the Portal de Archivos Españoles, pares.mcu.es, through a simple search on "lopez de mendoza grajales."

56. Gallardo, *Ensayo de una biblioteca*, 1: 419.

57. For example, Gómez Tabanera in *Pedro Menéndez de Avilés*, xxxvii, claims that Gonzalo Solís de Merás was from Tineo, but the *Biblioteca asturiana* only mentions that his uncle was from that town.

58. See the transcription in Ruidíaz, *La Florida*, 2: 529.

59. See "Acta de la traslación del cadáver de Pedro Menéndez de Avilés, Adelantado de la Florida, desde la villa de Llanes a la de Avilés, el año 1591" in Ruidíaz, *La Florida*, 2: 530–31. Perhaps the fact that Ruidíaz presented these two documents next to each other has contributed to the confusion. For a detailed analysis of the different theories regarding Solís de Merás's identity, see Ruidíaz, *La Florida*, 1: ccxxxvii–ccxxxix, which concludes that the reader should decide if these two men are the same person or not.

60. In the original "y lo mesmo dirá particularmente a Vuestra Majestad Gonçalo de Solís, que sirue a Vuestra Majestad, y por querer seruirme y se a hallado syempre conmigo en todas las jornadas que hize, sy no fue en ésta de Santa Helena, el qual, por ser mi deudo, entendido la jornada que yo en serujcio de Vuestra Majestad hazía, dexó el estudio de Salamanca, donde estaua acauando de pasar, y me fue a buscar a Cádiz, que contra mi voluntad se envarcó conmigo, que por ser casado no le quisiera traer." As far as I know, Eugene Lyon is the only one who knows of the existence of this letter, which he mentions in connection to Solís de Merás in *The Enterprise of Florida*, 96. The original was in the Archivo General de Indias under the heading Santo Domingo 168, but after my inquiries it was discovered that it was incorrectly catalogued, so it is now

in Santo Domingo 224, R1 N4. I have consulted a digital reproduction of the original at the Archivo General de Indias and a digital reproduction of its copy in the Stetson Collection, George A. Smathers Library, University of Florida. I am most grateful to Pilar Lázaro de la Escosura and James G. Cusick for their invaluable help.

61. The Revillagigedo copy has 113 folios, with the chronicle by Solís de Méras in ff. 1–109. Ferrera has 117, with the chronicle by Solís de Merás in ff. 1r–108v).

62. To my knowledge, the last two times that access was granted to the archive were in 1890–92, when Ruidíaz transcribed the manuscript, and in 1964, when Flagler College microfilmed part of the Revillagigedo collection.

63. Pérez Bustamante, "Fr. Bartolomé de Barrientos," 75, my translation.

64. Introduction to Connor, *Pedro Menéndez de Avilés*, xxi.

65. To mention just a few examples, f. 7r reads "9" and "104"; f. 13 reads "15" and "93"; f. 16r reads "18," "87," and "V." Since most folios are not numbered, and the rest as erratically as these, all numbers given here correspond to the order in which the folios appear in the microfilm at the St. Augustine Foundation.

66. Thanks to the discovery of the Ferrera manuscript, we now know that Revillagigedo is missing at least twelve folios: two folios corresponding to Ferrera ff. 41r (part), 41v, 42r, 42v, and 43r (part); two extending from the final lines of Ferrera f. 47v through half of f. 49r; two comprising Ferrera ff. 51v (last two lines), 52r, 52v, 53r, and 53v (four words); two comprising Ferrera ff. 56v (except first four lines), 57r, 57v, and 58r (except last four lines); one comprising half of Ferrera f. 67v, f. 68r, and a few lines of f. 68v; one extending from the last lines of Ferrera f. 71v to the last lines of f. 72v; and two running from Ferrera f. 83r (except the first few lines) to the first few lines of f. 85r. Ruidíaz's emendations in *La Florida* are at 1: 164–65 (only a paragraph supplied), 180–84, 194–95, 203–8 (including a chapter division), 234 (only eight lines supplied), 244 (only two lines supplied), and 272 (only a paragraph supplied), but in light of the discovery of this second textual witness, Ruidíaz's emendations can now be safely discarded as never having been part of the original chronicle.

67. A comparison of his edition with the microfilm shows that the order in which he copied the folios was, for example, 1r, 2r, 2v, 1v, a passage from Barcia, 3r, . . . Another problematic instance is the sequence of folios 55r, 56v (omitting two), coupled with the sequence 68v, 69r, 55v, 56r, 69v, . . .

68. Ruidíaz, *La Florida*, 1: 52–53, 55.

69. Ruidíaz, *La Florida*, 1: Advertencia preliminar.

70. Hudson, *The Juan Pardo Expeditions*, 305.

71. Gómez Tabanera, *Pedro Menéndez de Avilés*, xxxix, xxxixn13, my translation.

72. Revillagigedo, f. 31r (*apud* Ruidíaz, *La Florida*, 1: 95); Ferrera, f. 13v.

73. Ruidíaz, *La Florida*, 1: ccxxxv.

74. Gómez Tabanera, who never consulted the original manuscript, has stated that the chronicle "is more a diary than a chronicle, and it has been very carefully written and reviewed, perhaps hoping to leave it for posterity" (*Pedro Menéndez de Avilés*, xxxvii, my translation). Apart from the fact that Solís de Merás's lengthy narrative does not resemble a diary at all, a quick look at the facsimile of the Revillagigedo manuscript shows that the truth is quite the opposite of Gómez Tabanera's assertions, for the manuscript has not been carefully written, and the revisions are chaotic at best.

75. In the original, "El proceso adjunto es relativo a las jornadas y sucesos del Adelantado D. Pedro Menéndez de Avilés, de la conquista de la Florida, cómo fueron ganados los fuertes, la armada francesa y degollado Juan Ribao, general del rey de Francia con toda su gente, allanado y sugetado los indios y caciques de aquellas provincias, plantado en ellas la fe católica. Escrito por el Dr. Solís de Merás, cuñado de dicho Adelantado." Revillagigedo cover (*apud* Ruidíaz, *La Florida*, 2: 669).

76. Óscar Perea Rodríguez informs me that the pseudonym Gabriel de Cárdenas z Cano is an anagram of his real name, Andrés González de Barcia. However, one of the Cs has to be interpreted as a ç and used in the anagram as a z (which stands for the tironian note &) in order to use all the letters. The name, however, should be read as "Cárdenas y Cano," although some authors prefer to spell it the way it was printed. For a recent example, Gannon speaks of "Gabriel de Cardensa [*sic*] z Cano" (*New History of Florida*, xiv).

77. Barcia, *Ensayo cronológico*, 8: 45, my translation. The *memorial* is also referred to on pages 35 and 284.

78. Gallardo, *Ensayo de una biblioteca*, 1: 419.

79. Ruidíaz edits the petition mentioned above and titles it "Petition by Dr. Solís de Merás, author of the Memorial, requesting a copy of Pedro Menéndez's last will and testament" (*La Florida*, 2: 529). Once more, the title given to the chronicle is Ruidíaz's and not Solís's.

80. For the Spanish original, see the edition in part 3 of this volume. Words in *italic* represent my own description of the contents and do not appear in the manuscript. All folios are numbered on the front (recto), and all of them are paper. The folios measure 27.5 cm × 21.5 cm. The first three folios have not been numbered; numeration begins on the fourth folio, which has been numbered 1. In order to be consistent with the manuscript, I have kept this numeration in my edition, labeling the first three unnumbered folios 1*, 2*, and 3*, and beginning again with 1 on the fourth folio. Some of the folios have been numbered twice, but there is no alteration to the previous numeration (see, for example, ff. 6–8, 18, 21–23, 25, 30, 34–40, 42, 46–49, 51, 53, 57, 62, 67, 76, 81–83, 86–89, 97–102, 105, and 106).

81. Blasco Martínez, *Una aproximación a la institución notarial*, 24.

82. Martínez Navas, *Gobierno y administración*, 338.

83. Crespo-Francés, *Don Pedro Menéndez de Avilés*, 228; Álvarez de la Rivera, *Biblioteca histórico-genealógica asturiana*, 1: 57.

84. Hudson, *The Juan Pardo Expeditions*, 250. In this English translation he is called "Gonçalo del Ribero" (295).

85. Pezuela, *Ensayo histórico*, 118.

86. Mellén Blanco, *Pedro Menéndez de Avilés*, 301.

87. Letter from Philip II to Diego de la Rivera, 10 August 1581, in Álvarez de la Rivera, *Biblioteca*, I: 57. The so-called Tower of Báscones (or Palacio de Ferrera, but not to be confused with the palace in Avilés) is in the Asturian municipality of Grado. Its oldest structure is a defensive tower dating from the thirteenth or fourteenth century. The Álvarez Ribera family began the construction of the palace that is attached to the tower.

88. Ferrera, f. 108v.

89. The original folios are 1*, 2*, 1, 109–117.

90. See ff. 109v, 110r, 110v, 112v.

91. Ferrera, f. 111v.

92. Ferrera, f. 116v.

93. Revillagigedo, f. 39r (*apud* Ruidíaz, *La Florida*, 1: 116); Ferrera, f. 22v.

94. Words that have been omitted in both manuscripts and later inserted in Ferrera appear in italics: "y assi acordo de partirse de aquel puerto de ays a *seis* de nouiembre" (f. 29v); "e hirieron a *Pedro* de Ayala" (f. 44v); "alli me casé *fuera de la ley de graçia*" (f. 50v)—although the correction misses the point altogether; "y por capitan dellos a *el capitan* die[go de] Godoy" (f. 85r); "lleuo este socorro a la hauana a *los primeros* de Enero" (f. 85r); "dio horden el maestro de campo quando se fue a la florida *que fuese luego con su jente y que* llegando a sanct agustin" (f. 86r); "y descubriria aquella costa *hasta la laguna maymi*" (f. 86v); "que fue a *la Nueva Espa*[ña]" (f. 88r); "y por capitan dellos *a pedro pacheco buen soldado* y dexoles" (f. 96r); "y a Juan de Valdes y a *Pedro* de Ayala alferez del capitan Medrano e a *Diego* de salzedo" (f. 100r). For the three instances where no correction has been given, see ff. 85v and 100r: "a un puerto que esta en el sur de la Hauana que se llama [. . .] y por tierra llego a la Hauana que llego a tantos de [. . .]" (f. 85v); "y a Juan de aginiga y a alonso de Cabra y al licençiado [. . .] que era clerigo" (f. 100r).

95. Mellén Blanco, *Pedro Menéndez de Avilés*, 1, my translation.

96. See, among others, "se[r]" (f. 4v), "lo[s]" (ff. 4r, 5v, 6v, 26r, 32r, 71r), "su[r]" (ff. 29v, 3v, 6v, 7r, 27v), "francese[s]" (f. 13v), "po[r]" (f. 13v), "su[s]" (ff. 5v, 30v, 112r, 87r), "trinche[r]a" (ff. 7r, 7v), "ello[s]" (ff. 8r, 73v), "le[s]" (ff. 10v, 30v, 62r), "hace[d]" (f. 14r), "come[r]" (f. 24v), "rodilla[s]" (f. 29v), "esforçado[s]" (f. 38r), "la[s]" (ff. 42v, 70r), "alguno[s]" (f. 73v), "municione[s]" (f. 62r), "todo[s]" (f. 112v), "tabla[s]" (f. 72v), "aquello[s]" (f. 54v).

97. Indeed, the nature of these mistakes points to an oral rendering of the contents of the manuscript, for a scribe would not have omitted the final consonants of the words unless somebody pronounced them in that way.

98. Chapter VI in Barrientos includes a description of the land of Florida that co-incides with this one in a couple of paragraphs; see Mercado, *Menéndez*, 253–56. The "Description" edited here was partially edited in *La Florida*, 1: v–viii, by Ruidíaz, who mentioned that the original manuscript is in the archive of the conde de Revillagigedo.

99. All the letters begin with Philip II's list of titles and end with Diego de Ribera's sworn statement that they are faithful copies of the originals. In the main text of each letter, Ribera has taken different paragraphs from the *asiento* between Menéndez and King Philip, as well as other royal edicts, which can be consulted in Ruidíaz. See letter V, appendix IV; royal edict II, appendix V; and various paragraphs from the *asiento*, appendix VI, in Ruidíaz, *La Florida*, 2: 354–55, 383–85, 415–27. For additional translated primary documents, see Lyon, *Pedro Menéndez de Avilés*.

100. For the readings in Revillagigedo, see Ruidíaz, *La Florida*, 1: 52.

101. Gagliardi, "La biblioteca de Bartolomé Barrientos," n26, although the transcription errors should be attributed to Ruidíaz and not Mercado, who simply copied the earlier edition.

102. Connor, *Pedro Menéndez de Avilés*, 141n12.

103. See Connor, *Pedro Menéndez de Avilés*, 99, 101, 141, 142, 157, 164, 165, 166, 187,

219, 220, 239, 244, among others. Lines are missing on pages 192, 211, 212, and especially 242, where a whole paragraph has disappeared.

PART 1: *THE CONQUEST OF FLORIDA BY THE ADELANTADO PEDRO MELÉNDEZ DE VALDÉS*

1. In the original, the Adelantado is referred to variously as Pedro/Pero, Menéndez/Meléndez, and de Valdés/de Avilés. In the translation I have amended all variants to "Pedro Menéndez," as he is most commonly known, but since the Adelantado belonged to the house of Valdés I have retained this form when it occurs. The title of Adelantado—which I do not translate—referred to "a Spanish or Spanish colonial official, appointed to represent the king's interests in frontier areas in return for grants of authority and certain revenues and exemptions." Lyon, *The Enterprise of Florida*, 229.

2. The Order of St. James (Santiago), founded in the thirteenth century, was one of the four military-religious orders in medieval Spain together with those of Montesa, Calatrava, and Alcántara.

3. There are two captains with the same name on this list. See note 8 to the Spanish edition.

4. This captain is referred to variously as Esteban/Estébano and de las Alas/de las Salas. In the translation I have amended all variants to "Esteban de las Alas," as he is most commonly known.

5. In the original, Utina is referred to as Otina (and Ahotina, Aoctina, Hotina, and Ontina, once each), Mayaca as Mocoya (twice, Macoya), Saturiwa as Saturiba, Calibay as Calabay (once, Galabay), Emola as Emoloa. I have used Utina, Mayaca, Saturiwa, Calibay, and Emola as the preferred spellings in English.

6. An obsolete unit of measurement, the league had a variable value depending on the context (land or sea) and the country. On land, it originally referred to the distance a person could walk in one hour. At sea, it was the distance that a person standing on the deck of a ship could see.

The lagoon called Maimi/Maymi/Mayaimi is now Lake Okeechobee, but Menéndez was wrong about the Florida river system. According to Milanich, "what Menéndez planned was never realized; the river transportation system he envisioned did not exist. Although native dugout canoes might have been able to travel widely within and across Florida, Spanish boats could never do so. Even today a water route across Florida from the Gulf to the Atlantic remains only an unfulfilled dream" (*The Timucua*, 89–90). Still, Menéndez's belief in this internal river system was so strong that he carefully positioned each of his outposts within reach of a river supposedly connected to Lake Okeechobee (see detailed map in Milanich, *The Timucua*, 90).

7. The Bahama Channel, or New Bahama Channel, refers to the Straits of Florida, as opposed to the Old Bahama Channel, off the northeast coast of Cuba.

8. The Fleet of the Indies—Carrera de Indias, or Flota de Indias—was a convoy system adopted by the Spanish Empire to control the flow of goods between Spain, America, and the Philippines, as well as to protect the Spanish galleons from corsair attacks. The conquest and settlement of Florida, as we are told later on, was mainly motivated by the fact that foreign control of the Bahama Channel would pose a serious risk to the treasure fleet.

A general (or admiral general) of the fleet holds the highest rank in the Spanish Navy, and answers only to the king. The admiral of the fleet is the second in command, and his title is equivalent to that of general in the army.

9. Jean Ribault (1520–1565) was the leader of the 1562 French expedition to Florida which landed near the May River (St. Johns River) in present-day Jacksonville. He erected a stone column claiming the territory for France and then explored the coast northwards. When he arrived at Port Royal Sound, in present-day South Carolina, he built a fort on Parris Island named Charlesfort in honor of King Charles IX. After his departure for France, the soldiers killed the commanding officer, Albert de la Pierria, and all but one abandoned the fort and went back to France. A Spanish expedition led by Hernando Manrique de Rojas in late 1562 destroyed whatever was left of the fort and rescued the French soldier, Guillaume Rouffi, who was later given to the Adelantado as an interpreter.

10. The "affluent river" refers to the May River (St. Johns River), where René Goulaine de Laudonnière founded Fort Caroline on 22 June 1564.

11. Santa María la Real de Nieva is located in the province of Segovia, to the northwest of Madrid.

12. After a fire destroyed most of Valladolid in 1561, King Philip II moved the court to Madrid, transforming that city into the capital of Spain. The court was relocated again to Valladolid in 1601, but it returned to Madrid five years later.

13. The Real Consejo de Indias was founded in 1511 as part of the Council of Castile, and it became an independent entity in 1524. It was the main administrative organ of the Spanish Empire for America and the Philippines.

14. Álvaro de Bazán y Guzmán (1526–1588) is considered one of the best admirals ever to sail the sea. During the reign of Philip II he participated in many decisive battles, including Lepanto (1571) and the campaign to subdue Portugal (1581). The king conferred upon him the title of marqués de Santa Cruz in recognition of his merits.

15. A *zabra* was a sailing vessel resembling a small frigate. A *patache* was a small war vessel, used by fleets as an aviso and coast patrol. It carried men, stores, or orders from one ship to another, guarded the entrance of harbors, was a police boat or a customhouse tender. Connor, *Pedro Menéndez de Avilés*, 40n3.

16. The siege of Malta by Sultan Suleiman the Magnificent took place in May–September of 1565. Although the Turks were defeated, their naval power in the Mediterranean was not diminished at all.

17. The Monastery of Santa María de la Mejorada is located in the province of Valladolid, near Olmedo.

18. Cuba was the second island on which Christopher Columbus landed in 1492. Hispaniola (present-day Dominican Republic and Haiti) was also sighted by Columbus in 1492, while Puerto Rico was claimed for Spain on 19 November 1493, during his second voyage.

19. Francisco de Eraso (d. 1570) was one of the most important royal secretaries under Charles V. Philip II appointed him secretary of the Council of the Inquisition and the Council of the Indies.

20. "As a result of the great increase of trade with the West Indies, the Crown in 1503 determined to create a *Casa de Contratación*, a House of Trade, for its regulation and

encouragement. . . . This House of Trade consisted of three royal officials, a treasurer, a comptroller and a business manager, who resided in Seville and met daily to transact business. A chief pilot was added a few years later, the first to hold this office being Amerigo Vespucci. . . . It was responsible for the despatch of ships to the New World, and supervised, licensed and registered all emigrants to these parts. It was the watchdog over the laws relative to navigation, commerce and emigration. It was the government's adviser on economic conditions and policy in the colonies, and collected the duties on commodities imported from the New World." Williams, *From Columbus to Castro*, 48.

21. "The Spanish commercial monopoly was based in the first place on the designation of a single port through which all trade with the Caribbean, inward and outward, had to pass. In 1493 Cádiz, as Columbus had recommended, was designated the sole port of entry and departure for ships trading with the West Indies. . . . The restriction of the trade to a single Spanish port was reaffirmed. But Cádiz, despite its superior facilities, lost its monopoly to Seville, the wealthiest and most populous city of Castile." Williams, *From Columbus to Castro*, 47–48.

22. Pedro Menéndez sailed from Cádiz on his flagship, a one-thousand-ton galleon called *San Pelayo*, along with two shallops, four caravels, a galliot, a brigantine, and other small vessels. He also gave orders for sixteen more ships to sail from Avilés, Gijón, and Santander, totaling 2,646 men. Mercado, *Cartas*, 125n106.

23. The original reads "a storm called *furaca*," where *furaca* should be read as *furacán* > *huracán* (hurricane), but according to Mercado, "historians of Spanish Florida think that, because this storm lasted several days, it was not a hurricane but a storm from the northeast." Mercado, *Cartas*, 140n162, my translation. The Adelantado wrote to the Crown on 13 August 1565 explaining his unexpected arrival in Puerto Rico. Ruidíaz, *La Florida*, 2: 70–74; Mercado, *Cartas*, 126–29. He refers again to this storm in a letter written on 15 October 1565 (*Archivo de Indias*, est. 54, caja 5, legajo 6). Ruidíaz, *La Florida*, 2: 84–105; Mercado, *Cartas*, 139–57.

24. Diego Velázquez de Cuéllar founded the city of Havana on the southern coast of Cuba in 1515, but the settlement failed. In 1519 the town was moved, after several failed attempts, to its present location.

25. Santo Domingo de Guzmán is the capital and largest city in the Dominican Republic. It was founded in 1496–98 by Cristóbal Colón's brother Bartolomé, making it the oldest European city in the Americas.

26. It took the Adelantado two months to reach Florida on this first voyage, keeping in mind that the storm (hurricane) forced him off course and that he remained in Puerto Rico for a week. We are later told that the Adelantado made it back in seventeen days, when "he sighted the Azores Islands, having sailed an average of seventy-two leagues per day" (chapter 32, ff. 100r–100v).

27. The Te Deum, dating from the fourth century, is one of the most popular hymns in Christian liturgy.

28. These Indians belonged to the Timucuan group, which was defined by language. According to Milanich, "in the colonial period the Timucua were never united politically. The people we call the Timucua were a number of different independent groups who spoke dialects of the same language" (*The Timucua*, 41). These groups lived throughout much of northeastern Florida. For McCarthy, their territory extended "from

the east coast to the Aucilla River [and] had several hundred villages" (*Native Americans in Florida*, 111). For Bill and Dorcas Thompson the "Timucua tribes stretched from Jacksonville on the east coast to Tampa Bay on the west coast" (*Spanish Exploration*, 12).

29. A *maestro de campo* or *maestre de campo* was inferior in rank only to the captain general who appointed him, and served as a sort of chief of staff. Since he typically commanded a *tercio*—a regiment or corps—the term is here rendered as "brigadier general" or simply "brigadier," the translation favored by the nineteenth-century scholar Pascual de Gayangos.

The manuscript refers to the Adelantado's *maestro de campo* as Pedro Menéndez de Valdés on two occasions, although his most commonly used name is Pedro de Valdés y Menéndez de la Bandera (1544–1615). Therefore I have amended all variants to "Pedro de Valdés." The son of Juan de Valdés, the Adelantado's own brother, he was married to his cousin Ana Menéndez, the Adelantado's oldest daughter (see chapter 32). Throughout the whole narrative Pedro de Valdés, as the Adelantado's *maestro de campo*, will be his second-in-command and, at times, his lieutenant general in Florida and admiral of the fleet.

30. As Connor has explained, this sentence is misleading, since "the following day" refers to the day after the Adelantado found a good harbor, not the day following 28 August 1565 (*Pedro Menéndez de Avilés*, 83n5). The encounter with the French fleet and the founding of St. Augustine are recounted in a letter from Pedro Menéndez to the Crown dated 11 September 1565 (*Archivo de Indias*, est. 54, caja 4, legajo 16). The letter clearly specifies that the encounter with the French fleet occurred on 4 September. Ruidíaz, *La Florida*, 2: 74–84, esp. 76; Mercado, *Cartas*, 129–38, esp. 131.

31. Spain's conquest of the Canary Islands, off the coast of Africa, began in 1402 and was completed in 1495.

32. The French were located approximately twenty leagues north of Cape Canaveral, the place where the Adelantado first saw the coast of Florida. St. Augustine was founded eight leagues north of Canaveral, so it makes sense for the manuscript to mention that the distance between Fort Caroline (Fort San Mateo) and St. Augustine is twelve leagues. However, this distance must not be taken at face value, as it differs in other accounts and is only approximate. Father Francisco López de Mendoza Grajales, for example, states that "our fort [St. Augustine] is at a distance of about fifteen leagues from that of the enemy [Fort Caroline]" (*They Came and Remained*, 48).

33. Born in Las Morteras, Asturias, Diego Flórez de Valdés was, after the Adelantado, the most prominent Asturian sailor of the sixteenth century. He was a knight of the Order of St. James and admiral of Pedro Menéndez's galleons. Mercado, *Cartas*, 104n76.

34. This day commemorates the birth of the Virgin Mary. It was first celebrated officially in the seventh century. Although the syntax is confusing, the two instances of "on the following day" refer to 8 September 1565.

35. Although here and elsewhere I give *toneles* as "tons," it must be noted that the former is a little larger, as ten *toneles* are roughly equivalent to twelve tons. Connor, *Pedro Menéndez de Avilés*, 49n3. Crespo-Francés has also noted that "we have to differentiate between the larger English ton of 1,016.05 kilograms and the short one of 907.18 kilograms" (*Don Pedro Menéndez de Avilés*, 58, my translation).

36. As I have discussed in the introduction, miracles play an important part in the narrative, for the Adelantado is often presented as an agent of God. This sudden change

of weather—not at all uncommon in September, Florida's rainy season—is perhaps the most important "miracle," for it will tip the scales in the Spaniards' favor and seal the fate of the French. For other "miracles" related to the weather, see chapter 13 (f. 59v), when it begins to rain in Guale on 8 May 1566 after a drought of nine months, and chapter 19 (f. 74r), when it rains in Utina after a drought of six months. Keeping in mind that Florida's dry season lasts from October to May, both events—the long drought and the sudden rain—make perfect sense.

37. François was one of Laudonnière's mutineers from Fort Caroline (San Mateo). After he was captured in the West Indies and sent to Spain by Cuban government officials, Menéndez took him to Florida with him. Connor, *Pedro Menéndez de Avilés*, 92n10; Manucy, *Menéndez*, 40.

38. While *desposado* (espoused) can mean either betrothed or wed, Pedro de Valdés and Ana Menéndez were not yet married (see chapter 32 below, or the letter of Pedro Menéndez to the Crown dated 11 September 1565 [Archivo General de Indias, est. 54, caja 5, legajo 16], transcribed in Ruidíaz, *La Florida*, 2: 74–84, and reproduced in Mercado, *Cartas*, 129–38). Pedro de Valdés as *maestro de campo* was the land forces' second-in-command after the Adelantado; as *sargento mayor*, Captain Gonzalo de Villarroel was just behind.

39. In the ninth century, after the emerging Christian Kingdom of Asturias claimed to have discovered the tomb of St. James in the northwest of the Iberian Peninsula, the Apostle of Christ became such an important figure in Spanish historiography that he eventually became the patron saint of the country (celebrated on 25 July). At the Battle of Clavijo (844) the saint purportedly appeared in the midst of the fray to help the Christians defeat the Saracens. From that time on, Spanish forces would always cry out "¡Santiago!" or "¡Santiago y cierra España!" whenever they were in battle.

40. In a fortification, a cavalier or *caballero* is a platform that is set back from, and higher than, the outer wall.

41. The manuscript says that Cristóbal de Herrera is a "montañés," which can either mean that he was born in Cantabria or, more generally, that he was from the north of Spain. To be cautious, we should use the more general expression, but since most of the men in Pedro Menéndez's expedition were from the northern part of the country (Asturias and Vizcaya), it is quite certain that the expression indicates that he was born in Cantabria, for they would not use it to mean "from the northern part of Spain."

42. As the manuscript mentions, Jacques was Jean Ribault's oldest son. He was one of the few men who escaped the massacre that ensued after the capture of Fort Caroline. He was able to return to France aboard the *Pearl*.

43. The Cross of the Angels is a symbol of the Principality of Asturias, the Adelantado's native province, and it is displayed in the flag of its capital, Oviedo. It was donated to the cathedral of that town by King Alfonso II the Chaste (759–842) in the year 808. Its name derives from the legend that the cross was made by two angels disguised as pilgrims.

44. Here and elsewhere the numbers are approximate, as we have just been told that there were fewer than four hundred soldiers at the fort.

45. René Goulaine de Laudonnière (1529?–1574) had first traveled to Florida in 1564, a few months before Jean Ribault's second trip. He built Fort Caroline (San Mateo) at the mouth of the St. Johns River.

46. The Real Audiencia, here translated as High Court, was an appellate court in Spain and its empire.

47. If so, they did not stay long in St. Augustine before returning. In chapter 5 the Adelantado sends word to San Mateo to request more soldiers, and the brigadier dispatches Captains Vélez de Medrano and López Patiño, who arrive in St. Augustine on 23 October 1565.

48. This probably refers to an inlet, since there are no large rivers between St. Augustine and San Mateo.

49. Lyon, *The Enterprise of Florida*, 125.

50. This is the same strategy the Adelantado intended to use when he attacked Fort Caroline (San Mateo), should the French chase the Spaniards back to the woods. By positioning his men right outside the woods, the French would think there were more soldiers hiding in them.

51. Three of the ships from the French fleet were wrecked south of modern Daytona Beach, near Ponce de León Inlet. Milanich, *The Timucua*, 88. A few paragraphs below, we are told that four ships, not three, were shipwrecked.

52. Ferrera (f. 20r) mentions six hundred men, but the number is wrong. We are later told that the group was composed of 208 men. Ruidíaz has amended the number correctly: "dixo que 200 personas, capitanes e gente de Juan Ribao" (*La Florida*, 1: 110), but the reading does not coincide with either Ferrera or Revillagigedo.

53. Saint-Jean-de-Luz is a French town on the Bay of Biscay, very close to the Spanish border. This soldier is referred to as a *gascón* (from Gascony) because at the time Saint-Jean-de-Luz was inscribed into that historical region, which is now the southwestern corner of France.

54. If we follow the distances given in the manuscript, this figure—twenty leagues—is misleading. Since there are twelve leagues between San Mateo and St. Augustine, and the French were found four leagues south of St. Augustine, the correct distance between this place (south of present-day Daytona Beach) and San Mateo would be sixteen leagues.

55. The kings were "brothers" because Philip II had married Elisabeth de Valois, the sister of Charles IX of France.

56. Again, this distance is misleading. St. Augustine is not eight but four leagues to the north of this place, as we have been told by the Indians in f. 19v, by the group of Frenchmen in f. 21r, and by Pedro Menéndez in f. 25v.

57. Jean Ribault's ship, the *Trinité*, was wrecked near Cape Canaveral. Milanich, *The Timucua*, 88. According to the manuscript, the spot would be twenty leagues to the south of San Mateo (eight leagues south of St. Augustine). However, since this group of Frenchmen is now in the same place as the first one, the distance to San Mateo should be, again, sixteen leagues.

58. The distance should be, again, sixteen leagues, not twenty.

59. Ribault's words are obviously inspired by Genesis 3.19: "Revertaris in terram, de qua sumptus es, quia pulvis est, et in pulverem reverteris." The psalm "Domine Memento Mei," which Ribault recites before being killed, is problematic, as there is no psalm by that name in the Book of Psalms. The words are taken from Luke 23.42: "Et dicebat ad Iesum, Domine, memento mei, cum veneris in regnum tuum" (And he said to Jesus: Lord, remember me when You come into your kingdom).

60. The details regarding the capture of Fort San Mateo and the massacre of the French soldiers are specified in a letter written on 15 October 1565 (Archivo de Indias, est. 54, caja 5, legajo 6). Ruidíaz, *La Florida*, 2: 84–105; Mercado, *Cartas*, 139–57. In this letter the Adelantado mentioned that "when I was writing this letter, on the tenth of this month, I received news that the fort we had captured from the French had burned down because it caught fire one night." Ruidíaz, *La Florida*, 2: 101; Mercado, *Cartas*, 154, my translation.

61. When the Adelantado departed for St. Augustine, he promised to send two ships with supplies and artillery to the men in San Mateo. Upon his arrival in St. Augustine, learning that the French fleet had left the bar, he quickly dispatched the first ship, but we are not told about the second one.

62. The term *marranos* means "pigs," but in Spain it was also applied in a derogatory way to the *conversos*, the Jews who were forced to convert to Christianity in 1492 and who were always suspected of practicing Judaism secretly.

63. The date is, again, inaccurate. If the massacre at Matanzas Inlet occurred on 12 October 1565, and at the end of this paragraph we are told that Captains Vélez de Medrano and López Patiño arrived in St. Augustine on 23 October, it is impossible for the events in between to take place "twenty days" after the massacre. According to Lyon (*The Enterprise of Florida*, 128), this happened within two weeks.

64. Apparently Pedro de Valdés is now in St. Augustine, although we last heard of him when the Adelantado left him in San Mateo.

65. The ship was the *San Miguel*. Lyon, *The Enterprise of Florida*, 128.

66. "At this point the Adelantado entered a new and distinctive part of his kingdoms. As the marching men moved down the narrowing island they soon caught glimpses of the broad open waters of the Indian River. . . . The Spaniards had also entered a very different cultural area of the Florida Indians. The people who lived in this area, who were called the Ais, had built a long and stable culture organized almost entirely around the sea." Lyon, *The Enterprise of Florida*, 129.

67. The Ais were the same tribe that Ponce de León found in 1513. According to McCarthy, "the name of the tribe can be spelled in several ways: Ais, Aix, Aiz, Alis, and Jece," and their lands "extended south from Cape Canaveral into what is today Fort Pierce in St. Lucie County. They also lived to the west of there, on the mainland along the St. Johns River and along the Indian River, which used to be called the River of Ais. Their main village, which was near Indian River Inlet, probably had around it many towns, each with its own leader, and all were subject to one powerful leader" (*Native Americans in Florida*, 75).

68. At the beginning of chapter 7 we are told that the Adelantado departed from the port of Ais on 6 November 1565, so the date here is incorrect.

69. A real was a silver coin of 3.35 grams.

70. This is the Indian River gateway, which Pedro Menéndez called Puerto del Socorro. Mercado, *Cartas*, 158n221.

71. Captain Juan Vélez de Medrano was left here with two hundred men and fifty of the French captives (notice how the numbers differ from the manuscript). His appointment is found in the Archivo Histórico de Protocolos (Madrid), Protocolo 646, fol. 256–59. Lyon, *The Enterprise of Florida*, 130n51.

72. Bahía Honda is in the northwestern part of Cuba, on an inlet of the Florida Straits, west of Havana.

73. Francisco García Osorio de Sandoval was governor of Cuba from 1565 to 1567.

74. A *regidor* (literally, a ruler) was a member of a municipal council in Spain, Portugal, and the Americas. Juan de Rojas Hinestrosa was born in Cuéllar (Segovia) and was the son of Manuel de Rojas and Magdalena Velázquez. According to Lyon, he was related to the powerful Rojas family in Cuba: "In Pedro Menéndez' time, the most influential member was Juan de Rojas, whose kinfolk dominated the cabildo of Havana and occupied most of the other local posts of honor and privilege there. Rojas' wife, Doña María de Lovera, had demonstrated her close ties to Pedro Menéndez de Avilés by naming him in her 1563 will. . . . Juan de Hinestrosa, who had testified in Seville for Menéndez in his 1564 jailbreak case . . . served after 1565 as one of the Royal Officials in Havana" (*The Enterprise of Florida*, 82).

75. The Fleet of New Spain was based in Veracruz, and it traveled between Spain and present-day Mexico.

76. La Parra was in prison for three months. Connor, *Pedro Menéndez de Avilés*, 133n8. See the letter of Menéndez to the Crown dated 5 December 1565 in Ruidíaz, *La Florida*, 2: 105–25; Mercado, *Cartas*, 157–73.

77. Diego Flórez de Valdés, who had been the admiral of the fleet up to this point, was dispatched to Spain with messages to the king (see chapter 5, f. 27r).

78. In a letter written by Menéndez in Matanzas (Cuba) on 5 December 1565, he mentioned that he departed from Havana on the last day of November. Ruidíaz, *La Florida*, 2: 109; Mercado, *Cartas*, 160.

79. Matanzas is in the northern part of the island, fifty-six miles east of Havana.

80. San Francisco de Campeche is a town founded by Spaniards in 1540 on the Yucatán Peninsula of Mexico. Its name derives from the fact that it was built on the Mayan city of Kimpech. Puerto de Plata refers to present-day San Felipe de Puerto Plata, on the northern coast of the Dominican Republic. It was Christopher Columbus who named the mountain next to the city Monte de Plata (silver mountain).

81. Yaguana refers to the modern city and port of Léogâne, in Haiti, some twenty miles west of Port-au-Prince.

82. Both names refer to the Florida Keys. Speaking about Ponce de León's expedition to Florida, historian Antonio de Herrera y Tordesillas (1559–1625) mentioned that "on Sunday, the day of the Feast of the Holy Spirit, 15 May, they ran along the coast of rocky islets ten leagues, as far as two white rocky islets. To all this line of islands and rocky islets they gave the name of Los Mártires because, seen from a distance, the rocks as they rose to view appeared like men who were suffering. . . . On Wednesday they went in search of the 11 rocky islets that they left to the west. On Thursday and Friday they ran in the same direction until, on Tuesday, the 21, they reached the rocky islets, which they named Las Tortugas, because in one short time in the night they took, in one of these islands, 160 tortoises, and might have taken many more if they had wanted them." Davis, "Ponce de León's First Voyage," 19–21.

83. Tierra Firme refers to the northeastern part of South America. The Fleet of Tierra Firme was based out of Cartagena in present-day Colombia. New Spain, as mentioned above, refers to present-day Mexico, and its fleet was based out of Veracruz.

84. "The Caloosa were the most important group of Native Americans in South Florida. . . . They lived on the southwestern coast of Florida, from Charlotte Harbor down to the Ten Thousand Islands. The Calusa were very hostile to some of the other Indian groups in Florida, as well as to any Spanish explorers they encountered." McCarthy, *Native Americans in Florida*, 75.

85. A *bergantín* of the Adelantado's day, very unlike the brigantine of later centuries, was a two-masted vessel of shallow draft propelled not only by sail but by oars, generally ten or twelve pairs.

86. Pedro Menéndez Marqués had been appointed admiral of the fleet after Diego Flórez Valdés was sent to Spain. Since he too was later dispatched to Spain, it seems Diego de Amaya was now the new admiral.

87. Connor in *Pedro Menéndez de Avilés*, 145, translated this expression as "Ace of Diamonds," which is indeed equivalent to the Spanish card. I prefer to respect the original wording, since it is ironic for the soldier to receive a piece of gold worth seventy ducats in exchange for, literally, an "ace of gold."

88. The *vihuela*, a guitarlike instrument with six pairs of strings, was usually plucked, but the *vihuela de arco* was played, like the viol, with a bow. The Spanish word *salterio* can refer either to a psaltery, an instrument with plucked strings similar to the zither, or to a hammered dulcimer, with strings that are stretched over a trapezoidal sounding board and struck with handheld mallets.

89. The *estado* was a unit of height used most often in the measurement of wells, pits, and walls, according to the *Diccionario de autoridades* (1732). Its value was not clearly established and varied from country to country. In the Dominican Republic it equaled two Castilian *varas*, roughly 1.6 meters. An approximate value is also six or seven feet, similar to a fathom. In this context the chieftain's sister was seated about three feet from the ground.

90. Obviously, Chief Carlos did not get his name from Philip II's father, Charles I of Spain, as Solís de Merás is suggesting. Early Spanish and French chronicles refer to this tribe and its chieftain as either Carlos, Calos, Calus, or Caalus, so the confusion is due to the Spaniards' misinterpretation—or, rather, their erroneous pronunciation—of the name Calusa. In his *Memoria de las cosas y costa y indios de la Florida*, Hernando de Escalante Fontaneda (1535–1575)—who was shipwrecked in the Florida Keys at the age of thirteen and enslaved by this tribe—mentioned that Carlos was "a province of Indians, in the language of which the word signifies a fierce people, as they are called for being brave and skilled in war" (6).

91. Francisco de Toral (1502–1571) was a Franciscan missionary in New Spain and the first bishop of Yucatán from 1561 until his death. Luis de Céspedes y Oviedo (ca. 1530–1572) was the first governor and captain general of Yucatán from 1565 until 1571, when he was succeeded by Diego de Santillán y Pineda. Céspedes died the following year when the ship in which he was returning to Spain was lost. As it appears, de Toral did not hold the governor in much esteem: "He lacks schooling and has too many needs, and therefore, on one hand he is bound by his lack of knowledge, and on the other by his many interests, which have blinded him. To make it appear that there is justice, he afflicts and imprisons the poor because they have trod on the sun, while those who should be punished are walking free in the streets." Molina Solís, *Historia de Yucatán*, 1: 119n1, my translation.

Notice that the manuscript refers to Yucatán as an island, which is obviously a mistake.

92. A *fanega* or *hanega* was a measure of grain equal to 55.5 liters (approximately 15 gallons), but its value varied greatly in different regions of Spain.

93. According to Lyon ("The Florida Mutineers," 49–50), the key figures in the San Mateo mutiny were Sergeant Gutierre de Valverde of Captain Mejía's company, Gregorio de Robles, who was appointed "electo," Ensign Sargüero, Sergeant Goyán, and a soldier named Miguel de Mora, while the nominal leaders of the St. Augustine mutiny were Cristóbal Rodríguez and Sergeant Sebastián de Lezcano.

94. The frigate was *La Concepción.* Lyon, "The Florida Mutineers," 50.

95. The conquest of Peru had begun in 1532 with the expedition of Francisco Pizarro, who defeated the emperor of the Incas, Atahualpa.

96. For the daily rations on the armada captained by the Adelantado a few years later in 1568, see Pérez Mallaína, *Spain's Men of the Sea*: "Mondays, Wednesdays, Fridays, and Saturdays: a pound and a half (690 grams) of biscuit, one liter of water, one liter of wine, half a peck of a mixture (*menestra*) of horse beans and chickpeas for each 12 persons (150 grams per person), and one pound of salted fish for each three persons (153.3 grams per person). Tuesdays: a pound and a half (690 grams) of biscuit, one liter of water, one liter of wine, one pound of mixed rice and oil for each ten persons (46 grams per person), and half a pound (230 grams) of salt pork. Sundays and Thursdays: a pound and a half (690 grams) of biscuit, one liter of water, one liter of wine, one pound (460 grams) of salted meat, two ounces (57.5 grams) of cheese. Each month: One liter of oil and something more than a half liter of vinegar per person" (141).

97. Rodrigo Montes, from Oviedo, was the fort storekeeper. Lyon, "The Florida Mutineers," 51.

98. Saturiwa was the chieftain of one of the Timucuan tribes near San Mateo (ex–Fort Caroline). He was the only chieftain with whom Pedro Menéndez had to fight, although Pedro de Valdés also captured Emola, one of Saturiwa's subjects.

99. This paragraph is a bit unclear. The Adelantado allowed a few men to go to Spain to take care of their private affairs, warning the others about the dangers of rising up in rebellion after these men left. The bottom line is that the soldiers, including Captain San Vicente and his ensign Fernán Pérez, were to remain in the fort or else be sent to Spain as prisoners. However, both the captain and his ensign decided to embark and go to Hispaniola.

100. Christopher Columbus was the first European to set foot in Honduras, in 1502 during his fourth and last voyage, although the conquest of the territory did not begin until 1524 with the arrival of Gil González Dávila.

101. Triana, a western suburb of Seville, was home to sailors and artisans and was the traditional Gypsy quarter. The Muslim-era fortification called Castillo de Triana, later known as Castillo de San Jorge, became from 1481 to 1785 the Castillo de la Inquisición, seat of the feared Spanish Inquisition. Only a part of the original construction is extant today.

102. Havre de Grace is present-day Le Havre, a major port in Normandy in northern France.

103. Nicolas Durand de Villegaignon (1510–1571), with permission from the king of France, Henri II, departed from Havre de Grace in 1555 to establish a colony near pres-

ent-day Rio de Janeiro, in an effort to build a utopian colony of French Huguenots called France Antarctique. After several battles with the Portuguese, the French were finally expelled in 1567. Gómez Tabanera, *Pedro Menéndez de Avilés*, xxvii–xxviii.

104. This man is Guillaume Rouffi (or Rufin), who had remained at Port Royal, at the site of Charlesfort, after Ribault's soldiers deserted this colony and sailed to France in 1562.

105. Diego de Mazariegos Guadalfajara was governor of Cuba from 1556 to 1565 (right before Francisco García Osorio), as well as governor of the Province of Caracas from 1570 to 1576.

106. Guillaume is recounting events that took place before the arrival of the Adelantado. On 12 May 1564, Governor Diego de Mazariegos of Havana dispatched Hernando Manrique de Rojas to Florida to look for the French settlement of Charlesfort. There they saw that all the Frenchmen had abandoned the fort, with the exception of Guillaume Rouffi, a sixteen-year-old boy who, as the manuscript says, was later handed over to Pedro Menéndez de Avilés. Lyon, *The Enterprise of Florida*, 33–34.

107. Newfoundland—Terranova, Terra Nova, or Tierra Nova (New Land), initially called Tierra de los Bacalaos (Land of the Codfish)—was sighted as early as 1500–1501. The Portuguese explorer Gaspar Corte-Real told the famous cartographer Alberto Cantino about his own discovery of that land, and Cantino wrote about it in letters to the Duke of Ferrara on 17 and 18 October 1501. Gómez-Tabanera, *Pedro Menéndez de Avilés*, xx (although his dating of the letters is inaccurate).

108. Connor, following Barrientos, has explained this episode very clearly: "Ribaut's party, instead of going to ask the help of Orista (or Audusta), who had been so good to Ribaut's first settlers at Charlesfort, near Port Royal, in 1562, stopped on the way and remained with Cacique Guale, who drew them against their will into his war with Orista; so that the latter, from being the champion of the French, became their enemy and the friend of the Spanish" (*Pedro Menéndez de Avilés*, 167n7).

109. In the year 1566, Easter Sunday fell on 14 April, so Good Friday was on 12 April. Cappelli, *Cronologia*, 82.

110. It is unclear who the "six Christians" were. Besides the Adelantado's nephew Alonso and the ensign and their two servants, the three boy catechists were to have been left behind. Perhaps the Adelantado took one of the boys with him.

111. Madeira was sacked in October 1566 by Bertrand Montluc. Notice that the manuscript is describing future events, since at this point the date is May 1566. According to Taylor, "Funchal was paralyzed by the sudden raid made on it by three French vessels, filled with freebooters, under their leader De Montluc, who landed at Praya Bay. . . . The inhabitants, terror-stricken, barricaded their houses. . . . Montluc and his followers were of no religion whatever, though the Portuguese chroniclers call them Huguenots" (*Madeira*, 150).

112. A *visitador* was an officer appointed by the king in charge of visiting and inspecting the administration of justice in specific towns or territories. In the case of the American colonies, the *visitador* reported back to the Council of the Indies. Jerónimo de Valderrama, who was sent by Philip II as *visitador* of those lands in 1565, did not have a very good reputation, and (among other unpopular measures) he tried to increase the tribute paid by the Indians in New Spain. Cuevas, *Historia de la iglesia*, 2: 180–90.

113. The knights of the Order of St. James who were single took a vow of chastity, and those who were married promised to be faithful to their wives. Other than that, I have found no reference to the alleged custom of waiting "eight days," so the Adelantado is—once again—making excuses not to sleep with Doña Antonia. He was, after all, married to Ana María de Solís, but since he had to conceal from Doña Antonia that he was already married in Spain, the excuse of having to wait a week to sleep with her came in handy.

114. Alonso de Rojas "belonged to one of the largest extended families—and surely the most prominent one—in sixteenth-century Havana. One branch was headed by the brothers Alonso de Rojas and Diego de Soto or Sotolongo, who settled in the village around 1540 with their uncle Juan de Soto (or Juan de Rojas). Each brother came to head a dense network of relatives and kin who played important roles in the life of Havana. Alonso de Rojas represented Havana's town council before the Audiencia de Santo Domingo in the 1550s. He was elected regidor in 1564, 1568, 1570, and 1576." Fuente, *Havana and the Atlantic*, 190. For the dates of the appointments, see also Cowley, *Los tres primeros historiadores*, 1: 219–20.

115. A major port for the Spanish treasure fleet, Nombre de Dios is a city on the Atlantic coast of Panama founded in 1510 by Diego de Nicuesa.

116. Sanlúcar de Barrameda is a city in the Spanish province of Cádiz that served as a strategic port for the exploration and conquest of America.

117. Sancho de Archiniega (1531–1592)—also spelled Archinega, Archienaga, Arciniega, and even Achiniega—was a native of Portugalete in the province of Vizcaya. Beyond his command of the relief mission in 1566, little is known of him.

118. In chapter 14 we were told that Gonzalo de Villarroel was ill and that the Adelantado had to take him to Havana to be cured. In his place the Adelantado sent the brigadier from St. Augustine to San Mateo with orders to stay there until his own return from Havana.

119. There is an *instrucción* by Pedro Menéndez to his captains written in 1562 where he specified the passwords for each day of the week: "Sunday: The Most Holy Trinity; Monday: Saint John; Tuesday: Saint James; Wednesday: Saint Peter; Thursday: Saint Lawrence; Friday: Saint Christopher; Saturday: Our Lady of Victory." Ruidíaz, *La Florida*, 2: 410–13, esp. 411.

120. Juan de Ubilla was a prominent sixteenth-century sailor best known for having defeated the English privateer John Hawkins in 1568 at the Battle of San Juan de Ulúa off the coast of present-day Veracruz, Mexico.

121. For Mendoza Grajales, see the introduction. Jerez de la Frontera is a city and municipality in the Spanish province of Cádiz.

122. It is very strange that this captain should have the same name as the one killed by Saturiwa. Chapter 10 (f. 48r) said of Troche: "They seized him and his companion and took them to their chieftain, Saturiwa, who knew them very well. He commanded that [Troche] be ripped open and his heart taken out and pierced with arrows. The same was done to his comrade." Troche is mentioned once more in f. 82r below, and the wordings in Ferrera and Revillagigedo coincide.

123. Baltasar de Barreda may have been an ensign, but at this point he is captain of the fleet. Later on in the manuscript (ff. 81r, 85r, 85v, 94v, 95r, and 95v) he is always referred to as "Captain Barreda." See f. 80v below for a similar situation with Cristóbal de Herrera.

124. The River May (St. Johns River).

125. Utina was the chieftain of a Timucuan tribe that the French had first encountered in September 1564 when a group of soldiers sailed up St. Johns River. According to Milanich, "Utina, who sought to manipulate the French just as they wished to use him, convinced the French to send six or seven soldiers on a raid he was planning against Chief Potano. . . . Early in 1565 Chief Utina again convinced the French to send soldiers for another raid on Potano" (*The Timucua*, 85). Regarding the name of the tribe, for Milanich "Uti-na" means "my land" in Timucuan (46). Hoffman disagrees and says that it means "chief" (*Florida's Frontiers*, 50).

126. I have not found any information on this Indian chieftain called Peracho.

127. The Maymi or Mayaimi Lagoon refers to Lake Okeechobee. As Connor has explained very clearly, it appears that the Timucua told the Adelantado that the St. Johns emptied into Lake Okeechobee, which—additionally—was supposed to have a river flowing out of it to the west into Charlotte Harbor (Carlos) and another one flowing to the east, connecting it with Tequesta, near the present city of Miami (*Pedro Menéndez de Avilés*, 205n4).

128. The northernmost village and group vassal to Chief Saturiwa was called Caravay, sometimes appearing as Calabay, Sarabay, Saravay, or Serranay. The village was probably located on or near Little Talbot Island. Milanich, *The Timucua*, 49.

129. Although Ponce de León had traveled as far north as Chesapeake Bay, it was Lucas Vázquez de Ayllón who named it Bahía de Santa María (St. Marys Bay) on 29 September 1526. Don Luis de Velasco, who took his Christian name from the viceroy of New Spain, was called Paquiquineo. He was an Algonquian chief who had been picked up on an earlier expedition, taken to Mexico and Spain (where he met Philip II), and brought back to Florida in one of Menéndez's ships. In the fall of 1566 Menéndez had to allow Dominicans from Mexico and Don Luis to sail to Chesapeake Bay, but according to Hoffman, "the commentary record suggests Menéndez was unhappy about their voyage. Perhaps by prearrangement, the crew failed to find the entrance to Chesapeake Bay and sailed on to Spain" (*Florida's Frontiers*, 56–57). Years later, in 1571, Don Luis persuaded the Jesuits to establish a mission in his land, but in the winter he led an Indian attack that wiped out the mission, the only survivor being a small boy called Alonso Méndez, who was rescued by the Spaniards in 1572 and who informed them of all that had happened. Elliott, *Empires of the Atlantic World*, 10; Hoffman, *Florida's Frontiers*, 57; Mercado, *Cartas*, 36–37.

130. The Tequesta lived at the mouth of the Miami River near where downtown Miami now is. On the north side of the river stood their chief settlement, also called Tequesta. McCarthy, *Native Americans in Florida*, 108.

131. The first of the Juan Pardo expeditions took place from 1 December 1566 to 7 March 1567. The second one was from 1 September 1567 until 2 March 1568. The accounts have been preserved in four main documents: the "Long" Bandera Relation (Archivo General de Indias, Santo Domingo 224), the "Short" Bandera Relation (Archivo General de Indias, Patronato 19, R.20), the Pardo Relation (Archivo General de Indias, Patronato 19, R.22), and the Martínez Relation (Archivo General de Indias, Patronato 19, R.22). They have all been carefully studied, translated, and analyzed by Hudson in *The Juan Pardo Expeditions*, 205–96, 297–304, 305–15, and 317–21.

132. La Mona (from the Taino name Amona, in honor of their chieftain) is the largest of the three islands in the Mona Passage, a strait between Hispaniola (now the Dominican Republic and Haiti) and Puerto Rico. The settlement of San Germán in southwestern Puerto Rico was the island's second oldest, after San Juan, and was named after Germaine de Foix (1488–1538), the second wife of King Ferdinand of Aragón (1452–1516).

133. As with Baltasar de Barreda (chapter 29, f. 73v), Cristóbal de Herrera is referred to as an ensign, which he used to be, but at this point he is captain of the vessel. Later (f. 82r) he will be appointed general of the fleet sailing to Spain.

134. Guayanilla, on Puerto Rico's south coast, was originally named Guadianilla, after the Guadiana River in Spain.

135. Juan Ponce de León established in 1508 a settlement called Caparra which, a year later, was moved to a site called Puerto Rico (present-day San Juan). Note that, originally, the island was called San Juan Bautista and the town Puerto Rico, but the names began to be used indistinctly. Eventually the island was referred to as Puerto Rico and its capital as San Juan.

136. This Juan Ponce de León (1524–1591) was the grandson of the man who named Florida. He was the first Puerto Rican to become governor of the island.

137. Jean Bontemps was a French corsair who raided the coastal towns of present-day Colombia and Venezuela, sacking Cartagena de Indias in 1559. Landing on the island of Curaçao in 1571, Bontemps had to fight the brothers Antonio and Gonzalo Barbudo and was killed by an arrow. The Spaniards took his head to the High Court in Santo Domingo as a prize. Mercado, *Cartas*, 248n361.

138. The authorities began to encourage the construction of sugar mills as early as 1518. In Puerto de Plata, many Indians were given to Licentiate Ayllón, Francisco de Ceballos, Licentiate Juan Carrillo, and Pero López de Mesa. Iglesias, *La transferencia de tecnología*, 197. The abundance of sugar mills in Hispaniola was already noted in 1527 by chronicler Gonzalo Fernández de Oviedo: "in that island there are many varied and rich sugar mills, and the sugar is so good, perfect, and abundant, that every year the ships are laden with it" (*Sumario*, 16). As the manuscript mentions, Ceballos also owned a lot of cattle. According to López y Sebastián and del Río Moreno, the men who owned cattle in Hispaniola numbered no more than thirty, including "Pedro de Ceballos, who owned six thousand, and his uncle Francisco de Ceballos, with eight thousand" ("La ganadería vacuna," 35). The translations are mine.

139. For the arrival of these mutineers in Puerto de Plata, see chapter 10, where we were told that the pilot of the ship had given Ceballos a secret message from the brigadier, which he ignored.

140. The manuscript is referring to Alonso de Cáceres y Ovando, who was *oidor* from 1559 to 1572. The connection between Francisco de Ceballos (Cavallos, Zavallos, Çevallos) to the other prominent families of Hispaniola is difficult to determine. Francisca Colón (the daughter of Cristóbal Colón's grandson, also named Cristóbal) was indeed married to Licentiate Diego Ortegón, *oidor* of the High Court of Santo Domingo, but none of her sisters was married to any relative of Ceballos or the president of the High Court. Interestingly, a manuscript in the Archivo General de Indias (Patronato 18, N.1, R.9) describes the same family tree, but is unique in stating that Ceballos "has Licentiate Grajeda as father-in-law" (Utrera, *Historia militar*, 2: 159–60, my translation). Alonso de

Angulo Grajeda was president of the High Court from 1564 to 1566 (see Lugo, *Historia*, chapter 5), but there is no record of any of his daughters having married Ceballos. For the connection between the Grajeda and the Colón family to work, the text should read "a granddaughter of this president [was married] to a grandson of Don Cristóbal Colón," since Grajeda's granddaughter María de Rojas did in fact marry Luis Dávila Colón. As for Francisco de Ceballos, I could not find any records that mention the name of his wife.

141. Monte Cristo is now Monte Cristi, a town on the Dominican Republic's north coast. Puerto Real, identified by Mercado (*Cartas*, 133n137) as the Port Royal near Kingstown, Jamaica, was in fact a city on Hispaniola's north coast, near Cap-Haitien; important in the sixteenth century, it is long gone. See Deagan, *Puerto Real*.

142. Santiago de Cuba, on the south coast near the eastern tip, was founded by Diego Velázquez de Cuéllar in 1514.

143. Cabo de Cruz and Manzanillo are towns in the present province of Granma, in the southeast of Cuba. Bayamo was a port because the river Cauto allowed seagoing vessels to reach the city. Mercado, *Cartas*, 175n262.

144. Both the name of the harbor and the date when the Adelantado arrived in Havana have been omitted in both manuscripts, and in this case Ferrera has not amended the text.

145. This river is the Caloosahatchee, named after the Caloosa Indians. Connor, *Pedro Menéndez de Avilés*, 219.

146. The cruelty with which Carlos and his father had treated the Christians has already been mentioned in chapter 9.

147. Juan Rogel, who was born in Pamplona in 1529 and studied art and medicine at the University of Alcalá, became a Jesuit in 1553 and later lived in Cuenca and Toledo. Francisco de Villarreal, born in Madridejos in the province of Toledo in 1530, was secretary of the High Court in Granada and became a Jesuit in 1559. Zubillaga, *La Florida*, 328, 234; Mercado, *Cartas*, 37n82, 37n84.

148. In the "Description of the Land of Florida" at the end of the manuscript, a similar statement is made about the relationship between the French soldiers and the Indian women. The French "were on very good terms with the Indian women—the sisters, daughters, and wives of the chieftains—who had borne them some children." See chapter 34, f. 109r.

149. In the sixteenth century the Tocobaga lived along the Florida Gulf Coast from Sarasota to Tarpon Springs. McCarthy, *Native Americans in Florida*, 118.

150. The original has "patax" here but, as the account of the episode unfolds, twice calls this message-carrying vessel a brigantine.

151. In the original these officers are called *alguaciles*, which I have rendered as "constables," and *porquerones*, "bailiffs"—judicial agents in charge of detaining prisoners and taking them to jail (*Diccionario de Autoridades*).

152. Ferrera calls this soldier Hulano (Fulano), which is the name used in Spanish to refer to an unknown person. Ruidíaz transcribes "que se llamaba . . . , caballero de Trujillo," although Revillagigedo agrees with Ferrera. Ruidíaz, *La Florida*, 1: 295.

153. This soldier is mentioned in the "Long" Bandera Relation of the Juan Pardo expedition. See edition and translation in Hudson, *The Juan Pardo Expeditions*, 205–96, esp. 212.

154. Chief Emola was an ally of Saturiwa and Calibay who lived on or near the St. Johns River, to the southwest of Saturiwa's main village. Milanich, *The Timucua*, 49.

155. The Archivo General de Indias contains the proceedings on the insubordination of Captain Miguel Enríquez (Justicia 999, R.9, N.2) and of Pedro de Rodabán (Justicia 999, R.6, N.2). Lyon, "The Florida Mutineers," 58.

156. Flanders was one of the most troublesome holdings of the Hapsburg monarchs of Spain. By virtue of being duke of Burgundy, Emperor Charles I also became count of Flanders, but the European conflicts and the wars between Catholics and Protestants soon made this territory a hard one to control. The hostilities came to an end only with the Peace of 1648.

157. Terceira is one of the largest islands of the Azores group, which belonged then, as now, to Portugal. La Coruña was and is an important port city in Galicia, the northwestern part of Spain.

158. Cape St. Vincent in Portugal is the southwesternmost point of the Iberian Peninsula. According to Connor, a *fusta* is "a lateen-rigged lighter; a boat with a triangular sail" (*Pedro Menéndez de Avilés*, 239).

159. Pedro Menéndez arrived in Spain on St. Peter's Day, the same day on which he sailed for Florida two years before.

160. Viveiro, a town in the province of Lugo in Galicia, is some seventy miles from La Coruña.

161. La Concha de Artedo is located in the Asturian municipality of Cudillero.

162. The term in the text, "Mar de Levante," or Sea of the (Near) East, refers to the eastern part of the Mediterranean.

163. Gijón is the largest city in the Principality of Asturias, as well as its main port.

164. On the relationship between Ana Menéndez and Pedro de Valdés, see Lyon, *The Enterprise of Florida*, 224–25.

165. The term in the text, "Mar de Poniente," or Sea of the West, refers to the westernmost part of the Mediterranean.

166. Pedro Menéndez's complaint is not uncommon. In the words of Pérez Mallaína, "the unstable employment of the armadas' high command was one reason its members sought income beyond their official salaries" (*Spain's Men of the Sea*, 97).

167. The numbers do not match those in chapter 1. Folio 1v said there were four warships, not three, and five hundred soldiers, not four hundred.

168. Diego Venegas is buried in the Convento de Madre de Dios de la Piedad in Seville. On his tomb we can read: "Aquí yaze el licenciado Diego Venegas, primer oydor de la Casa de Contratación de Sevilla. . . . Falleció viernes 25 de diziembre de 1587 años, de hedad 66 años" [Here lies the licentiate Diego Venegas, first *oidor* of the House of Trade in Seville. . . . He died on Friday, 25 December 1587, aged 66 years].

169. Juan Menéndez de Avilés, the Adelantado's only son, was the general of the fleet of New Spain. He was shipwrecked near the Bermuda Islands on his way back from New Spain, shortly after departing from Havana on 11 August 1563. Mellén Blanco, *Pedro Menéndez de Avilés*, 52; Mercado, *Cartas*, 16n15.

170. Pánuco, present-day Tampico on the east coast of Mexico, was founded by Hernán Cortés in 1522 as Villa de Santiesteban del Puerto.

171. The seven settlements are St. Augustine, Santa Elena, San Mateo, Santa Lucía

(Ais), Tequesta, San Antón, and Tocobaga. However, shortly after the Adelantado's departure, the settlements of San Mateo, Santa Lucía, Tequesta, and Tocobaga were destroyed. Manucy, *Menéndez*, 85, 88.

172. In the first paragraph of this "Description" we were told that the Adelantado had built settlements in seven places, not eight.

173. The city of Veracruz, on the east coast of Mexico, was founded by Hernán Cortés in 1519.

174. Zacatecas, in north-central Mexico, was founded in 1546 after the discovery of its silver mines.

175. This paragraph and the next one recount events narrated at the end of chapter 29, when the Adelantado left detailed instructions on how to wage war on Saturiwa. We are now told that Captain Bayona had assisted Saturiwa in this war and later surrendered to Gonzalo de Villarroel. I have not been able to find any information on this French captain, who is not mentioned in Revillagigedo.

176. At this point Diego de Ribera has included five letters and royal edicts which I do not transcribe, as they can be found in Ruidíaz and Mercado. For their titles and contents, see the introduction.

PART 2: *LA CONQUISTA DE LA FLORIDA POR EL ADELANTADO PEDRO MELÉNDEZ DE VALDÉS*

1. The manuscript has three unnumbered folios at the beginning, which I have indicated with an asterisk. Of these, ff. 1*v, 2*r, and 2*v have been left blank.

2. MS: "del."

3. This is the only folio where the text is displayed in two columns.

4. MS: "el marques alonso menendez."

5. MS: "don pedro menendez de valdes." Although the name is correct, he is most commonly known as Pedro de Valdés y Menéndez de La Bandera. For this reason, and in order to avoid confusion with the Adelantado, I always refer to him as Pedro de Valdés.

6. MS: "casad con hija."

7. MS: "Curita."

8. Captain San Vicente is listed twice, perhaps because his brother is mentioned on f. 47r.

9. MS: "el capitan juan velez de medrano y albarado de medina del canpo." The manuscript has merged the names of these two captains into one, which in turn has caused two problematic variants in the text of both Revillagigedo and Ferrera (see below, ff. 17v, 18v). The name of Captain Diego de Alvarado appears in a letter from Pedro Menéndez to the Crown dated 11 September 1565. Ruidíaz, *La Florida*, 2: 82; Mercado, *Cartas*, 137.

10. MS: "Aoctina."

11. MS: "Toco Uaya."

12. Neither Ferrera nor Revillagigedo is divided into chapters, which I have supplied, although in many places I do not follow the order and divisions proposed by Ruidíaz, for the reasons discussed in the introduction.

13. MS: "md" (missing the abbreviation mark).

14. MS: "pasageron."

15. MS: "yndustriabas."

16. The letters "-tasen" appear as a catchword on f. 1r and are repeated on f. 1v.

17. MS: "costa y que se fuese."

18. With the exception of the first paragraph, most of the text of chapter 1 up to this point is repeated—with some variations—at the end of the manuscript (ff. 105r–107r).

19. The words "-pero viento" appear as a catchword on f. 1v, but are not repeated on f. 2r, although the narrative continues uninterrupted. As I have discussed in the introduction, from f. 2r to f. 108v the manuscript was copied by a different hand, which appears to be the same one that has amended several folios in Revillagigedo.

20. MS: "olonas."

21. MS: "çinco na nauios."

22. MS: "esperanca."

23. MS: "luega."

24. A previous number has been erased and corrected to "y quatro."

25. MS: "vien ento bonança."

26. Here begins chapter 10 in Ruidíaz's edition, La Florida, 1: 70, and therefore all the information contained on folios 1*r–3*v and 1r–3r in Ferrera does not appear in Revillagigedo, which begins with a different story about Pedro Menéndez's exploits before his expedition to Florida. As I have noted in the introduction, Ruidíaz has supplied much of the missing parts in Revillagigedo with text from Barcia's Ensayo cronológico, most notably parts of chapters 4, 6, 8, and all of chapter 9, which do not appear at all in either the Revillagigedo or the Ferrera manuscripts. In light of the discovery of this second manuscript, I believe Ruidíaz's emendations can now be safely discarded as never having been part of the original Memorial. Additionally, chapter 7 in Ruidíaz is located at the end of Ferrera (f. 107v), and half of chapter 8—what has not been taken from Barcia—appears on f. 105r. For other problems concerning Ruidíaz's emendations, see the introduction.

27. MS: "exerçioçio."

28. MS: "senas."

29. MS: "paresciendoles."

30. Revillagigedo is missing the word "dos" because the page is torn (see Ruidíaz, La Florida, 1: 73).

31. MS: "dicha."

32. MS: "y el enque yua."

33. MS: "dello."

34. MS: "en el en que el yua."

35. MS: "vros" (missing the abbreviation mark).

36. MS: "amostrassen."

37. MS: "antrada."

38. MS: "suplicando se lo."

39. MS omits. I follow Revillagigedo (apud Ruidíaz, La Florida, 1: 84).

40. MS: "aman derceha."

41. MS: "dieziendo."

42. MS: "passara."

43. MS: "compania."

44. MS: "reparo."

45. MS: "la gente que llego."

46. MS: "adelantado el qual respondio." I follow Revillagigedo (*apud* Ruidíaz, *La Florida*, 1: 91).

47. The word "nos" is repeated at the beginning of f. 12r by mistake, since it is not a catchword.

48. MS: "passada."

49. MS: "escuridiad."

50. For "abajandose" I follow Revillagigedo (*apud* Ruidíaz, *La Florida*, 1: 94), since the acidity of the ink has damaged the folio in Ferrera. For the rest of the sentence I follow Ferrera, since the version in Revillagigedo, "muy presto fue a lo alto" (*apud* Ruidíaz, *La Florida*, 1: 94), seems mistaken.

51. Ruidíaz transcribes "¿Quién va? . . . Francés?" but both manuscripts render the dialogue in French. Ruidíaz, *La Florida*, 1: 95.

52. MS: "reparo."

53. MS omits. I follow Revillagigedo (*apud* Ruidíaz, *La Florida*, 1: 95).

54. MS omits. I follow Revillagigedo (*apud* Ruidíaz, *La Florida*, 1: 95).

55. MS omits. I follow Revillagigedo (*apud* Ruidíaz, *La Florida*, 1: 96).

56. MS: "descibierto."

57. MS: "calose."

58. Revillagigedo: "los que mas presto pudieron entrar algunos franceses de las casas en camisa y otros vestidos salieron a reconoscer lo que era" (*apud* Ruidíaz, *La Florida*, 1: 97).

59. Revillagigedo: "el Adelantado a donde quedo como hubo pasado la mitad de la gente dixo a francisco de castañeda" (*apud* Ruidíaz, *La Florida*, 1: 97).

60. MS: "que se quedasse con toda la victoria." Even though this sentence is grammatical, it makes no sense in this paragraph. I follow Revillagigedo (*apud* Ruidíaz, *La Florida*, 1: 98).

61. Revillagigedo omits these last six words. See Ruidíaz, *La Florida*, 1: 98.

62. MS: "la granga."

63. The words "embiarian alguna fuesse alguna" have been changed in the manuscript to "embiarian por que fuesse alguna."

64. MS: "casas."

65. MS: "distinto."

66. MS: "villareal."

67. MS: "vista."

68. The transcription in Ruidíaz, "la puerta prencipal deste fuerte," is more correct, but it is not shared by either Ferrera or Revillagigedo. See Ruidíaz, *La Florida*, 1: 103.

69. MS: "distinto."

70. Ruidíaz, *La Florida*, 1: 104, transcribes "de Medrano é . . . de Alvarado," although nothing is missing in Revillagigedo or Ferrera. Remember that the names of Juan Vélez de Medrano and Diego de Alvarado were merged at the beginning of the manuscript, so I have added the name Diego to eliminate the confusion.

71. MS: "y soldados çiento dexaron." I follow Revillagigedo (*apud* Ruidíaz, *La Florida*, 1: 104).

72. MS: "recorrio a los."

73. MS: "ellas."

74. MS: "los de mes."

75. MS: "las."

76. Here begins chapter 11 in Ruidíaz, *La Florida*, 1: 107.

77. MS: "uañando."

78. MS: "se auian."

79. MS: "que auia auido mucha gente." I follow Revillagigedo (*apud* Ruidíaz, *La Florida*, 1: 110).

80. MS: "pudiesen en contar."

81. MS: "veynte de Juan de Ribau." I follow Revillagigedo (*apud* Ruidíaz, *La Florida*, 1: 110). Ruidíaz mentions that the soldiers were two hundred, which is correct, but this figure is not found in either Ferrera (which mentions six hundred) or Revillagigedo.

82. MS: "preguntole el Adelantado que a que venia el capitan dellos, dixo que le embiaua a ver que jente era." I follow Revillagigedo (*apud* Ruidíaz, *La Florida*, 1: 111), which is more accurate.

83. MS: "moças."

84. MS: "suecedido."

85. MS: "nuestro."

86. MS: "partiose." I follow Revillagigedo (*apud* Ruidíaz, *La Florida*, 1: 115).

87. Both Revillagigedo and Ferrera have left the name of this captain blank. A later hand has supplied it in Ferrera, where this captain had already been mentioned on f. 3v*. Ruidíaz, *La Florida*, 1: 116.

88. Here begins chapter 12 in Ruidíaz, *La Florida*, 1: 119.

89. MS omits. I follow *Revillagigedo* (*apud* Ruidíaz, *La Florida*, 1: 120).

90. MS: "panizuelo."

91. MS: "a quarto de legua."

92. The word "naua" has been corrected to "nueua" by the same hand.

93. MS: "alla."

94. MS: "y a todos hizo como a los demas." I follow Revillagigedo (*apud* Ruidíaz, *La Florida*, 1: 125) to avoid repeating the verb.

95. Here begins chapter 13 in Ruidíaz, *La Florida*, 1: 127.

96. MS: "y otro dicho dia." I follow Revillagigedo (*apud* Ruidíaz, *La Florida*, 1: 127).

97. Ruidíaz is missing the words "y se fuessen," but this does not agree with Revillagigedo. Ruidíaz, *La Florida*, 1: 127.

98. MS: "los françeses y moços que se hallaron." I follow Revillagigedo (*apud* Ruidíaz, *La Florida*, 1: 128).

99. Revillagigedo: "la gente que con el esta y otras injurias como marranos españoles" (*apud* Ruidíaz, *La Florida*, 1: 128).

100. MS: "y dentro de veynte dias que esto fue fueron degollados." I follow Revillagigedo (*apud* Ruidíaz, *La Florida*, 1: 128).

101. MS: "bachana."

102. MS: "Bernabe."

103. Revillagigedo is missing these last four words, and one of them is illegible in Ferrera. Ruidíaz, *La Florida*, 1: 130.

104. MS: "otros."

105. MS: "bachana."

106. MS: "bachana."

107. MS omits. I follow Revillagigedo (*apud* Ruidíaz, *La Florida*, 1: 132).

108. MS: "bachana."

109. MS: "sanct metheo."

110. MS: "para cada dia cada soldado."

111. MS omits. I follow Revillagigedo (*apud* Ruidíaz, *La Florida*, 1: 133).

112. Ruidíaz transcribes "diez," but Revillagigedo (*apud* Ruidíaz, *La Florida*, 1: 134) agrees with Ferrera.

113. The words "acordo el" are repeated at the beginning of f. 29v, but they are not a catchword.

114. MS: "assi." I follow Revillagigedo (*apud* Ruidíaz, *La Florida*, 1: 135). The abbreviation "anS" has been expanded differently in the two manuscripts.

115. MS: "bachama."

116. MS omits. I follow Revillagigedo ((*apud* Ruidíaz, *La Florida*, 1: 135).

117. Both Revillagigedo and Ferrera have left a blank for the day of the month, which a later hand has supplied in Ferrera. Ruidíaz, *La Florida*, 1: 135.

118. MS: "para que."

119. MS omits. I follow Revillagigedo (*apud* Ruidíaz, *La Florida*, 1: 136).

120. Revillagigedo: "y escarçeo de mar y corrian en popa e proa golpes de una mar e otra" (*apud* Ruidíaz, *La Florida*, 1: 136).

121. MS: "al."

122. MS: "que el en que yua."

123. MS: "al."

124. MS omits. I follow Revillagigedo (*apud* Ruidíaz, *La Florida*, 1: 137).

125. MS: "cacaue."

126. MS omits. I follow Revillagigedo (*apud* Ruidíaz, *La Florida*, 1: 138).

127. MS: "pudian."

128. MS: "en."

129. MS omits. I follow Revillagigedo (*apud* Ruidíaz, *La Florida*, 1: 140).

130. MS: "respondioles que no los tenia dixele."

131. MS: "distincto."

132. MS: "distincto."

133. MS: "quitole."

134. MS omits. I follow Revillagigedo (*apud* Ruidíaz, *La Florida*, 1: 143).

135. MS omits. I follow the transcription in Ruidíaz, although the word does not appear in either manuscript. Ruidíaz, *La Florida*, 1: 144.

136. MS: "ba hama hazer."

137. MS: "al."

138. MS: "las."

139. MS: "a la España."

140. Here begins chapter 14 in Ruidíaz, *La Florida*, 1: 149.

141. I have followed the narrative in Revillagigedo (*apud* Ruidíaz, *La Florida*, 1: 150) because the text in Ferrera (beginning with "y cada año") is out of order. Therefore, I have taken the first three lines of f. 35r and included them before the last four lines of f. 34v.

142. MS: "que en aquel fuerte en el puerto de guale."

143. MS: "unas personas."

144. MS: "hombre la saco."

145. Ruidíaz is mistaken when he transcribes "españoles y cristianos" (*La Florida*, 1: 151).

146. MS omits. I follow Revillagigedo (*apud* Ruidíaz, *La Florida*, 1: 152).

147. MS: "todo lo que passaua y todos puestos de rodillas adoraron la cruz dando gracias a nuestro señor y dela calidad de la tierra y condicion de los yndios." I follow the order in Revillagigedo (*apud* Ruidíaz, *La Florida*, 1: 152), which seems more appropriate.

148. Ruidíaz is mistaken when he transcribes "mujeres españolas e otros cristianos" (*La Florida*, 1: 152).

149. Ruidíaz is mistaken when he transcribes "españoles" (*La Florida*, 1: 152).

150. MS: "de otro."

151. MS: "estrado para en."

152. MS: "lleuo."

153. MS: "esforcado."

154. Ruidíaz is mistaken in both instances when he transcribes "quinientos" (*La Florida*, 1: 159).

155. MS: "que a aquel cazique ni a otro ninguno."

156. MS: "de nouenta a cien y años."

157. MS: "que eran dos christianos de los cautiuos." I follow Revillagigedo (*apud* Ruidíaz, *La Florida*, 1: 160).

158. MS: "tiseras y cuchillos cascabeles."

159. MS: "dancaua."

160. Ruidíaz has transcribed "4 ó 6," but this reading is not in the manuscripts. Ruidíaz, *La Florida*, 1: 163.

161. MS: "alcosse."

162. The text that follows on ff. 41r (partially), 41v, 42r, 42v, and 43r (partially) is missing in Revillagigedo. Ruidíaz in *La Florida*, 1: 164–65, has tried to supply this information with a paragraph from Barcia's *Ensayo cronológico*, but it is now evident that the manuscript is missing two complete folios.

163. MS: "saber su hermano y los mas yndios e yndias si sabian."

164. MS: "la yndio."

165. MS: "por."

166. Ruidíaz in *La Florida*, 1: 165, has edited the text as "mucho . . . procurar," but nothing is missing in the manuscripts, and the sentence is grammatical.

167. MS: "tenian."

168. MS: "indios y con."

169. MS omits. I follow Revillagigedo (*apud* Ruidíaz, *La Florida*, 1: 168).

170. MS: "porque si se."

171. MS: "Bachama."

172. MS: "los." I follow Revillagigedo (*apud* Ruidíaz, *La Florida*, 1: 168).

173. Here begins chapter 15 in Ruidíaz, *La Florida*, 1: 169.

174. MS: "camperche."

175. Both manuscripts omit the given name of Francisco de Toral, which I have supplied.

176. MS omits. I follow Revillagigedo (*apud* Ruidíaz, *La Florida*, 1: 169).

177. MS: "Julian."

178. Revillagigedo: "trece" (*apud* Ruidíaz, *La Florida*, 1: 169). On f. 46v we are reminded that the Adelantado has left three hundred men with Captain Medrano, so the figure in Ferrera is correct.

179. MS: "mas."

180. Both manuscripts omit the name Pedro, but a later hand has supplied it in Ferrera.

181. MS omits. I follow Revillagigedo (*apud* Ruidíaz, *La Florida*, 1: 170).

182. MS: "y ordenadas yendo y llegando." I follow Revillagigedo (*apud* Ruidíaz, *La Florida*, 1: 170).

183. MS: "la barca todos y el maestro de campo." The word "todos" has been added by a later hand in Ferrera, but I follow Revillagigedo (*apud* Ruidíaz, *La Florida*, 1: 172).

184. MS: "hizo descargo." I follow Revillagigedo (*apud* Ruidíaz, *La Florida*, 1: 172).

185. MS: "venidera." I follow Revillagigedo (*apud* Ruidíaz, *La Florida*, 1: 172).

186. MS: "los."

187. MS: "podria."

188. MS: "ataron." I follow Revillagigedo (*apud* Ruidíaz, *La Florida*, 1: 172).

189. Here begins chapter 16 in Ruidíaz, *La Florida*, 1: 175.

190. MS: "fue casado pensado y tratado doble." I follow Revillagigedo (*apud* Ruidíaz, *La Florida*, 1: 175).

191. MS: "Gancalo."

192. MS: "adrecar."

193. MS: "lo."

194. MS: "vino con la fragata." I follow Revillagigedo (*apud* Ruidíaz, *La Florida*, 1: 179).

195. MS: "los."

196. MS: "biuuir."

197. MS: "Goncalo."

198. A later hand in Ferrera has filled in the name "de Ledesma," then crossed it out and corrected it to "de Ganboa." Francisco de Ledesma is the recipient of a letter (Archivo de Simancas, Sala de Guerra, inventario 1, legajo 65) written by the Adelantado on 13 May 1557. Ruidíaz, *La Florida*, 2: 21–22; Mercado, *Cartas*, 89–90.

199. Revillagigedo is missing two folios, which correspond to the last lines of f. 47v and ff. 48r, 48v, and half of 49r in Ferrera. Ruidíaz, as usual, has supplied some of the text from Barcia's *Ensayo cronológico* in *La Florida*, 1: 180–84.

200. MS: "compania."

201. MS: "Goncalo."

202. MS: "Santa Elena."

203. MS: "tambien."

204. MS: "españa."

205. MS: "passeauan."

206. MS: "francisco perez e otros escriuian destos que auian hecho flaqueza tan perjudiciales." In Ferrera, the words "e otros" have been corrected by a later hand. Revilla-

gigedo: "querian ir a poblar e por estos cuentos que decian por las cartas que el capitan san vicente e fernando perez su alferez e otros escribian" (*apud* Ruidíaz, *La Florida*, 1: 186). Notice that the name of the ensign is wrong in Ferrera.

207. MS: "a a ella."

208. Here begins chapter 17 in Ruidíaz, *La Florida*, 1: 189.

209. MS: "me case fuera de la ley de graçia." Ferrera did not understand the words "abra de graçia," which refer to the French town of Havre de Grace, and left a blank, "me case . . . gracia." A later hand supplied the words "fuera de la ley," missing the point altogether. Revillagigedo has the name correctly (*apud* Ruidíaz, *La Florida*, 1: 191).

210. MS: "villaganon."

211. Some words are missing from Ferrera where there is a hole in f. 51r, but these are easy to supply from Revillagigedo (*apud* Ruidíaz, *La Florida*, 1: 191).

212. MS: "les."

213. MS omits. I follow Revillagigedo (*apud* Ruidíaz, *La Florida*, 1: 192).

214. Ruidíaz, *La Florida*, 1: 192, transcribes "alababan"—they praised—which does not make sense.

215. MS: "acudieron."

216. Revillagigedo is missing two folios, which correspond to ff. 51v (last two lines), 52r, 52v, 53r, and 53v (first four words) in Ferrera. Ruidíaz, *La Florida*, 1: 194–95, has supplied some of the text with a paragraph from Barcia's *Ensayo cronológico*.

217. The acidity of the ink has damaged the manuscript and one or two words are missing, although the sentence seems unaltered.

218. MS: "que los françeses con quinze personas dentro hauian llegado."

219. MS: "a aquellos."

220. MS: "labrancas."

221. MS: "pudiessen."

222. MS: "oristan."

223. MS omits. I follow Revillagigedo (*apud* Ruidíaz, *La Florida*, 1: 192).

224. Revillagigedo is missing two folios, which correspond to ff. 56v (except first four lines), 57r, 57v, and 58r (except last four lines) in Ferrera. Ruidíaz, *La Florida*, 1: 203–8, has supplied some of the text from Barcia's *Ensayo cronológico*, including a chapter division (chapter 18).

225. MS: "mayz y vellota pescado y ostrias cozido y assado."

226. MS: "camuças."

227. MS: "tienen."

228. MS: "alonso gomez." See the name of this captain on f. 82r below.

229. Here begins chapter 18 in Ruidíaz, *La Florida*, 1: 207, although his text has been taken from Barcia's *Ensayo cronológico*.

230. MS: "verso."

231. MS: "cacique que las."

232. MS: "quedado en hora buena." I follow Revillagigedo (*apud* Ruidíaz, *La Florida*, 1: 210).

233. MS: "con ello al adelantado y quando." I follow Revillagigedo (*apud* Ruidíaz, *La Florida*, 1: 211).

234. MS: "los."

235. MS: "dezian a aquellas."

236. Here begins chapter 19 in Ruidíaz, *La Florida*, 1: 213.

237. MS: "dandoles."

238. MS omits. I follow Revillagigedo (*apud* Ruidíaz, *La Florida*, 1: 215).

239. Here begins chapter 20 in Ruidíaz, *La Florida*, 1: 217.

240. MS: "se que quemo."

241. MS: "hacen."

242. MS omits. I follow Revillagigedo (*apud* Ruidíaz, *La Florida*, 1: 220).

243. MS: "los."

244. The words "dentro de ocho dias" are repeated at the beginning of 63v.

245. MS omits. I follow Revillagigedo (*apud* Ruidíaz, *La Florida*, 1: 224).

246. MS omits. I follow Revillagigedo (*apud* Ruidíaz, *La Florida*, 1: 225).

247. MS: "fuessse."

248. The ink has damaged the manuscript. I follow Revillagigedo (*apud* Ruidíaz, *La Florida*, 1: 228).

249. MS: "querian."

250. MS: "del buen entendimiento y del buen entendimiento de ella." The same hand has amended the text.

251. MS: "los."

252. MS: "y metio en el aposento donde estaua una vela encendida y el Adelantado." I follow Revillagigedo (*apud* Ruidíaz, *La Florida*, 1: 230).

253. MS omits. I follow Revillagigedo (*apud* Ruidíaz, *La Florida*, 1: 230).

254. MS: "el."

255. MS: "espertaua."

256. Revillagigedo is missing one folio (from halfway down f. 67v to the first few lines of f. 68v in Ferrera), for which Ruidíaz in *La Florida*, 1: 207, has supplied eight lines from Barcia's *Ensayo cronológico*.

257. MS: "nungun."

258. MS: "junio." The scribe has corrected it to "julio," which coincides with Revillagigedo (*apud* Ruidíaz, *La Florida*, 1: 235).

259. Here begins chapter 21 in Ruidíaz, *La Florida*, 1: 237.

260. MS: "en."

261. MS: "bendaño." Revillagigedo: "bendaña" (*apud* Ruidíaz, *La Florida*, 1: 239).

262. MS omits. I follow Revillagigedo (*apud* Ruidíaz, *La Florida*, 1: 240).

263. MS: "dos."

264. MS: "del."

265. MS: "estemos."

266. Revillagigedo is missing one folio (from the last lines of f. 71v to the last lines of f. 72v in Ferrera), for which Ruidíaz, *La Florida*, 1: 244, has supplied two lines from Barcia's *Ensayo cronológico*.

267. MS: "cuba y que."

268. MS: "teniendo." I follow Revillagigedo (*apud* Ruidíaz, *La Florida*, 1: 245).

269. Here begins chapter 22 in Ruidíaz, *La Florida*, 1: 247.

270. MS: "y que con."

271. MS: "dos naos la capitana y otras dos mayores."

272. MS: "çorita."

273. MS: "una aguja."

274. MS: "Ahotina."

275. MS omits. I follow Revillagigedo (*apud* Ruidíaz, *La Florida*, 1: 249).

276. MS omits. I follow Revillagigedo (*apud* Ruidíaz, *La Florida*, 1: 249).

277. MS: "querian."

278. MS: "fueron y los."

279. MS: "empecarian."

280. MS: "la aguja."

281. MS: "Galabay."

282. MS: "Hotina."

283. MS: "a."

284. MS: "ontina."

285. Ruidíaz, *La Florida*, 1: 258, transcribes "al fuerte . . . escondidos," but nothing is missing in the manuscripts.

286. MS: "vicioosa."

287. MS: "y."

288. MS omits. I follow Revillagigedo (*apud* Ruidíaz, *La Florida*, 1: 260).

289. MS: "los."

290. MS: "que esta questa." I follow Revillagigedo (*apud* Ruidíaz, *La Florida*, 1: 260).

291. MS omits. I follow Revillagigedo (*apud* Ruidíaz, *La Florida*, 1: 261).

292. MS: "luguar teniente."

293. MS: "consigo a los."

294. Revillagigedo: "ciento y cincuenta soldados" (*apud* Ruidíaz, *La Florida*, 1: 262).

295. Here begins chapter 23 in Ruidíaz, *La Florida*, 1: 263.

296. MS: "distinto."

297. MS: "rodrauan."

298. MS: "llegar."

299. MS: "alameña."

300. Here begins chapter 24 in Ruidíaz, *La Florida*, 1: 267.

301. MS: "de otra el." The words "de otra" have been written above the line but are superfluous, for there would be seven vessels, not six, besides the frigate and the brigantine.

302. MS: "rodrauan."

303. MS: "varrada."

304. MS: "seys mill."

305. MS: "presidentes."

306. MS: "señor que tenia."

307. The original spelling was "estorciones," but the same hand has corrected it to "estorsiones."

308. MS: "su magd."

309. MS: "acucar."

310. MS: "aeesta."

311. The original phrase was "partiose el Adelantado," but the same hand has amended it to "partiose la armada."

312. MS: "entra."

313. MS: "uista."

314. Revillagigedo is missing two folios, for which Ruidíaz has supplied five lines from Barcia's *Ensayo cronológico*. The original text in Ferrera ranges from f. 83r (except the first few lines) to the first few lines of f. 85r.

315. MS: "acucares."

316. MS: "yndias de frança."

317. The original word was "que," but the same hand has amended it to "y."

318. MS: "sobrinos."

319. MS: "çriado."

320. MS: "cabecas."

321. Revillagigedo, f. 92r (*apud* Ruidíaz, *La Florida*, 1: 272) omits: ". . . de Godoy." The Ferrera scribe has left a blank: "por capitan dellos a . . . diego doy," and a later hand has inserted "el capitan." Interestingly enough, in a letter written by Pedro Menéndez to the Crown on 29 November 1566, we find the same wording, "y por capitán dellos a . . . de Godoy." Ruidíaz, *La Florida*, 2: 165. Mercado's transcription of this letter in *Cartas*, 203, is a literal copy of the text in Ruidíaz, so the name is also left blank.

322. MS: "bronço."

323. MS: "mancanilla."

324. MS: "bayan."

325. Both manuscripts omit. Ruidíaz, *La Florida*, 1: 273, transcribes "a . . . de enero," as does Ferrera, although in this manuscript a later hand has inserted "los primeros."

326. This is the only instance in the manuscript in which a number has been indicated in Roman numerals, "xx."

327. MS: "bayan."

328. The name of the harbor and the date of the Adelantado's arrival in Havana have been left blank in both manuscripts, and the person who corrected specific instances in Ferrera did not amend the text here. Ruidíaz, *La Florida*, 1: 273.

329. The original word was "tres," but the same hand has amended it to "dos."

330. MS: "que auian traydo y la nao."

331. MS: "bayan."

332. MS: "el."

333. Both manuscripts omit this sentence, leaving a blank, but a later hand has completed the sentence in Ferrera: "que fuese luego con su jente y."

334. MS: "el."

335. Here begins chapter 25 in Ruidíaz, *La Florida*, 1: 277. Both manuscripts omit the sentence "hasta la laguna maymi," which a later hand has supplied in Ferrera.

336. Revillagigedo: "llegada la india en el bergantin a la habana" (*apud* Ruidíaz, *La Florida*, 1: 279).

337. MS omits. I follow Revillagigedo (*apud* Ruidíaz, *La Florida*, 1: 280).

338. Both manuscripts omit this fact. A later hand has filled in "la nueua espa" in Ferrera. Ruidíaz transcribes "que fue a . . . y le había dado" (*La Florida*, 1: 280).

339. MS: "compania."

340. The word "doña" is repeated at the end of f. 88v and the beginning of 89r, but it is not a catchword.

341. MS: "yndias."

342. MS: "yndias."

343. MS: "renidos."

344. Revillagigedo: "e otros dos indios e tres indias" (*apud* Ruidíaz, *La Florida*, 1: 284).

345. MS: "el."

346. MS: "lago." I follow Revillagigedo (*apud* Ruidíaz, *La Florida*, 1: 285).

347. MS: "tauila."

348. MS omits. I follow Revillagigedo (*apud* Ruidíaz, *La Florida*, 1: 287).

349. MS: "al."

350. MS: "quedaua."

351. MS: "carlos y acerto."

352. MS omits. I follow Revillagigedo (*apud* Ruidíaz, *La Florida*, 1: 292).

353. MS: "a abraços."

354. MS: "embarcar y para."

355. MS omits. I follow Revillagigedo (*apud* Ruidíaz, *La Florida*, 1: 293).

356. MS omits. I follow Revillagigedo (*apud* Ruidíaz, *La Florida*, 1: 294).

357. Ruidíaz, *La Florida*, 1: 295, transcribes "que se llamaba . . . , caballero de Trujillo," with an ellipsis where both manuscripts have "Hulano."

358. MS omits. I follow Revillagigedo (*apud* Ruidíaz, *La Florida*, 1: 295–96).

359. MS: "recogio y en."

360. Both manuscripts omit, but a later hand in Ferrera has added "a pedro pacheco buen soldado." The name is correct, and it refers to Pedro Gutiérrez Pacheco. Ruidíaz, *La Florida*, 2: 480.

361. MS: "el."

362. MS omits. I follow Revillagigedo (*apud* Ruidíaz, *La Florida*, 1: 298).

363. MS: "mocoya que lleuaua."

364. Revillagigedo: "se queria ir a san agustin" (*apud* Ruidíaz, *La Florida*, 1: 298). Both statements are correct. A few lines later, at the beginning of f. 97r, Menéndez tells his men that he is going to Spain ("él se había de partir luego a España"), but at the end of f. 97v we are told that the adelantado visits St. Augustine before going to Spain.

365. MS omits. I follow Revillagigedo (*apud* Ruidíaz, *La Florida*, 1: 299).

366. MS omits. I follow Revillagigedo (*apud* Ruidíaz, *La Florida*, 1: 299).

367. MS: "que."

368. MS omits these four insertions. I follow Revillagigedo (*apud* Ruidíaz, *La Florida*, 1: 300).

369. Here begins chapter 26 in Ruidíaz, *La Florida*, 1: 303.

370. MS: "puerto." I follow Revillagigedo (*apud* Ruidíaz, *La Florida*, 1: 305).

371. MS omits. I follow Revillagigedo (*apud* Ruidíaz, *La Florida*, 1: 305).

372. MS: "fuerça."

373. MS: "joada."

374. Here begins chapter 27 in Ruidíaz, *La Florida*, 1: 307.

375. The words "que tenian" are repeated at the end of f. 99r and the beginning of f. 99v, but not as a catchword.

376. Here begins chapter 28 in Ruidíaz, *La Florida*, 1: 309.

377. MS: "Espero." Revillagigedo: "Copero" (*apud* Ruidíaz, *La Florida*, 1: 309).

378. Revillagigedo: "Alonso" (*apud* Ruidíaz, *La Florida*, 1: 309).

379. Both manuscripts leave a blank for the given names of Pedro de Ayala, Diego de Salcedo, and the unknown licentiate. A later hand in Ferrera has added "Pedro" and "Diego" for the first two but has left the licentiate's name blank.

380. Revillagigedo: "melro" (*apud* Ruidíaz, *La Florida*, 1: 309).

381. MS: "enrriquez citados eran."

382. MS: "topan dos."

383. MS: "veyntiocho." I follow Revillagigedo (*apud* Ruidíaz, *La Florida*, 1: 311) because if Pedro Menéndez had sailed for twenty-eight leagues, he would have found himself in Avilés and not in the Bay of the Concha de Artedo, which is at a distance of twenty-five leagues from La Coruña.

384. MS: "en ellos que ni batel."

385. MS: "borde."

386. MS: "carmesi y con estandarte."

387. Here begins chapter 29 in Ruidíaz, *La Florida*, 1: 313. According to Ruidíaz, Revillagigedo would be missing information at the end of this "chapter," transcribing "y se admiraban . . . navegar tanta mar en tan pequeño bajel; e cierto es una de las cosas . . . que hasta hoy en la mar se han visto." Apart from the fact that the sentences are grammatically correct for the Spanish of the time, the discovery of the Ferrera copy proves that, indeed, nothing is missing in this folio.

388. MS: "tanto gallardete y piecas." I follow Revillagigedo (*apud* Ruidíaz, *La Florida*, 1: 315).

389. The following paragraph is left blank in Ruidíaz, *La Florida*, 1: 316, because the text is very difficult to read in Revillagigedo, f. 108r.

390. MS: "jornanda."

391. The following paragraph is left blank in Ruidíaz, *La Florida*, 1: 317–18, because the text is very difficult to read in Revillagigedo, f. 108r. The paragraph in Ruidíaz following this one has been supplied from Barcia's *Ensayo cronológico*, although Ruidíaz made a mistake in his edition and did not signal the beginning of this paragraph but only the end.

392. MS omits these last two instances. I follow Revillagigedo (*apud* Ruidíaz, *La Florida*, 1: 318).

393. MS: "enclauando."

394. MS: "esta."

395. This is the abrupt end of Revillagigedo (f. 109v). In his edition, Ruidíaz does not finish the sentence "los cuales entretenía como . . ." and supplies chapters 30 to 33 (*La Florida*, 1: 320–26), with text from Barcia's *Ensayo cronológico*. What follows in Ferrera corresponds to chapter 8 in Ruidíaz, a passage that is missing in Revillagigedo, and chapter 7 in Ruidíaz, in that order. Note that the text of the following five paragraphs in Ferrera has already appeared, with some changes, on ff. 1r–1v.

396. Here begins chapter 8 in Ruidíaz, *La Florida*, 1: 55–58, which is made up of text from Revillagigedo and from Barcia's *Ensayo cronológico*, to supply what the editor thought was missing.

397. MS: "forcoso."

398. MS omits. I follow Revillagigedo (*apud* Ruidíaz, *La Florida*, 1: 55).

399. MS omits. I follow Revillagigedo (*apud* Ruidíaz, *La Florida*, 1: 56).

400. MS: "luetranos."

401. MS: "real consejo del estado de guerra."

402. MS: "pateges."

403. MS: "los yndias."

404. MS omits. I follow Revillagigedo (*apud* Ruidíaz, *La Florida*, 1: 57).

405. MS: "florida y que se."

406. What is left of chapter 8, and all of chapter 9, is supplied in Ruidíaz, *La Florida*, 1: 57–67, from Barcia's *Ensayo cronológico*. The following paragraph in Ferrera does not appear in Revillagigedo.

407. MS: "vanegas."

408. MS: "magestad y habia."

409. Here begins chapter 7 in Ruidíaz, but the order is incorrect. Ferrera omits. I follow Revillagigedo (*apud* Ruidíaz, *La Florida*, 1: 51).

410. MS omits in these last two instances. I follow Revillagigedo (*apud* Ruidíaz, *La Florida*, 1: 51).

411. MS omits. I follow Revillagigedo (*apud* Ruidíaz, *La Florida*, 1: 52).

412. This is the end of chapter 7 in Ruidíaz, and in Ferrera the end of the narrative by Solís de Merás; what follows is the "Relación" and the letters included on ff. 109r–117v. As I have discussed in the introduction, if we were to follow the order proposed by Ruidíaz, the comment "as is mentioned before" would be out of place.

413. MS: "Puerto dela nueba es Paña."

414. MS: "al."

415. MS: "al."

416. MS: "liquidarban."

417. MS: "cauarias."

418. The word "yslas" has appeared as a catchword at the end of f. 109v.

419. MS: "panico."

420. MS: "pueblos que tiene."

421. MS: "los."

422. MS: "joada."

423. MS: "costa a vuestra."

424. The words "de todo" have appeared as a catchword at the end of f. 110r.

425. The words "que si" have appeared as a catchword at the end of f. 110v.

426. MS: "los."

427. The word "que" has appeared as a catchword at the end of f. 111r.

428. MS: "applantar."

429. MS: "riquecas."

430. The words "y sin" have appeared as a catchword at the end of f. 111v.

431. MS: "sealcaran."

432. The letters "-taleças" appear as a catchword on f. 112r and are repeated at the beginning of 112v.

433. The manuscript includes here the letters mentioned in the introduction, which we do not transcribe for reasons of space and because they can be found elsewhere. For the titles and contents of these letters, see the introduction.

Bibliography

Aguilar Sosa, Yanet. "La bibliofilia mexicana puede dejar su tragedia." *El Universal*, 8 February 2011. eluniversal.com.mx/cultura/64749.html.

Álvarez de la Rivera, Senén. *Biblioteca histórico-genealógica asturiana*. 3 vols. Santiago de Chile, 1924.

Barcia Carballido y Zúñiga, Andrés González de. *Ensayo cronológico para la historia general de la Florida: Contiene los descubrimientos y principales sucesos acaecidos en este gran reino a los españoles, franceses, suecos, dinamarqueses, ingleses y otras naciones entre sí y con los indios, cuyas costumbres, genios, idolatría, gobierno, batallas y astucias se refieren, y los viajes de algunos capitanes y pilotos por el Mar del Norte a buscar paso a Oriente o unión de aquella tierra con Asia; Desde el año 1512 que descubrió La Florida Juan Ponce de León hasta el de 1722, escrito por D. Gabriel de Cárdenas y Cano*. 1723. Madrid: Hijos de Catalina Piñuela, 1829.

Barrientos, Bartolomé de. *Life and Deeds of Pedro Menéndez de Avilés, Knight of the Order of Santiago, Captain General of Florida, wherein at Length Are Discussed the Conquests and Settlements of the Province of Florida and How They Were Liberated from the Lutherans Who Had Taken Power of Them: Composed by Master Barrientos, Professor of Salamanca*. In Callahan, *Menéndez de Avilés*, 245–396.

———. *Pedro Menéndez de Avilés, Founder of Florida, Written by Bartolomé Barrientos*. See Kerrigan, *Pedro Menéndez de Avilés*.

———. *Vida y hechos de Pedro Menéndez de Avilés*. In Crespo-Francés y Valero, *Don Pedro Menéndez de Avilés*, 251–379.

———. *Vida y hechos de Pedro Menéndez de Avilés*. See Martínez, *Vida y hechos*.

———. *Vida y hechos de Pero Menéndez de Avilés, caballero de la Orden de Santiago, Adelantado de la Florida, donde largamente se tratan las conquistas y poblaciones de la provincia de la Florida, y cómo fueron libradas de los luteranos que de ellas se habían apoderado*. In Mercado, *Menéndez de Avilés*, 233–376.

———. *Vida y hechos de Pero Menéndez de Avilés, Cavallero de la Hordem de Sanctiago, Adelantado de la Florida: Do largamente se tratan las conquistas y poblaciones de la provincia de la Florida, y cómo fueron libradas de los luteranos que dellas se avían apoderado*. In García, *Dos antiguas relaciones*, 1–152.

Bennett, Charles E. *Laudonnière and Fort Caroline: History and Documents*. Gainesville: University of Florida Press, 1964.

Blasco Martínez, Rosa María. *Una aproximación a la institución notarial en Cantabria.* Santander: Universidad de Cantabria, 1990.

Callahan, Laura, trans. *Menéndez de Avilés and La Florida: Chronicles of His Expeditions.* Edited by Juan Carlos Mercado. Lewiston, N.Y.: Edwin Mellen Press, 2010.

Cancio, Lorenzo de. *Cartas de Lorenzo de Cancio sobre la gobernación de Coahuila, 1761–1764.* Edited by Elviro Martínez. Monumenta Histórica Asturiensia 32. Gijón: Auseva, 1993.

Cappelli, Adriano. *Cronologia, cronografia, e calendario perpetuo: Dal principio dell'èra cristiana ai nostri giorni.* Edited by Marino Viganò. Milan: Ulrico Hoepli, 1998.

Cárdenas y Cano, Gabriel de [pseud.]. *See* Barcia.

Connor, Jeannette Thurber, trans. *Pedro Menéndez de Avilés, Adelantado, Governor, and Captain-General of Florida: Memorial,* by Gonzalo Solís de Merás. DeLand: Florida State Historical Society, 1923.

Cowley, Rafael, and Andrés Pego, eds. *Los tres primeros historiadores de la isla de Cuba.* 3 vols. Havana: Andrés Pego, 1876–77.

Crespo-Francés y Valero, José Antonio. *Don Pedro Menéndez de Avilés: Deuda histórica con un soldado ignorado de Felipe II.* Madrid: Safel, 2000.

Cuevas, Mariano. *Historia de la iglesia en México.* 5 vols. Mexico City: Patricio Sanz, 1921–26.

Davis, Frederick T. "Ponce de Leon's First Voyage and Discovery of Florida." *Florida Historical Society Quarterly* 14, no. 1 (1935): 7–49.

Deagan, Kathleen, ed. *Puerto Real: The Archaeology of a Sixteenth-Century Spanish Town in Hispaniola.* Gainesville: University Press of Florida, 1995.

Elliott, J. H. *Empires of the Atlantic World: Britain and Spain in America, 1492–1830.* New Haven, Conn.: Yale University Press, 2006.

Escalante Fontaneda, Hernando. *Memoir of Hernando de Escalante Fontaneda.* Edited and translated by Buckingham Smith. St. Augustine, Fla., 1861.

Fernández de Oviedo, Gonzalo. *Sumario de la natural y general historia de las Indias.* 1526. Madrid: Confederación Española de Gremios y Asociaciones de Libreros, 1992.

Ferrera manuscript. *See* Solís de Merás.

Fuente, Alejandro de la. *Havana and the Atlantic in the Sixteenth Century.* Chapel Hill: University of North Carolina Press, 2008.

Gagliardi, Donatella. "La biblioteca de Bartolomé Barrientos, maestro de artes liberales." *Studia Aurea: Revista de Literatura Española y Teoría Literaria del Renacimiento y Siglo de Oro* 1 (2007): N.p.

Gallardo, Bartolomé José. *Ensayo de una biblioteca española de libros raros y curiosos.* 4 vols. Madrid: Rivadeneyra, 1863–66.

Gannon, Michael V., ed. *The New History of Florida.* Gainesville: University Press of Florida, 1996.

———. Prologue to Manucy, *Menéndez,* n.p.

García, Genaro, ed. *Dos antiguas relaciones de la Florida.* México: J. Aguilar Vera, 1902.

Gómez Tabanera, José Manuel, ed. *Pedro Menéndez de Avilés y la conquista de la Florida (1565),* by Gonzalo Solís de Merás. Oviedo: Grupo Editorial Asturiano, 1990.

González de Barcia Carballido y Zúñiga, Andrés. *See* Barcia.

Grajales, Francisco López de Mendoza. *See* Mendoza.

Hoffman, Paul E. *Florida's Frontiers*. Bloomington: Indiana University Press, 2002.

Hudson, Charles. *The Juan Pardo Expeditions: Exploration of the Carolinas and Tennessee, 1566–1568*. 1990. Tuscaloosa: University of Alabama Press, 2005.

Iglesias Gómez, Laura María. *La transferencia de tecnología agronómica de España a América de 1492 a 1598*. Madrid: Ministerio de Industria, Turismo y Comercio, 2008.

Illescas, Gonzalo de. *Segunda parte de la historia pontifical y católica*. 1573. Madrid: Melchor Sánchez, 1652.

Kerrigan, Anthony, ed. and trans. *Pedro Menéndez de Avilés, Founder of Florida, Written by Bartolomé Barrientos*. Gainesville: University of Florida Press, 1965.

Kolars, Frank. *The Sea Tiger: The Story of Pedro Menéndez*. New York: Hawthorn, 1963.

Laudonnière, René Goulaine de. *Three Voyages*. Edited and translated by Charles E. Bennett. Gainesville: University Presses of Florida, 1975.

Léry, Jean de. *Histoire d'un voyage fait en la terre du Brésil, autrement dite Amérique*. La Rochelle: Antoine Chuppin, 1578.

———. *History of a Voyage to the Land of Brazil*. Edited and translated by Janet Whatley. Berkeley: University of California Press, 1990.

López de Mendoza Grajales, Francisco. *See* Mendoza Grajales.

López y Sebastián, Lorenzo E., and Justo L. del Río Moreno. "La ganadería vacuna en la isla Española (1508–1587)." *Revista Complutense de Historia de América* 25 (1999): 11–49.

Lowery, Woodbury. *The Spanish Settlements within the Present Limits of the United States: Florida, 1562–1574*. 1905. New York: Russell and Russell, 1959.

Lugo, Américo. *Historia de Santo Domingo desde el 1556 hasta 1608*. Santo Domingo: Librería Dominicana, 1952.

Lyon, Eugene. *The Enterprise of Florida: Pedro Menéndez de Avilés and the Spanish Conquest of 1565–1568*. Gainesville: University Presses of Florida, 1976.

———. "The Florida Mutineers, 1566–67." *Tequesta* 44 (1984): 44–61.

———, ed. *Pedro Menéndez de Avilés*. Spanish Borderlands Sourcebooks 24. New York: Garland, 1995.

Manucy, Albert C. *Menéndez: Pedro Menéndez de Avilés, Captain General of the Ocean Sea*. 1965. Sarasota, Fla.: Pineapple Press, 1992.

Martínez, Elviro, ed. *Vida y hechos de Pedro Menéndez de Avilés*, by Bartolomé de Barrientos. Monumenta Histórica Asturiensia 31. Gijón: Auseva, 1993.

Martínez Navas, Isabel. *Gobierno y administración de la ciudad de Logroño en el Antiguo Régimen: Ordenanzas municipales de los siglos XVI y XVII*. Logroño: Gobierno de La Rioja; Madrid: Instituto Nacional de Administración Pública, 2001.

McCarthy, Kevin M. *Native Americans in Florida*. Sarasota, Fla.: Pineapple Press, 1999.

McEwan, Bonnie G., ed. *The Spanish Missions of La Florida*. Gainesville: University Press of Florida, 1993.

Mellén Blanco, Francisco. *Pedro Menéndez de Avilés, Adelantado de la Florida: Datos genealógicos y nuevos documentos*. Madrid: Versus, 2011.

Mendoza Grajales, Fray Martín Francisco López de. *The Founding of Saint Augustine at Nombre de Dios: America's First Mission, 400 Years Ago, September 8, 1565*. St. Augustine, Fla.: St. Augustine Foundation, 1964.

———. *The Founding of St. Augustine: Memoir of the Happy Result and Prosperous Voy-*

age of the Fleet Commanded by the Illustrious Captain-General Pedro Menéndez de Avilés . . . Old South Leaflets 4.89. Boston: Directors of the Old South Work, 1897.

———. "Memoire of the Happy Result." In Bennett, *Laudonnière and Fort Caroline*, 141–63.

———. "Relación de la jornada de Pedro Menéndez de Avilés en la Florida." In Ruidíaz, *La Florida*, 2: 431–65.

———. "Relación de la jornada de Pedro Menéndez en la Florida." In *Colección de documentos inéditos relativos al descubrimiento, conquista y colonización de las posesiones españolas en América y Oceanía, sacados en su mayor parte del Real Archivo de Indias*, 3: 441–79. Madrid: Imprenta de Manuel B. de Quirós, 1865.

———. *They Came and Remained.* Saint Leo, Fla.: Abbey Press, 1964.

Mercado, Juan Carlos, ed. *Cartas sobre la Florida (1555–1574).* Madrid: Iberoamericana, 2002.

———, ed. *Menéndez de Avilés y La Florida: Crónicas de sus expediciones.* Lewiston, N.Y.: Edwin Mellen Press, 2006.

———. *See also* Callahan, *Menéndez de Avilés.*

Miguel Vigil, Ciriaco. *Noticias biográfico-genealógicas de Pedro Menéndez de Avilés, primer adelantado y conquistador de la Florida.* Avilés: La Unión, 1892.

Milanich, Jerald T. *The Timucua.* Oxford: Blackwell, 1999.

Milanich, Jerald T., and Susan Milbrath, eds. *First Encounters: Spanish Explorations in the Caribbean and the United States, 1492–1570.* Gainesville: University of Florida Press, 1989.

Molina Solís, Juan Francisco. *Historia de Yucatán desde la dominación española.* 3 vols. Mérida, Yucatán: Lotería del Estado, 1904.

Moore, Charles B. "Pedro Menéndez de Avilés y la tradición del modelo ficticio del conquistador en el *Memorial* de Gonzalo Solís de Merás (1565)." *Taller de Letras* 45 (2009): 103–18.

———. "La tradición literaria de las relaciones asociadas con el viaje de Pedro Menéndez de Avilés al sureste de Norteamérica en 1565." *Revista de Historia de América* 133 (2003): 103–23.

Pérez Bustamante, Ciriaco. "Fr. Bartolomé de Barrientos y su *Vida y hechos de Pedro Menéndez de Avilés.*" *Revista de Indias* 1 (1940): 73–88.

Pérez Mallaína, Pablo E. *Spain's Men of the Sea: Daily Life on the Indies Fleets in the Sixteenth Century.* Translated by Carla Rahn Phillips. Baltimore: Johns Hopkins University Press, 1998.

Pezuela, Jacobo de la, ed. *Ensayo histórico de la isla de Cuba.* New York: Imprenta Española de R. Rafael, 1842.

Pickett, Margaret F., and Dwayne W. Pickett. *The European Struggle to Settle North America: Colonizing Attempts by England, France, and Spain, 1521–1608.* Jefferson, N.C.: McFarland, 2011.

Revillagigedo manuscript. *See* Solís de Merás.

Ribault, Jean. *The Whole & True Discouerye of Terra Florida: A Facsimile Reprint of the London Edition of 1563.* DeLand: Florida State Historical Society, 1923. Reprint, Gainesville: University of Florida Press, 1964.

Roberts, Russell. *Pedro Menéndez de Avilés.* Bear, Del.: Mitchell Lane, 2003.

Ruidíaz y Caravia, Eugenio, ed. *La Florida: Su conquista y colonización por Pedro Menéndez de Avilés (Memorial que hizo el Dr. Gonzalo Solís de Merás de todas las jornadas y sucesos del adelantado Pedro Menéndez de Avilés, su cuñado, y de la conquista de la Florida; Cartas de Pedro Menéndez de Avilés; Bibliografía de la antigua Florida).* 2 vols. Madrid: Hijos de J. A. García, 1893.

Sánchez-Prieto Borja, Pedro. *Cómo editar los textos medievales: Criterios para su presentación gráfica.* Madrid: Arco, 1998.

Smith, Buckingham. *Colección de varios documentos para la historia de la Florida y tierras adyacentes.* London: Trübner; Madrid: José Rodríguez, 1857.

Solís de Merás, Gonzalo. "Conquista de la Florida." Manuscript in the archives of the marqués de Ferrera. Edited and translated in this volume.

———. Untitled *memorial.* Manuscript in the archives of the conde de Revillagigedo. Edited in Gómez Tabanera, *Pedro Menéndez de Avilés*; Mercado, *Menéndez de Avilés*, 34–232; Ruidíaz, *La Florida*, 1: 1–336. Translated in Callahan, *Menéndez de Avilés*, 33–244; Connor, *Pedro Menéndez de Avilés*.

Stone, Elaine Murray. *Pedro Menéndez de Avilés and the Founding of St. Augustine.* New York: P. J. Kennedy and Sons, 1969.

Taylor, Ellen M. *Madeira: Its Scenery, and How to See It.* London: Edward Stanford, 1882.

Thompson, Bill, and Dorcas Thompson. *The Spanish Exploration of Florida.* Philadelphia: Mason Crest, 2003.

Thompson, Kathleen. *Pedro Menéndez de Avilés.* Illustrated by Charles Shaw. Austin, Tex.: Raintree Steck-Vaughn, 1991.

Utrera, Cipriano de. *Historia militar de Santo Domingo: Documentos y noticias.* 3 vols. Ciudad Trujillo: Tipografía Franciscana, 1951–53. Reprint, Santo Domingo: Sociedad Dominicana de Bibliófilos, 2014.

Williams, Eric. *From Columbus to Castro: The History of the Caribbean.* London: André Deutsch; New York, Harper & Row, 1970.

Zubillaga, Félix. *La Florida: La misión jesuítica (1566–1572) y la colonización española.* Rome: Institutum Historicum, 1941.

Index

Death: of Adelantado, 12; of Menéndez Marqués, 160; of Ribault, Jean, 72–73

Doña Antonia (Indian woman): Adelantado, sex with, 96, 98–99, 136–38, 395n113; Adelantado asked to disembark with her by, 139; Adelantado baptizing, 98; Adelantado building house for, 139; Adelantado chasing after, 97–98; Adelantado cheering up, 136–37; Adelantado needing to safely return home, 135; Adelantado resented by, 180; Carlos greeting ceremony with, 139–40; as desiring to go home, 137; as good Christian, 136; Havana returned to by, 171–72; naming of, 98; as sister of Carlos, 93–100; as wife of Adelantado, 93–100

Editorial criteria, 28–31

Emola (Chief): as Saturiwa ally, 399n154; as Saturiwa Chief, 184; Saturiwa communicating with, 185

Enemies: García Osorio and Adelantado as, 11; Guale and Orista as, 115; Saturiwa and Adelantado as, 185

Enríquez, Miguel: Adelantado denouncing and charging, 186; Adelantado disrespected by, 186; as prisoner, 188, 190; Spanish soldiers injured by, 186

Ensayo cronológico (Barcia), 16, 379n48; Ruidíaz extracting from, 18

Eraso, Cristóbal de, 142

Eraso, Francisco de, 197–98, 385n19

Escalante Fontaneda, Hernando de, 2

Fear: of Adelantado by Calibay, 155; of Adelantado by Mayaca, 153; of Adelantado by Utina, 152; of French Lutheran fortification by Adelantado, 197; and love for Adelantado, 147; of mutiny by Adelantado, 108; of Saturiwa by Calibay, 155

Fernández Guerra, Aureliano, 3

Ferrera manuscript: as complete textual witness, 22; of *Conquest of Florida* account, 3–4, 17, 22; contents of, 22–23; copying of, 27; dialect discrepancies in, 27; events reiterated in, 18–19; facsimile of, *34*, *208*; genealogical data of, 377–78n5; good condition of, 22; inconsistencies in, 25; integrity of, 25; Revillagigedo manuscript inconsistent with, 19, 378n17; Revillagigedo manuscript strongly

connected to, 26; Ribera as scribe of, 23, 207–8; translation of, 28–29

Field commander. *See* Valdés, Pedro de

Fleet of New Spain, 87, 134, 142, 143, 391n75

Fleet of Nombre de Dios. *See* Fleet of the Indies

Fleet of the Indies, 8, 384n8

Fleet of Tierra Firme, 87, 142, 143, 391n83

Flórez de Valdés, Diego, 387n33; as artillery captain, 50; French Lutherans disconcerted by, 69

Florida: Adelantado desperate to save, 135; Adelantado taking possession of, 47; Adelantado voyage from Cuba to, 84; anniversary of, 1; climate of, 201–8; crops of, 202–3; description of, 201–7, 383n98, 400n172; enterprise and sources of, 12–15; explored by soldiers, 47; French Lutherans' settling, 201–2; good qualities of, 201–8; Indians' locations in, 201; map of Spanish settlements in, *xiv*; perilous coast of, 2, 38; Philip II attempting settlement, 2; Ribault arrival in, 37; settlements of, 203, 399–400n171; sighting of, 41, 377n1, 377n2; Spanish soldiers dissatisfied with, 379n36; Spanish soldiers required to be in, 109

La Florida (Ruidíaz y Caravia), 18, 19; transcription mistakes in, 19–20

Fort Caroline: attack survived by, 379n36; capture of, 42; Charlesfort replaced by, 11; Fort of France renamed, 207. *See also* San Mateo

Fort of France, Fort Caroline renamed, 207

Fort San Felipe, 124

Fort San Juan, 188, 203

Fort San Mateo, 59–60

François, Jean: as Adelantado French captive, 50, 54, 57, 388n37; Adelantado guided by, 54; Adelantado releasing, 58; as messenger, 58

French fleet, 387n30; Madeira captured by, 163; Valdés notified of, 162–63

French Lutherans: Adelantado attacking, 45, 56–57, 204; Adelantado blocking communication between Indians and, 44; Adelantado capturing fort of, 56–60; Adelantado communicating with, 45–46, 57–58, 65–66; Adelantado driving out, 37–38; Adelantado fearing fortification by, 197; Adelantado hail-

French Lutherans—*continued*
ing, 45; Adelantado killing, 57, 68, 73;
Adelantado offered money for safety
by, 67, 71–72; Adelantado offering safe
return to France for, 58; Adelantado
showing their dead to, 70; Adelantado
surrendered to by, 67; call to arms by,
69; Catholic faith, conversion to by,
80; confessions and communion of,
80; expedition against, 74–75; as false
Christians, 25, 116, 121–22, 126; fleeing
from Adelantado, 72, 75; Flórez de
Valdés disconcerting, 69; Florida settled
by, 201–2; fortifying of, 74; great fleet
being built by, 125; Guale as friend of,
113; Guale explored by, 114; Guale fort
of, 114; identification of, 45–46; Indians
directing Adelantado to, 42–43; Indians
trusting, 206; Madeira pillaged by, 125;
Orista threatening, 115; reinforcing
for attack, 49; shipwrecked, 65; slaves
released by, 207; Spanish soldiers fortifying against, 148, 149; Spanish soldiers
killing, 56–57; Utina manipulating,
396n125; Valdés finding escaped, 61;
Valdés finding fort of, 55
Frontera, Jerez de la, 12

García, Genaro, *Vida y hechos de Pedro
Menéndez de Avilés* transcribed by, 14
García Osorio, Francisco: Adelantado
arguing with, 82, 83, 84; Adelantado
asking money and supplies from, 82;
Adelantado denied help from, 142;
as Adelantado enemy, 11; Adelantado
not welcomed by, 81–82; Adelantado
recognizing danger in, 84; Adelantado
rejected by, 82–83; Barreda imprisonment by, 181–82; as Cuban governor, 11,
81; Spanish soldiers imprisoned by, 181
Gómez, Antonio, 123
La Granja, 57, 59
Guale (Chief): Adelantado frightening, 118;
Adelantado mediating between Orista
and, 117; Adelantado promised safety by,
119; Christianity desired of, 116, 126–27;
in country of, 112–19; as friend of French
Lutherans, 113; God asked for resources
by, 126; Orista enemy of, 115
Guale: Adelantado exploring, 112, 118;
Adelantado happily received in, 115, 125,

160; Adelantado negotiating peace in,
125; Christianity in, 160; as dry land, 117;
as French land, 113; French Lutherans'
exploring, 114; French Lutheran fort in,
114; Menéndez Marques staying in, 118,
129; Ribault, Jean, shipwrecked in, 113;
starvation in, 117
Guale interpreter: Adelantado commanding killing of, 128; Adelantado converting, 117; Alas strangling, 128; as French
Lutheran, 112–13; Indians converted by,
117; as traitor, 127
Guillermo (Frenchman): Adelantado accompanied by, 115; Adelantado receiving, 114; Adelantado trusting, 127–28;
as escaped Frenchman, 114; not captive,
116; Orista daughter married to, 121; as
schooled in Latin, 114

Havana: Adelantado voyage to, 79–84, 132,
182; as capital of Cuba, 79; Doña Antonia
returning to, 171–72; Fleet of New Spain
arriving in, 134; fortification of, 163;
Spanish soldiers celebrating Adelantado
arrival to, 81, 168
Herrera, Antonio de, 2, 377n1
Herrera, Cristóbal de, 164, 397n133
High Court: Adelantado advising, 61–62,
109, 163, 167; Adelantado received by,
163–64; Ceballos protected by, 166–67
Hinestrosa, Juan de: Adelantado consoled
by, 136; as treasurer of Cuba, 81, 100, 101,
136
Hispaniola: Adelantado defending Puerto
Rico, Cuba, and, 85; Adelantado reinforcing, 162; Adelantado voyage to, 162
Historia pontifical y católica, by Illescas, 13
House of Trade, 385–86n20; Adelantado
given money by, 38, 198–99; Adelantado
violating laws of, 8–9; prisoners sent to,
108, 111
Huguenots: first massacre of, 63–69; second
massacre of, 69
Hurricane: Adelantado hit by, 39, 386n23;
ships destroyed by, 39

Illescas, Gonzalo de, *Historia pontifical y
católica* by, 13
Imprisonment: of Adelantado, 199; of
Barreda by García Osorio, 181–82; of
Enríquez, 188, 190; of Recalde, 111; of

Rodabán, 188, 190; of Spanish soldiers by García Osorio, 181

Indians: Adelantado adored by, 43, 113; Adelantado baptizing, 98; Adelantado blocking communication between French and, 44; Adelantado communicating with Santa Elena, 121; Adelantado departing with, 98; Adelantado desiring Christian conversion of, 98, 116, 122, 170, 174, 177, 205; Adelantado directed to French Lutherans by, 42–43; Adelantado elder brother of, 91, 95, 122–24, 126, 154–55, 156, 178; Adelantado feasting with, 94, 122; Adelantado feeding, 47, 113; Adelantado friendship important with, 36, 172, 174, 196–97; Adelantado giving crosses to, 99, 115–16, 129, 155, 183; Adelantado giving gifts to, 76, 93, 94, 113, 123, 124, 129, 140, 151, 153, 154, 171, 204; Adelantado guided by, 75; Adelantado informed by, 64, 69, 74, 87; Adelantado in Guale encountering, 112; Adelantado loving, 97; Adelantado protecting women of, 97–98; Adelantado requesting calm from, 152; Adelantado trusted by, 37, 123, 202; as agile, 130; Alas given money by, 90; Alas going to Havana with, 100; captains killed by, 144; Christianity desired by, 98, 116, 122, 170, 174, 177, 205; Christians transformed into, 87, 88; cross kissed by, 99, 115–17, 183; Florida locations of, 201; Fort San Mateo burned by, 129; French Lutherans trusted by, 206; Guale interpreter converting, 117; money not understood by, 91; mutinies killing, 106–7; Ochoa murdered by, 144; of San Mateo and St. Augustine as treacherous, 130; of San Mateo as confident, 130; singing as sign of respect of, 92; Spanish soldiers given food by, 158–59; Spanish soldiers mocked by, 130; Spanish soldiers well received by, 42; of Tequesta desiring Christianity, 173; Valdés meeting, 42

Indian woman. See Doña Antonia

Italian Wars: beginning of, 7; Peace of Cateau-Cambrésis ending, 10; war strategies of, 7–8

Kerrigan, Anthony, 14, 380n50, 380n54

Killing: of Adelantado, Carlos planning,

90; of captains by Indians, 144; of French Lutherans, by Adelantado, 57, 68, 73; of French Lutherans by Spanish soldiers, 56–57; of Guale interpreter, Adelantado ordering, 128; of Indians in mutinies, 106–7; of livestock by Saturiwa, 184; of Ribault, Jean, by Adelantado, 72–73; of Spanish soldiers by poison fruits, 77; of Tocobaga, desired by Carlos, 175; of Tocobaga, refused by Adelantado, 175

Language: dialect differences in Spanish, 29–30; editorial criteria of, 29–31; seventeenth-century compared to modern Spanish, 29; spelling compared to pronunciation of Spanish, 29; translation from Spanish to English, 32; variant spelling of Spanish, 29

La Parra, Juan de, 82, 83

Las Tortugas, 87, 391n82

League: as misleading, 389n54, 389n56, 389n58; as unit of measure, 384n6

Los Mártires, 87, 100

Luna y Arrellano, Tristán de, 1–2

Madeira, 394n111; French fleet captured by, 163; French Lutherans pillaging, 125; as Portuguese island, 125

Maestro de campo. See Valdés, Pedro de

Manrique de Rojas, Hernando, 10

Marriage: of Adelantado and Doña Antonia, 93; of Adelantado and Solís, 6–7; of Castillo and Ribera, I., 24; of Philip II, 8

Martínez, Elviro, *Vida y hechos de Pedro Menéndez de Avilés* edition published by, 14

Matanzas, 85, 391n78, 391n79

Mayaca (Chief): Adelantado feared by, 153; Adelantado threatened by, 154; in country of, 151–56; Saturiwa as friend of, 153; village deserted by, 153

Maymi lagoon, 154, 155, 170–71, 384n6, 396n127

Mazariegos, Diego, 114

McAlister, Lyle N., 31

Memoria del buen suçeso, 12

Memorial (Solís de Merás). See *The Conquest of Florida*

Mendoza Grajales, Francisco López de: as expedition witness, 3, 16; journal of, 12, 15, 16; as vicar, 149

San Vicente, Juan de, 35, 105, 108–10, 379n43

Saturiwa (Chief): Adelantado desiring to meet, 184; as Adelantado enemy, 185; Adelantado forgiving, 205; Adelantado returning to country of, 184; Calibay fearing, 155; Emola as ally of, 184, 399n154; Emola communicating with, 185; livestock killed by, 184; Mayaca as friend of, 153; Troche and comrade murdered by, 107; war against, 186, 187

Seville, 9, 38

Sex: Adelantado and Carlos disagreeing about, 95; between Doña Antonia and Adelantado, 96, 98–99, 136–38

Singing, as form of Indian respect, 92

Slaves, 207

Solís, Ana María de, 5–7

Solís de Merás, Gonzalo: Adelantado expedition joined by, 16; Barrientos using narrative by, 13; Bibiloteca asturiana entry on, 15; as brother-in-law of Adelantado, 3, 15; as expedition witness, 3, 16; identity discrepancy of, 16; *memorial* by, 3, 15; Ribera, D., connected to, 24; son of, 15; as University of Salamanca student, 16; unsubstantiated evidence on, 15. See also *The Conquest of Florida*

Soto, Hernando de, 1–2

Spanish exploration, narratives of, 2–3

Spanish settlements, in Florida, *xiv*

Spanish soldiers: Adelantado cheering, 148–49; Adelantado Havana arrival celebrated by, 81, 168; Adelantado in Matanzas finding, 85; Adelantado insulted by, 53; Adelantado journey to Spain accompanied by, 189; Adelantado organizing rations for, 104–5; Adelantado preventing murder of, 173; Adelantado receiving insolence from, 53; Adelantado recruiting, 39, 199–200; Adelantado spoken of poorly by, 110; Adelantado thanks to, 148–49; Calibay protecting, 155; captains encouraging, 39–40, 51, 147–48; celebrating victory, 59, 64; commanders disrespected by, 102–3; as disheartened, 51, 78; Enríquez injuring, 186; exploring Florida, 47; as fatigued, 61, 77; fortifying against French Lutherans, 148, 149; fort San Juan constructed by, 188; French Lu-

therans killed by, 56–57; García Osorio imprisoning, 181; getting lost, 54–55; Indians giving food to, 158–59; Indians mocking, 130; Indians positively receiving, 42; mutiny crimes of, 195; mutiny lied about by, 195; opinions of, 73; Phillip II sending supplies with, 85; poison fruits killing, 77; as required to be in Florida, 109; Rogel loved by, 175; Rogel taught by, 175; speaking dishonestly, 110; starvation as struggle for, 76–78, 125, 132; stealing resources, 101; as stirred up, 104; victory encouraging, 64; water as obstacle for, 63–64

St. Augustine: Adelantado directing supplies to, 133, 390n61; Adelantado fortifying, 64; Adelantado returning to, 62, 129, 186; Adelantado sending supplies to, 189; as capital of Florida, 1; commander and officer capture in, 102; Indians as treacherous in, 130; Mendoza Grajales as vicar of, 149; Menéndez, B., as warden and governor of, 75; mutinies in, 101–11, 161; Valdés inspecting, 170

Starvation: in Guale, 117; as struggle for Spanish soldiers, 76–78, 125, 132

Storms, 39, 48–50, 53, 79–81

Supplies. *See* Resources

Tequesta (Chief): as Carlos ex-subject, 173; Carlos friendship with, 174; Indians of, desiring Christianity, 173; location of, 396n130; voyage to country of, 157–59, 172, 183

Tocobaga (Chief): Adelantado peace negotiations with, 174–78; Adelantado praised by, 177; Adelantado refusing to kill, 175; Carlos desiring to kill, 175; Christian captive of, 176; Christianity desired by, 178; in country of, 175; false Christians hated by, 176–77; loyalty to his gods by, 176

Translation: *The Conquest of Florida* errors in, 19–20; of Ferrera manuscript, 28–29; of Revillagigedo manuscript, 28–29; of Spanish names, 32; from Spanish to English, 32

Troche, Rodrigo, 107, 151, 395n122

Ubilla, Juan de, 147, 148, 150

University of Salamanca: Barrientos as

professor at, 3, 13, 16; Solís de Merás as student at, 16

Utina (Chief): Adelantado as friend of, 151, 156; Adelantado asked for rain by, 151; Adelantado's chieftain, understanding God as, 152; Adelantado feared by, 152; Adelantado meeting with, 155–56; Adelantado receiving humility from, 156; in country of, 151–56; French Lutherans manipulated by, 396n125; as humble, 156

Valderrama, Jerónimo de: Adelantado denied help from, 135–36, 142; Adelantado giving state of Florida update for, 134; Adelantado requesting meeting with, 134; Spain return of, 134; as *visitador*, 134

Valdés, Pedro de: Adelantado advised by, 55; Adelantado informed by, 144–45; Adelantado praising, 146; Adelantado rejecting passage to, 193; as Adelantado relative, 42, 50; Adelantado secretly followed by, 193; Adelantado sending upriver, 172; as afraid, 104; as brigadier, 35, 387n29; dealing with mutiny, 104; escaped French Lutherans found by, 61; family returned to by, 192; French Lutherans' fort found by, 55; getting lost, 55; history of, 192–93; as ill, 102; Indians met by, 42; Menéndez, A., married to, 42, 50, 399n164; notified of French fleet departure, 162–63; Phillip II thanking, 194–95; river tested by, 184; San German voyage by, 162; San Mateo and St. Augustine inspecting, 170; as San Mateo field commander, 103–4, 129; special forces organized by, 50; title defended by, 145–46; Zabal left in charge by, 144

Vázquez de Ayllón, Lucas, 1–2

Vega, Garcilaso de la, 2

Velasco, Don Luis de, 157

Vélez de Medrano, Juan, 101

Victory: Adelantado thanking God for, 59; Spanish soldiers celebrating, 59, 64; Spanish soldiers encouraged by, 64

Vida y hechos de Pedro Menéndez de Avilés (Barrientos), 12–13; Aguilar on whereabouts of, 14; different manuscripts of, 14; disappearance of, 13–14; García transcribing, 14; Kerrigan mentioning, 14; Martínez publishing edition of, 14; problems with, 13; source lacking in, 15

Villarreal, Father Francisco de, 172

Villarroel, Gonzalo de: as sick, 131; as warden and sergeant of San Mateo, 59–60, 102, 104; Zabal replacing, 131

Villegaignon, Nicolas Durand de, 112

War strategies, 43–45, 46, 54, 196–97, 389n50; of Italian Wars, 7–8; lack of resources inhibiting, 85–86; storms and weather helping, 48–50

Water, as struggle, 63–64

Women: Adelantado protecting Indian, 97–98; Adelantado sparing, 57

Zabal, Vasco, 143–44; Guale choosing to stay, 118; Villarroel replaced by, 131

Zurita, Juan de, 35, 151

David Arbesú is assistant professor of Spanish at the University of South Florida, Tampa, where he is also affiliated faculty of the Institute for the Study of Latin America and the Caribbean. He is the editor of *La Fazienda de Ultramar*, Spain's oldest translation of the Bible, and the author of two books, a critical edition of the medieval tale *Crónica de Flores y Blancaflor* and a verse translation of Spain's most popular theater play, *Don Juan Tenorio*.

CPSIA information can be obtained
at www.ICGtesting.com
Printed in the USA
BVOW03*2346120817
491667BV00008B/91/P

9 780813 061245